DEADLY ILLUSIONS

Also by John Costello

The Battle for Concorde (with Terry Hughes)
D-Day (with Warren Tute and Terry Hughes)
The Concorde Conspiracy (with Terry Hughes)
Jutland 1916 (with Terry Hughes)
The Pacific War
Vir... Under Fire – How World War II Changed Social and Sexual Attitudes
"And I Was There" – Breaking the Secrets of Pearl Harbor and Midway (with Rear
Admiral Edwin T. Layton and Captain Roger Pineau)
Mask of Treachery
Ten Days To Destiny

DEADLY ILLUSIONS

JOHN COSTELLO
AND
OLEG TSAREV

CROWN PUBLISHERS, INC.
New York

To the future hopes
and dreams of the
Russian People

Copyright © 1993 by Nimbus Communications, Inc. and Oleg Tsarev

Published by Crown Publishers, Inc., 201 East 50th Street, New York, New York 10022.
Member of the Crown Publishing Group.
Random House, Inc. New York, Toronto, London, Sydney, Auckland
Originally published in Great Britain by Century an imprint of Random House in 1993.
Crown is a trademark of Crown Publishers, Inc.

Manufactured in the United States of America

Library of Congress Cataloging-in-Publication Data

Costello, John.
    Deadly illusions : the KGB Orlov dossier reveals Stalin's master spy / John Costello and Oleg Tsarev. — 1st ed.
    Includes bibliographical references and index.
    1. Orlov, Aleksandr, d. 1973.   2. Spies—Soviet Union—Biography.   3. Defectors—Soviet Union—Biography.   4. Soviet Union. Komitet gosudarstvennoĭ bezopasnosti.
5. Espionage—Soviet Union—History.   I. Tsarev, Oleg.   II. Title.
DK268.072C67   1993
327.1247'092—dc20
    [B]   92-34137
                                                                                  CIP

ISBN 0-517-58850-1

10 9 8 7 6 5 4 3 2 1

First American Edition

CONTENTS

	Acknowledgements	vi
	Foreword	x
1	"People Like Us Hate the KGB"	1
2	"Sword and Shield"	13
3	"Industrial Help, Not Espionage"	55
4	"Dangerous Guesswork"	73
5	"A Complete Metamorphosis"	91
6	"Philby Will Be Called *SYNOK*"	114
7	"A Great Appetite for Agent Work"	141
8	"A Promising Source"	179
9	"An *Enfant Terrible*"	220
10	"Keep Out of Range of Artillery Fire"	248
11	"Forbidden Subjects"	267
12	"A Dangerous Game"	293
13	"In Constant Fear of Their Lives"	315
14	"Closely Guarded Secrets"	331
15	"A Professional to the End of His Days"	366
	Appendix I	390
	Appendix II	394
	Appendix III	406
	Appendix IV	412
	Appendix V	415
	Notes and Sources	431
	Afterword	487
	Selected Bibliography	511
	Index	519

ACKNOWLEDGEMENTS

Many former colleagues in the KGB and current friends in the Russian Intelligence Service who have contributed both directly and indirectly cannot be named for reasons which the reader will be able to appreciate. To them I extend a very special thanks. Ironic though it may appear, one of those who must be singled out is the last chief of the KGB. not only did General of the Army Vladimir Alexandrovich Kryuchkov approve the policy of making selected historical records public, but it was he who approved my collaboration with John Costello for this book. Another important initiator of this project is Leonid Vladimirovich Shebarshin, the former head of the First Chief Directorate of the KGB whose idea it was to write about Orlov and who nurtured and encouraged the book in its formative stages. It would not have been possible to navigate through the immense volume of records or assemble the material on which this book is based without the continuing help and patient advice of the Director of the Russian Intelligence Service Archive, Alexander Petrovich. Together with his two assistants, Colonel Vyacheslav Petrovich Mazurov and Colonel Dimitry Dimitrievich Vorobyev their advice and efforts have proved indispensable in this historic research effort into the files. Major-General Sergei Mikhailovich Golubev, the former Deputy Chief of the External Counterintelligence Directorate of the FCD warrants a mention for the special assistance he provided in the early stages of the project. The personal recollections of Alexander Orlov of distinguished retirees of the KGB, including Colonel Mikhail Alexandrovich Feoktistov, Lieutenant-General Pavel Anatolievich Sudoplatov and Colonel Boris Goodze, have contributed an invaluable insight and perspective. On many occasions in this voyage of historical discovery, I was grateful to be able to call on the resources of Volodya Merzlyakov, the knowledgeable curator of the KGB museum. The copying of the pictures in the Russian Intelligence Service Archive was provided by staff photographer Mikhail Mikhailovich Loginov and I should like to express my gratitude to him and many others at the Yasenevo headquarters for assistance in many matters, large and small. I owe a very special debt of gratitude to Colonel Yuri Georgievich Kobaladze, the head of the Press Bureau of the Russian Intelligence Service.

I wish to acknowledge the contribution made by John Costello whose inexhaustible energy and resourcefulness as a collaborator have been matched by his patience in dealing with our intelligence service and his grasp of how to transform raw historical data into a lively narrative. Finally, a note of personal appreciation is due to my wife Natasha, and to my daughter Xenia Olegovna Tsareva for the very professional skills that she devoted to the English translation of my original manuscript.

Oleg Tsarev

It is fitting that, first and foremost, I pay tribute to my co-author. Without Oleg Tsarev's patient efforts to bridge the chasm between secrecy and history this project would not have succeeded. I should also like to endorse the acknowledgements he has paid to his former colleagues in the KGB. Whatever the operational intentions of Vladimir Kryuchkov, history owes a debt of gratitude to the last chairman of the KGB. While he may be remembered as one of the conservative Soviet leaders who attempted to turn back the political clock on the democratic experiment in the former Soviet Union, it should not be forgotten that Kryuchkov was instrumental in authorizing this unprecedented collaboration which marked the first opening-up of the historical resource of the former First Chief Directorate Archive of the KGB. Once uncorked, the genie of historical truth can never be put back into its bottle of official secrecy as Leonid Shebarshin, the former head of the First Chief Directorate, appreciated only too keenly when he gave his personal endorsement to Oleg to work with a Western historian to set the record straight. I should like to express my personal gratitude to him and the Directorate of the Russian Intelligence Service for the ongoing support that they have given to this project which has established a new precedent for openness and objectivity in the study of intelligence history, not only in Russia, but the rest of the world.

I would not have been in a position to embark on such a controversial collaboration without the support and encouragement of my friends and contacts in the United States intelligence community. As in my co-author's case, some have requested that they remain anonymous. I thank them none the less not only for the confidence and consideration they have given to a 'Brit' whose fellow countrymen in the same profession have repeatedly voiced concerns about my being made privy to too much information that is denied by the restraints of the Official Secrets Act in Britain. Fortunately this exclusivity was not shared by their American counterparts and I have been generously received by officials at the CIA, FBI and NSA. Amongst the distinguished body of former intelligence officers whose assistance has contributed to this project, I would like to single out for having been especially generous with their hospitality, time and knowledge Walter Pforzheimer, Dr Ray Cline, Robert T. Crowley, Daniel Mulvenna and Hayden Peake. Although the alphabetical listing that follows cannot adequately acknowledge the individual contributions they have made, I should also like to express my personal gratitude to the late Russ Bowen, the late Laughlin Campbell, Elizabeth Bancroft, Shareen Brysaac, Marjorie W. Cline, George Constantinides, David Gaddy, Ruth Levine, Natalie Grant Wraga, Sam Halpern, Edward McCarthy, Helen Nears, Hank Schorreck, Robert Wade and Thierry Wolton.

While the Official Secrets Act continues to deny such extensive access to intelligence veterans in Britain, I am nonetheless grateful that I have been able to call on the knowledge of Robert Cecil, Colonel T.A.R. Robertson, Gervase Cowell, Oleg Gordievsky and the late Sir Dick White among others. Rupert Allason M.P. (Nigel West), Harry Chapman Pincher and James Rusbridger have also continued to be rooters-out of the truth and a fund of reliable information that might not otherwise have been prized from the closets of official British secrecy. It is often left to journalists to remind Whitehall of their responsibility to the public record and I applaud Richard Norton Taylor and Martin Walker of *The Guardian*, James Adams of *The Sunday Times*, David Twiston of *The Daily Telegraph* and Paul Greengrass for their contributions.

I am indebted to historians in academia whose rigorous scholarship sets the standard to which we non-academics – who some would dismiss as "airport bookstall historians" – aspire. Among the distinguished professors who have been generous with their support, criticism and encouragement are Arthur Schlesinger Jr, Robin Winks, Allen Weinstein, Warren Kimball and James Barros. I should also like to acknowledge the help and hospitality we have received from Verne Newton, author of *The Cambridge Spies* who is currently Director of the Franklin Delano Roosevelt Library, Hyde Park. A very special contribution has been made by Timothy Naftali of the John M. Olin Institute at Harvard, Andrew Barros of Sidney Sussex College, Cambridge University and Stephen Koch of Columbia University.

While I have not personally met archivists of the Russian Intelligence Service whose unseen efforts have made this book possible, I can vouch for the unique contribution that has been made by John Taylor. Once again I record my debt to this paradigm for all historical researchers and his National Archives colleagues: Terri Hamnet, Wilbur A. Mahoney, Eddie Reese, Rodney A. Ross, and Mary Jo Williamson. At the FBI in Washington the FBI Freedom of Information Office processed the Orlov and other files for release and in Britain the staff of the Public Records Office once again proved very helpful. The Library of Congress and the New York Public Library, the Butler Library at Columbia and the Dade County Library System at Miami Beach fulfilled my many requests for published works and articles with knowledge and alacrity. Joseph Gormley and Joanna Rubira of the University of Michigan provided information relating to Orlov's time at the Ann Arbor campus.

A very special "thank you" must go to Matthew D. Anderson, my assistant in New York, for his research forays to the New York Public Library in addition to the retyping and proofing of the manuscript, transcribing many hours of tapes and handling all the telephone and fax communications necessitated by my peregrinations between Moscow, London, New York, Washington and Miami. Once again I am personally indebted to many of my friends on both sides of the Atlantic for continuing to provide me with hospitality: Ken Nichols in Washington, Julia Wight and Laurence Pratt in London, and Harold Ketzer in Germany. I am grateful for the continuing logistical support of Robin Wight and Jerry Jantzi, the sound legal counsel of my attorney Gary Lazarus and the research assistance which has been contributed by Jasper Wight in Cambridge, Thierry Rance-Francius in France and Hans Zellweger in Switzerland.

To our editors: James Wade at Crown Publishers, New York – not forgetting his assistant Paul Boccardi – and Mark Booth at Random House UK and his assistant Andrea Henry, Nick Collins for his freelance editorial work and Dr Florian Marzin of Zolnay Verlag, our gratitude for all the effort they have put into transforming the manuscript into an impressive book. To our agents John Hawkins in New York and Michael Meller in Munich our thanks for the contractual engineering that has made this groundbreaking project possible. Finally, without the communications and transport facilities of British Airways, Federal Express, AT & T and MCI, this collaboration could not have been realized.

John Costello

FOREWORD

IT WAS AFTER six o'clock, well past the end of our working day in July 1990, as I stood outside my office on the second floor of the KGB headquarters building on Dzerzhinsky Square fixing the seal on the door required by security regulations.

I was cursing under my breath at the fiddling procedure necessary to thread a foot-long piece of cord through steel eyelets in the door and pressing the loose ends into the plasticine-coated tag on the frame, prior to stamping it with my personal seal. This crude but effective security device, which had come into use in early *Cheka* days, had miraculously survived all the technological progress of the twentieth century. But the stamp required just the right amount of spittle to make it come away cleanly after embedding the twine in the sticky plasticine. I had never been able to master the knack. There never seemed to be sufficient material on my tag. Either it evaporated or, as I used to joke, it had been gnawed away by the Lubyanka's mouse population looking for a sweet dessert after feasting away all night on top-secret KGB documents.

While wiping traces of "mouse delight" off my thumb, I heard a telephone in my office. From its distinctive ring, I knew that it was not the ordinary line, but the extension of the scrambler phone of the operational communications network used for secure calls. Tearing apart the laboriously fixed seal and unlocking the door, I rushed over to my desk to pick up the receiver. It was the Director of the Intelligence Service Archive, calling to ask if I would come out to see him. He had found something interesting that he would explain when we met.

"Interesting" to an intelligence service officer means urgent – or at least that has always been my experience. So it was with mounting curiosity that I drove out next morning to the First Chief Directorate headquarters. The operational nerve centre for Soviet foreign intelligence operations was located at Yasenevo in a complex of sixties Finnish-designed white and blue office blocks rising above the pine forest off the Moscow ring road.

After the round of security checks necessary, I found myself sitting in the Archive Director's airy modern office. After greeting me, he handed over a three-volume file bearing the code name "SCHWED" in handwritten Cyrillic capitals. The buff cardboard covers stamped with the number 32476 in administrative purple were browning with age. The brittle edges of the papers crumbled as I began turning them over with a rising sense of bewilderment.

"Well, do you think you would like to write about him?" asked Alexander Petrovich.

"I don't know," I said. "He was a traitor and I don't know how to approach the subject since we have not discussed such cases in public yet."

"Then you had better read his file thoroughly and we'll talk about it later."

Mikhail Sergeievich Gorbachev had been General Secretary for five years and *Perestroika* was beginning to filter through to the KGB which was finally participating in the new openness by releasing details of historically important cases no longer considered operationally significant. But this file was very different. It contained the records of a former Soviet General whom I had always regarded as the highest-ranking intelligence officer ever to defect to the West.

I was soon lost in the dossier. It was only when I heard the Archive clerk announcing that the reading room was closing that I tore myself away from its pages with great reluctance. I had been reading all day, with only a fifteen-minute lunch break, and by the end of that afternoon I concluded that my preconception had been wrong: SCHWED was no traitor after all.

Alexander Mikhailovich Orlov was the name by which the subject was best known, although his file indicated that in his career he had adopted a host of aliases and cryptonyms. His story was undeniably fascinating: he had been an early member of the *Cheka*, an underground Soviet "illegal" in the 1930s in many European capitals and he was the NKVD *rezident* in Republican Spain when he left his post in Barcelona in the summer of 1938 at the height of Stalin's political repressions. Then he had vanished for nearly fifteen years before erupting into public prominence in the United States in 1953 with the publication of his book *The Secret History of Stalin's Crimes*. In the twenty years that followed Orlov had played a subtle game of wits, first with the FBI and then with CIA interrogators. This enabled the Soviet agents he had recruited and former colleagues he could have identified to continue their clandestine operations against the West.

Orlov's case was therefore a classic: it was the record of a man squeezed between divided loyalties with very little room to manoeuvre. The narrow space in which he resolved his ethical and professional conflicts was a complex guileful conscience: the mind of a hardened and experienced intelligence officer who, on the one hand, gave the Americans just enough information to enable him to remain in the United States where he felt safe, and, on the other, did not betray Soviet agents whom he had trained and worked with. He succeeded in this challenging task by providing the CIA and FBI with a concoction of half truths, trivialities and disinformation which he skilfully passed off as a sincere confession. Just how cleverly he had deceived the FBI and CIA became evident to the KGB after a five-year search for Orlov, initiated in 1964, eventually resulted in two clandestine contacts with him in 1969 and 1971. The report of the KGB officer who conducted this operation proved beyond any doubt Orlov's loyalty to the Soviet intelligence service, its agents and his mother country. In 1972, shortly before he died the following year at the age of seventy-eight, this remarkable man, whose life had been twisted and bent by some of the stormiest events of the century, wrote his first letter home after a thirty-five-year-long exile in America. This survives in his file as an all-too-human epitaph to a man who had once been a prodigy, albeit a sometime evil genius of the twilight world of clandestine operations.

As I left Yasenevo that afternoon, I could not help reflecting that Orlov could have been a Le Carré character had he not been more real than any character in spy fiction. By the end of the day I knew that I had to dig deeper, to try to discover the complex individual whose astonishing career had only been hinted at in the files.

My interest in Orlov was personal as well as professional. After studying at the Moscow Institute of International Relations, in 1970 I joined the First Chief Directorate of the KGB. As I began training as a Soviet intelligence officer, I could never have dreamed that one day I would be the one who would make public one of the most interesting cases in the service's secret files. The confrontation of the Cold War was still the fact of life that was stressed repeatedly during our classes, and brought home by the example of one of those who lectured to us: Kim Philby. An agent cannot work without a cover, and, as this former British secret intelligence service officer who had begun his career for Soviet intelligence as a reporter reminded us, journalism is ideally suited for the purpose. The English were pioneers in this area of undercover operations in the 1930s and we learned from them. In 1974 I donned my cloak as a correspondent of the trade magazine *Sotsialisticheskaya Industria* and for the next five years plied a dual profession as a journalist based in London. Later I worked for *Pravda* for a year before joining *Isvestia*.

Undercover operatives posing as newspaper correspondents have been employed by every intelligence service in the world. This has long been well known in the West, but always denied by the Soviet Union. Indeed, the fact that there was an intelligence service operated by the KGB in peacetime was only admitted publicly for the first time in the summer of 1989, four years after the beginning of *Perestroika*.

Later that same year I decided to abandon operational work. I did so because I felt I had done everything there was to do. The clandestine game of intelligence has always been portrayed as more thrilling in fictional espionage than I ever found it to be in reality. As a day-in-day-out job, it can be gruelling and stressful because it demands of its players a round-the-clock concentration on every detail of their activity so as not to be caught off guard. After twenty years' active service in Europe, another foreign tour did not hold out the prospect of any further intellectual reward. I had, moreover, so grown into my cover of a journalist, that I wanted to devote myself to a full-time writing career.

So when the opportunity was presented to take up a position at the headquarters of the newly established press office of the KGB, I did not hesitate. The novelty that a secret organisation should set up a section to answer the inquiries of Soviet and foreign media at first appeared to be such a contradiction that those who were sceptical about the bureau's function were by no means all outside the KGB. It was an unusual function for me too. After years of denying my true profession, I was now openly acknowledging it. As I fielded a growing stream of calls from my new office overlooking the traffic circling round the forbidding statue of Feliks Dzerzhinsky I could not help wondering what he would have made of all this openness. If any doubt lingered in my mind as to whether Russian history was approaching a dramatic turning point, it was dramatically brought home to me on the night of 24 August 1991 as I watched from that same window the effigy of the founder of the Lubyanka being unceremoniously yanked from his granite pedestal by a crane before a huge crowd of cheering Muscovites packing Dzerzhinsky Square.

The two years that I spent in the press office at KGB headquarters did not mean I had cut my spiritual ties with the intelligence service. I remained in close contact with my friends in the First Chief Directorate whom I often met in the course of fulfilling a new brief. As part of the *Perestroika* policy instituted within the KGB, it fell to me to take the first steps to open up for the Soviet public some of the more notable secrets in our archive files. During my frequent visits to Yasenevo, I would spend hours researching the intelligence archives, looking for suitable material to illuminate the often shadowy and sinister role that our service had played in the murkier events of twentieth-century history. I worked through the Registry indexes, selecting those files to be retrieved by the archivists. They were the only ones permitted access to the repository, where rows of floor-to-ceiling steel cabinets housed seventy years of Soviet intelligence operations. The shelves were filled with grey and brown flip-top cardboard cartons, each containing two or three binders from the more than a third of a million individual cases and operational files. After several months' work we had reviewed the material which, from an operational and security standpoint might safely be made public. My first article was based on the files on Rudolf Hess, which from a historical point of view, I knew, would arouse great interest.

It was published in May 1990 and involved reports from Kim Philby, which coincided with a television documentary about this most famous British agent in the Soviet intelligence service. It related to reports he had supplied from his contacts in the Foreign Office on Hess's flight to Scotland in May 1941. These shed new light on continuing British efforts to keep secret the genuineness of Hess's intention to seek peace on the eve of the German attack on the Soviet Union. My version appeared in *Trud*, which was then the biggest Soviet daily newspaper, on 13 May. A report about it appeared the following weekend in the London *Sunday Times*. The sceptical article challenged the veracity of the information that Philby had relayed to Moscow and cast aspersions on the KGB's motivation in releasing such information. The inference was that my *Trud* article was yet another Soviet exercise in disinformation.

I regarded this assertion as very unprofessional, even for a journalist, since it was highly unlikely that in 1990 a Soviet intelligence officer would be put up to signing his own name to false information. But I could hardly blame my British colleagues for their scepticism since it was only to be expected after so many years of Cold War confrontation and mistrust. But not everyone who read the report was inclined to be so dismissive. The records of the British interrogation of Hitler's deputy and their intelligence records, which surely contain the true background to the Hess affair, have remained officially secret, and it was not long before letters started reaching the KGB press office about the assertions made in my article. One well-known British historian visiting Moscow later told me his colleagues were divided in their views on the behind-the-scenes events of May 1941. While most supported the official British version that Hess's flight was the lone act of a madman, there were some who did not think it too far-fetched that he might have been lured to Britain by a renegade MI6 operation, as was indicated in intelligence reports received from Soviet penetration agents such as Philby. Without access to the contemporary MI6 records – which the British Government still declines to release – it will be impossible to establish the final truth of the Hess affair with historical certainty.

The reaction to my article about Hess's flight however made me keenly aware that any release of the KGB records would be a controversial and frustrating exercise. Not only was there an inherent disinclination to believe information in the Soviet intelligence files, but many historians had built their reputations on what they had written and I realised how strongly they would resist accepting a new theory – even if it was supported by documents with impeccable authentication. New evidence must surely be the touchstone for the true historian who must be prepared to admit that an earlier interpretation was misconceived, if hitherto unavailable records can be shown to pass the test of veracity.

The revision of the hitherto accepted version of the case of Alexander Orlov was an ideal opportunity to use the archive for a historical purpose. This is because it would not only alter the West's understanding of a major Soviet intelligence figure, but also the perceptions of Orlov held by many KGB veterans. The former NKVD *rezident* and security adviser to the Republican Government in Spain has long been regarded as a traitor, but I had learned that it was only because of his disloyalty to Stalin that he was branded a defector in 1938 and he had remained a figure of scorn until the end of the Cold War because of the "need to know principle" on which the service operated. Only a handful of the most senior officers ever saw his KGB dossier, owing to the extremely sensitive information it contained.

Orlov was considered to be a traitor as a result of such indisputable facts as his flight from Spain in 1938 and his resurfacing to unmask Stalin in the United States in 1953. This opinion, held by many in the Centre at the time, had become part of the indisputable history of our service, to be repeated unthinkingly in the corridors and lecture rooms of the KGB. It had been a view which I too had inherited – that is until three months after the publication of my article on Hess, when I was presented with the Orlov files as the proposed subject for my second article from the KGB archival records. When I had digested the facts of the case it became clear that he was neither a traitor, nor a defector in the true sense of the word. Historically it would be more correct to describe Orlov as a refugee from Stalin's terror, a fact I found acknowledged in his contemporary file by the use of the code name FUGITIVE. Significantly those originally charged in 1938 with investigating his case also used the words "non-returner", a surprisingly mild term at a time when scores of Soviet intelligence officers were being recalled to be shot for alleged treachery as part of Stalin's grim purge of the NKVD. The reason for this contemporary distinction in Orlov's case became obvious as I read deeper into his dossier: he had been responsible for the recruitment of Philby and other members of the so-called Cambridge "Group". These and other agents he had worked with he never betrayed in his American exile. Indeed some of them had continued to provide extremely valuable service for the KGB right on into the early 1960s.

This was the ultimate test of Orlov's loyalty – and it reveals why he was never regarded as a traitor by those who knew all the facts at the time of his flight from Spain in 1938. While it is hard to read the minds of those who had to live and act more than half a century ago in the madness of Stalin's despotism, it appears that even he had concluded that the fleeing General could be relied on to keep his secrets after Orlov had sent an extraordinary letter to Nikolay Ivanovich Yezhov, the then NKVD chief. The fact that the intended manhunt for the fugitive General was dropped before it even began, on orders received from the very top of the Soviet hierarchy, the Central Committee – that is Stalin himself – is an indication that the pact which Orlov had offered was tacitly accepted. The General would not talk in return for the NKVD not taking action against him or his relatives in Russia.

It was shortly after I realised the true significance of Orlov's communication, that a letter from New York was delivered to my desk at the Lubyanka. John Costello, a British historian and writer, was requesting copies of the Hess documents quoted in my piece for *Trud*. Although he too cast doubts on their reliability because he did not see how Philby, who was not in the Foreign Office or London at the time, could have reported on the secret debriefing of Hitler's deputy, it was clear that he had researched the case and found inconsistencies in the official British version. More importantly, his letter revealed that he had recently obtained, under the Freedom of Information Act, an October 1941 report from the US Military attaché in London which appeared to duplicate a briefing on Hess given by Churchill's intelligence aide Major Desmond Morton, which had reached Moscow through a Soviet channel.

Costello appeared to have obtained American independent corroboration for at least some of the points made in my article. I reported his letter and request to Leonid Vladimirovich Shebarshin, who as head of the First Chief Directorate had the authority to release the documentation. I noted that in principle there ought not to be any problem in releasing copies of the paraphrased cables known as *spravkas* of Philby's May 1941 reports naming his Foreign Office source. Nor was there any reason to keep secret that other important reports on Hess had been received from Colonel Frantisek Moravetz (Moravic), who, unknown to the British, fed the MI6 information he received as the head of Czech military intelligence in London to the Soviet *rezident* in London throughout the Second World War. The documents in question had already been effectively declassified by the publication of quotes from them in *Trud* and Shebarshin agreed Costello could have copies of the documents. Xeroxes were sent to him via the diplomatic bag to the Soviet United Nations Mission in New York, in November. I later learned that his astonishment at receiving my package was almost as great as that of the experts he immediately consulted in Washington. They concluded that the documentation was almost certainly genuine and the first officially declassified pages of First Chief Directorate files ever supplied to a Western historian.

At the same time as Costello was becoming aware of his serendipitous research breakthrough, I was putting the finishing touches to my article revealing the true story of Alexander Orlov. It was published in two consecutive instalments, the first appearing in *Trud* on 20 December 1990 to mark the seventieth anniversary of the founding of the Soviet intelligence service. Later that day I paid a courtesy call on Shebarshin, who was in his office at 2 Dzerzhinsky Square, before attending the annual celebratory meeting of intelligence officers and veterans at the KGB club. I presented him with the office copy of *Trud*, only to have him wave it away.

"I have seen it already. Why don't you write a book?" was how my Director greeted me, somewhat dismissively.

"A book about Orlov?" I asked, doubting that he was serious, since he had not looked up for more than a few moments from the paperwork that preoccupied him on his desk.

"Yes," Shebarshin replied firmly.

"But there is not enough material for a book in the files that I saw," I murmured.

"Alexander Petrovich can surely take care of that," he declared, as if the Archive Director would easily be able to take care of what was only minor administrative detail. Then he congratulated me on the article and went back to his papers.

A few days later, when I was researching my next article, which was to be about the Berlin branch of the Soviet wartime network the Gestapo codenamed *Rote Kapelle*, I received a call from Alexander Petrovich at the Archives to say I could now come and see some new material on Orlov. This time he produced seven more thick volumes covering his work as chief of the NKVD "illegal" *rezidenturas* in Paris and London. The material was fascinating and absolutely unknown before. I asked for this batch of files to be sent by courier to my office at the Lubyanka. (Such a transfer of documents was possible at the time, but since August 1991 the strict security regulations intended to protect the records have made it impossible to remove any material from the Intelligence Service Archive.)

Putting off all other work, I spent several days buried in the hundreds of pages of fascinating new material. I discovered that these records included, among many other items, Orlov's correspondence from the London "illegal" *rezidentura* which he had directed from the summer of 1934 to the autumn of 1935. In his own handwriting I read details of his plans for Philby, Maclean and Burgess. They were all recruited under his directions by Arnold Deutsch and Ignaty Reif (not to be confused with the better-known Ignace Reiss), a Soviet undercover intelligence officer in London whose involvement in the Cambridge "Group" was previously unsuspected. After Reif had been forced to leave Britain by the Home Office, Orlov then had personally controlled the original members of the Cambridge network – or "Group" as it was referred to in the contemporary records. The files unlocked the final secrets of the origins and early successes of one of the most fascinating intelligence operations and social phenomena of the twentieth century.

It was at this time that I first met John Costello, when he came to Moscow in January 1991 to examine the Hess dossier personally. In the course of two days of discussions, I showed him the Hess and Moravetz files and translated many of the documents for him. I also gave him a summary of the main points of my December articles on Orlov and mentioned my research into the *Rote Kapelle* files. When he asked me what my next project would be, I told him that I had been asked to write a book on Orlov which would also require a review of the FBI and CIA documentation of his interrogations after he emerged from fifteen years of hiding. Costello volunteered to assist, explaining about the Freedom of Information Act and how to file requests for American documents.

Our initial meetings took place on the Friday and Saturday of the first weekend in January 1991 and Costello was due to leave on Monday afternoon. But early that morning he rang me up in my office and said that he would like to return to the Lubyanka headquarters to discuss something urgent with me. When we met, he said that he had spent most of Sunday thinking over the Orlov story. He found it such a fascinating revelation that he proposed I consider teaming up with him to write Orlov's story for a Western audience. The unusual combination of a serving KGB officer and an independent historian was pragmatic, and, above all, very attractive in terms of meeting the criteria of objectivity and balance. I told him that I needed to seek the approval of my superiors.

So I reported Costello's proposal to the Chief of Intelligence, and subsequently to the Chairman of the KGB, Vladimir Alexandrovich Kryuchkov. Both he and Shebarshin reacted favourably and on 16 January 1991 I received full authority to go ahead with the joint book project. That week Costello had returned to Moscow after I had obtained permission for him to shoot a short video film of the so-called "Black Bertha" file, named from Hess's reported nickname among homosexual circles in Berlin and Munich. Costello was very anxious to incorporate the relevant Soviet documents in his forthcoming book *Ten Days to Destiny* and asked me to assist in this process by explaining, to camera, the contents of the files and why the KGB had decided to release the material to him. This left us little time to discuss the Orlov project since it was the eve of the Gulf War so finding a television camera crew was difficult because they were all covering the diplomatic shuttling back and forth between Moscow and Baghdad.

We did, however, agree that we would try to have a sample chapter of the Orlov book worked up by the publication date of *Ten Days to Destiny* three months later. Given the controversy that the KGB's Hess material was expected to create, I was given permission to go to the West to explain the significance of the records. It would also give me the opportunity to meet interested publishers and to explain the KGB's new approach to history, which involved making public certain documents that would shed light into some of the darker corners of important intelligence operations. Although the British Government denied my request for a visa, I was later able to travel to the United States, where I received an exceptionally warm welcome from former members of the American intelligence community. They were intrigued to hear about how Orlov had deceived them and offered to assist us with the project. In between a hectic week of press and television interviews, Costello and I met with the Crown publishing group, whose Vice-President James Wade expressed enthusiasm for the project. Crown was an appropriate and ironic home for our book, since its parent company, Random House, had in 1953 published Orlov's sensational memoir, *Stalin's Secret Crimes*.

Only a month after I had addressed a meeting of the National Intelligence Study Center in Washington on the changes that had taken place in the KGB, I found myself briefing the Western press in Moscow as the Soviet Union underwent a far more dramatic transformation than could ever have been predicted. The political changes flowed thick and fast following the attempted August *putsch* against President Gorbachev. KGB Chairman Kryuchkov was arrested, but neither his fate nor the restructuring of the KGB affected the Orlov collaboration, which he had authorised.

The fragmentation of the USSR and the reconstitution of the Russian Republic under Boris Yeltsin did, however, result in the break up of the 75-year-old state security *apparat*. The First Chief Directorate was separated from the KGB, becoming under its new director, Yevgeny Maximovich Primakov, the SVRR or Russian Foreign Intelligence Service.

As one of the former KGB intelligence officers who stayed in the Service, I moved to its newly created Press Bureau. Housed in a turn-of-the-century mansion in a leafy Moscow back street that had once been the luxurious residence of Viktor Semyonovich Abakumov, a former NKVD chairman, my office is now far from the bustle of the former KGB headquarters building on Lubyanka Square. Yet even so, by May 1992 the increasing demands of working on the Orlov book led me to the conclusion that I had to have more time of my own for writing. The research for this book had by then extended into scores of files, which under the strict new regulations could not be removed from the Archive. This necessitated frequent trips to Yasenevo headquarters to check and recheck documents and I found that I could not achieve the level of commitment needed for this project in my spare time. So I decided to take "early retirement" while remaining a part-time consultant with the service, in order to complete *Deadly Illusions*.

This book is, as the observant and well-informed reader will quickly appreciate from the source references, the result of many months of delving in the still secret intelligence files on both sides of what was once termed the Iron Curtain. Apart from the seven volumes of Orlov's personal files, with the diligent assistance of the SVRR archives staff I have had to extend my researches into hundreds of other personal and operational case files, by no means all of which were obviously connected directly our subject's work.

That my work has had to be so extensive was a forcible reminder to me of the sheer extent of Orlov's knowledge and involvement in Soviet intelligence operations. The depth to which I have now dug into the archival records explains certain discrepancies in dates and facts from those used for my Orlov articles in *Trud*. Originally I was granted access to only three files, but soon found that contrary to my first impression when I began this project, no single case file gives the full and complete story of any particular subject. This became very evident in the case of Philby's early career and Orlov's operations in Spain. To pull a single file, or set of files and trust – as I did when I wrote my newspaper articles – that they will provide all the information necessary to write up a case, is a great error.

The reason is that intelligence records cannot be considered "archives" in the traditional historiographic sense of the word. They would represent a great challenge to scholars accustomed to the order of the diplomatic records of the Public Records Office in London or the National Archives in Washington because they are collections of operational documents compiled to serve the practical needs of running agents. Some of the reports in the files are not even stitched into the bound volumes in chronological order; others were extracted and have been placed into another case file relating to that operation, or in some cases turn up under an entirely different subject. It is therefore only by lucky chance that you can find the end of a paper trail without spending many hours – and even days – reviewing irrelevant material.

Many of Orlov's reports are either undated, or worse, misdated. Frustratingly, this is typical for the Soviet intelligence files of the 1930s when the practice was for the incoming report from a *rezidentura* to be cut into separate pieces containing specific sets of information. Each section was then inserted into the relevant agent's file, without any cross-referencing by date, or subject, by the desk officers. This was of course not due to any deeply laid plot but to simple administrative inefficiency. Soviet intelligence officers of that time never thought that their files would become a historical source, since it was never anticipated that even a formal institutional history would ever need to be written. The contemporary records were only kept to satisfy immediate and practical needs. Some of the most sensitive operations, such as acts of political terror in Stalin's times were deliberately left unrecorded, so as not to leave any trace after an assassination was committed. This, as I found, was the case when Orlov masterminded the compromising, arrest and kidnapping of Andreu Nin. It was only possible to recreate the sequence of events that led to the murder of the bespectacled Spanish Marxist leader at Orlov's direction in the summer of 1937 when I discovered a correlation between three separate documents that at first glance seemed unconnected – but which taken together added up to a smoking gun.

In telling the story of Orlov, the Russian Foreign Intelligence Service has decided to follow the FBI and CIA practice of not disclosing the names of Soviet agents who may still be alive and who have not been previously identified. Wherever this was the case, I was authorised only to release their codenames. (Operational information of this nature is also excluded from requests under the Freedom of Information Act regarding FBI and CIA reports, so the RIS is doing no more and no less to conceal such sources.) Where some of them have been identified, either because of a transparent codename, or from information obtained from other records, the responsibility for accuracy has therefore been entirely assumed by my co- author. For a somewhat different reason, certain names have been withheld from the appendix attached to Orlov's letter to the chief of the NKVD in July 1938 listing all the operations he had either participated in, or knew about. Many of these relate to operations which have yet to be researched properly and have been omitted so as not to provoke premature and unwarranted speculation. To wait for the release of these subsidiary details would have meant leaving this manuscript to collect dust – and this we thought would be unfair to the reader and to this unique effort to serve history. When and if this data becomes available, such information as can be safely and responsibly released will be incorporated in subsequent editions of this book.

Yet even if we cannot provide all the answers, this project has been an unprecedented collaborative effort in the recording of intelligence history. Since it relies on documentation from both sides of what has been called the Looking Glass War, it comes as close as anyone has ever come to a complete telling of a classic Soviet intelligence case. As the first exercise of this kind to be made from the operational archives of the Russian Intelligence Service, I can guarantee that where information is provided from historic files, it is specific and faithful to the spirit and wording of such documentation. Where operational considerations have made it necessary for us to withhold data or names, I have so stated.

The responsibility and research has been a daunting task for both my co-author and I, but it has also proved a stimulating experience. As a former intelligence officer, trained to 'keep it in the family' for security, I remained true to the injunction by having my daughter, Xenia translate my part of the manuscript as I wrote, from Russian into English. Finishing the translation of yet another chapter, she would keep asking me, 'Dad what's going to happen next?'

I hope that readers of this book will share some of the excitement that this member of Russia's younger generation experienced at discovering a small but fascinating aspect of our country's formerly very secret history.

OLEG TSAREV
Moscow, February 1993

I

"PEOPLE LIKE US HATE THE KGB"

O N FRIDAY, 14 November 1969, a passenger wearing a dark grey overcoat alighted from the morning Chicago train at Ann Arbor station and hailed a taxi. At the intersection of State and South University Streets the cab stopped. The man got out and joined the students hurrying to classes on the sprawling University of Michigan campus. The icy wind blasted snow flurries in from Lake Huron, rattling the bare branches of the trees on the sidewalk outside Lorch Hall as he entered through the glass swing doors of the six-storey Law and Economics building. No one paid any special attention to the short figure whose coat was a bit too stylishly cut – although he conspicuously did not fit in with faculty or students. Pausing before the notice board posting the day's classes, he scanned the list, then set off along the ground-floor corridor.[1]

In one of the lecture rooms, an elderly man was addressing the class of students. Though he had aged heavily, his features were easily recognized by the visitor from the photographs in a thirty-year-old administrative file, which described him as: "Medium height, athletic build, nose slightly broken, balding head, hair turning grey. Wears a short moustache, also grey. Very resolute features and manners. Walk, gestures and speech sharp; steady eyes. Has an excellent command of English with an American accent. Speaks German more or less fluently, can express himself in French and Spanish."[2] The moustache had long since been shaved off, the head was almost bald and the elderly man's Yankee twang was pronounced. Age had also taken its toll of his athletic physique, endowing him with an academic stoop. But there could not be the slightest doubt that this was his target.

Satisfied, the visitor carefully closed the door and checked his watch. Fifteen minutes remained before the class was scheduled to end, when he planned to introduce himself to the lecturer. The train ride from Chicago had been long and chilly, so he walked back down the corridor in search of a bathroom.

Less than ten minutes passed before the man in the dark grey overcoat returned to the lecture room. To his dismay he found it empty. Silently he cursed himself for giving priority to a call of nature; the miscalculation cost him an opportunity to make a low-key contact with the man he had travelled half way across the globe to find. He had the home address and phone number of the lecturer, but as a careful and methodical investigator, he decided he would get confirmation from the university register. But he did not pursue his inquiries in the Economics Faculty, he crossed over to the adjoining Department of Physics to ask for a list of resident and visiting lecturers. There he found that the name of Alexander Orlov was one of the few listed as attached to the Law Faculty that did not bear any academic qualifications. Apartment 703 at 400 Maynard Street was the residence of the lecturer, only a few blocks away according to the city street map.

The Baird carillon had already chimed midday over the campus as the visitor set out along State Street, then heading down William Street, where a right turn brought him into Maynard Street, and to the eleven-storey apartment house. It was a plain concrete box: advertised as "quietly comfortable" in the *Yellow Pages*, its apartments offered temporary homes to visiting lecturers and graduate students.

Walking slowly past the canopied entrance of Maynard House, he observed that a doorman of forbidding bulk manned the desk. This visitor did not wish to be announced for fear of putting Orlov on the alert, so he ducked into the stationery store next door. By peering through a conveniently placed rack of greeting cards, he was able to keep watch on the entrance to Maynard House while waiting for an opportunity to make an unannounced entry.

When he spotted three boys crossing from William Street opposite, the man stepped quietly out of the shop. Then he saw a kitten walking along the sidewalk. Scooping it up, he called out to them just as they reached the entrance to Maynard House, "Does this cat by any chance belong to you?" One of the boys immediately came forward to claim his pet and the stranger handed it to him with a friendly caution about the danger traffic posed to a wandering cat. Then, as the boys politely held open the door for him, he switched the topic to baseball. From his years in the United States he knew that you could strike up conversation with anyone about America's favourite spectator sport. As they made their way through the lobby to the elevators he busily engaged them with his views on the outcome of the recent World Series. The burly doorman, assuming the man was with the boys, did not challenge him. Nor did he notice how closely the stranger in the dark overcoat scanned the names on the lobby mail boxes as the group waited for the elevator.

Stepping into the car, one of the boys pressed the seventh-floor button. This prompted the man to select number eight to keep up the pretence that he was a resident. As they got off, he said farewell to the boys, rode to the top floor, then rode the elevator back down to the seventh floor. The corridor was deserted and within moments he was standing before the front door of 703, the residence of the lecturer who had been the subject of a five-year-long man-hunt.

The visitor tapped lightly on the door, then he carefully positioned himself out of the line of vision of the spy hole. His precautions were justified by the clanking of three deadbolts being turned back. Warily the door was opened until it was caught by a heavy safety chain. Framed in the narrow gap was the slightly broken nose and bright hazel eyes of the old man who had been lecturing earlier.

"May I speak to Mr Orlov?" the visitor politely inquired.

The occupant was visibly startled. "Who are you?" he demanded.

"I am Feoktistov, Mikhail Alexandrovich," the caller announced. "Can I come in? I have a letter for you from an old friend."

The elderly man unhooked the heavy door chain with obvious reluctance. The visitor quickly pushed his way inside, forcing his host to retreat into the living room of the apartment. Face to face, the stranger announced that he was carrying a message from Nikolay Prokopyuk, an old acquaintance from Barcelona.[3] Taking an envelope from his coat he handed it to the old man who adopted a defensive posture, denying he knew anybody by that name. He suggested that the visitor must be mistaken, but just as he was about to hand back the unopened letter, a woman burst into the room. Her grey hair, pulled into a tight bun, accentuated her thin features and hostile expression.

"Who are you?" the bird-like woman demanded. When the visitor announced he was a Russian bringing a letter from an old friend, she launched into a torrent of ferocious protests.

"Please do calm down," said Feoktistov, as he put his hand into his overcoat pocket to produce his passport.

Fearful that the stranger was reaching for a gun, the gaunt woman tensed like a startled cat. He proffered the green diplomatic passport embossed with the hammer and sickle identifying its bearer as a Soviet employee of the United Nations Secretariat in New York.

"Sasha, this is a KGB agent, he's come to kill us!" the woman screamed in Russian, her eyes filled with hate, her voice with fear. With a piercing shriek she dashed from the room. She returned with a pistol in her trembling hand, her forefinger coiled around the trigger. "I'm going to shoot you! You came to kill us," the woman shouted, her voice quivering with terror and rage. "Sasha, give the letter back, it's poisoned."[4]

In a desperate effort to calm them, the visitor seized the letter from the old man and tore it open, vigorously rubbed the envelope and its contents between his palms and then licked both hands. "You see, if the letter were poisoned," he declared, "I wouldn't have done that."

Twenty years later Feoktistov, retired KGB officer, smiled with wry amusement as he recalled the melodramatic scene in which he found himself staring down the barrel of a loaded gun. He was interviewed in his Moscow flat, eight months after the monolithic KGB had been dissolved following the abortive August coup of 1991. The silver-haired veteran of the Soviet intelligence service had been originally reluctant to discuss how he had tracked down and confronted Maria Orlov and her husband Alexander, the highest ranking officer ever to flee to the West from the Soviet intelligence service. Feoktistov only agreed to talk about the encounter after repeated assurances from Oleg Tsarev that he had seen the Orlov dossier and had official permission to discuss the case.

It was from the pages of this same secret KGB file that Feoktistov said he had been briefed, before masterminding the extended operation that led him to the Ann Arbor apartment. He reflected that neither the KGB records nor his operational directive prepared him for the fiercely protective role Maria Orlov had developed during thirty years of American exile. So, when he was confronted by a pistol-packing wife, he could do little more than protest as she bustled her husband from the room.

"But, Maria, I want to talk to him," Alexander Orlov persisted.

"No, he will destroy you," Maria countered, trying to push her husband out of the room.

Feoktistov recalled how the old man had turned to him and said, "I want to talk to you. Phone me right away from the call box across the street." Maria had then ordered Feoktistov to stand against the wall with his hands raised. "She frisked me as expertly as any police officer," he observed with a smile.

"You know very well who you came in search of," Mrs Orlov declared. "People like us hate the KGB," she continued, her bitterness rising to the point of hysteria. "We would kill you if we could. We are going to inform the American authorities at once."

"Calm down, Maria Vladislavna," Feoktistov said he had repeatedly urged the distraught woman. He assured her that the Orlovs were no longer regarded as traitors in the Soviet Union and that neither he nor the KGB meant them any harm. He tried explaining several times that his visit was simply to deliver a letter from her husband's old colleague from their days in the Spanish Civil War. Feoktistov also said that he had news from Maria's sisters in Moscow. Did she not want to hear about them?

"I don't want to hear anything about my sisters from you," Mrs Orlov retorted. "We'll drop my sisters."[5]

"Do you not care for your sisters any longer?" Feoktistov doggedly persisted.

"I know how Soviet citizens receive letters from abroad and then are accused of all sorts of things because of the association," Mrs Orlov shot back. But the mention of her sisters, whom she had not seen for over thirty years, appeared to trigger Mrs Orlov's memory. According to Feoktistov, she suddenly asked him the name of his uncle. When he told her it was Dimitri Petrovich Feoktistov and that he had been deputy to the head of administration services to the Council of People's Commissars, she said she had known of him.

Feoktistov, observing a recent *Pravda* newspaper on the table beside an ink-stained copy of the Soviet magazine *Communist*, took advantage of the lull that had overtaken Mrs Orlov's rage to try to win her over. Obviously the Orlovs took a keen interest in the Soviet Union, he said, pointing to the Russian journals. Maria insisted that it only extended to borrowing copies of the newspaper and magazines from a local library, before launching into a denunciation of the postwar Soviet leaders. She singled out Nikita Khruschev's comment during his visit to the United States that he would like to retire to an American farm if the Central Committee would permit it. This, Maria declared, was a "very anti-patriotic statement and not worthy of the leader of a great nation". From this Feoktistov concluded that Mrs Orlov was obviously a staunch Russian patriot. It had given him hope, he said, that he might yet win her trust. This would not be easy, however, for Mrs Orlov, brandishing the pistol, had by then forced him to back out of the apartment and into the corridor. Feoktistov became thoroughly alarmed when one of the neighbours suddenly came out into the corridor. When Maria Orlov managed to tuck the gun beneath her apron, he feared it might go off accidentally.[6]

"Apart from Sasha, I have no one," Mrs Orlov raged on, telling Feoktistov how their ailing seventeen-year-old daughter had died in 1940, only two years after they had been forced to flee from Stalin's murder squads to the United States to hide. He also learned how the Orlovs had eked out a frugal existence for fourteen years. As their cash reserves dwindled, she told him how they had been forced to subsist largely on a diet of cornflakes. They had not been able to live normally until 1953, when they received money from Orlov's book *The Secret History of Stalin's Crimes*, which made sensational headlines after its serialization in *Life* magazine. Her tirade is recorded in the report Feoktistov dutifully sent to Moscow and which constitutes part of his KGB dossier. The Orlovs' heartbreaking tale of hardship was not the important information Feoktistov had been commissioned to obtain, but these were the only details of significance that he could send to Moscow following his return to New York. Surprisingly, his report contains no mention that Mrs Orlov had threatened him with a gun. This, Feoktistov explained, was because he withheld this fact so as not to jeopardize the possibility of a second meeting with the Orlovs.[7]

"Although our conversation was tense," Feoktistov recalled, "at times she had started to withdraw, only to stay, as if something were drawing her to me." So his report stated that, towards the end of the hour-long stand off, he believed he had succeeded in melting some of the ice of Maria Orlov's mistrust. He failed however to persuade her to permit him to meet her husband again that day, so judging that he had learned all he could that afternoon, Feoktistov ended the confrontation by passing on one sister's regards and assuring her that she was well and had a good job in the Soviet Union. This only provoked Mrs Orlov's hostility. It "could not possibly be true", she snapped.

"You have wrecked all our plans. You've messed things up for us," Mrs Orlov shouted as she retreated into the apartment. But Feoktistov did not lose the significance of her parting comment: "But none the less I have come to respect you a little."

Maria Orlov then abruptly closed the door in Feoktistov's face. As he headed for the elevator, he heard the heavy deadlocks being snapped back into place behind the door of apartment 703. Until he stepped into the lobby, he said he was unsure whether Orlov's angry wife had raised the alarm and he would be walking into the arms of the police. The entrance, to his relief, was empty – except for the building's uniformed attendant, who ignored him as he walked out of the front door.

Out again on State Street, Feoktistov pulled up the collar of his overcoat against the wind and headed for the campus. He scouted for a telephone, found a booth that appeared safe from surveillance and dialled 665 4781. Significantly, it was Orlov who answered. In contrast to his openly hostile wife, the old man quickly made clear his willingness to communicate.

"Oh, dear, hello again, I am so sorry that Maria didn't let us talk and I couldn't receive you," Feoktistov recalled Orlov had told him, his plaintive voice indicating that there was no hostility towards him. According to Feoktistov, the most revealing moment came when Orlov asked, "Tell me, are you my colleague?"

Feoktistov regarded Orlov's question as highly significant. Speaking carefully, he attempted to reassure Orlov that he was indeed still regarded as a loyal comrade by those "old friends who knew him". Feoktistov pursued this idea by assuring the old man that his mission truly was to pass on a message from "old friends" who wanted to thank him for being "a true patriot". All in Moscow wished him "good health" and wanted to inquire after his "well-being". Feoktistov then asked if a meeting between them was possible. Orlov answered equivocally by saying, "Let us speak on the telephone."

It had been more than three decades since the old man had last been in contact with a member of the Soviet intelligence service, and Feoktistov used the opportunity to draw all he could from Orlov's memory. In the summer of 1938, when he was at the pinnacle of his career as Stalin's trusted secret police chief in Spain, Orlov had fled to the United States. Promoted to the special rank of Major of State Security by order number 832/A of 14 December 1935, Orlov had been a recipient of the Order of Lenin, with the rank equivalent to a Brigade Commander in the Red Army. In contemporary ranking this was equivalent to a General Major, or a one-star Brigadier General in the US army. Historically, therefore, Orlov remains to this day the most senior Soviet intelligence officer ever to defect to the West. In this capacity he had carried with him many secrets and the names of members of Soviet underground networks. What Feoktistov hoped to learn was whether Orlov had betrayed any of those agents to his interrogators in the FBI and CIA. He therefore responded encouragingly to Orlov's invitation: "What do you want to know?" "Talk about everything, your life, your health, your work," Feoktistov said he had urged.[8]

"I'm in good health, but our life here is dull," Orlov observed, carefully declining to speak about anything over the telephone except generalities.

"I don't work now and I have never had any permanent position in America," Orlov complained. "They don't trust people of our sort."

Orlov's assertion about the Americans was not surprising. The Soviets also never fully trusted their own defectors from the West. Nonetheless in what Feoktistov believed was an attempt by Orlov to reassure the KGB through him that he had not sold out to the Americans, Orlov had embarked on a justification of his public statements.

"As you know, I have written two books," Orlov told Feoktistov, describing *The Secret History of Stalin's Crimes* as "a cry from the soul in which he had attempted to expose the true facts regarding a tyrant's rise to power. This Orlov told him was historically important since this information had derived from his personal knowledge as a ranking officer of the Soviet intelligence service. Other key facts had been provided by Stalin's wife's brother, Pavel Alliluyev, with whom he had worked in Germany in the late 1920s. Furthermore, Orlov said that he had himself known Stalin personally before his posting to Spain, serving on the committee which briefed the Soviet dictator and the Politburo on foreign intelligence.

"I do not know any more than I wrote," Orlov assured Feoktistov, "but you can be certain that I made none of it up." His blood-chilling account of Stalin's crimes had made headlines around the world in 1953 by detailing how the Soviet secret police had orchestrated the Moscow show trials which began the Great Purge. The book's publication had also brought Orlov to the attention of the FBI after he and his wife had spent fourteen years as fugitives hiding in the United States.

A Handbook of Counter-Intelligence and Guerilla Warfare, which appeared ten years later, attracted none of the public attention of his first work, Orlov said, but he assured Feoktistov that in it he had drawn only on well-known cases and had not given any secrets away. "It was based purely on technical data," which he "thought might be translated in the Soviet Union and would become useful as a practical guide". In this way, he told Feoktistov, he had intended "to provide a little service to my country".

Feoktistov suggested that he would appreciate an autographed copy. But Orlov ignored the KGB officer's ploy to get himself invited back to the apartment to collect it and so have a chance for a more personal chat. Nor was the General prepared to be any more explicit about what he had divulged to the Americans concerning his career in the secret service of the Soviet Union.

"Strictly speaking our telephone conversation terminated when I pressed for a personal meeting and discussion," Feoktistov commented. According to his account, Orlov had responded evasively that it would not be "profitable to fix a date then and there", but that he would be "welcome to come back and talk at some later date".

"I took a Greyhound bus from Ann Arbor to Chicago that afternoon and then went by plane back to New York," Feoktistov added, recalling how, when he came to write up his report for Moscow – which he signed with his code name GEORG – he had "described Maria's over-reaction to my visit less colourfully". He had stated in his report that she was "highly strung" and that he considered her reaction was due to a "certain instability in her character". As he put it in his interview: "I never thought that she would really have shot me or I would have behaved in an entirely different way!"[9]

Feoktistov deliberately left Orlov with the impression that he would return to Ann Arbor before the end of 1969. Yet the KGB file shows he did not receive permission from Moscow to try to re-establish contact with Orlov until nearly three months later. But in February 1970, when Feoktistov drove back to Michigan, he found to his dismay that the Orlovs had left Ann Arbor shortly after his visit. This was confirmed by the Law faculty and neighbours at Maynard House. Neither they nor the doorman could provide a forwarding address.

Stalin's former spymaster and his wife had gone to ground again, and Feoktistov had returned empty handed to New York to pass the word to Moscow that it would be necessary to start the hunt for the Orlovs all over again. Resuming his cover work as an English interpreter attached to the Soviet delegation to the United Nations, the Soviet intelligence officer waited for instructions to come from the Centre, as the KGB headquarters was known. Nearly two years passed before Feoktistov was authorized to pick up the trail once again. The reason for this long delay in resuming the operation, in his opinion, was Moscow's concern that the Orlovs' flight from Ann Arbor indicated their alarm at having been found by the KGB after thirty years. While the Orlov files do not offer any reason for the delay, it is clear that they had no wish to frighten the General into making a clean breast of all his secrets to the FBI and CIA. This would have been a far more damaging outcome to Feoktistov's mission than waiting until the reassuring dust of time had settled again around the Orlovs.

The FBI records reveal that the unexpected arrival at their apartment of a KGB agent had indeed "messed things up" as Mrs Orlov had predicted. Feoktistov's appearance had put them in a dangerous dilemma as Orlov himself would explain to him at their second meeting two years later. He had to consider the possibility their unannounced visitor was an FBI provocation agent posing as a KGB officer to trick him into betraying the secrets that he had so far withheld. Orlov told Feoktistov in 1971 that he had had no choice in 1969 but to report their encounter with the Soviet intelligence officer to the FBI.

The Orlovs' apparently ambivalent loyalties explain why the report they gave the FBI was very different from the account filed by Feoktistov. Although the full version has yet to be declassified, a summary published in the records of the US Senate has Mrs Orlov describing her valiant two-hour "battle of wills" which she claimed took place in the seventh floor corridor of Maynard House.[10] According to their version, the Orlovs never permitted the KGB agent to cross the threshold of their apartment. Nor did Orlov ever inform his American protectors that it was at *his* invitation that the KGB agent had later telephoned him. According to Orlov's account, he had immediately hung up on Feoktistov after he had called to make an angry reproach for refusing to admit him into their apartment. Mrs Orlov also omitted to tell the FBI how she had pulled a gun on the KGB man. This is all the more curious, since she suffered from a heart condition and had made much of the exacerbation of her medical state caused by her fears that their discovery was a prelude to their assassination by the KGB. With their whereabouts now known to the KGB, the Orlovs followed advice to leave Ann Arbor and go underground again for their own protection.

"If the Soviets have an ulterior motive with respect to the Orlovs, it has not been reflected to date," the FBI decided. As a UN employee Feoktistov was not subject to travel restrictions and his approach was "not illegal" since he had not tried to "recruit or intimidate" the Orlovs. As this report reveals, the FBI had no reason to doubt that the Orlovs were telling the whole truth about what transpired between them and the KGB officer. The secret knowledge Orlov might have possessed about the Soviet intelligence apparatus in 1938 had by 1969 been degraded by the passage of more than thirty years. But the FBI did not rule out the possibility of an assassination of the couple to settle old scores. The ever present fear of the long arm of Soviet vengeance had forced the Orlovs to live under an assumed name for fourteen years of their exile. When the couple testified in 1955 and 1957 before the Senate Internal Security Sub-Committee they were given no publicity and to the end of his life, all Orlov's official correspondence was conducted through his New York attorney.

Alexander Orlov's death in 1973 was marked by a tribute from the US Senate. Senator James O. Eastland eulogized Stalin's former spy master, whose residence in America had been legitimized by special act of Congress, as "one of the most important witnesses" ever to testify during the time he chaired the Senate Internal Security Sub-Committee. Describing Orlov as "the highest ranking officer of the Soviet State Security (now the KGB) ever to come over to the side of the Free World", Eastland announced that he had left behind him "a priceless legacy – in the form of his testimony about the inner workings and objectives of the Communist conspiracy and about the activities of the Communist apparatus in the related fields of espionage and subversion". "If there was any defect, it was not in General Orlov," Eastland said, "but in the utterly immoral system he had renounced." "This former Soviet intelligence officer has made an unforgettable impression." Even the word "defector", the Senator declared, was "ironically inappropriate when linked to Orlov's name".[11]

Just how ironical and inappropriate it was to describe Orlov as a defector emerges from the KGB files detailing the significance and extent of the Soviet espionage secrets which the former Russian General *deliberately* concealed from the Americans. These expose Senator Eastland's eulogy, published by special direction of the Senate under the title *The Legacy of Alexander Orlov*, as a mistaken tribute. Truly reliable Soviet defectors came over to the West after a fundamental shift of allegiance, and the ever present questions all counter intelligence officers have to ask are, "Are they for real?" or "Are they sent?" In Orlov's case there is now every reason to doubt that Stalin's spy master ever defected in the proper sense of the word. None of the documents obtained under the Freedom of Information Act (representing just a fraction of hundreds of hours of debriefing he gave the FBI and CIA), give any indication that he ever came close to revealing what he really knew about the inner workings of the Soviet espionage apparatus. Despite the fact that much of this material remains classified, it is self-evident that Orlov did not expose Kim Philby or any of the penetration networks his KGB dossier shows he had a direct hand in establishing before his "defection", since some of the agents he had recruited continued operating for the Soviets well into the 1960s. Indeed, there is now every reason to believe that what information he did supply was a carefully judged deception intended to conceal, rather than reveal, his most important secrets. Despite the tributes paid to him by Senator Eastland, Orlov never truly recanted his faith in Lenin's Communist Revolution. He was never a defector, but only an escapee from Stalinism.[12]

Even amongst the FBI and CIA officials whose professional business it was to debrief and consult with Orlov over the years, there was always the suspicion that he had held back some of his most important secrets. While it was usual for defectors to keep information in reserve to buy a future meal ticket, Orlov appeared especially reticent. His FBI and CIA interrogators have admitted being troubled about Orlov's extensive knowledge of Britain. He always claimed to have absorbed this from British documents passed to Moscow by Soviet agents working in London during the 1930s. His detailed knowledge of the location and appearance of London's government buildings was unlikely to have come simply from reading reports in Moscow. But Orlov would never admit that he had ever set foot in England – and he always remained unhelpfully vague about the Soviet intelligence operations he had been involved in throughout Europe before his posting to Spain in 1936.[13]

The nagging doubt remained that Orlov, who had repeatedly proclaimed his anti-Communism and his loyalty to the United States, might be holding back the names of Soviet agents out of a sense of loyalty. The American counter-intelligence officers, who reviewed the Orlovs' reports of their meeting with Feoktistov, apparently never suspected that the real reason behind the KGB's attempt to re-establish contact with their exiled General after so many years might have been to make sure he had not betrayed his most closely held Soviet intelligence secrets.

The KGB's many volume dossier on Orlov not only reveals for the first time what those secrets were, but why the decision was taken – after the lapse of a quarter-century – to track him down. These files, which until 1990 were accessible only to the most senior echelons of the Soviet intelligence service, are the *true* legacy of Alexander Orlov.[14]

If enduring loyalty to the ideals of Lenin's Revolution, and personal loyalty to colleagues and agents, was what really held Orlov back from divulging some of the most important aspects of his remarkable career as a Soviet intelligence officer, then it is a historic irony that these secrets were to be eventually revealed by the collapse of Communism in the third Russian revolution to take place this century. The KGB dossier on Orlov contains an astonishing legacy of international espionage and deception, personally orchestrated on a grand scale by a master of the art who ended up as an exile from the motherland he set out to serve.[15] It shows how his adherence to the vision of Communism ultimately proved to be as deadly an illusion for Alexander Orlov as the deceptions that he spent half a lifetime weaving against the West.

2

"SWORD AND SHIELD"

Igor Konstantinovich Berg was the pseudonym Orlov had assumed most often in America to disguise his true identity as one of the most important exiled veterans of the Soviet intelligence service. False identities had long been a professional accoutrement for a man who, in his career as a Soviet spy master, had worn a succession of different aliases rather as a man pursuing a more mundane occupation wears a different tie each day to work. His FBI file alone indicates he had used at least eight names whilst living under cover in the United States. If the number of aliases are a measure of a spy's versatility, then the dozen more pseudonyms which appear in his KGB dossier are an indication of the complexity of Orlov's deception. But, for the purposes of unravelling the story of his remarkable career, he will be Alexander Mikhailovich Orlov, the alias he used for his last assignment as the Soviet secret police chief in Spain – and the one by which he is best known to history.[1]

Orlov told Feoktistov that it was Stalin who had personally assigned him that pseudonym. But, in his sworn statement to the Immigration and Naturalization Service, he asserted that: "The name of Orlov was given to me by Maxim Litvinov, the Foreign Minister, because on the way to Spain I had to cross Hitler's Germany [and because] the name of Nikolsky was known to the German Gestapo."[2] This is just one of the discrepancies to have surfaced in unravelling Orlov's story. The presumption is that he did not want to reveal that he knew Stalin personally, and wanted to appear less important than he actually was. While there are many significant conflicts of fact between the version he gave the Americans and the documentation in the KGB files, on his date of birth and real name, there is no disagreement. He was born in the Byelorussian town of Bobruysk on 21 August 1895 into the family of Lazar and Anna Feldbin, who gave their son the names Leiba Lazarevich. According to his FBI file, he had a sister who later became a dentist in Moscow, but who died in 1918.[3] Their father was one of the many children of a family of

Askenazim Jews who had migrated from Austria to the forested hinterland of European Russia at the turn of the eighteenth century, shortly before Napoleon's ill-fated march on Moscow.[4]

The defeat of the French ushered in a brief period of relative freedom from the Tsar's pogroms for the growing Jewish community in Russia, during which Orlov's paternal grandfather built up a flourishing timber business, becoming a pillar of his Bobruysk synagogue and one of its leading benefactors. In 1885 he travelled to Palestine with a delegation of Russian Jews to purchase land during the *Aliya Rishona* – the first emigration inspired by the rallying call "*Beth Ya'akov lehu venelha.*" ("House of Jacob, let's go".) Grandfather Feldbin had made a large contribution towards the purchase of a tract of marshland named the Gates of Hope in anticipation that it could be drained for building a settlement. In the final years of his life Orlov was fond of proudly recalling that his family's contribution to the state of Israel was the site of the flourishing town of Petah Tikva.[5]

While Orlov was growing up during the last decades of Tsarist rule, his family maintained their strong religious commitment despite renewed pogroms and anti-Semitism. Russian Jewish families who aspired to build a better life faced waves of persecution and discriminatory laws shutting religious minorities out from the upper reaches of the Imperial bureaucracy, professions and armed services. The Feldbins passed on their faith to their children as something more than a precious spiritual heritage: for Orlov it became a mainspring of personal resilience and determination of character. It enabled him to survive the difficult times after his family chose to remain in Russia, after the abortive revolutionary uprisings of 1905, when many of the Feldbins' aunts, uncles and cousins decided to join the growing exodus to the United States.[6]

Among those emigrants from Bobruysk who were to prosper in America were many cousins who had been his boyhood companions, the most prominent of whom were Isaac Rabinowitz, who became a trustee of New York's Brandeis University, and Nathan Koornick, who became a prosperous businessman. When Orlov later found himself an exile in America, he found his old friends, such as his classmate Boris Rosovsky, were there to turn to for support.

As a boy, Rosovsky recalled Orlov as a popular playmate: adventurous, outgoing, and a born leader. A sepia picture of Orlov in his early teens stares out from the first volume of his KGB dossier. Taken by a Bobruysk photographer, it is a stiff but revealing portrait of a young man in a high-collared but noticeably worn jacket with neatly parted hair, full lips and prominent ears. His slightly quizzical expression and assured stare suggests that even as he entered his teens

Orlov was not lacking in self-confidence. According to Rosovsky he was "a very bright student in school", who also "excelled as a painter". His closest boyhood companion told the FBI how Orlov was "very much of an athlete and was a good soccer player". He recalled how Orlov had developed a teenage "crush" on his sister, even though there was a great social gap between them. Orlov's parents were "rather poor", his father was only an agent in the timber trade, while the Rosovskys were wealthy, owning a number of factories. Their son notes, however, that the Orlovs were "very religious" and their house "was always immaculately clean".[7]

Orlov had gravitated, in the way that children do, to spending time in the more luxurious surroundings of the Rosovsky home. He appears to have been impressed by the difference in their social standing, always asking his friend's mother if he could see the table whenever it was set for important guests. Boris remembered how his best friend Leiba "held a certain resentment or jealousy" for the wealth enjoyed by the Rosovsky family, "but at the same time he was always a gentleman who spoke what he had in mind in a very nice manner". Their friendship continued through their teens and Rosovsky explained how Orlov had saved him from drowning when he fell, fully clothed, into the Bobruysk river one summer's day in 1913 when they were out boating. Orlov's physical courage was never foolhardy, according to Rosovsky, but was allied to a sharp intellect, which impressed the rabbi who taught them the Torah and enabled him to shine academically at school.[8]

Orlov remained close friends with Rosovsky until 1915, when the wartime economic decline prompted his father to give up the timber trade and move to Moscow in search of more lucrative work. Orlov's scholastic ability and aptitude for drawing enabled him to win admission to the Lazarevsky Institute where he distinguished himself not only in academic subjects but also in the subsidiary art course. The educational establishment founded by the Armenian brothers Lazaryan groomed its students for entry into the Imperial diplomatic and consular services. Later it became the Soviet Institute for Oriental Languages.[9] It was there that Orlov became fast friends with Zinovy Borisovich Katsnelson, another cousin, with whom he lodged in the family's small apartment. Zinovy was no less well endowed with academic ability. After they both graduated near the top of their class, they abandoned the pursuit of art for a more solid career by enrolling in the University of Moscow Law School, one of the renowned academic institutions of Tsarist Russia. No sooner had they begun their jurisprudence course than their studies were interrupted in 1916 when they were both drafted into the Tsar's army. Neither saw any action in the war itself. During the year before the Revolution that they served as private foot soldiers they were fortunate to be assigned to the 104th regiment, a reserve unit stationed far behind the front line, in the Urals. [10]

As a boy, Orlov had entertained dreams of growing up to lead a dashing cavalry regiment, only later to find that his aspirations were frustrated because Jews could not aspire to a commission, let alone join the elite regiments of the Tsar's army. But the opportunity for him to pursue that yearned-for military career opened up in February 1917 with the reforms introduced by the Provisional Government after Tsar Nicholas II had been forced to abdicate, after the first Russian Revolution. In March 1917, second lieutenant Feldbin was passed out of the 2nd Warrant Officers' Schools and by May he cast his lot in with the radical revolutionaries by joining a faction of the Russian Social Democratic Workers Party. Orlov did not enrol with Lenin's Bolsheviks, but another element making up the RSDWU led by Solomon Abramovich Losovsky who later became secretary general of the *Profintern* (the Red International of Trade Unions). As a member of Lozovsky's so-called Group of Internationalists, Orlov made many useful contacts in the revolutionary movements and picked up a sound knowledge of English, German and French. But as the questionnaire in his personal file indicates, he did not become a member of the Communist Party of Bolsheviks until 1920, when his sponsor was V. A. Ter-Vangayan, a veteran Marxist who had become his friend and political mentor. [11] Nonetheless, his activist credentials indicate that his commitment to the second Revolution that brought the Bolsheviks to power in October 1917 was a true expression of his ideological commitment, rather than expedient opportunism.

"I believed in the programme and the promises of Lenin," was how Orlov later justified his decision to become a Bolshevik. "I saw in his programme remarkable progress compared with the feudal regime of the Tsar, when ninety-five per cent of the people were illiterate and there were constant religious persecutions of minorities." [12] In common with many Jews who were to play a leading role in the birth of the Soviet state, Orlov's decision to join with the revolutionaries was an instinctive reaction to the Tsarist pogroms. He may not have played a significant part in the October Revolution which enabled Lenin's minority Bolshevik Party to seize control of the government, but, as for many of his contemporaries who lived through this tumultuous period, the upheaval was akin to a spiritual rebirth, not just for Russia, but also personally. Although Orlov would later denounce Stalin and the excesses of his tyranny, to the very end of his life he maintained faith in the Grail-like ideals of the Marxist-Leninist revolutionary doctrine. [13]

As a Revolutionary soldier, Orlov's loyalty was rewarded with a minor appointment in the administration Lenin set up with the objective of bringing the Russian Government and vast bureaucracy under the control of his minority Bolshevik party. From November 1917 until the middle of 1918 Orlov served as chief of the Information Service of the Supreme Finance Council. A civilian bureaucrat's life apparently had little appeal for Orlov, as his file reveals that the next year he rejoined the military. In the new Red Army, as part of the Bolsheviks' policy of reinforcing their control by introducing educated party members, he became part of its officer corps which was reconstructed according to the directives of the People's Commissar for War, Leon Davidovich Trotsky.[14]

A bloody civil war had erupted in 1918 after three separate White Russian armies under Admiral Kolchak and Generals Denikin and Yudenich ignited open rebellions against the Bolsheviks as they set out to restore the Tsarist regime by marching into the Russian heartland from Siberia, the Caucasus and the Gulf of Finland. Orlov's service record shows that in September 1920 he was posted to the 12th Red Army on the south-west frontier of European Russia as an investigator and executive officer with the Special Department (military counter-intelligence). Here he had his first chance to demonstrate his cool-headedness under fire fighting against the invading Polish army. The legitimacy of this foreign military incursion was supported by the so-called anti-Bolshevik Russian People's Army recruited by Boris Savinkov, a Social Revolutionary Party leader and former member of the provisional Government. An implacable enemy of Lenin, Savinkov's goal, like that of the other White commanders, was to smash the Red Army and oust the Bolsheviks, with the aid of Polish forces.[15]

The Russo-Polish war brought Orlov rapid promotion to commander of guerilla operations in the south-west during a series of campaigns in which he successfully directed irregular units against the Polish army and its White allies. He personally led operations into enemy territory occupied by the Poles on hit-and-run raids that dynamited bridges, railway tracks, power installations and telephone and telegraph lines. The deeply forested countryside of south-west Russia was ideal operational terrain for irregular forces to advance stealthily through the woods and infiltrate round the enemy's rear. These sabotage missions were co-ordinated with the 12th Army, which relied on Orlov for intelligence obtained by these raids. Some of his expeditions behind enemy lines were conducted solely with the objective of gathering the enemy's maps, war plans and other data on the strength and disposition of Polish forces. Orlov's guerilla forces would then set out to capture an enemy staff officer who would be interrogated for additional information.[16]

The most valuable informant captured by Orlov's irregular operations proved to be his opposite number, Colonel Senkovsky, the commander of the Polish guerilla forces. As Orlov told it, the Red Army was in full retreat at the time and Senkovsky had arrived at the front personally to direct the infiltration behind the Russian lines of forty Polish and anti-Bolshevik White Russian officers. When captured, they revealed that they were on their way to take command of 8,000 Ukrainian rebels and deserters who were hiding in the forests. The timely capture of Senkovsky thwarted the Polish plan to marshal this force for an attack on the 12th Army's rear. But for Orlov and his men, this might have resulted in a major defeat and Orlov's counter-intelligence coup brought him a glowing commendation from headquarters for helping turn around a desperate military situation.

Another important operation in which Orlov was involved as a member of the Special Department of the 12th Army was the capture of Ignaty Ignatievich Sosnovsky. As one of the leading agents of the Polish Military Intelligence Service, he was not only an important catch but was also successfully "turned" by the Soviets against his former commanders. After the war, using the name Dobrzyhnsky, he served as a Soviet undercover agent until he was accused of treachery and shot in 1937.[17]

Orlov frequently operated behind enemy lines personally directing operations amidst the birch forests, where his courage and willingness to put his own life on the line in dangerous operations proved an inspiration to the forces under his command. It was during these closely fought guerilla operations against the anti-Bolshevik and Polish forces in the struggle for the heartland of European Russia that Orlov also made friends who were to prove valuable allies over the years. One was his driver, Max Besanov, who later became a trusted source after he was made Stalin's personal chauffeur.[18] The first-hand experience gained from directing operations during the Russo-Polish war made Orlov one of the Red Army's acknowledged experts on counter-intelligence and guerilla warfare. His timely production of intelligence had played a vital role in checking the bid by the Polish army to advance towards Moscow in the summer of 1920.

Under Trotsky's energetic leadership, the Red Army emerged triumphant by exploiting the division and lack of co-ordination in the strategies of their White Russian opponents. Orlov's guerilla operations had also contributed to the Bolshevik victory, that enabled Trotsky's relatively meagre forces to secure Russia from both internal and external attack, by the end of 1920. As the 12th Army's counter-intelligence chief, Orlov also had responsibility for rooting out counter-revolutionary groups which sprang up like mushrooms in the 12th Army's rear.

Orlov's war record brought him to the attention of Feliks Edmundovich Dzerzhinsky, the founder of the Soviet secret police apparatus, who, as head of the Special Department on the south-west front, had frequently visited the 12th Army. The *Cheka*, as it became known, was the ancestor of the KGB and was formed and charged with the mission to "search for and liquidate all counter-revolutionary or sabotaging policies and activities throughout Russia". The "Peace and Land" policy that gave the peasants control over their plots ensured that the Bolsheviks were more widely supported than the Whites in this struggle for the heart of the Russian nation. Their success at outmanoeuvering the more numerous, but less united claimants to power, was evident from the rapid and practically bloodless establishment of Soviet authority by the end of November. Yet by December 1917 they faced a growing threat as rumours began reaching Moscow of former Tsarist officers organizing in the Urals and the Don River region. The pending strike by civil servants of Petrograd instigated by the Constitutional Democrats (*Kadets*) also threatened to raise the spectre of starvation and paralysis. The impetus that gave birth to the *Cheka* was therefore more practical than ideological, as Lenin called for the mobilization of a force to counter the threat to his Party's authority. In the prevailing atmosphere of chaos and crumbling of civil authority there was a pressing need for law enforcement as the flood of demobilized and disaffected troops returned from the front. Only the exercise of a strong central power could hold the fragmented country together: the question was whether this dictatorship would be established by the Red or White. It was Lenin who moved swiftly to gain the upper hand for the Bolsheviks by establishing a political police force, although he himself appears to have conceived of the *Cheka* as only a temporary expedient to deal with the immediate threat of a White-organized subversion and the challenge to his Party in the Constituent Assembly mounted by the more numerous Mensheviks and Socialist Revolutionaries.

The *Cheka* emerged from a commission created by the Bolshevik Party's organizing genius, Feliks Dzerzhinsky, following the directive he received from the People's Commissars (CDC) of 19 December 1917 to counter the strike planned by Petrograd civil servants. Although Lenin's directive charging the commission with overseeing the campaign against subversion included action against counter-revolutionary elements which expanded its activity into the political sphere, the *Cheka*'s mission was originally intended to be temporary during the period of active confrontation. It was only after Dzerzhinsky's report on subversion in the Council of People's Commissars on 20 December that *Sovnarkom* added this to his brief by voting to approve the creation of the *Extraordinary Commission for Counter-revolution and Subversion*. It was to consist of just eight people. The decree initially empowered the *Cheka* to conduct preliminary investigations, confiscation of property, expulsion from the capital, deprivation of bread coupons and the publication of lists of saboteurs in the press for public denunciation. The power to bring in court sentences was not given to the *Cheka* until 21 February 1918 when Petrograd faced the threat of an advance by German forces. Internal as well as external forces now menaced the Bolshevik regime. When Lenin had dissolved the Constituent Assembly in January 1918, he had turned to the *Cheka* as the "special apparatus" of the "organization of the armed people" to suppress all opposition to the Bolsheviks, proscribed as "counter revolutionary". The stage was therefore set for Dzerzhinsky's state-controlled police force to play a leading role in securing the survival of the Soviet state by assuming the repressive mantle and ruthless terror of the Tsar's hated *Okhrana*.[19]

Anticipating "a fight to the finish" against superior political odds, Dzerzhinsky called for "an organ for the revolutionary settlement of accounts with counter-revolutionaries".[20] Receiving the "no-holds-barred" authority he had requested, he began settling accounts with the anti-Bolshevik opposition with a clinical remorselessness born of his personal hatred of the class from which he had sprung. The founder of the *Cheka* was the son of a well-off family of Polish landowners who in his own words had "trained himself to be without pity" for the bourgeoisie. As a young man he had exorcized an adolescent vocation for the Catholic priesthood by becoming a zealous socialist revolutionary. A slight, ascetic man of Spartan habits, Dzerzhinsky had the sleeves of his tunic jackets cut short deliberately to display the deep manacle scars on his slim wrists, a personal stigmata from his years of imprisonment in Tsarist jails. While he drove round Moscow in an appropriated Rolls Royce car, he was driven by a zealous belief in the necessity of preserving the "quasi religious" purity of the Marxist revolution, ascribing it to his determination to "embrace all mankind with my love, warm it and to cleanse it of the dirt of human life".[21] Dzerzhinsky's fanaticism was fired by his consuming hatred of the bourgeois class. His avowal to bring about its destruction was fired by the twelve years of his adult life that he spent in the custody of the Tsar's secret police enduring its exquisite repertoire of torture.

The ordeals Dzerzhinsky experienced in this furnace of pain and suffering had forged this quietly spoken man with a neat goatee into "Iron Feliks", a tireless and fanatical defender of the Revolution, whose penetrating hard blue eyes "made you feel that he could see into your very soul".[22] Although he had formerly condemned the brutality he had personally suffered under the *Okhrana*, Dzerzhinsky had spared no effort to refine the lessons he had so cruelly learned and apply them to securing Bolshevik rule. Under his direction, *agents provocateurs* were recruited to penetrate, expose and liquidate nests of counter-revolution. In accord with Lenin's sanctioning of "a special system of organized violence" the *Cheka* enabled the Bolsheviks to establish a Communist dictatorship *over* rather than *of* the proletariat by ruthlessly rooting out and destroying all opposition.[23]

The *Cheka* as symbolized by its original emblem, considered itself to be "the sword and shield of the Revolution". This entailed defending the new state against the external enemies of Communism as well as crushing all internal opposition. But the first major *Cheka* operation against a foreign power – the assassination of the German Ambassador Count Mirbach in Moscow in the summer of 1918 – was not even authorized by Dzerzhinsky. It was a clumsy attempt by the Central Committee of the Left-Social Revolutionary faction to protest against the draconian peace terms imposed by the Germans at the Treaty of Brest-Litovsk, which Lenin had accepted as the price of extricating Russia from World War I. The assassination brought discredit on the *Cheka* – and the temporary resignation of Dzerzhinsky. But he was soon restored to the command reacting to this setback to his authority by purging the dissident elements and imposing a control that was henceforth to be absolute and unyielding.[24]

The Mirbach assassination that brought Russia to the brink of war with Germany again served to permit Dzerzhinsky to resort to the most draconian measures to guard the Revolution against the threat posed by hostile capitalistic foreign powers. The *Cheka* was expanded rapidly after Britain and France in the summer of 1918 led the international military expeditions to Siberia and Archangel in an effort to strangle the infant Bolshevik regime shortly after its birth. Their secret interventions, while not nearly so extensive and sustained as Soviet propaganda claimed, none the less enabled Dzerzhinsky to inflate fears of a massive foreign threat following the *Cheka*'s first major counter-intelligence victory in the summer of 1918. This was the discovery of the so-called Envoys' Plot. It was uncovered by Dzerzhinsky's agent, Colonel Edouard Berzin, who had successfully penetrated the British secret service networks in Russia. The calculatedly inflammatory name given to the plot derived from the exposure of the role played by Robert Bruce Lockhart, British consul general in Moscow during World War I who after the Revolution had become the head of a special liaison team that maintained a presence in Petrograd even though Britain's government would have no official links with Soviet Russia until 1924. In the best tradition of the "great game" of espionage for which MI6 was legendary, Lockhart had arranged to bribe with secretly provided British money the commander of a contingent of Lettish troops who would instigate the armed overthrow of the Bolsheviks.[25]

One of the leading players in the operetta-like plot that played right into Dzerzhinsky's hands was Sidney George Reilly, who, in March 1918, had been dispatched to Russia as an adviser to Lockhart's mission with the rank of captain in the British Secret Intelligence Service (SIS), – popularly known as MI6. From the confessions provided by Reilly himself, after he was captured by the Soviets six years later, it is clear that the career of this eldest son, born in 1874 to an Odessa shipping broker by the name of Mark Rosenblum, was remarkable enough even without the encrustation of legend applied by later generations of spy writers and television producers.[26]

After an education outside Russia that included a philosophy degree at Heidelberg and another in chemistry from London's Royal Institute of Mines, Reilly married an Irish girl. He adopted her father's surname along with her Catholic faith and British citizenship, to become a "thoroughbred Englishman". Allegedly he was recruited by British intelligence in 1897, while Reilly's thirst for adventure and wealth took him half way around the world before he returned to his native land in 1909. There he became one of the promoters of aviation, founding a society known as Krylya and building the first aerodrome in Russia. By 1915 he was living in New York, where the outbreak of World War I enabled him to enrich himself as an arms dealer. The following year, his passion for flying led him to volunteer as a pilot in the British army. He served in the Royal Flying Corps until January 1918, when he transferred to full-time undercover work for British intelligence.[27]

Using his mother's maiden name of Massino, Reilly operated out of the British legation in Vologda, conducting missions to Petrograd, Murmansk and Moscow. Exploiting the political turmoil of the civil war with a natural talent for deception and disguise, Reilly was soon running extensive underground operations in Russia for Lockhart and MI6. Using forged documentation, he managed to get himself appointed a commissar for the transportation of automobile spare parts during the evacuation of Petrograd, commuting to his apartment in Moscow on the special train reserved for Bolshevik officials. Dispensing several million roubles to the clergy through Patriarch Tikhon, Reilly's plotting culminated in his bribing of the commander of a Lettish division of riflemen, Berzin, who had been introduced by Reilly to Lockhart as a potential leader of a military putsch to overthrow the Petrograd Revolutionary Government.

When the plot was uncovered by the *Cheka* penetration agents, Reilly managed to evade the wave of arrests that put Lockhart and his fellow conspirators – including a US State Department official of Russian-Greek descent with the unlikely name of Xenophon Kalamatiano – into the cells of the building on Moscow's Lubyanka Street that served as *Cheka* headquarters.[28] While the Anglo-American conspirators languished, Reilly made good his escape with a panache that he would later boast of to his Soviet interrogators:

> Having finished the liquidation of my affairs in Moscow, on 11 September 1918 I departed for Petrograd in a railway car of the international society in a compartment reserved for the German embassy, accompanied by one of their legation secretaries and using the passport of a Baltic German. I spent about ten days in Petrograd, hiding in various places, to liquidate my network there and also search for a way to cross the Finnish border – I wanted to escape through Finland. I was not able to do this, so I then decided to go through Revel. I departed Petrograd for Kronstadt after receiving from the German consulate a "Protection Certificate" which was issued to natives of the Baltics. I had, in addition to this document for exiting Petrograd for Kronstadt, a pass issued to one of the Petrograd Workers Committees in a Russian name. There was a launch with a Finnish captain already awaiting me at Kronstadt, on which I spent the night. I set off for Revel . . . In Revel I took up residence in the Hotel Petrograd using the name of Gregory Berman, an antiquarian who had left Russia after a misunderstanding with Soviet authorities . . . After ten days I departed secretly on the launch for Helsingfors, and from there to Stockholm and London, where I arrived on 8 November.[29]

Living up to the nickname "Ace of Spies", with which Reilly was accredited sixty years later in a popular television series, he was safe in Britain when the diplomatic row over the so-called Envoys' Plot reached its climax. Lockhart was then released from prison, in exchange for Russian envoys to Britain, including Maxim Litvinov, who had prudently been seized by the British Government as hostages. Washington had not moved so smartly. The unfortunate

Kalamatiano did not get out of a Russian prison until August 1921.[30] In the meantime the State Department official found himself one of the four principals sentenced to death on 3 December 1918 along with Lockhart and Reilly, against whom *in absentia* judgements were passed by the Supreme Military Tribunal.

The trial enabled the Bolsheviks to portray their new-born Socialist state as under dire threat from within and without by capitalist plotters and spies. The opportunity for inflating this propaganda scare was afforded by the assassination attempt made on Lenin by a member of the Social Revolutionary Party named Fanya Kaplan. Both incidents added urgent credibility to Dzerzhinsky's proclamations for strong measures to protect the Revolution from massive and well-organized hostile forces.

The mounting threat to the Bolshevik regime in the chaos of the civil war brought what their White Russian opponents called the "Red Terror" as the *Cheka* cracked down with an accelerating campaign of raids, arrests and executions of those opposing the regime. Reacting to the threatened breakdown of the regime's authority, Lenin authorized Dzerzhinsky to unleash "organized terror" that he deemed necessary for "terrorizing the enemies of Soviet power in order to strangle crimes in their germ".[31] The bloody terror waged by both sides was a step by step escalation of civil violence in reaction to a growing threat of subversion – both real and perceived. According to Lockhart the British military intervention provided both the climate and excuse for Dzerzhinsky to accelerate the ruthlessness of his counter revolutionary activity. "I only believe that our intervention increased terror and bloodshed," he reflected in his autobiographical account, a view echoed by Volodya Merzlyakov, the surprisingly youthful historian of the Russian Intelligence Service. His own access to the classified records of the *Cheka* has given him a unique – and remarkably dispassionate – grasp of the conflicting forces that forged Dzerzhinsky's iron-handed secret police apparatus. The internal records of the *Cheka* have convinced Merzlyakov that neither the harshly condemnatory Western analyses, nor the previously self-serving vindications published under the former Soviet regime adequately explains the true story which, until now, has been inaccessible to outsiders.

"The Bolsheviks had to walk through a corridor of tough and uncompromising circumstances," Merzlyakov concludes. While not a justification for the ruthlessness of the *Cheka*, it does help to explain the apparently excessive brutality orchestrated by Dzerzhinsky in the violent years following the Revolution.[32] The "Red Terror" certainly helped the Bolsheviks emerge victorious from the life-or-death struggle, but the toll in human life was enormous. In addition to the battle casualties on the fighting front against the White Russians and their allies, the internal repression orchestrated by the *Cheka* with the militia units of the Red Guard resulted in the deaths of a quarter of a million Russians.[33] Nor were the "extraordinary measures" curtailed after the autumn of 1920, by which time the Red Army had secured effective control of Russia. Dzerzhinsky's "extraordinary commission" had by its demonstrable effectiveness earned a permanent role for itself by making it possible for the Bolsheviks to crush their internal rivals and proclaim themselves *the* legitimate Communist Party.

The *Cheka* had by now expanded massively and was on course to becoming a state within the state, with its own army, bureaucracy and local *Chekas* in the provinces. The expansion of the secret police apparatus was unprecedented, even for Russia, which had a long tradition of such organizations since the *oprichniki* of Ivan the Terrible in the sixteenth century. After starting out with just twenty-three men in December 1917, the *Cheka*'s total strength was approaching a quarter of a million just three years later. Of these 137,106 comprised internal troops and 94,288 frontier guards. Over 30,000 made up the so-called civilian staff, amounting to a secret police force that outnumbered the peak strength of the Tsar's *Okhrana* by more than two to one.

As the principal apparatus for enforcing the authority of the Bolsheviks, the *Cheka* now became a central element of Lenin's regime. The need for "extraordinary measures" to rein in the masses was found to be greater than ever as the economic dislocations of the civil war provoked widespread discontent in the Russian peasantry. Rebellious movements amongst the national minorities were fuelled by the disbanding of a large part of the Red Army and Dzerzhinsky was, therefore, able to persuade Lenin to ignore criticism of the *Cheka*'s growing authority and operations. He continued to inflate the size and scope of its octopus-like organs, setting up the Foreign Department known as the INO (*Inostrannyi Otdel*) to conduct intelligence operations, and its subsidiary counter-espionage division known as the KRO, formed to counter foreign subversion.

Among the former Red Army counter-intelligence officers selected to play an important role in the post-civil war *Cheka* was the twenty-five-year-old Orlov. His abilities had been favourably reported by Artur Krystianovich Artusov, the new KRO Counter-Intelligence chief who had encountered Orlov in his wartime service as the *Cheka*'s Special Department chief with the 12th Army units during the

Russo–Polish war. When Orlov requested a transfer to Moscow in December 1920, his request was quickly approved and he was seconded into the *Cheka*'s burgeoning force, which had assumed responsibility for the defence of Soviet frontiers from the Red Army troops.

At the beginning of 1921 Orlov was posted to Archangel as head of investigations and counter-intelligence in the *Cheka*'s Frontier Department of Northern Russia. He was a member of what was now one of the Soviets' elite forces, which inculcated a fierce loyalty by instilling a pride in their organization's defence of the Revolution. Incorruptible and puritanical, it was already enshrining its institutional traditions such as paying its officers on the twentieth day of the month, in recognition of 20 December, the date of the *Cheka*'s foundation – a practice later adopted by the KGB.[34]

Since Orlov was an operational officer who would come into contact with foreigners, he was required to adopt a new name according to the strict rules laid down by Dzerzhinsky to protect organizational security. So Leon Feldbin became Lev Lazarevich Nikolsky – the first of a long string of aliases. This was the name by which Orlov was known during his counter-intelligence investigations at the White Sea port of Archangel, which Dzerzhinsky had singled out as a place to hunt down foreign spies planted during its occupation by an Allied expeditionary force at the beginning of the civil war.

It was during the early months of Orlov's first tour of duty with the frontier troops in northern Russia that he married Maria Vladislavna Rozhnetsky in Archangel on 1 April 1921. His bride was a strikingly beautiful and intelligent woman from Kiev, eight years his junior who had been allowed to quit her job as an archivist with the Foreign Ministry to become a full-time medical student. She had joined the Party at sixteen and had begun work for the Soviet Government in 1919 before volunteering for service with the Red Army as a clerical assistant with the General Staff of the south-west front, where she had first met Orlov. Unusually for a romance that blossomed under war conditions, their devotion was to prove an enduring union: a relationship which survived the disruptions of Orlov's career, providing them both with an emotional sheet-anchor for almost half a century.[35]

In the fall of 1921 the newly married couple returned to Moscow from Archangel. There Maria enrolled in the medical school of the Second Moscow University, while her husband returned to law school and then took up his appointment as a civilian investigator in the Criminal Collegium of the recently established Soviet Supreme Court. Officially he had terminated his association with the *Cheka*, but in reality this was simply a device that Dzerzhinsky employed to permit selected *Chekist* protégés to acquire the legal qualifications and the respectability that would assist them in their service careers. It was also the Communist practice to assign *Chekists* and Party officials to work in the civilian bureaucracies in order to strengthen the political reliability of their staffs. So, by resuming his part-time studies in Moscow Law School, Orlov was eventually able to graduate with a law degree three years later.

At the Supreme Court, Orlov served under the direction of Nikolay Vasilievich Krylenko, a prominent Communist lawyer and Party official. Although not fully qualified himself, Orlov none the less assisted with the formulation of the first criminal code introduced in the Soviet Union. His contributions can be traced from his articles which appeared in the 1922 issues of *Soviet Jurisprudence Weekly*. It was while Orlov was helping to give birth to the obdurate legal underpinning of the Soviet state that his own daughter, Veronika, was born on 1 September 1923.[36]

In his capacity as an assistant prosecutor and investigator of "economic crimes", Orlov later recalled how he often found himself making presentations in the same courts as Andrei Vyshinsky, a former Menshevik who had jumped on the Communist bandwagon after the Revolution. Twelve years later, as the Party's tame Rector of the Moscow University Law Faculty, Vyshinsky became notorious as the stage manager of Stalin's show trials. When they were working together on the Supreme Court, there was no shortage of cases to prosecute. The famine and dislocation induced by two and a half years of civil war would soon force the ever pragmatic Lenin to backpedal on War Communism by introducing the so-called New Economic Policy that partially restored capitalism and invited investment from the West.[37]

Guarding against the profiteering this encouraged, and rooting out offenders became another justification that Dzerzhinsky made for keeping intact the mighty apparatus he had built against the demand for clipping the wings of the *Cheka* which had been voiced by delegates to the Tenth Russian Communist Party Congress in March 1921. This critical forum coincided with the rebellion at the Kronstadt naval fortress, west of Petrograd. Directed principally against the *Cheka*, the insurrectionists denounced the "mass executions and bloodletting" of the Communist regime. The list of grievances published by the sailors, whom Lenin himself only four years earlier had called the heroes of the October Revolution, protested against the "bayonets, bullets and torture chambers" of the *Cheka*, which they unfavourably compared with the worst excesses of the *oprichniki* of Ivan the Terrible.[38] With a ruthlessness that Ivan himself would have envied, a 50,000 strong force of *Cheka* and Red Army troops savagely crushed the rebellion. Survivors who fled to Finland were induced to return with the promises of a pardon – only to be dispatched to concentration camps set up by Dzerzhinsky as an integral part of his growing empire of terror. The rebellion was made the pretext for another expansion in the powers of the *Cheka* after the Party Congress had outlawed the opponents of bureaucracy, the workers opposition and the Democratic Centralist Group. Dzerzhinsky now was able to order that deviations in the Party were to be reported not only to the Control Commission, but also to the *Cheka*, putting the security service inside the Party apparatus and making it the principal mechanism for suppressing dissent.

The Kronstadt Rebellion, which accelerated Lenin's decision to introduce the New Economic Policy thus halting the requisitioning of agricultural produce from the peasants, resulted in a cosmetic concession to Dzerzhinsky's critics. After the end of the civil war Lenin had at first believed that the *Cheka* had fulfilled its role so its powers were curtailed by a 23 December 1921 resolution of the Ninth All Russian Congress of Soviets. This stated that the "strengthening of the Soviet power, internally and externally permits the restriction of the sphere of activity of the All Russian Extraordinary Commission and its organs . . ." Its power of "out of court" sentencing was withdrawn after the Congress decided to review its status and the result of this review was the abolition of the *Cheka* and its rebirth on 6 February 1922 as the State Political Directorate, or GPU from its Russian title *Gosudarstvennoye Politicheskoye Upravleniye*. It was established under the People's Commissariat for Internal Affairs (*Narodnyi Kommissariat Vnutrennikh Del* – the NKVD) whose commissar was now none other than Dzerzhinsky. The administrative sleight of hand therefore enabled "Iron Feliks" to retain both the apparatus and its control with only the loss of the *Cheka*'s authority to order summary justice and imprisonment. But Lenin's declaration of May 1922 that the "law should not abolish terror; to promise that would be a self-delusion", followed by his order for the suppression of the Menshevik Party, ensured that before the year was out the GPU had repossessed the powers of summary execution that had made the *Cheka* such an effective instrument of repression.[39]

The culmination of Dzerzhinsky's power as a secret police chief came in 1924 with the adoption of the first constitution of the USSR. The GPU had in 1923 been renamed the Unified State Political Directorate (*Obyedinyonnoye Gosudarstvennoye Politicheskoye Upravlenye*) or OGPU for short when it was removed from the direct control of the Internal Affairs Commissariat. Dzerzhinsky had then resigned as the NKVD commissariat's chief, but his authority over the secret police remained absolute because the OGPU, since 1922, had been constituted as an independent commissariat in its own right. The additional measure of authority this gave Dzerzhinsky in the Soviet regime was confirmed shortly after Lenin's death on 21 January 1924, when the OGPU chief was named Chairman of the Supreme Council of National Economy and a candidate member of the Politburo.

The institutionalization of the vast OGPU apparatus that Dzerzhinsky had created ensured that it became a permanent organ of the Soviet state. But his burdensome new duties and the jockeying for position to become Lenin's successor which now consumed the members of the Politburo obliged him increasingly to delegate the day-to-day running of the OGPU to his two deputies, Vyacheslav Menzhinsky and Genrikh Yagoda. Dzerzhinsky was also having to confront critics from within the Party, because the vast power of the state security apparatus made some members of the Central Committee very uneasy. A revealing memorandum to Menzhinsky that came to light after the 1991 Russian coup shows that even "Iron Feliks" had to "take into consideration that such attitudes exist", as he wrote in response to a stinging critique of the OGPU from Nikolay Bukharin.[40]

"It would be the greatest political blunder if the Party yielded on the fundamental question of the GPU and gave new life to the Philistines," Dzerzhinsky advised Menzhinsky in an "eyes only" letter of 24 December 1924. Complaining that Bukharin's liberal attitudes "would mean a victory for Trotskyism and a surrender of our positions", he nevertheless was moved to instruct his deputy that: "To counteract these attitudes we need to review our practices, our methods and eliminate everything that can feed such attitudes. That means we [the GPU] must become quieter, more modest, we should use searches and arrests more carefully with better incriminating evidence; some of the arrests (NEPism, official misconduct) should be limited, or made under pressure or by mobilizing party organizations in these affairs."[41]

One of those whom Dzerzhinsky assigned to investigate such "misconduct" was Orlov, who, in 1923, had been summoned to the OGPU head's office and asked to handle the investigation for the prosecution of a corruption case involving the conversion of state property to the private gain of the accused. Orlov presented his findings to a special Politburo meeting which was attended by both Stalin and Dzerzhinsky. While the thoroughness of his investigation was impressive, Stalin argued successfully for the rejection of Orlov's not guilty verdict. It was his contention that the more politically expedient death sentence would serve as a powerful deterrent to other economic criminals. Nevertheless, Dzerzhinsky was so impressed by his hand-picked investigator's fearless presentation that he insisted Orlov he brought back to OGPU headquarters and offered a post in the Economic Directorate, known as the EKU.[42] His cousin Zinovy Katsnelson was already one of the senior officers of the Frontier Guard Division, so it is quite possible he helped facilitate Orlov's promotion.

Orlov's service record that is to be found in the first volume of his personal file states that in 1924–5 he was appointed assistant to the chief of the EKU while simultaneously occupying the post of head of its Section VIII. He moved into an office reserved for OGPU section chiefs in its Lubyanka headquarters. The palatial six-storey building had once housed the All Russian Insurance Company, but by this time its whimsical gables and pastel stucco facade had become a grimly ironical architectural statement given the fear this building inspired in most Russians. A photograph of Orlov from this time wearing a fashionable pin-collar shirt, with tousled but thinning hair and neat moustache suggests more the image of a slightly harassed scoutmaster than a rising star of the Soviet secret police. As a twenty-nine-year-old lawyer, Orlov can hardly have been unaware of the sinister reputation of the organization in which he was a rising official. Working alongside Andrei Ivanchikov as assistant to Grigory Blagonravov, the chief of the Economic Directorate, Orlov supervised five subsidiary departments. According to Orlov's later testimony to the US Senate, he had been charged by Dzerzhinsky with the "control of industry and trade" with special responsibility for "combating corruption". One of the five sections under Blagonravov was V, headed by Lev Mironov, which monitored foreign businessmen with a view to exploiting those who were granted investment concessions in Russia under the New Economic Policy. Another of Orlov's departmental associates was Briantsev, whose Section IX handled the Economic Directorate's extensive list of domestically targeted secret informers. But the most influential of Orlov's comrades in the Economic Department was his cousin Katsnelson.[43]

As assistant to the chief of the directorate, Orlov had access to those sectors which opened a whole new OGPU area of secret operations. With Dzerzhinsky now the commissar responsible for running the Soviet economy, he increasingly turned to the OGPU Economic Department for help and to devise operations for luring Western investors into believing that there were huge profits to be made investing in the Soviet Union. Firms in Britain, France and Germany were thought to be gullible and greedy enough to believe in the fictional prospectuses drawn up by Katsnelson, who had established himself as one of Dzerzhinsky's principal troubleshooters in this operation. Refinancing the Soviet industrial base was one of the major priorities of the New Economic Policy. To drum up business, Russian trade missions had been sent abroad to set up shop, even though the Soviet Union was denied diplomatic recognition as an international pariah whose main export was Communist Revolution. The promise of fat profits to be made by exploiting the vast market of the Russian proletariat proved an irresistible lure for many Western governments.

Foreign trade, therefore, became the key which the Soviets used to unlock the door to full membership of the international community. Ironically the country they believed was their main adversary – Britain – was the first to be taken in. The Anglo-Soviet trade accord was signed in London in March 1921, following a year of hard bargaining between Moscow's envoys and the Government of Prime Minister David Lloyd George, who hoped it would help restore Britain's fortunes as well as the popularity of the Liberal Party. Within a year Germany, Italy, Sweden, Norway, Austria and Czechoslovakia had followed suit. To achieve this success the Commissariat of Foreign Trade had worked hand in glove with the Foreign Department of the *Cheka*, whose importance in the OGPU increased as its force of overseas agents expanded to exploit these breaches in the West's defences.

Until 1929 the INO or Foreign Department of the OGPU was under the control of Mikhail Abramovich Trilliser, whom Orlov characterized as "an ascetic old Bolshevik who had served a term of ten years hard labour at the brutal Tsarist prison camps called *katorgas*". Like his original boss Dzerzhinsky, the long years of incarceration had cut a hard edge on Trilliser, who had been a professional revolutionary since his teens. Under his direction the Foreign Department exploited the overseas *rezidenturas* as beachheads for intelligence and industrial espionage.[44]

Trilliser's successor was the Counter-Intelligence Department (KRO) chief Artusov, Orlov's early mentor. The burly son of an immigrant Swiss cheesemaker, Artusov was one of the most fertile minds in Dzerzhinsky's original organization. Four years senior to Orlov, with whom he forged a close friendship during the Russo-Polish war, the KRO chief was an inventive genius when it came to devising deception and provocation operations. It was also Artusov who, when chief of the *Cheka*'s Counter-Intelligence Department, had masterminded some of its most daring and rewarding deception and provocation operations.[45] These were the so-called *Sindikat*

(Syndicate) and *Trest* (Trust) operations that snared thousands of White Russians and deceived not only the British but also the French and Polish intelligence services. The elaborate web of conspiracies, woven largely at Artusov's direction, involved setting up a network of OGPU agents masquerading as White Russian counter-revolutionaries. From the Soviet point of view "Operation Trust" was a so-called "active measure" designed to be a lightning rod strategy to discharge the threat of constant terrorism and subversion by channelling the efforts of the White Russian emigré organizations into accumulating their forces in anticipation of a decisive overthrow of the Bolshevik regime.[46]

Critical to the success of the strategy was the influence the OGPU gained over Grand Duke Nikolay Nikolayevich, one of the principal figures in the White Russian leadership operating from Paris. This had been achieved early in 1923, according to an August report from Alexander A. Yakushev, the OGPU agent posing as a senior Trust official who had arrived in France on 18 August to make contact with General Yevgeny Miller and General Holsmann. Yakushev had quickly wormed his way into the confidence of the two ranking White Russian military leaders in exile, who arranged for him to meet the Grand Duke the following week. Their conference on 24 August lasted for three hours, according to Yakushev, who reported how they had discussed the situation in the Soviet Union and how the Trust and the Whites could co-ordinate plans and tactics for bringing about a *coup d'état*. Yakushev proposed that MOR, the Russian acronym for the Monarchist Organisation of Central Russia, would eventually be transformed into the Monarchist Party of Russia. Its political council would become the central committee to select the restored Tsar on the basis of who was best fitted as "the bearer of the supreme ideals of monarchism", for whom it would then act as adviser and nominator of Government members. Yakushev reported that the Grand Duke assured him "not only do I agree, but will not stop consulting you, or make a step without you, not only now, but in the future and will always seek your advice".[47]

The inveigling of Grand Duke Nikolay Nikolayevich helped pave the way for the Trust and the related Syndicate operations to become a remarkably successful stratagem, which helped the Soviets buy relative internal peace until the deceptions were exposed in 1926, six years in which they were able to consolidate their control over the sprawling Soviet Union.

The complexity of interlocking operations was such that the contemporary Trust file compiled by the NKVD alone comprises some thirty-seven volumes. Even historians of the Russian Intelligence

Service who have examined the records are left reeling by the files full of code names, which changed so often that they give the many interlocking deception operations the complexity of a symphonic score. These reveal that another major theme of the Trust was to orchestrate the feeding of disinformation to the Poles and, through them, to the British to provoke them to send agents like Reilly to attempt to subvert the Bolsheviks. Another important theme was a skilfully directed hoax to siphon not only cash and backing from emigré Whites, which might otherwise had gone to financing insurrections, but also to expose and entrap the surviving anti-Bolshevik underground in the Soviet Union.

Operations were also launched to promote a positive image abroad of the Soviet Union. One of these involved arranging for the publication in the West of a book entitled *Three Capitals*, written by Vasily Shulgin, a well-known monarchist supporter. The Trust arranged for him to be smuggled into Russia for what he believed was a secret fact-finding tour. His travelling companions were OGPU agents, who manipulated both what he saw and the impression he fed back to the Whites.

> "Shulgin, when reporting his impressions to the emigrés, said that, when he had set out on his trip, those who knew about it predicted he would suffer the same fate as Savinkov. Reviewing his impressions and drawing conclusions about MOR, he now says that, having met with more than twenty members of the Trust, he finds it hard to imagine that they could all be specially selected Bolshevik agents. None of them betrayed it by their attitude and actions and this had encouraged him to revise his suspicions."[48]

One of the principal targets of Soviet deception operations was Boris Savinkov, the implacable anti-Bolshevik Socialist revolutionary who had proved adept at fomenting uprisings and guerilla operations in Russia during the civil war. When his Russian People's Army had been defeated in 1920, Savinkov had taken refuge in Poland, where he headed the Russian Political Committee that began preparing for further incursions. With access to the still extensive anti-Bolshevik network in Russia, he proved a sharp thorn in the side of Moscow. Artusov's so-called *Sindikat* 1 operation was specifically directed at penetrating and neutralizing Savinkov's operations.

It began in the winter of 1921. Savinkov, who was then in Poland received a visit from Alexander Eduardovich Opperput (whose real name was Staunitz-Upelnitz), a representative of the Western regional

Committee (Byelorussia) of the Union for the Defence of the Motherland and Freedom. He succeeded in persuading Savinkov to revive the cause in preparation for igniting a fresh round of rebellions and Opperput became privy to the names and organizational structure of Savinkov's networks. Then in May 1921, Opperput was arrested as the Union for the Defence of the Motherland crumbled under the assault of the Soviet secret police. Unknown to Savinkov, Opperput – who also used the alias of Pavel Ivanovich Selyaninov – was then turned by the *Chekists* and he became one of the Trust's leading *agents provocateurs.*[49]

After forty members of the White underground had confessed in a round of well-publicized Moscow show trials, Savinkov was forced to leave Poland because of vigorous Soviet diplomatic protests to Warsaw. He then set up a new base of operations in Paris, this time funded by the British and French. In 1924 Savinkov became the principal target for *Sindikat* II, when two emissaries arrived from the USSR, posing as members of one of the surviving anti-Bolshevik underground groups. They presented a letter of support from a former aide and thereby succeeded in persuading the suspicious White leader of their *bona fides* and sought to persuade him to return to Russia to head a new underground movement against the Communists.

One of those whom Savinkov summoned to assist in his campaign was Sidney Reilly, who, after his escape to London in 1918, had returned to the Crimea later that year as a political officer for southern Russia on General Denikin's staff. After acting as an adviser to the British Government at the Versailles Peace Conference, Reilly had then continued to serve as an adviser to MI6 on Russian affairs, relaying intelligence from the Russian emigrés assisting Savinkov. At the end of 1920 he had helped organize an expedition to Byelorussia before returning to London, where, by 1922, he had come to the conclusion "that a more expedient means of fighting consisted in the agreements with the Soviet authorities that opened the doors of Russia to English commercial and trade ventures".[50] To this end he had returned to New York to pursue business interests, abandoning his first wife to marry Pepita Bobadilya, the Spanish-born widow of an English playwright. It was not surprising, therefore, that Savinkov should turn to Reilly to become the principal fund-raiser for the new operations he was provoked into mounting by the *Sindikat* agents. One of these *agents provocateurs* was Andrei Pavlovich Fedonov of the so called Liberal Democrats Organisation, a *Cheka* front, who had been introduced to Reilly by Savinkov. In disregard of Reilly's cautions, Savinkov agreed to be smuggled across the Soviet border on 15 August 1924 – only to end up in the interrogation cells of the basement of Dzerzhinsky's Lubyanka headquarters building. Within two weeks he had made a full confession and agreed to co-operate with the OGPU. This he did by calling upon his followers in the anti-Bolshevik underground to "bow before the power of the workers and peasants and recognize it without reservations".[51]

Savinkov's recantation and co-operation saved him from the firing squad. He received the relatively light sentence of ten years' imprisonment, which led some of his followers to conclude he had indeed been "turned" by his captors. When he fell into the inner courtyard of the Lubyanka a year later, it appeared to others that he had been pushed to his death. This, is not, however, the case according to the first-hand version given to Boris Goodze, a veteran OGPU and later GRU officer, who was serving at headquarters at the time. He recalls being told how Savinkov was indulging in a drinking bout with a group of *Chekists* in an upper room of the Lubyanka when he arose from the leather sofa and walked to an open window overlooking the courtyard. Whether he then fell out because of his stupor, or jumped was not clear to those present. But an OGPU officer by the name of Grigory Syroezhkin was just in time to catch him by the ankle. His arm, which had been weakened by a youthful wrestling injury, did not have the strength to hold on, however, and Savinkov plunged to the courtyard below.[52]

The success of the two "Syndicate" operations in drawing the fangs of surviving anti-Bolshevik underground members was exceeded only by the "Trust" deception. Artusov's bogus "Monarchist Organization of Central Russia" at the heart of this operation had been initiated in 1921 and continued running until 1927. Its financial transactions operated under the cover of the Moscow Municipal Credit Association, a financial trust fund supposedly established by undercover White dissidents under the dispensation of the New Economic Policy. Its principal targets were the influential Russian emigrés' organizations in Berlin and Paris, calling themselves the Russian Monarchist Council and the Russian General Military Union. Posing as Trust emissaries OGPU agents duped the head of the monarchist organization in France, the former Tsarist General Alexander Kutyepov, into betraying his contacts inside Russia. At the same time the inflated promises that investing in the Moscow trust would help bring down the Soviet Government enabled the OGPU's agents in France and Germany to penetrate the targeted emigré groups and sow dissension and suspicion.

The Trust soon grew into an international scam that also succeeded, through the Poles, in duping British intelligence and, to varying degrees, the secret intelligence services of half-a-dozen other European nations until it was exposed in 1927 as a huge hoax. Its most celebrated victim was Sidney Reilly, who, only a year after Savinkov's fatal journey had travelled to Helsingfors to meet with Trust agents. The deception had been carefully orchestrated by Artusov on the basis of disinformation that fooled Finnish intelligence and in January 1925 Yakushev, the OGPU agent posing as a senior Trust official travelled to Finland. He was accompanied by a former colonel in the Tsarist army by the name of Schukin, who was the OGPU agent posing as the Trust's Leningrad representative. In Finland they met Nikolay Bunakov, a White activist who had links to British intelligence and who wanted one of their agents – Sidney Reilly – smuggled to Moscow for a reconnaissance mission. Dzerzhinsky, who had earlier cautioned the initiators of the deception operations not to get mixed up with the British secret services because they were "as sly as foxes and they'll sniff you out" finally authorized an exception to be made to entrap Reilly.[53] Artusov's foreign counter-intelligence agents were accordingly instructed to lure the British spy back to the USSR, where he could be arrested and interrogated before the *in absentia* death sentence on him was carried out.

So important was this operation regarded that Soviet intelligence records show that it was supervised by Genrikh Yagoda. Reilly had already met with Trust representatives in Paris a year earlier; their *bona fides* having been vouched for by General Kutyepov and by Savinkov, before his capture the previous year. After Kutyepov had held a preliminary meeting with the undercover emissaries from Moscow, Reilly arrived in Helsingfors in the middle of September 1925, where he met Yakushev and Schukin.

"The first impression was unpleasant," according to Yakushev's report of his encounter with Reilly. "His bulging dark eyes expressed something biting and cruel; his lower lip drooped deeply and he was too slick – the neat black hair, the deliberately elegant suit." After Reilly's initial reluctance to travel with him and Schukin into Russia, Yakushev reported that he had persuaded the British agent to change his mind. The actual entry into Russia involved wading across the Sister river, which required the still elegantly dressed British agent to unwind and then rebandage the varicose veins on his legs.[54]

Having provided Reilly with a Soviet passport in the name of Nikolay Steynberg, the party made their illicit way across the frontier on 26 September. Their crossing was made near Vyborg, where the Finnish General Staff had arranged to turn a blind eye to a "window" across the frontier to keep in touch with the anti-Bolshevik resistance. It was pouring with rain, according to Yakushev, as they reached Peschanoe station, where they took the first train to Leningrad.

At a rendezvous at the Leningrad apartment of Schukin, Reilly met with Vladimir Andreyevich Styrne, an OGPU counter intelligence officer who was posing as a representative of the Moscow Trust council. That evening Reilly and Yakushev, accompanied by an unsuspecting White Guard emissary named Mukalov-Mikhaylov, left for Moscow where they arrived the next morning. Reilly was then driven by car to a dacha in Malakhuvka, where he expected to meet the Trust's leaders. After a hearty meal, they all gathered in a glade in the forest for security. Reilly promised to send some $50,000 for the penetration of the Communist International (Comintern as it was known) and the theft of art treasures. According to Yakushev's report, he was also offered a personal introduction to Winston Churchill if he came to England. Then, as dusk was gathering, Reilly bade the group farewell and got into the car he believed was to take him to Moscow's October Station to catch the night train back to Finland.

The driver and his two escorts were OGPU agents, who had been detailed to take the British agent straight to the Lubyanka. But while on the road back to the city, Reilly requested to be taken to a safe house where he could write to his English contacts to confirm that he really had been in Moscow. The OGPU guards then drove him to the apartment of the Trust agent, Opperput, on Maroseyka, from where he was taken, not to the railroad station, but handcuffed into cell 73 in the Lubyanka.[55]

While Reilly displayed cool self-possession during his first hour-long interrogation under the direction of Yagoda, another OGPU team set out for Leningrad. The following day, at the border near the village of Alakulya, where Reilly was scheduled to cross back into Finland, the Russians staged a fake incident. An exchange of fire, involving the arrest of the courier, Toivo Vyachi, and the supposed shooting of Reilly and Schukin was arranged. Two bodies were then loaded into a truck which had been driven up to the Russian side of the border in full view of the Finnish guards. The charade continued at an emergency meeting of the Trust's council in Moscow, where the OGPU counted on genuine White conspirators to relay news of Reilly's death back to the White emigrés in Helsinki. Some, however, refused to believe that Reilly really was dead, contending that he had merely been wounded and was being held in hospital under interrogation. This widespread belief was encouraged by Reilly's wife. She maintained that her husband survived after betrayal at the hands of the Trust, putting, as we now see from the Soviet records, the whole operation in jeopardy. The fear that the longer Reilly remained alive the greater the risk that their elaborate deception would unravel, spurred OGPU interrogations of their captive. To encourage him to open up Reilly was repeatedly reminded that he was under the death sentence passed on him seven years earlier.

Reilly quickly appreciated that his best chance of survival was to play for time by not revealing all at once the information about his undercover activities that Dzerzhinsky wanted in the hope that the British would arrange for his release. This is clear from the notes later discovered secreted in his clothing, bed and in cracks in the wall of his Lubyanka cell where he kept a personal record of his interrogations in anticipation that he would be able to make a full report to British intelligence on *Chekist* methods on his return to England. Preserved in the OGPU archival records, Reilly's disjointed notes of his ordeal provide a moving testament of how his courageous stubbornness was gradually eroded by the effective psychological techniques applied by his captors:

30 October. Late in the day. Changed into Soviet clothes. All personal clothing taken away. Managed to keep a second blanket. Was sleepy. Ordered to take an overcoat and cap. Room downstairs near bath. This iron door. Present in the room are Styrne, his comrade, stout jailer – young fellow (from Vladimirskya province), bailiff, possibly someone else. Styrne informed that GPU Collegium reviewed the death sentence and that only if I do not agree [to co-operate] will the sentence be executed immediately. Said this did not surprise me, my decision remains the same and that I am ready to die . . . Asked by Styrne, didn't I want time for reflection? Answered that this is their affair. They gave me one hour. Taken back to cell by young man and keepers helped. Prayed . . . made small package of my personal things, smoked some cigarettes, and after 15–20 minutes said I was ready . . . Explained again my decision and asked to make a written declaration in this spirit and that I am glad that I can show them how an Englishman and a Christian understands his duty. Refusal . . . they said that no one will know about it after my death. Then a lengthy conversation began, persuasion as usual. After approximately three quarters of an hour a heated conversation for 5 minutes. Silence, then Styrne called the bailiff and left. Kept waiting about 5 minutes, during this time loading weapons in outer rooms and other preparations. Then they came to the car. Inside were the bailiff, his soldier, young fellow, chauffeur and guard. Short trip to garage . . . Very cold . . . Endless wait . . . I decided that apparently I will be taken somewhere beyond the city . . . Adjournment 20 hours was communicated. Terrible night. Nightmares.[56]

Reilly spent much of that night, according to OGPU reports, alternately crying and praying before a small picture of his wife. The minutes of that day's interrogation session reveal why: he had finally broken and agreed to co-operate fully with his captors. The full text of the letter he penned that day was an abject submission to all their demands:

To the Chairman of OGPU
FE Dzerzhinsky

After the discussions that have taken place with V. A. Styrne, I express my agreement to co-operate in sincerely providing full evidence and information answering the questions of interest to the OGPU relating to the organization and personnel of the British intelligence service and as far as it is known to me what information I have relating to the American intelligence and likewise about those persons in the Russian emigration organizations with whom I had dealings.

Moscow, the Inner Prison,
30 October 1925
[Signed] Sidney Reilly[57]

The dam of Reilly's resistance had finally burst. For the next six days Styrne's debriefing records confirm that the "Ace of Spies" spilled the details of his many operations, including his visit to Churchill and his final mission for MI6 which had led to his trip to Helsinki.

"Hungry all day," Reilly noted on 3 November. "Summoned about 9 in the evening. Letter and messages from Styrne through Feduleyev. Six questions: Miller, Kils, the German's work, our co-operation – what kind of materials do we have concerning the USSR and the Comintern? China?"[58] Next day he recorded that he was "very weak" when he was summoned to another interrogation at 11 am which lasted until 5 and then, after a break for dinner, until 2 am the next morning. This time the questioners probed Reilly for information on Scotland Yard's operations against the Russian Trade Delegation in London and whether British counter-intelligence had really managed to insert their penetration agents into the All Russian Co-operative Society (ARCOS) in London.

"Calmed down with regard to my own death – I see great developments in the future," Reilly noted after the day's ordeal was over.[59] His hopes were to be dashed the next day. Yagoda concluded that prisoner No. 73, as he was known, was now engaged only in spinning out what information he had to buy time, in the hope that the British would arrange his extradition. Moreover, much of the information he supplied had already been duplicated by Trust's other penetration agents. Concern grew that any leak that Reilly was alive and giving depositions could expose the whole operation and endanger the lives of those OGPU operatives involved abroad in the Trust deception. Taking all this into consideration, it was decided that nothing more was to be gained by delaying the execution of the British agent.

Shortly after eight o'clock on the evening of 5 November 1925 a black car sped out of the inner courtyard of the Lubyanka, heading for the woods on the north-eastern outskirts of Moscow, beyond Sokolniki. Inside were Reilly and four OGPU officers, Feduleyev, Syroezhkin, Dukis and Ibragim. They had told prisoner No. 73 he was being taken for an outing. Reilly was therefore off guard three-quarters of an hour later when the driver of the car feigned mechanical trouble at a prearranged spot near Bogorodsk. Feduleyev suggested that they stretched their legs while the problem was dealt with.

"Leaving the car, I walked on No. 73's right, Ibragim on his left and Comrade Syroezhkin followed some ten steps behind," Feduleyev wrote in his official report. "After walking some 30–40 steps, Ibragim, from slightly behind us, shot No. 73, who let out a deep breath and fell without a cry." After shooting him again in the chest, they covered Reilly's head with a bag and drove him back to the Lubyanka. Telling the attendant that it was the body of a man hit by a tram, they carried Reilly's corpse to the medical office, where it was photographed clothed and naked. "The whole operation was completed by 11 in the evening of 5/11/1925," Feduleyev's report concluded. Four days later Reilly's corpse was secretly buried.[60]

Reilly's widow placed a mourning notice in *The Times* of London on 15 December, but she had still not given up hope that he was alive in a Moscow prison. Two years later, in February 1927, Pepita Bobadilya wrote a plaintive letter to the Soviet Ambassador in Paris requesting proof of her husband's death. When the request arrived at OGPU headquarters, it was assumed was that it was made not by the grieving widow but by British intelligence seeking to find out when its agent had died as a clue to how many of their secrets he might have been persuaded to betray.

Soviet records reveal that Reilly, who had been elevated – largely as a result of his own boasts – into Britain's master spy, had in fact given very little away that was not already known to the OGPU after his grovelling letter to Dzerzhinsky, promising that, in return for his life, he would become a turncoat and serve the Revolution by revealing all he knew about the British and American intelligence services. More importantly Reilly's capture by the OGPU had scored an important victory in disposing of the legendary master spy who had sold his services to the British – and to half a dozen other European intelligence services.

The thirty-seven volumes of Trust operational files reveal that Reilly was only one of the victims of a series of interlocking operations which amounted to a strategic deception on a scale never before attempted. For nearly six years the Soviets racked up success after success until the whole edifice was exposed two years after Reilly's death. The archival records show how, by early 1927, the Trust-induced, step-by-step gradualist strategy of the Russian monarchists' movement in Paris was already being overtaken by the more aggressive policy of terrorism advocated by General Kutyepov's deputy, General Yevgeny Miller. He had undercut the "wait-and-see" approach advocated by the OGPU agents under the guise of the Monarchist Organization. The decline of the influence of their agents prompted the OGPU chiefs at the beginning of 1927 to wind up the Trust operation. But the Soviet plan for orderly phasing out of their Monarchist Organization so as not to expose the monumental scale of the deception was to be frustrated by the untimely defection to the West of one of its leading protagonists.

Opperput, who, though not an officer of the OGPU, had become one of the most prominent of the Trust agents, learned of the impending termination of operations and decided that he might personally profit by changing sides and selling information before the final shut down. On 13 April 1927 he crossed the Finnish border and exposed what remained of the deception exercise including the fact that inflated information about the strength of Soviet military dispositions had for years been fed through Trust channels to Polish, Finnish and Estonian intelligence services in order to deter military intervention by the Western powers.[61]

After the deception had been blown, the equanimity with which Stalin reacted came as a surprise to the OGPU chiefs. Instead of the anticipated outburst, he announced that it was all for the good. The Trust and Syndicate deceptions had been dependent on presenting the Soviet Union as constantly prepared for fighting a civil war. While helping deter Western military intervention, Stalin said it did not give encouragement for anyone to do business with them and he announced that this was now a major objective.[62]

During its remarkable six-year run, the victims of the Trust deception had included not only Reilly but also thousands of White

Russians in the Soviet Union and Europe who realized too late that their networks had been riddled and betrayed from within. The Trust provocation had also duped many European intelligence services, demonstrating both the Communist regime's infiltration of Russian emigrés' groups and providing a timely warning that should have alerted the West that the OGPU had expanded its external intelligence gathering and penetration operations. Yet it was a lesson that went largely unheeded by European and United States authorities, who had been misled into believing that even if the Soviet regime could not be overthrown, then at least Stalin was now ready to do commercial business with the West. This was a posthumous victory for Dzerzhinsky, who before his death in 1926 had combined his roles as chief of both the state security apparatus and the Supreme Council on the National Economy by successfully deploying the OGPU to further Soviet foreign policy and economic interests.

Since the state security organization was not yet rigidly compartmentalized, Orlov, as a rising member of the Economic Department and as a friend of Artusov who had run Trust, would presumably have been privy to its broad objectives. Although the Syndicate and Trust operations had been run by the Counter-intelligence Department (KRO) the opportunity for exploiting their broader objective – to assist in the raising and channelling of foreign capital into the rebuilding of the Soviet industrial base – was the responsibility of Orlov's department.

One of the important outcomes of the Trust deception was the degree to which it prompted White emigré organizations to obtain increased secret funding from the intelligence services of various Western governments who were bankrolling them. This was achieved by the activities of Trust agents, who reinforced the impression that Lenin's New Economic Policy (NEP) heralded the eventual abandonment of Communism and the restoration of the capitalist imperative. It was one of the functions of the OGPU Economic Directorate (EKU) Department VIII, which was under Orlov, to lure gullible capitalist entrepreneurs to find hard currency desperately needed by Soviet industry. His primary responsibility, he later recalled, lay in "protecting the foreign trade of the Soviet Union from the pressures and abuses of the world cartels and other organizations of monopolistic capital".[63]

Western businesses and corporations, Orlov discovered, justified exacting unusually large profits and fees because Russia's credit was "none too good".[64] Such uncertainty, however, did not stop the scramble by Western capitalists for massive Soviet contracts at prices they believed they could dictate. It fell to Orlov's investigators to uncover their price fixing, so that they could be beaten down before the contracts received official Soviet authorization. This put him at the centre of a growing overseas espionage operation, since it was his department that monitored all such potential deals. This was achieved through OGPU officers attached to ARCOS in London and its sister operations in Europe. These Soviet trading outposts were rapidly transformed into beachheads of economic and industrial espionage. Tapping into the financially booming Wall Street was another important target of the OGPU's clandestine effort to raise hard cash. American investors – with their eyes on the prize of the potentially vast Soviet market – quickly fell victim to belief that the NEP signalled the impending demise of Communism. Lobbying by the business leaders of the US Government led to the Soviet trade mission establishing its first base of operations in the New World. The corporate front opened its doors for legitimate business in New York in 1924. Its acronym was AMTORG with its headquarters in Moscow,

Orlov was a member of the Economic Department responsible for overseeing AMTORG before he left Moscow at the end of 1925. His posting was prompted by the need for his expertise in guerilla warfare to command the OGPU frontier troops in Transcaucasia where he was charged with ensuring that the borders were effectively sealed off to prevent outside incursions that would disrupt Soviet operations to put down the growing disturbances among the perennially fractious Georgians. His appointment had the blessing of a native son, Stalin, who as Secretary General of the Communist Party had a keen personal interest in quelling the insurrections as he connived and manoeuvred the Politburo to consolidate his power after Lenin's death the previous year.[65]

Headquartered in Georgia's Black Sea resort of Sukhumi, Orlov as a brigade commander had six regiments under his control. But his 11,000 troops had to be spread very thinly. Policing the Soviet Union's extensive southern borders with Persia and Turkey was no easy task, since the wild mountainous terrain had for centuries been the refuge of bandits and insurrectionists. In this difficult posting Orlov demonstrated his flair for organization by getting the maximum effect from the minimum of resources. Dealing with the insurrectionists required working closely with the regional OGPU chief, Lavrenty Beria, a member of Stalin's "Georgian mafia" whom Stalin later promoted head of the secret police *apparat*.

Photographs taken during his duty in Sukhumi show Orlov the front-line soldier, bullet-head shorn of all hair and mustachioed with the barrel chest of a stocky prize-fighter. Obviously in the peak of physical fitness, he posed with his favourite horse, looking very much the assured commander of a brigade of frontier troops.

Orlov was accompanied on this posting by his wife and three-year-old daughter, Veronika. Called Vera by her doting parents, the child had inherited her father's sharp intelligence and her mother's good looks. She was the apple of her parents' eyes. For the first and only time he and Maria had the opportunity to pursue the happiness of a normal family life in the relative tranquillity and comfort of the Black Sea republic. Georgia's vineyards and bountiful small farms had largely escaped the ravages and the famines of the civil war. But even in this Soviet oasis of plenty and year-round warmth, far from the snows and intrigues of Moscow, tragedy stalked the Orlov family.

While out boating on a Tiflis lake one spring afternoon, Orlov had been unable to row his family ashore fast enough to prevent them all being soaked by a sudden rain squall. Vera developed a shivery cold and high temperature. At the time her parents brushed it off as nothing more bothersome than a lingering childhood bout of flu. Only later, after they had returned to Moscow the following year, were the Orlovs shocked when their doctor diagnosed rheumatic fever as the cause of Vera's failure to make a full recovery. Her prognosis was bleak, as the disease which damaged the heart was then incurable.[66] As the years passed and their only child's health progressively worsened, the devotion of her parents grew more intense. Orlov became increasingly fixated on his daughter's predicament and never gave up hope that, if not in Russia, then in some other country they might find a doctor who could cure his afflicted child.

The opportunity to get Vera abroad for medical treatment could well have been one of the factors behind Orlov's move to the Foreign Department of the OGPU in 1926. As a result of the steady expansion of the Foreign Department's control over Soviet external intelligence and subversion activities, the empire-building Dzerzhinsky had since Lenin's death sought to consolidate the intelligence operations. This brought the OGPU into conflict with the Communist International, whose primary mission was subversion.

The Comintern, as it was termed in Soviet jargon, had been Trotsky's brainchild. Set up under the chairmanship of Grigory Zinoviev, it had been packed by Moscow with international Communists eager to execute Lenin's grand design for Comintern to ignite national Communist parties in a chain-reaction global revolution. But the collapse of the Communist insurrection in Germany in 1923, which Zinoviev had precipitately ordered, proved only the most glaring demonstration of the stubborn refusal of the international proletariat to combust spontaneously. Nor had

Comintern proved any more successful when it came to handling espionage operations. While Zinoviev may not have been the actual author of the notorious letter purportedly written by him in 1924, it certainly echoed the general tenor of the intercepts of the Comintern cables by urging the British Communist Party to keep up the pressure on the Labour administration in preparation for the anticipated revolution. Its sensational publication, on the eve of the 1924 General Election in Britain, helped the Conservatives to topple the country's first Labour government, rebounding on Moscow to add to Zinoviev's discredit.[67]

The Comintern's failure to export the revolution was compounded as much by wishful thinking and poor intelligence as by the lack of enthusiasm of the international working classes. So, with Stalin's support, Dzerzhinsky before his death had used the OGPU Foreign Department to chip away at Comintern. He had obtained the Central Committee's authorization for INO chief Trilliser to veto any activities that threatened Soviet security and won the power to co-opt Comintern personnel to further OGPU intelligence activities. This steady erosion of his rival's fiefdom was encouraged by Stalin, who was one of Lenin's political heirs together with Zinoviev, Trotsky and the Moscow Party chief, Lev Kamenev. The uneasy quadripartite leadership had fragmented, when Stalin's machinations resulted in the expulsion of Zinoviev, Trotsky and Kamenev from the Central Committee of the Communist Party. This left the ambitious and wily Party Secretary as Lenin's sole heir.[68]

Stalin's bid for dictatorial power succeeded, because he maintained his alliance with the head of the state security apparatus, despite the demise of his ally Dzerzhinsky in July 1926 from a heart attack. The OGPU's network of secret police informers, its legion of intelligence agents and its own armed forces effectively came under his direct control when the succession passed to the first deputy chairman, Vyacheslav Rudolfovich Menzhinsky, a Russified Pole. But the heir to "Iron Feliks" was not cast in the same unyielding metal.

Menzhinsky's aesthetic manner was accentuated by gold *pince-nez* and his lack of a commanding presence, and a worsening heart condition denied him the stamina necessary to run such a large organization. What Dzerzhinsky's heir lacked in authority, he compensated for in his pliant submission to orders from the "Big Boss", as Stalin now became known.

Menzhinsky's own lack of ruthlessness was more than compensated for by his deputy, Yagoda. Aggressive, energetic and brutal, he now became the new driving force of the OGPU, while his chief was reduced by his angina to playing the role of the

Lubyanka's languishing diva who was obliged to receive visitors unable to rise from his office couch. If Stalin did not fully trust Yagoda, it suited his purpose that the pliant OGPU chief relied on his deputy to direct the full force of the secret police apparatus to crushing the larger land-owning peasants. After the 1927 termination of Lenin's NEP experiment with capitalism, these *kulaks*, along with other "profiteers", became the new demons to be exorcized from the Soviet state. It was Yagoda who organized and dispatched the armed OGPU squads into the Russian countryside to impose ruthlessly Stalin's collectivization of farms, while other OGPU units were brought in to supervise the rigorous industrialization demanded by the first Five-Year Plan.

The "sword" of the awesome state security apparatus Dzerzhinsky had forged now began cutting down the vestigial remnants of the very Revolutionary ideals it had originally been formed to shield. Once Stalin had installed himself as the undisputed leader of the Soviet state he was in a position to control the OGPU. After Dzerzhinsky's death, it was too late, as Trotsky discovered, to rally his forces. First banished to Alma Ata in Kazakhstan and then cast out into exile in Turkey, Trotsky was eventually to be murdered by an agent of the Soviet secret police apparatus that kept Stalin in his despotic authority until his death in 1953.

Orlov, like many other ranking officials at the Lubyanka, would also live to rue the day he so tamely acquiesced to this seizure of power by the Big Boss. But in common with all those for whom loyalty to Lenin's ideals had been the driving impulse of their professional careers, even the most prescient OGPU chief failed to appreciate the deadly significance of Stalin's betrayal of the Revolution until it was too late. The old guard *Chekists* were reduced to acting as obedient nursemaids of the Soviet state, dutifully administering Stalin's brutal prescriptions until they found themselves obliged to swallow the same poison. Orlov and the other veteran *Chekisty* had by that time become so much a part of the system that its inertia prevented them from stalling this sinister shift in the course of the Revolution. In Orlov's case, Stalin's assumption of control actually resulted in an advancement of his career. This came about because the OGPU had to devote more and more effort to feeding the insatiable appetite of the Big Boss for the secrets of foreign governments. The rapid expansion after 1926 in the scope of Soviet foreign intelligence operations provided Orlov with the chance to find his true calling.

In the summer of 1926 Orlov took up his first foreign appointment in Paris under the alias of Leon Nikolayev. According to the French entry stamp, his passport was that of a diplomat who was accredited to the Soviet Trade Delegation. This was Orlov's cover for his intelligence role as the "legal" *rezident* in France, as he admitted in a 1965 debriefing conducted by the CIA at the request of the French counterintelligence agency *Direction de la Surveillance du Territoire* (DST) whose domestic mandate approximates to that of the FBI in the US and MI5 in the UK.[69]

According to Orlov, his responsibility as OGPU *rezident* involved not only supervising security and watching over the political reliability of the Soviet embassy and Trade Delegation staff, but also collecting and forwarding intelligence. The OGPU agents worked alongside but not directly with the military *rezidentura* which was maintained and staffed by the military intelligence arm of the Red Army. While the Red Army focused its efforts on obtaining intelligence primarily of a military nature from its own network of informers and spies, the OGPU *rezidents* spread their net much wider.

As the OGPU representative in France, Orlov commanded one of the largest Soviet intelligence networks in Europe outside Berlin, which until the Nazi take-over of Germany in 1933 had been their principal base of operation. This was an unusually important post to be assigned to an officer as relatively inexperienced as Orlov and it attests to the regard in which he was held in the OGPU. According to his CIA debriefing Orlov indicated that he was in fact operating under the wing of Iakov Kristoforovich Davtian. He was the former chief of the Foreign Section of the OGPU, who under the alias of Davydov was accredited to the diplomatic staff of the Soviet mission at the same time in 1926. Christian Rakovsky was the Ambassador, but Orlov observed that the real power in the embassy was in fact wielded by Davtian. Rakovsky's authority, according to Orlov, had been seriously eroded because he had become the target of continual harassment by former White Russian officers with the assistance of right-wing French politicians campaigning for the restitution of France's considerable pre-war investments in Russia. Their interventions in Parliament would eventually lead to a rupture of diplomatic relations and thus to the recall of Rakovsky on Stalin's orders.

Orlov revealed to the CIA that it was Davtian who was responsible for recruiting Herbette de Monzie, who he characterized as a "pillar of the French political establishment". It was de Monzie who Orlov admitted alluding to in his *Handbook* as one of the political leaders in a "country in Europe" who maintained secret contacts with the Soviets and who acted as a go-between with the "agents of influence" in Parliament.[70] Shortly after leaving Paris, Davtian was rewarded by promotion to ambassadorial rank and the task of manipulating their agents in the French Parliament was taken over by a Soviet named Yelansky. Significantly, Orlov told the CIA in 1965 that he could not give any precise information on the actual identity or the party of the French parliamentarian "in the pocket" of the Soviets. It is significant to find that he insisted particularly that de Monzie's name not be communicated to the French although the DST files show that this is what the CIA promptly did!

Orlov also told the CIA that Dimitri Mikhailovich Smirnov, whom he knew affectionately as "Dima", was his assistant in the *rezidentura* in Paris in 1927. He was a former Pole, whose cryptonym was VICTOR and who operated in France under the alias of Dimitri Mikhailov. It was he, Orlov disclosed, who recruited the White Russian General Diakanov in furtherance of the Centre's objectives of penetrating emigré organizations in Paris. Smirnov, who succeeded Orlov in 1933 as "legal" *rezident* became one of his closest service colleagues. Yet for all his skill as an intelligence operative, Orlov disclosed that his friend was deceived by his wife and that the son born to the couple in Moscow in 1932 was actually sired by Fydor Alexandrovich Karin, a protégé of Artusov who had formerly been *rezident* in Germany under the cryptonym JACK.[71]

Orlov's other assistant at the Paris *rezidentura* was Dimitri Lordkipanadze, a Georgian whom he knew from his duty in Tiflis. Using the pseudonym of Zagarelli, he was on a special mission under Stalin's direct orders to induce a famous Menshevik, N. V. Ramishvili, who was then in Paris, to write a book on the revolutionary movement in the Caucasus. Stalin hoped thereby that his own contribution to the Bolshevik movement would emerge sharply from this work. But Lordkipanadze's failure to carry off the assignment earned him what was ultimately to prove the fatal enmity of the Soviet dictator.[72]

It is evident that while Orlov provided the CIA with some details of the personnel and organizational structure of the Paris *rezidentura*, others were deliberately misleading. But it is equally clear from what he supplied the French that he did not add much to his published account of his time in the Trade Delegation's operation when he wrote that his job was to focus on economic intelligence and espionage operations. This, as he himself wrote, "had little to do with studying the economy of foreign countries, but was created for the purpose of exercising state control over the Soviet export and import operations, and of protecting the foreign trade of the Soviet Union from the pressures and abuses of the world cartels and other organizations of monopolistic capital". When Orlov arrived at the Soviet Embassy that then – as now – was housed in an historic *hôtel* in the rue de Grenelle, the OGPU was in the final stages of taking over the intelligence functions and "active measures" that had formerly been carried out through the Comintern network. They included penetration and provocation operations, the cultivation of sympathetic Communists as informers and running active agents. According to Orlov, misinformation – or disinformation as it is now called – was also on an OGPU *rezident*'s agenda.[73] "The matter of deciding what information or rumours, if any, should be deviously planted within earshot of a certain foreign government is a question of high policy in itself and must be subordinated to the specific aims pursued by the Soviets' highest policy makers," Orlov later observed. "Misinformation is not just lying for the sake of lying: it is expected to serve as a subtle means of inducing another government to do what the Kremlin wants it to do or to frighten and bluff a foreign government into inaction or into the making of a concession to the USSR."[74]

The example that Orlov gave in his *Handbook* of an operation involving the French General Staff stated that they were supplied with pages from a German army report indicating that Hitler was planning to reoccupy the Rhineland, which had been demilitarized under the Versailles Treaty, as a prelude to an invasion of France eighteen months later. When the DST followed this up, the CIA elucidated from Orlov that the successful deception operation had been run by Boris Berman who directed the Disinformation Section at the Centre. Orlov, significantly, said he could not recall the details, indicating only that it was his belief that the channel used to plant the information was a Soviet agent named Oumansky who was personally connected with Pierre Laval. Oumansky was a Russian Jew who was a dedicated Communist. According to Orlov, after Oumansky had accompanied Laval to Moscow, the French politician who would later head the notorious wartime Vichy government gave him a gold watch as a souvenir. Yet when he was pressed for more substantive details, Orlov said he knew nothing more about the operation. He insisted he had only once met Oumansky by chance, in a compartment aboard the *Red Arrow* express train from Leningrad to Moscow.[75]

The information that Orlov supplied was tantalizingly inconclusive for the French. So too was his response when questioned about the secret police officer of an unidentified European country, who, he had stated in his *Handbook,* had informed the Soviets that "an influential cabinet member" was a "partner in a big narcotics ring". (This was in fact France's Minister of Justice.) Although Orlov admitted to the CIA that this startling information had been received "between 1926 and 1928" during the years when he was *rezident* in France, he claimed neither to recall the name of his informant in the French police nor to be able to identify him from a list of names supplied him by the DST.[76]

Orlov's apparently contrived memory lapses when it came to providing the crucial missing elements of these French cases is typical of the way he avoided answering the CIA's questions on the cores of these important cases. By 1965 when he was questioned at the request of French counter- intelligence such details were of purely historic importance and nearly three decades had passed since he professed his defection from the Soviets. Orlov in this – as in so many other cases – never really had the intention of making a clean breast of his ancient secrets. From what he did admit, however, it is clear, that during his first overseas posting he had been deeply involved in many important operations. Orlov had also learned "on the job" how to be an effective player in the clandestine games of intelligence. Although he had evidently arrived in Paris with a sound grasp of the so-called rules of *Konspiratsia* that governed Soviet intelligence operations from his counter-intelligence work, his time in France brought Orlov face to face with confronting the practicalities of undercover operations in a foreign country. Even in the Twenties, a Soviet intelligence officer had to deal with a confusing *argot* of espionage terms some of which would become familiar during the Cold War from the spy-fiction genre of writers such as John Le Carré.

"Tradecraft", as it was later to become known, has a special vocabulary for the language of Soviet espionage. This ranged from such obvious euphemisms as "meets" for clandestine rendezvous and "legends" for cover stories, to the arcane "*duboks*" or "dead drops" for sites for leaving messages, "books" for passports and "compatriots" for foreign Communists. A "*klichka*" was a code name; a "*podstava*" (literally "insert") was a "plant" or provocateur; a "*vnutrennik*" (literally "insider") was the name given to penetration agents and "*raschet*" (literally "final account") was the term applied to the physical liquidation of a hostile agent. Orlov, as a Soviet intelligence officer, also had to master all the practical tricks of the trade including how to throw off police surveillance by making convoluted journeys – switching public transport between buses and taxis was a favoured method. When it came to passing documents to contacts, libraries and the dark interiors of cinemas were favoured. According to Orlov, the OGPU in the 1920s and 1930s favoured particularly the use of the surgeries of "trusted dentists and physicians", which were the preferred sites for really important meetings.[77]

Distinguishing provocation agents from genuine informants required a sixth sense, according to Orlov. To make the point he related in his *Handbook* an incident that occurred in a Paris café during an exploratory "meet" with a high official of the French Ministry of

Commerce. The encounter, he tells us, was arranged in order to take stock of the bureaucrat, who had for some time been dropping hints to the Soviet trade delegate in France that he was prepared to co-operate with the Russians. As an earnest of his sincerity, the Frenchman had passed over a file of classified data concerning the trade policy of his government towards the Soviet Union. On the face of it he appeared a potentially valuable source, but there was something about the circumstances of this particular "walk-in"'s direct approach which had triggered the Soviet officer's suspicions. Instinct told him that he should exercise extreme caution following up the approach. To this end he took care to dispatch two of his most trusted agents to observe from the side-lines the meeting which he arranged should take place in the very unsuspicious surroundings of a busy Parisian bistro.[78]

The precautions taken proved fully justified. Orlov related that as soon as the Soviet officer sat down, he noticed two men a few tables away. "Those two men look like police agents," he says the officer remarked provocatively to the French official, who dismissed his concerns rather too quickly: "To me they look like typical middle men, brokers, I should say, who conduct their business from cafés."

After the Soviet officer had left, watching agents reported that the French Ministry of Commerce official had immediately gone over and sat down with the two men and engaged in an animated discussion. They had overheard a remark about the Comintern and various references to Russia and Russians, before one of the Frenchmen had then paid the bill and all three men had left in the same taxi!

In 1965 Orlov revealed to the CIA that the name of the French official was "Welman or Velman" whose responsibilities at the Ministry involved commercial affairs with the USSR. Orlov had become suspicious when he began turning over French papers that proved to be worthless. He said he had personally taken over the case in 1927 and insisted that Welman bring documentation relating to commercial treaties to a rendezvous at the Café Osner. This he did, insisting that they must be returned to him by the following day. Welman, who was normally punctual, was however late making this second meeting. This led Orlov to believe that he might have gone to the police and that a trap was being sprung for him.[79]

"Have you brought the papers?" Orlov recalled was Welman's first question. Convinced that the French police had their rendezvous under surveillance, as he described in his *Handbook*, he had taken steps to avoid being caught red-handed. He therefore told his French contact that he had not got the government documents with him and that they were in the hands of another of his colleagues who was awaiting them in another restaurant in the Bois de Boulogne.

They took a taxi there which enabled Orlov to have his own agents check that there was no surveillance at this second location. He then arranged for papers to be handed back, but left immediately afterwards. Orlov claimed that he had never told Moscow Centre of his suspicions. Although Welman had continued supplying documents over the next several years, Orlov remained convinced that this was one of a dozen cases where he was dealing with a double agent. Confirmation of his suspicion, he said, was that although the French documentation appeared at first glance to be very significant, on close examination it was of no real value. This suggested that in the parlance of espionage it was "chicken feed", low-grade information specially prepared by France's counter-intelligence service.[80]

"Thus," Orlov noted with a satisfaction that appears a little too self-congratulatory, "the crude attempt of the French police to plant a 'double' was nipped in the bud."[81] He also conceded that such close encounters with a rival intelligence service held a "peculiar kind of fascination" for him. While he had been taught to regard foreign intelligence officers as professional spies, Soviet officers thought of themselves as "revolutionaries carrying out dangerous assignments of the Party". Nevertheless there existed what he described as a "feeling of kinship". Encountering a foreign intelligence agent gave him, Orlov wrote "the same thrill and curiosity with which two enemy pilots sight each other over the wide spaces of the sky".[82]

Nor was Orlov's cloak-and-dagger work as an OGPU *rezident* in Paris restricted to operations against external enemies. He related how he was personally charged with picking up the pieces of some of the mistakes made during the early years, when Soviet efforts to build underground networks led to the dispatch of agents quite unsuited to setting up under cover as businessmen. Such efforts had proved a costly failure because, as he pointed out, most OGPU agents had no business acumen. Too many of the firms, which had been set up on a lavish scale in order to make the operative appear prosperous, proved disastrous failures when it came to luring potential agents. Moreover, the temptation provided by the abundance of funds to set themselves up in espionage which were provided by the local Soviet trade delegation had frequently turned undercover agents into embezzlers on a grand scale.

One of the first tasks Orlov had to tackle was an investigation of Yury Praslov, whose case he described in general terms in his *Handbook*. According to the details that Orlov provided the CIA – and which were passed on to the French DST in 1965 – Praslov was the first Soviet "illegal" *rezident* to operate in France. "He was an authentic

member of the service sent there to work under commercial cover,"
Orlov told the CIA, revealing that Praslov's operational code name was
KEPP. Although he could not be specific about the date when Praslov
first began operations he did furnish the CIA with details about the
investigation he conducted in 1926–7 when he was *rezident* in Paris
operating under the cover of the Trade Delegation.[83]

Praslov had been sent to Paris with a Latvian passport and
businessman "legends" in order to establish an export-import firm in
France. Orlov was not able to recall – once again – the name of the
company which Praslov had opened in a lavishly decorated headquarters. He did tell the CIA that he operated in France with another
agent named Bogwood, whom he had once encountered in Turkey.
According to Orlov it was Bogwood who had blown the whistle on
Praslov, resulting in the Centre's decision to order an investigation of
his comrade's commercial front. Orlov discovered that despite the
hiring of a large staff, Praslov's operation had failed to get either a
single business transaction to its credit – or to recruit one agent. He had
then turned for help to Mikhail Lomovsky, his friend who had been
the head of the Soviet Trade Delegation. He had agreed to assist
Praslov by turning over to Praslov's concern a huge volume of goods
exported from the Soviet Union – from which Praslov promptly
creamed off a large commission.[84]

The cosy business association between a supposed Latvian national
and the Russians not surprisingly attracted the interest of the French
counter-intelligence service. So close was the surveillance of Praslov's
firm by the *Sûreté Générale* that it prevented him from embarking on
any espionage operations. In the meantime the large volume of the
business passing through the Trade Delegation had put tens of
millions of francs at Praslov's disposal. After embezzling two million,
this Soviet agent was seized with remorse and decided to balance his
books with the assistance of luck and the gambling tables of the Casino
de Deauville.

When confronted by Orlov's demand to see the firm's books, a rueful
Praslov admitted he had lost nine million francs at the Casino, and he
told Orlov that he was ready to go back to Moscow "to be shot".
Praslov would undoubtedly have been liquidated on his return – had not
Stalin personally intervened with Trilliser. Praslov happened to be the
brother-in-law of one of the Big Boss's henchmen, so his appeal
prompted Stalin to an uncharacteristic act of magnanimity when he
ordered the former *rezident* to a concentration camp for five years.[85]

From first-hand experience of cases such as Praslov's, Orlov learned
how Soviet foreign intelligence operations were still amateurishly
ineffective. This was reinforced by the string of debacles in the spring

of 1927 that exposed the real weakness of the OGPU's foreign intelligence operations. That March the Poles had exposed a spy ring in Warsaw run by a White Russian general, then the Soviet trade mission in Istanbul was uncovered as an espionage front. In April a police raid on the Soviet consulate in Peking produced a large haul of incriminating espionage documents, and then the Swiss arrested the eighth member of a French spy ring run by Jean Cremet, a senior member of France's Communist Party. In May, a group of Austrian Foreign Ministry officials was arrested for supplying secret documents to Moscow. But the biggest coup against the Soviets, however, came when that month the British, acting on a tip-off from an informer, mounted a massive raid on the Soviet ARCOS headquarters in the City of London. The operation produced indisputable documentation that the Russian Trade Delegation was operating as the cover for one of the off-shore nerve centres in a global Soviet network of intelligence and subversion.

The impact of the ARCOS raid had a very direct affect on Orlov. After Stanley Baldwin, the British Prime Minister, announced the expulsion of both the trade mission and the Soviet embassy, the Paris *rezidentura* was ordered to take over the responsibility for running what remained of Soviet intelligence operations in Britain. The heart of the problem, he concluded, according to his *Handbook*, was that placing the OGPU's *rezidenturas* in the embassies and associated trade delegations made them lightning rods when disaster struck and their agents were uncovered. Discovery of the networks left the Soviet diplomats open to accusations of improper conduct, while their contacts in the local Communist Parties were branded as spies masquerading as a political party.

"Each time a spy ring working for the Soviets was exposed the trail led straight to the Soviet embassy with all the resulting adverse publicity," Orlov observed of the Soviet intelligence apparatus in the late 1920s. "What the Soviet Government wanted was to reorganize its intelligence operations on foreign soil in such a manner that if some of its agents were caught, the trail would not lead to the Soviet embassy, and the Soviet Government would be able to disclaim any connection with the exposed spy ring."[86]

Orlov experienced the problem at first hand when he was sent at the beginning of 1928 to serve as control chief of the Soviet Trade Delegation in Berlin, the principal European base of the growing Soviet foreign intelligence apparatus.

3

"INDUSTRIAL HELP, NOT ESPIONAGE"

WHEN ALEXANDER ORLOV departed for his new posting in Germany, he was obliged to leave his ill wife behind in Paris. Maria joined him later as a secretary in the Trade Delegation where she was soon elected the service member of the Party Committee.[1]

Orlov arrived in Berlin shortly after his thirty-third birthday, in January 1928, four years after a succession of Moscow-inspired Communist insurrections in the Weimar Republic. The Revolution may have failed to take root in Germany's postwar experiment with democracy, but the personal freedom embraced by the Weimar parliament had given the green light to a revolution in intellectual and sexual expression. The former capital of the strait-laced German Reich had become the hedonistic centre of Europe. Social behaviour had undergone a revolutionary change even as the frontiers of drama had been extended by the biting satires of Bertolt Brecht. The playwright's collaboration with the composer Kurt Weill brought the smash hit *Threepenny Opera* to the stage just two months after Orlov's arrival in Berlin. Sexual conventions were openly flouted in the erotic cabarets of the Kurfürstendamm. Its movie houses titillated audiences with *risqué* performances and Marlene Dietrich's portrayal of the *femme fatale* Lola Lola in *The Blue Angel* soon made her the city's most famous erotic export.

To a newcomer to Berlin in the late 1920s outward appearances were deceptive. Whether it was the flamboyant transvestite chorus line of the Eldorado cabaret club on the Mozartstrasse or the Russian diplomatic staff working at the Soviet trade mission on the Lindenstrasse, nothing in a city which acted as a magnet to hedonists and spies was quite what it seemed on the surface. Orlov himself became a part of that deception by assuming a false identity. His passport named him as Lev Lazarevich Feldel, an accredited trade counsellor.[2] But his real mission was not commerce, it was espionage, although this would not have been apparent to anyone who visited his office in the *Handelsvertretung die Sowjetunion*, as the Soviet trade mission's headquarters was known to the Germans. Housed in a monumental building a block from the Reichsbank and a short walk from the Soviet embassy on Unter den Linden, the Trade Delegation served as an imposing front for intelligence gathering.

Throughout the Weimar years, before the Great Depression brought the gangs of Nazi Brownshirts on to its streets with their raucous calls for Hitler to restore authoritarian power, Berlin was the spy capital of Europe. The *Handelsvertretung* was the nerve-centre for Soviet European espionage operations. The impressive size of the Trade Delegation's headquarters was an outward manifestation of the secret dimension of the conspirational relationship that had been forged between the USSR and Germany after the Weimar Republic had broken with the rest of Europe in 1922 to strike a deal with the Soviet Government. The Treaty of Rapallo, which had been signed in that year at the Italian seaside resort, had not only granted the Bolshevik regime *de jure* recognition, but had also granted them "most favoured nation" status. Opening the public door to an increasing volume of trade had also permitted the Soviets to set up espionage operations under the cover of Germano-Soviet commercial firms conducting legitimate business. Among the most prominent were *Deruta Deutsche-Russische Transport Gesellschaft*, the German/Russian Oil Company and *Garantie-und-Kredit-Bank für den Osten* AG. These were front operations modelled on Wostwag (*West-Oesteuropaeische Warenaustausch Aktiengesellschaft*), the Berlin trading firm founded in 1921 by the Ehrenlieb brothers, Aaron and Abraham. These two Polish-born military intelligence staff officers were assigned Red Army funds to set up their business front at 19 Schiffbauerdamm.[3]

The Rapallo agreement, which had inaugurated an era of close commercial collaboration between the Weimar Republic and the Soviet Union, also contained a set of secret clauses that enabled Germany to circumvent the restrictive edicts imposed by the Versailles Treaty. These were intended to keep the German armed forces demilitarized, but, throughout the decade before Hitler came to power, German navy, army and air force personnel secretly worked and trained in Russia. Working alongside Soviet technical experts, military personnel were able to continue development work on submarines, aircraft and tanks, an activity that was specifically banned by what many Germans resentfully regarded as the Versailles *diktat*.

One of Orlov's most important responsibilities at the Trade Delegation was to supervise the secret military contracts and purchases that the Soviet Union had made with Germany. In 1929, his principal subordinate in this clandestine arms dealing operation was Pavel Alliluyev, whose appointment had been authorized by Soviet Defence

Commissar Klement Voroshilov. Orlov was one of only a handful of top officials who knew that the man Moscow had sent to supervise the inspection of airplanes and motors purchased from Germany was the brother of Stalin's second wife, Nadezhda Alliluyeva. During the two years that they worked together in Berlin, Alliluyev became a close confidant and trusted friend from whom Orlov learned a great deal of first-hand information about the byzantine inner workings of the Kremlin. Alliluyev had lived in an apartment there since 1919, when his sister, a darkly beautiful seventeen-year-old whose strong will matched her striking oriental beauty, had married the forty-year-old Stalin. Their tempestuous marriage was to end tragically with Nazdezhda's suicide in 1932, a year after Alliluyev returned to Moscow from Berlin. Orlov would later learn directly from Alliluyev, whom he encountered again in Paris in 1937, that, despite the rumours that Stalin had shot her in a rage, his sister had in fact turned a revolver on herself to escape an unbearable marriage after a particularly stormy argument with her tyrannical husband.[4]

Stalin's decision to dispatch his brother-in-law to work under Orlov in Berlin was an indication of the importance he gave to the clandestine co-operation which brought the Soviet armed forces access to German weapons technology. As long as Stalin exploited the Russo-German relationship to re-equip the Red Army and air force, the collaboration served to reinforce the anti-French attitude of Russia's traditional European foe, Germany. This resentment reached boiling point when France's army of occupation in the Rhineland had moved into the Ruhr in 1923 after the Germans failed to meet their war reparations payments. But the hidden price Stalin exacted from Germany for this marriage of military convenience was a massive infiltration of Soviet agents into Germany.

Moscow's hopes of fomenting a second Bolshevik Revolution in Germany collapsed in the abortive Communist insurrections in various parts of the country in October 1923, but in the aftermath of what was a Comintern-inspired debacle came a dramatic increase in the espionage operations of the Fourth Department of the Red Army (RU) and the Foreign Department of the OGPU. To further the goals of Stalin's Five-Year Plan, the RU and OGPU agents operating from the *Handelsvertretung* launched a combined assault on the technological secrets of German industry. Their operations were directed towards stealing the patented chemical processes of the mighty I.G. Farben, purloining modern steel-making technology from Krupp and Rheinmetal, obtaining the engineering blueprints of Borsig and Mannesmann, and acquiring the latest developments in the electrical industry from AEG and Siemens. The officials of the Soviet Trade

Delegation – which acted as the principal clearing house for legitimate contracts and the cover for Soviet espionage networks – recruited staff and infiltrated Communist sympathizers into Germany's world-renowned scientific research establishments such as the Kaiser Wilhelm Institute, Berlin's Technical High School and the Luftfahrt-forschungs Institute.[5]

Orlov's part in many of the key operations was critical. He had arrived in Berlin just after the announcement of the targets of the first Five-Year Plan to rebuild the Soviet Union as a modern state. Stalin's impossible industrial goals had been set with scant regard to human cost or productive capacity – and Germany was the obvious source from which Russia could obtain the technological skills and scientific know-how for stoking Soviet industry. This was an essential part of Orlov's mission, and his past as OGPU intelligence chief in the Paris Trade Delegation involved him in a new brand of espionage operation which, at this juncture in the history of the USSR, became as important as military intelligence or political subversion.

"Its purpose was to assist in the industrialization of the Soviet Union by stealing production secrets – new inventions, secret technological processes, etc," Orlov later wrote, explaining how "the Soviet intelligence organizations abroad began to recruit into their networks engineers and scientists, and inventors working in the laboratories and plants of the largest industrial concerns."[6] According to Orlov, when he arrived in Berlin, the Soviet Union was already committed to buying large quantities of machinery and even whole plants from the West to fulfil the goals of the Five-Year Plan. Negotiations were under way with the Germans to purchase the patents of industrial processes, with German engineers contracted to go to Russia to instruct and train Soviet technicians in the new methods. But the price demanded for this technical aid was so steep that Stalin had instructed the OGPU to give priority to its agents to organize the stealing of the inventions and patents.[7]

The response was the establishment in 1929 of a new industrial intelligence division in the INO, the Foreign Department of the OGPU. Its mission was to obtain by illegal means what the Commissariat of Foreign Trade could not arrange through legal contracts or economical licensing of German industrial processes. It was operated in league with the Economic Intelligence Department, for whom Orlov commanded a large staff at the *Handelsvertretung* in Berlin. The huge building with its staff of Russians and sympathetic Germans was commensurate with its mammoth legitimate commercial turnover of hundreds of millions of marks in foreign trade.

In the years before Hitler came to power in 1933, the financial health of many famous German firms such as BMW and Junkers was critically dependent on their contracts with that section of the Trade Delegation anodynely designated The Engineering Department. This was the cover operation which arranged for the export to the USSR of German armaments banned by the Versailles Treaty. The personnel of this department, both Soviet and German, were carefully vetted by the OGPU officials strategically posted in the Personnel Department of the *Handelsvertretung*, who hired outside collaborators with the help of trusted members of the Communist Party of Germany (KPD).

The Red Army's Military Intelligence Department had also provided funds for the Lowenstein brothers, two German jewellers with secret connections to the KPD, to rent a store in Ritterstrasse which backed on to the Lindenstrasse office block. This provided clandestine access for Soviet agents on active industrial intelligence operations to the *Handelsvertretung* offices of Orlov and his GRU comrades. Subsidiary networks were also run from a satellite Trade Delegation office in Hamburg.[8]

"Sometimes the theft of all the necessary formulas, blueprints and instructions was sufficient to enable the Soviet engineers and inventors to reconstruct a complicated mechanism or to duplicate a production process," Orlov records.[9] But, despite this success, he noted how often the Soviets found that the human element – a special skill and engineering instinct – was missing when it came to duplicating a complex industrial process. Then it was necessary, according to Orlov, to find the appropriate German or other foreign engineers and induce them with financial rewards to go to Russia to train Soviet technicians. It was the Trade Delegation which then arranged for these trips to the Soviet Union to be carefully concealed by having German nationals travel via third countries using false papers. These were supplied by the OGPU's so-called *pass apparat*, the clandestine passport "factories" which the Soviets maintained in Germany and other European countries, operated by skilled forgers known as "cobblers" because they utilized the stitching and eyelet machines and dyes used by shoe menders to manufacture passports.[10] A "new" passport identity was necessary to conceal the fact that a particular German scientist or engineer was making an unauthorized visit to the Soviet Union.

"The fees paid by the Russians for such trips ran sometimes as high as $10,000 for a few days work," according to Orlov, who noted that, nevertheless, "the savings to the Soviets amounted to millions".[11] The example Orlov himself drew on to illustrate the success of his German operation was the detailed account he provided of how the OGPU stole the process for manufacturing industrial diamonds.

Increasing Soviet demand for the diamonds used in cutting tools essential to the expanding oil industry and metallurgical projects of the Five-Year Plan had led to Krupp's offer to supply their newly invented *widi*, as the artificial stones were known (from the German *wie diamant*, "like diamond").[12]

The Soviet Commissariat of Heavy Industry had immediately purchased a sample batch of *widi* for testing in drilling operations. When the hardness and high cutting-ability of the artificial diamonds had been established, the Commissariat decided to buy the production patent rights and contract with Krupp to build a plant to produce them in the Soviet Union. But when the two senior directors of the German firm arrived in Moscow, they drove too hard a bargain. Once the staggering price was announced at a Politburo meeting, Stalin, according to Orlov, had declared to OGPU chief Menzhinsky: "The bastards want too much money. Try to steal it from them. Show what the OGPU can do!"[13] The challenge was accepted and the appropriate orders went to the Trade Delegation in Berlin. The first step in what Orlov described as a "difficult assignment" was to locate the plant producing *widi* and discover the names of the inventor and engineers in charge of production.

The German selected for this mission was Dr B., as Orlov named his agent, a scientist at the Technical High School in Berlin. Through a professional colleague, he was able to discover that the Krupp plant making the industrial diamonds was located on the outskirts of Berlin. By going there and chatting with factory technicians in a *bierstube* near the works, and claiming he was working on a treatise on hard-metal alloys, they recommended he talk with the foreman in charge of the process, whose name was Cornelius. With the assistance of a Berlin police praesidium inspector, who, Orlov revealed, was also a secret Soviet informant, the home address of Cornelius was made available to Dr B. He then went to see the Krupp foreman and plied him with drinks and dinner. Flattered by the attentions of so eminent a scientist, Cornelius talked freely about the furnace in which the *widi* were formed under great heat and pressure. Its inventor was an engineer for whom Orlov used the pseudonym of "Worm", who, he said, had recently been fired by Krupp after he had set out to build another furnace for one of the industrial giant's competitors.[14]

"Worm" had been blacklisted by Krupp's, which effectively meant he could not get another job in the industry and he was, therefore, an easy target for the Soviets. Orlov related how Dr B. had only to pose as an intermediary for a Swedish firm interested in setting up an industrial diamond plant to break Krupp's monopoly to arouse "Worm" 's interest. For a 10,000 mark fee, he agreed to write a full technical report on the process. However, as an ardent member of the Nazi Party, "Worm" stipulated that he would only co-operate with the Swedes on condition they did not sell the diamonds to the Russians.

Working assiduously on Mrs "Worm" 's avarice with offers of an additional 1,000 marks a week and secretly paying her an allowance to buy clothes, Dr B. won her support. This became critical when word came from Moscow that, in addition to "Worm" 's production blueprint, they needed to have the inventor on hand for the construction and operation of the furnace, which revolved at high speed and temperatures to generate the great heat and pressure required to transform the graphite particles into industrial diamonds. Orlov noted how it took a week of badgering by the wife before "Worm" would agree to accept a two-year contract to work in Russia. The inventor then insisted on living in a first-class hotel in Moscow with a chauffeur-driven car as well as a contract for his former assistant from Krupp's. Mrs "Worm" continued to receive a separate allowance from the Soviets, which proved crucial in keeping her husband in Russia after he contracted rheumatic fever. Although his letters home were full of his hatred of the Soviet Union, his wife's newly acquired taste for high living in Berlin ensured that her husband fulfilled his contract in order to provide the Five-Year Plan with industrial diamonds at bargain-basement prices.[15]

Not all the OGPU's efforts to steal German technology proved as successful. Orlov recounted how, in 1929, a scheme dreamed up by Abram Slutsky, who was then deputy chief of the Foreign Department, backfired badly. It involved using an OGPU agent who was ostensibly fleeing the Soviet Union to set up a bureau of patents in Berlin. The firm's heavily advertised "positions available" and its manager's pretended anti-Soviet stance were expected to attract a flood of useful inventions as well as the chance to bribe and subvert inventors working for the German military. The agent whom Slutsky selected was the cousin of a German director with the UFA film studios, a man whose status would help establish the *bona-fides* of the bureau, which was set up in a lavish Berlin office suite with a $40,000 slice of OGPU funds.[16]

Orlov, recalling Praslov's failure in France, viewed the whole scheme with great scepticism, noting also that it cost $30,000 a year to keep the fake patent office in business. It proved a poor investment. No intelligence of any significance was gained by the operation and, from the flood of crazy inventions that poured into its offices, the only weapon which came into the bureau's hands was a small model of an artillery piece. The Commissariat of Defence had already received the blueprint of this owing to their secret agreement with the German

General Staff. The bureau also attracted police surveillance, leading to its being wound up in 1930. Unusually for the OGPU, Slutsky's agent who ran it was permitted to retire in Germany after giving assurances that he would not make any revelations to the authorities.[17]

Another Berlin intelligence operation which Orlov described in a way that suggests he was its instigator, started with high expectations, only to turn sour. This was the courting of a Russian- born German pencil manufacturer who had lost his factory and extensive holdings in the Revolution. After fleeing to Berlin with his family Mr C., who was identified only by his initial, was by 1931 living with his daughter in very straitened circumstances when he was approached by a representative of the Soviet Commissariat of Light Industry. He was made an offer it was thought he would not refuse – to return at a handsome salary to supervise the construction of a new pencil manufacturing plant in Moscow. The impoverished German industrialist jumped at the opportunity to restore his family fortune, but he soon found out that the offer was not made simply because Soviet schoolchildren suddenly needed his gold-embossed pencils. It was a lucrative bribe made only because the Centre had learned that his daughter was the personal secretary to the Japanese *chargé d'affaires* in Berlin and that she often worked for the Ambassador himself. According to Orlov, the OGPU lacked high-level sources of Japanese intelligence, so the chance of obtaining such access could not be passed up. However, when the father was told by his Soviet contact that his business deal was dependent on him persuading his daughter to bring home confidential Japanese military and diplomatic papers, he told his wife. The scheme collapsed when she protested violently that her daughter "would never be a spy".[18]

A painstakingly laid plan to exploit female sources which, Orlov noted, *did* succeed brilliantly was initiated in 1929, when one of his agents became romantically involved with a young secretary at the German Foreign Ministry. A blonde Nordic beauty who was a Nazi sympathizer, she was none the less unwittingly lured into becoming a valuable source for Soviet intelligence. Her lover persuaded her to bring him secret diplomatic dispatches to the Nazis by declaring he was an ardent follower of Hitler. Many successes were achieved by deceitful love affairs, but as Orlov observed, some even ended up in lasting marriages. He recalled how his former boss Artusov had chuckled over one particular case, observing: "This couple will have an interesting story to tell their grandchildren when asked how they happened to get married."[19]

Orlov would later justify his conduct of Soviet industrial intelligence operations in Berlin before the US Senate Committee, by asserting that in 1931 the Economic Department of the OGPU had estimated that the industrial cartels and trusts of the West which traded with the Soviets were overcharging by up to seventy-five per cent for goods and services supplied to Russian plants.

"I must confess that it was I," Orlov testified in 1957, "who in 1930 discovered the existence of a so-called gentlemen's agreement or bloc among the electric companies of the world."[20] He told the Judiciary Sub-Committee how one of his agents in Germany had provided him with dramatic confirmation in the form of a confidential memorandum sent out by the General Electric Company of the United States. "I remember a document signed by Vice President Mindor, a letter addressed to the German AEG company," Orlov said in his 1955 testimony, referring to a letter from a director named Bleiman to a director of the Swiss firm Brown Boveri which he said contained "a list of prices that ought to be charged to the Soviet Union, ostensibly because the Soviet Union's credit was no good". He explained that this revealing document had been obtained with the help of a pro-Communist German employee of AEG. It proved crucial, according to Orlov, in helping the Soviet Union eventually to break up this cartel that he said rigged "sixty to seventy per cent higher than normal prices" for electrical generating equipment and heavy motors supplied to the USSR.[21]

Just how effectively the Soviet intelligence *apparat* succeeded in their industrial espionage operations in Germany during Orlov's tenure at its Lindenstrasse nerve centre is evident from a 1930 report of the Union of German Industries. The *Reichsverband der Deutschen Industrie*, as it was known, had set up an office to combat industrial espionage, which estimated that annual losses by the end of the decade amounted to over 800 million marks or nearly a quarter of a billion dollars a year. Counter-espionage efforts mounted by German industry had little success because the Soviets had managed to plant a German Communist as a secretary in its head office. A contributory factor was the unwillingness of the Foreign Ministry of the Weimar Republic to upset relations with the Soviet Union. This led to the espionage cases that were uncovered in the 1920s not being rigorously prosecuted. Light sentences of a few months' imprisonment were the norm – even for the most flagrant offenders – and cases were hushed up to avoid public criticism of the German-Soviet pact.[22]

The mounting level of espionage activity from the Soviet Trade Delegation became too embarrassing to ignore. Towards the end of Orlov's posting, the Berlin police headquarters, which had established a special division to counter industrial espionage, revealed a threefold jump in reported espionage cases between 1929 and 1930, from 330 to over 1,000. Many were traced to Communist workers who were an essential element in the well-organized network charged with gathering industrial information and secrets under the direction of Soviet officials in the *Handelsvertretung*. It turned out that the Soviet Trade Delegation was more often than not linked to, or directly involved in too many of these cases to be ignored. The official rejections of complicity issued from the Soviet embassy and the Trade Delegation had become so frequent that the newspapers began referring to the patently ironical "the expected denial" or "the inevitable denial" from the Soviet spokesmen.[23]

"Is it not time that less politeness and more energy were shown?" chided the *Frankfurter Zeitung* in 1931. This demand followed the Soviet Trade Delegation's denial that one of their officials, Glebov, had contracted an Austrian engineer named Lippner to steal petrochemical secrets from the I.G. Farben plant in Friedrichshafen. The call for action became a clamour later that year, after a Communist trade union leader named Erich Steffen and twenty-five engineers from the I.G. Farben Industrie chemical plants in Frankfurt and Cologne were arrested. A month in jail persuaded Karl Dienstbach, the local official of the Communist Revolutionary Trade Union opposition, the RGO, to make a full confession of how Steffen's network was stealing information for the USSR.[24]

The German Foreign Ministry refused to sanction demands from Steffen's prosecution that the police search the Lindenstrasse offices. But Moscow was sufficiently alarmed at the potential for exposure for an official of the Soviet embassy whose code name was ALEXANDER, to be detailed to arrange Steffen's defence under the cover of a Communist front organization. But the attempt to smother the affair by buying the silence of the defendants and witnesses backfired when Steffen's secret letter ordering his RGO officials to describe their actions as "industrial help, not espionage" fell into the state prosecutors' hands.[25]

The public outcry over the affair and the relatively light ten- and four-month sentences handed down to Steffen and the other leaders of the Soviet espionage ring aroused a political furore. The Nazis made political capital out of the Government's leniency and the case led to a stiffening of the penalties for industrial espionage. A decree "for the defence of the national economy" was signed into law by President Hindenburg on 9 March 1932, increasing to five years the maximum penalty for stealing German industrial secrets for a foreign country. After Hitler became Reich Chancellor the following year, the death penalty was introduced for industrial espionage.[26]

The culmination of the Soviet industrial espionage scandal came with the assassination in Vienna on 27 July 1931 of Georg Semmelmann. Formerly an employee of the Soviet Trade Delegation's Hamburg office, he had for eight years been a trusted operative of the OGPU who had served jail time and been expelled from various European countries. But in the spring of 1931, the Centre concluded that the German girl whom Semmelmann had married made him a security risk and immediately dismissed him. Resentful at being cut off from his well-paid post with the *Handelsvertretung*, Semmelmann promptly announced his intention of suing his late employers. He then tried to put pressure on his former Soviet masters by writing to an Austrian newspaper threatening a series of sensational articles on Soviet espionage operations in Berlin and Vienna.[27]

Semmelmann's promise to reveal details of the Soviet intelligence services' illegal passport factories and their manipulation of the KPD to further military involvement in industrial espionage brought a swift response by the agents of Moscow. Andrei Piklovich, a Serbian Communist claiming to be a medical student, went to Semmelmann's apartment and shot him dead before calmly surrendering to the Austrian police. At his trial, which took place against the backdrop of demonstrations inspired by Communists in his support, the self-confessed assassin was acquitted and set free after his brazen admission that his shooting of Semmelmann was prompted by the "war to the end against capitalist rule". If Semmelmann had been allowed to live, Piklovich asserted that he would have betrayed many "proletarian fighters".[28]

Orlov, in his capacity as the Berlin Trade Delegation's senior intelligence officer, was vulnerable long before the Semmelmann affair burst into the headlines. The decision to recall him to Moscow in the April of 1931 appears to have been directly related to the mounting number of Soviet espionage scandals involving the Berlin *Handelsvertretung*. Pressure for a full police investigation of the Soviet operations had been building since January 1930, when the *Berliner Tagesblatt* had carried a news story linking the Soviets to the circulation of forged US $100 bank notes in the German capital under the sensational headline, "Who Counterfeits The Dollars?"[29]

"I learned about this operation of counterfeiting $100 bills in 1930," Orlov would later admit, testifying that he had found out that the operation was "directed by Stalin personally". He revealed that it had involved the purchase of a German bank to facilitate the distribution of the millions of forged American dollars. Since Orlov at the time was not only one of the ranking Soviet intelligence officers in Berlin, but had overall responsibility for economic operations, he must have known a great deal more about the carefully laid OGPU scheme than he ever admitted in his appearance before the Senate Internal Security Sub-Committee. The operation had begun the year after Orlov had arrived in Berlin, when in 1929 the Soviets had acquired control of the Berlin private banking house of Sass & Martini. The deal was effected through a front, a Canadian group, who then immediately sold the venerable finance house to a Mr Simon. He acted as an intermediary for Paul Roth, a former Communist member of the Berlin municipal council who was later discovered to be in the pay of the Soviet embassy.[30]

"The chief customer of the bank was a man by the name of Franz Fischer," Orlov disclosed. He himself claimed never to have met the OGPU operative who, towards the end of 1929, deposited $19,000 in forged US currency in the bank. According to Orlov, the forgeries deceived the untrained eye because they had been "well fabricated" by the Russian engraving and printing offices. What he did not, however, reveal in his 1957 testimony to the Senate Internal Security Sub-Committee was how Soviet agents had cultivated members of the staff of the US Government Bureau of Engraving and Printing in Washington DC to obtain genuine US bank note paper stock. Indeed, it was not until the Deutsche Bank had shipped the first batch of bills to the Federal Reserve bank in December that careful examination of the old-style $100 bills revealed minute telltale discrepancies in the engraving of the digits and in details of Benjamin Franklin's head.[31]

After the US Treasury issued a global alert on the forged $100 bills on 23 December, the Berlin police raided the premises of Sass & Martini. In its vaults they discovered more American bills and their subsequent investigation quickly uncovered the duplicitous Soviet ownership of the bank and the role played in passing the bogus bills by Fischer, who had since vanished. He was identified as yet another former employee of the Soviet Trade Delegation in Berlin, who had worked in the automobile section.

The scandal forced Stalin to abandon his counterfeit currency scam, whose Napoleonic scale became apparent during the next five years as the bogus US currency surfaced all over Europe, China and South America like pernicious oil slicks from the hoard of forged $100 bills. In December 1932 the FBI arrested Dr Valentine Burtan, an American heart specialist who was a Communist, together with his accomplice, a former German aviator posing as "Count" Enrique Deschow von Bülow. They were charged with passing $100,000 in spurious bills to Chicago banks and mobsters. The two were convicted and sentenced to fifteen-year prison terms, but the real mastermind behind the final act of the bizarre plot to flood the United States with counterfeit currency had made good his escape to Russia. He was later to be identified as Nicholas Dozenberg, one of the original founders of the Communist Party of the United States and a long-term Soviet underground agent who had operated a Soviet front company in the United States registered as Roumanian-American Films.[32]

The counterfeit American currency operation only survived as long as it did, Orlov insisted, because of Stalin's direct involvement. He testified that he knew the scheme had originally been planned by the *Valuta* section of the OGPU. Besides attempting to round up all the genuine US dollars privately held by Soviet citizens, it was decided to supplement this by printing $10 million of the counterfeit bills to raise hard currency to support the Five-Year Plan. As Orlov pointed out, it had been a reckless venture that demonstrated that the Soviet dictator had no regard for cost effectiveness. It was, he said, a "bizarre, foolish operation, because after all, nobody could distribute more than $1 million." But in a telling indication that he knew more about the affair than he disclosed, Orlov told the Senate Sub-Committee that, before leaving Berlin he had personally interviewed a "noted criminal" from Shanghai who had been arrested while in possession of a hoard of the counterfeit $100 Benjamin Franklin bills.[33]

"I was just curious to see a real common criminal for the first time in my life," was how Orlov justified his action to the American Senators in 1957. He said that he found the Chinese gangster, whose name he perhaps too conveniently could not recall, had purchased his release from the Berlin police by bribing them with half his store of forged currency. Given Orlov's track record in Soviet underground operations, such a disarmingly naive excuse appears far too disingenuous and unprofessional. He might have realized at the time that Stalin had ordered the OGPU to off-load the fake dollars on supposedly less sophisticated Chinese and South American banks once the counterfeit currency operation was uncovered, after the raid on the Soviet-owned Berlin banking house which served as the original outlet for the operation.[34]

Newspaper headlines accusing the Soviet Government of involvement in the fake US currency racket inflamed public indignation and served to focus the German police investigation on the activities of the Soviet Trade Delegation. Orlov's recall shortly after the scandal broke was a characteristic damage-control reaction by the Soviet intelligence *apparat*, removing their principals from the eye of a storm.

Orlov was particularly vulnerable to suspicion because of his previous posting in Paris, from 1926 to 1928, where in January 1930 there had been a sensational kidnapping of a General Kutyepov.

During his tour of duty with the Trade Delegation in the French capital, Orlov would have learned how the OGPU agents had penetrated the entourage of the chief of ROVS (*Russky Obshche-Voyensky Soyuz*), as the White Russian Military Union was known, who had long been a prime Soviet target. One of his leading associates was General Nikolay Skoblin, who had been recruited by the OGPU and opened the way to the penetration of ROVS and the kidnapping. After Kutyepov had disappeared from the streets of Paris, it later transpired that he had died from a heart condition aboard the Soviet steamer to which he had been taken after being chloroformed by his Soviet abductors.[35]

Orlov admitted to the FBI that he had learned about the General's abduction and manner of death when he returned to Moscow for a briefing at the Centre. Although he claimed to have known nothing about the operation until two months after the kidnapping, he told US Senators in 1957 that he learned the details only after his recall in 1931. He said he had been in Artusov's office when the chief of the Foreign Department took a telephone call from Yasha Serebryansky, Kutyepov's kidnapper, who had been arrested in Romania while on another "executive operation", as the OGPU then referred to its kidnapping and assassination missions.[36] Artusov had expressed concern, according to Orlov, that Serebryansky might reveal the operation and the location of the General's burial site. This, he explained, would have exposed the members of the OGPU's penetration network to discovery by the French police. Their subsequent investigation into the Kutyepov affair, although inconclusive, had been spurred on by well-informed revelations about the subversion and espionage operations run from behind the high, whitewashed walls of the Soviet legation in the rue de Grenelle.[37] These allegations were made by Grigory Bessedovsky, who in October 1929 was the Soviet acting *chargé d'affaires* when he made a dramatic escape over the embassy wall, pursued by gun-toting OGPU security guards. Bessedovsky had been a close friend of Orlov during his first posting in Paris. According to what he told the CIA, the diplomat's defection had been mishandled by Yanovic, Orlov's successor as *rezident*, after the Centre had dispatched a former docker named Roisenman to investigate Bessedovsky's loyalty after allegations that he was a disloyal Ukrainian nationalist. According to Orlov Roisenman had ordered Bessedovsky to "put a bullet in his head". Bessedovsky knew a great deal about Soviet clandestine operations in France and gave away a great deal to the French police. Although he did not know it at the time, Orlov said that he later discovered that as a result of their close friendship, his cover as Nikolayev was the only item that Bessedovsky withheld in his debriefings.[38]

The stories of Soviet abduction, assassination and espionage plots filled the headlines of the world's press – and the investigatory files of European police and counter-intelligence bureaux. These could well have given Orlov cause to reflect on the drawbacks of running espionage operations from inside the Soviet embassies and trade delegations in Paris and Berlin after he returned to Moscow in April 1931, and so have helped reshape Moscow Centre's overseas operations. As he later observed: "What the Soviet Government wanted was to reorganize its intelligence operations on foreign soil in such a manner that, if some of its agents were caught, the trail would not lead to the Soviet embassy, and the Soviet Government would be able to disclaim any connection with the exposed spy ring."[39]

Orlov told his American debriefers that on his return to Moscow Artusov, his boss, had proposed that he go abroad again immediately to fence the crown jewels of the Romanovs, but that he had managed to decline the mission.[40] The OGPU records, however, give no indication that Orlov or anyone else was ever tapped for such an operation at this time and that his principal job was head of Section VIII, the economic intelligence department of the INO. In this capacity he could have contributed to the recasting of the way in which the Soviet intelligence *apparat* conducted its foreign operations. He had not only first-hand experience of the Paris and Berlin stations, but was also at the Centre when the so-called "illegal" *rezidenturas* were established to run the OGPU operations abroad through underground stations having no connection with the legations and trade missions. Orlov was therefore at the Lubyanka during the dramatic expansion in the scale of the OGPU's internal operations to enforce the collectivization of Soviet agriculture.

What was proclaimed as the "Second Revolution" was initiated on Stalin's orders when, heedless of the terrible human and financial cost, the armed troops of the state security forces were dispatched throughout the USSR to terrorize the peasantry and workers. The OGPU played a leading role in imposing the collective farm policy as well as pressuring industrial workers to meet the impossible goals set by the first Five-Year Plan. The forced collectivization caused the terrible famine of 1932–3 which led to spontaneous peasant opposition and uprisings against the Party in the hitherto productive farmlands of the Ukraine, revolts that were savagely repressed by OGPU troops.[41] Although Orlov was involved in the reform of foreign operations, during two years at Moscow Centre he would, as a senior *Chekist* with many contacts in other departments, have been aware of the monumental suffering and brutality being inflicted on the starving masses as Stalin employed the OGPU to enforce Party *diktat*. A quarter of a century later he would cite this knowledge as one of the factors which contributed to his decision to defect in 1938.

"Since 1931, when the brutal policy of farm collectivization caused a famine in the USSR, I was completely disillusioned in the Communist Party and the Kremlin's policies," Orlov stated at his 1954 examination before the US Immigration Service.[42] What he did not explain was why it took six more years for him to rebel, or why he had continued to serve with equanimity in the upper reaches of an increasingly dehumanized secret police. Nor did Orlov ever admit to sharing in any measure the collective responsibility that the members of the OGPU certainly bore for acquiescing in Stalin's take-over of their *apparat*. Like many of the other old-guard revolutionaries, Orlov appears to have remained aloof and blinkered by his aspiration to Leninism until it was too late to affect the tyrannous course of Stalinist repression; he then chose to flee when the reign of terror turned on the loyal *Chekists* like himself.

In the FBI interrogations of Orlov that have been declassified, he carefully evaded revealing any details of the role he had played during the crucial years when Stalin imposed his personal authority over the OGPU. His service records show that Orlov had actually headed Section VII of the Foreign Department, which was responsible for co-ordinating economic intelligence. But he would tell the Immigration and Naturalization Service inspector in 1954 that, from 1931 to 1933, he "worked in an export flax trust for the Soviet Union" where he "was in charge of personnel about two years". He did admit that he had travelled to the United States with a passport bearing the name Lev Leonidovich Nikolayev, arriving in New York aboard the German liner ss *Europa* on 23 September 1932. The visit, he said, was simply an official one arranged with the Soviet Trade Delegation by General Motors, four of whose executives attended his admission hearing and posted a $500 bond that he would observe the terms of his three-month visa.[43]

The records of the special inquiry held by immigration officials in New York on 26 September 1932 confirm that Nikolayev – as Orlov claimed to be – denied having any American relatives. But, when questioned by the Immigration and Naturalization service in 1954, he admitted he had "found two" by ringing up dozens of familiar names in the telephone directory and "asking if they were born in Russia". FBI investigators later established that Orlov had, in fact, contacted a far wider circle of old Bobruysk friends than he admitted. They also discovered that he must have lied at the 1932 immigration hearing by declaring that he was not a Communist. Orlov would later justify this deceit by claiming he was only observing standing Soviet instructions which forbade any of their officials to disclose any affiliation with the Communist Party.[44]

Orlov's operational mission, if any, during his three months in the United States in the fall of 1932 is not detailed in his KGB dossier which only reveals that the purpose of his trip was to obtain a genuine American passport to use for his underground missions in Europe. He would tell the FBI how he visited a General Motors automobile assembly plant in Detroit and looked up his Jewish cousins in New York. But it is now clear that his movements were never properly established, although investigators did discover at the time that Orlov had enrolled on a year-long English language course at Columbia University as Nikolayev. This was clearly inconsistent with the requirements of his three-month visa and US Immigration records show that he sailed for Europe aboard the ss *Bremen* on 30 November.[45] It may be a significant clue to his activity that Columbia University happened to be the *alma mater* of Americans who became Soviet agents: it was whilst at Columbia that Elizabeth Bentley and Whittaker Chambers, amongst others, admitted that they had become members of the Communist Party of the USA.

While contemporary Soviet records have not yet been found that link Orlov to any specific recruiting operations, his file contains genuine American identification papers. The red-covered passport No. 566042 bearing the State Department seal and signature of Henry L. Stimson was issued on 23 November 1932 in the name of William Goldin. Describing the bearer as 5 ft 8 in with black hair and brown eyes and having been born in Russia on 20 July 1899, it states his occupation as SALESMAN. The confident attitude of a dapper, bespectacled Orlov sporting a neat moustache and a broadly striped silk tie in the photograph identified by William Goldin's signature reflects the satisfaction he must have felt at assuming his new American identity.[46]

Orlov deliberately deceived the American authorities again when he claimed in 1954 that he did not work "for about a year" after his return to Russia from his visit to America, before he "began working for Intourist". He also said that he had been "director of the Visa Department" before becoming "deputy chief of railways and sea transport of the NKVD" in 1935, occupying this strange post until the summer of 1936, when he was posted to Spain.

This, as Orlov well knew, was only partially true since it was a common administrative practice in the Soviet intelligence service to "park" an officer just returned from overseas in another more lowly internal service department or directorate until another posting abroad, or until a commensurate position in the Foreign Department was freed for him.[47] In fact the Soviet archives reveal that after a second abortive mission to Paris in 1933 to set up a new underground station to penetrate French military intelligence, Orlov went on to play a major role in the development of one of the Soviet Union's most important penetrative operations: the Cambridge network in Britain. Then, as Stalin's secret police chief in Spain Orlov is shown by the documents to have acquired detailed knowledge of and been personally involved in the recruitment of agents who served in the Berlin section of what the Germans dubbed the *Rote Kapelle* – the Red Orchestra of Soviet underground agents whose secret communications with Moscow helped determine the course of World War II.

The insights that Orlov had into these two historically most significant espionage networks were arguably the most important secrets he successfully concealed from the FBI and CIA. It is therefore an appropriate juncture at which to halt the narrative account of Orlov's remarkable career in order to examine the new evidence in the KGB archives about the Berlin section of the wartime Soviet espionage network. This was the so-called Red Orchestra, which haemorrhaged secrets to Moscow by clandestine radio transmissions from Communist agents all over the Third Reich. During the most critical period of World War II, this network was controlled singlehandedly by one of Orlov's closest associates, his former assistant, Alexander Korotkov.

4

"DANGEROUS GUESSWORK"

THE BERLIN SECTION of the *Rote Kapelle* had its genesis, according to the Soviet records, in the visit of a pro-Communist delegation of German academics to Moscow in August 1932. As head of the Economic Intelligence Section VII of the OGPU it can be assumed that Orlov would have received notice of the visitors who were leaders of an association opaquely called the Society for a Planned Economy.[1] The secretary of this pro-Soviet group, which had been formed on the pretext of studying the planned economy of the USSR under the banner of *Arbeitsgemeinschaft zum Studium der Sowjetrussichen* or ARPLAN for short, was a thirty-one-year-old academic named Arvid Harnack. A government official from the province of Thuringia who had taken a doctorate in economics from Giessen University, Harnack was the scion of a distinguished Baltic family who had settled in Darmstadt, where his father was a professor at the *Technische Hochschule* and his uncle was a respected German theologian, after whom the well-known institute Harnack-Haus had been named. But in common with many young Germans who graduated from *Gymnasium* in the years immediately after World War I, Harnack passed up university at eighteen to join the *Freikorps*. These freewheeling paramilitary bands of nationalistic young Germans, many of them demobilized and unemployed war veterans, were later to become Nazi storm troopers. Armed and led by disgruntled officers of the defeated *Reichswehr*, the violently anti-Bolshevik *Freikorps* terrorized the Poles and Balts in the disputed eastern territories of Weimar Germany. In March 1920 a certain Captain Erhardt led the *Freikorps* units which ousted the Republican Government from Berlin in a putsch that briefly installed Wolfgang Kapp, an extreme right-wing politican, as German Chancellor.[2]

Shortly after the Berlin insurrection had been put down, Arvid Harnack grew disgusted with the bully-boy violence of the *Freikorps*. After being captured in a clash with the Communists in Silesia on his release he left his unit in order to pursue a belated academic career, graduating four years later with distinction in legal studies. After receiving a Rockefeller Foundation scholarship he continued his post-graduate studies in Britain and the United States. At the University of Wisconsin in Madison he met a vivacious American student named Mildred Fish, who was to become his wife. By then a Social Democrat, Harnack began to take a deep interest in the workers' movement. Within two years after his return to Germany in 1928, he was awarded a doctorate of philosophy at Giessen. By 1931 Harnack and his wife had become committed Marxists. After studying the history of Lenin's plan for building a Socialist state in the USSR, he had completed the transition from right-wing patriot to fervent, if not openly avowed, Communist.[3]

In common with many German intellectuals in the decade before Hitler came to power, Harnack chose not to wear his Communist political sympathies on his sleeve by openly joining the KPD (*Kommunistische Partei Deutschland*). Instead he became a member of the ARPLAN Society and a year later, in 1931, joined the *Bund Geistiger Berufe* (BGB), the so-called Union of Intellectual Professionals, one of the "cover" organizations set up by the KPD to extend its influence among academics, scientists and civil servants. According to a contemporary report received by the OGPU from Comintern sources, the BGB had been formed with the aim of "spreading ideological influence in those circles of the intelligentsia that, for various reasons, were hesitant to join a mass movement". It had been specifically constructed to appeal to German nationalists by its founder Professor Friedrich Bernhard Lenz, who according to the Comintern report, "sympathized with the Soviet Union and whose intensely patriotic views convinced him that only by allying with the USSR could Germany escape the consequences of the Treaty of Versailles and provide for the restoration of the former power of the German state".[4]

While Harnack and the other members of the German delegation were in Moscow in 1932, they were carefully scrutinized as potential underground agents by Soviet intelligence officers assigned to VOKS, the Russian acronym of a Soviet organization styling itself the "Association for the Maintenance of Cultural Relations Abroad". This organization sponsored national societies for cultural relations, and it had associates in many European centres of learning including Oxford and Cambridge, drawing its membership largely from the Communists and the left-wing. The group had maintained close links with a Soviet diplomat in Berlin named Alexander Hershfeld, and the contemporary records show that the Centre's interest in Harnack increased after he joined the staff of the Ministry of the Economy in April 1935.

The Nazi seizure of power had convinced those in German left-wing intellectual circles that only with the help of the USSR would they turn the tide against National Socialism. This set the stage for Harnack's career as a Soviet source which began when the Centre earmarked him for recruitment as an undercover agent. The mission was assigned to Hershfeld. The minutes of the chief of the Fifth Department of the Chief Directorate of State Security (GUGB) of the NKVD (as the OGPU was renamed after its reorganization as a department of the Interior Ministry in 1934) indicate that Artusov issued instructions on 15 July 1935 "to consider and expedite preparations for Harnack's recruitment".[5]

Hershfeld may not have been a professional intelligence officer, but Artusov decided that, because the diplomat knew Harnack personally, he was qualified to undertake the initial sounding out. The critical first meeting took place in Berlin on 8 August 1935, lasting "for about three hours", according to Hershfeld. His subsequent report to Moscow related how Harnack had gone to great lengths to clarify the conditions of his co-operation with Soviet intelligence and how he intended to combine it with his Party and anti-Fascist activities. Since this was contrary to the Centre's rules, Harnack was told that he would have to abandon such potentially risky activity and break off his secret association with Communist fronts by severing all ties with the now outlawed KPD. Hershfeld reported that he had explained in great detail to Harnack how dangerous it would be to try to continue with his open anti-Fascist activities and that, by going underground, he could achieve far more in the struggle against Hitler.[6]

Harnack consented to the Soviet terms and was assigned the code name BALT in the NKVD's underground network of German informants. Alexander Belkin, a regular intelligence officer whose NKVD cryptonym was KADI, was dispatched to Berlin as Harnack's first control officer. Belkin was also a close colleague of Orlov, who later became his deputy in Spain. It was through an exchange of messages with the Centre in the spring of 1938 about Harnack and another initial member of the Berlin network, that Orlov knew the full extent of the development of the Soviet penetration of the Nazi Government.[7]

Belkin had been the midwife of Harnack's network of high-level sources covering German industry and the military, many drawn from his associates in the pro-Soviet ARPLAN and BGB groups. Harnack was encouraged to spare no effort to establish a cast-iron cover for his underground activities. This he achieved by joining the National Socialist Union of Lawyers, becoming the leader of the section in his own ministry. He was also elected to the Herren Club, an exclusive professional circle of prominent German manufacturers, aristocrats, bureaucrats and high-ranking officers from the army, navy and air force. Many would in turn become valuable sources of the intelligence Harnack started passing, via Belkin, to Moscow.

Harnack's rapid rise to prominence as a valued Soviet source was assisted by his wife Mildred, who was head of the Union of American Women in Berlin, and a close acquaintance of Martha Dodd, the daughter of the US Ambassador to Germany.[8] The couple's widening circle of diplomatic friends increased his value to the NKVD and at the same time enhanced his position in the Economic Ministry office, where his main responsibility was US-German trade relations. His extensive contacts not only made him more valuable to the Soviet intelligence service but it also provided Harnack and his wife with a convincing disguise for their clandestine work for Moscow. Outwardly they gave every appearance of being the perfect Nazi couple. The success of their cover was confirmed by LIZA, the code name of a trusted NKVD intelligence source in Berlin who provided the Centre with an independent assessment that began with a shrewd estimate of Mildred Harnack:

> She is bold, tall, blue eyes, large figure, typically German-looking, [although] a lower-middle-class American, intelligent, sensitive, loyal, very much the German *frau*, an intensely Nordic type and very useful. He came from a good family, German theologian and philosophy background, middle-class, well educated of a well-to-do family. He is also blond, blue eyed (wears glasses), of medium height, stocky and when last seen very Nordic looking. They were intensely cautious in their technique of making contact, diplomatic in the extreme with other people, giving every impression of being highly trained and disciplined. Both of them maintained good contacts with Nazi women and men. Arvid was not suspected at the time and had an important post in the ministry. I am sure that, unless I have been profoundly deceived, they are completely reliable and trusted people from our point of view.[9]

Just how well the tempo and future direction of the key Berlin section of "The Red Orchestra" developed can be judged from the extent of Harnack's NKVD file. Captured Gestapo records, on which all previous assessments by Western intelligence agencies and historians of the *Rote Kapelle* have been largely based, had not reflected either the early origins or the true extent of the Soviet intelligence operations in Germany. The contemporary records show that Harnack became an important NKVD source two years earlier than previously suspected by the Gestapo, who assumed he was the ringleader of the network run by Soviet Army intelligence when they arrested him in 1942. Moreover, many members of the Berlin groups escaped the Gestapo round-up and were not betrayed by Harnack or any of those who were caught and interrogated.[10]

The Harnack agent file contains a remarkable diversity of information supplied by him during the three years after his recruitment. Some of his most important informants were former acquaintances in the BGB group, including Baron Wohlzogen-Neuhaus, a senior representative in the technical department of the OKW, the military supreme command known as Oberkommando Wehrmacht, who was assigned the code name GREEK. Others were Hans Rupp, a leading accountant of I.G. Farben Industrie, whose cryptonym was TURK; Tizien, an emigré White Russian manufacturer with high-level contacts in OKW and the code name ALBANIAN; and Harnack's step-nephew, Wolfgang Haveman, a naval intelligence officer in the High Command of the *Kriegsmarine*, who was given the code name ITALIAN. Harnack, who was given the new code name CORSICAN, was an important source in his own right. In the Ministry of the Economy in Berlin he held the official rank of *Regieurungsrat*, which gave him access to all the documentation and reports pertaining to the foreign trade of the Third Reich.[11] With his access to such a wide network of informants to draw upon, Harnack was able to provide Moscow with a growing stream of high-grade intelligence before World War II. Its importance can be judged from a contemporary summary of the information received by the Centre from Harnack by June 1938:

Valuable documentary materials on the German currency and economy, secret summary tables of all Germany's investments abroad, the German foreign debt. Secret lists of goods liable to importation into Germany. Germany's secret trade agreements with Poland, Baltic countries, Persia and others. Valuable materials concerning the secret foreign service of the German Ministry of Propaganda. The foreign policy department of the Party and other organizations. Also documentation concerning the currency financing of the different German intelligence services, etc . . .[12]

Apart from the intelligence directly from Harnack himself and the sources in his own network, his NKVD dossier shows that he had identified and assisted Soviet undercover agents to target and recruit other important independent agents. One was Karl Behrens, who worked in the design department of AEG, Germany's pre-eminent heavy electrical engineering contractor. In 1935 Harnack put Soviet intelligence in touch with this secret Communist sympathizer. Assigned the Russian cryptonym LUCHISTY (German STRAHLMAN), Behrens was to provide many technical blueprints that assisted the Soviets to develop their electrical engineering industry.[13]

The impunity with which Harnack operated while building up his network owed much to the Centre's ability to monitor the Gestapo through their agent Willy Lehman. But the reports of this key informer, whose code name was BREITENBACH, and the information reaching Moscow from Harnack were disrupted in the summer of 1938 by the consequences of Stalin's purge of the NKVD, that swept away thousands of the *Cheka* old guard.[14]

Orlov avoided the bloody fate that mowed down many of his contemporaries in the Foreign Department by making good his flight from Spain while the recall and execution of some of the NKVD's most experienced field officers wrought havoc with the running of its underground agents. One of the most badly hit was the Harnack network; five of the eight intelligence officers in Berlin were recalled to Moscow and shot for alleged treason. Virtually every officer who was involved in the NKVD's "legal" and "illegal" field stations in Germany fell victim to Stalin's paranoia. The operation of the Berlin networks ceased completely as far as supplying information to Moscow Centre was concerned. Harnack and other German sources found they were cut off from any contact with the Soviets. Considering the importance of the information they were supplying from the heart of the Third Reich at a time when Stalin was negotiating an alliance with Hitler, it is evident that the Big Boss had sliced off his nose to spite his face. The Great Purge had effectively cut the Kremlin off from accurate intelligence on German foreign policy intentions during the two years leading up to Hitler's decision to plunge Europe into war.

Harnack waited, in vain, fifteen months from June 1938 until September 1940, for the prearranged telephone call that would summon him to meet his new Soviet control officer. It was not until the morning of 17 September that his contact with Moscow was restored when a tall, thin man knocked at the door of his Berlin apartment at Woyrschstrasse 16.[15]

The early caller, who introduced himself as Alexander Erdberg, was an NKVD intelligence officer who, that August, had been posted under diplomatic cover as a Third Secretary to the Soviet embassy in Berlin. This is the Russian agent who was incorrectly identified by the Gestapo and later cited in *The Rote Kapelle: The CIA's History of Soviet Intelligence and Espionage Networks in Western Europe 1936–1945* as "the Russian who recruited Arvid Harnack around December 1940 in Berlin".[16] But, as the NKVD file shows, by that date Harnack, code-named CORSICAN, had been a Soviet agent for more than five years.

Access to the NKVD records puts the *Rote Kapelle* in a new perspective. On the basis of the captured Gestapo files it had been assumed that this important Soviet network in Germany was primarily a military intelligence operation run by the Red Army. Now it is clear that its most important element, the Berlin network, was an NKVD operation. The Soviet archives also reveal that Orlov's former assistant Alexander Korotkov was Alexander Erdberg. Known as SASHA to his comrades, Korotkov's first operational posting in 1933 – as the following chapter will recount – was as Orlov's deputy in the "illegal" NKVD field station in France. Korotkov's file reveals that the route by which he had become a top-flight Soviet intelligence officer was unusual, even in those exceptional times. He had started his career in the Lubyanka headquarters as an elevator operator in the headquarters maintenance department. Recommended to the Foreign Department by Yagoda's personal secretary, Veniamin Gerson, with whom he used to exercise at the NKVD sports club known as Dynamo, Korotkov nonetheless survived the purges that cost his friend his life and sent his mentor Orlov into exile. He rose through the Lubyanka hierarchy and in the early 1950s he became head of the Illegals Directorate of the KGB.[17]

Korotkov had learned his tradecraft as an agent handler with Orlov in Paris, subsequently working in Germany before "visiting" Norway and Denmark in 1939. A tall, thin man, his apt first operational cryptonym was DLINNY, the Russian for "long". Korotkov proved as resilient as his wiry physique. Following the purging of Yagoda in 1936, his friendship with the secretary of the deposed NKVD chief put him under a cloud of suspicion that dogged Korotkov's career until 1939, when he was peremptorily discharged from the service. He reacted in a way that few of his contemporaries dared, by challenging the decision to dismiss him. In a letter to the NKVD chiefs he questioned the reason for his dismissal and to his surprise the notice was withdrawn. Within weeks Korotkov was entrusted with one of the most important missions of his career, when he was posted to Germany with the aim of reviving Moscow's contact with CORSICAN. He was also charged with restoring the Centre's links to another Berlin network which can only be identified by its code name FÜRST, in addition to reviving Lehman, their source in the Gestapo, code named BREITENBACH.[18]

Orlov's former assistant arrived on Harnack's Berlin doorstep that September morning in 1940. Korotkov assured CORSICAN that he was "a friend of Hershfeld" who badly needed Arvid's help. According to his report to Moscow, Korotkov found Harnack very guarded and suspicious that the caller might be a Gestapo provocateur. That is why Erdberg, as Korotkov called himself, did not pursue any questions at this first encounter. Instead he proposed that they make a rendezvous a few days later before bidding CORSICAN goodbye.

That same afternoon Korotkov sent an encyphered telegram from the Soviet embassy on Unter den Linden to Moscow. It reported that he had succeeded in restoring contact with CORSICAN and he proposed meeting Harnack by car and driving him in secret into the Soviet embassy, where they could talk without risk from the Gestapo.[19]

Korotkov's plan was approved and as soon as Harnack realized that he was dealing with a genuine Soviet intelligence officer, he explained the reason for his cautious reaction at their first meeting. Six months earlier in March he had been subjected to investigation by the secret police after the Berlin Gestapo had received an anonymous tip-off that there was a *Regierungsrat* at the Imperial Ministry of the Economy who had formerly been a Communist sympathizer. The Gestapo, according to Harnack, had conducted a very thorough investigation of him because he was a State Secretary in charge of trade policy at the American section, with the authority to see and sign secret documents. Thanks, however, to the iron-clad cover he had constructed for himself, he was perceived to be a model Nazi bureaucrat and the Gestapo investigators quickly ran into a dead end. The allegations were dismissed as a malicious attempt to bring Harnack into disrepute.[20] The experience had been harrowing. The Gestapo's well-wisher, as Harnack knew only too well, had tugged at a thread that could have unravelled his network and endangered the lives of dozens of secret Soviet sympathizers in the upper reaches of the Berlin Government. The anonymous informant had come dangerously close to exposing one of the NKVD's most important sources of intelligence in the Nazi Government. This made both Harnack and his Soviet control officer very careful about how they arranged future contacts. Their concern proved justified. The CORSICAN file shows that by 1940 Harnack's network had grown to encompass sixty strategically placed sources, of whom fifteen were absolutely reliable anti-Fascists, as Korotkov told Moscow:

> CORSICAN, after losing contact with us in 1938, continued his proselytizing work among the intelligentsia along the established lines of the BGB, avoiding any connections to the KPD. With the assistance of his wife, he has personally vetted old acquaintances from the Union, carefully selecting and drawing in new recruits. At

present, within the larger circle, centres have been formed, each of which is dedicated to the education and training of a small group. Although CORSICAN himself cannot personally vouch for every person, every one of these sixty people, the whole network is drawn exclusively from people who have the same background, think alike and come from the same social strata. CORSICAN's description of the way that they camouflage their operations is that, while not all of the members of the circle know one another, something of a chain exists. CORSICAN himself tries to remain in the background although he is at the heart of the organization. The aim of them all is to prepare personnel to occupy administrative posts [in the German Government] after the *coup d'état*. CORSICAN himself has had no contact with the Communist Party.[21]

Korotkov's report on CORSICAN's organization aroused concern at Moscow Centre because Harnack's violation of the compartmentalization required for NKVD underground networks had increased its vulnerability to exposure and penetration by the Gestapo. There was also the concern that Harnack was primarily building his network as a secret anti-Fascist conspiracy and only secondarily exploiting it as a source for Soviet intelligence. What Korotkov did establish and convey to Moscow was that Harnack would never have agreed to abandon his crusade against Hitler simply to become a channel for the transmission of the secrets of the Third Reich to the USSR. This was eventually accepted by the NKVD chiefs, who instructed their man in Berlin to conduct "a very careful treatment of Harnack so that a wall of distrust did not arise between him and his operator".[22]

The Centre realized that there was no other choice but to run the risk of running CORSICAN's network on Harnack's terms. By the autumn of 1940 events had reached an historic turning point, following the fall of France that June, which had left Hitler master of Europe. The RAF may have saved Britain from invasion by beating back the *Luftwaffe* in the Battle of Britain, but an unconquered England was an encouragement for Germany to turn eastwards. Stalin knew that the Nazi-Soviet Pact signed the previous year was little more than a brutally cynical marriage of convenience. Reports were already reaching Moscow from Soviet undercover agents that, even as Hitler continued sending out peace feelers to Britain, he was preparing for an eastern *Blitzkrieg* to carry out his long-promised crusade to rid the world of Bolshevism.[23]

Barely one week after contact was re-established with the CORSICAN network, on 26 September 1940 Korotkov received from Harnack what was the first firm intelligence report that military preparations for an attack on Russia were under way:

An officer of the supreme command of Germany (OKW) has told CORSICAN that by the beginning of next year Germany will be ready for war with the Soviet Union. A preliminary step will be the military occupation of Romania, which is planned for the near future. The objective of the campaign will be to occupy western European Russia along the Leningrad–Black Sea line and the creation on this territory of a German vassal state. The remainder of the USSR is to be constituted into a state which is friendly towards Germany. At a conference of the Economic Warfare Committee, its chairman, Rear Admiral Gross, dropped hints that the general operations against England are being postponed.[24]

The yellowing hand-written note appended to Korotkov's crypto-gram in the NKVD file indicates that the Chief of the Directorate for State Security had immediately transmitted this alert to the RU RKKA (later GRU), the Intelligence Directorate of the Red Army. CORSICAN's file shows that the flow of accurate military information on German preparations for war against the Soviet Union increased dramatically after December 1940, when Harnack recruited a *Luftwaffe* lieutenant into his network. This important new source was Harro Schulze-Boysen. He was the thirty-one-year-old son of a career navy captain from Kiel, the great-nephew and a godson of Admiral von Tirpitz, who had been the driving force behind the Kaiser's naval ambition and the architect of Germany's World War I battle fleet. But the young Schulze-Boysen had eschewed military service to study law and politics at the Universities of Freiberg and Berlin, where he had been inspired by humanist ideals. He joined the nationalistic Order of Young Germany (*Jungedeutsche Ordnern*) before becoming a Socialist, when he made a point of living in a workers' tenement in the blue-collar district of east Berlin. The experience led him to embrace Communism and, in 1932, he began publishing an openly anti-Nazi magazine *Der Gegner* (*The Opponent*). This led to his arrest in 1934, following Hitler's ban on left-wing opposition parties and trade unions. Schulze-Boysen was interrogated at Gestapo headquarters, where one of his editors had died under torture. He himself served only a short term of incarceration in a concentration camp before he was freed through the intervention of Hermann Goering, who happened to be a close friend of the Schulze-Boysen family.[25]

The experience served not only to increase Schulze-Boysen's opposition to the Nazis, but also taught him the need of going underground by appearing to embrace Nazism. On Goering's recommendation he enrolled in the School of Transport Aviation, where he graduated as a flight observer with distinction and then obtained a post in the Air Ministry. His fluency in foreign languages enabled him to pursue a career in the *Luftwaffe* counter-intelligence bureau, where his rapid rise through the ranks of the Fifth Department of the General Staff was assisted by Goering. The future *Reich Marschall* was the guest of honour at Lieutenant Schulze-Boysen's 1936 wedding, when he married Libertas, the grand-daughter of Count Oldenburg und Hertfeld, who had been a close friend of Kaiser Wilhelm II.

Despite her aristocratic lineage, Libertas Schulze-Boysen was an intelligent, internationally educated woman who shared her husband's hatred of the Nazis. She wholeheartedly helped him form a clandestine anti-Fascist circle in Berlin whose leading members were Gisella von Pollnitz and Walter Küchenmeister, a self-educated art historian and Communist Party member whose KPD contacts included Kurt and Elizabeth Schumacher, who became part of the CORSICAN network. After receiving word that the Nazi secret services were planning to foment a Trotskyist rebellion in Barcelona in 1937, Schulze-Boysen and Gisella von Pollnitz conspired together to deliver a secret warning in French – to disguise its source – that was handed in to the Soviet embassy in Berlin.

Arvid Harnack had first come into contact with the like-minded Schulze-Boysen in 1935, but it was not until five years later that they began their secret co-operation. By that time the *Luftwaffe* lieutenant headed a group of some twenty people united in their determination to work for Hitler's overthrow. Among those in Schulze-Boysen's circle who had direct access to military secrets of the Third Reich were a ranking counter-intelligence chief in the Air Ministry named Gertz and a Major Gregor, a secret Communist who was a liaison officer for Goering responsible for contacts with the Ministry of Foreign Affairs. Another prominent source of Schulze-Boysen's was code-named SCHWED (not to be confused with Orlov, who had the same cryptonym), a captain whose name is not given in the files but who served as an *aide de camp* to Field Marshal von List, the commander of German troops in the Balkans.[26]

The military information which Schulze-Boysen began relaying through Harnack to Moscow was soon to become so important that, on 15 March 1941, the Centre instructed Korotkov to make direct contact with SENIOR – the code name assigned to Schulze-Boysen – to encourage him to form his own independent network.

"Last Thursday CORSICAN brought us together with SENIOR," Korotkov reported from Berlin on 31 March. "SENIOR realizes perfectly well that he is dealing with a representative of the Soviet Union, and not the Party. He gives the impression that he is fully prepared to tell me everything he knows. He answered my questions without an evasion or intention of concealing anything. Moreover, he had prepared for the meeting and had put down on a piece of paper certain points to pass over to us." At the same time Korotkov was careful to take Harnack's advice about how to handle Schulze-Boysen.[27] "CORSICAN had warned us of the necessity of accepting that SENIOR, as he put it, is a fervent Decembrist who should be left with the feeling that his Party work, which he worships, should not become mere espionage," the Centre was told. "Contrary to CORSICAN, who makes great plans for the future and trains his people for the time when the Communists come to power, SENIOR seems to us to be a more energetic person who concentrates on the need for action to achieve and bring about the changes which CORSICAN dreams of."[28]

After the NKVD had established direct contact with Schulze-Boysen, the CORSICAN and SENIOR files show that relieving Harnack of his role as an intermediary made the work of both sources more productive. It was through the Harnacks that Schulze-Boysen established contact with the author and playwright Adam Kuckhoff. His wife Greta had been another German student at Wisconsin University and Kuckhoff was the leader of another anti-Fascist circle identifying itself as "Creative Intelligentsia". Through Harnack's cousin they also established links with the Social Democrat secret opposition to Hitler led by Karl Goerdeler, the former mayor of Leipzig, who was to be executed for his part in the July 1944 plot against Hitler. Another member of Kuckhoff's circle was Adolf Grimme, a leading Social Democrat and associate of the trade unionist named Wilhelm Leischer, whose own underground opposition group included Berlin's *Polizei-Präsident* Graf Wolf von Helldorf, who had assembled a damaging dossier on the Nazi leadership.[29]

The potential value of such a group to Soviet intelligence was considerable. On orders from the Centre, Korotkov arranged with Harnack to meet Kuckhoff on 19 April 1941. The playwright readily agreed to co-operate with the Russian in supplying information and was assigned the cryptonym OLD MAN. His network became the third major element in the Berlin section of the *Rote Kapelle*, as revealed by a chart in the CORSICAN file. The decision to tap the intelligence sources provided by these interlocking groups of anti-Nazi conspirators was not taken lightly in Moscow because their amorphous and divisive nature violated the strict security rules under which the NKVD customarily operated their underground espionage rings. But the exigency of the spring months of 1941, which brought increasingly ominous indications of an impending attack on the Soviet Union, explains why the Centre allowed Korotkov to act as the contact man for all three networks using the cryptonym STEPANOV in his secret communications with Moscow.[30]

When it came to passing on military intelligence in the run up to the German invasion on 21 July, the SENIOR files show just how accurate a source of intelligence Schulze-Boysen was. His access to strategically valuable military information derived from his work at the Air Ministry, where he processed secret intelligence reports received from Germany's air force attachés. The depth and detail of the intelligence he passed on to Korotkov was not simply to do with the *Wehrmacht* but also provided the Soviets with an insight into German intelligence against the United States, as is evident from a May 1941 report received from the Berlin field station:

> SENIOR knows for certain that the American air attaché in Moscow is a German agent, he communicates to German intelligence information which he, in his turn, receives from contacts in the USSR and American citizens working in Soviet industry. STEPANOV requests caution when using this information as SENIOR is one of the few people who knows that the American is a German agent.[31]

The Centre checked the information about the US air attaché in Moscow and wired back an affirmation to Korotkov that "SENIOR's report about the American air attaché has been partly confirmed by our information". It was through Schulze-Boysen that Moscow learned that the Persian military attaché in Berlin had contracted his services to the British as an intelligence agent and that the Germans had broken the Persian code system – after bribing a rug seller to steal it in return for a licence to import and sell his carpets in Berlin.[32]

The NKVD files also disclose, in the run-up to the German attack on the Soviet Union, the accuracy and range of the intelligence warnings CORSICAN and SENIOR supplied. It is astonishing to find that they were all dismissed by Stalin. The list of summaries of their reports received by the Fifth Department of the Chief Directorate of State Security from September 1940 to June 1941 amounts to eleven pages in the CORSICAN dossier, providing an intelligence blueprint of the forthcoming German invasion.[33]

As January 1941 began the Soviets received warning that the *Luftwaffe* was about to make intensive reconnaissance flights over the frontier and Leningrad. In the following weeks Goering transferred the Russian sector to the active section of the air force staff, while the army began distributing maps of industrial targets in the USSR. By March news came that Hitler had decided on a spring date for the invasion because the Russians would not be able to burn the still-green wheatfields which the Germans intended to harvest. OKW predicted that the Red Army would be able to resist the *Wehrmacht* for little more than a week before it would be smashed and the Ukraine occupied to deprive the Soviet Union of its industrial base. Confirmation was also sent to Moscow that the campaign against Britain had been postponed, signalling an eastward movement of German forces. By April Schulze-Boysen had told Moscow that the Luftwaffe battle plans had been completed and would focus on destroying railroad junctions in the western part of the USSR and on knocking out the Donetsk coalfield and the aviation plants in the Moscow region. By May it was clear that the attack, originally scheduled for that month, had been postponed by at least four weeks. In June word was received from CORSICAN that the operation was imminent when he sent a list of the German officials who had been appointed to take over the economic management of the conquered Russian territory.[34]

Finally, just five days before the German *Panzer* divisions rolled across the Russian frontier at dawn on 22 June, after one of World War II's most murderous artillery barrages, Korotkov relayed to Moscow from SENIOR the *Luftwaffe* order of battle in an ominous and explicit final warning that concluded: "All German military measures for the preparation of an armed attack on the Soviet Union have been fully completed and the blow can be expected to fall at any moment."[35] So important did the NKVD chiefs consider this cryptogram that it was sent directly to Stalin as soon as it was received. Testimony to the cynicism with which the Soviets' supreme leader reacted to this warning is the obscene dismissal of the 16 June report which had been passed on verbatim to him by the deputy NKVD chief Vsevolod Nikolayevich Merkulov: "To comrade Merkulov. You can send your 'source' from the German air force staff to his whore of a mother! This is not a 'source' but a disinformer. J. Stalin."[36]

How, it must be asked, could Stalin possibly have rejected this final and explicit warning? It confirmed months of specific reports from CORSICAN and SENIOR which reinforced other intelligence of German invasion preparations that the NKVD files show the Centre received from agents in Germany, Poland, Romania, Britain and even the United States. It seems incredible that both the Kremlin *and* the Red Army could have been taken by surprise by Operation Barbarossa, as Hitler had christened his crusade against Russia.

Stalin may have had grounds for rejecting as "provocation" the alerts of the impending attack that Churchill had relayed to him, warnings based on carefully disguised ULTRA intelligence derived from intercepts of the German *Luftwaffe* ENIGMA code machine signal traffic.

Since he dismissed the corroborating stream of accurate intelligence relayed to Moscow from agents such as Harnack and Schulze-Boysen, this must raise fresh questions about the factors behind the intelligence debacle that constituted the Soviet Union's "Pearl Harbor". The new revelations serve to accentuate the conundrum which was debated on both sides of the Iron Curtain for half a century. Was Stalin so mesmerized by his secret admiration for Hitler that he was blind to the possibility that the *Führer* would stab him in the back? Or did the intelligence directorates of the NKVD and the GRU misread and misconstrue the evidence of the impending attack just as their American counterparts did before Japan's surprise attack on the Pacific Fleet base on 7 December 1941?

The Soviet archival records which have now become available suggest that both factors contributed to the disastrous failure of the Kremlin leadership. The evidence of the CORSICAN and SENIOR agent files certainly suggests that Stalin had unambiguous evidence of the impending German attack. But other NKVD records also show that the reports reaching the Kremlin about Hitler's intentions were clouded by the Soviet mind-set over how to evaluate secret intelligence and an astute disinformation operation conducted by the *Abwehr*.

Stalin was not alone in his inclination to disbelieve the intelligence of impending war coming in from Berlin. By June 1941 it had reached the level of hearsay and street gossip in Berlin. The "secret" was relayed to Moscow not only from their trusted sources in the upper reaches of the Third Reich such as CORSICAN and SENIOR, but the same information was coming from rumours picked up by the wives of Soviet technical specialists working in German armaments plants. Because of the Soviet belief that *razvedka* (secret intelligence) was the only accurate source, both Moscow Centre and the Kremlin questioned what sort of secret preparations to attack Russia there could be if it was the subject of women's gossip and was even being written about by the Berlin correspondents of American newspapers.

The failure to properly assess the relative value of intelligence sources was at the root of the confusion overtaking the Centre during the critical countdown to war. The flood of information overwhelmed the Soviets' capacity to analyze it – just as happened in Washington six months later in the days prior to the attack on Pearl Harbor. The miscalculation in each case was the result of too much information from too many sources, rather than too little from too few. This led to fatal misjudgements in both instances because preconceptions were allowed to overrule sound analysis. In the Soviets' case the blindness arising from conflicting information is revealed in the operational instruction sent to Korotkov on 5 April

1941. "Recently we have been receiving agents' reports about the German preparations for an attack from all directions," the Centre told their Berlin *rezident*. Since the British and American press stories reinforced the warnings of CORSICAN and SENIOR by predicting an attack on the Ukraine, the Moscow analysts had received "so many agents' reports about Germany's supposedly secret preparations to attack that this, together with the volume of discussion in the Anglo-American press, raises the possibility that a deliberate disinformation campaign is being conducted".[37] Whether this was the result of the Germans themselves trying to put pressure on the Soviet Union or an Anglo-American ruse to disrupt German-Soviet relations was unclear.

It is now evident that the confusion in Moscow intelligence evaluation was aggravated by active German disinformation measures. When the concentration of troops, tanks and aircraft along the eastern frontier of the Third Reich reached proportions that could not be disguised or denied, the Gestapo made use of one of their penetration agents to feed a false explanation of the build-up directly to Moscow. Postwar interrogation of a Soviet prisoner of war named Siegfried Müller, who had been a member of the Gestapo's 4D Department in 1941, revealed that the Russian section of the *Abwehrstelle* Berlin had been running a Latvian journalist named Orest Berlinks. Unfortunately for the Soviets, he was considered a most reliable source by Amayak Kobulov, the NKVD *rezident* in Berlin.[38]

According to Müller's postwar interrogation report, Berlinks was such a valuable channel for feeding false information to Soviet intelligence that Hitler and Ribbentrop had prepared his reports themselves. While this may have been an exaggeration, the contemporary NKVD records confirm that in April 1941 the Centre had specifically directed Kobulov to find out the reason for the movement of such large masses of troops and armaments to the Russian border.[39] The answer Kobulov got from Berlinks, who claimed it was the "official" explanation given to him personally on 4 March 1941 by a Colonel Blau of OKW, was that "during [the First] World War we managed by colossal shifts of troops to disguise the real intentions of the German High Command".[40]

Since, against the Soviet yardstick of *razvedka*, this was supposedly genuine "secret" information obtained through a trusted source, when it reached Moscow it was given added credibility because it fitted in with Stalin's own convictions. Nor did it conflict with the undeniable evidence of the German build-up on the borders of Russia which Stalin believed was a gigantic military bluff by Hitler. To further confuse the Soviets, the German secret services also used other channels to leak hints that any military operation against Russia would be preceded by German claims on the Ukraine, couched in the terms of an ultimatum. This disinformation was also disseminated throughout the ministries of the Third Reich with the intention of bringing it to the notice of foreign governments through hints dropped in diplomatic channels.

The CORSICAN file confirms that Harnack fell for this disinformation, reporting to Korotkov in April 1940 that: "At a meeting of responsible officials of the Ministry of the Economy, press representative Kroll declared, 'The USSR will be asked to join the Axis and attack England. As a guarantee, the Ukraine will be occupied and possibly the Baltic [states] also.'"[41] Moscow's assumption that some ultimatum would precede any German military operation was reinforced the following month by a report relayed from SENIOR: "First Germany will present an ultimatum to the Soviet Union claiming wider export privileges as a reprisal for Communist propaganda. As a guarantee of these claims, German emissaries must be stationed in industrial and economic centres and the factories of the Ukraine. Certain Ukrainian regions are to be occupied by the German army. The delivery of this ultimatum will be preceded by a war of nerves whose object will be to demoralize the Soviet Union."[42]

Repeated German denials of any intention to attack was another ploy which Soviet records show was misread in Moscow when they were received from SENIOR, who was highly regarded as a source of *razvedka*. Referring to secret documents passing through his hands at the beginning of June, Schulze-Boysen had informed Korotkov that "German military attachés abroad, also ambassadors, have been given instructions to disprove rumours about any armed conflict between Germany and the USSR".[43] His information appeared to corroborate his report that the German air attaché in Moscow had sent for his wife and children to join him.[44] Such intelligence tended to reinforce Stalin's conviction that he must not be intimidated by Hitler in what appeared a gigantic game of military bluff – so he therefore waited for the ultimatum of German demands that never came. The cleverly directed contradictory signals reaching Moscow during May and early June 1941 served to dilute and divert the logical inferences to be drawn from the stream of accurate intelligence of a German invasion that CORSICAN and SENIOR had been relaying for months. This is confirmed by the comment Korotkov appended to the report he relayed from Harnack at the beginning of June. It listed the names of the Germans who were appointed to manage the economic districts into which Hitler intended to carve up the USSR: "How far this belongs to the sphere of rumours now circulating in Berlin, or is really a preparatory measure of German intentions, or an exercise in bluff is difficult to say."[45]

Such confusion was inevitable at NKVD headquarters because the Foreign Directorate, at that time, had no specialized analytical department capable of separating disinformation from accurate intelligence. This, as Orlov had discovered at first hand, was a major structural weakness in their set-up because Stalin insisted on being his own intelligence analyst of last resort. "Dangerous guesswork" was how the Big Boss had dismissed any interpretative efforts by underlings. He evidently believed that only he was equipped with the omniscience to divine the true significance of intelligence reports. That is why Stalin, according to Orlov, had repeatedly cautioned his intelligence chiefs to keep away from hypotheses and equations with too many unknowns.[46] "An intelligence hypothesis may become your hobby-horse on which you will ride straight into a self-made trap," was Stalin's maxim as far as intelligence estimation was concerned. "Don't tell me what you think, give me the facts and the source!" And as contemporary documentation shows, that is just what the NKVD chiefs did in June 1941. They passed on to Stalin's Kremlin office the raw cryptograms from Korotkov and other agent runners in practically the same form as they were received – without any comment or assessment of their significance or relative reliability. Those to whom the assessments were addressed, usually Stalin or Molotov, acted as their own intelligence analysts. Theirs was the responsibility for drawing the fatally flawed conclusion that Hitler was bluffing when he was not.

The *Führer*, too, was also misled by the *Wehrmacht*'s intelligence estimates that the massive German onslaught against the Red Army could crush the Soviet Union into defeat in a six-week campaign. The invasion did send the Soviets reeling and forced the withdrawal of their diplomats, closing the NKVD's "legal" field station in Berlin, and compelling it to go underground. The CORSICAN and SENIOR networks, which had succeeded in getting valuable intelligence to Moscow before the German attack, had communications restored sporadically until September 1942, when the Gestapo moved in and their leading members were arrested, summarily tried and executed (see Appendix II).

While the NKVD files on Harnack, Schulze-Boysen, Kuckhoff and the other Berlin agents disclose that some of the most compelling warning chords of the cataclysm of June 1941 had been sounded by their section of the *Rote Kapelle*, they were lost on the tone-deaf ears of Stalin. But their "musicianship" was to provide information to the Red Army that contributed to Hitler's ultimate defeat.

5

"A COMPLETE METAMORPHOSIS"

"ALL ESPIONAGE," Alexander Orlov wryly observed in his *Handbook*, "is equally illegal as far as the laws of the [target] countries are concerned."[1] But, no doubt reflecting how he himself had commenced his career as an "illegal" in the spring of 1933, he acknowledged the dangers inherent in such operations. In his previous postings as a Soviet intelligence officer Orlov had been a "legal" resident in the country, directing the work of its *rezidentura* as an official member of the embassy staff or Soviet trade delegation. Now he was to direct the work of an underground *rezidentura*, concealing his Russian identity by entering the foreign country with false papers and residing there as an "illegal".

"The Soviet officers went 'underground' disguised as businessmen or people of other professions, concealing their identity under the cover of false foreign passports and other tricky devices."[2] Orlov wrote from personal experience, although he was careful to omit that he himself had ever been involved in such activity. The nature of his new assignment as an "illegal" on a special mission in France reflected the change that had taken place in the way the Soviets conducted their overseas intelligence-gathering operations. The NKVD archives reveal that until the late 1920s most Soviet operations abroad were directed from the Soviet embassies and trade missions. However, a string of setbacks had followed the 1927 British police raid on the All Russian Co-operative Society headquarters in London, which led to the expulsion of the entire Soviet legation from Britain. Truck loads of captured documentation were removed from ARCOS offices together with the intercepted cables to the embassy, whose cypher the British had broken, that revealed how official Soviet diplomatic and trade missions were used as the front for intelligence-gathering operations.[3] In the aftermath of the damage which resulted from the ARCOS affair, from an earlier raid on the Soviet consulate in Peking and from the folding up that April of a Communist spy ring in France, Moscow was forced into a dramatic revision of both its overseas espionage operations and its cypher systems. To protect its diplomatic communications from code breaking the Soviets adopted the so-called one-time cypher pad system which was thenceforth used by the NKVD to insulate their intelligence operations from the diplomatic service.

"What the Soviet Government wanted", according to Orlov, "was to reorganize its intelligence operations on foreign soil in such a manner that if some of its agents were caught, the trail would not lead to the Soviet embassy, and the Soviet Government would be able to disclaim any connection with the exposed ring."[4] So the Soviet intelligence services in the early 1930s came up with a new *modus operandi* based on the so-called "illegal" *rezidentura* which was completely divorced from Soviet embassies and trade delegations. The "illegal" apparatus operated underground and under cover, establishing its own secret channel of communication with the Centre in Moscow. So successful did this type of operation become that Orlov tells us it was adopted by the Soviet military intelligence as well. "The underground *rezidenturas* gradually took over the major part of the intelligence activities abroad," wrote Orlov, who noted that the "legal" *rezidenturas* were not dismantled entirely because the chiefs of Soviet intelligence "had a change of heart and decided that it would be advantageous to Soviet intelligence to observe the national scene through two independent sets of agents to check the information supplied by one against the data received from the other".[5] But the "legal" *rezidents* were ordered to abstain from risky operations that might damage the prestige of the Soviet Union. The 1930s therefore saw the golden age of the so-called "Great Illegals" thanks to the pioneering effort of Orlov and his contemporaries who set about the task of building underground networks all over Europe.

"The underground *rezidenturas* were given broad discretional powers and extensive scope of activities," Orlov recorded. The difference between "illegal" as opposed to "legal" operations was that "Soviet intelligence officers in charge of the secret network no longer enjoyed the immunity of the Soviet embassy and the privileges of the diplomatic passport, nor the facilities of the diplomatic pouch, in which stolen secrets could be easily channelled to Moscow."[6] This put the NKVD officers involved at greater personal risk.

"The transition of Soviet intelligence to underground methods of operation was not easy," Orlov recalled. Apart from losing diplomatic protection and assurances that, if they were caught, the Soviet Government would launch vigorous protests to secure their release, another problem was the shortage of intelligence officers who knew foreign languages well enough to pass for nationals of foreign countries. To meet the demand the NKVD launched a rigorous training programme, which included instruction preparing officers for acquiring legitimate occupations and business cover that would enable them to spend many years in the country in which they were to operate.

This in turn required establishing new identities for agents and thus this was the responsibility of the passport desk of the Foreign Department of the NKVD. It was their job to obtain and doctor genuine passports of foreigners who had emigrated to the Soviet Union or to fabricate the passports of a foreign country. To produce forgeries that could pass close scrutiny by watchful immigration officers required the manufacture of stamps, covers and documentation which drew on the expertise of highly skilled experts at the Soviet government engraving offices. However good the forgery, it could be detected by reference to the passport serial numbers held by the country of origin. It was for this reason that all Soviet *rezidenturas* were instructed to obtain, by fraud or bribery of officials in passport offices, the genuine article. American passports were of especial value to the Soviet intelligence service. Not only did the United States have a prestige which caused European police agencies to treat them with respect, but the inability of its bearer to speak perfect English did not arouse suspicion because America was the adopted homeland of so many Russian and European immigrants.[7]

Like many Soviet "illegals", Orlov had already obtained a genuine American passport by subterfuge. One way this was done, he explained, was by obtaining photostat copies of the birth certificate of a baby who had died in infancy whose age would have approximated to the agent's. Two witnesses only were required to attest to a passport applicant's identity by swearing a notarized oath that they had known the subject for five years. Naturalization papers of a recent immigrant of the same age and background could easily be "borrowed" for a fee and passed off as an agent's own in a passport application. This was the method Orlov himself had used to obtain his American passport in November of 1932 under the cover of an official visit sponsored by General Motors.[8]

Orlov's American passport in the name of William Goldin was obtained through a fraudulent application with the aid of an underground Soviet agent in New York whose code name was SOUND. Equipped with a freshly minted proof that he was an American businessman whose thick Slavic accent could be conveniently explained by his immigrant status, Orlov could well have been recalling his own personal experience when he wrote of a Soviet intelligence officer who was eager to try out his new identity as soon as he boarded the boat in which he sailed from New York back to Europe at the end of 1932.[9] He recounted two incidents by which this "very same officer of the NKVD" learned that careful homework was necessary to polish a legend before he could pass as an American.

"A furrier", Orlov wrote, seemed an appropriate answer for the undercover Soviet intelligence officer to give when a group of card players on the liner asked his profession. It proved a mistake with the New York ladies who questioned him about "prices on various grades of mink". The figures that he plucked out of the air "made the ladies' eyes pop out" and they began avoiding him, suspecting that "he was a thief or a crackpot".[10] The second incident occurred after the boat docked in Cherbourg and the officer travelled to Paris, checking into the Grand Hotel with his American passport and speaking French, in which he was fluent. "The room clerk happened to be an American from Brooklyn; he was glad to welcome a compatriot in English and asked a question or two about the crossing." Taken by surprise, the would-be American became confused and uttered a "nondescript sentence in English which the clerk did not understand". Attempting to extricate himself from the mistake only resulted in stuttering confusion and he checked out of the hotel the next morning, returned his American passport to the Soviet embassy for safekeeping and made an application to Moscow to study English for three months.

The lesson to be drawn from this unidentified officer's experience, Orlov pointed out, was that an "illegal" had to have a reasonable command of the language and knowledge of the "native city" of his new identity. But, as he himself observed, "a thorough investigation will almost always puncture his false identity, no matter how well it is camouflaged".[11] That was why he said that underground operatives were under standing instructions from Moscow to "withdraw from the field" if they learned they were under surveillance by the authorities. As Orlov acknowledged, all "illegals" like himself who had previously served as Russian "legals" had an Achilles heel – one which he himself referred to as a "serious blunder of policy on the part of the NKVD". They were at risk because their new identities could be uncovered if they were recognized by former acquaintances or alert border officials. He cited the example of his former colleague Dmitri Smirnov, the "legal" NKVD *rezident* in Paris as a secretary of the Soviet embassy, who was travelling through Poland with Greek papers when an alert Polish border official recognized him as the man who had travelled to France only a year earlier on a Soviet diplomatic passport.[12] While Orlov's command of English was limited, he was able to get by with his American passport, but Smirnov's cover was blown because he had not one word of Greek. None the less, as Orlov noted, Moscow Centre often had no option but to take such risks. There was an acute shortage of senior officers like himself "with the high training, experience and stamina for underground service". Then, too, there was a certain egotism on his part. As he put it, "The dangerous work in the underground is surrounded in Moscow with such an aura of heroism that many an intelligence chief, irrespective of his previous service abroad in an official capacity, tries to get the hazardous assignment as a matter of honour and personal pride."[13]

The Centre selected Orlov as one of its experienced operatives in the spring of 1933 to manage an ambitious scheme to penetrate the French General Staff. This was a challenging assignment. Most Soviet intelligence operations in France, as in Britain, had been transferred to "illegals" since 1927, the year which witnessed the disasters of ARCOS and the partial break-up of a widespread Soviet espionage network led by the French Communist Jean Cremet. As a result of these twin setbacks, the counter-intelligence operation of the French *Sûreté Générale* had stepped up its activities against Moscow's undercover operations in France. For four years they searched without success for the leader of the ring, a Russian native masquerading under a dozen aliases, the most improbable of which was General Muraille. A fiery Bolshevik of the old Leninist school, he had gone "underground", aided by his ability to speak French like an Auvergne peasant. "Paul/Henri/Albert/Boissonas" proved an elusive agent of the GRU, providing them with a vast array of military blueprints and samples of new weapons until he was finally caught and convicted of espionage in 1931. The officers of the *Sûreté Générale* were already aware of the scale of Soviet operations in France. These increased dramatically in 1933 after Hitler's rise to power in Germany resulted in the Nazi ban on Communists which forced Moscow to abandon Berlin in favour of Paris as the nerve centre of both their operations in Western Europe.[14]

The moving force behind the shift to underground operations was Artusov, Orlov's friend, then the head of the Counter-intelligence Department (KRO) who had succeeded Trilliser in 1930 as chief of the Foreign Department. He brought to the task of reorganizing the Department's overseas operations all the ingenuity that had characterized the brilliantly successful Trust and Syndicate deceptions, of which he had been one of the principal architects. So, when it came to preparing for Orlov's first underground operation, Artusov himself put the finishing touches to the operational plan before it was submitted in March 1933 to Menzhinsky, the chief of the Directorate of State Security of the NKVD.

The contents of the plan were so secret that Artusov took

extraordinary measures – even for the closely compartmentalized
NKVD – to limit access by those who were not directly concerned.
Typists and office clerks were excluded. The records reveal that the
operational orders were handwritten for security and, because of its
secrecy, it was not registered. Because of this omission, it was given
no official file number and no classification. But its title spoke for
itself: "Penetration into the Second Bureau of the French General Staff
and its Network in the USSR."

Orlov's principal target was to be the intelligence department, the
legendary *Deuxième Bureau*, where his mission was defined as "to
carry out recruitments in its most important sections". These were
listed in order of priority as the north-eastern section (which directed
the field stations "working immediately against the USSR and located
in the countries adjoining the Soviet Union") and the technical section
"where the personal files of sources are concentrated".[15]

The operational plan listed the members of Orlov's four-man illegal
group by code name, starting with his own, the Russian word for
"Swede", and ending with his wife's, which was JEANNE:

1. *Rezident* – SCHWED
2. Assistant – DLINNY
3. Courier – EXPRESS
4. Technical assistant and local courier – JEANNE

The designated location of their base of operations or field station
was "a Swiss town adjoining France". Until further notice, it was
decided that his cover was an American seeking medical treatment at
one of the sanatoria for which the area round Lake Geneva was
famous. Three months were deemed necessary for Orlov's "perfecting the English and French languages and also for setting up the
courier and his family".[16] The main point for communications with
the Centre was set up through a cypher clerk of the Soviet consulate in
Milan, to whom communications would be sent using the courier
EXPRESS.

"The personal photo of EXPRESS is being sent to Milan," explained
Orlov's operational plan. "The cypher clerk in Milan has been
provided with a special code for these communications," it ordered,
setting down that "In extraordinary and unforeseen circumstances
(EXPRESS's illness; his being exposed, etc.) the pass code for the cypher
clerk will be 'I have brought you Vladimir Fedotov's regards' together
with the display of US $1 banknote No. A. 60884782D."[17] Vienna
was set as the emergency point of communication with the same pass

code but a different banknote bearing the serial number X25782760B.

Orlov was to carry both his genuine United States passport in the name of William Goldin and an Austrian one in the name of Leo Feldbin. Although it was unusual for "illegals" to be sent abroad with their family, Orlov's wife was an exception which had been granted because of his sick daughter and because Maria functioned as a member of the team. She and Vera travelled under her Austrian passport made out for Marguerite Feldbin. EXPRESS would use an American passport in the name of Arnold Finkelberg and would be assisted by the former Lubyanka elevator operator, Korotkov. He had been assigned the pseudonym DLINNY for his first operational mission and was already *en route* to Switzerland. To avoid the rigorous passport controls at frontier railway stations, it was planned that the couriers should use special tourist trip tickets, which avoided the need for such inspections. This would also help to keep down the cost of the operation since the general expenses of Orlov's "illegal" group, code-named EXPRESS after his courier, were set at a mere $1,500 a month.

The plan for the EXPRESS group's penetration of the *Deuxième Bureau* was to be assisted by a French defector – a former source in the General Staff who was distinguished by his flaming red facial hair. Code-named KADU and referred to by Orlov only as "Red Beard" he had been recruited in 1932 by another Soviet "illegal" operating in France whose name was Theodore Mally. It was KADU who claimed, through an NCO named Lagrange, to have the chief of the *Deuxième Bureau* "in his pocket". According to Orlov's 1965 statement to the CIA, he had learned in Moscow that Lagrange had written some indiscreet letters for his chief which he arranged to pass on to the Soviets together with other revealing correspondence. But "Red Beard" evidently became over-confident and slipped up and was in danger of being exposed in December 1932 when the Centre ordered that he should be brought out from France under cover to Moscow where he continued to be a valuable source of information.[18]

The "exfiltration" of KADU had abruptly cut the Centre off from its intelligence source in the heart of the French General Staff. But he had left behind a colleague who, he advised "would be ready to help" Soviet intelligence if they contacted him. The French defector had supplied a detailed description, drawing attention to his telltale lameness. The name of this officer was also known, but KADU did not have his address or any other particulars besides anticipation of this French sympathizer's co-operation. Orlov code-named him FRIEND in his secret reports to Moscow Centre.

Orlov assumed his American identity of William Goldin for Operation Express, entering France on his illegally obtained US passport. While this genuine document would have stood any scrutiny, Orlov himself could not. He was too well known in Russian emigré circles in Paris because of the contacts he had made while working there between 1926 and 1930 as an official of the Soviet Trade Delegation. This was why Switzerland was selected as the base for his underground group. But before he could assume the role of an itinerant American businessman, Orlov had to brush up his English and his French. So he set off for Vienna in the late spring of 1933, where he devoted most of his time to perfecting his English. He enrolled for private lessons with a British professor who was later to cross his path with most unpleasant consequences. To this English-man, Orlov presented himself as a Russian, living in Austria under his Soviet passport in the name of Leo Nikolayev at the Schloss Pension at 27 Hauptstrasse in the suburb of Hinterbrül bei Wien. On completing his language course, he wired a cryptic cable to ARTUR (Artusov), his boss at Moscow Centre on 13 June 1933: "On 1 July I change my status into a new one and leave for my place of work. SCHWED"[19]

The NKVD records show that Orlov left for Prague, accompanied by EXPRESS, on 27 June. There he and his courier collected their "new books", as foreign passports were called in the contemporary jargon of the Soviet intelligence service. This was standard practice. An underground operative never went directly to the country in which he was to operate, but travelled on either his Russian passport or on a "temporary" foreign passport which was not considered safe enough for permanent residency, to an intermediate country. There he would collect a new passport, which had been sent into the country via diplomatic bag to the Soviet embassy. It was in the intermediary country that "a complete metamorphosis" of an agent could take place. "He sheds his old identity, leaving all possible traces behind, takes his false passport, and becomes a new person," was how Orlov described the process. "From there he starts to 'swim', as the Soviet lingo goes, and travels to the country of his assignment."[20]

Orlov's metamorphosis into William Goldin, citizen of the United States of America, took place in Prague. Then he left for Geneva, travelling via Berlin, where he had a meeting with a German who used the code name STAHL who had worked for the local NKVD rezidentura as an agent. Orlov found that STAHL was most eager to leave Germany. As a Jew, he considered that now the Nazis had come to power it would be increasingly difficult for him: he was in some danger as a result of "an unpleasant situation" which had arisen from the part he had played in the operation to obtain the secret of the process for making industrial diamonds. STAHL's role as one of the intermediaries in the affair had prompted a police investigation and he assured Orlov that he had no intention of submitting to Nazi justice. He said he was to leave shortly for Paris, where he offered to make his services available, claiming he had come across some valuable intelligence. As Orlov reported it to the Centre, STAHL "through his old acquaintance Rybnikov, the owner of a bookshop at 3 rue Langier, has supposedly discovered an officer of the north-eastern section of the French General Staff".[21]

Orlov clearly lacked confidence in the reliability of both STAHL and his information, but he could not afford to reject his offer of a lead. On the one hand, as an intelligence officer with a defined mission, Orlov was clearly tempted by the opportunity of making contact with a source who might lead him to his target, while, on the other hand, he had sound reasons for not trusting STAHL. In addition to the large fee he demanded, the German agent had a bad track record with his control officer in Berlin, which Orlov alluded to in the report he made to Moscow Centre: "Concerning the use of STAHL in general, I should point out that, owing to certain circumstances, if I had at least one other single recruit or local personnel at my disposal, I would turn him down. These circumstances arise from his extraordinary animosity (which expressed itself during our last meeting) against the comrade that had controlled him."[22]

Weighing up the pros and cons of using STAHL overcame Orlov's uneasiness about him: he judged that the importance of his mission outweighed his personal reservations and justified enlisting him. So he set a rendezvous for them in Paris for 10 July, allowing time for him to establish his base of operations, as directed, in Geneva. It was a decision he came to regret when the true nature of the game played by STAHL became apparent a few months later.

On arrival in Paris, Orlov found drawbacks after having operated as a "legal" in the city five years earlier. An anonymous anecdote in his *Handbook* reveals how he had to learn the hard way that there had been inevitable changes in the city, which he failed to take into account, such as the demise of a favourite restaurant. He relates how a Soviet intelligence officer had arranged with Moscow to cable another *rezident* to come to a meet at the Brasserie Duval. When he arrived for the rendezvous, a piano showroom occupied what had been the Duval's location on the rue de la Madeleine. An inquiry of a nearby *gendarme* revealed that the restaurant had closed many months before.

"Amazing," the policeman told the Soviet officer. "You are the second tourist who within five minutes has asked me about the Duval restaurant." With that he pointed out the contact reading a theatrical poster only a dozen paces away.[23]

Orlov's first report to Moscow from Paris appears to reflect this incident and reveals his increasing unease over the agent's trustworthiness. His telegram records that he did not head straight for the rendezvous he had arranged, but first took a detour through the narrow streets surrounding the chosen location. Only after Orlov had assured himself there were no suspicious people in the vicinity who might have been French police or counter-intelligence officers of the *Sûreté Générale* did he sit down at a café table. From there he was able to observe the opposite side of the street, where his contact was scheduled to pass by at the prearranged hour.

STAHL, according to Orlov, appeared approximately on time on the appointed side of the street, walking from right to left as instructed. Intently watching from inside the café for any signs of tension in STAHL's face or gait, Orlov found nothing to arouse his suspicions. But he prudently chose to let another couple of minutes go by before making a move. When no surveillance agents followed STAHL up the street, he slipped out of the side door of the brasserie, quickly caught up with him and exchanged the agreed code word salutation.

"I have something interesting for you," STAHL declared a little too self-importantly, according to Orlov. "Do you remember me telling you about an officer from the General Staff. Well, he calls on the '*Biblioteka MAYAK*' for Soviet newspapers and magazines. The sister of the owner of the library, Nina Garnitskaya, brought us together."[24]

At Orlov's suggestion they crossed the street to another nearby café to continue their conversation. Over a glass of wine STAHL explained that the targeted officer's name was Vladimir Alexandrovich Rykovsky, a former White Guard officer. A Ukrainian from Poltava who had become a French citizen, he was described as a tall, heavy man nearing forty with a large crooked nose, unusually small ears, dark hair with grey streaks and a small bald spot. "He speaks softly and slowly, but self-assuredly," STAHL told Orlov. "Nina told me that on Tuesdays and Fridays he calls at the library for Soviet military publications and stays there from 11 am to 1 pm. I arrived there at the given time and she introduced us to one another as I am an immigrant too."[25]

"What gave you the idea he works in the General Staff?" Orlov asked, reporting that STAHL had claimed that: "All the material on the intelligence work on the Soviet Union is concentrated in his hands. He is the connecting link between the centre of the French intelligence in the Soviet Union and the Paris Centre, I mean the General Staff. His chief is a Frenchman of captain's rank. He goes about in a

Rolls Royce and, according to certain indications, lives above his means."[26]

"Did Rykovsky really tell you all this the first time he saw you," asked Orlov, only to be assured that, "Nina Garnitskaya did." The librarian, who had evidently known the subject for some time, had informed STAHL that the Captain was a frequent caller at her library. To support his claim, STAHL handed over a doubly folded piece of paper containing Rykovsky's address and cover name: "JUAN, 12 rue Moren, Mongérome par Paris, telephone number 87."[27]

"I think a person like that will only work for money, though it's early to say anything for certain yet," Orlov reported he had cautioned STAHL, advising him, "You take care of him."[28]

Orlov noted that the mention of money had prompted STAHL to give a lengthy explanation of his pressing need for a cash advance. He said that his property in Germany, including a country house, had been confiscated by the Nazis and he needed to meet the heavy expenses of establishing a new home in Paris. He concluded with a passionate monologue claiming to have borrowed large sums to pay off those who knew of his involvement with the Soviets, "otherwise they will betray me lock, stock and barrel".[29]

Despite an uneasy suspicion that his agent might be embroidering a hard luck story to extort money, Orlov decided he had no choice in the circumstances but to hand over the envelope he had prepared. It contained a large wad of French banknotes, which represented a sizeable chunk of the $1,500 he had been allotted to fund that month's operations. His suspicions about STAHL after this first meeting were sufficiently aroused for him to make the long train journey to and from Milan to his designated communication point. He handed over a lengthy report about his concern over STAHL, requesting to know what Moscow Centre could tell him about the man Rykovsky.[30]

Returning to Paris to keep his second meeting with his agent, Orlov learned that STAHL had spoken to Rykovsky on behalf of "a friend of his" who, he claimed, was a prominent Nazi who would like to receive information about the USSR from the French. Rykovsky could give no immediate help, but, in STAHL's opinion, his reaction had been reassuring. He also reported that he had been given a freelance assignment by the French General Staff which involved sifting through "advertisements" published in the Soviet press that they believed might contain encyphered messages. STAHL went to considerable lengths to assert how he believed Rykovsky could be a very valuable Soviet source, again asking Orlov to supply him with more money. At their next meeting a few weeks later, STAHL announced that Rykovsky was now ready to supply French documents, but had insisted that he would do so only in exchange for the information which Germany possessed about the Soviet Union. Again STAHL demanded another large payment for his services.[31]

The suspicion that STAHL had set him up for a scam was now inescapable, but Orlov admitted to the Centre that he was still hesitant to confront the agent because nearly two months into the operation, his own efforts to locate FRIEND as a way of penetrating the French General Staff were moving at a snail's pace. Until he had received Moscow's response to his request for information about Rykovsky, he was unwilling to risk a breach with his grasping agent, who offered the only possible line into the target. He did, however, make plain his concern at the lack of progress he was making with Operation Express.

The report Orlov sent to Moscow on 5 September 1933 stands as a vivid catalogue of the problems confronting a Soviet "illegal" operating underground in hostile territory and a revealing documentation of both technique and jargon. It was as close as Orlov – a tough and careful NKVD operative – ever came to criticizing his superiors by indicating that he was ready to abandon a mission. His report made clear that his group needed the services of a Frenchman to recruit native contacts. This "breeding", in service jargon, he argued was now essential to making progress with this tricky penetration operation. As he told Moscow Centre:

Except for STAHL, a person without any experience in my new sphere and a stranger in this country, I have not got a single genuine Frenchman for "breeding" through whom I could orient myself and feel about for new acquaintances without immediately scaring them off by my alien citizenship and foreign appearance. Without such a person, in the first instance I have to play the role of a secret agent myself.

I consider the average French would do it better because: (a) I am a foreigner in France and (b) I have not got a "firm" [a cover], I cannot strike bargains with anyone. My position is purely that of an American "who prefers rest in Europe to the loss of money under the blows of the US crisis".

I tried to get close to some people, but with no success. I have become acquainted with a German official in the League of Nations named Henssler. He can't give [me] anything. I have got to know the wife of a Paris architect Altman (the husband is the son of the famous painter). She was de Moncy's mistress four years ago. She is easy to cultivate, but what is her influence on de Moncy now? According to the evidence, it is very weak. As to the cultivation of

Rykovsky, it cannot yet be considered a definite success. That is why I believe it to be my duty to raise this question now, at the end of two months. It is hard for me to invest foreign currency on the organization of an operation that doesn't promise success. I am, therefore, requesting you to consider making the following adjustments:

1. To recall me and reorganize the operation around a team which has already proved itself made up of EXPRESS (a good courier, a real foreigner); DLINNY (who has mastered the language and can "wear" a passport), his wife (who knows German and French perfectly).
2. Or to assign me at least one reliable Frenchman from one of our other groups.
3. Or to risk only me (to secure the safety of all my other people) and give it to Mally's man. He may muck it up, but he may just do a good job.
4. Or reduce the [budgetary] allocation considerably, so that, in the event of my assignment's failure, the waste of currency will not be perceptible.
Any one of your decisions will be law for me.[32]

SCHWED

Orlov's operational code name resulted in him being referred to cryptically by his comrades as "the Swede", although he had never been to or had anything to do with Sweden. His reference to the "man" recruited by his fellow "illegal" Theodor Mally was heeded by Moscow. When Orlov received the Centre's answer early in 1934, he learned that the heavy cost was not a consideration for the NKVD chiefs who were determined that he press ahead with the plan to penetrate the *Deuxième Bureau*. Accordingly, the Centre complied with his request for additional support, informing him that his group would be strengthened by the addition of an agent code-named JOSEPH together with the French agent of proven reliability who is identified on the files only as B 205.[33] There was, however, disturbing news concerning STAHL's alleged contact on the French General Staff, Rykovsky. The Centre reported that "his name is unknown to KADU. *Deuxième Bureau Intelligence* (SR) does not have agents in Paris (that is, working in Paris). The *Deuxième Bureau Counter-intelligence* (SCR) has no agents at all, but works through the *Sûreté Générale*. Rykovsky is hardly a member of the *Deuxième Bureau* staff and by no means an officer."[34] An additional comment from Mally noted that "according to the archive materials on English agents in Turkey in 1928 a certain Rykovsky worked for Christie on the Russian matter."[35] This added another disturbing element to Orlov's dilemma, since Christie had been identified as an MI6 officer who headed the "passport bureau of the British Embassy in Athens [and] who worked from there against Turkey and the USSR".[36]

After receiving this unsettling information from Moscow, Orlov recast his plan to take account of two possibilities. As he reported to the Centre, either Rykovsky was not what he said and STAHL was an operative of Britain's intelligence service, or STAHL had invented the story of Rykovsky belonging to the French General Staff to draw money out of him. He postponed his intended showdown with STAHL after his agent stunned him with a report at their next meeting of what appeared to be a very promising new turn of events. This came when STAHL announced that he had been able to make the acquaintance of Marshal Pétain, the French military hero of the Great War whose dogged defence of the Verdun Fortress had saved France from the German offensive of 1916. He told Orlov that MARSHAL, as he was referred to in the NKVD cables, had introduced him to Pierre Taitinger, a right-wing member of the Chamber of Deputies who was the editor of the newspaper *Jeunesse Patriote*.[37]

STAHL's new contacts were of special interest to Orlov and Moscow because this right-wing group supported the fiercely anti-Bolshevik aims of the large White Russian emigré circles in Paris, who were the target of a separate Soviet penetration operation. The focus of the Centre's operation had been directed against the leaders of the Russian Combined Services Union, the so-called ROVS, who were the hard core of the exiled veterans who had fought the Red Army in the civil war. After the 1930 kidnapping of General Kutyepov from a Paris street corner in broad daylight, his successor as the head of ROVS, the bearded Tsarist General Yevgeny Miller, became an informant for the *Deuxième Bureau*. He was also a prime target for Soviet intelligence until he, too, disappeared in another sensational abduction in 1937.[38]

The chain of connections that STAHL now claimed to have made were of great interest to Orlov and the Centre, the more so since he reported that Taitinger had introduced him to an officer of the *Deuxième Bureau* named Curgess, who had put STAHL in touch with one of his colleagues named Junod, whom Orlov's agent described as a "captain with an order in his buttonhole". He had not only promised STAHL assistance in getting French citizenship papers, but claimed that STAHL's professed anti-Bolshevik views and willingness to help these right-wing officers had now made him a welcome visitor at a secret office maintained by the *Deuxième Bureau* near the Jardin du Luxembourg. STAHL told Orlov that he had been more than ten times to this office, whose secret entrance was located at 75 rue de l'Université. The porter there had been given standing instructions always to show him into the ground-floor office located on the left of the front door, from where its small window looked directly out on to the street.[39]

What at first persuaded Orlov to believe STAHL was secret information obtained from the former French General Staff officer who was now advising the Centre in Moscow. According to the defector KADU, the main building of the General Staff headquarters was at 235 rue de l'Université, but he confirmed that the *Deuxième Bureau* maintained their most secret offices further down the same street at No. 75. Orlov reported to Moscow that he had decided to use this inside knowledge to test STAHL, by taking up his offer of providing visual proof of his remarkable coup in penetrating the offices of the General Staff's counter-intelligence department.

"We have arranged with STAHL today that at 4 pm sharp, he will be looking out into the street from the window of No. 75," Orlov informed the Centre early in January 1934. "The time was fixed by me. He expects me to walk along the street at the appointed hour to make sure that he is there. Of course it won't be me who'll walk by, but it will be interesting to make sure of his permanent access there. If STAHL can be trusted then his effort should be regarded positively, but I almost have proof that he had not seen MARSHAL himself six weeks ago, but saw only General Miller, who was the one who brought him to No. 75."[40]

On the appointed day it was not Orlov, but EXPRESS, his courier in the "illegal" group, whom STAHL did not know, who walked by No. 75 and observed STAHL looking out of the window. Now that he had apparently proof provided that his German agent really had delivered on his promises, Orlov prepared to congratulate him, but he was saved from handing over another substantial sum of money by the Centre's communication which arrived in the nick of time to expose an elaborate fraud, which despite his own better judgement, he had nearly fallen for. Once again it was information provided by KADU that saved Orlov from making what might have been the biggest error of judgement of his entire career. The Centre reported that STAHL's contacts Junod and Curgess were not known to KADU, but he speculated that Curgess could be an intelligence officer named de Colbert Turgis, who might have truncated his own name as a pseudonym. From KADU too came additional hard facts about the internal topography of 75 rue de l'Université, which put a very different light on STAHL's claims to have penetrated the inner sanctuary of the *Deuxième Bureau*. As KADU described it, to the left of the entrance was a small room with a table, at which the porter had visitors fill out their requests for a pass to the building. Two metres from the door of the small room was a large glass door leading to the intelligence department. Three steps up and behind it, via a small landing and through a door on the left, stairs led down into a large room. It was in this room that, according to KADU, informants whom the *Deuxième Bureau* had reason not to trust were customarily received and, if necessary, arrested.[41]

This information now prompted Orlov to make a radically different assessment of EXPRESS's sighting of STAHL in the ground-floor room at No. 75. Nor did it escape Orlov's attention that STAHL, despite his important new contacts in the *Deuxième Bureau* had never again mentioned how he was cultivating Rykovsky. He concluded that he must confront his agent with the discrepancies in his story, his decision to have a final showdown reinforced by reports he had received from his own agents, who had kept the entrance at No. 75 under close surveillance in the hope of establishing contact with FRIEND, the officer with a limp. Many weeks of watching had not only failed to identify any such officer, but it had also confirmed that the entrance at No. 75 was used mainly by civilian office cleaning staff. Although KADU had confirmed that a secret door led from the intelligence department into the General Staff building, it was only open in office hours and not used as a general entrance. Mally, while unable to join Orlov in Paris yet, had confirmed that STAHL's appearance in the ground floor window was no proof at all that he had been received into the intelligence section of the *Deuxième Bureau*.[42]

The final straw that broke Orlov's patience with STAHL came when he received information that his agent had approached the Soviet Trade Delegation in Paris with the offer to sell "an important invention". According to an NKVD undercover agent named ROSANNE, who was operating with Orlov's former colleagues in the trade mission, STAHL wanted a large sum of money for the secret of turning ordinary paper into waterproof paper. As Orlov angrily reported to Moscow: "He started the whole story with the Trade Delegation behind my back, thinking that I'm cut off from our official organizations and he would succeed in pulling the wool over the eyes of the Trade Delegation to make a little money and keep it secret from our organization."[43]

Following this disturbing discovery, Orlov decided he could no longer postpone a final confrontation with STAHL. He began, according to his report, by asking the German to describe Marshal Pétain. Even though STAHL managed to give a completely inaccurate description of one of the most famous figures in France, he tried to protest that it did not matter whether he saw the real man or a plant because he said that he believed it was the Marshal. He tried to defend his position by saying that, whatever the man's identity, it had enabled him to get into the *Deuxième Bureau*. "You saw me in the window of No. 75, didn't you?"[44]

In answer to Orlov's questions on why it was that he was so readily received by the *Deuxième Bureau* STAHL replied that he had given "two descriptions of warfare gases of great importance to the 'Firm'," knowingly using the term employed by NKVD officers. "When I asked if he could give us copies of these reports, he answered that the copies were at his house and that we could have them at any time," Orlov reported. "When we came to get them, he did not give them to us on some silly pretext. Such copies obviously do not exist."[45]

Sensing that the canny STAHL was ducking his challenge, Orlov himself resorted to a bluff. He declared that he knew that STAHL's property in Germany had not been confiscated by the Nazis, as he had earlier claimed. Visibly shaken that Orlov was so well informed, STAHL confessed that he made up the story about the confiscation to gain sympathy and money. His confession of his deceit made the nature of his intention to cheat the Soviet intelligence service obvious.

Orlov reported the outcome to Moscow Centre, recommending STAHL's "liquidation". In this context the term meant cutting off all ties, rather than physical elimination, for which the contemporary NKVD term *"raschet"* would have applied in the case of an agent who had cheated.[46] Moscow gave its consent without hesitation.

After ridding his group of the double-dealing agent, Orlov was determined to make up for lost time by redoubling his group's efforts to discover ways to penetrate the *Deuxième Bureau*. "Having finally received in your last letter the confirmation of our reports that No. 75 was isolated from the rest of the offices, we instituted surveillance of the main entrance," Orlov informed Moscow early in 1934. "For the last ten days we have determined the addresses of two lame men, but a check of their names on their apartment doorbells showed that neither of them is FRIEND."[47]

Since STAHL had repeatedly misled Orlov, it is improbable that he would have continued the search for the sympathetic French officer if he had not had independent corroboration. This was just the start of the hunt for the lame man. In the course of the next few weeks Orlov's men shadowed and checked the addresses of eight limping men who left the main entrance of the French General Staff building in the rue de l'Université. All of them proved false leads. The watch on the headquarters building did give Orlov a new idea after his men had observed how many young women were on the staff.

Why not, Orlov reasoned, seek a way in through one of them? He outlined his scheme in a letter to the Centre, proposing that he use

French agent 205, who was now working under Mally, to recommend a couple of trustworthy young Communists who could establish contact with the female secretarial staff of the *Deuxième Bureau*.

Moscow was initially against involving the local Party in espionage operations lest it backfire. Orlov then appealed to the Centre, drawing their attention to how successfully a similar operation had worked. "I was utterly disappointed by your ban on using one or two Frenchmen to cultivate female staff as it had been done in case 238."[48] The names of those involved in the case are not in Orlov's file. Such an operation, Orlov contended, could work with a secretary of the *Deuxième Bureau*.

"Your prohibition on the use of one or two young Frenchmen for the cultivation of women officials, as in case number 238, has upset me greatly," Orlov responded. "We need Frenchmen," he argued, giving the reason why he believed his scheme would produce the desired result. "I did not mean for them all to be 'compatriots'," Orlov explained, seeking to defuse the issue of using Communist Party members by stating that it was his intention that they should merely recommend trustworthy and absolutely reliable Frenchmen.[49] He argued that, in the current political situation, where the left and the right wings in France were at loggerheads, it would be relatively easy to exploit the right-wing sentiments of the type of women who worked in the *Deuxième Bureau*. His plan called for the targeting of these Frenchmen on to selected secretaries of the "Firm". One way to achieve this was for such a man to pose as a member of the Young Monarchist's Union and use this to play on the rightist sensibilities of the target by telling her "every Royalist's duty is to struggle against the danger of Socialism in the French establishment", painting a picture of a "formidable struggle against the Communist menace and particularly against the USSR".

Orlov pointed to the recent stir made by the Royalist demonstrations in the streets of Paris and the revolving door character of recent French Governments in response to the threat of Fascism. Such a stratagem, he contended, would succeed in obtaining valuable information from women who "otherwise might be intimidated by the thought of spying for a foreign country, but who would pass information to French patriots".[50]

The Centre this time assented to Orlov's scheme, even though it refused to sanction the use of French Communists. With only French recruits at his disposal, he had to rely on Agent 205 to cultivate the targeted secretaries working in the General Staff headquarters. The records show that "205" did indeed manage to get acquainted with one of them well enough to begin her cultivation in the spring of 1934.

While awaiting developments in the main French operation under his direction, Orlov was tapped by Moscow Centre to go to Rome in December 1933.[51] An indication of his standing at the Centre was that he was the undercover agent entrusted with supervising the operation to turn a member of Mussolini's Government into a secret Soviet collaborator. The Centre had received word from Boris Berman, an NKVD officer who operated in Rome under the alias of YELMAN, that an appropriate financial inducement could secure the services as an informant of the Minister of Corporations Giuseppe Bottai, who was a leading figure in the Fascist Grand Council. Artusov, who was then the INO chief, assigned his trusted friend Orlov to this mission because the importance of the potential source required that Stalin be personally informed.[52]

Using his American passport, Orlov travelled under cover to Rome via Lugano on 12 December to make a personal assessment of the prospective recruit. Returning three days later, he filed a positive report on the probable success of the operation to Artusov.[53] An anecdote in his *Handbook* evidently relates to a personal reminiscence of a weekend trip made to Capri, to the favoured island resort of Roman socialites. The hotel which he booked into was very full and he was asked by a waiter if he would mind sharing a table. His dining companion turned out to be a young Polish diplomat who was serving as a Second Secretary in Poland's Vienna embassy. They struck up a friendship, taking walks and swimming together; they became constant companions.

"It is of course possible," Orlov reflected, too archly not to have betrayed that he was clearly the individual involved, "that the Soviet intelligence officer tried to cultivate a little friendship with the Polish diplomat with an eye to his possible recruitment at some later date into the Soviet net." But his cultivation of the diplomat almost proved fatal to his cover when he encountered him again unexpectedly in awkward circumstances, when Orlov was recalled to Moscow to make a personal report on the Italian operation. To avoid having a suspicious Soviet border stamp on his pristine American passport, Orlov travelled to Moscow on his Soviet passport. He was, therefore, alarmed to encounter the Polish diplomat, who had joined the first-class compartment of the Eastern Express when it stopped at Schlesische Station in Berlin en route to Warsaw. The young man was delighted to rediscover his American friend. Orlov had to revert to his former cover and, thinking quickly, explained that he was going to Moscow to make the connection with the Trans-Siberian express for Tokyo. To preserve his cover, Orlov knew he would have to shake off his enthusiastic friend before the passport inspection at the Polish border. This, he recorded, was difficult on a speeding train, but he succeeded by excusing himself from the dining car and secreting himself in the third-class carriages during the border stop.[54]

Orlov may have succeeded in saving the cover essential to his operation as the Paris underground *rezident*, but the Italian operation went sour. After reporting to Moscow and receiving Stalin's approval for the operation, it was decided that the recruitment of Bottai by handing over the authorized $15,000 inducement could most safely be accomplished during the Minister's forthcoming visit to Germany. Under the guise of an officially arranged meeting with Mikhail Lubimov, the head of the Soviet Trade Delegation in Berlin handed the Italian the envelope full of high denomination US bills. "When he saw that he had only $15,000 in the envelope, he decided it was better to go and tell the story to Mussolini," Orlov recalled in his 1957 testimony to the US Senate. He explained that after the Duce had protested "unofficially" to the Soviet Ambassador at the attempt to bribe one of his ministers, Stalin's reaction had been characteristic: "Too little money – next time you ought to try $50,000."[55]

It was shortly after this Italian interlude that Orlov discovered what at first appeared to be another opportunity to penetrate the *Deuxième Bureau*. Because it seemed to have presented itself purely by chance, like many such intelligence opportunities, Orlov decided to follow up the report of Alexander Korotkov, who had enrolled in an anthropology course at the Sorbonne as a Czechoslovak using the name of Rajonetsky as cover. Orlov's deputy, whose code name was DLINNY, had made friends with a French student who appeared to be an avid reader of the Socialist newspaper *Populaire* and so poor it seemed that he was after a while forced to drop out of the Sorbonne. For three months Korotkov lost contact with his friend. Then he encountered him again apparently by chance while strolling along avenue de l'Opéra. The young Frenchman explained that with the help of his fiancée's father he had got a job as a photographer at the *Deuxième Bureau* copying maps and documents – although he was still earning too little to get married.[56]

When Korotkov informed Orlov of the encounter, it appeared that cultivating the French student would offer a long-coveted key to gaining access to the secrets of the *Deuxième Bureau*. The chance nature of the association seemed to rule out the possibility of a trap and, since the initiative was left to Korotkov, it did not seem possible that the man was a "plant". Orlov therefore advised his assistant to pursue his friendship. A check on the fiancée's father revealed that he was indeed a former army sergeant who worked at the War Ministry as an office manager. Orlov requested permission from Moscow Centre to go ahead with the operation, and to accelerate the move towards recruitment he instructed Korotkov to finance the purchase of an engagement ring for the Frenchman, with the promise of a loan that would enable the young couple to marry.[57]

Orlov was confidently awaiting the green light from Moscow to go ahead with his operation when an officer of the *Sûreté Générale* who had been a Soviet informant until the previous year, until a falling out with the "legal" *rezidentura*, decided to resume contact with his Soviet controller. As chief of the narcotics violations section, he had access to secret service files. He had alerted the Soviets to the corrupt Minister of Justice and had passed on the police records of the Kutyepov kidnapping. Now this source produced another memorandum which showed that the *Sûreté Générale* had been informed by one of its undercover agents in the French Communist Party that a certain Czechoslovak residing in Paris and attending the Sorbonne was a Soviet national and an agent of the NKVD. The *Sûreté* had dispatched a young agent to enrol in the same anthropology course and make the acquaintance of the suspected Soviet agent.

What Orlov acknowledged as a "brilliant piece of counter-intelligence work" was brought to his attention in the nick of time when the "legal" *rezident*'s report was relayed to him by Moscow.[58] The Centre ordered a halt to the recruitment of the Frenchman and instructed that Korotkov be sent temporarily out of the country. As it turned out, averting this trap set so skilfully by the *Sûreté* also proved to be Orlov's final operation as an "illegal" in France. Fate intervened to prevent him remaining in Paris long enough to achieve his mission of penetrating the *Deuxième Bureau* of the French General Staff.

On a sunny April day in 1934 Orlov happened to be walking down a busy Paris street when somebody behind him called out, "Lev", in a loud voice. Resisting the natural inclination to turn round and see who was hailing him as Lev Nikolsky – the alias he had used six years before in the Soviet Trade Delegation – Orlov hurried on. As William Goldin, a citizen of the United States of America, he had to ignore the summons. With many Russian emigrants in Paris named Lev he hoped that the caller might have made a mistake. But a few seconds later a hand on his shoulder caused him to freeze in dismay as he realized the man who was looking him in the face had not made a mistake.[59]

"Lev, wait, don't you recognize old friends?" an unkempt individual demanded in an insolently apologetic tone. The man who had stopped him in his tracks was no stranger, but a former comrade named Vernik, who had worked alongside him in the offices of the Trade Delegation six years before when Orlov had used the organization as cover in his previous incarnation as a "legal" Soviet intelligence officer.

Orlov reported that he gave a cursory acknowledgement, after Vernik had identified himself, announcing that he had given up working for the Trade Delegation to take unauthorized leave in Paris. He confirmed what Orlov already knew: that his former comrade, who had defected in the late 1920s, had been branded as a traitor by the authorities in Moscow. By his shabby appearance and his unshaven face which had grown prematurely old Orlov could see that life had not been easy for Vernik since he had deserted his post.

"Maybe you'll treat me to a glass of wine for old time's sake so we can have a chat," Vernik suggested with hope in his voice. Trapped in a difficult predicament, from which he knew there was no easy escape, Orlov agreed.[60]

While they were walking to a nearby café, Orlov realized it was highly unlikely that Vernik could know that he was in France illegally posing as an American. He probably believed that Nikolsky was still on an official trade mission and this was the line that he held to during their twenty minutes of stilted and difficult conversation. In the course of it Vernik complained how hard his life had become. He said he was convinced now he had made a mistake by breaking off with the Soviet Union and pleaded with Orlov to help him return to his homeland and find a job there. To slough off this unwelcome acquaintance from the past as quickly as possible, Orlov promised to aid him before excusing himself by claiming a pressing business appointment.

Hurrying away from the fateful encounter, Orlov recognized that his operation as an "illegal" in France had been dealt a fatal blow. He knew that Vernik's defection would have come to the attention of the *Sûreté Générale* and that he might well have become an informer. There was no time to be lost in packing his bags and quitting Paris. After contacting his deputy Korotkov, who had just returned to Paris, Orlov left for Switzerland, leaving DLINNY to send emergency notification to Moscow: "SCHWED ran across Vernik by chance. He asked where and what SCHWED was doing. SCHWED has decided to leave Paris for a while to see how things will turn out."[61]

The reports reaching Moscow from the Soviet Trade Delegation in Paris were not auspicious. When Orlov failed to call Vernik as promised, the latter had begun a desperate hunt for him, enlisting the aid of other Soviet defectors and finally even telephoning the

Delegation and pleading for information about "Nikolsky" with officials who were his former comrades. When news of Vernik's persistence was communicated to the Centre, they issued instructions that their "illegal" *rezident* in Paris must give up his station. Meanwhile, after several weeks in Switzerland, Orlov had returned to Paris in anticipation that there would be no repercussions from his chance encounter with Vernik. It was with resignation that Orlov prepared once again to leave France. On 8 May 1934 he sent a message to Moscow through the prearranged emergency channel: "Today, according to your instructions I am leaving for Switzerland. SCHWED."[62] So it was not to Orlov, but to his successor that the honour fell of recruiting FRIEND, who became the Soviets' first "mole" in French military intelligence.

For Orlov, a new assignment awaited him in Vienna. His bad luck in Paris was to be compensated for when he was ordered to leave Austria for London on a new mission. It was to open a new chapter of his operational life – a hitherto unknown English one – which, as the NKVD archives reveal, marked the crowning achievement of his work for the Soviet intelligence service.

6

"PHILBY WILL BE CALLED *SYNOK*"

ORLOV ARRIVED IN Vienna after his hasty departure from Paris to learn that his next mission was to take over the running of a group of "illegals" in England. In the NKVD files can be found the original of the 19 June 1934 letter that the Centre sent to Austria three days after his arrival in the capital.

"During the past two months," Orlov was informed, "we have received two letters from MARR written in secret ink which we have not been able to develop."[1] One of his first tasks would be to establish a more reliable form of communicating with the Centre. The "invisible" writing in chemical ink between the lines of a seemingly innocent letter sent through the mail had been the preferred method used by Ignaty Reif, who for nearly a year had been running the NKVD *rezidentura* in London. Reif was a Russian "illegal" who is not to be confused with his better-known comrade Ignace Reiss, another Soviet "illegal" of Polish extraction who was murdered in Switzerland in 1937 after defecting from his network in Belgium. The code name MARR had been assigned to Reif before he landed in England in April 1934. As far as can be established, he was never identified as the "illegal" Soviet intelligence chief in Britain by MI5. His NKVD file shows that he had the status of acting *rezident* because the London operation was still being run as a subsidiary of the *rezidentura* in Paris.

Reif, under the alias Max Wolisch, had entered Britain on 15 April 1934 on a stolen Austrian passport No. 468302 issued in Vienna in 1933. The neatly cropped photograph on his aliens registration certificate issued by the Bow Street police station shows a round-faced individual with the alert, bespectacled eyes of a schoolteacher. He described himself as a commercial "representative" whose business was with the Scandinavian countries. This was to camouflage the frequent trips he made between London and Copenhagen which was the communication base for Reif and the NKVD couriers from Britain to make contact with Moscow without MI5 surveillance. He gave his address as 17 Talbot Square, Hyde Park, a brisk ten-minute walk from the Soviet embassy in Kensington Palace Gardens.[2]

Orlov's instructions marked a switch in the Centre's policy towards their London station. In contrast to Reif, he was to assume direct responsibility for the "illegal" group and, as *resident*, report directly to Moscow. His original orders required him to base himself in Copenhagen, from where, it was contended, he would run not only a network in Britain but also operations in the Baltic states, from where the British intelligence service controlled its agents operating in the Soviet Union.[3] Yet even before Orlov made his first visit to England by way of Stockholm, landing at the port of Harwich on 15 July 1934, difficulties were emerging in the offshore operation of the "illegal" networks in Britain from Denmark. Not least was the commencement of a new operation in England that was foreshadowed by the seventh paragraph of Orlov's letter of instruction, which reported that Reif had just enlisted a potentially important British recruit.

"At the time of the dispatch of this letter to you," the Centre advised, "we have just received from MARR – who is in Copenhagen at the moment – the following information which has just reached us by telegraph. The son of the Anglo agent Philby, Ibn Saud's counsellor, has been recruited by the group."[4]

Harry St John Bridger Philby, called Jack by his close friends, was a former British Government adviser who was one of the leading Arabists and desert explorers of his day. The prospect of his son being brought under Soviet control immediately made his recruitment an important operation for the NKVD chiefs, not just because his father was now an adviser to the ruler of Saudi Arabia. They believed – wrongly – that he must also have been an agent of Britain's Secret Intelligence Service. In reality Philby senior had been dismissed from the Colonial Office in 1924 for being at "loggerheads" with the Government, as it was described in a confidential MI5 report that noted how he had "several times acted in deliberate defiance of official policy".[5]

St John Philby was the son of a Ceylon tea-planter who cast himself in the mould of a great English eccentric. His life-long love affair with Arabia was the mainspring of a deep personal rebellion against the British Government which would almost lead to his internment as a Nazi sympathizer after he had spoken out against Winston Churchill, proclaiming that Hitler was a peacemaker, in a wartime parliamentary election. Eventually it led him to renounce Christianity in favour of Islam, taking the name Abdullah and marrying as his second wife a Saudi slave girl. St John Philby had never concealed from his son his contempt for the British ruling class or his wilful betrayal of its mannered principles when he felt called on by a higher personal destiny. The paradox of the father's divided loyalties was, as his NKVD file attests, inherited by his son, who by the age of twenty had already determined to follow the family tradition of duplicity.

Harold Adrian Russell Philby was born at Ambala in the Punjab on New Year's day 1912 during his father's service in India. Nicknamed Kim after the wily Irish boy raised among Indians who was the spy-hero of Rudyard Kipling's eponymous tale of imperial derring-do, life for Philby *fils* was to imitate fiction. His childhood was spent in awe of a famous father who was more often than not absent exploring the Empty Quarter of Arabia. His father's obsession with the alien attractions of Islam was to be matched by his own infatuation with Communism, which was the culmination of a political rebellion forged during his education at his father's old school and *alma mater*, Westminster, and Trinity College, Cambridge.

Kim Philby was not driven, as were so many of his generation, by poverty and social deprivation to embrace Communism. He hailed from a background of privilege and was schooled in the establishment of Britain's ruling class, and it stamped him for life. Though he adopted an alien political philosophy, like his father who kept up his membership of London clubs, young Philby never foreswore the institutional comforts. In his retirement in Moscow he admitted a yearning for the accoutrements of an English gentleman's life – the deep leather armchairs of the Pall Mall clubs, Coleman's mustard and Worcestershire sauce – and he religiously completed the day-old Times crossword puzzle every day.[6]

The roots of Kim Philby's Communism make all the more intriguing the revelations of the former KGB files, that detail the actual mechanism by which the Soviet intelligence service managed to induct so loyal a recruit. The process by which he and other scions of the British Establishment transformed themselves into underground Soviet agents whose names were to become synonymous with treachery has been the subject of fascination, investigation and speculation ever since 23 January 1963. On that night Philby vanished from Lebanon after he failed to turn up at the British embassy in Beirut. He had been working as a correspondent for the London *Observer* newspaper, a job which was rumoured to be his cover for continuing to work as an agent for MI6, as Britain's Secret Intelligence Service is popularly known from its pre-World War I military nomenclature, before it came under the control of the Foreign Office.

Philby's treachery[7] and the astonishing extent to which he had deceived his former colleagues in the British and American intelligence services was to become shockingly apparent six months later when he surfaced in Moscow to publicize his betrayal by admitting he had become a Soviet penetration agent long before he joined MI6 during World War II. The image of Britain's vaunted Secret Intelligence Service received another dent when it emerged that Philby's decision to flee to Moscow had been prompted by the bungled mission assigned to Nicholas Elliott, a former MI6 colleague, who had flown to Beirut to extract an admission of guilt and arrange for Philby's return and immunity from prosecution in return for a full and secret confession. The damage that Philby had inflicted on the British – and by implication on the Cold War operations of the Central Intelligence Agency to which they were tied by the special relationship – was extensive.

Philby's wartime career in MI6 had taken him into the upper reaches of British intelligence, culminating in his appointment to lead its anti-Soviet operations in its postwar Section IX. The belief that he was being groomed eventually to head the entire organization was reinforced in 1949 when he was assigned as liaison officer in Washington, a progress that was only derailed in 1951 following the defection of two Cambridge friends.

To the embarrassment of the British, it was the Americans who took a hard-line attitude over suspicions raised by Philby's links with the diplomats Guy Burgess and Donald Maclean. In May of 1951 both men fled to Moscow from London after receiving a tip-off that MI5 was closing in on them. Investigations by the FBI and CIA pointed to Philby. Washington demanded his recall after an investigation into allegations that he was the "third man" in the Cambridge spy ring. Lack of concrete evidence and cool bravado enabled Philby to survive interrogation by MI5. What he could not dispel, however was the cloud of circumstantial suspicion which made it impossible for him officially to stay in the service. With help from influential friends, Philby returned to journalism and, in 1955, had the satisfaction of a public exoneration from Prime Minister Harold Macmillan, who made a parliamentary statement denying that the former ranking MI6 officer was the "third man".

Official credibility was left in tatters after Philby's 1963 defection. Over the following sixteen years rumours continued to multiply that more of the Kremlin's British "moles" had burrowed their way into the upper reaches of British intelligence and the diplomatic service. The appalling dimension of one of the most spectacularly successful penetration operations in the history of espionage emerged in 1979, when Prime Minister Margaret Thatcher confirmed the existence of another agent of the Soviets' Cambridge espionage network. That bombshell detonated with the publication in dogged defiance of

English libel law of *The Climate of Treason* by the respected BBC journalist Andrew Boyle.[8]

The "fourth man" – as the US edition of Boyle's book was aptly titled – alluded to a spy in Buckingham Palace cryptically referred to as "Maurice", who was named in Parliament as Sir Anthony Blunt, one of Britain's most respected art historians, adviser to the Queen and former Surveyor of the Royal Picture Collection. Stripped of his knighthood in the public furore, Blunt, it was revealed, had confessed shortly after Philby's defection in return for a promise of secret immunity from prosecution. He, too, was a Cambridge graduate, who admitted being recruited and acting as a talent scout for the Soviets before joining MI5 during the war. Blunt's unmasking laid bare the hypocrisy of the British ruling Establishment's code of self-preservation. It led to a spate of allegations that other Soviet "moles" had benefited from this official reluctance to disclose the true degree to which the agents of the Kremlin had taken advantage of the edifice of privilege and class which constituted the so-called British Establishment.

Many of the distinguished Cambridge and Oxford contemporaries of Philby, Maclean, Burgess and Blunt who had become enamoured with the gospel of Marx in the 1930s fell under suspicion that they too might have betrayed their country to Moscow. The notion that there were scores of Stalin's Englishmen still to be unmasked also gathered credence from the popularity of the cynical webs of fictional Cold War espionage woven by John Le Carré. "Mole hunting" became a lucrative cottage industry for British journalists and writers cashing in on the public's appetite for spy stories. Rooting out the upper-class turncoats who had been manipulated by the sinister Karla-like Soviet masterminds enhanced the awesome reputation of the KGB and also satisfied a national psychological need to find the scapegoats whose treachery explained Britain's rapid postwar decline. When the British Government in 1987 sought to muzzle the former MI5 "mole hunter in chief", Peter Wright, to prevent the publication of his book *Spy-catcher*, the author's testimony gave further grounds for the belief that Soviet intelligence had recruited a legion of high-flying young Englishmen to betray their country.[9]

"It is simply not correct to say that the extent of penetration was thoroughly investigated," Wright declared in defence of his 1987 headline-grabbing affidavit that only the tip of a massive iceberg of Soviet penetration had so far been exposed.[10] Despite repeated official denials, the British Government's refusal to make public *any* MI5 investigatory records during their long and ultimately futile actions to enforce the oath of official secrecy on Wright in Australia and in the

European Court only added to the mountain of press speculation. If Orlov had still been alive, on the evidence of his KGB dossier he would certainly have relished the uproar which resulted from an operation he orchestrated fifty years earlier. Paradoxically, as the granite edifice of the Soviet Union began to crumble under the thaw induced by President Gorbachev's *glasnost*, the British Government retreated behind the archaic battlements of the Official Secrets Act, which was modified to make it harder for journalists or parliamentarians to discover the truth of intelligence cases.

The irony of the situation cannot have been lost on Philby as he read his copy of *The Times* in Moscow. In 1988 his masters in the KGB took it as a cue for a final curtain call to draw attention to and pay tribute to, his achievements. It was with obvious relish that Philby set about fanning the flames of speculation by granting an exclusive interview to a British journalist in the relative luxury of his large Moscow apartment, whose 12,000-book library would not have disgraced a Fifth Avenue apartment. Appropriately for the era of new Soviet "openness", Stalin's veteran English spy posed for photographs, not in uniform, but sporting carpet slippers and a monogrammed Cambridge-blue cashmere sweater. Beaming benignly for the camera, he cheekily held up a copy of *Spycatcher*, then still a banned book in his native land.

Philby took the opportunity to declare his unshakeable faith in Communism, declaring that he "had no regrets" and "would do it all over again". To prove his point he pulled out a tray full of Eastern Bloc medals, singling out his Order of Lenin, which he insisted was the equivalent to one of the better orders of British knighthood. "My loyalties were always to one side – the KGB," Philby asserted, expressing confidence that history would prove him right. "I want my bones to rest where my work has been,"[11] he concluded. His wish was to be granted three months later, following his death on 11 May 1988 from congestive heart failure. After lying in state in the gloomy marble entrance hall of the KGB officers' club, Philby's remains were interred in the Kuntsevskoye cemetery, Moscow, under a granite memorial emblazoned with a single gold star. The obsequies in the Soviet press paid tribute to his lifetime of "exceptionally delicate work" and his carefully unspecified "heroic" accomplishments were described only as "multifaceted and global in their geographic scope".[12]

Neither the obituaries, nor Philby himself, shed more light on the central enigmas of his long career than he had been permitted to reveal by the KGB in his published autobiography. The readers of the London *Sunday Times* had learned more from his final interview in 1988 about his still-strong addiction to the life-style of the English gentleman than they did about the heroic deeds he had performed for the Soviet intelligence service. He had declined to the end to give details about his recruitment or work by pleading that he was obliged to remain silent about "KGB operational matters".[13]

The veteran Soviet agent's last public performance was in marked contrast to the detailed assistance he had given to a generation of young KGB officers, to whom he was known by the code name TOM. (Among them was Oleg Tsarev, who found Philby always helpful and considerate. Tsarev first met TOM in 1974, when, as a serving intelligence officer, he was required to disguise his real name and call himself Alec, which was the name to which Philby personally dedicated the copy of *My Silent War* he gave to Tsarev). Yet even as one of the great heroes of the Soviet intelligence service, Philby himself was never permitted access to his own voluminous case file. He therefore never knew some of the essential details of his relationship with the Soviets. Indeed Philby could never have envisaged that so soon after his death the secret records to which even he was denied access are being declassified, including his own first-hand account and debriefing given to the KGB after his defection. Now, for the first time, it is possible to piece together the process by which the first and succeeding members of the Cambridge network really were recruited. The central and hitherto unknown role played by Orlov explains why Philby was always so guarded about revealing who it was that had masterminded what was to grow into one of the most celebrated spy rings in modern history, whose importance is only now beginning to be measured. Recently declassified FBI and US State Department records confirmed that Donald Maclean betrayed British Government secrets and Anglo-American atomic policy decisions which accelerated the Soviet acquisition of nuclear weapons and helped to shape the course of the Cold War.[14] Guy Burgess, the "third man" to be brought into the ring, helped extend to Oxford a network of Soviet underground agents whose efforts on behalf of Moscow became global when its members crossed the Atlantic to penetrate the Roosevelt administration. Other "Oxbridge" recruits of Stalin were to pass to the Soviets ULTRA military intelligence derived from intercepted German and Japanese coded messages which helped save the Red Army from defeat in World War II.[15]

"The Three Musketeers", according to a letter in Maclean's hand, was the nickname by which he, Philby, and Burgess liked to identify themselves, a recognition of the fact that under Orlov's direction they were the three original founding members of the Cambridge network.[16] Their enormous importance could not have been foreseen by the Centre or by Orlov when he arrived in Britain in July 1934.

Nor does it appear that it was simply chance which brought this particular Soviet "illegal" to London. Orlov himself provides clues that it was he who played a central role in developing the whole concept of recruiting disaffected university graduates as penetration agents. Pointers to the genesis of the scheme, which appears to have owed something to his experience of running underground networks in Europe, can be found in his *Handbook*. This revealing insider's guide to the strategy and tactics of espionage was written, as the author himself proclaims in its foreword, in an effort to reconstruct his 1936 manual which laid out "the base rules and principles of Soviet intelligence". The original manual, according to Orlov, was "the only textbook for the newly created NKVD school for undercover intelligence officers and army officers at the Central Military School in Moscow". He asserts he was a member of the faculty and had lectured for a number of years "as a sideline" before producing its original manual: *Tactics and Strategy of Intelligence and Counter-Intelligence*, based on "all the most important cases of intelligence and counter-intelligence work in the NKVD".[17]

Yet nowhere in his extensive KGB dossier is Orlov credited with the authorship, although he claimed to have produced it "at the beginning of 1936". Possibly he may have written some chapters of a teaching manual during his spell in Moscow from the end of 1935 to September 1936 which may later have been proscribed after his flight from Spain, when Orlov was branded a 'traitor'. But it is fact that no veteran who studied at the Central Military School before 1938 can recall his textbook – and it is even more curious that not a single copy survives.

What is significant about Orlov's claim, however, is his assertion that he had written it immediately after his return to Moscow from London where we now know that he had acted as midwife and first director of the Cambridge penetration network. Orlov was careful in 1964 to omit any hint of his own involvement when he reconstructed the alleged manual as his *Handbook of Intelligence and Guerilla Warfare* under the indirect patronage of the CIA. But in the context of his personal dealings with Philby, Maclean and Burgess, his writings assume a new importance – especially those passages that can be read as indirect credits to himself for developing the operation that recruited disaffected high-flying Cambridge graduates to serve Moscow. Its objective, he informs us without naming the targeted universities, was to cultivate potential recruits who, by virtue of their academic attainment could be counted on to rise rapidly to the senior echelons of government service and whose dedication to serve Communism would guarantee that Moscow would eventually be supplied with a steady stream of high-level secrets. The need for such informants, Orlov explained, was essential because Soviet intelligence, and especially Stalin, were wedded to the concept of *razvedka* as the only "true intelligence" – that is information "procured by undercover agents and secret informants in defiance of the laws of the foreign country in which they operate".[18] Moscow had laid down the fundamental principle that "important secrets of foreign states can and should be procured directly from the classified files in the government departments of those states and from foreign civil servants who agree to turn over state secrets to the Soviet Union". The dilemma that confronted the Soviet intelligence service in 1930 was that most of the sources they had already recruited were low-level employees of foreign ministries and intelligence services. While the information received from cypher clerks and secretaries in the British Foreign Office was valuable, the informants lacked access to the higher decision-making echelons. Orlov tells us that all the efforts made to win their informants promotion had been "spotty and far from satisfactory".[19]

"Only in the early 1930s," according to Orlov, "did one of the chiefs of the NKVD intelligence hit upon an idea which solved this most difficult problem as if by magic". His curiously elliptical explanation that the unidentified officer concerned "approached the problem not only as an intelligence man, but as a sociologist as well", suggests that he had more detailed knowledge of how the scheme evolved. Orlov was one of the few ranking NKVD officers of the time in Moscow who was equipped with the necessary operational experience to know that "in capitalistic countries lucrative appointments and quick promotions are usually assured to young men who belong to sons of political leaders, high government officials, influential members of parliament", for whom "promotion was almost automatic". Given Orlov's involvement in developing the Cambridge penetration network, which was based precisely on this principle, it is clear that he was referring to his own first-hand experience when he wrote: "It does not surprise anyone if a young man of this background, fresh from college, passes the civil service examinations with the greatest of ease and is suddenly appointed private secretary to a cabinet minister and in a few short years assistant to a member of the Government." How else but from direct access could he have known that the Centre "no longer worried about attaining promotions for their charges"?[20]

"Their promotions came automatically," Orlov wrote, self-congratulatorily, noting how "the NKVD chiefs looked forward with great anticipation to seeing some of the new recruits in ambassadorial posts a few years hence." Although no names were mentioned in the *Handbook*, this appears to be a reference to the subsequent careers of the Three Musketeers. His familiarity with the tactics used to build the Cambridge network is apparent from his detailed description of how "the NKVD *rezidenturas* concentrated their energy on the recruitment of young men of influential families". Philby, Maclean and Burgess are not named, but surely they were the models Orlov had in mind when he wrote that "the main theme on which the NKVD based its appeal was to young men who were tired of a tedious life in the stifling atmosphere of their privileged class". The secret of hooking them for clandestine Soviet service depended on a skilful angler's knack of choosing the right moment to strike. That was when their youthful idealism enabled them to be caught and directed into underground work – or, as he put it, "when the young men reached the stage when their thinking made them ripe for joining the Communist Party, they were told that they could be much more useful to the movement if they stayed away from the Party, concealed their political views and entered the 'revolutionary underground'."[21]

Orlov demonstrated a profound grasp of the psychological factors involved in the successful cultivation and recruitment of Philby and his comrades. Their intelligence and background did not make them easy catches, but it was Philby himself who acknowledged, some thirty years later, just how well his former mentor had played on the conflicting political currents facing a left-wing Cambridge graduate in the 1930s to persuade him to dedicate himself to the service of the Soviet Union. "It is a matter of great pride to me that I was invited, at so early an age, to play my infinitesimal part in building up that power," Philby observed in his KGB vetted autobiography. "How, where and when I became a member of the Soviet intelligence is a matter for myself and my comrades. I will only say that, when the proposition was made to me, I did not hesitate. One does not look twice at an offer of enrolment in an elite force."[22]

Philby may not have hesitated to take up an invitation to serve in an elite force, but the NKVD records show that the irresistible offer held out to him was not what he made it out to be since it was actually made without the authority of Moscow. The communications problems with the "illegal" station in London left the Centre unaware – and unapproving – of the initial approach to Philby that led him to become a Soviet agent. As a result, the usual lengthy process by which the local *rezidentura* submitted detailed reports on a potential candidate's suitability and then awaited the Centre's analysis and approval before sounding out his willingness to co-operate was accelerated.[23]

Now that the details of Philby's recruitment can be unravelled from the NKVD records it is evident that had it not been for the failure of chemical ink communications, which necessitated Reif, the "illegal" Soviet *rezident* taking the first steps towards his recruitment on his own initiative, the delays in waiting for Moscow approval would have been fatal to the recruitment. Philby would have proceeded with his plans to join the Communist Party of Great Britain. This in turn would almost certainly have ruled him out as a candidate because of the Centre's aversion to tapping for recruitment as penetration agents anyone who had become a fully fledged Party member with records vulnerable to police investigation. That Philby had approached the CPGB before his first meeting with Reif is itself confirmation that he had not, as previously believed, been recruited in Vienna. This is corroborated not only by the NKVD archival records, but also by the 283-page deposition on his recruitment and career that Philby provided for the KGB in 1985. This first-hand memoir tells how on his return from Vienna in the spring of 1934 he went to the headquarters of the Communist Party of Great Britain to register as a member *before* he was approached by Reif.[24]

"My decision to go to Austria was taken before I had decided to join the Communist movement," Philby explained, stating that his trip to Vienna had originally been motivated by his decision to pursue a diplomatic career after graduation. "Knowledge of the German language and culture was a condition of joining the Foreign Service,"[25] he said in his confessional deposition. If for no other reason than it was given in confidence to the KGB, his secret memoir is a more credible version of the truth than his coy and malicious published account, *My Silent War*. In his KGB deposition he describes how he attempted to reconcile his ambition to be a British Ambassador with his intense ideological commitment to Communism made shortly before his graduation. He said he had leaned steadily leftward from his support of the Labour Party at Westminster and industrious canvassing for them at Cambridge, where, despite a stutter that prevented him making speeches, he had become Treasurer of the University Socialist Society. He describes his Socialism as having been reinforced by his studying of economics after he switched Tripos subjects, after a dismal third class in History Part I in the exams at the end of his second year. He had embraced Marxism, he explained, more out of frustration than disgust at the rout of the Labour Party in the 1931 election, and he admitted it was not until his final term at Cambridge that he was truly convinced that Communism was the solution to Britain's political dilemma.

"I decided to work in some way for the Communist movement during my last week in Cambridge," Philby declared. "The actual process of my coming to this decision lasted about two years. In part the approach was rational and in part emotional." That his was not a blinding light on the road to Damascus conversion but the result of long and personal agonizing is consistent with what he wrote in his published memoir. "Naturally I had my doubts and hopes – and self-criticism," Philby admitted to the KGB. "But my self-examination and the influence of events in world affairs led me to this decision. I did not see any way to avoid the issue. Either I must take this decision or give up politics as a whole." He said that his decision was taken only after "an analysis of Marxism and, of course, study of the Great Depression".[26]

"One evening I reflected in my room at Cambridge," was how Philby recalled his moment of decision. "I sat down in an armchair and I took the decision there and then. It was a decision for life, but at that time it was known only to me and I declared it to no one but myself."[27] Philby sanctified his conversion to the new faith by spending the £14 prize Trinity awarded him for his upper-second in Part II of the Economics Tripos (Cambridge University Honours Examination) on the Communist bible: the complete works of Karl Marx.

Once Philby had decided to dedicate his life to serving the Revolution, he sought the advice of someone he trusted to put him in contact with those who could receive him into the new faith and provide direction for his missionary zeal. That person was Maurice Dobb, one of his economics supervisors, a junior fellow of Pembroke College. He was the Cantabridgian John the Baptist of Marx, preaching the decline of capitalism and the triumph of Communism. A patient and plausible teacher, as the British co-author of this book can personally attest, Dobb had inspired generations of undergraduates with his eloquence since May 1932, when he had carried the Cambridge Union Debate that "This House has more hope in Moscow than Detroit". One of the prominent early members of the British Communist movement, Dobb had never hidden his passionate commitment to the Revolution. His tersely reasoned articles and books promoting the Soviet Union were so widely read that they infuriated King George V who, in 1925, had vainly sought to have this "Bolshevik" corrupter of his loyal young undergraduates banished from his university.[28] But academic freedom triumphed and Dobb was later to become a full professor and a fellow of Trinity College after promising not to engage in subversive activities. He had little choice. He cut such a provocative figure that MI5 records which surfaced in the United States archives show that he was constantly under surveillance and his mail was frequently intercepted. It was only long after Dobb's death that Philby revealed that he was the Cambridge don who had been instrumental, not in recruiting him as had often been speculated, but in setting him on the road which eventually took him to Moscow.

"I have been watching you for several years. I have seen your movement in this direction and I'm very glad you have come to this decision." Philby said Dobb told him when he asked how to go about getting himself confirmed as a fully-fledged Communist.[29] In what may be a sinister pointer to a more significant role played by Dobb than he or Philby ever admitted, Dobb did not then direct his former pupil to the CPGB headquarters in London. Instead he gave Philby a letter of introduction to an executive of the International Workers Relief Organization known as MOPR from its Russian acronym for *Mezdunarodnya Organinzatsyr Pomoshy Rabochym*, a Communist front based in Paris. Philby notes in his KGB memoir how Dobb conspiratorially required him to memorize its addressee, whom he recalled had an "Italian sounding name".

This could have been Louis Gibarti, the alias of a prominent Comintern agent named Ladislas Dobos, whom Dobb knew from his contact with MOPR.[30] Dobb would have omitted Gibarti's name from both the letter and envelope for fear of losing his Cambridge fellowship, had the introduction to such a prominent international Communist been traced back to him by the ever watchful MI5.

Armed with Dobb's letter and a volume of Marx, Philby left Cambridge for London, where his father gave him £50 for proof-reading the galleys of *The Empty Quarter*, the latest account of his exploration of the Arabian desert. This was then a princely sum, enabling Philby to purchase a motorbike, on which he set off for the Continent to observe for himself the struggle between Socialism and Fascism. He chose Vienna, which had become the frontline of the conflict after Hitler rose to power and the Nazis sought to influence Austrian politics. The city had become the cockpit of a bitter political war between the urban Socialists and the right-wing in the coalition that controlled the Government. The Austrian Chancellor, Dr Engelbert Dolfuss, alarmed at the increasing power of the Nazis, manoeuvred to negotiate an accommodation with Hitler. But to do so he had to meet the demands of his right-wing allies that he crush the alleged Communist-led insurrection in the working-class district of his capital. Both sides had raised and equipped private forces and the situation on the streets of Vienna in the summer of 1934 had become explosive.

When Philby reached Paris en route to Austria, he used Dobb's letter to gain access to the MOPR leadership.[31] Learning that Philby was heading for Vienna and eager to assist the struggle against the Nazis, Gibarti – if as seems likely, it was he who advised the young Englishman – provided an introduction to Georg Nepler, the leader of the Austro-German Immigrant Help Committee.

On arrival in Vienna Philby related how he went to see Nepler, who was a musician by profession, "a Marxist by belief and a Communist by Party membership". In his spare time he directed the Help Committee, which, he told Philby, gave assistance to any and all refugees from Hitler no matter whether they were Communists or Social

Democrats. After Nepler had established to his satisfaction that his visitor really was genuinely dedicated to Communism, he asked what he thought he could do to help their cause.[32]

"I'm ready to do anything you need," Philby declared, recalling how he had asked Nepler to "recommend a place to stay where I wouldn't have to fear the surveillance of the landlord". He was given the address of "a very close comrade" named Litzi Friedman, whose parents lived in the centre of the city which had until recently been the crowning glory of the Hapsburg Empire. Frau Friedman's dedication to the Revolution was beyond doubt, Nepler explained: she had been jailed for two weeks the previous year for Communist activity because the Party had been banned in Austria.[33]

When Philby arrived at the home of Israel and Gisella Kohlman, Litzi's parents, who lived in a large apartment house at 9 Latchkagasse, they took him in as a lodger. Within a short time he had fallen for the vivacious charms of their plumpish daughter. Two years older than the reserved young Englishman, Litzi was an independent-minded divorcée who had only recently left her Zionist husband, Karl Friedman, whom she had married at the age of eighteen. There was a gypsy-like allure in the dark eyes of Litzi, that added a powerful sexual appeal to their shared commitment to the Communist faith. Against the background of Vienna's political turmoil, with its strikes and police patrols necessitating clandestine meetings of Party cells, the adrenalin of adventure enhanced the thrill of Philby's first romance as the two lovers shared the dangers of membership of the illegal Communist underground.

Litzi arranged for Kim to become treasurer of her Communist cell. He wrote political pamphlets and collected money, proudly recalling how potential donors reacted to his English accent generously with higher than average donations of ten Austrian schillings. Some of the cash was used to buy arms when violent confrontations broke out between the police and the urban Socialists. As Philby put it, "the Nazis had the support of forty per cent of the population, the same proportion as the Social Democrats, with the balance of twenty per cent in the hands of Dolfuss".[34] Vacillating between such conflicting demands, the Austrian Chancellor found it impossible to sustain his political balancing act in a country where the divisiveness between left and right was intensified by the stream of political and religious refugees fleeing from Hitler's regime.

Taking their cue from their German comrades, the Austrian Communist Party had gone underground and was following Moscow's directive to make ready for armed resistance in their working-class strongholds. Philby arrived to find preparations underway for manning the barricades to protect the Karl Marx and Goethe Hof, the large, modern workers' housing developments on the outskirts of the city. It seemed to him that he had arrived on the brink of a cataclysmic showdown between the forces of Fascism and Socialism, recalling with pride in later years how he played his part in the great struggle, assisting victims of Nazism by smuggling them out illegally into "safe" European countries. Food, money and clothes were needed to keep this "underground railway" system operating. The Comintern played a leading role in this effort, establishing in Paris a Committee for Aiding Refugees from Fascism, which operated alongside the MOPR. Philby worked as a courier for these groups, using his British passport for protection and cover for his illegal Party missions.

"Usually I took a large envelope with me which contained a large number of papers together with a parcel wrapped in brown paper. I hadn't any idea what was inside, it could have been money, it might have been instructions, it could have been private letters between a husband and wife,"[35] was how Philby described these missions, which he assured the KGB he had undertaken confidently. "My main work at that time was to help Vienna's city communists of MOPR. I could help them in a very active way because I had a British passport. You probably have no idea how prestigious a British passport was at that time in countries like Austria, Czechoslovakia and so on because everyone would assume that a British traveller was either a Lord or a diplomat with a pocketful of money. It was sufficient to show your British passport to gain admittance anywhere . . . and as soon as I joined their organization its leader said, 'It is a stroke of fortune that he has a British passport, he can help with channels of communication.' My contact in the MOPR city committee was, at that time, a charming lady of 50 or so by the name of Mitzi Frischau. She was the one who would give me courier assignments between Prague, Vienna and Budapest."[36] Frischau kept him in ignorance of what those packages contained, which, he was assured, was for his own protection. "If I had been arrested and asked what was in the envelope and parcel," Philby asserted in his secret memoir, "I would simply have replied that a friend of mine had asked me to bring them with me and that I didn't know what was inside." If he had been stopped, his cover was that he was simply carrying them to a destination he had written down. "I would have taken out my wallet and searched for the address," he explained, "and as naturally as possible declared, 'Oh, God, I have left it in Vienna.' "[37]

Conceding that such a story might not have worked if he had been stopped by the Austrian police, Philby reflected that, in comparison to his later exploits for the Soviet intelligence service, the alibis concocted by the Viennese Communists were "only on the amateur and unconvincing level". He said he had been given a bunch of mimosa blossom as an "identity ticket" during one trip to Prague. The flowers had crumbled to yellow powder before he reached his destination, but this had not mattered to his contact. Primitive though his "tradecraft" was then, Philby told the KGB that he did not recall a single incident which put him in real danger. He insisted that he had been unafraid even after Dolfuss's crackdown in Vienna in the spring of 1934, when Government artillery shelled the Karl Marx Hof. Hundreds were killed and wounded in four days of bloody street fighting before the workers' insurrection was ruthlessly crushed, forcing many comrades to make good their escape to avoid arrest. Philby admitted that he did not fire any shots in the battle, not through any lack of valour on his part. He explained he had been detailed to a machine-gun crew, but his group never received its weapon, so his principal activity during the fighting was as one of the couriers maintaining communication with the underground Communist cells.[38]

Britain and France demonstrated their indifference to what the British Foreign Secretary dismissed as a "mad little civil war". Their unwillingness to intervene diplomatically to save Viennese Socialism from extermination by the Nazi pressure left Philby more convinced than ever that only the Soviet Union offered any hope of saving Europe from sliding into the totalitarian abyss of Fascism. At the same time he was realistic enough to realize that the insurrection's failure foreshadowed the eventual usurpation of the Dolfuss government by the Nazis and annexation of Austria by Germany. He decided to pull out, although it was to be four years before the *Anschluss*, when Hitler's open Mercedes Benz drove triumphantly through the cheering Viennese crowds jamming the swastika-bedecked Ringstrasse.

"I left Austria a more convinced Communist than I had arrived there," Philby assured the KGB in 1985, stressing that his decision to leave was made not out of consideration for his own safety, but because of concern for his comrades in arms. He said that, while his "almost diplomatic" status was guaranteed by his British passport, he feared that Litzi would be rearrested and sent to a concentration camp if she remained in the city.[39] "If the Nazis had come, she would have been done away with; that was why I decided to marry her, give her a British passport, return to England and from there to carry on my Party activities,"[40] Philby said, recalling how they were married in a hasty ceremony in Vienna town hall on 24 February 1934. Once Litzi had obtained her British passport two months later, they set off across the Austrian border, heading west across Germany, with his wife riding pillion on his motorcycle. Passing through France en route for the Channel ports, the newlyweds stopped off in Paris for sightseeing. Though neither knew it at the time, Philby's path crossed that of Orlov for the first time, shortly before his own hurried departure for Switzerland. Ironically, it was when Orlov reached Vienna that he received the secret instructions from Moscow that eventually brought him together with Philby.

Arriving in London, Philby initially began making plans to renew his links with the Communist Party after he set up temporary home with Litzi at his mother's home in Acol Road in the north-west London district of Kilburn. The long-suffering Dora Philby found her son's Austrian wife to be a hard and domineering woman whom she suspected of being the prime inspiration for her son's now openly avowed Communism. But Party work would not provide them with any income. Short on funds and long on ambition, Philby decided to use his Cambridge degree and Trinity connections to get into the Government bureaucracy. In common with many of his contemporaries, he sat for the Civil Service examination.

"I do hope [Kim] gets a job to get him off this bloody Communism," Philby's mother wrote to his father in Jeddah. "He's not quite extreme yet, but may become so if he's not got something to occupy his mind."[41] But her hopes, and her son's desire to pursue a career in the Foreign Office were both dashed after he visited Cambridge. There he enlisted the aid of his former tutor and appealed for funds to help his Viennese comrades. The Socialist Society was more forthcoming than Dennis Robertson, a senior fellow of Trinity who had been his economics tutor. He was lukewarm when asked for a reference to support Kim's Foreign Office application. Despite his long friendship with St John Philby, Robertson regarded his son's espousal of radical Socialism as too profound, so he felt he had to caution the son that he would be obliged to warn the selection board of the Foreign Office that his former student's "sense of political injustice might well unfit him for administrative work".[42] Knowing that this aspersion on his left-wing views would damn his chances of making a career in government, Philby decided to abandon his effort to get into the Foreign Office and announced his intention of working for the Communist Party.

Ironically the Communist Party of Great Britain also had doubts about Philby, but for other reasons. It hesitated to welcome with open arms this Cambridge educated product of the British privileged class. According to what Philby himself told the KGB, if his ideological zeal had not burned so fiercely, his enthusiasm to serve the Revolution would have been cooled by the frosty reception he received at Party headquarters. At the dingy King Street office building overlooking Covent Garden produce market he encountered the scepticism and suspicions of a pettifogging functionary. His contempt for the narrow-minded insularity of the CPGB was still fierce fifty years later when he told the KGB how he was confronted with hostile questions about who he was, where he had been and why he wanted to join the Party. The desk-bound official appeared to disbelieve Philby's account of how he had just been risking his life for the Revolution on the barricades of Vienna.

"Well, we must verify this. The Party is illegal in Austria and that's why we may have some difficulty," Philby was told. "Come back in about six weeks."[43]

"Had I joined the Party before I would not have been the Kim Philby who is talking to you now!" he assured the KGB when he dictated his memoir for them in 1985. The bureaucratic brush-off was taken as a personal affront, although Philby reflected that the Communist Party's reluctance to admit him marked a turning point in his life. That month-and-a-half's delay saved him from joining the CPGB and so establishing a police record that would probably have ruled out his recruitment by Soviet intelligence. Though an ardent disciple of Lenin to the end of his life, Philby would look back with relief on his abortive visit to King Street, which, along with his participation in the London May Day that year, he observed, was the "last Communist action" he ever openly undertook.[44]

It was while Philby was kicking his heels in frustration at the British Communist Party's reluctance to enrol him that he was spotted as a potentially valuable recruit for the Soviet intelligence service by a London-based talent scout for the NKVD. In his published autobiography Philby declined to reveal anything about the actual mechanism of his recruitment, declaring that it was no business of his readers. He fudged the issue by telling his own children on one of their visits to Moscow that he was "recruited in 1933", the implication being that he had become a member of the Soviet intelligence service in Vienna, when he was "given the job of penetrating British Intelligence".[45] In the interview Philby gave the *Sunday Times* shortly before his death he was still evasive about revealing when and where he was recruited, and dropped hints which contradicted his earlier claims.

"My work in Vienna must have caught the attention of people who are now my colleagues in Moscow, because almost immediately on my return to Britain I was approached by a man who asked me if I would like to join the Russian intelligence service," Philby cryptically declared.[46] His assertion can now be seen as just another attempt by the "first man" of the Cambridge network to throw investigators off the scent by laying a false trail. In fact his file reveals the identity of the Austrian who had spotted him and introduced him to the Soviet officer who tapped him for recruitment by the mastermind who had arrived to run the "illegal" NKVD station in London.

The NKVD records show that it was Alexander Orlov who really was the *éminence grise* of the Cambridge network. Philby successfully managed to confuse the trail. None of his American interrogators so much as suspected that Orlov had ever been to Britain, and certainly no MI5 officer has even so much as hinted in private or public that he was the long sought after animator of one of the most successful spy networks ever recruited by Soviet intelligence. Orlov may not have initiated the first stage of the approach to Philby, but he supervised and was ultimately responsible for directing Philby as a fully-fledged Soviet intelligence agent. As the NKVD London *rezident*, often out of touch with Moscow, Orlov was responsible for authorizing the process which transformed the ideologically-driven young English-man into a disciplined agent equipped with the expertise and psychological resources for carrying out his assigned mission of penetrating the British intelligence services. The eighteen volumes that make up Philby's file detail how Orlov was also directly involved in inducting the two other recruits making up the "Three Musketeers", who formed the nucleus of the Cambridge network.[46]

Philby did not reveal the identity of any of those involved in giving birth to the Cambridge network. When *My Silent War* was published in 1968, Orlov was alive and in contact with the CIA, who had never learned about his role as the animator of the Cambridge spies. At that time, as his KGB file reveals, Orlov, even after thirty years as an exile in the United States, was still performing a valuable role by not betraying the identity of any of the Soviet penetration agents he had run. What Philby did not know was that even as he was writing his carefully tailored autobiography, the KGB was mounting an under-cover operation to locate and re-establish contact with Orlov and persuade him to return to Moscow. A "double defection" by Orlov at that time in the Cold War would have notched up another propaganda coup for the Soviet intelligence service. So Philby, bound by the strict rules of *Konspiratsia*, was not permitted by the KGB, who approved every word of his manuscript, even to hint how he had been recruited.

Orlov, therefore, was not only considered a potentially useful asset but there was also a need to protect the other Soviet agents he came to London to run, including the identity of the Austrian woman who had spotted Philby and by whose efforts he was dissuaded from joining the Communist Party. From his own interrogations in 1952 Philby, as we shall see, knew that this particular operative, whose code name was EDITH, had fallen under suspicion. Moreover she was still alive in 1968 and living in England at the time his book was published.

Edith Tudor Hart was the real name of the Soviet agent who turns out to have been the long sought missing link in Philby's recruitment. Edith, as her NKVD file reveals, was far more than a run-of-the-mill operative. Born in 1908 into the Suschitsky family, Edith, as a former member of the Vienna Communist Party, had arrived in London in 1933 after escaping prosecution for her illegal Party activities. Like her friend Litzi Friedman, she had sought refuge by marrying an English medical doctor named Alex Tudor Hart, who sympathized with the Comintern. An accomplished photographer, who had photographed the poverty of the Vienna slums for left-wing magazines, she had soon established a successful London studio with a growing reputation for children's portraiture.[47]

It was not, however, for her photographic skills that Edith Tudor Hart was brought into the NKVD's London underground network. Her file discloses that she had been active in the Communist underground in Vienna in 1929 and served as one of the trusted "cultivation officers" of the London "illegal" *rezidentura*. Her job was to spot sympathizers who were potential candidates for recruitment, like Philby. Although shortsighted, which led to her being criticized for not being careful enough, she established a reputation as a very loyal and resourceful comrade who carried out important assignments for Moscow.[48]

It was Edith Tudor Hart, who had also known Litzi Friedman in Vienna, who invited her old comrade to tea shortly after the Philbys had returned to London in May 1934. Litzi brought along her husband, since he was at a loose end while waiting impatiently to hear whether he would be accepted into the Communist Party. Over the teacups the couple gave vivid first-hand accounts of action on the Vienna barricades. Philby announced that the experience had made him more determined than ever to find some way of continuing to work for the Party in England, despite, as he told it, the off-hand way he had been treated at CPGB headquarters.

Philby's ardour and the cool manner with which the reflective pipe-smoking young Englishman recounted his underground courier missions impressed Tudor Hart. Although it later became part of the Philby legend that he had smuggled comrades to safety through the sewers of the Austrian capital, he admitted in his KGB debriefing that although he learned such operations had been conducted, he himself was not personally involved in them.[49] However, his connections to the British Establishment, through his well-known father (whose criticism of British policy in the Middle East was becoming more outspoken) fired Edith Tudor Hart's interest. She did not tell him so at the time, but as an undercover Soviet agent she saw at once that Kim, rather than Litzi, could be turned into a potentially valuable asset for the Soviet underground network to which she belonged. Moreover, she decided to move quickly to forestall Philby from joining the CPGB.[50]

The Soviet "illegal" to whom Edith Tudor Hart reported about Philby was an Austrian named Arnold Deutsch who had worked with her in the Vienna underground. He assured the Centre: "I knew her from Vienna in 1926. She is about thirty. She married an English doctor and in May came to Britain. She works as a photographer and has a studio. She is one of the most celebrated children's photographers in England. I met her soon after my arrival in Britain. She immediately agreed to work for us."[51]

Deutsch himself was not Austrian, but a Czech by birth, whose parents had moved to Vienna in 1908 when he was four years old. Deutsch possessed unique qualifications and a talent for "illegal" work that had brought him to the attention of Moscow when he joined the Communist Party as a student at Vienna University. A handsome man with twinkling blue eyes and fair curly hair, Deutsch was far from the stereotype middle-European trader's son raised in the Orthodox Jewish quarter of Vienna. A brilliant student who had studied chemistry, philosophy and psychology before he was twenty-four, he had been awarded a doctorate with distinction for a thesis on silver salts. His study of Marxism had persuaded him to become a Communist, like his wife Josefine, whom he married in 1929. On the eve of the Vienna uprising, in January 1932, the Deutsches had travelled to Moscow, where Arnold was assigned to the International Department of the Comintern. In August that year he joined the Foreign Department of the NKVD, when he began instruction in the duties of a special agent in the Soviet intelligence service. His wife, "Fini", worked from 1931 to 1935 with the International Department of the Comintern, using the cover name Liza Kramer. After qualifying as an underground radio operator, she would later rejoin her husband in London in February 1936.[52]

It was as a husband and wife team that the Deutsches operated in London, although they had travelled separately on their own Austrian passports. Arnold assumed the legitimate cover of an academic researcher attached to London University.[53] On the surface Deutsch was just another aspiring professor from Vienna, the home of psychology, who soon acquired a wide circle of friends in the British academic community. None of them ever suspected that the amiable and clever young academic, who entertained so frequently at his spacious flat on Lawn Road, at the heart of Hampstead's intellectual community, was being funded by and operating under the directions of NKVD headquarters in Moscow. Nor did any of his academic associates guess that Deutsch was operating under a series of operational aliases including STEPHAN, LANG and ARNOLD. OTTO was the code name Deutsch customarily used with the British contacts he cultivated during the four years he operated as one of the principal lieutenants and aides of the London "illegal" station.[54]

It was Deutsch with whom Edith Tudor Hart urgently consulted in late May or early June 1934 to discuss how to expedite the approach to Philby before the six weeks expired and he returned to Communist Party headquarters. Philby was a perishable commodity, and that was why they decided to rush through the normally lengthy procedure and careful checks that the Centre insisted upon before approving the first covert approach to a potential agent. According to her report on Philby's file, through her own contacts with the Austrian underground Tudor Hart ran a swift check and, when this proved positive, Deutsch immediately recommended to Reif, the acting *rezident*, that he pre-empt the standard operating procedure by authorizing a preliminary personal sounding out of Philby.[55]

Moving a recruitment along so fast was not without risks and Reif knew that he was courting the disapproval of the cautious chiefs at the Centre if the operation went sour. But yet another breakdown in communications with Moscow provided him with the latitude he needed to justify acting on his own initiative to authorize Deutsch to arrange a clandestine "meet".

Philby's ignorance of Moscow's rigorous vetting requirements is evident from the account he gave the KGB of that first meeting with Deutsch. He recalled the elaborate precautions that Tudor Hart had taken to ensure that he was not being tailed during a contact with a Soviet underground agent. Of the meeting that changed his life Philby said: "An acquaintance of mine whom I used to know in Austria found me and asked whether I wanted to meet a very important person who could be of interest. Of course I answered 'Yes' without hesitating. And in two or three days we set out on a long trip about the City, taking a taxi, going down into the Underground, walking on foot, hailing a cab suddenly and then changing to another taxi."[56] Philby, apparently through lapse of memory, alluded to his having met Edith Tudor Hart in Vienna, which the NKVD reports show was another case of his memory being in conflict with the records. But she was the one who accompanied him on the June morning when they criss-crossed

London several times on their way to meet Deutsch. She, he remembered, had chided him for trying to short-circuit the elaborate rules of *Konspiratsia* developed by the NKVD, which were intended to throw off any shadowers and that turned an otherwise simple journey into a "very complicated trip which lasted several hours".

"It ended around mid-day in Regent's Park with 'our man' there sitting on a bench," Philby said, recalling how Tudor Hart had introduced him to this unidentified person as "the man we spoke of" before she walked swiftly away. This, he said – incorrectly as the record reveals – was the last he ever saw of her.[57]

"Good afternoon," was how Philby remembered introducing himself. His proffered hand was grasped with a conspiratorial firmness by the anonymous man, who "began asking about my views and all my activities". Since he was obviously a native of central Europe, it did not strike Philby as odd that, as they sat on a bench in a London park, their conversation slipped into German, a language in which Philby welcomed the opportunity to prove he was now fluent. Nor did he recall any surprise that this stranger appeared to know a great deal about him.

"I didn't ask him any questions about himself," Philby added, "and really I didn't know then where he came from, whom he represented – the Soviet Union or the Comintern."[58]

"I know that you'd like to join the Communist Party," Philby said he was told by the shortish, bright-eyed man, who cautioned him: "You'll become one of many thousands of Communists. You will have a direct link to the working class, a direct link. However, you are a bourgeois by education, appearance and origin. You could have a bourgeois career in front of you – and we need people who could penetrate into the bourgeois institutions. Penetrate them for us!"[59]

Philby, in his KGB memoir, claimed to have swiftly sized up the purpose of their talk. "The main thrust of the conversation was that he was offering me a very interesting future, very exciting work and prospects so that I, while occupying interesting positions, would supply information which a Communist could not usually get access to," Philby declared. "In other words, you've just politely asked me whether I will consent to be a deep penetration agent."[60]

"That is exactly what I'd like to offer you," responded Deutsch, according to Philby. Whether or not an "illegal" as well trained and shrewd as Deutsch would have talked about "deep penetration" when he reported only that they had agreed on anti-fascist work is open to doubt, but Philby said that he did and that he "found the offer fascinating". So far there had been little to stir his adrenalin in Britain, which had run at a high level during his months in Vienna. Adrift in in his native country, that had denied him the opportunity of a prestigious Foreign Office career to support ego and wife, it is not hard to understand the irresistible appeal of this invitation offered in an afternoon encounter with a Soviet intelligence officer on a bench in Regent's Park.

"My future looked more romantic now," Philby recalled, carefully adding for the benefit of his KGB audience: "A little later I realized that my work wouldn't always be defined as 'romantic', but would be difficult, humdrum and very hard. I did not know it then – and even if I had known it, maybe I would still have given the same answer I did then. 'I agree,' I said – and we arranged to meet again in two weeks."[61]

Only after Deutsch had reported positively on the outcome of his meeting with Philby did Reif advise the Centre of the potential new candidate for cultivation. He reported that he was confident that they had discovered a potentially very useful and trustworthy recruit for "the organization", as he put it in his monthly letter to Moscow in June 1934, signed with his cryptonym MARR and written from Copenhagen shortly after his initial cablegram:

In future Philby will be called SYNOK. Through Edith, who is known to you, who had worked for some time under ZIGMUND in Vienna, we have established that the former Austrian Party member, who had been recommended to Edith by our former Vienna comrades, has arrived in Britain from Vienna, together with her husband, an Englishman. He is also known to Arnold. Edith has checked their credentials and has received recommendations from her Vienna friends. I have decided to recruit the fellow without delay – *not for "the organization", it is too early for that, but for anti-Fascist work* [emphasis added]. Together with Arnold and Edith, I worked out a plan for Arnold to meet with SÖHNCHEN before SÖHNCHEN moved to his father's flat. Arnold Deutsch's meeting with SÖHNCHEN took place with all precautions. The result was his full readiness to work for us.[62]

After his first meeting with Deutsch, as Reif's cable indicates, Philby had not only been sounded out as a potential NKVD asset but had also been given a code name. This was SYNOK in Russian, but the NKVD records show that their London "illegals" preferred to use German rather than Russian. Not only was it the spoken language they all shared, but in the event of surveillance or interception of their communications the use of German would serve to disguise their Soviet connection. So Philby was usually referred to in correspondence by the German diminutive SÖHNCHEN, whose English equivalent is SONNY as in "Sonny Jim". But his report makes it very clear that Reif referred to the Centre the question whether to proceed further in recruiting Philby for "the organization" since it was "too early" a stage for SÖHNCHEN to be considered for anything more taxing than general "anti-Fascist work". This was in line with two stages of NKVD recruitment procedure. They were by no means instantaneous and, as Philby's file shows, he was not considered an inducted agent under discipline and capable of operational tasks for many months. The recruitment was not completed until *after* Orlov had taken up direction of the London *rezidentura* and the files make it clear that it was he who played the supervisory role in the process, eventually meeting with SÖHNCHEN six months later.[63]

The precise dates of Philby's recruitment are not clear from his file. Philby's own recollection was that his first meeting with Deutsch in Regent's Park took place "at the end of May or in early June 1934".[64] This corroborates Reif's report to Moscow Centre number 2,696, which is undated, but from its numerical sequence was telegraphed by cypher from Copenhagen in early June. The "acquaintance" from Vienna whom Philby states that he knew in Austria was Edith Tudor Hart. So, while Philby was not, as has so often been claimed, recruited in Vienna, the "Austrian connection" *did* play a significant role in bringing him into contact for the first time with the Soviet intelligence service.[65]

Philby was careful never even to hint at the role played by Tudor Hart and disguised her role and that of Deutsch when, in his interview in 1988, he conceded that his recruiter was "not a Russian, although he was working for the Russians".[66] Apart from the need to protect the Austrian connection, he appears to have been particularly anxious to play down the significance of Deutsch. Although he himself never had access to his own or OTTO's files, the KGB, for reasons that Deutsch's dossier makes obvious, were most anxious not to reveal that he had been one of their star recruiters. The NKVD records show that Deutsch had brought them no fewer than seventeen important British agents to serve Stalin during the time he operated in London between 1934 and 1937. Only a handful have ever been identified by the British, and they included recruits he made at the Universities of both Oxford and Cambridge.

Philby's deposition for the KGB also discloses that he had a particular justification for not giving any clues that could put Tudor Hart at risk of prosecution. He told the KGB how MI5 suspicions about her had almost prematurely unmasked him as a spy during the intense interrogations he underwent in 1952 for his suspected tip-off of Burgess and Maclean. The moment of crisis came during his confrontation with the legendary police investigator Arthur Skardon, who had shattered the cover of atomic spy Klaus Fuchs. Philby recalled for the benefit of the KGB how he had been saved by his ice-cool demeanour when the questioning turned to his connection with Tudor Hart, who had fallen under MI5 suspicion

"Skardon's technique during the interrogation was such," according to Philby, "that he used to start a conversation on some general and abstract subject, for instance about China or America, then suddenly inject a small question into the conversation." This was how his interrogator had deftly slipped in a seemingly innocuous reference to Edith Tudor Hart, about whom Philby had already been questioned by Dick White of MI5.

"Edith Tudor Hart was that same woman who had introduced me to OTTO, everything had started with her," Philby told the KGB. "Indeed White asked me about her. Of course, I had met her about ten times, but I responded to White: 'Edith Tudor Hart? Was that the name you mentioned? No I don't remember her.' "[67] When White had said that Philby might be "interested to know" that, as an espionage suspect, her phone had been tapped and that MI5 had intercepted a call to her husband at home telling him to destroy negatives of a photograph she had taken of Philby, he claimed he had eluded the trap by saying that many people had taken his picture and that he had no specific recollection of Tudor Hart.[68]

"Skardon bore in mind this very episode in the previous interrogation with White," Philby said, observing how in a calculated aside, the canny police interrogator had interjected: "Yes, I forgot to ask you, you told Dick White that you had not met a woman called *Elizabeth* Tudor Hart."[69]

"Tudor Hart, oh, yes, I remember him asking about her, but I haven't met the woman," Philby said he responded. He told the KGB that he had almost been caught off guard. Skardon had evidently hoped to catch him out if he had corrected him by responding: "Not *Elizabeth* Tudor Hart, but *Edith* Tudor Hart."[70]

"Such minor tricks could get on one's nerves and lead to confusion," Philby observed with the self-effacing confidence of a veteran Soviet agent for whom the lesson had helped him survive more than one such trap. It was, he said, to settle this old score that he had deliberately included in *My Silent War* the photograph of him as a pensive young man smoking a pipe which had been taken by Tudor Hart shortly after his return from Vienna. "The negative really was destroyed, but I kept the photo," he chuckled, pointing out to the KGB with relish that "neither Dick White nor anybody else managed to prove that it was Tudor Hart who had taken it".[71]

Looking back on his long career as a Soviet intelligence agent, Philby could be forgiven for preening his ego by underlining for the benefit of a new generation of KGB officers the sang-froid that had made him such an accomplished spy. But learning the "tradecraft" that was essential to his success and survival began only after Philby had been tapped for the first stage of his recruitment by Reif. Contrary to his later assertions, the NKVD records confirm that Philby's actual induction into the Soviet intelligence service did not take place immediately or follow automatically after his first meeting with Deutsch in Regent's Park. It was not until after Orlov arrived in London in July that the process of transforming this promising candidate into a Soviet agent was effected under the supervisory direction of the new chief of the London station.

7

"A GREAT APPETITE FOR AGENT WORK"

"THE SONS of many distinguished public figures sympathize with the Communist Party and work for it, we will have a list of them before long." This was the assessment included in the first report Orlov relayed to Moscow in July 1934, shortly after he assumed command of the "illegal" *rezidentura*.[1]

Naming friends and associates who shared a sympathy for Communism was standard Soviet procedure for testing the willingness and suitability of candidates being considered for recruitment, but in Philby's case it assumed a special significance because Orlov's primary mission was to organize the penetration of the British Intelligence Services. It was also Soviet practice to order potential recruits to break off all contacts with open Communists and instructions had already been issued to Philby by Deutsch to have nothing more to do with British Communist Party headquarters in King Street. Given the way they had spurned his original application, this directive must have given Philby some satisfaction although he cannot have relished being told to dispose of all his left-wing books and pamphlets, including his prize collection of the works of Karl Marx. But to establish his political respectability he was instructed to take every opportunity of demonstrating that he had grown out of his "student" Socialism. To reflect the bland conservatism of the British Establishment Deutsch advised Philby to set about finding a respectable career to pursue, one which would ultimately enable him to be of assistance to Moscow.[2]

When Orlov landed at the port of Harwich on the east coast of England on 15 July 1934 he appeared to be an American entrepreneur arriving to open an import office in London. He had travelled via Stockholm where his US passport was newly stamped with the UK visa he had obtained from the British consulate four days earlier.[3] At the same time, however, Orlov's file reveals that he was facing a conflict between his loyalty to the NKVD and his family obligations. After he had returned to Moscow via Ostend on 25 July to make a report on the London station, he wrote a personal request to Artusov, the head of the Foreign Department, asking to be relieved of his foreign duties due to the poor health of his daughter who needed constant attention. His request was turned down and Orlov returned to London the following month to assume the running of what was to become one of the Soviet Union's most important intelligence operations.[4]

The NKVD archive records of the London "illegal" station disclose that Orlov inherited a network of productive British agents, including an academic at London University whose code name was PROFESSOR. He was to prove a less valuable source for Orlov than three of Deutsch's recruits, BÄR (BEAR), ATILLA and NACHFOLGER (SUCCESSOR). Their code names appear frequently in his reports from London, but since none was uncovered by the British, the Russian Intelligence Service – in line with the practice of the FBI and CIA – has decided that it would be inappropriate to identify them for this book.[5]

Anticipating that the exploitation of the NACHFOLGER group and the development of his own network of agents would take considerable time and effort, Orlov returned to London prepared for a long sojourn in Britain. Mindful how his cover had been blown in Paris, he appears to have been determined this time to develop a cast-iron "legend" as a legitimate cover for his clandestine operations. For this reason he took yet another route back to England, arriving at Newhaven on 18 September after crossing the Channel from Dieppe. As an American importer/exporter such frequent foreign trips would be unlikely to invite surveillance by MI5 and the ever-alert Special Branch of the Metropolitan Police.

William Goldin was the "legend" under which Orlov operated in Britain as the NKVD *rezident* in London. As far as can be established, neither his cover nor his connection with the Cambridge spies was ever suspected by the British authorities. Had MI5 records contained any trace of Goldin/Orlov, he would surely have been unmasked by Peter Wright's investigation and been named in *Spycatcher*. Significantly, he reveals that Edith Tudor Hart had also fallen under MI5 suspicion, but only as a "carrier" not as the Soviet agent who had talent-spotted Philby.[6]

One reason why Orlov's cover worked so well was that he was operating with the genuine American passport he had obtained illegitimately during his trip to the United States two years earlier. He had also worked up and completely adopted the persona of William Goldin, an Austrian-born immigrant to the United States who spoke English with an accent. Outwardly there was nothing to indicate that Orlov/Goldin was not the legitimate businessman he claimed to be, and to stamp his "legend" with credibility he set up an import/export business with funds allocated by Moscow for the purpose.

In accordance with British law, the NKVD front proclaiming itself "The American Refrigerator Company Ltd" – as headed notepaper in Orlov's dossier announced – had an English director named M. S. Stansfield. It is ironic, in the light of Orlov's secret mission, that his company's address was Imperial House at No. 84 Regent Street, only a hundred yards from Piccadilly Circus, traditionally regarded as the heart of the British Empire. The actual entrance to its fourth-floor office suite was situated just around the corner from the famous Café Royal, in a quiet colonnaded arcade known as Air Street. Appropriately for an espionage cover, The American Refrigerator Company's office was a floor above the offices of the London branch of Hollywood's Central Casting Bureau, the British headquarters of Encyclopaedia Britannica and the Duckerfield School of Dancing.[7]

Goldin's neatly printed business cards listed the American Refrigerator Company's telephone number as Regent 2574. It conducted a legitimate business importing the best models of US-made electric freezers and took out advertisements promoting its products in the trade papers. As managing director, the bespectacled Mr Goldin kept punctual office hours, joining the throng of commuters in the Underground as he travelled to Piccadilly Circus Station from the furnished flat he rented just north of Bayswater Road. To protect his cover the Centre arranged for Orlov's wife and young daughter to travel to London separately, using an Austrian passport in the name of Frau Feldbiene. Since Maria had again been detailed to act as one of the *rezidentura*'s liaison officers, the strict rules of *Konspiratsia* required that they did not live together openly as man and wife. As Maria Feldbeine, Mrs Orlov set up separate home in a nearby flat, a short ride by Underground from her husband's home.

The strict security precautions with which Orlov cloaked his personal and professional life were soon to prove their value when a slip-up by another Soviet "illegal" agent led the Vienna police to discover that the Austrian passports issued to Maria Feldbeine, Max Wolisch and Ignaty Reif had been fraudulently obtained using false birth certificates. Orlov's NKVD file attributes this to the "carelessness" of a fellow agent who he himself obliquely referred to in connection with this incident in his *Handbook*. Without a hint of how it related to his own operations, Orlov wrote that this slip-up, which "caused a great deal of trouble to NKVD intelligence", occurred in 1934 when "a top flight intelligence officer by the name of Mally" was assigned to underground work in the USA.

Mally's genuine Austrian passport, issued in the name of Paul Hardt, which he had "obtained by fraud in Vienna", was stamped "not valid for travel in the United States".[8] When he applied to the US consulate in Paris in Autumn 1935 for a visa, rather than come face to face with consular officials, Mally checked into the Hotel Carlton, where the head porter was accustomed to arranging visa and first-class travel for guests. However, not even a request from such an exclusive establishment as the Carlton persuaded the American clerk at the consulate to process the necessary paperwork, in the light of the travel ban in the passport. Word was send back that "Mr Hardt" must visit them in person. This alarmed Mally. Telling the Carlton that he had cancelled his plan to travel to America, he asked them to get his passport back. The US consulate declined, insisting that its owner had to collect it in person. Mally, by now convinced he was being shadowed, checked out of the hotel and informed Moscow that he would have to abandon both his Austrian passport and his mission. The US consulate then sent the unclaimed passport back to Vienna, where an investigation, according to Orlov, "revealed that the passport had been issued fraudulently to an unauthorized person by a bribed official". The issuing officer was arrested. When the report of this reached Moscow, the Centre became concerned that their hapless Austrian agent would confess to issuing a string of other passports. An alarm went out to all underground agents ordering that all those with Austrian passports issued in the same series must leave the countries in which they were residing without delay: among them were Reif and Orlov's wife and daughter.[9]

"Thus, a seemingly innocent incident ended in the disruption of the intelligence work on a wide front," wrote Orlov. What he did not explain in his *Handbook* was that his "illegal" station was one of those most seriously affected. Reif himself did not leave quickly enough to avoid a summons in January 1935 to report to the Home Office. Had the British learned about the missing batch of passports? If they had, it is all the more surprising that he was not taken into police custody. The summons was addressed to Max Wolisch, the alias on his Austrian passport. But, much to his relief, after a round of questioning by an official at the Home Office, Reif was not charged with passport fraud, but simply advised to arrange for his prompt departure from England by 15 March 1935. As Reif reported it to Orlov, on the desk of the Home Office examiner he had observed a "bulging file" stamped "Wolisch", suggesting that his alias had been the focus of a considerable investigation by British authorities.[10]

Orlov expressed his concern to the Centre about Reif's encounter with the British authorities in a letter of 24 February 1935. "They, it seems, have been digging around but could not come up with anything concrete and decided to get rid of him. Had they been in possession of some concrete material against him they would not have sent him out of the country, but finished him off," Orlov reported, adding: "For this or other reasons, I think that his passport is not suitable for working in other countries."[11] As Orlov explained in his *Handbook*, "The mere fact that a person has a false passport may be punishable according to law, but to convict him of espionage more weighty proof is required".[12] Nonetheless, the London station chief had to tell Reif that he had no choice but to comply with the British order to leave. After learning of Moscow's agreement, in his next letter he expressed concern that Maria was also in danger of being exposed. "Your information that the network supplying us 'books' [passports] one of which MARR [Reif] had, has failed has made me very worried. As you know, my wife has a book of the same country MARR had. With a 'book' of the same kind PAUL has already once failed in Paris. My wife's 'book' is registered in the appropriate organization with all the details. That is why I have decided to send my wife and daughter back home."[13]

The emergency that had precipitated the abrupt departure of two members of his "illegal" *apparat* obliged Orlov to undertake a drastic restructuring of the NKVD's London field station. In February 1934 he alerted the Centre in a cryptic letter, sent by ordinary mail, of his concern that Deutsch had also come under surveillance by MI5. As a precaution he had assumed responsibility for handling BÄR, NACHFOLGER and ATILLA and had taken over control of Philby and his two Cambridge friends who he had recommended for anti-fascist work. One was Donald Maclean, who had been assigned the code name WAISE (ORPHAN). The other was Guy Burgess, who Orlov had only just advised Moscow was a homosexual, for whom he had chosen the ironically appropriate pseudonym MÄDCHEN (LITTLE GIRL).[14] The nucleus of the Cambridge group by February 1935 had already passed through the first of the stages of the recruitment process – but only Philby was considered to have reached the second stage and ready to become a probationary agent of the Soviet intelligence service.

It was indicative of the seriousness of the crisis that until the alarm was over and Deutsch could safely share the burden, Orlov had single-handedly to assume responsibility for the schooling of the "candidates for recruitment", as such trainees were known in the NKVD, as well as running the station's other active agents. Together with Reif and Deutsch, he had constituted the management of the "illegal" London station. According to Orlov's own account, he had to remain "closed-mouthed and on constant guard with almost everyone else – only the resident director and his chief assistant know the whole network and all the operations". While it was "important to know everyone of them by sight", he stressed that a *resident* also had to make himself familiar with "the biographical data of each informant, his occupation and place of work, how he had been recruited, his accomplishments for Soviet intelligence and their degree of reliability". It was he who held the "key" to every informant in the form of a special password that the *rezident* would use to warn them of an emergency. But, as Orlov noted, it was only on very exceptional occasions that a *rezident* would actually contact "the most valuable and reliable informants".[15]

The decision to take over sӧhnchen personally, as well as the two other Cambridge candidates for recruitment, marked an important milestone in the formation of the "Three Musketeers". Deutsch's operational history of what he termed the "Cambridge Group", which he compiled for the NKVD chiefs on his return to Moscow three years later, contains an explanation of why Philby was selected as the "first man" of the network. The penetrating assessment of Philby made by Deutsch shows that his study of psychology had given him a keen insight into the character and attributes necessary for qualifying as a fully fledged Soviet agent:

> sӧhnchen comes from a peculiar family. His father is considered at present to be the most distinguished expert on the Arab world. He has a command of several Arabic dialects and has himself become a Muslim. He is an ambitious tyrant and wanted to make a great man out of his son. He repressed all his son's desires. That is why sӧhnchen is a very timid and irresolute person. He has a bit of a stammer and this increases his diffidence. He is a typical armchair scientist, well read, educated, serious and profound. He is a clumsy person emotionally and does not easily get close to people. Often he is simply afraid to talk because of his speech defect, unwilling to make a fool of himself. It is difficult for him to tell lies. sӧhnchen has studied Marxist teachings thoroughly and he generally studies everything thoroughly, but he would always say that he knows little. He has a profound knowledge of history, geography and economy – and at the same time likes and understands music. He is undoubtedly a sentimental person, but, owing to his upbringing and the whole life of the English bourgeoisie, this side of his character is rather corrupted. He is a shy person and does not know how to handle money in the sense that he does not know how to arrange his own budget. However, he handles our money very carefully. He enjoys great love and respect for his seriousness and honesty. He was ready, without questioning, to do anything for us and has shown all his seriousness and diligence working for us. He is a kind and mild person. His temperament inclines him to pessimism and that is why he needs constant encouragement.[16]

The notion that Philby was a closet sentimentalist who was sucked into his career of espionage because the hard-boiled Soviets nurtured him with the reassurance that his distant and impervious father had failed to provide is too simplistic an explanation as to why he chose to betray his country. But as Deutsch's analysis suggests, his juvenile deprivation of paternal affection may well have contributed to his vulnerability to Soviet recruitment.

Orlov certainly appreciated the advantages of the psychological carrot over the Freudian stick when it came to grooming potential spies like Philby and his friends to work secretly against their country. For all his hard-nosed resolution Orlov had a sensitive touch when it came to inspiring loyalty in his subordinates – whether his Bobruysk playmates or the soldiers he had led on the Polish front. He also knew better than to rush the process.

After spending ten days in London after his initial arrival we find that he had returned to Moscow to report personally on the prospects for his "illegal" group. Arriving back again in London on 18 September, it was then that he began monitoring the assignments Philby was given by Deutsch as part of the testing process to which all potential agents were subjected. After providing a list of Cambridge friends who might be amenable to cultivation, Philby's next goal was to find a career which would facilitate his anti-fascist work, which was all he was told about his secret mission at the time. Deutsch reported that Philby had shown not only responsiveness to disciplined control, but also the determination necessary to carry out rudimentary intelligence tasks, to order and precisely as instructed.[17]

Philby, in his KGB memoir, provided a graphic picture of how this process of preparing a Soviet agent was conducted by Deutsch, whom he knew only as OTTO:

> As to training it was mostly verbal instruction. He went on and on instructing me first and foremost in questions of security. Even in those matters he had a very human approach. Once I told him: "Look, you have said it ten times already."
>
> "Ten? Well, that's not enough. I've got to tell you the same thing one hundred times, no less."
>
> I must say that in those days, without electronic devices, the ways and means of providing security were primitive enough and simple. In various services they differed not so much in form as in the degree of their application. We had no complex equipment. We simply had to observe the rules. And that not even for 100 per cent but 200 hundred per cent. Double and redouble our caution, that was our rule![18]

There was, however, a major drawback to the Centre's plan for

Philby which required that after he had proved his willingness to do anti-fascist work he could be recruited for the intelligence service. When Orlov assumed direct responsibility for running Philby in February of 1935, this particular Cambridge graduate had no prospect of a Government post and was hardly an ideal candidate to become a penetration agent in the British intelligence apparatus. Philby was an outsider with little prospect of joining the trusted circle of reliable chaps from which the secret services drew most of their recruits. MI6 in particular was a self-perpetuating clique that enlisted new men through a shadowy old-boy network of snobbish senior officers who did most of their recruiting from leather armchairs in the exclusive clubs of Pall Mall and St James's. Although qualified by social class and education, Philby had effectively blackballed himself from this circle by his espousal of left-wing Socialism. So he had to opt for an altogether less gentlemanly route into the Whitehall fraternities: to cultivate Government contacts by becoming a respectable journalist.

This was no easy task for a Cambridge graduate with no experience or previous inclination for writing. But Philby demonstrated a persistence and ability to achieve an assigned objective by ferreting out his father's friends in the newspaper and magazine business, until he found a post with the *Review of Reviews,* a small-circulation news journal whose liberal standpoint afforded him the perfect cover for reconstructing his political image. The magazine's proprietor, Sir Roger Chance, a Cambridge contemporary of Kim's father, recommended Philby to his editor, William Hope Hindle, as an assistant. Selecting and subbing news reports afforded Philby little access to Government secrets, but the mundane work did give him the chance to demonstrate his political dependability by authoring such anodyne articles as "Three Years of Protection", "Weights in the Balance" and "Japan's Pacific Islands". Just how well Philby succeeded in his Moscow-directed mission of burying his past is clear from the impression that he left on Chance as being "vaguely liberal". He would be recalled as a "decent young man with a sense of humour and no recognizable political views, quite unlike his father".[19]

Orlov's reports also show that while Philby was polishing his cover as a politically correct journalist, he was also advancing the Centre's primary goal by making the initial approach to his Cambridge friend Donald Maclean. When Philby met the London *rezident* for the first time to discuss his friends, it was a demonstration not only of Orlov's faith in SÖHNCHEN but also of the trust in which he was now held. Philby responded warmly to Orlov's encouragement at the meeting. Although not referred to by specific date in the NKVD records, from Orlov's reports to the Centre, the encounter that marked SÖHNCHEN's passing stage 2 of the recruitment process to become a probationary agent in the Soviet intelligence service can be bracketed to late December 1934.[20]

"It was OTTO that introduced me to Orlov," Philby recalled of Deutsch's arranging for their open-air meeting in Regent's Park on a chilly afternoon, as bundled-up children in perambulators, pushed by uniformed nannies, fed bread to the squabbling ducks on the nearby boating lake. At the time Philby was not aware that this was his first face-to-face meeting with the head of the London "illegal" station. There was no mention of Orlov's status and he was introduced to Philby only as Bill.[21] The accounts of the "Three Musketeers" on file in Moscow show that they referred to Orlov as "Big Bill" to distinguish him from "Little Bill", since Reif had also identified himself as "Bill" when he had earlier met Philby and his friend Maclean.[22]

"It was again in the park," Philby stated in his secret memoir for the KGB, recalling how he met Orlov "maybe ten or twelve times" during the next nine months. In contrast to Deutsch and Mally, who later took over as "illegal" *rezident*, he characterized Big Bill (whom he would later come to know as Orlov in Spain) as a "prototypical NKVD man" who gave the impression of being a "stern man, but very polite and courageous". Orlov in his turn appears to have treated Philby more like a son than an operative. "He had a paternal attitude towards me," recalled his protégé. "As for me, I had the feeling that he was the true chief of all this business from Moscow and my attitude towards him was that of a hero. This did not mean that I rated badly or had any less respect for OTTO [Deutsch] or THEO [Mally], it was just that at this time a real Russian, a Soviet man, had come. To put it another way, I considered THEO and OTTO to be Communists, but rather that I thought of Orlov as a Bolshevik."[23]

The obvious admiration which Philby had for Orlov suggests that he came to view him as the empathetic paternal figure he had lacked in his real father, St John Philby, an often absent paterfamilias who had been quick to criticize and slow to encourage his son. As Deutsch's assessment makes clear, Philby had been left with a keen sense of inferiority about his own self-worth, the outward manifestation of which was a nervous stammer and excessive diffidence. Philby had learned to turn his speech impediment to his advantage. It gave him an endearing appearance of vulnerability which, allied to his ingratiating manner, camouflaged his dissimulation. Orlov's sympathetic handling of the young Englishman reinforced Philby's dedication to serve the Revolution, a humanitarian approach that paid off. It is not without significance that Orlov chose to stress this aspect of his work in his *Handbook*.

"Unlike Western intelligence services, Soviet intelligence treats its informants with genuine solicitude," wrote Orlov. "This solicitude for the informant is based more on considerations of self-interest than on moral or humanitarian grounds," he noted, and was essential in securing their loyalty. For Philby and the other original members of the Cambridge network, this solicitousness was an article of faith. As far as agents were concerned, according to Orlov, the NKVD "never violates its promise not to divulge their identity or services on behalf of the Soviet Union, and it rushes to their aid whenever they are in trouble". Such attentive nurturing, he emphasized, was adopted not for humanitarian reasons but because the Soviet intelligence service very early on "came to the conclusion that such a policy toward the informants benefited its cause and contributed to its success".[24]

Yet Orlov, for security reasons, never rated a place in the pantheon which the postwar KGB reserved for the so-called "Great Illegals" of the Soviet intelligence service. Their achievements in the 1930s and 1940s creating underground networks is commemorated in a historical room at what was the KGB First Chief Directorate building at Yasnevo, on the Moscow ring road, that now serves as the headquarters of the Russian Intelligence Service. Deutsch is among Orlov's contemporaries whose portraits decorate the walls of this memorial. Many of them were to fall victim to Stalin's purges, but their reputations were rehabilitated and restored to the pantheon of KGB heroes in the 1950s. Orlov however, remained "officially" a traitor to the Soviet public until 1990, when, on the personal directive of the KGB Chairman, Vladimir Kryuchkov, selected sections of his dossier were finally unlocked from the secret vaults and made available to this book's co-author for his newspaper article.[25]

Orlov's full dossier provides conclusive evidence that he was the most remarkable of all the "Great Illegals". Ironically, until Tsarev's piece about him appeared in *Trud* marking the 1991 anniversary of the founding of the Soviet Intelligence Service, Orlov was celebrated in the West, but despised in the Soviet Intelligence Service as a defector.

Now that Orlov's career can be accurately documented, he can be seen to have been a much more pivotal figure in the history of twentieth-century intelligence than has hitherto been assumed. If only for the part he played in the recruitment of the original members of the Cambridge network and then keeping this secret throughout his long American exile, Orlov deserves an honoured place in the memorial room. He himself had hinted as much in the *Handbook*, which can now be seen to have been written as a cryptic testament to this feat.

"The recruitment of new informants into the underground network is the most hazardous and difficult of all activities," Orlov wrote in this book. "From the very first step the agent finds himself at a serious disadvantage, because, by proposing to a person that he become a spy for the Soviets, the agent exposes his own role even before that person has given his reply." This explains why the Centre insisted that its *rezidents* and their lieutenants put potential recruits like Philby through a two stage process involving a rigorous series of checks to establish "who these people are, where they are, and what they are; their views and beliefs, private lives and ambitions, their moral character and weakness, and above all their potential value as sources of information".[26]

According to Orlov, candidates for recruitment were motivated towards becoming spies for a variety of reasons including idealism, money, career and other motives of personal gain, romantic entanglements, love of adventure, the need to conceal a crime, homosexual deviation and other vices. "From the point of view of human motivation," Orlov observed "a rich variety of reasons, calculations and emotions guide people into undertaking espionage." Contrary to popular belief, however, he asserted categorically that blackmail was not a satisfactory recruitment tool since it led to resentment and could boomerang because the recruiting officer's fate was always in the hands of the agent. He himself said he had learned "to be straightforward with them all" and that this was the best way to secure the "co-operation and devotion" of a source.

"The skilful builder of a network who selects and lures people into the adventures of intelligence and guides them in the endless battle of wits," Orlov reflected, "bears considerable similarity to the creative novelist – with one major difference – the novelist traces on paper the emotions and actions of imaginary characters. The builder of the spy net inspires and directs the feelings and actions of real people." For a novelist an unconvincing plot resulted only in bad reviews, but, as Orlov pointed out, "if the creator of an intelligence scheme allows himself to introduce illogical and unbelievable combinations, his plans will fall through and his live characters will soon find themselves behind bars".[27]

Given Philby's dismal career prospects at the beginning of 1935, it attests to Orlov's judgement of this potential agent's ability that in one of his reports to the Centre, he stated unequivocally that penetration of MI6 was the ultimate goal for which he was "leading SÖHNCHEN out on to a wide road of work for the Soviet intelligence service".[28] It is also an indication of Orlov's rating of Philby that both he and Deutsch were always ready to offer encouragement to the often disillusioned young probationary, reassuring him that even his job as a lowly journalist was leading him towards the "wide road" of more important work for Moscow.

"Week after week, we would meet in one or other of the remoter spaces in London," Philby recorded. "I would reach the rendezvous empty handed and leave with a load of painstaking advice, admonition and encouragement." He paid tribute to "the infinite patience shown by *my seniors* [emphasis added] in the service, a patience only matched by their intelligence and understanding". While he did not name those "seniors", we now know that Orlov from the beginning of 1935 was the one who ensured that he was "endowed with much of the required mental equipment" for what Philby termed his "serious work".[29]

Orlov's own 1935 reports to Moscow suggest that Philby was deliberately misleading in his published autobiography. The NKVD files reveal that, far from going to his meetings in Regent's Park and other open-air locations empty handed, within six months SÖHNCHEN was tapping his Whitehall friends for information which he then passed on to his Soviet handlers. Even before the end of 1934, when he was still in the first stage of his recruitment, Philby's file shows that he fed Deutsch confidential Government information obtained from his father and from a Cambridge associate who was working for the War Office. Amongst the reports was one containing the Saudi Arabian Ambassador's answer to the Foreign Office, consenting to the building of an RAF base in the Near East, which had evidently been purloined from St John Philby's official correspondence. He was also relaying military information gleaned from a renewed friendship with Tom Wylie, an old Trinity College friend from Cambridge who was then the Resident Clerk in the War Office. Wylie was a homosexual confidant of Guy Burgess, who was a regular participant at the dissolute parties in Wylie's spacious flat behind the guarded portals of the War Office in Whitehall.[30]

Wylie was the source – probably unwitting – of a secret internal War Office review of the British army's military intelligence apparatus, which was photographed and dispatched via Soviet courier to the Centre on 12 July 1935. Since it contained many references to names of army intelligence officers, it proved especially useful to Moscow. The Centre's estimate of Philby's potential value can only have been raised considerably when they learned from SÖHNCHEN that Wylie had recently been promoted to the post of private secretary to the Permanent Under Secretary at the War Office, Sir Robert Cready.[31]

"The preliminary agent outline included SÖHNCHEN's approach to his university friend, a certain Wylie," Orlov informed Moscow. As Resident Clerk, a lack of access to high-grade military intelligence had not qualified Wylie himself to be cultivated as an agent, but his new position led Orlov to request Moscow's permission to use Philby to cultivate Wylie for his network. "Ministers come and go with the frequent changes of cabinet," Orlov explained, "that's why Ministers have Permanent Under Secretaries to direct the work of the ministry for the portfolio irrespective of parliamentary and party struggle."[32]

Enclosed was the invitation card Wylie had sent Philby for an official dinner at his new apartment in the War Office building. "Those who attended were, for the most part, military," Orlov reported, relaying Philby's account of how an intoxicated Wylie had boasted of his closeness to military intelligence officers. "Wylie is very affably disposed to SÖHNCHEN, knows about his 'left' ideas in the past, which [Wylie] in his cups had blurted out to one of the [army] quartermasters from the Middle East with whom he was engaged in discussion, with SÖHNCHEN, about Ibn Saud." Orlov reported that Philby had seized on his friend's gaff to deny his "former infantile views". This, Orlov wrote, encouraged the army officer into an even franker disclosure about British military forces in the Middle East, which Philby had duly relayed to him.[33]

"Wylie is an able, educated fellow, but, like most of the polished sons of this country, a pederast," Orlov cautioned the Centre, when reporting that he had "told SÖHNCHEN that his task was not to undertake anything in the nature of an approach [to Wylie], merely to resume friendship with him".[34] Corroboration that Orlov had indeed targeted the War Office Secretary for recruitment is in subsequent reports in which he referred to Wylie by the code name HEINRICH. Burgess later assumed the assignment of cultivating Wylie until his outrageous behaviour caused Moscow to order the abandonment of his recruitment. The War Office, however, continued to turn a blind eye to his flagrant life-style throughout World War II!

By the summer of 1935 SÖHNCHEN was already operating as a trusted Soviet agent, even if he did not realize he was working for their intelligence service. His status – and that of Burgess and Maclean – is confirmed by the financial records for the month of June, which Orlov, as station chief, submitted to Moscow to justify the substantial disbursements he was drawing to support his expanding *rezidentura*. The ledger sheet with entries in Orlov's hand is further evidence of the high degree of control with which the Centre supervised its far-flung underground empire. It also provides a unique view of the housekeeping required to maintain an NKVD "illegal" station, as well as its composition and relative ranking in importance of Orlov's network of British agents.

SCHWED (Orlov) paid himself £120, while STEFAN (Deutsch) received £80 and the "illegal" station's courier PFEIL received £56. One of Orlov's agents code-named ATILLA received £36 remuneration for information supplied. His significance and that of another – as yet unidentified – British Government source code-named NACHFOLGER (who received £15 that month) is evident from their entries before that of the "Three Musketeers" from Cambridge. Burgess, not surprisingly in view of his extravagant lifestyle, was paid £12 10s 0d, making MÄDCHEN the top-grossing agent of the Cambridge group. He received thirty shillings more than the £11 for SÖHNCHEN (Philby) and the £10 paid to WAISE (Maclean). On a *pro-rata* basis Philby was receiving expenses from the Soviets amounting to only slightly less than his £4 a week editorial pay or about half the annual £375 salary

Maclean got paid as a Third Secretary in the Foreign Office.[35]

Actual operational expenses for Orlov and Deutsch were £57 and £17 18s 0d. PFEIL got £3 12s 0d. ATILLA received 5s, and 5s 6d was paid to EDITH (Tudor Hart). For travelling to Copenhagen and back with twenty-two days in hotels Orlov drew £10 12s 10d. PFEIL, who must have made several round trips to Denmark, was reimbursed £3 12s 0d. Payments to Orlov's cover business amounted to nearly £110, including the purchase of a refrigerator but not including £95 9s 0d for telegram costs, among which were two cables Orlov sent to the USA, presumably in connection with The American Refrigerator Company Ltd.[36]

The "expenses" cost of running the London "illegal" station amounted to around £500 a month (over $2,000 at 1934 exchange rates). This translates to over $50,000 in contemporary terms, by no means an insignificant sum. So, even though Orlov's mission of penetrating British intelligence was a long-term goal, the Centre was clearly anticipating a substantial return to make such a heavy investment. This was not least among the factors that spurred Orlov to make every effort to develop schemes for making Philby a more productive agent. One such operation used his cover as a journalist in a bid to lure into the network as sources Government secretaries who responded to a "situations vacant" advertisement in *The Times*.

Exploiting the romantic aspirations of women for sources of secret information was a favourite ploy of Orlov's, as he reveals in his *Handbook* in which he wrote of "the constant efforts by the Soviet intelligence to enrol into its service young women who work as secretaries, stenographers, code clerks and administrative assistants in important departments of foreign governments". Government secretarial staff were a particular target of all intelligence services, he noted.[37]

"Young women dream of love and marriage," according to Orlov who observed chauvinistically that suitable women could be cultivated by arranging for introductions to "young men with good looks, manners and education" who were already serving the Soviet intelligence service. He may have had one of the "Three Musketeers" in mind when he reported his hope that "the sponsored romance blossoms into a love affair" through which "a suitable confidence game is devised in order to explain to the girl why her Romeo wishes to read the secret documents which pass through her hands".[38] In many cases Orlov wrote that he had found that it was not even necessary for the boyfriend to inveigle the secretary into supporting the lofty ideals of Socialism: the woman's passion in such a romantic entanglement was sufficient to betray military and political secrets.

In his 24 February letter to the Centre Orlov reported on the case of a female operative code-named BRIDE who he and Reif were exploiting very carefully to cultivate a Foreign Office diplomat.[39]

Philby, in his capacity as assistant editor of the *Review of Reviews*, was instructed by Orlov to book newspaper advertisements for typists/stenographers. The "required experience" of handling economic and political literature was designed specifically to appeal to the daughters of respectable middle-class families who made up the greater proportion of trusted secretaries in the Whitehall ministries which the Centre had targeted for penetration.

"Out of the sea of responses taken out of the postbox by us," Orlov informed Moscow on 24 April 1935, "a steno-typist from the central secretariat of the Admiralty seems the most suitable candidate. To become better acquainted with her, SÖHNCHEN accepted her for evening work in his editorial office. Now we have before us the task of finding a 'lover' for her. You will appreciate that the outcome of such an affair is always unpredictable."[40] Moscow, however, decided that Orlov's romantic scheme presented too much risk for his star recruit. This is clear from the hand-written endorsement on the letter, "Using SÖHNCHEN for recruitment – categorically to be forbidden."[41] The Centre's refusal to allow Philby to recruit Whitehall secretaries is additional indication that, by the summer of 1935, he was already marked out for the NKVD's long-term aim of penetrating the British intelligence service.

Rebuffed by Moscow, Orlov then set about trying to devise another scheme that would bring Philby closer to achieving this formidable goal set for him. The succession of plans he submitted to the Centre are notable both for their ingenuity and their adventurousness. One of the most original of his proposals was sent to the chiefs in Moscow after he learned from Philby that Emir Saud, the heir presumptive to King Ibn Saud of Saudi Arabia and the commander of his army, had met St John Philby during his visit to London in the summer of 1935 to ask his advice about an English teacher.

"I jumped at the prospect of Emir Saud looking for a teacher as an opportunity for bringing SÖHNCHEN into play at the highest level," Orlov wrote Moscow, enthusiastically outlining his proposal that Philby offer himself for the job. "In two months he could leave [for Arabia] with the Emir, where he would live in the palace as one of the family."[42] The friendship of his father with Ibn Saud was so close that St John Philby spent at least a couple of hours every day in the King's palace. Philby *père* also believed his son would be a natural choice for the language teaching post and so it was Orlov's intention, that having secured the job, Philby *fils* would then approach another of his friends whom he knew worked for MI6. According to his plan, Kim would inform "ANNA (the well-known English intelligence officer Lockhart who is known to Philby) or ROSS (the principal of the School of Slavonic Languages)" – known MI6 contacts – that as "a devoted Englishman" he believed it was his duty to report on what he would see and hear at Ibn Saud's palace. Since he would expect to be an interpreter for important documents, Philby would inquire if he could be informed of which areas would be of interest to the Government and, using his most diffident manner and "with an innocent look, without mentioning any names, target the intelligence service".[43]

If the British intelligence service failed to take the bait, Orlov proposed that Philby would arrange to fall ill at the last moment and not travel to Jeddah. But, if they were hooked and Philby was invited to become an MI6 informant, he would proceed to Saudi Arabia. He would "work there like a slave for about six months for the intelligence service, that is write frequent reports about every movement in the palace, about every guest, depicting everything in interesting terms".

"By the way, read SÖHNCHEN's article in the enclosed magazine," Orlov added. "He's a clever, intelligent fellow." According to his plan, Philby would do everything to show his suitability to become a full-time intelligence officer by favourably impressing his MI6 contact, who would be an undercover officer on the staff of the British embassy in Jeddah. Philby would then entertain the official, showing himself to best advantage in order to get good references on his file with the British intelligence service.[44] There was also another advantage to such a posting, Orlov noted:

> Here I would point out that SÖHNCHEN's former left-wing politics would not preclude the intelligence service using him in Arabia. Since there is no Communism there, to suspect him of Communist aims in the presence of Ibn Saud would hardly be logical.[45]

The intention, as Orlov relayed it to Moscow, was that after six months establishing his "legend" as a reliable MI6 informant in Saudi Arabia, Philby "falls ill because of the rigorous climate and returns home". Then Philby, "after a decent interval," would resume his career as a journalist and travel to the Soviet Union on assignment. Before leaving for Russia, he would take care to resume contact with British intelligence to tell them how he had access to important information about the USSR, which would lead to a renewal of his invitation to work for MI6 as a freelance agent. "By feeding him stories as a journalist and with some information from the intelligence service, we could get SÖHNCHEN out into his large role," Orlov assured the Centre. "His personal qualities would assist a plan like this. He is educated, clever, modest, taciturn when needed – and the main thing is that *he is one of us by his ideas.*" As he confidently put it "The success of the whole legend hangs on just one incalculable link – that is whether the [British] intelligence service will accept him."[46]

"I think they are likely to," Orlov predicted. Slavatinski, one of the ranking NKVD chiefs, agreed, noting on Orlov's report "I don't think his intelligence service will refuse the services of SÖHNCHEN." Moscow's go-ahead was relayed to their London *rezident*, but, before the plan could be put into operation, it collapsed when the Emir selected another teacher.[47]

Orlov's belief that MI6 would not turn down Philby's offer to work for them led him to develop another, similar strategy when another opening occured shortly after Philby and his wife Litzi returned to London from a 1935 summer holiday in Spain, to an unexpected job offer from his father's old employer, the Indian Civil Service. It was proposed that he become a press liaison officer at a large salary in New Delhi. "A special point I would like to single out in the enclosed material is a personal letter from the Indian Minister of Home Affairs addressed to SÖHNCHEN," Orlov informed the Centre. Philby had told him that he did not know the Minister in question, but discovered that he had been recommended by a journalist acquaintance who was a sub-editor on *The Times*.[48]

"I instructed SÖHNCHEN to take up this position," Orlov advised the Centre, even though Philby was still awaiting the outcome of the negotiations over his salary. Permitting Philby to go to India was a risk. It meant not only losing the information he provided from his contacts in Whitehall but also the opportunity to uncover more candidates for the network in England. Regarding this point Orlov was "frankly doubtful" of any possibilities that would yet "swim up" in the near future. He was of the opinion that it would be no great loss if Philby were to give up his "current work". His preference was for letting SÖHNCHEN take up the Indian posting, which could offer Philby opportunities he would not get in London for working with British intelligence.[49]

Orlov justified his conclusion in four ways. Regrettably, the first and obviously the most important reason has had to be deleted from his declassified report because the Russian Intelligence Service is still unwilling to reveal the identities or targets of the other key agents Orlov was running at the time.[50] His second point was that Philby's "productive work is limited just to cultivating Ibn Saud's [London] base". The third was that "the cultivation of HEINRICH [Wylie] can be transferred to MÄDCHEN [Burgess]". Fourth, he argued that "because SÖHNCHEN is still remembered as a fellow with 'left' ideas, it makes his opportunities for easily obtaining the post of secretary to an important person difficult, etc".[51]

"A year of SÖHNCHEN's work at the Indian Ministry of Home Affairs will put an end to his past 'left-wing' reputation," Orlov continued, reminding Moscow that SÖHNCHEN's abilities had "developed strikingly in understanding his tasks and agent work". Philby, he believed, had a real chance to make himself indispensable to the Indian Home Affairs Ministry and at the same time become "a valuable informant for the intelligence service". Orlov also contended that, in his capacity as a press officer, Philby would be in a position to recruit other journalists and be able to curry favour with the Indian constabulary. As a Government bureaucrat, Orlov pointed out, Philby could become very influential. By serving for a year as "the Government's dog" in New Delhi, Philby would inevitably come into renewed contact with the British intelligence services. This contact with MI6 could then be reactivated if Philby were to travel to Russia "at his own initiative", where he could continue to offer his services, as he put it, "under our direction". It was, therefore, he said, worth sacrificing Philby's less valuable work in London for a year "for the sake of even greater work and prospects in the following years".[52]

"I repeat once again that SÖHNCHEN has developed strikingly," Orlov concluded. "He is a very dedicated person with a keen appetite for agent work and he will make a great and valuable worker in the future."[53] Under the capable direction of Orlov Philby was shortly to demonstrate his chameleon abilities by becoming a German sympathizer. "Such was the main course of my work," Philby would later tell the KGB. "It was not very interesting but was important enough. I appeared to be absolutely pro-Nazi and it was a very bitter experience."

Orlov's dispatch, dated 12 September 1935, seeking Moscow's approval for Philby to go to India, was the last one that he sent from London. Shortly afterwards, one of those chance accidents occurred that serve to remind ordinary folk that the world is a small place, but which deal a fatal blow to the career of an undercover intelligence officer like Orlov living in a foreign country under an assumed identity. For the second time in just over two years his past unexpectedly caught up with him, when he was hailed by an old acquaintance. According to the 9 October report that the Centre received from their agent code-named SCHORR in Copenhagen, he had just received a letter from Orlov advising that he had bumped into the man who had given him English lessons when Orlov was living openly as a Soviet citizen in Vienna. The encounter had taken place in the house where Orlov rented a bed-sitter, obliging him not merely to vacate his rooms for temporary residence in a nearby hotel but also to make plans for leaving England, because the meeting had destroyed his "legend" as an American businessman named Goldin.[54]

Orlov was too old a hand at the "illegal" game to believe he could continue working under cover in London without putting his whole network of agents in danger. So he took immediate steps to relinquish the running of the "illegal" station and to wind up his business affairs without arousing suspicion. On 10 October he received instructions from Moscow to pull out which arrived in the form of a prearranged emergency message: "Lotti must leave for the south."[55]

In the circumstances the Centre decided that this was not the time to dispense with Philby's services in London. Deutsch happened to be on home leave at the time, so after a briefing from Orlov, who arrived in Moscow on 29 October, he returned to London to inform SÖHNCHEN to turn down the Indian appointment. In accordance with standard NKVD practice, Philby would not have been told the reason for Orlov's sudden departure, only that he had been recalled to Moscow.

Over two years were to elapse before the two would re-establish their relationship working for the Soviet cause on opposite sides of the battle lines of the Spanish Civil War.

Shortly after Orlov's departure from London, Philby's journalistic career took a turn which was to play a crucial role in securing for him the political credentials that would eventually make him acceptable to the British intelligence service. Deutsch had by then resumed his role as control officer shortly after Philby reported that Wylie had introduced him to a friend named Talbot, the editor and publisher of an obscure magazine called the *Anglo-Russian Trade Gazette*. This struggling periodical was the organ of an association of British financiers who had business interests in pre-Revolutionary Russia. Its editor, therefore, was suspected by the Centre of being a contact of British intelligence.

Since 1917 these businessmen had been trying to salvage their investments in Russia by lobbying MPs through their magazine and letters. As a second decade after the Revolution rolled by, with the British Government proving as intractable in their willingness to make restitution as Lenin's heirs, the *Gazette* was losing its backers and readership. When Talbot met Philby, he explained that his magazine and its right-wing leaders were dying off. He was planning to resuscitate it as an Anglo-German periodical with financial backing from Berlin, which was keen to promote trade and harmonious relations with Hitler's Reich. In Philby's KGB memoir he relates how he found the idea rather interesting, but not for the same reasons as those of its proprietor. Talbot had divulged that he himself was too old to start a new magazine and he was looking for a young editor.

"Why a young one?" Philby said he had asked innocently, only to be assured, "So that he does not ask for too much money!" This made it plain that Talbot was considering him for the post of editor. When Philby was offered a substantial increase over the £4 a week he was receiving at the *Review of Reviews*, after consulting with OTTO, he shook hands with Talbot and gave in his notice to William Hindle.[56]

"It seems to me," Philby would later reminisce, "that it was this consent of mine which was the beginning of my actual work for the Soviet Union."[57] While it was certainly true that he was entering a new phase of usefulness to Moscow, Orlov's reports show that by the autumn of 1935 SÖHNCHEN was no longer a probationary Soviet agent. He had, in fact, been providing the Centre with information about the extent of British support for Hitler since the beginning of 1935. As the editor of a pro-Nazi magazine, it must have seemed to Philby that for the first time since Vienna he was entering the enemy camp as a spy when he joined the Anglo-German Fellowship. This was an organization of City bankers, right-wing parliamentarians and society figures who, since 1932, had joined together to lobby the British Government for a *rapprochement* with Nazi Germany.

Philby had also made good connections with officials of the German embassy and soon became a regular visitor at the lavish receptions in its chandeliered salon in Carlton House Terrace and he was on hand when Joachim von Ribbentrop arrived in London in the summer of 1936 as Germany's new ambassador. The former liquor and champagne salesman caused a diplomatic sensation by giving the Nazi salute to the King at Buckingham Palace instead of the usual bow. So it is not surprising that Philby was looking distinctly ill at ease in white tie and tails among the swastika-decked tables in the official photograph of a banquet at the Dorchester Hotel on 14 July hosted by the Anglo-German Fellowship for visiting Nazi dignitaries.[58]

Cambridge friends were appalled that Philby had, in their view, become an admirer of Hitler. His explanation that he was only editing the Fellowship's journal for the money was an unconvincing excuse that did not justify his shift of political allegiance. But this scepticism reinforced the cover Philby was establishing to mask his secret services to Moscow as he passed reports to Deutsch that alerted Stalin to the true extent of unofficial contact between Britain and Germany. He had learned through his contacts in the Fellowship how many financiers, manufacturers and import and export specialists had a vested financial interest in cementing good relations with Hitler and the Third Reich. Philby visited Berlin frequently, travelling to the German capital about once each month and spending a week there meeting Nazi officials. His friends at the German embassy in London arranged for him to be given red-carpet treatment at the request of Ambassador Ribbentrop who Hitler would install as Reich Foreign Minister in 1938. Philby recalled how difficult it was to hide his contempt when he met top subordinates of Joseph Goebbels in the Nazi Propaganda Ministry. Productive though such encounters were for the Soviet intelligence service, he remembered them as psychologically onerous.[59]

"Suddenly I found myself among people whom I hated," Philby told the KGB. "Because of my deep antipathy toward them, strictly speaking, I saw it as my duty to do what I was doing."[60]

One particularly galling personal moment came when he encountered a former Communist acquaintance from Vienna who asked bitterly, "Tell me please, when you were in Austria, were you already working as a police informant against us?"[61] Philby ducked the question, recalling that he had learned to deal with such encounters philosophically. It helped to steel him, he said, for the more rigorous demands of leading the double life of an underground intelligence officer.

"The task is to shape yourself, not the image of a Nazi," Philby recalled Deutsch as counselling him before his first trip to Berlin. He was told to adopt the guise of "an independent thinking Englishman who perceives Hitlerite Germany as a fact of middle European life in the mid-1930s and who is trying to derive from it economic as well as cultural benefit for his own country". This advice from OTTO stood Philby in good stead when he was confronted with the conflicting loyalties and double life thrust upon him by the demands of Moscow Centre. It also reflects Deutsch's skill as a control officer that he was able to convey to his charge an appreciation of the psychological rigours of a secret agent's life and the mental gymnastics necessary to alleviate some of the stress.[62]

Philby's first-hand experience of the smug brutality of the Nazi regime served to reinforce his own dedication to Communism and his belief that he was helping Moscow work towards the ultimate destruction of Hitlerism. This hardening of purpose was observed by Deutsch who reported that SÖHNCHEN was now ready to make whatever sacrifices were necessary to fulfil his mission. His opinion was endorsed by Mally, the new chief of the London "illegal" station who had arrived in Britain in April 1936 to take over control of the Cambridge group. By then it included Philby and Maclean as well as Burgess whose induction into the second stage of serving Soviet intelligence had already been authorised by Moscow.[63]

Mally was another of the "Great Illegals" whose portrait was hung by the KGB in a place of honour in its historical room. Orlov, who was by this time exercising a supervisory role over the Cambridge group from Lubyanka headquarters in Moscow, believed that Mally was exceptionally qualified to bring his work with Philby and his comrades to fruition. He knew Mally well and in his *Handbook* paid tribute to his successor as London *rezident* whom he called a "top flight NKVD intelligence officer". In *Stalin's Crimes* Orlov fondly recalled his friend who had a "strong, manly face and large, childlike blue eyes".[64] Mally's tall frame and engaging appearance reinforced his natural charm. His cultivated air of cosmopolitan intellectuality made a powerful impression on Philby and his Cambridge comrades, who "worshipped him".[65]

According to Orlov, Mally had travelled "on a genuine Austrian passport, obtained by fraud in Vienna" until 1935, when his carelessness disrupted operations for a time. But Mally was neither Austrian nor Russian. He had been born a Hungarian. A former chaplain in the Austro-Hungarian army, he had abandoned Christianity for Communism in the Tsarist prisoner of war camp in which he was incarcerated until 1917 following his capture on the Carpathian front. Whilst suffering the privations of the camp Mally lost his faith in God and found allegiance to Bolshevism. After the Revolution, he served with the Red Army in the civil war, before being selected by Dzerzhinsky for the *Cheka* at about the same time as Orlov. Mally, too, had operated underground in Austria, Germany and France, according to the NKVD records, frequently using a Dutch passport in the name of Willy Broschart. He was a talented member of the NKVD's select echelon known as the "Flying Squad": a band of "illegal" intelligence officers who took on especially dangerous assignments. According to MI5 records, Mally's arrival in England was noted by the authorities, who had been alerted that he and his wife were travelling on suspect Austrian passports in the names of Paul and Lydia Hardt.[66]

Mally reported to Moscow using the cryptonym MANN, but he was known to Philby and the other Cambridge recruits as THEO.[67] He shared Deutsch's belief that sooner or later Britain would have to fight Germany and instilled this conviction in Philby, who was told that the impending war would enable him to fulfil his ultimate mission of joining British intelligence. As a result, he never lost sight of his ultimate goal and did not become too rabidly pro-Nazi. Had he done so, Philby might have found himself on the list for internment when the war eventually did break out – this was the fate of the editor named Carroll who succeeded him when the magazine was renamed *Nazi Leaflet*.[68]

Philby's tenure as editor of the Anglo-German trade magazine had already become uncertain in the autumn of 1936 when Mally reported to the Centre that his agent SÖHNCHEN was coming under increasing pressure from both the Fellowship and Goebbels's officials in Berlin to adopt a more openly pro-Nazi editorial line in his articles. Following an October trip to Germany, Philby informed Deutsch that his contact at the Ministry of Propaganda had hinted that he was about to be fired.

As Philby recounted the exchange to the KGB in 1985, he said that it left him in no doubt that he would soon have to look for a new job:

> I met my contact in the Ministry of Propaganda who said: "I believe it's your last visit to us, Kim."
> "Why?"
> "You see, we have decided to change the financing of the magazine. We would like to deal with another ranking group in Britain and we're taking upon ourselves all the publishing expenses."
> "Do you mean that you're going to publish a hundred per cent Nazi magazine in Britain?"
> "Yes," said my contact. "It's more convenient for us."
> "But you'll hardly get anywhere," said I.
> "Well, that's our problem. We have taken this decision and we will act accordingly. In any case you will not be getting any more money from us."[69]

Philby discussed this disturbing development with Deutsch on his return to London. To his surprise, OTTO did not seem at all upset.

"To hell with them," was Mally's reaction. "This is just in time, because you're going to Spain."

Philby later recalled he was not at first averse to the idea, because ever since his childhood he had been interested in the country. His affection for the Iberian peninsula had been reinforced by his recent vacation there with Litzi, although he knew that his next trip would be no holiday jaunt.[70]

Battling armies had supplanted bullfights as the Spanish blood sport reported by foreign journalists. They flocked to Spain to cover the grisly civil war which had erupted in mid-1936, after General Francisco Franco's Fascist forces had launched a military rebellion against the left-wing Republican Government. When Hitler and Mussolini sent arms, troops and aircraft to assist Franco in crushing the new legitimate Government and state, the Republicans appealed to the democracies for help. An indifferent Britain and nervous France sought to avoid clashing openly with Germany and Italy. All the help the so-called Loyalists received from the democratic countries was unofficial. The International Brigade, a rag-tag army of international volunteers whose Socialist and Marxist convictions led many to their deaths among the Spanish olive groves, came from England and other European countries, besides including a large contingent from the United States calling itself the Abraham Lincoln Battalion. Stalin had answered the appeals from Madrid that summer, not out of conscience, but to further Soviet ambitions. He grudgingly dispatched arms and military advisers – including Alexander Orlov, now a General-Major – to assist the Spanish Government with counter-intelligence and guerilla warfare operations.[71]

"Where am I going? To Madrid, Barcelona, Valencia?" Philby recalled asking Deutsch, assuming that he would be assigned to the Republicans. He was surprised and somewhat dismayed to be told, "Oh, no! You are going to the opposition. On which side could Kim Philby, an English journalist and sincere friend of Nazi Germany be?"

The Centre's decision to send Philby to Spain under the cover of a freelance right-wing British journalist was not planned solely for the purpose of using him to gather news and intelligence about the state of military and political affairs in Franco's camp. "I was told that my trip was very important to gather information," Philby recalled, "but what was even more important was to gain a reputation and establish myself as a journalist to obtain a more important job."[72]

As with the abortive Saudi Arabian and Indian schemes, the goal of using Philby to penetrate MI6 was to be advanced by attracting the interest of the British intelligence service in using him as an informant. That was why SÖHNCHEN was instructed that he had to earn a reputation as a brilliant and fearless reporter. Where better to achieve this than reporting from the battlefields of Spain, which, by the autumn of 1937, had become the front line of the great struggle against the military forces of Fascism?

Philby recounted to the KGB that neither Deutsch nor Mally could do much to brief him for his mission, since neither had ever been to Spain. To the outside world Philby had to make it appear he was off to report the war as a freelance journalist, paying his own way in the hope of receiving compensation from the publication of articles which he would dispatch from the front. In reality, NKVD records show that his trip was entirely financed by the Soviet intelligence service. But since his "legend" required that Philby earn a living by selling his stories, he had elicited accreditation from the *Evening Standard* newspaper of London. By the time of his departure, he also claimed to represent two press agencies, London Central News and Continental News Service as well as the German magazine *Geopolitics*, to which he had been a contributor. His contacts at the German embassy also put him in touch with the Duke of Alba, the former royalist Spanish Ambassador who was now Franco's representative in London. He furnished Philby with a letter of introduction to his son, Pablo Merry del Val, who was the Nationalist head of military censorship.[73]

"My immediate assignment was to get first-hand information on all aspects of the Fascist war effort," Philby declared in his published autobiography. His NKVD file discloses that he was charged with a more sinister mission.[74] The object of all the paperwork he had been given was not, it turns out, simply to enhance his opportunities as a freelance journalist. It was intended to get Philby into the heart of Franco's entourage where Moscow was planning to use him to set up the assassination of the General.[75] It is not clear from the files so far examined whether the NKVD chiefs intended SÖHNCHEN to be Franco's executioner or merely the agent who opened the door for others to deliver the lethal blow. Given Philby's relative inexperience, it is more likely it was the latter, since the assassins were to be saboteurs from the units Orlov was training for the Loyalists.[76]

One indication of the Soviet-inspired plot against Franco appears in a communication in April 1937, when Mally reported to Moscow Centre that he had personally briefed SÖHNCHEN on the need "to discover the system of guards, primarily of Franco and then of other leaders". Philby was instructed to report on vulnerable points in Franco's security and recommend ways to gain access to him and his staff "by observing the control over those visiting him or his headquarters, his (their) excursions into the streets, their daily schedule, their home addresses or the locations of the places they frequent, where they sleep, where they eat (whether they eat in restaurants) – in short, all that is needed to act". Of secondary interest was the "number of German and Italian troops arriving in the Nationalist camp".[77]

Philby recalled in his KGB memoir that he was so eager to go to Spain that he was ready to depart within "two weeks" on 20 January 1937.

The records, however, show that he actually left London on 3 February 1937. Philby recounted how Mally gave him an address in Paris to which he was to send, by mail, his intelligence reports. He was also provided with a code sheet with which to encypher them, printed on thin but durable paper which he could crumple and swallow to prevent its discovery.[78] His NKVD file also discloses that SÖHNCHEN had an emergency channel of communications for passing intelligence reports through his wife (who later went herself) to Lisbon, where he had collected his visa from the so-called Franco Agency. Litzi was under orders to stay in Portugal and remain in contact with the Soviet courier network there while her husband made his way, at the end of February, to the Nationalist stronghold of Seville.[79]

"I gathered information for our people which I sent to France," Philby recalled of his mission. "It concerned mainly the military situation, military plans of Franco, armaments, troop movements, it also included political information." This information would eventually end up in Orlov's hands as the NKVD chief in Spain and he would pass it over to the Republican Government. "I began writing my letters to the Paris address about two weeks after my arrival in Seville," Philby told the KGB. "I tried to write letters every week. There was enough military action I could observe for myself. I could see with my own eyes the temporary aerodromes which were under construction. I could watch the troop transfers and I could deduce from their tabs and shoulder flashes what kind of troops they were – and in addition I had established some contacts with Italians. They were so fond of talking and boasting that I didn't have to ask questions."[80]

No one suspected that the diffident young English reporter with the stutter who teased Franco's military staff with pedantic questions was a Soviet agent. Philby, however, recalled how he very nearly was uncovered when, after a couple of weeks in Seville, he decided one day to take a train to Cordoba to see a bullfight. Unaware that he was entering a restricted military area, he found himself arrested and questioned by the military police, who ordered him to turn out his pockets. Only his quick-witted decision to let his wallet drop on the floor gave him the opportunity to fish out and swallow the incriminating code sheet while his accusers were scrambling for his papers on the ground.

In describing the incident with great relish in *My Silent War*, Philby omitted to relate the sequel. It is the account he gave to the KGB which reveals that he had then to write to his Paris contact to request a new code sheet.[81]

"The difficulty lay in the fact that we didn't have a code word for the word 'code'," Philby explained. "That was why I wrote in the letter I had 'lost the book I had been given' and asked them to send me a new one."[82] Only much later, long after his return from Spain, was he to discover that the address he had been given – Mademoiselle Dupont, 78 rue de Grenelle, Paris 6 – was that of the Soviet embassy in Paris. Had the Spanish postal censors been alert, they could have started an investigation which would certainly have led to his arrest as a spy. It would not have been difficult for Franco's military intelligence service to have identified the British reporter and his espionage activity from the Spanish postmarks that coincided with the battlefront. The simple code he used to encypher his reports in these letters to Paris could easily have been broken, exposing the true contents of the letters which he continued to mail over a period of two years from all the areas of intense military activity. The Soviet intelligence service would later acknowledge that this glaring error endangered their agent at the very outset of his long career. But fate smiled on Philby, in contrast to the bad luck experienced by Orlov, that had obliged him to abandon his *rezidenturas* in England and France. Now the "legal" NKVD station chief in Madrid, Orlov was the ultimate recipient of the intelligence reports whose steady flow was restored after SÖHNCHEN received a new code sheet.

It came as a great surprise for Guy Burgess, Philby said in his KGB debriefing, to find that it was his friend Kim to whom he had been dispatched, in response to Philby's emergency request for a new "book" in a seemingly innocuous letter suggesting a rendezvous in Gibraltar. Burgess had previously been made aware that Philby was working for Soviet intelligence. As the next chapter will describe, the circumstances of Burgess's recruitment had been highly unusual and the security of the Cambridge network had been more compartmentalized that it became under Mally, who took a relaxed view of the rules of *Konspiratsia*.[83]

The reunion of the Cambridge duo took place in the bar of the Rock Hotel, where Burgess handed over a new code sheet and a further supply of money. The pair dined together and talked through the evening. To a casual eavesdropper at the next table it was just English gossip. Later, in the privacy of Burgess's room they continued their exchanges into the small hours of the morning, as Philby briefed Burgess with the latest information on Franco's military headquarters and operations for relay, via Mally, when Burgess returned to London.[84]

It was shortly after their meeting in Gibraltar that Philby received a summons to return to London for debriefing on the first three months of his first overseas mission. He was subjected to questioning by

Deutsch, who, he recalled, raised his hackles by suggesting at first that his performance of his duties was less than satisfactory.

"Weren't you ashamed of writing such dull letters to such a beautiful woman as Mademoiselle Dupont?" Deutsch demanded teasingly.

"Try and write an interesting letter yourself when you have to communicate something serious in every fifth word," Philby said he responded, complaining that the lack of interest was the fault of the peculiar code system that he had been given to disguise his military reports.[85]

Well aware of Philby's deep psychological need to be praised, Deutsch reacted with a grin and a pat on the back. "Notwithstanding, your information was of great importance and the Centre thanks you for it."[86] Deutsch then made it clear to him that Moscow was becoming concerned about his ability to carry out his mission to arrange for the assassination of Franco. Their orders required that he return to Spain, but this time as a correspondent of a major newspaper or magazine. This, they believed, would give him better access to Franco and his military staff, who were currently headquartered in the western province of Salamanca. To land such a reporter's job, Mally instructed Deutsch to advise Philby that he should get an article published that would bring him to the attention of London's leading newspaper editors.

When Philby expressed reservations about the whole assassination plan, Deutsch reassured his obviously troubled agent with praise for what he had accomplished so far. He left it to Mally to relay his concern to the Centre that they were requiring too much of Philby. This he did in his report dated 24 May 1937:

> The fact is that SÖHNCHEN has come back in very low spirits. He has not even managed to get near to the "interesting" objective. But I think or rather feel from my talks with him that, even if he had managed to make his way through to Salamanca, even if he had managed to get near to Franco, then – in spite of his intention – he would not have been able to do what was required of him. Though devoted and ready to sacrifice himself, he does not possess the physical courage and other qualities necessary for this [assassination] attempt.[87]

While Mally made very plain to Moscow his belief that his agent was unsuited psychologically and physically for his part in the assassination plan he also took it on himself to allay Philby's concern by ridiculing the NKVD chiefs for wanting to pursue such an absurd plan.

Deutsch later wrote that this was a bad error on Mally's part since criticizing the Centre tended to undermine an agent's confidence in its authority. That he was highly critical of the manner in which Mally had disparaged the chiefs in front of Philby is evident in the report he wrote in 1939, after his return to Moscow, on the Cambridge group:

> This was the case when MANN [Mally], according to the Centre's order, was given the task of ordering SYNOK [Philby] to assassinate Franco, although MANN knew that SYNOK would not be able to cope with this assignment. When the Centre continued to insist on this operation, he communicated the task to SYNOK, but in such a way that SYNOK saw that MANN himself did not take this assignment seriously. Such behaviour undermines the Centre's authority in the eyes of these people – the more so since they have a natural tendency to cynicism, which they have inherited from their class and the general attitude of the British intelligentsia. That is why they should always see our officers display an unshakeable confidence in the Centre, because only in this manner will they be able to overcome this attitude inherited from their bourgeois class.[88]

"However, as has happened in the past, we did not receive any answer at all from the Centre to the serious questions they asked. This put us in difficulties with our sources," Deutsch also complained, asking rhetorically, "Why did the Centre assign tasks for these people which could not be properly justified to them?"[89]

Such strong criticism of the NKVD chiefs in the Lubyanka was highly unusual for a Soviet intelligence officer. It was indicative of Deutsch's and Mally's strong feelings on the subject, although it is not clear from the records whether it was their report that persuaded the Centre to drop Philby from their assassination plot, or whether it was Orlov, exercising his authority as NKVD chief in Spain who intervened on SÖHNCHEN's behalf. The dispute, nevertheless, offers a revealing insight into certain vulnerabilities in the character of Philby, denting the myth of his icy calculation and ruthless dedication in executing orders from Moscow.

While the Centre pondered SÖHNCHEN's brief, Philby produced a penetrating article on the Spanish Civil War unencumbered by the chains of Franco's censors. Then he took it to his father, who happened to be in London, for a critique and advice on how to get it published.

"You should start at the very top and send it to *The Times*," Philby said his father told him. For once he exerted himself on behalf of his son and sought out a friend who was an Assistant Editor on *The Times*. The friend informed him that there was an opportunity for

Kim because the paper had just lost two of its correspondents in Spain: one had died in an automobile accident and the other had quit, disgusted at having his reports emasculated by Franco's pernickety censors. Philby's reportage and analysis impressed Barrington Wood and resulted in the offer of an assignment to which every British journalist worthy of his typewriter aspired. In his reminiscences for the KGB Philby vividly recalled how his father had telephoned him with the news.

"I have just met with the assistant editor of *The Times*, Barrington Wood, in my club," Philby senior boomed down the line. "He has informed me that you wrote a very acceptable article and they'll be glad to publish it. More than that, they would be happy if you'll agree to go back to Spain as a regular correspondent." When Philby indicated that he would be delighted to accept, his father, true to form, announced that he had already taken that decision for his son.[90]

At the ripe age of twenty-five Philby had achieved a plum assignment as one of the two *Times* correspondents in Spain. He remembered that it was with some trepidation that next day he arrived in the hallowed offices of *The Times*, where Ralph Dickens, the Foreign Editor, introduced him to the Editor, Geoffrey Dawson as "the son of the Arabist Philby". In the presence of one of the most powerful figures in the British Establishment of the time, Philby was carefully deferential, recalling that he found the fifty-year-old bachelor Dickens "a little bit pompous, but essentially a kind person". It was Dawson, Philby noted; who had then proposed that he spend a couple of weeks in *The Times* offices to acquire the finer points of the august newspaper's prim editorial etiquette before he set out to return to Spain.[91]

The Times correspondent's post came with a £50 a month allowance for "special expenses while acting as a correspondent with General Franco's army".[92] The assignment also put Philby within striking distance of the British intelligence service, since it was common practice for senior British correspondents to be tapped for information by MI6. So while Philby served a brief apprenticeship under Dickens's tutelage, Mally enthusiastically informed Moscow headquarters that SÖNNCHEN had achieved their objective. This was sent just before he departed from London for good at the beginning of June 1937.[93]

Philby was scheduled to leave London for Spain by 4 June, but it was not until 4 September that Deutsch eventually received specific instructions from the Centre for SÖNNCHEN personally to re-establish contact with Orlov. The arrangements were made through the NKVD's "legal" *rezident* in Paris, Georgy Nicolaevich Kosenko, whose code name was FIN.[94]

Ten days later Philby travelled to Biarritz the elegant spa on the French Atlantic coast to make his first rendezvous in two years with Orlov. In the café of the Miramar Hotel they arranged that they would meet at least twice a month at Narbonne to exchange military and political intelligence according to a prearranged schedule. This quiet French town just north of the Spanish frontier was selected because Orlov could easily travel there from Republican territory and Philby would also not arouse suspicion by taking his breaks from front-line duty. A French train ran from Bayonne, a town situated in the north-western section of the frontier with Francoist Spain, along the border to Narbonne. Its coaches were much sought after by journalists travelling to and from the front enjoying the magnificent vistas of the Pyrennees and the excellence of the dining car.

In the intervals between his bi-monthly meetings with Orlov in Narbonne, it was arranged that Philby would continue sending military intelligence to FIN in Paris. "The greater part [of the information] I recorded in detail on paper in France and handed it over to Orlov," Philby later recalled for the KGB adding that additional intelligence was "forwarded down the line through channels which I knew nothing about".[95] His reports were to be written in invisible ink using photographic chemicals rather than the clumsy code. Since these could be purchased in any pharmacy, Orlov advised him that they would cause no suspicion if they were found during a police search. Using the Soviet embassy in Paris as a mailing address continued to put Philby unwittingly at risk, but the French police, who were now more alert to the clandestine operations of the Soviet intelligence service. But they never picked up the trail. Even if they had intercepted his letters to the Soviet Embassy, it is unlikely they would have relayed the information to Franco's headquarters, because in the 1930s Europe was so riven by political and national divisions that their police forces and security services rarely co-operated. The French secret service, however, did from time to time assist MI5 in cases of Communist subversion and Philby regarded it as another stroke of providence that the Centre's slip-up over his channel of communication with Orlov was never uncovered.[96]

The closest to disaster Philby came was on New Year's eve 1939, when the car in which he was travelling with three other journalists from Saragossa to the battleground at Teruel took the full blast of an artillery shell. Bleeding and stunned, he was none the less able to walk calmly away from the wrecked vehicle with only cuts to his forehead and wrist. Observers reported that Philby was no less phlegmatic when he described for the readers of *The Times* their correspondent's close brush with death, an event that took the lives of his three companions. Two months later he was personally decorated for his bravery when Franco, the man whose assassination Philby was supposed to arrange, pinned the Red Cross of Military Merit on his chest.[97]

If Orlov did indeed have a hand in persuading the Centre that Philby was of far greater potential value to Soviet intelligence as a live penetration agent than a dead hero, then there was a brutal irony to the incident which only he and his protégé would have appreciated. The shell which came within inches of ending his life had been made by Soviet workers and had been fired by one of the Russian artillery pieces that General Orlov had been responsible for delivering to the Republican army.

Philby, by his own account, had many other opportunities for getting close to Franco during his second tour in Spain. Before leaving London, he had once more visited the German embassy, which alerted their legation in Spain to assist a Fascist "sympathizer". As a *Times* correspondent, he was regarded as an important adjunct to the pro-Franco propaganda machine. Philby encouraged his German contacts in this belief, playing up his acquaintance with Ribbentrop, which he found useful in strengthening his position and widening his contacts with the influential Nazi acolytes of the Falange Party in Franco's entourage.

"I made the utmost use of him [von Ribbentrop] when I was in Spain," Philby recounted to the KGB, wryly explaining that "even though my five-minute meeting with Ribbentrop had given me no important information, it had the greatest influence on my working relationship with people of lower rank than him, but of high enough rank for me. As soon as they learned that I had been received by Ribbentrop they behaved far more freely in front of me and discussed matters which they would not have dared talk about to a journalist who had not had the honour of being received by Ribbentrop."[98]

Philby's tactic proved successful in helping him ferret out military intelligence of value to Orlov and the Republicans. In particular he recalled the "friendship", as he described it, that he struck up with Major van der Oster, the *Abwehr* chief in Spain.[99] Confirmation of the extraordinary degree to which Philby enjoyed the confidence and favour of the Falangist authorities appears in the NKVD records. It reached Moscow by way of WAISE, the code name Orlov had chosen for Maclean.

Maclean was by then a Third Secretary at the Foreign Office Western Department, handling material relating to Spain. He was, therefore, delighted to come across a June 1937 docket in which

Philby's name cropped up in a memorandum of Lord Cranborne. The Under Secretary of State had reported on a meeting with the Duke of Alba, Franco's emissary in London, to hear complaints about the negative attitude of the British press to the Franco regime. Cranborne had pointed out that this was due in no small part to the hostility of Falangist military censorship – to which the Duke responded that he anticipated that this would all change now that *The Times* had sent a brilliant young journalist named Philby to cover the battlefront in Spain.[100]

Nor did Philby disappoint the Spanish Duke, or the many right-wing British readers of *The Times*, most of whom sympathized with what they regarded as Franco's holy crusade against Bolshevism. For a correspondent with such strong Communist beliefs, it nonetheless generated great psychological stress to have to report the rising tide of Nationalist victories in 1938, as Franco's forces drove eastward across the Aragon front to Catalonia. In six months he had rolled up the Republican forces until the advance was finally stalled in summer heat along the Ebro river. Philby was obliged to tell his readers how, with the aid of Luftwaffe bombers, Franco's soldiers were gaining the upper hand as Italian-made tanks enabled them to outgun and outfight the Loyalists. The International Brigade, despite backing from Soviet officers, was losing badly, as the mangled bodies of dead and wounded comrades littering the contested highways and olive groves mutely attested. Republican corpses and abandoned Russian-made arms now greatly outnumbered Nationalist losses and casualties. As the destruction of men and Soviet *matériel* on the viciously fought Catalonian battle front mounted, Philby suffered, too. He told the KGB that it was especially painful to witness the growing number of brutal executions of Communists accused on trumped-up charges of plotting to assassinate Franco.

"This was probably the worst time of my life," was Philby's memory of 1938, when he was obliged to report on Franco's accelerating tide of victories. "It's almost impossible to describe, it was an awful time. In my articles I tried to suppress any emotion. I sought to report only cold information."[101] His professed objectivity did not impress the Republicans' embassy in London, which protested the "falsehood and propaganda" being promoted by *The Times*. Yet for all the psychological angst in his KGB memoir, Philby did not deny himself the comforts of a long love affair with a glamorous divorcée. Significantly his KGB memoir contains no mention of Lady Frances ("Bunny") Doble. It does, however, include his reminiscences of some lighter off-duty incidents in which he participated.[102]

One such incident involved Philby's encounter with a fellow British newspaper correspondent, Winston Churchill's son Randolph, whom he characterized as "a larger-than-life show-off like Guy Burgess" but, as he put it, "in a capitalist way". He recalled how one evening he was sitting at the same table in a crowded San Sebastian restaurant. Churchill, in his booming voice, was denouncing all Spaniards for their lack of valour on the battlefield when he was interrupted by an officer whose uniform bore captain's insignia.

"You may be interested to know there are many people here who speak English. Please would you keep your voice down," a well-spoken Spanish officer cautioned Churchill, much to the delight of Philby.

"Who the hell are you?" Churchill roared back. When the captain calmly announced he was an officer in the Spanish army, Churchill boorishly demanded to know why he was not at the front. Philby recalled how he and the rest of the group had a difficult time trying to defuse the unpleasant situation by discreetly assuring the officer in Spanish that his loud-mouthed accuser was "nuts".[103]

Philby's KGB memoir also contains an account of a curious conversation with his wife Litzi after his second tour in Spain, when he returned to London for a brief rest in the autumn of 1938. She asked him to report to his Soviet contact that she had "met someone who knows of a man who knew a scientist who was engaged in researching a completely new form of energy". Litzi explained that, although she did not understand it very well, it was a source of energy so potent that it could be compared to one lump of coal fuelling a train all the way from Vladivostok to Moscow. According to Philby's account given over four decades later to the KGB, he had asked Burgess to arrange for his wife to meet a Soviet comrade in London so that she could relay this curious report to Moscow.

"I still wonder whether it wasn't Fuchs," Philby told the KGB debriefers in Moscow after his defection, noting that he had never heard any more about it. Even though he was a trusted agent, Philby was never enlightened as to whether his wife's report had helped bring the Soviets into contact with Klaus Fuchs, the German emigré physicist who later helped Moscow obtain vital secrets about the atomic bomb.[104]

Such information was regarded as of less immediate importance to Moscow than Philby's mission at Franco's military headquarters. His intelligence had become crucial to Orlov's stategy for using guerilla forces to halt the accelerating Nationalist advance. As the Republican military situation deteriorated in 1938, Orlov became increasingly dependent on the intelligence he received from SÖHNCHEN, at their meetings across the French border, to judge where to deploy most effectively his specially trained ambush and sabotage units. By his own account, Philby's respect for Orlov increased as the outcome of the Spanish Civil War turned against the Republicans in spite of Soviet military intervention.

"A man of action," was how Philby remembered Orlov at this critical juncture of the Civil War. "He was energetic – I would even say a desperately energetic character. For instance he liked to always go about armed – probably as the result of his desperate energy and extravagantly romantic attitude towards his profession."[105] He provided a vivid picture of an incident which shows that even facing a collapsing military situation, Orlov had not lost his grim sense of humour or his thirst for adventure. It occurred during a meeting at Perpignan, when Philby had been dutifully waiting in this small French town at the foot of the Pyrenees. A large car screamed to a halt in the square. A heavily built man in a raincoat emerged. It was Orlov. But, as he crossed the square to greet him, Philby noticed that he was moving in an awkward and suspicious manner.

"What's the matter with you?" Philby asked. Orlov nonchalantly denied that there was anything amiss with him, but, when assured that his walk was clumsy and suspicious, he lifted the flap of his trench coat to reveal hanging at his side a large black sub-machine gun worthy of a Chicago gangster.

"So I have been unmasked after all," Orlov said, exploding with laughter. Philby was told to wait and the General climbed awkwardly back into his car, its tyres kicking up a small cloud of dust as it screeched out of the market square. After half an hour Orlov returned. He got out of the car, this time walking easily. Grinning from ear to ear, he pulled back his coat to show Philby that he was no longer toting his heavy weapon like a cowboy pistol. He then sat down and told Philby how always keeping the sub-machine gun at his side had saved his life. Orlov gave a hair-raising account of an incident that Philby later put on record for the KGB.[106]

According to Philby, this had occurred during an exceptionally oppressive afternoon when Orlov decided to do what all Spaniards do when it becomes so hot that even the swarms of summer flies take a siesta. Stretched out on a hotel bed, naked except for a sheet, Orlov said, he had quickly dozed off, but not before he had laid his trusty sub-machine gun at his side with its safety catch off. He was only half-conscious when he was aware that the door to his room was being opened. Although not properly awake, Orlov instinctively grabbed his weapon and emptied the ammunition clip before he was fully conscious of the situation. He found that he had literally stopped dead in their tracks two men who had entered the room. He assured Philby that he had later discovered they had been commissioned to kill him – but whether they had been sent by Franco or his enemies in the NKVD he said he never ascertained.[107]

Philby never forgot this anecdote with which his Russian mentor underscored that a Soviet intelligence operative could never afford to let down his guard – even when asleep. Its impact was all the more powerful because Orlov told it to Philby at one of their last meetings before his dramatic flight from Spain in July 1938. For the second time Philby was abruptly left to his own devices by Orlov. According to standard practice, the Centre arranged for SÖHNCHEN only to be informed that his long-time mentor had been recalled to Moscow. The NKVD records show that the only member of the network to learn the truth about his "defection" was Orlov's immediate subordinate at the Barcelona field station.[108]

When Orlov disappeared, Philby had known him for a little more than four years. Yet in that time Orlov's forceful personality and stern schooling had played an important part in equipping him with the skills he needed to function and survive as a Soviet underground agent. It was not until fourteen years later that Philby learned of Orlov's fate in his sensational revelation about Stalin in *Life* magazine. Since it was clear that he had chosen to come forward himself and had not been unmasked he did not fear for his own exposure. "He never said a single word about me," Philby observed, "even though of course he was interrogated in a very thorough way by the CIA and FBI and was in constant contact with them."[109] Even if Philby and the two other Cambridge "Musketeers" had known in 1938 that Orlov had fled to the West, it is unlikely they would have spent sleepless nights worrying whether they would be unmasked. They held Orlov in such high esteem that they simply would not have believed Big Bill might ever betray them, or abandon his commitment to the ideals of Lenin's Revolution.

What did upset Philby in the weeks following Orlov's abrupt departure from Spain, as he readily admitted to his KGB debriefers, was having to report each Nationalist success as Franco's forces remorselessly ground down the Republican army's defence line along the Ebro front. What he was witnessing was the desperate last stand of the Loyalist armies. The beginning of the end came when the front crumbled in November and within two months Franco took Barcelona. Philby celebrated his twenty-sixth birthday miserably as the first newspaper correspondent to enter the former Republican stronghold. Stalin's reluctance to commit Soviet arms and men on the same scale as the Germans and Italians meant that the Republican army had never been able to match their Nationalist enemies tank for tank and gun for gun or to compete with the air power of the Condor

Legion sent by the Luftwaffe. Yet Philby, it seems, did not hold any grudges against Stalin for his miserliness as he reported the triumph of the Fascists who took Madrid at the end of March two months later, as the Spanish Civil War fizzled to an end. Nor was Philby's commitment to Soviet Communism shaken by the reports of the ruthless purges that Stalin had orchestrated in the Soviet Union. For the ideologically blinkered, it was too easy to dismiss the reports of the Moscow show trials as propaganda. As a Soviet intelligence agent Philby's only concern was serving the cause of Communism – no matter how ruthless its complexion – as the only hope for defeating the Fascism that he regarded as a far greater evil.

Witnessing the triumph of Franco in Spain was for Philby a truly bitter defeat and a wrenching personal experience. But he knew better than most of his contemporaries the danger of the Nazi menace. Hitler was on the advance again as the epicentre of the great struggle shifted back from Spain to northern Europe. With the ink hardly dry on the previous autumn's Munich Agreement, in the spring of 1939 Germany had absorbed into the Reich a large swathe of the emasculated state of Czechoslovakia. The Führer now threatened war unless Poland acceded to his territorial demands on the Baltic port of Danzig and the corridor leading to it, which had been ceded to Poland in the Versailles Treaty. With the British and French Governments belatedly guaranteeing Polish sovereignty, Europe was mobilizing for war even as the diplomats scurried about in a desperate bid to avert a showdown with Germany.

It was against this grim background that Philby lost his battle with *The Times* to retain his special £50 a month expense account. In disgust he packed his bags, writing in a memo to *The Times* in July that it was no longer necessary for the newspaper to maintain two full-time correspondents in Madrid. Spain was no longer fertile territory for a journalist – or for an undercover Soviet intelligence agent. After bidding farewell to his mistress Bunny Doble, Philby arrived back in London to find public air-raid shelters being hurriedly thrown up in London parks and Whitehall being sandbagged in anticipation of German air-raids should war break out over Poland. At *The Times* he was promised the post of chief military correspondent with British military headquarters in France. Philby was, therefore, able to view the prospect of war with some relish because it would enable him to send military intelligence to Moscow bringing him a step closer to achieving his ultimate objective. He recalled during his KGB debriefing the injunction that Orlov had given him thirty years earlier: "Give your consent to any work that you consider useful, but always keep in mind that your goal is the British intelligence service."[110]

Within a year of war breaking out in Europe that autumn that advice was to be vindicated, at the end of May 1940. Shortly after Philby arrived back in Britain along with the British Expeditionary Force evacuated from the beaches of Dunkirk, he received a summons from the Foreign Editor of *The Times*.

"You have been called for by the War Office, a certain Captain Sheldon wants to see you," was how Dickens gave Philby the news which he had been awaiting so long.[111] The summons enabled him to take his first official step into the British intelligence apparatus. After six years Philby had finally "got on to the wide road", as Orlov had put it. By then in exile and unaware of the "first man's" achievement, before Orlov left Moscow for Spain in 1936 he had had the satisfaction of reading secret British Government papers obtained by the "second man" of his Cambridge network. Two years before Orlov was forced to flee from Stalin's vengeance, the second of his "Three Musketeers" had become a fully operational Soviet "mole" burrowing into the entrails of the British Foreign Office.

8

"A PROMISING SOURCE"

"KGB OF THE USSR – First Chief Directorate. Second Department. TOP SECRET – Do Not Hand Out Without Second Department's Permission" is stamped in black Cyrillic capitals on the cover of the first file of Donald Maclean's multi-volume operational dossier. That its original worn brown NKVD cover has been replaced by the KGB is an indication of the heavy use of file No. 83791 on the British agent whose code name was HOMER. Beneath its ironically appropriate Cambridge-blue new cover is the yellowing front page of the agent file, which records that Maclean's first cryptonym was WAISE.[1]

That his file commences in January 1935 is proof that Maclean was the "second man" in order of recruitment, in the Cambridge spy network. The very thickness of the first two volumes of reports is itself an indication why WAISE came to be regarded by Moscow as an even more valuable and productive source than the "first man", Philby. Its opening pages, moreover, corroborate what Philby told the KGB in his secret memoir: that he put Maclean at the top of the list of Cambridge Communist contacts that he had compiled in the summer of 1934.[2]

To fulfil his first mission for the Soviet intelligence service, Philby had gone to Cambridge to prepare the ground. Like the sinister uninvited fairy at a royal christening party, he arrived during the first week of June, when, even at the height of the Great Depression, the university was *en fête*. The picture-postcard college courts with their close-cropped lawns were the setting for all-night balls during "May Week" in the first week of June. The festivities marked the end of another academic year after the conclusion of Tripos examinations. By day slender racing shells competed in the May Bumps on the lower River Cam, while less sporting types spent their afternoons lazing on lawns leading down to the Backs, as the upper river is called. Their sport was watching the punters in their striped college blazers and straw boaters grappling with twenty-foot poles. With more or less skill they propelled the snub-nosed punts loaded with giggling girlfriends under ancient bridges – their summer frocks damp from the dripping leaves of overhanging willows.

The spectacle of revellers still in evening attire at midday swaggering along King's Parade would have been a powerful inducement to Philby on his secret mission to undermine the British Establishment. Cambridge during May Week was nothing but a prolonged "coming-out party" for the sons and daughters of Britain's ruling class. During a time of mass unemployment, their hedonism still confidently celebrated their accession to their appointed places on the rungs of the ladder that led to the ruling elites in government, the law and other professions. This flaunting of the social and economic divisions between Britain's upper- and lower-class citizenry proved to be an appropriate milieu for Philby to renew contact with former Marxist comrades, plotting in their clandestine Communist cells to tear down the fabric of this bastion of educational and social privilege. His mission was to observe and search out those with dedication and determination. What he was seeking were young men whose Communist idealism was a powerful enough incentive to betray their class and country by secretly serving the great social and economic experiment pioneered by the Soviet Union.

Philby found no shortage of potential candidates. In 1934 Communism had become the fashionable political hair shirt worn by many Cambridge undergraduates who wanted to sweep away forever the May Balls, champagne and punts. Devotees of the gospel of Marx, they sided with the workers. What they yearned for was a revolution that would banish all the trappings of the privileged class as abruptly as Lenin had dispossessed the squabbling politicians of the Provisional Government and disposed of the last vestiges of the Tsar when his Bolsheviks stormed the Winter Palace at St Petersburg seventeen years earlier.

"The Russian experiment has aroused a very great interest inside the university," a senior fellow of St John's College had observed at the beginning of the decade.[3] The supposed "scientific" rationale of dialectical materialism had a magnetic appeal to an academic community dominated by the physicists, biologists and chemists who had made Cambridge one of the world's leading centres of science research. The obsession with scientific rationalism that made Cambridge University, after World War I, a natural recruiting ground for the Soviet intelligence service, was as much a product of the centuries-old tradition of radicalism as of the scientific age. Cambridge owed its very existence to dissent. It was founded by a group of thirteenth-century clerics who broke with the discipline of the Oxford academies to establish Chaucer's "Canterbrigge" in the remote fens of East Anglia. The humanistic teachings of the philosopher Erasmus and the later, Lutheran exiles from Catholic Europe, established the university as the intellectual pivot of the English Reformation. The self-analytical Puritanism of Cambridge graduates such as John Milton and Oliver Cromwell helped lay the foundation stones for rational Cambridge minds like Isaac Newton, the seventeenth-century mathematical genius who mapped the scientific boundaries of the modern universe. It was from Cambridge also – a century-and-a-half later – that Charles Darwin set out on his voyage of discovery that led him to develop a scientific rationale for the origin of species. In the University's famed Cavendish Laboratory J. Clerk Maxwell's experiments in the mid-nineteenth-century on electromagnetic theory opened the door for J. J. Thomson's research into the electron as the twentieth century dawned. On the eve of World War I Ernest Rutherford had established the structure of the atomic nucleus and paved the way for his pupils, John Cockcroft and E. T. S. Walton, who eventually split the atom in the Cavendish Laboratory on the eve of World War II, to raise the curtain on the nuclear age.

The 1920s and 1930s were the golden years of Cambridge scientists, whose worldwide reputation between the wars had inevitably attracted the interest of a Soviet Union desperate to catch up with the advanced technology necessary to build a Socialist workers' paradise. One of Russia's leading physicists, Pyotr Kapitsa, had arrived from Leningrad in 1930 to pursue his research at the Cavendish Laboratory. The presence of Kapitsa and other Soviet scientists such as George Gamow, together with the proselytizing of Communist economist Maurice Dobb, encouraged the notion amongst the Cambridge intellectuals of scientific bent that Lenin truly had revolutionized the role of science in post-Revolutionary Russia.[4]

It was the belief that a new age had dawned Red that encouraged the Marxist views of leading members of the Cambridge scientific establishment, among whom were chemist J. D. Bernal, biochemist J. B. S. Haldane and physicist P. M. S. Blackett. The pro-Soviet sympathies of this powerful coterie of scientific intellectuals inevitably influenced their pupils in the debates that took place in the Union, the Socialist Society and the elite secret undergraduate clubs such as the Heretics and the Society of the Apostles. As Britain's economy sank inexorably deeper into the seemingly intractable morass of the Great Depression of the 1930s, it was tempting for many in this academic ivory tower to believe Moscow's propaganda that capitalism was doomed because science was serving only the narrow interests of the ruling class. In the Soviet Union, by contrast, the Revolution, according to the propagandizing Dobb, had abolished class to ensure that scientific effort truly was serving the needs of a brave new egalitarian social order.

"The political climate of the period was very favourable," Orlov noted in carefully general terms, in his *Handbook* published in 1963. He would recall how it had been his experience that "the young generation was receptive to libertarian theories and to the sublime ideas of making the world safe from the menace of Fascism and of abolishing the exploitation of man by man".[5] Such a simplistic ideology had transformed the naive Marxism of many adolescent rebels from a badge of naive defiance against the oppressive prefectorial discipline of their boarding schools into a passionate political commitment. Philby and his Cambridge comrades, however, were driven less by juvenile inclinations to *épater les bourgeois* than by a conviction that they had discovered an intellectual rationale that provided the panacea for Britain's social and economic inequality. The Communist experiment appeared to hold out to them and their generation the promise that the future could after all be salvaged from the Great War's political and economic wreckage inherited from their parents.

"To be a dialectical materialist means to think of things and our ideas of them not as static, rigid, eternal entities, but as changing, developing, interacting," proclaimed Alister Watson, a brilliant research fellow of King's College in a 1934 *Cambridge Review* article. Provocatively his piece praised "the tactics of Lenin, which have converted Marxism into the 'official philosophy' so much hated and scorned".[6] Watson's defiant defence of Communism provides an insight into the rationale that had captured some of the brightest analytical minds of his Cambridge generation. Others had come to the same conclusion by way of practical experience, including Philby and his Trinity contemporary David Haden-Guest, the son of a Labour MP, who had abandoned his philosophy studies to observe at first hand the stuggle between Fascism and Socialism. After a spell of imprisonment in Germany for taking part in anti-Nazi demonstrations, Haden-Guest had returned to Cambridge a militant Communist to complete his studies and proclaim the ideology of the future. He was to die fighting for his beliefs with the International Brigade in the Spanish Civil War, like his charismatic contemporary John Cornford, who became a martyred hero for this Cambridge generation. Others such as Jimmy Lees, an ex-miner on a trade union scholarship and a founder member of Trinity's first Communist cell, had arrived at the colleges favoured by blue-blooded young aristocrats with the fire of Communism coursing through their working-class hearts.[7]

The so-called "Red cells" of Cambridge, although they might contain paid-up, card-carrying Party members like Lees, were "unofficial" in the sense that they were not under the control of the King Street headquarters. Membership in them did not require a green CPGB membership card, an important factor that Philby had been told to take into account when he compiled his list of potential candidates for Reif and Orlov. When he returned to London, as Philby explained in his KGB memoir, he had already drawn up a roster of potential recruits from which he made a final list of seven names. The original list was not forwarded in full to Moscow, but we know that at least two names on it – Maclean and Burgess – were to become Soviet intelligence agents during the time Orlov was head of the London "illegal" station from July 1934 to October 1935.[8]

According to Philby's KGB confession, he deliberately put Maclean's name at the top – and Burgess's at the bottom – of that list, indicating his own rating of their potential. Maclean was considered a prime target for recruitment not, he stressed, simply because they were old Cambridge friends, but because by the time of his graduation in 1934 he was one of the most active members of his underground university cell and likely to succeed – where Philby had failed – to fulfill his intention of entering the Foreign Office.

Donald Duart Maclean certainly had all the makings of a future British ambassador. Athletic and six foot four, the twenty-year-old was the quintessential image of a handsome young Englishman who with an effortless air of superiority strode out from the Trinity Hall pavilion to bat first in cricket matches for his college. Endowed by nature with striking good looks, and with a boyish sensuality that hinted at a certain sexual ambivalence, Maclean was also blessed with a fine intellect. When Philby had looked up Maclean during his May Week visit, he learned that his old friend had just taken a distinction in the final examination of the Modern Languages Tripos. He was even more pleased to find that Donald had decided to forego an academic career and was intending to enter the Foreign Office to become a diplomat. Moreover he was confident of successfully passing the Civil Service Examination and Interview Board since he possessed not only impeccable grades, but also politically powerful family connections. His father, the late Sir Donald Maclean, had been a barrister who had given up a successful law practice to become a Liberal MP and later a Cabinet Minister in the National Government. At the time of his father's death from a heart attack two years earlier in the summer of 1932, the elder of his three sons was rebelling against the paternalistic authoritarianism of Sir Donald who had inherited from his Scottish Presbyterian parents a dour belief that the Bible was the revealed, literal word of God.[9]

Young Donald had resolved to nail his faith to the Communist Manifesto after what he considered was his father's betrayal of political principle in accepting a post in the Coalition Government of Tories and Liberals formed in 1931 by the turncoat Labour leader Ramsay MacDonald. But he raised his personal red flag of rebellion at Cambridge only after his father's death. According to his close school and college friend James Klugman, only then did Donald become "cheerfully open now about his unreserved allegiance to the Communist cause".[10]

James Klugman was in a position to know. He had been an active member of the Party since their days together at Gresham's School, a nonconformist educational establishment that had also produced W. H. Auden. The poet's iconoclastic verses celebrated in parodying with wickedly classical metaphor the crumbling of capitalism for Maclean's generation, as it reached adulthood during the political and economic turmoil of the 1930s. Frustrated at the apparent inability of the politicians to offer any solution, Auden and his generation of left-leaning intellectuals were angry because of their justifiable conviction that the British Government did not seem to care that Fascism was triumphing in Europe. To Philby, Maclean and their Cambridge comrades, the only hope of saving European civilization from sinking into a terrifying abyss of totalitarianism was for Britain to join the scientific social experiment represented by the Soviet Union.

Maclean was not the only Cambridge undergraduate who naively considered going to the Soviet Union to do his bit to further the Revolution. His doting mother, Lady Maclean, had in her bereavement dismissed as a flight of youthful aberration her son's abrupt declaration that as a Communist it was his duty to go and work in Russia as a teacher or farm worker. She continued to promote the idea of a diplomatic career for her son by asking favours of her late husband's friends in the highest levels of the Government. Becoming a teacher, or driving a tractor on a collective farm, was a romantic aspiration entertained at that time by many undergraduate Communists. But it demanded the sacrifice of a career and creature comforts that few of the "young gentlemen" were willing to give up. At Cambridge they were attended by an army of deferential college servants who waited on them in hall, while "bedders" and "gyps" cleaned and fetched and carried for them, even polishing their shoes. They had grown too accustomed to the privileged life to opt for spartan living conditions on a collective farm. Even the most ardent member of the University Socialist Society secretly preferred the theory to the practice of Marxism. Few members of the Trinity College Communist cell ventured into the town's working-class neighbourhood of Hills Road to sell the Daily Worker. They took to the streets to parade their political views only when a protest march of the unemployed from the shipyards of the north to London passed conveniently near the centre of town.

Cambridge Communist demonstrations were no more violent than the annual clashes with the right-wing boat club and rugby-playing "hearties" at the November Poppy Day parade. Political protests were restricted to barracking the cinema newsreels and the genteel picketing of Trinity College hall when the servants went on strike to try to get one of the most richly endowed institutions in England to increase their miserably low wages. Only a very small minority of Communists had first-hand experience of bullets, broken bones and jailings from manning the political barricades in Europe. The searing tales told by Haden-Guest and Philby of street fighting in Germany and Austria were far removed from the experience of their Cambridge comrades. Their harrowing tales did, however, serve to reinforce the conviction of a growing number of leftward-leaning undergraduates that only the teachings of Lenin and the discipline of the Comintern could muster the forces of Socialism to defeat the assaults of the Nazi storm troopers.

"What they wanted was a purpose in life and it seemed to them they had found it," Orlov observed of the impact of Communism on the disaffected generation of students of the 1930s. Although he did not name them when he wrote his *Handbook*, he might have been describing his Cambridge "Musketeers" when he wrote how their burning purpose had to be kept concealed, heightening the drama of the adventure on which they embarked. For these young, upper-class Englishmen whose recruitment he had supervised, there was also the powerful stimulus generated by possessing secret knowledge, that while enjoying careers of privilege and perks within the citadel of Britain's cosseted class-system they were secretly nurturing the revolution that would tear those walls down. "The idea of joining a 'secret society' held a strong appeal for the young people who dreamed of a better world and heroic deeds," Orlov noted. "By their mental make-up and outlook they remind one very much of the young Russian Decembrists of the past century, and they brought into Soviet intelligence the true fervour of new converts and the idealism which their chiefs had lost long ago."[11]

The revolutionary "Decembrist" fervour that had so impressed Orlov was present in Philby and, to an even greater extent, in the "second man" of the Cambridge network. In selecting Maclean for cultivation after receiving Deutsch's report, Orlov found that he was in many respects a better candidate to fulfil the objective of the NKVD's penetration strategy. In contrast to the "first man", whose political reputation had become a hindrance to entry into the upper echelons of the British Government, Maclean's genteel brand of Communism was combined with glowing academic qualifications and political connections that could be guaranteed to gain him admittance into the Foreign Office.

It was during Orlov's initial trip to London in July that the NKVD records show that Philby was assigned the mission of sounding out Maclean. It is intriguing to find that all the original members of the Cambridge network received code names that disregarded the strict rules of *Konspiratsia* that all NKVD agents were expected to follow. With the exception of SÖHNCHEN (SYNOK = SONNY), the founding group's pseudonyms bent the rules of strict security. Each related to an easily identified attribute of the agent, such as Maclean's cryptonym WAISE (ORPHAN), that alluded to his father's recent death.[12] This is corroborated by Deutsch's account of the origins of what he called "the Cambridge Group" to be found in the London *rezidentura* records, which document the first steps in Maclean's recruitment.

"It was SCHWED's [Orlov's] plan to recruit WAISE [Maclean] and MÄDCHEN [Burgess] through SYNOK [Philby]," according to Deutsch. "SYNOK got instructions to sound out WAISE:

a. to determine his opportunities and contacts.

b. to find out if he is prepared to abandon active party work and begin working for us like SYNOK."[13]

"SYNOK fulfilled our assignment with a positive result for us," Deutsch records, noting that "WAISE expressed his readiness". What actually transpired behind these matter-of-fact phrases can be reconstructed from Philby's own secret memoir. This recounts how he invited Maclean over to his flat in Acol Road, Kilburn, during one of Maclean's visits to London, to sound him out without giving away his purpose. In what was a slip of memory Philby stated his meeting with Maclean as having taken place in December 1934, but as Reif had reported their first contact to Moscow on 26 August, this critical discussion must have occurred five months earlier[14]. In it, Philby had carefully steered the conversation around to ascertaining that his friend was intending to continue as an active Communist after he came down from Cambridge. Carefully steering the conversation to his friend's declared intention to continue working for the Party, Philby asked how Maclean thought he could remain an active Communist while pursuing a career in the Foreign Office.

"If you are going to sell the *Daily Worker* there, you're not going to be there very long," Philby recalled advising his Cambridge comrade, noting how he dropped a cryptic hint, "But you can carry out special work there for us." This aroused Maclean's interest and Philby moved on to explain in very general terms his own contact with the Soviets and how his friend could also help the Communist cause by passing on information from Foreign Office documents which would aid the Soviet Union. Philby records that Maclean immediately wanted to know whether he would be working for the Soviet Government or the Comintern?[15]

"Honestly I don't know but the people I deal with occupy very senior positions and work in a very important organization," Philby said he had responded. So great had his own enthusiasm been for becoming an undercover agent that when Philby was approached by Deutsch, he recalled that he had not even felt it necessary to ask this question himself. Philby therefore advised Maclean that he did not know anything more than that "they are connected with Moscow".[16]

Maclean remained silent and thoughtful according to Philby, who recalled that he then asked whether he could talk the whole thing over with his friend Klugman, who had been his Communist mentor since they had begun their political rebellion at school. "If you do that, you can forget our talk," Maclean was told by Philby. He explained that his Soviet contact had made it very clear that those who wanted to provide secret assistance to Moscow could not have any dealings with or links to Party comrades because of the need for absolute security. Maclean would have to break off all links with anyone like Klugman who was a card-carrying CPGB member. This caused his friend some hesitation. and it was two full days before Maclean came back to him to let Philby know that he was prepared to accept the conditions.[17]

The NKVD records indicate that Maclean's acceptance of Philby's invitation was mid-August 1934, the month during which Orlov was in the Soviet Union, having returned at the end of July to brief Artusov on the situation at their "illegal" London station. So it fell to Reif, as acting *rezident*, to relay Philby's positive report on Maclean to Moscow. To do this he crossed the North Sea again to Denmark to communicate with the Centre via the "legal" station in the Soviet embassy in Copenhagen. His cable of 26 August 1934 announcing a favourable outcome of the approach to Maclean appears as a paraphrased *spravka* in the first volume of Maclean's Soviet file: "MARR reports that SÖHNCHEN has contacted his friend, the latter has agreed to work, wants to come into direct contact with us. MARR asks for consent."[18] Moscow, however, would still not sanction any direct contact with Maclean. The Centre cabled back to Reif in Copenhagen in response to his cable No. 55/ 4037 a terse instruction to "abstain from direct contact until the check has been run to determine his opportunities. In the meantime use him through SÖHNCHEN."[19]

This caution reflected not only the strict rules of the *Konspiratsia* but also the tight control NKVD headquarters kept on the operations of their "illegal" stations. Their refusal to consent to an approach to

Maclean was, it appears, in part because they had not been kept up to date on developments in London as a result of a continuing communications problem. The station's previous reports had been photographed and the undeveloped rolls of film concealed in boxes of ladies' face powder, which were smuggled out to Copenhagen by PFEIL, one of the female couriers assigned to Orlov's London group. However, when these arrived in Moscow, it was found that they were largely unreadable because of improper exposure, so the chiefs at the Centre had no idea of the rapid progress Reif and Deutsch were making in the cultivation of the embryo Cambridge group. Had Orlov himself been on hand in the Lubyanka, he might have overcome the Centre's hesitancy over Maclean, but, when Reif's request arrived at headquarters, he was away from Moscow visiting his family.[20]

When Orlov returned to London on 18 September, he himself took the decision to establish direct contact with Maclean, entrusting the mission to Reif, who conducted the first meet with Maclean in mid-October 1934. It was successful, as Orlov's November report to Moscow confirms: "We have contacted SÖHNCHEN's friend WAISE, whom we wrote to you about. He has broken off completely with his compatriots and he intends to become a member of the highest [Government] circles and, since his connections are excellent, he is expected to obtain a high-level position."[21]

Orlov was careful to assure Moscow that Maclean had already cut off all his ties to the Communists – "compatriots" in NKVD jargon – prior to entering his name for the British Civil Service Board examinations. Obtaining a Foreign Office post was a highly competitive process by which even Cambridge graduates were required to take a preliminary interview, sit a tough examination and then be quizzed by a selection panel.

Maclean and his comrades did not have to sit an examination for the Soviet intelligence service and so were unaware of the two stage vetting procedure which involved an equally rigorous selection process. After being talent-spotted candidates for selection were discreetly contacted and cultivated with tasking missions before they were ready to go on to stage two, when, as "candidates for recruitment", they were put under training. By the end of 1934, Philby was already in the second stage of this process and Maclean was about to become a "candidate for recruitment" with a series of tasks aimed at discovering his appetite and ability to perform clandestine operations. They were conducted with a view to establishing the repertoire of psychological attractions which would be necessary to bring him and keep him under the discipline of his assigned control officer. According to Reif's account, written after his return to Moscow in 1939, by January 1935, he was satisfied that Maclean had made the break with his Communist circle of friends irrevocably and had "put a cap on his work as a 'compatriot'."[22]

Some of Maclean's Cambridge "compatriots" from his Communist cell found it hard to accept his gradual withdrawal from their friendship. Guy Burgess, in particular, regarded it a symptom of his friend's weakness and refused to allow him to break with the Party, taking it upon himself to try to bring him back to the Communist fold. Maclean's Cambridge contemporary and biographer Robert Cecil, to whom Donald had frequently boasted of his Communist ideals, found it strange that he had suddenly cut himself off from his former comrades just before he began cramming for his Civil Service examinations. Cecil, who was not a member of the Communist cell he admitted he was once approached to join, recalled the occasion when he was present as Lady Maclean solicitously enquired of her son if he intended joining a political demonstration by London workers.

"You must take me for a bit of a weathercock, but I've now given all that up," was Maclean's response – much to his mother's relief.[23] At the time Cecil simply assumed his friend had turned over a new political leaf in response to the entreaties of Lady Maclean, who was still busily lobbying her husband's former ministerial colleagues to ensure that her beloved son was accepted into the diplomatic service.

Cecil, who himself became a career diplomat, was later to conclude, correctly, that Maclean had, in fact, been responding to instructions from Moscow. This is confirmed from a report made shortly after Reif's enforced departure from London: "In February 1935 passed SIROTA [Russian for WAISE] over to SCHWED." This confirms that Orlov himself had direct contact with Maclean who then began carrying out missions under the "training" phase of his recruitment. While studying for the Civil Service Commission examinations at Scoones, the preferred "crammer" of well-connected graduates who chose a Foreign Office career, the Centre demanded evidence that WAISE really would measure up to the demands they intended to make of him. They therefore instructed their London *rezident* to assign him some specific intelligence missions. Orlov was told "to use WAISE, even though he has not yet obtained the position that interests us. Send your concrete proposals."[24]

Meeting with Maclean, Orlov proposed that he should obtain information for the anti-fascist cause by exploiting family contacts with the Establishment and high officials in the Government. This he suggested could also help further his future career in the Foreign Office. Maclean, like Philby, was still unaware that he was being tapped by the Soviet intelligence service.

"WAISE is preparing for his Foreign Office examination," Orlov reported back to Moscow, listing the various steps Maclean had taken to fulfil their directive: "He has also become a member of the

'Women's Club', where women, mainly the secretaries of the ministries and political organizations, are concentrated." The so-called club, according to Cecil, was probably one of the large Whitehall canteens that catered to the staff of Government ministries. It served Orlov's purpose to jolly along the Centre by inflating the effort Maclean was supposedly making, by including the trivial reference that WAISE had "made the acquaintance of the secretary of Foreign Secretary Sir John Simon's wife, her maiden name is Halpin".[25]

It is doubtful if Maclean achieved anything more than a nodding acquaintance with Lady Simon, but of far more significance was the list of names Orlov provided in the final section of his report, which notes that WAISE "has become friendly with a Foreign Office official Shuckburgh. The latter is working in the Spanish section, presents no special interest, but through him he has made contact with other members of the Foreign Office."[26]

Dismissive though Orlov initially was of Evelyn Shuckburgh, who was then in the Western Section of the Foreign Office, Maclean's Cambridge contemporary at King's College was to become a useful, if unwitting, source for Maclean during his early career. He was a "high-flyer" who went on to become Assistant Secretary General of NATO and later British Ambassador to Italy. At the time, however, Orlov reported that it was not Shuckburgh, but an unidentified American journalist who had introduced Maclean to a Foreign Office official named Oliver Strachey, brother of the celebrated Bloomsbury intellectual and biographer of Queen Victoria, Lytton Strachey.

"Strachey's connection with the 'secret department' has been confirmed by two other sources," Orlov noted cryptically. He was of far more interest to Moscow since he was then a Foreign Office codes and cyphers expert. Strachey would later go on to break the German *Abwehr* traffic in World War II, which was designated, in recognition of his effort, "ISOS" – "Intelligence Source Oliver Strachey". The "secret department" was a reference to the British code-breaking operation. (The assumption of the British co-author is that it was from his agents NACHFOLGER and BÄR that Orlov received confirmation that Strachey was associated with the SIS). Since MI6 was also the recipient of code-breaking intelligence, it appears that this was what Orlov meant by the "secret department" of the Foreign Office. This is further corroborated by another reference to it in relation to Maclean having made "the acquaintance of a certain Carew-Hunt, also an official of the Foreign Office secret department".[27]

Robert Carew-Hunt was a Russian-speaking MI6 officer who happened to be its leading expert on the Comintern and one of the Foreign Office's trusted authorities on the Soviet Union. He was to become a wartime associate of Philby when he joined MI6 during the war – and later actually became his subordinate when Philby was promoted in 1945 and put in charge of anti-Soviet operations in Section IX.[28]

Orlov's next report elevated the Centre's interest in Maclean because the penetration of MI6 was the ultimate objective of the Soviet intelligence service and his already demonstrated ability to make contact with some of its key members made WAISE a potentially useful agent. That their attention was now focused on Maclean is evident from the 9 March 1935 response to Orlov's letter:

> Concerning WAISE, your information about him gave great satisfaction. With regard to him, our main aim is to use him to penetrate the Foreign Office. We request that you steer him firmly in that direction because WAISE, through his connections, has an excellent chance of being appointed to the Foreign Office. His new contacts, Halpin (in future to be code-named VASYA) and especially Shuckburgh (MANYA) and Strachey (SONYA) – since they are officials of the secret department of the Foreign Office – are extremely interesting to us.[29]

Under the sub-heading "Our general intentions for WAISE", the Centre then went on to map out their expectations for Maclean, who they assessed was "undoubtedly a promising source demanding special attention. The more so, because your July reports indicate that he is really well disposed towards us and works not just for material reward. The latter circumstance, however, should not be construed as instructions not to pay him, especially since he will probably need financial support in connection with the fact that he is getting a post with the Foreign Office."[30]

With Moscow pinning such high hopes on Maclean, Orlov took steps through his deputy Reif to ensure that their expectations were fulfilled. Concerned that good grades might not be enough to get Moscow's candidate into the Foreign Service in the light of his previous left-wing record, Orlov advised Maclean to obtain as many recommendations as he could from influential family friends to alleviate any lingering suspicions that he might not be a suitable chap to become a British diplomat. According to Orlov's report, it was Lady Maclean who turned up trumps for Moscow by enlisting the support of the Conservative leader and Prime Minister, Stanley Baldwin, which Reif reported on his return to Moscow. "Since Baldwin is a personal friend of the Maclean family, WAISE's mother succeeded in getting a letter from him," Reif advised the chiefs in the Lubyanka. "I saw the letter personally in which he writes that he is willing to help WAISE with all his influence to pursue a diplomatic career. The letter also mentions that a certain person in the

Foreign Office has been advised by Baldwin that he's personally interested in WAISE's advancement."[31]

When it came to the examination, Scoones had Maclean so well prepped that he was graded in the first dozen in the Civil Service examination. Cecil, who went through the same process the following year, pointed out that it was the Foreign Office Interview Board which was the real hurdle to be overcome. This committee of leading members of the diplomatic service and their wives made short work of any young man whose manners or political views were suspect and not deemed appropriate for a British diplomat. Maclean, who had the advantage of his family friends nonetheless had to anticipate questioning about his Cambridge Communism. Since he would not be able to deny the record, his best strategy was therefore to admit it – and thereby turn his apparent frankness and honesty to his advantage. Towards the end of the interview, when the inevitable question came up, Maclean was ready for it, later taking credit for instantaneous inspiration rather than what was more probably a carefully rehearsed act.

"I did have such views – and I haven't entirely shaken them off," was Maclean's disingenuous response. The board members, he would later boast to family friends, must have been impressed by his show of honesty, because he saw them nodding approvingly to each other as they thanked him for answering their questions. The board was fortunately predisposed in his favour. Its chairman, Richard Chatfield, was an old friend of his father, as were Lady Rumbold and Lady Bonham Carter, both formidable influences on the board's decision.[32]

Maclean learned officially on the eve of Orlov's hurried departure from London in October 1935 that he had passed with flying colours and was one of the half dozen successful candidates invited to join the Foreign Office. So Orlov left London knowing that the "second man" of the Cambridge group had been successfully inserted into the British Government. As proof of his triumph, Orlov carried with him a photograph of the letter Maclean had received from Lord Simon, personally congratulating him on his acceptance into the Foreign Office. The Foreign Secretary would not have been so fulsome in his praise for the newest recruit to his staff if he had known that his letter would be read with glee in the Lubyanka. Orlov and the Foreign Department congratulated themselves that the newest recruit to His Britannic Majesty's diplomatic and consular service could now be inducted as a fully-fledged agent of the Soviet intelligence service. As Reif himself had attested, Maclean was now a "[Soviet] Union agent who had devoted himself to our work even more willingly".[33]

In contrast to Philby, Maclean was fresh from university and lacked the political baptism of fire which had forged the former's burning ideological commitment to Communism. But the Soviet recruitment of this academically gifted and suave, well-bred young Englishman attests to the skills of Orlov and his lieutenants to sniff out, enlist and redirect the loyalties – on a permanent basis – of the disaffected offspring of the British upper class. This was no mean feat for a Russian timber merchant's son operating in the entrails of an alien society. He knew nothing and cared less about the cricket matches, genteel tea parties and waspish social etiquette of the young men who he trained to serve the Soviet intelligence service. Much of the credit goes to Deutsch, whose reports on the Cambridge group demonstrate a profound analytic grasp of the individual psyches and motivation that made them the first of Stalin's Englishmen.

In the little more than three years that Deutsch operated with the "illegal" group in London he had a personal hand in the selection and recruitment of no fewer than seventeen British agents.[34] A search through the archives of the seventy-five-year history of the Soviet intelligence service reveals that few other officers came close to matching Deutsch's record. Testimony to his unerring ability to pinpoint the characteristics of a potential recruit that could be exploited to bring the candidate under disciplined control are evident in the penetrating psychological assessments he constructed of the members of the British underground network. His assessment of Maclean, in particular, shows not only why he proved a model Soviet recruit but also indicates some of the psychological "handles" that he detected in the original members of the Cambridge group that enabled them to be turned so effectively to the service of Moscow. It is appropriate to quote Deutsch's analysis at some length, because it underscores the four character elements – an inherent class resentfulness, a predilection for secretiveness, a yearning to belong, and an infantile appetite for praise and reassurance that were considered essential to turn these young Englishmen into Soviet spies:

WAISE [Maclean] is a very different person in comparison to SYNOK SÖHNCHEN, i.e. Philby]. He is simpler and more sure of himself. He is a tall, handsome fellow with a striking presence. He knows this, but does not make too much use of it because he is too serious. He was an active member of the Communist Party at Cambridge and has undertaken a wide variety of Party work, from distributing the newspaper to picketing factories that were on strike. He came to us out of sincere motivation, namely that the intellectual emptiness and aimlessness of the bourgeois class to which he belonged antagonized him. He is well read, clever, but not as profound as SYNOK. He is honest, and at home became accustomed to a modest life-style because, even though his father was a minister, he· was not a rich man. He dresses carelessly like SYNOK and is involved in the same Bohemian life. He takes an interest in painting and music. Like SYNOK, he is reserved and secretive, seldom displaying his enthusiasms or admiration. This to a large degree is explainable from his upbringing in the English bourgeois world, which is first and foremost conditioned always to display a reserved appearance. He lives without a wife, though it would not be difficult for him to find someone. He explained it to me by the fact that he had an aversion to girls of his own class and so could only live with a woman who is also a comrade.

Reif once told him a dirty joke and WAISE told me afterwards of his astonishment that a Communist could speak so shabbily and mockingly of women. WAISE is ambitious and he does not like anybody telling him he has made a mistake. He is a brave person and ready to do anything for us. In money matters he is irreproachable. He did not want to take money from us, but in some cases he needed it. However, he does not know the value of money and is not economical. Neither he nor SYNOK know for certain which organization they are working for. We simply told them that it was for the Party and the Soviet Union. This was absolutely clear to them. They felt closely connected with the Party, which was corroborated by the fact that each month, out of the money they received from me, they reserved a sum for the Republicans in Spain and for the MOPR [International Workers Relief Organization].

Our relations were based on Party spirit – we were on first name terms. Since WAISE was cut off from Party life, I frequently bought him Party newspapers and books which he kept locked up at home. After reading them, he returned the volumes to me. Usually I gave him books as a present; this gave him great pleasure. He likes to be praised for our work, since it provides him with the acknowledgement that he is doing something useful for us.

WAISE, SYNOK and our other agents in England have grown up in a climate in which the legality of our Party is upheld in an atmosphere of democratic illusions. That is why they are sometimes careless and our security measures sometimes appear exaggerated to them. If any relaxation of security were permitted on our part, they would become even more undisciplined. That is why, when running them, we should stick strictly to the essential security measures even at the risk of cutting faintly ridiculous figures. It is especially necessary to stress our adherence to these principles in front of them. Our revolutionary cause has an absolute hold and authority over them. That is why they rate our officers only from this point of view.[35]

Deutsch's analysis highlights the degree of immaturity in the British recruits, who were willing to "do anything for us" in return for "being praised for their work". Ideologically motivated against the bourgeois class though they certainly were, it is surprising to find that Cambridge graduates were not more questioning of what appears to have been the visceral appeal of serving the Revolution. But, as Orlov himself put it, saving the world from the horrors of Fascism won for the Soviet Union the loyalty of "aimless young men", tired of a tedious life in the stifling atmosphere of their privileged class, searching for a sheet anchor of personal faith in troubled times.[36]

The tragedy for both Orlov and his recruits was that the "Great Illegals" were not really representative of what Soviet Communism came to be under Stalin. All the spymasters, with the exception of Deutsch, were soon to be liquidated, imprisoned or forced to flee like Orlov from a totalitarian tyrant's mindless and self-aggrandizing brutality. The reason Deutsch managed to escape the purge of the NKVD old guard was that, as his file shows, he was more of a technician than a revolutionary like Orlov. He survived only to be lost at sea in November 1942, when the steamer carrying him to America to begin a new phase of his underground work was torpedoed by a German U-boat.[37]

Deutsch's considerable technical expertise was put to the test when Orlov made his hasty departure from London in October 1935, leaving his lieutenant with the delicate task of managing WAISE during his first months as a probationary operational Soviet intelligence agent in the Foreign Office. Maclean's appointment to the Western Department gave him direct access to secret papers and reports relating to British policy in the Netherlands, Spain, Portugal and Switzerland in addition to those on the League of Nations. Moscow might have been better pleased if bureaucratic chance had placed Maclean in the Northern Department, which conducted relations with the Soviet Union, Scandinavia and the Baltic states. But Maclean quickly remedied this by making friends with a ranking official of that department named Labouchère, who, Deutsch reported, was un-wittingly giving "help with transference" of information.[38] To keep up to date with what was going on in Britain's relations with France, Germany and Belgium WAISE was able to tap his Oxford acquaintance Anthony Claude Rumbold, the son of British diplomat Sir Horace

Rumbold, who was then a Third Secretary in the Foreign Office Central Department. Tony and Donald lunched regularly together at the Travellers' Club in Pall Mall. Maclean would promptly relay any information he had gleaned to his Soviet contacts.

"I gave instructions that during the first few months he was to get to know the lay-out of the Foreign Office and the department he was working in," Orlov minuted in a March 1936 memorandum for Abram Abramovich Slutsky, the chief of the Foreign Department. During the nine months he was in Moscow before his posting to Spain, the NKVD records show that Orlov continued to monitor and have a hand in directing the Cambridge group. He was, for example, especially insistent that Maclean should not be made fully operational "until he had familiarized himself thoroughly with the routine of transferring and keeping secret documents and possible ways to remove them". Maclean was not to take out any materials at this stage from the Foreign Office, but advised to "confine himself to supplying us with brief information about the character and contents of the papers passing through his hands".[39]

From Orlov's office in the whimsically monumental Lubyanka headquarters, the espionage he influenced had as its focus the ground-floor room in London's Foreign Office where Maclean occupied one of the desks in the Western Department. The grand Victorian Venetian-style Palazzo in Whitehall that housed the nerve centre of British overseas power was sardonically referred to in NKVD cryptograms as ZAKOULOK (the back alley), an allusion to its arched courtyard entrance off Downing Street.

"The preceding months of preparation confirmed that WAISE enjoys free access to all the documents that pass through his department," Orlov reported on 26 March to Slutsky, alerting him to the fact that he now judged Maclean ready for full activation. "Quite a favourable situation for removing documents and photographing them has come to light," he noted, in what was soon to be proved by WAISE to be an understatement.

"There was bugger-all security," Robert Cecil commented scathingly, observing that, when he joined the Foreign Office the following year, "there was not even a security officer".[40] It was more of a club which conducted confidential business on an honour system in the quaint belief that gentlemen did not read mail that was not addressed to them. Since those who were not considered gentlemen had supposedly been weeded out by the rigorous selection process, confidentiality was taken on trust. Cecil recalled that once papers and secret reports arrived in the Western Department from the Registry, there was no set security procedure and very little attempt made to keep even the most sensitive documents locked up. The department consisted of three rooms. One was occupied by its head with an adjoining office for his secretary, opening into a large room where Maclean and the other junior officials, ranked on entry as Third Secretaries, had their desks. They were responsible for sifting and processing all incoming telegrams to be read and commented on by the Second Secretaries, who, would if necessary, pass the more significant up the line of seniority to the department head. Because all but the most secret documentation passed up from base to apex of the bureaucratic Foreign Office's administrative pyramid, even a fresh-man Third Secretary like Maclean had free access to all the department's most sensitive material. Security was classified according to the colour the Registry used for the jackets enclosing the papers. "White jackets", as the buff manilla folders containing the bulk of the documents were perversely known, were all supposedly confidential. Secret and higher classifications were denoted "green jackets" from their distinctive green banding. "Red jackets" with the crimson banding contained the secret intelligence reports from MI6. "Blue jackets", the most secret of all Foreign Office papers, enclosed reports obtained from breaking foreign codes and cyphers. These "BJS" were referred to with prep-school humour as "black jumbos" and were supposed to go straight to the head of the department.[41]

"Only the head of the department had a lockable press in which he was supposed to keep these most secret papers," Cecil recalled, noting how little attempt was made to lock up even the BJS. They would frequently be left on the head of department's desk if he went to the lavatory or popped out for a meeting, or to the canteen. Security was so lax that even documents stamped "secret" could be removed from the office for working on at home. No approval was needed at that time and, because the Foreign Office operated on trust, there were no undignified searches or security checks at the exits to cast an aspersion on the honour of its gentlemen diplomats.[42]

The anticipation of the chiefs at the Centre rose steadily through the early months of 1936 as their "mole" in the Foreign Office began relaying to the eager eyes in Moscow some of the British Government's most closely held diplomatic secrets. The NKVD archives disclose that this was not the first occasion the Soviet intelligence service had obtained access to confidential Foreign Office cables. Two cases of previous penetration – never admitted by the British – confirm that Maclean does not deserve the honour of being the first Soviet agent to penetrate the inner sanctums of the Foreign Office. This accolade actually belongs to an employee of the Communications Department named Ernest Holloway Oldham, a "walk in" to the Soviet embassy in Paris in 1929. A disaffected employee attached to a British trade delegation, Oldham offered to sell a Foreign Office cypher system for £2,000 only to find himself thrown out on his ear by the *rezident*, a less than sophisticated Soviet intelligence officer by the name of Vladimir Voynovich. A former docker with a longshoreman's lack of vision he evidently suspected a British provocation plot. When Moscow identified the codes as genuine, Voynovich was reprimanded. The Centre dispatched an experienced "illegal", Dimitry Bystrolyotov, to re-establish contact with Oldham and apologize for his rough treatment. The painstaking search took this Russian colleague of Orlov's almost a year. When HANS, as Bystrolyotov was code-named, finally located the cypher clerk in 1930, he paid him £2,000 and put Oldham and his wife (who according to his report had seduced him) under Soviet control. Espionage proved too much, however, for Oldham. He resigned shortly before committing suicide in suspicious circumstances in 1933. Because of British secrecy, the significance of the Oldham case has remained undisclosed and underestimated. The truth, as revealed by NKVD, files is that Oldham was not just a code clerk but a cypher expert who developed codes and was therefore able to provide Moscow with a great deal of information on security and secret traffic systems. The resourceful Bystrolyotov, who operated under the alias of Hans Gallieni in England, had also obtained from Oldham not only the keys to unlock a considerable volume of British cypher cables but also the names of the other paid members of the Communications Department who became targets for Soviet recruitment.[43]

One of the names passed to Moscow by Bystrolyotov was Captain John Herbert King, who was attached to the British League of Nations delegation in Geneva. Estranged from his wife and saddled with the burden of maintaining a free-spending American mistress, King was living way beyond his means. He became vulnerable to cultivation with Soviet money through expenses-paid Spanish holidays arranged by Henri Christian (Hans) Pieck, a Dutch artist, who was one of the NKVD's roster of agents in The Hague who were being run by Mally, the Centre's so-called "flying illegal". When King returned to London late in 1934, he began supplying Pieck with Foreign Office cables under the illusion that he was helping his friend's Dutch banker compile information on international trade relations. Assigned the code name MAG, King soon graduated to become a very valuable source for the Centre with his wholesale removal of copies of the Foreign Office cables he encoded, a role he continued to play until he was exposed by the Soviet defector Walter Krivitsky in the autumn of 1939. Information gleaned from Oldham and King enabled the Centre, with Maclean's help, to kick the door into the Foreign Office and its secrets wide open.[44]

The WAISE dossier reveals how, from the beginning of January 1936, when he handed his first bundle of Foreign Office papers to Deutsch, Maclean smuggled out an ever growing volume of documents. These were photographed overnight and handed back, to return the next morning. The volume soon became so great Deutsch instructed Maclean that, whenever possible, he should bring the documents out on a Friday night to give the overworked photographer of the "illegal" station two days to work before the papers were returned on Monday morning. The quantity and quality of the intelligence flowing from this source to Moscow picked up dramatically as Maclean gained both in expertise and confidence. No one in his office appeared to bother about the increasing amount of documentation he was ostensibly taking home to work on in his Chelsea bachelor flat in Oakley Street, a stone's throw from the Thames.

The reservoir of Foreign Office intelligence Maclean tapped opened up such a flood of documentation that Deutsch was soon overwhelmed. Following Orlov's departure, he had assumed the burden of heading the London "illegal" station and found it increasingly difficult to service Maclean in addition to taking care of the network, vetting new recruits and handling all the technical matters. Orlov's response to this overload on Deutsch was to send the INO Chief Slutsky a memorandum which concluded, "Taking into consideration the importance of the above-mentioned material and information that has fallen into our hands, in addition to the importance of other cultivations and recruitments that could benefit our field stations abroad, I consider the question of the Foreign Department's assigning an experienced and talented underground *rezident* to head the field station in the British Isles to be extremely pressing."[45]

Theodore Mally, one of the Centre's top agents, had by then been despatched to England under the cryptonym MANN in January 1936 with sole responsibility for handling the material supplied by MAG, the code clerk King. The Chiefs did not immediately authorize him to give assistance to Deutsch's group. But, since Mally was a proficient and capable "illegal" who had experience in both counter-intelligence and agent operations, Orlov eventually prevailed on the Foreign Department. Mally was recalled to Moscow for briefing with Orlov and, by April 1936 had returned as the newly designated London *rezident* with responsibility over Deutsch for the running and development of the Cambridge group.

The veteran NKVD operative was soon complaining that Maclean's material was swamping his relatively small and overworked team. As Mally reported to Moscow on 24 May 1936:

Tonight WAISE arrived with an enormous bundle of dispatches, of which MAG [King] had supplied only a few. Only part of them have been photographed, which we have marked with a w, because we have run out of film and today is Sunday – and night-time at that. We wanted him [Maclean] to take out a military intelligence bulletin, but he did not succeed in doing this. On Saturday he must stay [on duty] in London and we hope that he will be able to bring out more, including those which he has not managed to get out yet.[46]

When the films containing the copies of Maclean's latest haul of Foreign Office documents were developed in Moscow, after being smuggled out by the courier PFEIL to Copenhagen, Orlov was impressed by their importance. "There is reason to believe we have run across a branch of British military intelligence which is operating in a number of countries and also the Soviet Union," Orlov reported to Slutsky. He stated that the documents he had just seen persuaded him that "we are closing in on one of the branches of the British intelligence service".[47]

The reason for Orlov's elation is clear from the memorandum he sent Slutsky summarizing the most significant information which reached Moscow Centre from Maclean. To show that WAISE was tapping into MI6 sources he cited the Foreign Office report "about the state of German ordnance factories with exact figures of armaments production of each plant given separately" and another "describing the mobilization plans of various countries, Germany, Italy, France and the Soviet Union". The Centre had investigated how the Foreign Office knew about "mobilization of Soviet industry as recently carried out in 1932 in the Far East", from his previous report, telling Orlov that it pointed to a British spy operating somewhere in the upper reaches of the Kremlin apparatus.[48]

Maclean had also forwarded a report of "the army supply committee on the organization of British industry for war purposes before and after hostilities begin, about procurement for government arsenals and plants, and about the adaptation of private industry and transport companies for a smooth transfer of the country to a state of war". Included in its appendices was a top secret report by Britain's Imperial Defence Committee on the preparations needed for conducting war in the Far East together with "a directive for recasting the plans for conducting war in Europe [against Germany] in the five-year period [from 1934 to 1939]". Yet another appendix detailed British army procurement in the event of war with the USSR. Maclean had also passed on complete minutes of the Imperial Defence Committee meeting of 20 December 1936 attended by Prime Minister Baldwin, the service ministers and the military chiefs of staff.[49]

"From among those present," Orlov noted, "Sir Maurice Hankey [the British Cabinet Secretary] should be singled out, who, according to WAISE, was the official responsible for running military intelligence against a number of countries, or alternatively was in charge of processing the information as it comes in." Orlov emphasized that this meeting had discussed such matters as "radio broadcasting during wartime, measures for defending Government buildings against air attacks, securing the safety of the principal ordnance plants by transferring them to safe areas, the state of ammunition procurement of the army and navy, tanks, fuel – and the shortage of oil supplies of the navy". The Imperial Defence Committee, the highest military council in Britain, had decided that "the shortage of fuel should be kept absolutely secret, since its disclosure would lead to serious political complications". Orlov drew attention to the section on the operational readiness of the German air force, which challenged Winston Churchill over the validity of the data he had received from the British Air Staff. The Imperial Defence Committee had decided that the information at the core of the dispute "had been obtained from an exclusive, secret source – and that was why there was a necessity for handling them especially carefully to prevent their disclosure".[50]

Another document that Orlov picked out for special attention was the minutes of a conversation between Hitler and the British Ambassador in Berlin in which they discussed a proposal for a secret pact for exchanging technical data between Britain, Germany and France on the strengths of their air forces. "Hitler declared that he agreed to a mutual exchange of data with England," according to the British report, but was adamant about not sharing the information with the French because the Führer had declared, "if France were trusted with these materials, they would immediately fall into the hands of the arch enemy, the Soviet Union".[51]

The scope of the secret British reports Maclean passed to Moscow was not only extensive, but also of enormous importance. The papers ranged from an industrial assessment on the state of German war industry to the instruction issued by Sir Robert Vansittart, Permanent Under Secretary at the Foreign Office, concerning involvement of the Soviet embassy in Montevideo with a recent insurrection in Brazil, and from pages of the so-called "War Book" for mobilizing Britain on the eve of hostilities to a report on the "surveillance over foreigners and hostile individuals".[52]

Of greatest interest to the NKVD chiefs was that Maclean had begun to tap into some of the most closely held secrets of Britain's code-breaking operations. From the so-called "blue jackets" that should have been securely locked in the head of department's safe, Maclean was able to provide confirmation that the British had not made any progress in decrypting the Soviet cypher systems. This must have been reassuring news for Moscow Centre and the NKVD's signals intelligence operation, which worked jointly with the Fourth Department of the GRU. With Maclean supplying the plain text of dispatches and King providing access to the encyphered versions, it can be assumed that the Soviet cryptanalysts were able to continue intercepting and eavesdropping on much of the British Government's most secret radio traffic. The degree of their success must still be a presumption, because historic signals intelligence records are still as closely guarded secrets in the Russian Republic as in Britain.

The Soviet signals intelligence effort was extensive. How much it was stimulated by the reports that Maclean supplied is a matter for speculation. But it is clear he passed on to Moscow details of the progress the British were making in their assault on the encyphered communications of the Soviet Union and other countries, including the United States. It remains British government policy to adhere to the fiction that Britain's code breakers never attempted to read the communications of friendly countries during peacetime, but the contents of the NKVD files demonstrate how false that position is. Maclean's material provided proof of this activity by the Foreign Office's top secret intercept and code-breaking facility, known by its acronym GC & CS – Government Code and Cypher School. He not only informed Moscow that the British were reading Comintern telegrams, but also passed across reports which confirm that the BJS frequently contained intelligence from decyphered American, German and French diplomatic cryptograms.[53]

Maclean was not only able to confirm that the Soviet diplomatic cyphers withstood a sustained British attempt to crack them, but also helped to ensure that such efforts remained fruitless. His timely warning in 1936 put paid to any chance of success of a major assault on Soviet traffic by GC & CS, who set up an elaborate scheme to try to break the veil of secrecy of the one-time pad cypher system of the Soviet embassy in London. He leaked to Mally the documents he had seen arranging for the planting of "inspired" questions concerning the Soviet Union raised in Parliament by a co-operative Conservative MP. Duly briefed on the real purpose of the questions, the Foreign Secretary gave an unusually lengthy and detailed answer. The GC & CS code breakers counted on their ability to intercept the encyphered text in which the Soviet embassy was expected to transmit the parliamentary exchanges verbatim to Moscow. By comparing it with the original, the cryptanalysts hoped to break out, word by word, the values of the Soviet cypher pads. Although this would not have provided any long-term access to the one-time-pad system that had been introduced after the British raid on ARCOS, as a result of Maclean's tip-off, the Soviet embassy cypher clerks were instructed in future to take special care to paraphrase all reports of ministerial statements. With their agents Maclean and King in place in the Foreign Office, the Centre would have received an early warning if the British code breakers had been able to make any substantive progress towards unscrambling Soviet cryptogram traffic.[54] The code breakers in Moscow were no doubt also intrigued by Maclean's reports on Strachey's work for GC & CS and his mention of "an enciphering machine which absolutely excludes the possibility of decryption and spares the necessity of using codes".[55]

Within six months of entering the Foreign Office, Maclean was therefore making an important contribution to Soviet intelligence on a very broad front. This represented a triumph for their penetration strategy. Apart from the intrinsic value of the intelligence itself, it is evident that Maclean's operation was also assisting Soviet counter-intelligence operations. Specific data in Foreign Office reports on the USSR gave the NKVD vital clues in hunting down and neutralizing spies who were operating undercover in the Soviet Union for the British. NKVD records show that in 1936 Maclean's reports resulted in an investigation which uncovered one of these traitors in the People's Commissariat of Foreign Affairs.

Could this have been the MI6 source Anthony Blunt, in 1964, admitted betraying in 1941? It is possible that he was the mysterious "Gibby's Spy", first publicly identified by Peter Wright, who in 1933 was a member of Anastas Mikoyan's commissariat and who was recruited by Harold Gibson, an undercover MI6 officer with the British embassy who had been to school with the commissariat secretary in Moscow before the Revolution. This is consistent with an SIS report that Maclean passed to the NKVD in March 1937 which led to the discovery of a British agent in the Commissariat of Foreign Affairs. The evidence in NKVD files suggests that "Gibby's Spy" had, in fact, already been betrayed by Maclean and that Soviet intelligence had "turned" the commissariat secretary to feed false information to the British until Blunt inadvertently stumbled across this successful double deception operation.[56]

From other "green jacket" MI6 reports obtained via Maclean the NKVD was alerted to the fact that by March 1937 British intelligence had succeeded in penetrating the entourage of Willi Münzenberg.[57] This expatriate German Comintern leader was the architect of many of the Communist "front" organizations including the League

Against Imperialism, The Workers' International Trust and The World Committee for the Relief of the Victims of Fascism.[58] Among the most successful "fronts" was the League Against Imperialism which, like the others Münzenberg created, was part propaganda and part intelligence-gathering. Such operations sprang up like red mushrooms after Münzenberg had been forced to leave Berlin in 1933.

Maclean's intelligence also enabled the NKVD subtly to assist Stalin's foreign policy machinations by trading to the Germans and French tip-offs about sources in their own ministries who were leaking information to the British.[59] Maclean had become so valuable and so productive a source that in the spring of 1936 the London *rezidentura* advised Moscow to establish a special routine for handling him. "I stress once again to you that WAISE should be transferred into a separate branch," Mally urged Moscow Centre in a 24 May report from London.[60] As the *rezident* with responsibility for ensuring that this heavy stream of documentation was passed as rapidly as possible to Moscow, he personally urged Orlov and the chiefs to run Maclean through an exclusive and independent channel.

"Keep WAISE as the apple of your eye, give him your maximum attention and care," was the Centre's initial response.[61] Several weeks later the London *rezident* was told he would shortly be sent an experienced "illegal" code-named HANS who was then settling his personal affairs in Moscow. This was Bystrolyotov who, like many of the "Great Illegals", was a contemporary of Orlov. Another colourful character who could have stepped straight out of a Hollywood spy film, Bystrolyotov was a handsome lady-killer who spoke several European languages and combined a dashing manner with great personal courage. He was adept at assuming the character of the alias he adopted for his undercover work, passing himself off as Hungarian Count Hans Gallieni in England and an English milord on the Continent. Along with Mally, he had been a member of the Soviet intelligence service's elite "flying squad" of agent runners who slipped back and forth across European frontiers using a clutch of false passports and identities to evade the security police of a dozen nations. His personal NKVD file records how he had recruited a string of valuable agents in Italy, France and Czechoslovakia in addition to Oldham and King in Britain.[62]

Bystrolyotov had in his time come face to face with the bullets of hostile counter-intelligence agents, but his courage and quick wits could not save him from Stalin's brutal toady Nikolay Ivanovich Yezhov, who had become chief of the NKVD. Before Bystrolyotov's scheduled June departure from Moscow for Copenhagen to cross the North Sea to England to take over the running of Maclean, Yezhov began his purge of "illegal" cadres of the Soviet intelligence service. Bystrolyotov, like many of his comrades in the old guard, was arrested on a pretext and convicted of "espionage for the benefit of foreign states". Sentenced to hard labour in a Siberian *gulag*, he only secured his release sixteen years later, after Stalin's death.[63]

In the meantime Orlov continued monitoring Maclean's output in Moscow, as WAISE in London continued to meet regularly with Mally or Deutsch to hand over large bundles of documents, mostly culled from the "green" and "red jacket" Foreign Office documentation. They were then photographed in the apartment of HERTA, another code name used by the female courier PFEIL. They were returned to Maclean the next day, so that he could take them back the following day. For the most secret "blue jackets" containing signals intelligence, which Maclean could only obtain access to during office hours, he had been given a roll-reflex camera so that he could photograph them himself *in situ*. The operation was extremely risky, but Maclean managed to pull it off without being caught.

Moscow's "ORPHAN" in the Foreign Office was more than simply a passive conduit through which the Centre was able to scoop up a small mountain of secret British documents. Maclean was also supplying information that helped the London *rezidentura* learn about the command structure and senior personnel of Britain's internal counter-intelligence organization, the security service better known as MI5. In August 1936, for example, a report signed by its head, Sir Vernon Kell, passed across Maclean's desk and he passed it on to Mally. Mally then promptly informed Moscow Centre that "Kell is the head of the secret section MI5. MAX [a second pseudonym for the War Office secretary Wylie] confirmed this to MÄDCHEN [Burgess]. We have established Kell's address and will immediately put him under surveillance to learn where he goes to work."[64]

Shadowing the chief of MI5 enabled the NKVD *rezidentura* to identify other senior members of Kell's staff who entered its headquarters near the Victoria and Albert Museum in London's bustling Cromwell Road. Orlov continued to stress, however, that MI6 was the principal target for the Cambridge group. Maclean scored a "hit" on 8 October 1936, when he reported that an SIS officer named David Footman had come to see him at the Foreign Office. This, as the next chapter will describe, created an opportunity for putting Burgess into play to get the Cambridge group's first foot inside the door of the British Secret Intelligence Service, shortly after Orlov had left the Centre in Moscow for Spain.

After Maclean had achieved a year of unbroken success, the London "illegal" station suffered a succession of setbacks in 1937. In June Mally was recalled to Moscow, another victim to the so-called "*Yezhovchina*" – the blood bath that resulted from the wave of trumped-up treachery charges fomented by the NKVD chief. His flamboyant style made him an easy target for the accusations of Trotskyite sympathies. Mally preferred martyrdom in Stalin's purge rather than inviting disgrace by fleeing, only to risk being gunned to death by the NKVD's hit squads. This was the fate which was shortly to overtake his old friend and GRU "illegal" Ignace Poretsky, who operated under the cover name of Reiss.

"They betray their own people," Mally told Reiss, who he met on his way through Paris that summer, according to his widow's published account. As a former priest, Mally acknowledged that he did not have a chance, but Mrs Poretsky declared he "decided to go there because nobody can say: 'That priest might have been a real spy after all.' "[65]

Mally's fate was to be found guilty of Trotskyism and shot. But his fatal summons to Moscow can now be seen to have been instrumental in saving the Cambridge group from being prematurely uncovered by MI5. One of their penetration agents, a plucky secretary from the Ealing Ladies Hockey Club named Olga Gray, had been infiltrated into Communist Party headquarters. Her hard work and seeming political reliability had brought her to the attention of Percy Glading, a Communist former Admiralty employee who was part of an espionage network run by the London *rezidentura* at the Government-run Woolwich Arsenal armaments factory and research establishment. Using the alias Peters, Mally had meetings with Glading in a Holland Park house in April 1937 that were reported on by Gray. Her information on other members of the ring enabled MI5 to identify Mally and Deutsch as Soviet intelligence agents. Their surveillance continued for more than nine months, but until the British Government permits access to the historic MI5 records it will not be clear why Special Branch waited until 21 January 1938 to arrest Glading and his accomplices in the Woolwich Arsenal spy ring. By this time both Mally and Deutsch were long gone from British soil.[66]

Evidence that MI5 was closing in came when the NKVD "illegal" station in London suffered its second blow after Deutsch's three-year British residency permit to study psychology expired. He was called in by the police for an interview and told to leave the country. The Centre's fear that their "illegal" network in London had finally come to the attention of MI5 was heightened after they had received a report from Edith Tudor Hart in June 1938 that she had been visited by two officers of Special Branch. They had enquired if she had bought a Leica camera in 1936. She told them she could not remember as she was a professional photographer who acquired many cameras in the course of her work. When they showed her an invoice made out to a Dr Hart of 63 Acre Lane SW2, she admitted she lived at that address but "obviously this was not my name". The police had then asked her to sign a statement that she had not bought the Leica, which she had declined to do without first consulting her lawyer. The officers had left and she heard nothing more. But when Anthony Blunt checked Edith Tudor Hart's MI5 file in May 1941, he found that she had indeed been under surveillance in the 1930s as an active Austrian Communist immigrant.[67]

For Deutsch to have attempted to prolong his stay in England would have put at risk not only the Cambridge group but also the other underground agents whom he had been running, including the as yet unidentified NACHFOLGER, ATILLA and BÄR. So the Deutsches and their child packed their bags and left before the expiry date on his permit to avoid arousing any further suspicion. His file in the NKVD records, however, reveals that Deutsch returned secretly in November 1935 under a new alias to spend ten days cauterizing the arteries of communication of the decapitated *rezidentura*'s network of agents.[68]

For nearly six months until the spring of 1938 Maclean and the other members of the Cambridge group were left without a control officer. Before Mally was sentenced to death by the Military Collegium of the Supreme Court on 20 September 1938 (after he had been found guilty on trumped up espionage charges brought under article 58 section 6 of the Criminal Code), there was a vindication of sorts for the former London *resident* when his proposal for setting up an entirely separate "illegal" channel to handle Maclean was approved by the Centre. That spring Yezhov had approved a policy change that switched direction of overseas intelligence operations back to the control of the "legal" NKVD *rezidentura* in Soviet embassies. His purge of the "Great Illegals" had, in fact, left the NKVD chief little choice but to reverse the decade-old policy of insulating the overseas networks from the "legals" who operated under the cover of diplomatic staff.

Grigory Grafpen, the "legal" NKVD *resident* who was the next to take over the networks of the former "illegal" London station was not cast in the same mould as his predecessors. In place of the cultivated Mally, the intellectual Deutsch and the inspiring Orlov whose cosmopolitan experience had given a flavour of inspired adventure to the Cambridge group, they now had to take orders from a strong-willed NKVD officer whose cultivated manner and smart suits helped him pass for one of the Soviet diplomats in the gloomy Victorian mansion overlooking Kensington Gardens that served as the USSR's embassy. Known by the code name SAM, in April 1938 he took over responsibility for running the Cambridge network and Deutsch's Oxford recruits. Maclean, however, never had any direct dealing with Grafpen, although his file shows he had been given instructions on how to contact WAISE in an emergency. This involved telephoning Maclean at his flat before 9.30 a.m. or after 10.30 p.m. with the request, "Hello, it's Bill here, wouldn't you like to go to the theatre?" one day before the intended meet. The prearranged rendezvous was the Charing Cross underground station where Grafpen would identify himself by carrying a copy of the *Manchester Guardian* newspaper and make the statement, "I have not seen you for a long time, Donald". Maclean, who was to have a copy of *Esquire* magazine in his hand, would respond with, "Have you got any news of Theodore?"[69]

The charade was never necessary because the Centre had selected a young female agent in her late twenties to be his control officer. Her relative youth and Russian birth meant that this specially trained officer was one of the few qualified members of the NKVD at the time to have been spared the accusations of treachery and Trotskyist conspiracy which had decimated the ranks of the "illegal" officers.

The first meet between Maclean and his new Soviet handler was arranged to take place in the Empire Cinema on the east side of Leicester Square in London's West End on 10 April 1938. Assigned the code name of NORMA, her file gives the exchange she used to identify herself as an NKVD officer:

"Did you see my friend Karl?" NORMA asked Maclean who had been briefed to respond, "Yes, I saw him on 7 January."[70]

NORMA is not identified, nor are details of the cover she used in London because she later successfully ran other operations that the Russian Intelligence Service is not yet willing to reveal. She had arrived in England only a few weeks earlier and had set herself up in a flat in Bayswater, north of Hyde Park, favoured by Soviet agents because it offered both proximity to the Soviet embassy and plentiful cheap accommodation for itinerants in the flats and hotels of the once stately Victorian terraced houses of the area. Her first choice of a ground-floor flat, whose windows could be looked into from the street, did not meet with the approval of SAM, who was a stickler for security. Declaring that it was too easy to put under surveillance, Grafpen instructed her to move to a more secure flat on a higher floor. A *rezident*'s instructions had to be followed to the letter under the iron

regime imposed by Yezhov. Failure to follow the strict rules invited
instant recall to the Lubyanka. For a blunder that could be construed as
treachery the preferred method of establishing accountability was a
bullet in the back of the head.[71]

NORMA was in no doubt about the importance of her mission. She
was to be the sole contact for LYRIC, as Maclean was now referred to in
the NKVD traffic. An expert in photography and secret communications this conscientious woman hailed from a new generation of
Soviet intelligence officers who had been specially trained as go-
betweens for running agents. For NORMA the Revolution was only a
childhood memory. A dark-haired and attractive woman, she was
only four years older than her charge. NORMA was the fifth NKVD
officer he had encountered in four years, a fact Maclean pointed out in
an autobiographical report written at the request of the Centre in
November 1942. Indeed, before NORMA arrived to take command of
his secret life, Maclean admitted that he had known little about the
personal identities of the agents who had been running him.

"One of your people who I worked with was known to me as Little
Bill," Maclean wrote, reflecting that "I did not know his real name
and cannot help you establish it apart from the fact that, as I believe, he
later returned to his normal work in the paper industry".[72] He was
never to learn that the man was Ignaty Reif, whose only connection
with the paper industry was as a member of a logging detail in a
Siberian prison camp during the eight-year sentence of hard labour he
received during the purge. "Then came Big Bill", who, Philby had
told him, had "later worked in Spain". But it is clear that Maclean
knew neither Orlov's real name nor Mally's because he told Moscow
Centre that he remembered the latter only as a "tall Hungarian named
Theodore" who was a "former monk", who preceded Deutsch,
whom he described as a "Czech and a scientist" who called himself
OTTO or STEPHAN.[73]

Maclean's first encounter with NORMA was evidently quite a
surprise. Her NKVD file shows that the Centre had authorized SAM on 4
April to set up the meet and six days later Grafpen wired Moscow:
"NORMA's contact with LYRIC has been established."[74] Within a matter
of days, Maclean had brought a large batch of Foreign Office
documents to NORMA's flat, where she photographed them before he
took them away. The undeveloped rolls of film were then passed by
NORMA to Grafpen for shipment via the embassy diplomatic bag to
Moscow.

One of the justifications for Moscow Centre selecting a pretty
young woman as Maclean's control officer was that their frequent
late-night meetings would be unlikely to arouse suspicion that their

relationship was anything more than a natural romantic attachment. But within only a few weeks NORMA turned "legend" into real-life romance in the best traditions of a melodramatic spy thriller.[75] Orlov was to note in his *Handbook* how "idealistic young women" who worked as NKVD agents frequently "acted as a powerful stimulus" for young upper-class men. "Brought up first by a governess as sissies and later sent to exclusive private schools," he believed that such young men were "charmed by the daring young Amazons and their intellectual associations often blossomed into romances". Orlov could never have known about the affair Maclean had with his female control officer, a liaison that was to prove dangerous for them both.[76]

NORMA conducted her affair with LYRIC in defiance of the strict security regulations of the Soviet intelligence service. In her file is a report which shows that she had committed the cardinal sin of revealing Maclean's cryptonym to him during their pillow talk. In the normal course of events the Centre might never have learned about NORMA's indiscretion had Maclean himself not mischievously exposed it. He did so in a letter that he gave her in a sealed envelope to forward to Moscow along with his first batch of Foreign Office material. When the package was opened, it caused consternation at the Centre which cabled instructions to the London embassy ordering their *rezident* to investigate this serious breach of security. Grafpen, at his meeting with NORMA, demanded to know how Maclean knew that he was code-named LYRIC. She broke down and confessed that they had fallen desperately in love. Not only did she admit telling Maclean his cryptonym, but she had also given him hers. Back to the Centre went SAM's report on NORMA's failure, along with her profuse expressions of regret at being such a thoughtless comrade and causing such a dangerous slip-up.[77]

NORMA's romance with WAISE put the Centre in a quandary. To recall her might well upset the smooth progress of one of their best intelligence assets, through whom the NKVD was monitoring the British reaction to Hitler's demands as the crisis over Czechoslovakia came to the boil in the summer of 1938. Europe was preparing for war and Yezhov could not afford to deprive Stalin of such valuable first-hand intelligence, especially since his own authority was coming under challenge by Lavrenty Beria, who, in July 1938, had just been appointed deputy chief of the NKVD.

If NORMA were recalled to Moscow for disciplining, Yezhov would be blamed for cutting off Stalin's direct line into the British Foreign Office. So Yezhov endorsed the decision not to break up the romantic couple lest it alienate Maclean and render him uncooperative. The Centre accordingly instructed SAM not to interfere with the lovers beyond issuing a stern caution to NORMA not to reveal the new and more prosaic cryptonyms assigned to the couple as a security precaution: ADA and STUART.[78] It is interesting to note that although ADA's affair with Maclean continued for another year, she never updated her lover on his new cryptonym. Obviously Grafpen had made it clear to her that it was more than her life was worth to betray their cryptonyms again. Proof of her fidelity can be found in Maclean's 1942 autobiographical report, in which he noted that he had been given "a sweet-sounding code name, LYRIC. Not having any contradictory information, I suppose I still bear this name now."[79]

Maclean's handwritten letter dated 25 April 1938 which, but for Hitler's warlike threats, might have earned NORMA a one-way ticket back to Moscow, sits in his NKVD file. The purple notation of an NKVD official records that it was received in Moscow five days later in the diplomatic bag from London. Its "Dear Comrade" salutation leaves the identity of the addressee ambiguous, but, from its deferential tone and reference to both OTTO and THEO, it cannot have been addressed to either Deutsch or Mally. Nor is it likely that Maclean would have adopted its chatty tone to address the NKVD collectively. The inference can be drawn from such clues that Maclean believed he was writing to Orlov, the one NKVD officer at the Centre who was most familiar with the details of his career. The letter is also revealing for the insight it provides into Maclean's *modus operandi*. In its entirety it provides a fascinating historical snapshot of how the "Three Musketeers" – as Maclean alluded to himself, Burgess and Philby – regarded themselves as very important special agents of Soviet intelligence:

Dear Comrade,
This is to say first of all how glad I am to be in touch and working again. As you will have heard, I have no reason to think that my position is not quite sound, and I think the arrangements which we have made for work should be all right. The trial of Glading will doubtless have increased watchfulness on the part of the authorities. Certain warnings have recently been issued in my office, possibly as a result thereof, namely that "green" [i.e. secret] papers, should as far as possible not be taken out of the office, and that "red" [i.e. most secret] papers should *never* be, and also that blotting paper used to blot confidential papers must be carefully destroyed!

With regard to the work, I will let you have, as before, all I can, which will be chiefly the printed dispatches & telegrams, & such secret reports and particularly interesting papers as come my way. This time we are sending some dispatches & a good many telegrams; it would be useful to know how many of the latter you would like – a lot of them are I think of little value. We have also sent a memorandum by Collier, head of the Northern [Russian] Department about British policy generally in regard to Spain, together with the comments thereon of the high Foreign Office authorities. The document is, I think, of considerable interest. Collier takes the more or less left-wing anti-Fascist line which, as you will remember, he has long followed, but all the rest of them who comment, Halifax, Momsey, Plymouth & Cadogan, are as was to be expected, unanimously in favour of the present policy of conciliation with Italy & consequent acceptance of a Franco victory. Vansittart, who, as you will see, does not comment, is believed to share Collier's views, at least in part (as indicated in the memorandum), but it appears that his advice is not much sought since Eden left. I may be able to tell you something more on this point later.

With regard to myself, I am being assigned, as you now I think know, to the Paris embassy as a 3rd Secretary, in all probability in the middle of next October. I do not really know how easy or difficult it will be to do our work in Paris, but I think & hope that it will be much easier than at most places to which I might have been sent. I am therefore pleased – provided that you are too. I shall have to go away for the regular holiday in the summer and have arranged provisionally to do this in September, which leaves about 4 clear months for work here. It would also mean in effect that I should go straight from my holiday to Paris. I shall stick to this arrangement unless you prefer some other.

I have seen Kersakoff (OTTO will know who I mean), who was back here for a few days some 3 weeks ago: he is very anxious to be put in touch again & says that the same applies to others who are in Paris.

I heard yesterday that the 3rd Musketeer has had a breakdown of some kind and has had to go away for 2 months. I have not seen him myself for many months so do not know if this is likely to be true, but I shall be sorry if it is.

I don't think I have anything more to say at present, except to send my best greetings to OTTO & THEO, to any other I may know, and to yourself.

LYRIC

PS Please let me know if there are any particular things you want to know about & I will do my best. I deal myself only with Spain, as before.[80]

Maclean's letter, from its reference to "Kersakoff" and other members of the group, clearly indicates that he possessed an unusually wide knowledge of other agents' identities. This implies that Orlov, Mally and Deutsch had been unable to observe the rules of *Konspiratsia* that Moscow demanded. The founding members of the Cambridge group were so close that it was inevitable that each knew of the work of the others.[81] While it has proved impossible to trace Kersakoff from the NKVD records, it can be inferred that Maclean's reference to the "3rd Musketeer" is an allusion to Burgess. This is clear from the MÄDCHEN NKVD file, which records that a bad dose of syphilis was the cause of their agent's breakdown in health in January 1937. He was hospitalized for a painful course of mercuric chemotherapy, which was the only effective way to kill the syphilitic spirochete in the days before penicillin.[82]

To paraphrase the famous oath of Alexandre Dumas's legendary Musketeer trio: "Exposure of one, exposure of all", as far as Philby, Maclean and Burgess were concerned. But it is clear that LYRIC's letter must have caused the Centre less concern over this inherent flaw in the Cambridge group's security than worry that, unless a replacement could be found for Maclean in the Foreign Office, they would be cut off from a vital intelligence source when he took up his post at the Paris embassy.

The NKVD records show, however, that this was not the blow it might have been. Before leaving London in 1936 Deutsch had alerted the Moscow Centre to the Foreign Office practice of sending all Third Secretaries to overseas embassies after two years in Whitehall.[83] Moscow had responded that their interest was best served by Maclean continuing to work as long as possible in London, where he had access to a far wider range of documentation in the Western Department than he would in any British legation. In anticipation of Maclean's inevitable overseas posting, the ever resourceful Deutsch had hurried along the induction of other Cambridge recruits.[84]

Maclean's replacement in the Foreign Office was code-named MOLIÈRE. In accordance with its policy the Russian Intelligence Service released only the cryptonym of the "sixth" man recruited to the Cambridge group. But from the transparency of the initial codenames of the Cambridge group it has been concluded that MOLIÈRE was John Alexander Kirkland Cairncross, who was writing a thesis on the French playwright. The son of a Scottish ironmonger, Cairncross, after taking a degree at Glasgow University and studying at the Sorbonne, in 1934 won a scholarship to Trinity College, Cambridge, to take the Modern Languages Tripos. While not an open Communist, a visit to Germany in 1935 had hardened his studiously left-wing convictions into a firm belief that Hitler could only be stopped if Britain made an alliance with the Soviet Union. Cairncross admitted that he was spotted and approached as a potential candidate for the Soviet intelligence service by the "fourth man" of the Cambridge network, Anthony Blunt who had himself been recruited by Burgess. Blunt then acted as the NKVD resident talent scout. As Cairncross's French supervisor, Blunt had been able to make the initial approach successful despite what Cairncross described as their mutual distaste for one another.[85]

Blunt passed his pupil on to Burgess, whom Cairncross admitted finding "fascinating, charming and utterly ruthless". It was Burgess who cultivated Cairncross and who recommended him to Deutsch. By 1936, after he graduated with first-class honours, Cairncross had already broken all contacts with Klugmann and the Cambridge Communist circle. Nor did he need to cram like Maclean before sitting the Civil Service examination. He passed out the head of the list, his academic brilliance overcoming his lacklustre performance in the Interview Board. Cairncross then became a Third Secretary in the American Section of the Foreign Office in the autumn of 1936, a year behind Maclean.[86]

Cairncross maintained that his decision to enter the Foreign Office was his own and not influenced by the Soviets. This is confirmed by the NKVD Maclean files which contain Mally's letter of 9 April 1937 reporting that MOLIÈRE had been recruited and would be contacted at the end of May – this was some six months after he had actually entered the Foreign Office.[87] The file also shows that MOLIÈRE did not supply Deutsch with documents until 9 September 1938. Since he moved to the Treasury a few months later, Cairncross asserted to the authors that whatever information he did pass on to the Russians at this time was "minor and neutral". But as his code name suggests, Cairncross admits that he was more suited to pursue an academic career in sixteenth-century French literature than Government service.[88]

Unable to find a niche for himself within two years, Cairncross had worked his way through the American, League of Nations, Western and Central Departments of the Foreign Office. When Maclean left Whitehall for Paris in September 1938, MOLIÈRE appears to have been slated by Moscow to take over as the Soviets' principal "mole" in His Majesty's Foreign Office. But only until the end of the year, when he moved to the Treasury, much to Grafpen's annoyance and Moscow's displeasure. Cairncross said he justified his move by explaining that his background denied him the chance of fitting in with the clubby Establishment cliques of the Foreign Office.[89]

Grafpen and his *rezidentura* in the Soviet embassy who had taken over the running of Cairncross and the expanding Cambridge group had in the meantime to arrange for handling Maclean in Paris. Appreciating the practical necessity for keeping the ADA and STUART relationship intact, the Centre decided that ADA, despite her slip, should be assigned to France so as not to lose access to Maclean's intelligence gathering. The Czechoslovak crisis was then racing towards its shameful dénouement at Munich that October, when the British and French Governments sold out that country for a guarantee that proved as worthless as the scrap of paper bearing Hitler's signature.

"NORMA came to Paris to work for me and continued working until my departure from the embassy in June 1940,"[90] Maclean wrote in his NKVD autobiography, in which he also recorded how much he regretted that his ability to supply important intelligence had been greatly diminished with his posting to France. There were few opportunities for serious espionage in the stately rooms of the Paris mansion on the rue Faubourg St Honoré that served as the ambassadorial residence and chancery. Maclean sent word via ADA that "he was doing little" for Moscow and that upset him. The freshman Second Secretary found the endless round of diplomatic dinners and receptions irksome and pointless, the more so as Britain and France teetered on the brink of war with Germany over Czechoslovakia. His disgust on reading the secret diplomatic cables revealing the degree to which Chamberlain and Daladier abandoned Czechoslovakia was exacerbated by the rapturous welcome with which the Munich claims of "peace in our time" were greeted in the *salons* of Paris. By the end of the year Maclean was spending more and more of his off-duty hours immersing himself in the Bohemian circles of the *Café Flore* and *Aux Deux Magots*, the famous Left-Bank cafés, a convenient walk from his bachelor apartment. There he would pass hours drowning his frustration in alcohol and a fug of Algerian tobacco smoke in the company of the writers and Socialist intellectuals who mixed Marxist dialectic with *anis*.

"Work in Paris is a complete change for him in many respects," Maclean's control officer reported to the Centre at the end of 1938. Her report, which reads more like a *cri de coeur* from an anxious paramour, vented her fears that Maclean was undergoing a deep personal crisis:[91]

While in London he could act as he liked. He had his friends and the opportunity to read a lot. Things are different in Paris. He leads a completely different social life. He must attend dinners and receptions. His whole life is concentrated around the embassy. He hates this atmosphere, but at the same time must work in it. I know that he is a very good comrade and the new environment will not detract from his performance. But I think that a letter from home will be a great pleasure to him in this situation. He has great confidence in me and often shares his thoughts with me. That is why I know that a letter will mean a great deal to him. I brought instructions for work and sometimes personal letters. That is why I know what an impression they produce on him.[92]

What Maclean's mistress and Soviet control officer meant by a "letter from home" was written encouragement from Moscow. A note penned by Deutsch was duly received by him. ADA noted in her next report that it had temporarily raised Maclean's spirits and that he passed on his thanks to OTTO. But Maclean's performance, in his own eyes and in Moscow's, continued to decline through 1939, when the war clouds gathered over Europe. Hitler's threat to Polish territorial integrity frightened Britain and France that spring into rashly giving the unconditional guarantees which London and Paris found themselves reluctantly called on to honour when Germany invaded Poland in September. The devil's pact that Stalin made with Hitler that August did not shake Maclean's conscience deeply enough to cause him to question his blinkered loyalty to Moscow. After hostilities broke out in Europe in September 1939, the stress Maclean was under increased.

The "Phoney War" was entering its fifth month when the crisis between ADA and STUART came to a dramatic head in January 1940. Using a prearranged signal, ADA called for an urgent meeting with her superior, an NKVD officer code-named FORD, operating from the Soviet embassy. He found himself confronted with a melodramatic situation for which he was quite unprepared. That he did his best to try to defuse an explosive *menage* of espionage and passion is evident from the report he wrote to the Centre. Its terse and awkward phrases reflect this officer's embarrassment at being called upon to solve a situation which was more emotional than operational. The disjointed and awkward paragraphs of FORD's report only hint at the drama that must have been played out in the stormy confrontations which had taken place between Maclean and ADA:

At the meeting ADA related the following: she had noticed recently that STUART had become close to some woman, though he himself did not tell ADA anything about it. Having noticed a number of changes about his behaviour and the arrangement of his room, ADA decided to ask STUART about it straightforwardly. The latter was surprised that ADA knew about it and confessed that he had become intimately close with – loved a young American woman. This American woman, Melinda Marling – is of liberal ideas – the daughter of well-to-do parents living in the United States without any particular interest in politics.

STUART admitted to ADA that he had told Melinda Marling about his membership of the Communist Party and about his link with us "in the spy business".

STUART assured her he had not given away ADA's name to his sweetheart, though he told her that he contacted us through a certain woman . . . ADA informs that, according to her observations, STUART's action is explained by "boyish lightmindedness" and that, as before, he works with us sincerely and with enthusiasm.[93]

When the Paris *rezident*'s report reached Moscow, the staff working for Pavel Fitin, the forbidding new head of the Foreign Department, must have handled FORD's report like a grenade with its safety pin pulled. The need to keep Maclean as a source required that they direct ADA to back away from her emotional tangle without losing control of the British diplomat. This was no easy task for the jilted lover/control officer. What she reported in her emotional distress as her agent's "boyish lightmindedness" for the American woman had already developed into powerful attraction. Maclean had literally fallen head over heels for Melinda Marling, a spirited girl wise to the ways of the world. In an autobiographical essay in his NKVD file Maclean explained why he told her he was a spy: "When we first met each other, she had no reason to think that I was anything more important than an ordinary official of the British diplomatic service. After some time she came to the conclusion that my way of life as a diplomat made our relations impossible and she left. I told her about the reason why I led such a life. Then she came back and we have been together ever since."[94]

Maclean's resolution of his love triangle was only temporary. With Hitler's *Blitzkreig* about to overwhelm France, Moscow could not simply recall ADA and let Maclean's ardour cool. An accommodation was, however, worked out, and their cosy arrangement was permitted by the Centre until German *Panzer* divisions rolled across the Seine and the British legation began to leave the City of Light.

The rumble of artillery fire rolled over Paris like distant thunder on 10 June, when Melinda and Donald were married in a hurried ceremony. The honeymoon couple bade farewell to ADA and left Paris forty-eight hours before the Champs Élysées echoed to the jackboots of Hitler's victorious legions. A week later the new Mr and Mrs Maclean were evacuated from Bordeaux on a British destroyer whilst Hitler personally dictated armistice terms to the French Government. ADA managed, with the help of the Communist underground, to return safely to Moscow. She was not punished and her file cryptically records her return "to foreign intelligence work".[95]

Maclean, who returned to a new desk job in the Central Department, resumed pilfering Foreign Office secrets as soon as contact with Moscow was restored. This time he was placed under the direction of VADIM, the operational crytonym of Anatoli Gorsky, who had replaced Grafpen as the NKVD *rezident* at the Soviet embassy. Gorsky, a former cypher clerk, was a short bespectacled man with "angry eyebrows" but a "dry business-like manner", according to a former colleague.[96]

Now that VADIM's firm hand directed WAISE, he began to pass an ever growing volume of secret documents and telegrams. Although it had been claimed that it was Cairncross who first alerted Stalin to the possibility of an atomic bomb, the Soviet records reveal that it was in fact Maclean. The first indication of the work of Britain's top-secret Uranium Committee was received from Maclean in September 1941. This is confirmed by a September 1941 cryptogram received from Gorsky which stated: "I am informing you very briefly about the contents of a most secret report of the Government Committee on the development of uranium atomic energy to produce explosive material which was submitted on 24 September 1941 to the War Cabinet." Technical details followed and it was Maclean who was identified by Gorsky as the source of the report on the Uranium Committee in a second cryptogram. This was sent separately according to the security rules that sources and information were not to be identified in the same telegram.[97] The apogee of Maclean's work for Soviet intelligence, however, came at the end of the war, following his appointment to the British embassy in Washington in 1944. His special security clearance gave him access not only to American atomic secrets but also to the top-level strategy councils of the White House when President Truman established NATO.

Maclean's NKVD records show that he was one of Stalin's most valuable spies. His access to the decisions at the highest levels of the Anglo-American councils which planned Allied military and economic strategy gave the Kremlin an inside track advantage during the early years of the Cold War and during the beginning of the Korean War.[98] The volume of shelf space occupied by Maclean's operational files in the vaults of the Russian Intelligence Service at Yasenevo is tangible proof of the staggering return achieved by the "magic" penetration scheme to which Orlov had acted as midwife and sometime director.

In what must rank as the most eloquent testament to just how singlemindedly the Cambridge agents performed for Moscow Maclean's letter written from blitz-ravaged London on 29 December 1940 states: "This work has the same importance for me as for you – if not even greater importance because it is my life I live for it. I will try, as hard as I can not to do anything to endanger it. I can't say that I like my work. But I admit that it is one of the uses in our great struggle to which I am most suited and I intend to stand by it until I am relieved of it."[99]

Maclean's value to the Soviet intelligence service can also be gauged from the volume of secret British material he supplied to them. Quite apart from its operational value, the physical quantity is staggering. The NKVD archives show that the products of his espionage from the time he entered the Foreign Office in 1935 until June 1940, when he left France, amounted to forty-five boxes – each containing over 300 pages of stolen documents. This was no mean achievement for a twenty-eight-year-old, considering that at the end of these five years he was only one-third of the way through his active and productive career as a Soviet intelligence agent. For sheer volume, therefore, Maclean's achievement was only exceeded by that of the "Third Musketeer"; but the NKVD files on Guy Burgess reveal just how wild a card Orlov introduced into his Cambridge pack when he authorized the recruitment of the "third man".

9

"AN *ENFANT TERRIBLE*"

GUY FRANCIS DE MONCY BURGESS has been the subject of myth and legend ever since his dramatic defection to Moscow in 1951. He stalks the pages of the biographies of his literary contemporaries, the files of the FBI and doubtless the unreleased secret archives of MI5, larger than life and far more scandalous than any fictional author would ever have dared to portray a spy. Burgess was made a scapegoat and accused of being the principal recruiter of the network, according to testimony given by its "fourth man", Anthony Blunt, the "fifth man", Michael Straight and "sixth man", John Cairncross.[1] Even Philby in his public utterances found it convenient to portray Burgess as the animator of the Soviets' Cambridge network. Supposedly he deployed his insatiable homosexual appetite and formidable intellectual charms to seduce a score of friends and acquaintances into becoming agents of Moscow, brilliantly camouflaging his sinister mission with his debauchery, garlic-laden breath and dirty fingernails.[2]

The Orlov dossier finally establishes that Philby came first, Maclean second and that Burgess was not, as so many have claimed, the "first man", but the "third man" to be recruited into one of the most successful of all the Soviet underground spy networks. But the NKVD files reveal that the decision to permit him to join was taken by Orlov more out of necessity than by choice. The reason for his reluctance was that Burgess was the last of the seven names on the list of Cambridge contacts Philby had recommended as potential candidates.[3] According to his KGB memoir, Philby had such strong reservations about the suitability of his Trinity contemporary for undercover work that he had put a row of four question marks after Burgess's name.

"While Burgess is of course a very ideologically strong man, his character is that of an '*enfant terrible*'," Philby recalled advising Orlov.[4] This was an understatement. Anyone at Cambridge in the early 1930s could have cautioned Orlov that Burgess was so notorious a character that any association with him would threaten a secret organization's security. But, as will be seen, both Orlov *and* his opposite numbers in the British intelligence service found it useful to exploit the talent of this Rabelaisian intriguer.

Boyishly good-looking with a terrier's eyes and sense of mischief, Burgess revelled in excess. Flagrantly homosexual and unashamedly a Communist, Burgess made himself a hero of the Cambridge left by organizing a strike of the Trinity College servants and driving his car like a battering ram during student demonstrations. Like many libertines his principal weapon was an outrageous and infectious charm honed by an amusing, sparkling wit and repartee.

Goronwy Rees, an Oxford contemporary who was not homosexual, but at whom Burgess made a pass before eventually tapping him for the Soviets, described him as a "kind of Figaro figure, ever resourceful in the service of others in order to manipulate them to his own ends".[5] Burgess indulged in his friends, as he did in sex, politics and alcohol – to excess. His indiscriminate trail of male seductions suggests he was attempting to submerge a deep sense of his own masculine sexual inadequacy. He liked to claim that his perversion was the result of the childhood trauma he had suffered at the age of eleven, when he had to extract his hysterical mother from beneath the corpse of his father who had suffered a fatal heart attack in the act of copulation.[6] This was such a typically exaggerated piece of self-justification that it is curious to find he never alluded to it in his KGB debriefings.

What can be established from the biographical record is that Burgess was born in 1911, into the family of a career naval officer whose death in 1925 left his mother free to remarry. Her second husband was a retired army colonel named John Retallack Basset, who gambled heavily on horses and whose winnings were often lavished on a stepson who quickly learned how to manipulate adults for favours. Burgess had established himself a precociously well-read and bright pupil at Eton, still Britain's most famous boarding school, when his mother arranged for him to complete his education at Dartmouth Naval College. As he later told the KGB with characteristic immodesty, he "considered himself too clever" to serve in the navy. Playing up an eyesight defect resulted in his discharge from Dartmouth and the transfer of Burgess back to Eton. From there he went up to Cambridge University in 1930, carrying with him a deep resentment against the ruling elite of Eton, who declined to elect such a flagrant sexual pervert to the society of school prefects known as Pop. At Trinity College Burgess read history, achieving distinction in the first part of the Tripos only to flunk his final exams three years later, for which his sympathetic college tutor arranged a face-saving *aegrotat*. This "consolation degree" did not earn him any honours, but it did permit him to continue his university studies as a postgraduate researcher and salaried college supervisor in history.[7]

Burgess proved himself an undisciplined intellectual, who squandered his academic brilliance in alcoholic overindulgence and passionate dedication to left-wing politics. While still in his first undergraduate year Burgess had become a member of one of the underground Communist cells at Trinity. Marxism was an especially powerful opiate in the debates of the society of the Apostles, a semi-secret intellectual fraternity which tapped Burgess for its ranks in 1932.[8] His election was engineered by Blunt, a former homosexual lover four years his senior, who was then a junior fellow of Trinity, researching the history of art that was to take him to the pinnacle of that profession. Blunt was a member of the first Marxian generation of Apostles which included Dennis Proctor, Alister Watson, Hugh Sykes-Davies and Richard Llewellyn-Davies. Burgess was a more than usually ardent convert. Lord Rothschild, who was also elected shortly afterwards, complained that, whenever Burgess was present, "We talk endlessly in the Society about Communism which is rather dull".[9]

Burgess embraced a more red-blooded Marxism than the purely intellectual strain affected by his close friend Blunt; his was an ideological conversion rather than a wearing of Communism as a badge of fashionable left-wing commitment. As an historian Burgess claimed to have made a profound theoretical study of the works of Marx, Engels, Lenin and Stalin. His fondness for demonstrating his grasp of dialectical theory by quoting from the standard texts impressed both Orlov and Deutsch.

Blunt may have employed Marxist analogies in his waspish column as art critic of the *Spectator* magazine but his own conversion was more anaemic, and more cerebral than emotional. "The events that took place in Germany impressed themselves on even such an isolationist as I was, and I dimly started to understand my position was not entirely satisfactory," Blunt explained in an autobiographical essay written for the NKVD in 1943:

> Subjects which I knew such as history and art history did not only represent an interest for me, but also gave me a direction to the true understanding of these subjects from the scientific point of view. This feeling gradually grew in me thanks also to the influence of Burgess, Klugman, John Cornford and the others who belonged to this group [of Communists]. In the end I was fully convinced by the

truth of the Marxist approach to history and other subjects familiar to me. The Communists thought that I was a hopeless man.[10]

Blunt, as his NKVD file reveals, admitted his intention was to conceal rather than flaunt his Communism. Burgess, on the other hand, brandished his like a banner to demonstrate how he had distanced himself both ideologically and spiritually from his bourgeois background. Espousing a Bohemian life-style, dressing scruffily, drinking to excess and revelling in homosexual adventures, Burgess by his final undergraduate year was as celebrated in Cambridge for his outrageous behaviour as for his political convictions. By day he preached the gospel of Communism and by night he bedded whichever don, undergraduate, college waiter or town sales clerk took his fancy. To his more reserved homosexual friends he prescribed sex with "rough trade" as the remedy for releasing their bourgeois inhibitions. Burgess would therefore not have been the candidate of choice for the Soviet intelligence service whose potential agents were usually selected on the basis of their self-discipline, dedication and ability to conceal themselves.

Significantly, Philby had put Guy at the bottom of his list too, apparently because he suspected his friend might be too flamboyant and mercurial a character to work secretly for the "anti-fascist" underground. That Burgess featured at all was because of his ability to charm and his articulate dedication to Communism. These qualities must have impressed Orlov too, for his NKVD file indicated that he had discussed Burgess as a potential recruit as early as August 1934, when he went back to Moscow after taking stock of the London *rezidentura*. He had then recommended having Burgess approached during a trip he was making with a Cambridge group to the USSR until "a check through our 2nd Section established that he had already left the country, so it was decided to approach him on the ISLE. [NKVD jargon for Britain]".[11] By the time that Orlov had returned to London in September, Maclean was already in he first stages of his recruitment process and the question of whether to mount a serious cultivation of Burgess did not arise until several months later. As Philby recalled in his KGB memoir, he attended a meeting towards the end of 1934 at which he said that his views on the suitability of Burgess were canvassed by Orlov and Deutsch.

"Orlov was an extremely hard man," according to Philby's account in which he admitted, "I honestly did not know what to do" because he was "new to the business". According to Philby, Orlov was of the opinion that Burgess might prove useful and directed him to consider how best to sound out his friend Guy.[12] The Soviet intelligence service had discovered that homosexuals could be tapped to become valuable sources of information since they were obliged by draconian criminal penalties to live part of their lives in secret. Fear of exposure was so great among the homosexuals in Western government service that the process of making contact rarely involved a risk even if the Soviet approach was rejected.

"Considerable success was achieved by the Soviet intelligence service among foreign diplomats tinted with homosexual perversion," Orlov wrote in his *Handbook*, noting that the high concentration of homosexuals in Western diplomatic services had enabled Soviet intelligence to make "ample use of these unstable individuals". It had been found that homosexuals were able to approach other members of the diplomatic corps and were "remarkably successful". Fear of exposure meant that, even if they declined to co-operate, such diplomats would never denounce their recruiters to the authorities. "The Soviet intelligence officers were amazed at the sense of mutual consideration and true loyalty among homosexuals," Orlov wrote.[13] So, although Burgess might never make a diplomat, he would have realised that such a promiscuous graduate would have access to the shadowy Whitehall homosexual network which introduced young men from Cambridge into the discreet all-male coteries found in Britain's diplomatic establishment. After Orlov and Reif reviewed the pros and cons of enlisting the seventh man on Philby's list, they decided in October 1934 to first recruit Maclean only to find that Burgess proceeded to force the issue in a manner uniquely his own.

Burgess and Maclean were close friends; some even suspected that Guy, true to form, had seduced Donald, who would himself later admit having indulged in homosexual adventures. Whether or not they went to bed together, they were close comrades in underground Communist cells. When Maclean, dutifully following Deutsch's instructions, tried to cut all ties with the Party, he found it impossible to shed Burgess.

"And if Guy set his mind on achieving something, there was no heavenly or diabolical force that could stop him from doing it," Philby observed, recalling how Burgess insistently taxed Maclean. He had reported his concern at the time to Deutsch that Guy would simply not let go, refusing to accept that his Cambridge comrade could just stop being a Communist.[14] "It is simply impossible and I don't believe you," Burgess had insisted. According to Philby's KGB memoir, he eventually succeeded in wearing down his friend's defences until Maclean promised he would, after all, keep working for the Party. In doing so, however, he had to explain to Burgess why it was necessary for him to appear to have broken with Communism. This confronted Deutsch and Orlov with a serious dilemma. By revealing that he was secretly working for Moscow, Maclean had made himself a hostage to Burgess's discretion and created a potentially dangerous situation for their embryo Cambridge network. For as Philby reported, Burgess was not only an *enfant terrible*, but also an inveterate gossip.

Alarmed at the possibility that Burgess might unwittingly expose his friend, Philby let Deutsch know his fears that Guy would not be able to resist letting his comrades into the secret that he knew all about what Maclean was really doing: that although he was denying it openly, Donald was still a Communist. After receiving Deutsch's report, Orlov decided that they now had no option but to take Burgess into their "illegal" network in order to shut him up.

Late in December 1934, Maclean arranged for Deutsch to meet Burgess to sound him out. Philby recalled how Burgess was impressed and flattered by his proposal. The appeal to his love of intrigue made Burgess jump at the chance of joining his friend Maclean in the band of three who had been invited to work secretly for Moscow and the Revolution. His friend's face, Maclean reported, had lit up with joy at the meeting with Deutsch when he announced that he was "honoured and ready to sacrifice everything for the cause".[15]

The assignment by Orlov and Deutsch of the cryptonym MÄDCHEN [Little Girl] set the seal on the recruitment of Burgess as the "third man" in the Cambridge network – which NKVD records confirm remained a tightly-knit group of three for the next two years. They also show that Orlov might never have brought Burgess into his network but for the faulty negative films on which his reports were copied for couriering undeveloped, for security, to Moscow. This difficulty continued to plague his communications with the Centre until the end of January 1935. Since his "illegal" station was therefore effectively out of touch with Moscow, Orlov made an independent decision to recruit Burgess.

The Centre reacted with surprise and displeasure when a new code name, MÄDCHEN, cropped up without warning in Orlov's January report. Not only had they not given permission for direct contact to be made with Burgess, but, because the first three members of his Cambridge network were close friends, his was a serious breach of the rules of *Konspiratsia*, that required that agents be compartmentalized from one another. Voicing their concerns, Moscow fired off a reprimand to London that ordered Orlov not to proceed with the recruitment of Burgess.[16]

"You are puzzled who MÄDCHEN is and order to break [with him]," Orlov responded in a letter of 12 July 1935. "I have ordered STEPHAN [Deutsch's code name] over the phone to suspend contact with him in implementation of your directive." Trying to smooth ruffled feathers at the Lubyanka, he expressed his surprise at "this misunderstanding".[17] "I'm beginning to suspect that our letters are not reaching you in full or maybe part of them has not been fully understood," Orlov wrote, explaining that Burgess "was recommended by SÖHNCHEN [Philby] and WAISE [Maclean] who describe him as a very talented and adventurous chap capable of penetrating everywhere". He himself vouched for Burgess, who he said was "a former compatriot of a Cambridge group [i.e. member of a university Communist Party cell], an extremely well-educated fellow, with valuable social connections, and the inclinations of an adventurer. Though I rate him lower than SÖHNCHEN and WAISE, I think that he will come in useful."[18]

Protocol now satisfied, the Centre deferred their reservations concerning the group's shared knowledge of their Soviet connection and lifted their ban on the cultivation of Burgess as a probationary agent.

As the development phase of Burgess's recruitment began under Deutsch's supervision, he came to regard Orlov's judgment of MÄDCHEN's potential usefulness as correct. Despite initial concerns about how to bring such a headstrong and unruly candidate under disciplined control, he found his task easier because Burgess had "joined the Communist Party on the basis of a theoretical study of Marxism". According to Deutsch's evaluation, "the Party work was something of a salvation for him, especially its life and purity". Burgess, he discovered, was "a very temperamental and emotional man and he is easily subject to mood swings".[19] Deutsch found him "well educated and extremely well read, but he is superficial. He speaks very well, willingly and a lot." MÄDCHEN's character was "completely the opposite" of Philby's and Maclean's, he concluded in the psychological profile of Burgess he wrote in Moscow in 1939:

Many features of his character can be explained by the fact that he is a homosexual. He became one at Eton, where he grew up in an atmosphere of cynicism, opulence, hypocrisy and superficiality. As he is very clever and well educated, the Party was for him a saviour. It gave him above all an opportunity to satisfy his intellectual needs. Therefore he took up Party work with great enthusiasm. Part of his private life is led in a circle of homosexual friends whom he recruited among a wide variety of people, ranging from the famous liberal economist Keynes and extending to the very trash of society down to male prostitutes. His personal degradation, drunkenness, irregular way of life and the feeling of being outside society was connected with this kind of life, but on the other hand his abhorrence of bourgeois morality came from this. This kind of life did not satisfy him. His homosexuality he explains as not inborn because he can also live with women. He learned it at Eton because everyone is engaged with homosexuality there, so he simply joined in. The pupils there lived several to a room and the class masters use their superior position to seduce the young boys."[20]

It was the homosexual connection, as Orlov anticipated, that proved to be one of the most exploitable assets Burgess brought to his "illegal" group. This was evident in his first assignment to all probationary candidates to supply a list of friends and contacts. Burgess, with his customary excess, provided a roster of over 200 people in a four-page letter. His list ranged from acquaintances at Cambridge like Dennis Proctor and Professor G. M. Trevelyan to Lord Keynes and Dennis Robertson. From his Foreign Office contacts Burgess nominated Peter Hatton and Con O'Neil. He included Lord Camrose and Joseph Ball of the Conservative Research Department, plus, for good measure, Conservative MPs Harold Nicolson, Major Jack Macnamara and Angus Hambro. Among his purely homosexual contacts he included Werner von Fries, an attaché at the German embassy, Tom Wylie at the War Office and a man named 'Back', whom Burgess recommended as a "lumpen proletarian and a pederast".[21] Burgess's list attests not only to his predatory nature but his charm for older men that provides a revealing insight into the web of homosexual connections that extended from Cambridge into the upper reaches of the British military, academic and governing establishment. What the Centre made of such an eclectic roster is not indicated in the NKVD files, but the list was especially valuable to an experienced Soviet intelligence officer like Orlov, who immediately set about exploiting the potential Burgess had opened up.

One name which attracted his immediate interest was that of Dennis Proctor, a fellow left-wing member of the Apostles who, after graduating in 1931, had entered the Civil Service and by 1935 was a Private Secretary to the Prime Minister, working from Stanley Baldwin's office. According to Burgess, Proctor was one of the senior Apostles known as Angels who frequently attended the Cambridge gatherings of the society. Since Burgess had assured Deutsch that Proctor shared his ideological viewpoint, although he had never been a Communist at Cambridge, it raised the prospect of establishing a penetration agent inside the Prime Minister's residence at 10 Downing Street. Orlov therefore wasted little time in getting Deutsch to instruct Burgess to try to bring Proctor under cultivation. By February 1935 Orlov requested Moscow's approval for the approach with the confident prediction that the possibility of MÄDCHEN succeeding was "very great".[22]

Lacking any detailed background information on Proctor, the Centre was at first disinclined to believe Orlov's reports on the value of the intimate nature of Burgess's relations with his friends. They promptly vetoed the proposed cultivation of Proctor. Four months later they would change their minds and authorize the cultivation of Wylie. Proctor's name appears in NKVD files only as Baldwin's secretary. That he was considered only a marginal candidate is indicated by the fact that he was never assigned a code name like Wylie.[23]

Tom Wylie, another target Orlov singled out from Burgess's list, was an old university friend of Philby. A fellow member of the "homintern", as the left-wing Cambridge homosexuals came to be known, Wylie was then Secretary to the Permanent Under Secretary of War. Orlov informed Moscow that he had assigned Philby the task of cultivating Wylie "without undertaking anything essential", but after the Centre objected to using Burgess to approach Proctor, Orlov put a check on this operation too.

"Anticipating that along with the secretary of B[aldwin] who is a great friend of MÄDCHEN, you would take the same view of Wylie's case, I will also ban his cultivation," Orlov reported, advising Moscow that he had "restrained myself for the time being from making any plans for him". Nevertheless he suggested that they should reconsider. As he tactfully put it, "the thought flashed through my mind that possibly we could send Wylie MÄDCHEN, who is also a cultured pederast and an adroit chap who would – according to the mysterious laws of sexual attraction in this country – conquer Wylie's heart".[24] Orlov's assurances of MÄDCHEN's capacity as an *homme fatal* evidently persuaded the Centre, because this time they did not object to his plan. Burgess quickly effected an intimate relationship with Wylie, who was code-named HEINRICH (subsequently MAX) in NKVD records. But, although there is evidence that Wylie put Burgess in contact with military intelligence officers, the Centre halted the recruitment process of MAX when it was decided that he was too great a lush and homosexual philanderer to make a Soviet agent.

The NKVD files disclose that during his development, Burgess was for the same reasons also considered a risky candidate for recruitment by the somewhat puritanical chiefs in the Lubyanka. According to Deutsch, there was some justification for their hesitancy:

> MÄDCHEN has imagination and is full of plans and initiative, but he has no internal brakes. He is, therefore, prone to panic easily and he is also prone to desperation. He takes up any task willingly, but he is too unstable to take it to its conclusion. His will is often paralyzed by the most insignificant of difficulties. Sometimes he lies, not maliciously, but because of fear of admitting some minor error on his part. In relations with us he is honest and does everything

without objections and sometimes produces an impression of a person who is too readily subdued. Though he dresses very scruffily, he still likes to attract attention. This is a generally characteristic feature of his. He craves to be liked and only reluctantly acknowledges his weaknesses. This accounts for the fact that he suffers because some of his friends who used to know him as a Communist now think that he has ceased being one.[25]

It appears that it was this intense craving for acceptance that persuaded Deutsch and the Centre that they now held a psychological key to bringing Burgess under control despite his inherent lack of discipline. MÄDCHEN's emotional craving for praise made it more difficult for him than it had been for Philby and Maclean to make the required break with his circle of friends in the Communist underground at Cambridge. Deutsch would therefore have been relieved at the decision Burgess made in the summer of 1935 to abandon his attempt to get a fellowship with his thesis on a Marxist interpretation of the Indian Mutiny. Quitting Cambridge however required that Burgess find some way of replacing the £440 he was earning as a supervisor and turn his talents to a career which would enable him to be of use to the Revolution.

Initially Burgess turned to his friend Victor Rothschild, who provided him with a stipend as a financial consultant. In reality it transpires that Burgess helped out with a Rothschild-backed publication of surveys on economic and political matters being run by a German Communist emigré named Rudolf Katz.[26]

In November 1935 through contacts in the Whitehall homosexual network Burgess obtained a post as personal secretary to the newly elected pro-German MP Captain John Robert Macnamara. The following spring Burgess with his friend Wylie and a Church of England archdeacon, the Venerable J. H. Sharp, set off on a homosexual junket through Germany. The party sated both their political and sexual appetites with members of the *Hitlerjugend* in a manner that would surely have shocked the Foreign Relations Council of the Church of England, which had sponsored Macnamara's trip. They would have been even more alarmed had they known that compromising photographs of the MP and the Archdeacon with their arms around a succession of handsomely endowed specimens of Aryan manhood were later delivered by Burgess to Deutsch. They are preserved to this day in the MÄDCHEN file in the Russian Intelligence Service archives.[27]

As Macnamara's aide, Burgess moved for a time in the same

Anglo-German Fellowship circles as Philby. It was also through this pro-Hitler group that he was introduced to Edouard Pfeiffer. This former Secretary General of France's Radical Socialist Party was an *homme de confiance* of Prime Minister Edouard Daladier in his dealings with the French right wing. Off duty, Pfeiffer was active in the French Boy Scout movement. He managed to mix sex and conspiratorial politics in a manner Burgess found irresistible. He relished recalling the night he attended a reception at Pfeiffer's Paris apartment where French Government officials in evening dress were playing table tennis, with a muscular cyclist lying stark naked as a net.[28]

Pfeiffer was no less enamoured of the boyish charms of Burgess and he arranged for him to contribute articles to a Nazi-financed Paris periodical.[29] Having made his professional entry into journalism Burgess tried a probationary job in *The Times* editorial office in May 1936. He obtained the introduction from Roger Fulford, another member of the homosexual network, who was one of the newspaper's correspondents and who later became a ranking MI5 officer. But Burgess quickly tired of the routine of editing newspaper copy and quit after a month. Then, in October 1936, with the help of Professor Macaulay Trevelyan, the eminent Trinity historian, he landed a job at the British Broadcasting Corporation. The glamour and novelty of being a radio talk show producer suited Burgess's flamboyant personality and provided an outlet for his flair for the spoken word.

Mally, who was now head of the "illegal" station in London, decided that here was an opportunity to exploit Burgess's new-found respectability and access to the airwaves to identify and cultivate members of the British intelligence service. Shortly before his departure for Moscow in October 1935, Orlov learned from the agent code-named PROFESSOR that British intelligence officers were taught Russian at London University's School of Slavonic Studies. He had also established that one of the school's principal language teachers, Elizabeth Hill, was a relative of General Miller, who led the anti-Bolshevik Russian General Military Union, which was headquartered in Paris. In June 1935 Orlov had therefore instructed Burgess to apply to the school to study Russian. He was briefed to make the acquaintance of Hill and, by attending her classes, to discover and befriend those of her pupils who were MI6 officers in training. Deutsch was soon able to inform Moscow that the scheme had been put into operation.

"This plan is successfully being fulfilled," Orlov had reported to the Centre on 12 July 1935. "MÄDCHEN went to the Institute of Slavonic

Studies asking them to recommend him a teacher. The university luckily sent him to Hill, who gave him one lesson privately. The next step will be for him to ask her to put him in a group or to pair them with other pupils so that he may get a better ear for pronunciation and to make lessons livelier. Thus we count on approaching other pupils since MÄDCHEN knows how to make friends."[30]

Orlov's original confidence that Burgess could be successfully harnessed to serve the interests of the Centre was not misplaced. A year after Orlov left London Deutsch was able to report that the cultivation of Lisa Hill had progressed after she had heard one of Burgess's talks on BBC radio and he had dangled before her the prospect of inviting her to make a broadcast. Before its popularism in the age of television, the BBC held a cachet for British academics. Soon the unsuspecting Professor Hill was sharing confidences with Burgess to such an extent that, by early 1936, Deutsch was able to report to the Centre that MÄDCHEN had confirmed that so many intelligence officers attended the School of Slavonic Studies that he described it as "the centre of work of the local firm", as MI6 was referred to by the London "illegals".[31] Burgess had by now also learned that the school's director was a former MI6 officer who was planning to return to the Soviet Union "with the intention of renewing his work". He was able to report that the director's secretary was "known to be a Communist" and that Professor Hill herself had "probably very good relations with the people who work here and is ready to take part in it [the MI6 plan]".

Hill's close links with MI6 were confirmed when Burgess found out that she was the sister of Brigadier George A. Hill, the celebrated military intelligence officer who operated in Petrograd just after the Revolution with the legendary Sidney Reilly under the code name IK 8. In his colourful memoir, *Go Spy Out the Land*, Hill extravagantly claimed to have become a friend of Trotsky and helped him found the *Cheka*. Burgess had also established that Hill herself had formerly worked for MI6 and that she too might soon resume an active role by travelling to Moscow. To this end he discovered that the Professor was ingratiating herself with left-wing university students sympathetic to the Soviet Union.[32]

The mission of Burgess at the School of Slavonic Studies was only a partial success because he was unable to cultivate any MI6 officers on the language course. But it demonstrated to the Centre that Burgess could be a useful agent. That they now regarded MÄDCHEN as suitable to become a fully-fledged agent is indicated by the fact that he was selected as the courier to carry a new code sheet and money to Philby in Gibraltar.[33]

The "third man" in order of recruitment of the Cambridge group therefore became the "first man" to achieve Orlov's goal of making direct contact with the British secret intelligence service. The opportunity for Burgess to achieve this had opened up, shortly after Orlov had been posted from the Lubyanka to Spain in the autumn of 1936, when Maclean reported in October that an MI6 officer named David Footman had come to see him at the Foreign Office. Mally immediately decided to use Burgess to cultivate Footman.[34]

Explaining his strategy to the Centre, Mally went to considerable lengths to allay any concern that Moscow might still have about the operational abilities of MÄDCHEN in view of his "disorderly way of life". According to his report, Burgess "now has become more serious. He is not shy, on the contrary, he is slightly daring; whatever assignment you give him he will squeeze in anywhere. If you tell him, 'You must make friends with this or that person', he will do it very quickly. Nor does he impose himself on the person in question, but manages to arrange it so that this individual of interest to us would invite him himself."[35] Deutsch also added his own endorsement that Burgess was now ready for his first serious mission as an undercover agent by asserting that MÄDCHEN "could make friends with and achieve the acquaintance of almost anyone".

Deutsch first reported the contact with Footman in 1936, but it was not until his letter to the Centre of 25 July 1937 that he suggests Burgess should cultivate the MI6 officer. The ten month delay before Burgess could put the scheme to cultivate Footman into operation was due to his bout with syphilis at the beginning of 1937.

After his long treatment and convalescence, Burgess had used his cover as a BBC producer to make contact with the target MI6 officer again in the summer of 1937. This he did through Footman's literary agent in connection with the intelligence officer's two recently published novels, *Balkan Holiday* and *Pig and Pepper*, which had both been *succès d'estime* in London literary circles. He had received the Military Cross in World War I, joining the Secret Intelligence Service after serving in the Levant consular service. Footman was by then one of MI6's leading Soviet experts and, as well as writing novels, this talented intelligence officer managed to pursue scholarly studies of Russian history.[36]

Flattered to be invited by the BBC to discuss the possibility of making a radio broadcast about his latest book, Footman sent word that he would be happy to meet Burgess. The latter was able to ensure that their relationship got off on a firm footing by offering him a higher than usual fee.

"At last I managed to invite Footman for a dinner," Burgess gleefully informed Deutsch. "As the result of a successful and friendly conversation I became close enough for him to invite me to lunch tomorrow."[37] Their first encounter was at the Langham Hotel, opposite Broadcasting House in Portland Place. Long a dowdy office annex of the BBC, the Langham Hotel has now been restored to its pre-war glory as a Hilton Hotel. No commemorative blue plaque yet identifies it as the historic location of Burgess's first operation against MI6 for the Soviets, but NKVD records indicate it is worthy of one.

Unknown to Burgess at the time, one of the "illegal" station's trusted female agents staked out the meet. This double check on MÄDCHEN's first important mission was conducted by a female agent code-named GYPSY, who watched to see how he fulfilled his first important mission. "The meeting took place in the lobby of a hotel," Deutsch reported, reassuring Moscow that "GYPSY immediately recognized MÄDCHEN, who was very agitated as he later told me, he was afraid that Footman might not turn up. The meeting took place precisely as we had agreed with him and he later told me about it."[38]

Deutsch's report reveals Burgess's determination to show that he took his first mission as a Soviet undercover agent very seriously indeed. He was careful to omit no physical or biographical detail about Footman that he felt might be useful to Moscow:

He is an intelligent, quiet man of the English type, but quick, smart and elegant. He is 6 feet tall. He is slim, dressed like a Foreign Office official. Thin dark hair, dark eyes, manly face, long narrow mouth, a small back of head. One of his hands (upper wrist) has plentiful black scars looking like small black spots. I've learned something about his past. Approximately in 1920–1924 he was a vice consul in Egypt. Then he was doing the same job in Belgrade. Later he left the consular service and was a representative of a number of large companies in the Balkans. He was doing this for some years and then again joined the Civil Service, where he is working now, that is in the Passport Control Office. We talked for a while about this organization. The Passport Control Office, according to him, keeps watch over foreigners and complications in the passport service. I've checked that through another civil servant – Proctor. F[ootman] is always on his guard. But I think he liked me and this is what I was after."[39]

Not content with a written report, Burgess also deployed his skills as a caricaturist to sketch Footman in profile. This he handed over to Deutsch together with the MI6 officer's home address, which he had written out in his own hand on a sheet of paper bearing the heading of a Mayfair car dealer. The originals of both documents were forwarded by Deutsch to Moscow, where they are bound somewhat incongruously into MÄDCHEN's file.[40]

Footman was then taken to lunch by Burgess and persuaded to prepare two radio programmes for the BBC. Hinting at the underlying nature of the relationship he was aiming to exploit, Burgess archly reported that "we became very friendly". Although it is not clear from the NKVD files just what the precise nature of their relationship was, it was evidently not restricted to the BBC studios. Burgess was clearly on intimate enough terms to become a trusted informant for Footman, who, the following year, began giving him freelance missions for MI6.[41]

One of the first of these missions Burgess undertook for British intelligence was in May 1938 when he volunteered the services of his current boyfriend, Jack Hewitt, who happened to be working as a switchboard operator in the Goring Hotel. Konrad Henlein, the Nazi leader of the Sudeten Germans, was to stay at his hotel during discussions with the British Government about Hitler's claims to northern Czechoslovakia. Hewitt, under the direction of Burgess, monitored all the German's telephone conversations.

"It was all a bit of a lark," according to Hewitt, who recalled how, after eavesdropping on Henlein's calls, he had reported the details to Burgess and Footman in a Westminster pub behind the Broadway Buildings office block that was then MI6 headquarters.[42] Evidently MI6 found Burgess useful enough to employ him that summer in a second undercover operation after he had been invited by his friend Pfeiffer to act as a confidential courier for Daladier's secret letters to Chamberlain. "The communications of a confused and panic-stricken patriot to an ignorant provincial ironmonger," was how Burgess later described the exchanges in which the two prime ministers formulated their plans to defuse the Czechoslovak crisis by appeasing Hitler.[43] Every time Pfeiffer returned from Paris, Daladier's letters would be taken by Burgess to the suite MI6 maintained in the St Ermin's Hotel, where they would be photographed while he translated them for Footman, whose French had become rusty.

The NKVD's grand design for penetrating British intelligence came close to succeeding in mid-1938, when Burgess learned that there was a vacancy in the Passport Control Office, the cover MI6 used for its officers posted to Britain's overseas embassies. Footman agreed that Burgess was a suitable candidate during a lunch at which they discussed the possibility of Burgess leaving the BBC to work as a full-time intelligence officer. It was to further this objective that a week later Footman introduced Burgess to E. P. G. Norman, the former SIS head of station in Prague, one of the principal pre-World War II bases of British intelligence operations against the Soviet Union. This meeting took place in the Royal Automobile Club, a columned building in Pall Mall which Burgess reported was a favourite watering place for MI6 officers who, he noted, had open accounts in its restaurant. During the lunch it emerged that Norman was sizing up Burgess for a mission to Italy. His task would be to discover what Mussolini's attitude to Spain would be now that Franco's forces appeared to be winning the Spanish Civil War.[44]

"You don't have to do it yourself," Burgess reported that Norman told him, explaining how he would be expected to perform under-cover intelligence operations.[45] He said he had expressed his willing-ness to undertake the mission and, when Norman warned that as a BBC journalist he would arouse suspicions, he volunteered to ask his friend Lord Rothschild to arrange some cover job with the Italian branch of the family bank in Rome. This appealed to Norman, who also disclosed that Rothschild was already working on a secret scientific project for the War Office in Cambridge. This, he said, would make it easy for MI6 to approach him about Burgess.

Footman told Burgess at their next meeting that he had made a very good impression on Norman, although it had later been decided that his cover for the Italian mission would present a problem. He said he had agreed he was not exactly cut out to pass as a banker and instead suggested that he might pose as a lecturer since he knew so many people in the academic world. Adopting what he reported to his Soviet control officer as a "casual matter-of-fact manner", he took the opportunity to mention to Footman that as an undergraduate he had himself been a Communist and that he did not want to hide it from him. Footman's reaction was better than Burgess dared hope. The MI6 officer said this opened up new possibilities if the Italian mission did not work out.

"I have an excellent idea," Footman declared, according to Burgess, telling him how his experience and contacts would be of great use to "our boys in the anti-Communist section". He promised to arrange a meeting with the head of the MI6 counter-intelligence section.[46]

Footman was as good as his word. Shortly afterwards he introduced Burgess to Major Valentine Vivian, the chief of Section V, who would later be persuaded to bring Philby into MI6. Described by Burgess as a "fragile man" of 5 ft 10 ins with vertical lines in his fingernails and a stomach ulcer that kept him from drinking alcohol, his grotesque drawing of Vivian makes him appear even more dyspeptic than he really was. What had impressed Burgess about the officer who was later to become deputy chief of MI6 was his encyclopaedic knowledge of Marxist theory and a grasp of Comintern politics that left even Burgess overwhelmed.

"It was unpleasant for me," Burgess reported, "that, with the exception of the account of the Seventh Comintern Congress, I had read very little about the current trends in Marxist theory since 1934, when I left the Party." He said that Vivian had advised him to broaden his knowledge because: "Theory is necessary for action," and to achieve this Burgess was told he would have to be grounded in it before he could be considered as an undercover MI6 agent in the British Communist movement.[47]

"Legal Party members are not dangerous, so you shouldn't work among the activists," Vivian advised Burgess. This was a matter for the police and Special Branch. He therefore asked Burgess to consider cultivating people who were not members of the Party such as Victor Gollancz, the publisher and founder of the Left Book Club, who MI6 considered "very important and very dangerous". Another was a young undergraduate named Dennis James, who according to Special Branch, "has been a true revolutionary since the age of sixteen".[48] Vivian indicated that, "both in Oxford and Cambridge there is a secret Party membership that has to be uncovered".

It must have sent a shiver down Burgess's spine wondering how much the British secret services knew about the Cambridge cells. Vivian was certainly aware that "in the BBC there was an underground Communist organization", and one MI6 was determined to root out. "You will have to find out who its members are", Burgess was told by Vivian, unsuspecting that his intended "witch-hunter" was himself a secret member of the Communist coven. Relishing the irony of the situation, Burgess reported that he had not been able to resist the temptation of declaring innocently that he really could not understand what the Communists were up to in using such people.[49]

"Neither can I," Vivian agreed, emphasizing his belief that the "latest directive of the Comintern is extremely left wing". It was at this point in the conversation that Burgess recalled that Vivian had abruptly checked himself for indiscreetly letting it slip that the British had been intercepting the Comintern directives from Moscow. Conspiratorially, Vivian had then turned to Footman and apologized for having spoken out of turn in revealing this secret. Burgess was gratified and reassured to be able to report that the MI6 counter-intelligence chief had then told him that, although the recently intercepted Comintern directives were top secret, they were about to be published and he would get a copy. The lunch concluded with Footman and Vivian confidently assuring Burgess that his main task as an undercover British agent would be to get into the Party and arrange to be sent to Moscow.[50]

In a written report Burgess drew up after the meeting it can be seen that, in effect, he confirmed the *raison d'être* of the Soviet penetration strategy. "Does F[ootman] suspect me? I think he doesn't," Burgess asked rhetorically. "Why? Class blinkers – Eton, my family, an intellectual. I must stress that I have always told you: 'Avoid people like me. We are suspect for historical reasons.' Now I say, 'Only people like me are beyond suspicion.' "[51]

Burgess, however, had still to overcome the Centre's suspicions. If Orlov had still been monitoring the Cambridge Group in Moscow, his intervention might have accelerated his penetration. But, with all the "Great Illegals" liquidated, imprisoned in the *gulags* or put to flight, there was apparently no one at the Centre with the vision to approve the exploitation of the coup Burgess had single-handedly pulled off. It also irked the chiefs in the Lubyanka to learn that MÄDCHEN had chosen to act entirely on his own initiative during the hiatus after the recall of Mally and Deutsch had left the Cambridge group temporarily without a control officer.

The disruption caused by the purge of the "Great Illegals" meant that Burgess was out of direct contact with Moscow after Deutsch's departure, in October 1937, for nearly ten months. His NKVD file shows that the Centre's link with MÄDCHEN was restored in Paris in August 1938 through PIERRE – the cryptonym of Leonid Eitingon – who was then serving as Orlov's deputy in Spain. Eitingon continued running Burgess, requiring both to travel to Paris until the Centre decided, in March 1939, that Gorsky, the new London "legal" *rezident*, should take over control of MÄDCHEN. It was therefore through Eitingon that Burgess pressed Moscow to let him fall in with Vivian's plans.[52]

The Centre, however, repeatedly said "no" to MÄDCHEN acting as an MI6 "mole" in the Communist Party of Great Britain. The Foreign Department of the NKVD disapproved a scheme that was considered too risky for someone as mercurial as Burgess to pull off.

The NKVD did not consider itself responsible for guarding the security of the worldwide Communist movement. The view prevailed in the Lubyanka that, if authorization were given for Burgess to accept Vivian's offer of becoming a plant in the CPGB, it would distract him from the main target: the British Government's intelligence apparatus aimed directly at the Soviet Union. When Burgess was informed that Moscow had forbidden him to carry on with his penetration for MI6, he protested. Evidently ignorant of the rule that a Soviet underground agent unquestionably accepted instructions from the Centre, he fired off a "Dear Comrade" letter to Moscow questioning the wisdom of their decision.

"An anti-Communist whom I met later told me that he used his son, an Oxford undergraduate, as a spy in the left-wing student movement," Burgess wrote, cautioning that "it is most probable that in this way they can place somebody in Oxford or Cambridge and will be able to discover me and the others known to you. I give this example only to show and to stress that it will be better if a person doing this work is our man who will have the opportunity to cover the people that we need or to present facts in such a way that they will look unimportant or are misleading."[53]

"If they do it to us, why can't we do it to them?" Burgess pleaded. But the narrow-minded Foreign Department Chief Slutsky found his challenge impertinent and refused to reconsider the decision. Burgess was told very firmly by Gorsky to drop his cherished plan to become an undercover Communist working for MI6. "According to your directive I told F[ootman] that I don't think that I could ever again become 'left' and work as a provocateur in the British Communist Party," was how Burgess dutifully reported his compliance with Moscow's orders. He said he thought he had made his excuse convincing by telling MI6 that the Communists would distrust him too much. "This is of course true," Burgess observed, his tongue very much in his cheek when he admitted, "I have very successfully in the last five years built up a reputation for myself as a drunk, trouble-maker, an intellectual and a Fascist renegade."[54]

With characteristic persistence, however, Burgess's letter sought the Centre's approval for another scheme. He presented it as though the idea had been initiated by Vivian although it is more likely that it was the product of Burgess's own fertile mind. "F[ootman] however asked me if it is possible to get in touch with the Russian embassy in London," Burgess reported, contending that this would give him another unique opportunity to become a full-time British intelligence agent. His justification was that Vivian had given him some material for a book on the Russian terrorist movement. "I will acquaint myself with the subject and then write a letter to the embassy asking them to help me in collecting new material for the book," Burgess explains, saying that he would use it to establish a relationship with Ivan Maisky, the Soviet Ambassador to London, who, Vivian told him, was a great academic. "Then I could go to Moscow, if the British wish and the Russians invite me, to go on with my work."[55]

Once again the Centre gave a firm "no". Deutsch, who was then in Moscow advising on the running of the Cambridge group, may well have contributed to the rejection of the schemes submitted by

Burgess. That is certainly the inference to be drawn from the profiles he drew up highlighting what he saw as flaws in MÄDCHEN's ability to execute such difficult operations:

> At first he dissipated his activity, often acting on his own initiative without asking us and because he was inexperienced he made mistakes. We tried to slow him down and therefore it seemed to him that he was doing very little. If he does something wrong in his work for us, he will come and tell us everything. There was such a case. Until November 1935 I was on holiday in the USSR. He has a very good friend, an American comrade [unidentified], who at that time came to London for his holiday and he [Burgess] told him that he was doing special work. When MÄDCHEN met me he told me about that and was in very low spirits because he was tortured by remorse for what he had done. First he tried to explain what he did by the despair that he experienced because of the lack of contact with us. But later he acknowledged that he had done it because of his desire to boast.
>
> MÄDCHEN is a hypochondriac individual and always thinks that we do not trust him completely. That can be accounted for by a principal feature in his make-up – internal instability. It should be stated that in the time he has been working for us he has improved immensely in this regard. He has repeatedly tried to persuade me that we are his saviours. Hence his alertness and fear of making a mistake that could bring his dismissal from our work. I demonstrated my trust to him by the fact that I do not consider him a stranger, but our comrade.[56]

Such a cautious assessment would hardly have encouraged the Centre to put the whole Cambridge group at risk by allowing someone as mercurial as Burgess to become a penetration agent in MI6. The level-headed and operationally-tested Philby was the one they had in mind for this mission. They did not raise any objection, however, to Burgess operating on the periphery of British intelligence as a freelance agent. This Burgess succeeded in pulling off himself as a result of an introduction Footman gave him to Major Laurence D. Grand, the head of D Section of MI6. This section had been established in March 1938 to prepare ways for "attacking potential enemies by means other than operations of military force". In contemporary parlance, this was the "dirty tricks" section of SIS, which operated under the cover of the Department of Statistical Research at the War Office.

"My first assignment from Grand was to work on the Jewish question and Palestine," Burgess wrote in his letter to Moscow dated 19 December 1938. He explained that his task had been "to activate Lord Rothschild" in a political manoeuvre intended "to split the Jewish movement" with a scheme whose purpose was to "create an opposition towards Zionism and Dr Weitzmann". The intention was to isolate and neutralize the Zionist leader so that the British Government could strike a deal with the Arabs. Burgess duly solicited Rothschild's support for establishing a Jewish community in an area between Lebanon and Egypt. It was believed that this would divide the Zionist lobby and at the same time act as a buffer to any Italian territorial adventure north into the British protectorate of Egypt from their newly seized colony of Abyssinia.[57]

Burgess's reports in his NKVD file show that he then assisted Grand in producing anti-Hitler propaganda broadcasts under the ostensibly independent Joint Broadcasting Commission. They were actually commissioned by MI6 for beaming to Germany from radio stations in Luxembourg and Liechtenstein. While supervising their production, Burgess picked up and passed on to Moscow a warning that British Government policy was directed more against the Soviet Union than the Third Reich.

"The broad intention is to work with Germany wherever possible and ultimately against the USSR," Burgess reported for Moscow's benefit in early 1939. Since he had signed the Official Secrets Act in order to have access to the Foreign Office reports necessary for his propaganda work, Burgess was able to feed a stream of accurate policy intelligence to Moscow. The MÄDCHEN NKVD file, for example, reveals that on 3 August 1939 he reported the conviction of the British chiefs of staff that "a war between Britain and Germany can be easily won" and that the Government therefore had no need to conclude a defensive pact with the Soviet Union. Such inside information reaching the Kremlin from Burgess could only have reinforced Stalin's conviction that the British and French Governments were not seriously interested in a treaty. Evidence that this was a vital factor in bringing about the Nazi-Soviet pact appears in a report provided by Burgess just before Ribbentrop's visit to Moscow to sign the accord which cleared the way for Hitler to go to war over Poland.[58]

"In Government departments and talks with those who saw the documents about the negotiations [between the British Government and the Soviet Union] the opinion is that we have never intended to conclude a serious military pact," Burgess told his NKVD controller. "Prime Minister's office openly says that 'they thought they could avoid a pact with the Russians'. (The actual words used by the secretary of Horace Wilson.)"[59]

After war had broken out in September 1939, Burgess continued to supply a stream of useful intelligence. His reports reveal he lived up to Mally's estimation that he would prove a "*Mädchen für alles*" (a maid of all work); they range from details of Grand's scheme for assassinating Hitler to his masquerade as Mr Francis, the go-between of MI6 in a plan to enlist Labour Party support for fomenting a Swedish miners' strike to deprive Germany of coal supplies. Until early 1940 Burgess acted as Grand's adviser on a part-time basis, while he also worked as a BBC talks producer. He served as a contact with the Ministry of Information before leaving the BBC, when the German *Blitzkrieg* on the West began in April 1940. Then he went to work full time for Grand to assist with the setting up of a training school at Brickendonbury Hall. This was the special training camp where British agents were taught how to conduct subversive operations, which was to be the forerunner of the wartime Special Operations Executive.

"I thought it was a good way of acquiring for myself a more central position," Burgess explained in the memoir he wrote for the KGB reporting how he had used his job for "learning the names of the agents who were sent abroad and establishing contacts with the officers of SIS and MI5 who I invited to the school to deliver lectures".[60]

"Guy Fawkes College", as Grand's brainchild was known, also served as the vehicle for getting Philby his first intelligence related job during the summer of 1940 when Grand's training school was shut down. It was Burgess, ironically, who then found himself out of a job while Philby, then a *Times* correspondent, was transferred to SOE, the "Special Operations Executive" that Churchill had ordered to be set up after the fall of France to train saboteurs to "set Europe ablaze". From SOE Philby would make the transition into MI6 the following year to begin the mission for Moscow for which he had been groomed by Orlov. But the "Third Musketeer", Burgess, who had helped engineer his friend's entry into the SIS with assistance from Vivian, found himself out in the cold.

Burgess had no choice then but to return to his old job at the BBC although he continued to undertake freelance missions for his friends in British intelligence. With the encouragement of his Soviet control officer, Burgess had enlisted the aid of Footman and Blunt – who, thanks to Lord Rothschild's sponsorship, was now in MI5 – to try to enter the counter-espionage section of the security service. Burgess struck up a close personal friendship with Guy Liddell, a divorcé who enjoyed the company of Burgess's homosexual coterie on their regular outings in blacked-out London to wartime music halls. But when it came to getting a job in MI5, however, Liddell made no bones about wanting to "keep that man out of my office".[61] He did, however, assign one of his assistants, a Trinity contemporary of Burgess named Kemball Johnston, to operate Burgess as a sub-agent.

Burgess's first mission for MI5 was to recruit Erich Kessler, a homosexual Swiss journalist turned diplomat Burgess had seduced in 1939. Code-named ORANGE, Kessler – as the NKVD files confirm – proved a useful source of intelligence for both MI5 and the Soviet intelligence service on German dealings with the Swiss. So, too, did agent TOFFEE, a prominent Free Hungarian exile named Andrew Revoi, who was recruited as an MI5 source with the aid of Burgess's homosexual charms.[62]

The protean character of Burgess, as confirmed by his NKVD dossier, helped him to peddle his unique services as a homosexual lure to the simultaneous advantage of both the Soviet and British intelligence services. But his loyalty always remained with Moscow. His MI5 profile remains a closely guarded official secret in Britain, but it is unlikely that it contains a radically different assessment of his potential value as an undercover operative than the summary that survives in the Soviet archives:

> *Mädchen's future potential.* He has a wide circle of contacts. He can make friends with almost anyone. But his initiative must be contained almost all the time and he must be controlled very rigidly. Every assignment which is given to him should be defined in every minor detail. It is also necessary to keep a watch on his private life, on his friends and so on. He understands that we must know this and willingly tells us about that. It is very important that our officers who will be in contact with him know that they must be, in all respects, a model for him. He needs unconditional discipline, authority and adherence to principles. It is necessary to teach him all the time the rules of security.[63]

Keeping Burgess under "unconditional discipline" was the key to his successful exploitation. This was a task for which Deutsch had briefed both Grafpen and his successor, Gorsky, at the Soviet embassy. In his thirties when he was promoted from cypher clerk to NKVD intelligence officer in 1939 after training in Moscow, Gorsky had concealed a native shrewdness behind a pair of cold blue eyes. He was known to the "Three Musketeers", as HENRY. Philby found him "dry" and Gorsky was scorned by Blunt as "flat-footed and unsympathetic".[64]

While Gorsky may have lacked the charisma of Orlov, the charm of Mally or the intellectual fascination of Deutsch, he proved adept at devising missions that exploited the peculiarly versatile talents of Burgess. For example, on 14 October 1942 he put up a new plan to Moscow for deploying MÄDCHEN in a renewed attempt to recruit Dennis Proctor for the Soviet intelligence service. He reported that

HATA (the Ukrainian word for a peasant hut, which was the NKVD code name for MI5) was, for a reason not explained, relying on Burgess to obtain financial information from his friend Proctor, then a high official in the Treasury.

"In the event that Proctor is HATA's agent and is connected with it through MÄDCHEN, he would undoubtedly tell the latter much more than he has done up until now," the London *rezidentura* reported. Furthermore, he said that if the plan for recruiting Proctor was to succeed, then he believed that "MÄDCHEN may have the chance to become involved in working for HATA on other prominent Englishmen". He requested permission to encourage Burgess to get himself into MI5 "so that we could use these agents in our own interests, unwittingly, through him".[65]

Once again Proctor was to prove an elusive target. Despite Burgess's assiduous efforts as a factotum for the British secret services, he could not provide Moscow with the same level of access to MI5 secrets as was available through Blunt. Apart from providing valuable insights into how MI5 conducted their operations, the wartime MÄDCHEN file contains only documents received from Grand, including the weekly information bulletins based on Foreign Office intelligence information from the SIS.

It was not until Burgess managed to gain a post in the Foreign Office in 1944 that he finally had the opportunity to pass over thousands of secret documents. His Soviet archive file does show, however, that Burgess had laboured long and faithfully to demonstrate his willingness to assist Moscow by seeking out and acquiring, often on his own initiative, valuable sources of new information.

"MÄDCHEN always thinks he does too little for us and therefore is tortured by remorse," was how Deutsch described Burgess's powerful motivation. He was so eager to please the Soviets that he had even responded to an appeal to tidy up his careless appearance because he "realized that if he was working for us he could not go about dressed as he was". Deutsch noted how after one dressing-down MÄDCHEN had started to "look after himself", and stopped drinking so heavily. As a result of his bout of syphilis in the spring of 1937, he had even claimed that he had "stopped living with males", declaring his intention "after his recovery" to consider getting married.[66] This was of course a promise Burgess could never have fulfilled; it proved to be just another of his chameleon-like self-delusions. But, by playing Figaro for his friends and contacts in MI5 and MI6, he gained the confidence of many of their officers in the most senior cadres. He memorised and transmitted to the Soviets the names of key members of the British secret services as well as their foreign intelligence agents. All this information Burgess methodically catalogued and passed on to Moscow, along with useful insights into the operational housekeeping of the British intelligence services. The sheer volume of information in NKVD records leaves little doubt that out of the "Three Musketeers" MÄDCHEN was by far and away the most energetic of the trio. As Deutsch's psychological profile makes clear, he performed not out of expectation of any material reward, but in the belief that he was serving an ideological conviction and "that he is doing special work which corresponds with his vanity".[67]

"It's a very high mark for our work that after six months I can tell you about them [MI6], but after six years of work with you I cannot tell them anything about you," we find that Burgess observed in a letter he wrote to Deutsch in Moscow in July 1939.[68] Their success at concealing their operation must have been very gratifying to Moscow Centre. The willingness to serve an unseen master so unquestioningly was remarkable and it was a tribute to the original team of "illegals" who cultivated and recruited them. None of the Cambridge group, with the exception of Philby, who in his KGB memoir says that he knew Orlov by name in Spain, ever learned the real names of the controllers who ran them (or were even fully aware that they were Soviet intelligence officers and not diplomats). They did not even know whether their Soviet contacts were permanently living in Britain or just coming from abroad specially to attend meetings with them. This impression was sustained, because sometimes, when the members of the Cambridge group were travelling outside Britain, the controller had meetings with them on the Continent in locations such as Paris.[69]

Significantly it was Burgess, in his enthusiasm, who was the only one who appears to have grasped the grand scale of the NKVD's penetration operation. He came to believe that he had played a central part in the evolution of the scheme for recruiting "moles" who would burrow into the British Government and intelligence apparatus. This emerged from his memorandum "Work Among Students for the Preparation of them for the Civil Service" that he wrote and forwarded to Moscow on 12 March 1939. In it he set down the rationale of the Soviet penetration scheme developed long before Burgess had become one of its first recruits:

The organization of work among university students is of the greatest importance because, through this work, we could control the regular inflow of people who are going to enter the Civil Service and whom it would be possible to recruit before they become too well known and to arrange for them to secure posts in one or another branch of the Civil Service. Two of the most important universities are, of course, Oxford and Cambridge. To conduct such work there we need somebody who is in close contact with students.[70]

The reports Burgess sent to the NKVD show that he thought of himself as the talent scout for an "Oxbridge" network because he continued to offer successive suggestions for enhancing and strengthening the operation. As his control officer reported to the Centre in 1938:

> The kind of work which he would do with great moral satisfaction and with absolute confidence in its success and effectiveness is the recruitment by us of young people graduating from Oxford and Cambridge Universities and preparing them to enter the Civil Service. For this kind of work he has such assistants as TONY in Cambridge and GROSS in Oxford. MÄDCHEN always returns to this idea at every meeting, motivating it by the argument that only this kind of agent can give us truly trustworthy information.[71]

The references to TONY, and GROSS are the original code names given to Anthony Blunt and Burgess's friend Goronwy Rees. That neither bore German cryptonyms like the "Three Musketeers" indicates that Blunt and Rees were not among the first generation of Cambridge recruits. Blunt's rather too obvious code name was later changed to JOHNSON in wartime cryptograms from the NKVD *rezidentura* in the Soviet embassy. But it was as TONY and in collaboration with Burgess that his induction coincided with the second phase of the expansion of the Cambridge group into a network. The actual date of Blunt's introduction to the Soviet intelligence service can now be accurately determined from Deutsch's history of the Cambridge group, in which he noted: "In the beginning of 1937 MÄDCHEN introduced me to TONY."[72]

"I and A[nthony] B[lunt] always worked on the basis that with consistent, adroit effort we should try each year to find a really trustworthy and reliable comrade," Burgess himself recorded in his 1952 debriefing for the KGB,[73] pointing out that Blunt evolved from talent scout to a key wartime source for the Soviets. As a senior MI5 officer Blunt had access to ULTRA intelligence, so he was able to pass on to Moscow some of the most important military secrets in Britain. But in his own diffident autobiographical essays for the KGB Blunt consistently sought to downplay the significance of his first years as a Soviet agent.

"To characterize my activity in the period since 1937 up to the beginning of the war, I did almost nothing," Blunt wrote to Moscow in 1943, describing his own role as the Centre's talent scout. "I started to do our work and also tried to do a rather difficult task – that is to create the impression that I did not share the views of the left wing, while on the other hand to be in the closest contact with the undergraduates of the left wing so that I could spot talent – the people who were of interest to us. As you already know, I recruited the following comrades: M.S. [Michael Straight] and L.L. [Leo Long]. I was also asked to establish contact with C. [Cairncross] and I did that for G.B. [Burgess]."[74]

The Russian Intelligence Service declines to identify Blunt's third recruit whose code name was ABO and who has never been exposed. It has no such reservations about Michael Whitney Straight who confessed in 1963 to the FBI. His code name was NIGEL. He was a member of the Trinity underground Communist cell and the scion of an American industrial and banking dynasty, and the fifth man in order of recruitment. For a time Straight was a Soviet wartime source in the US State Department, but by the end of 1942 he broke with Moscow and was eventually to expose Blunt twenty-one years later. Leo Long, code name RALPH, was a Trinity scholar from the working class who was also a member of the same Communist cell and, like Straight, was an Apostle. He became an important wartime source for Moscow in British military intelligence. MOLIÈRE was John Cairncross, who, as we have seen, replaced Maclean for a time as the Centre's principal source in the Foreign Office in the autumn of 1938. He then moved to the Treasury, before taking up a wartime post at GC & CS at Bletchley Park. Cairncross has admitted to passing critical ULTRA intelligence to Moscow on German military dispositions on the Eastern Front, which earned him a Russian medal for helping the Red Army win the battle of Kursk in 1943.[75]

The recruits Blunt and Burgess tapped from the class of 1937 marked the second stage in the expansion of Orlov's original Cambridge group. They were added to the following year by another code-named MAYOR, whose identity continues to be protected because he never confessed and was not identified as a Soviet agent. Since GROSS (Goronwy Rees) was recruited through Burgess, he was not considered a member of the Oxford ring by the NKVD, but part of the Cambridge group.[76]

First approached by Burgess and Blunt in 1936, Rees broke away in 1939 in protest against the Nazi-Soviet Pact. None of the members of the Oxford network have ever been positively identified. For this reason the Russian Intelligence Service judges it prudent to keep their identities a secret. What the NKVD records do confirm, however, is that its principal organizer was given the cryptonym SCOTT. The development of the Oxford group began in 1936, and was built up by Deutsch based on his success with the Cambridge group.[77] The NKVD files indicate that SCOTT and its other founding members like Rees were cultivated and recruited primarily by Deutsch and Mally.[78] But, whatever Orlov learned about the Oxford recruits before he went to Spain, as with his first-hand knowledge of the Cambridge group, to which he had acted as midwife, Orlov was to take the secrets to the grave.

"KEEP OUT OF RANGE OF ARTILLERY FIRE"

THE SPRING OF 1936 saw the apogee of Orlov's career as one of Stalin's ranking spy masters. From his desk in Moscow Centre he was monitoring the operations of the Soviets' potentially most valuable underground espionage networks: the Cambridge group and its associated Oxford offshoot. He was also giving lectures on counter-intelligence and intelligence at the Central Military School in Moscow, where NKVD agents were trained. Although no copies survive, Orlov later told the Americans that he had written a manual entitled *Tactics and Strategy of Intelligence and Counter-Intelligence* which he said was produced as the basic text for the "spy schools" that trained Soviet and foreign recruits in the tradecraft of espionage.[1]

Orlov's authority was recognized by his appointment in the spring of 1936 to the six-man council which advised the Foreign Ministry and the Politburo on operations and foreign intelligence derived from secret documents obtained by Soviet spy rings operating abroad.[2] This so-called "Little Council" drew its membership from the State Security *apparat*, Soviet Military Intelligence and the Commissariat of Foreign Affairs. It produced intelligence assessments for the Politburo and Foreign Ministry. This influential body was chaired by A. N. Poskrebyshev, the chief of Stalin's secretariat, and included Georgy Malenkov, Yezhov's deputy in the Cadres Department of the Central Committee, who was later to become the Soviet Premier.[3]

Participation in the "Little Council" brought Orlov to Stalin's personal attention because once a week the committee met to prepare a full report on their overseas intelligence operations against foreign governments for the desk of the Big Boss. It was Orlov's task to assemble secret foreign diplomatic communications obtained by Soviet agents – including those obtained by Maclean. The Big Boss insisted on receiving his copy of the report before a copy was sent to the Foreign Ministry to keep one step ahead of Vyacheslav Molotov, the Soviet Foreign Minister. From what Orlov later told

Feoktistov, he was frequently consulted personally by Stalin on actual operations during 1936.[4]

This access to inner circles of the Politburo put Orlov in a unique – and ultimately dangerous – vantage point. At the beginning of 1936, Stalin launched his all-out bid to eliminate potential opposition to his rule. From the heart of Lubyanka headquarters, where the operation was initiated, Orlov witnessed at first hand the beginning of what was to be known as the Great Purge.

"Early in 1936 about forty NKVD men were summoned for a special conference by the chief of the Secret Political Department, Molchanov," was how Orlov vividly recalled the blood-letting had been initiated. The assembled high-ranking officers were astonished to be told that "a vast conspiracy had been uncovered, headed by Trotsky, Zinoviev, Kamenev and the other leaders of the opposition". The conspiracy, according to Molchanov, had been growing over many years, nefariously establishing "terrorist groups in almost all the big cities and had set itself the aim of assassinating Stalin and the members of the Politburo and of seizing power". Priority was to be given to mounting a full-scale investigation, with Stalin personally supervising the task, assisted by Nikolay Yezhov, the Secretary of the Central Committee of the Communist Party.[5]

The enormity of the announcement staggered even the most hardened NKVD officers present. "How could it be?" Orlov remembered they asked one another as they filed out of the meeting. How could such a huge conspiracy have been uncovered without their participation or knowledge since the NKVD maintained extensive secret networks of informers? Despite their scepticism, they had no choice but to go along with the investigation mapped out for them in great detail by Stalin and Yezhov. The plan was to bring to court the principals, who would be confronted with fifty co-defendants culled from 300 of those already convicted for opposing Stalin. Confessions of complicity were to be obtained for stage-managed trials by a process that Orlov characterized as "a severe inquisitorial work-over".[6] He wrote that Yagoda was charged by Stalin with gathering evidence to be used in staging a public trial of the leading conspirators, Kamenev and Zinoviev. Since the death of Menzhinsky in July 1934, Yagoda had headed the state security *apparat*, known as the NKVD, the acronym of the *Narodnyi Kommissariat Vnutrennikh Del* (People's Commissariat of Internal Affairs), in which it was now incorporated and of which he was also the Commissar.

"The whole scheme was worked out in detail by Stalin and Yezhov," Orlov wrote, with its "practical execution entrusted to Yagoda".[7] The view of many of the old-guard *Chekists* in the NKVD was that Stalin was bent on taking his final revenge on Lenin, whose last testament had included warnings about the insidious ambitions of the Party's ambitious General Secretary. Now that Stalin effectively controlled the secret police he intended to use them to liquidate the last of Lenin's close associates who dared to criticize him. He was purging the old-guard leaders of the Communist Party committees, and had begun with the suppression of the Society of Old Bolsheviks in 1935, the year when he had ordered Soviet history books to be rewritten to inflate and glorify his own role in the Revolution.

Orlov had also learned on his return to Moscow from London in the early part of 1935 how the Big Boss was suspected by many of his *Chekist* comrades of having been deeply implicated in the murder of Sergei Kirov, the chief of the Leningrad Soviet. Bluff and outspoken Kirov had been a charismatic figure whose popularity and outspokenness in the Politburo made him a potential rival to Stalin until his assassination on 1 December 1934. He was shot by a deranged gunman named Leonid Nikolayev, who, it turns out, had been supplied with both a weapon and a pass to gain access to the closely guarded office in the palatial Smolny Institute, formerly a finishing school for the daughters of the nobility. This curious sequence of events had raised whispers of Stalin's complicity.

It is doubtful if Kirov had ever posed any immediate threat to Stalin who made his murder the expedient pretext for launching a broad purge of the Party. This task of investigating and "explaining" Kirov's assassination Stalin had assigned to Yagoda. Nikolayev and thirteen others conspirators had duly been summarily shot that December, together with hundreds of alleged White Guardist plotters. But, in an astonishing reversal the following month, Yagoda had dramatically announced that the NKVD investigation had uncovered the "real" culprits. He named them as Kamenev and Zinoviev, Stalin's former comrades in the Politburo who were arrested and subjected to a punishing round of interrogations before their secret trial in January 1935. Despite the state prosecutor's inability to produce any proof of their involvement in Kirov's murder, they were sentenced to five- and ten-year prison terms after Yagoda had bullied them into admitting "political and moral responsibility" in order to save their families.[8]

On Yagoda's orders, Kamenev and Zinoviev, early in 1936, were taken to the Lubyanka cells from their prison to be re-interrogated with the object of extracting a new confession to lend credibility to Stalin's allegations that they were part of a huge conspiracy against him instigated by Trotsky. The "investigation" failed to produce the desired results as quickly as Stalin expected. Not until May were suitable "confessions" obtained from fifteen prisoners, whose

HOME TOWN BOY: The postcard view of Bobruysk in 1907 shows the less-than-affluent surroundings which were the boyhood home of Leiba Feldbin (Alexander Orlov) whose self-confidence was captured by a local photographer at about the same time. The moustache he grew as a student in Moscow, gave a Chaplinesque appearance to the young Revolutionary who was appointed by the Bolshevik's to the Supreme Finance Council in 1918.

COMBATING THE COUNTERREVOLUTION: The bloody civil war pitted the Red Army (*background*: a cavalry charge on the Polish front in 1921) under its commissar Leon Trotsky (*top right*) against the White armies of the anti-Bolshevik forces and their foreign allies. The interrogation of prisoners on Russia's southwest frontier (*below left*) as military counterintelligence officer brought Orlov to the attention of Feliks Dzerzhinsky (*top left*) the head of the *Cheka* who was charged with the waging of a ruthless war against the forces of counterrevolution and subversion.

DECEIVERS AND DECEIVED: The *Trust* and *Sindicat* web of interlocking operations involving OGPU agents Opperput/Selyanov (*opposite page top left*) was one of the most successful, and targeted the White Russian military leadership in exile. General Kuteypov's (*inset above right*) plans to ferment uprisings in the USSR were neutralized and he himself kidnapped in 1930 six years after the balding Boris Savinkov (*background centre*: with Alexander Kerensky to his immediate right) had been lured back to Moscow and imprisoned. In 1925 OGPU officer Alexander Yakushev (*inset above left*) masterminded the snaring of the legendary Sidney Reilly (*opposite top left*) in a *Trust* plot which ended with the corpse of the Ace of British spies (*opposite below left*) on display in the Lubyanka sick bay.

RISING STARS OF THE OGPU: Even off-duty at Sekumi on the Black Sea coast of Georgia in 1925, a shaven-headed Orlov (*above*) projects a stern authority of a commander of the Transcaucasia border forces. Another veteran of the *Cheka* was the bearded Mikhail Trillisser (*below*) who served in the Soviet Far East and later became head of the Foreign Department which directed Orlov's espionage operations.

The original
Lubyanka building
formerly the
headquarters of the
pre-Revolutionary
'All Russian
Insurance Company'
as it appeared in
1926 when
Vyacheslev
Menzhinsky (*below*)
succeeded
Dzershinsky as OGPU
chief when Trilliser
(*centre right*) was
chief of the INO.

Josef Stalin was
a pall bearer at
Dzerzhinsky's
funeral along
with Genrikh
Yagoda (*second
from left*) the
future OGPU
chief who
walked a
respectful pace
behind Lev
Kamenev (*fourth
from left*) one of
the Politburo
victims of the
purge that he
would later
orchestrate for
'The Boss'.

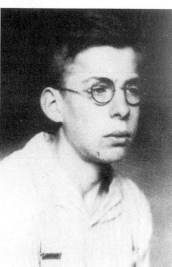

Alexander Korotkov (*centre left*)
Orlov's former assistant ran the
Berlin section of the *Rote Kapelle*
which had its genesis in a trip to
Moscow in 1932 by the pro-Soviet
academics (*bottom left*) of the AR-Plan
Group. Its two principal networks
were codenamed SENIOR led by (*top
right*) Arvid and Mildred Harnack
and the CORSICAN group of Harald
and Libertas Schultze-Boyzen (*below
right*) photographed on their yacht
with Kurt Schumacher. The
network's clandestine radio operator
was Hans Coppi (*above left*).

PLAYERS IN THE BERLIN SECTION OF THE RED ORCHESTRA: Albert Hoessler (*above left*) a former German member of the International Brigade who was recruited at Orlov's secret spy school in Spain. Parachuted into Prussia in 1942 to re-establish contact with CORSICAN and SENIOR he was betrayed to the *Gestapo* and shot. Erika von Brockdorf (*above right*) one of the female members of the CORSICAN network paid with her life for her part of the communist underground opposition to Hitler. Adam Kuckhoff (*below left*) the leader of the third element of the Berlin section of the *Rote Kapelle* was code-named OLD MAN. Willy Lehmann (*below center*) was the Soviet source in the *Gestapo* whose code-name was BREITMANN, Kurt Schulze (*below right*) was another prominent member of the Soviet Berlin network whose code name was BERG.

RECRUITERS OF THE OXBRIDGE SPY RINGS: Operating under the direction of the be-spectacled Ignaty Reif (*above left*) the illegal NKVD *resident* in London who operated under the alias of Max Wolisch the Austrian academic Arnold Deutsch (*above right*) made the first Soviet contact with Kim Philby (*opposite page right*) on a bench in Regent's Park in June 1934. Within a month Orlov (*opposite left*)

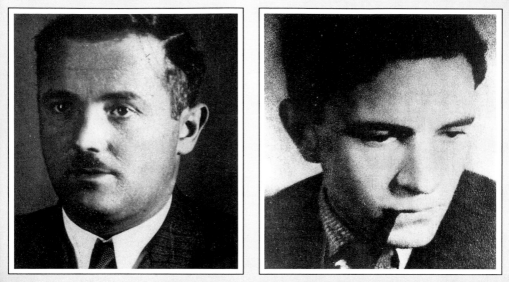

had arrived to take over as chief of the London station and he assumed overall responsibility for the cultivation of the 'First Man' of the Cambridge 'Group'. Their effective undergraduate recruiting techniques were later to be extended from Cambridge to Oxford University.

THE AMERICAN REFRIGERATOR CO., LTD.

CABLES :
AMFRIG, LONDON
TELEPHONE :
REGENT 2574

W. GOLDIN, U.S.A
M. S. STANFIELD

IMPERIAL HOUSE (OFFICE 48)
(ENTRANCE AIR STREET)

84. REGENT STREET.
LONDON. W.1.

193

Take one to relieve congestion.

PHONE: REGENT 2574.

William Goldin,
DIRECTOR

AMERICAN REFRIGERATOR Co. LTD.
Imperial House (Office 48)
80/86. Regent Street, London. W.1.

This passport is good for travel in a
countries unless otherwise limited.
This passport is valid for two years fro
the date of issue unless limited to a short
period.

William Platt

DEPARTMENT OF STATE
WASHINGTON

Auto Renewal on page 1

4   5

THE SECRET SOVIET SPY STATION: Behind the business façade of AMFRIG in a fourth floor office overlooking London's busy Regent Street, Orlov operated undetected by MI5 as an American entrepreneur with a genuine US passport (*left*) in the name of William Goldin. Before he handed over his British agents to Theodore Mally (*below right*) in 1935, Philby (*centre*: lecturing a class of KGB trainees forty years on) had brought in Donald Maclean (*below centre*) and Guy Burgess (*below left*) into the ring who called themselves 'The Three Musketeers' of the Soviet's Cambridge network.

'DISPOSING OF THE ENEMIES OF THE BIG BOSS': The domesticity of Stalin's summer residence in Yalta (*above*) with his daughter Svetlana on the lap of Lavrenty Beria the deputy head of the NKVD was in stark contrast to the bloodthirsty Purges that were liquidating their opponents. Controlled by Nikolay Yezhov (*below left*) assassination squads under the direction of Mikhail Spiegelglass (*below centre*) roamed Europe. Hit-lists were based on the exaggerated reports of NKVD penetration agent Mark Zborowsky (*below right*) who had become a trusted member of the exiled Trotsky's entourage.

CRATIONS IN SPAIN: Orlov's assistant Alexander
lkin (*above left*) who had been running the
RSICAN network in Berlin before he came to
ain to help direct the secret spy school in Spain
ich recruited the American Lincoln Brigade
unteer Morris Cohen – alias Peter Kroger
ove right) – for a career of espionage. The 1937
ing of NKVD defector Ignace Reiss (*right*) by
zhov's murder squads was a fate that Orlov
w he risked when he decided to flee to
erica in 1938 from Barcelona where he had
self directed the liquidation of Andres Nin
ow left) along with dozens of his fellow Spanish
rxists. Orlov's deputy Leonid Eitingon (*below
t*) who in 1938 made frequent trips to Paris to
Guy Burgess, two years later masterminded
assassination of Trotsky in Mexico.

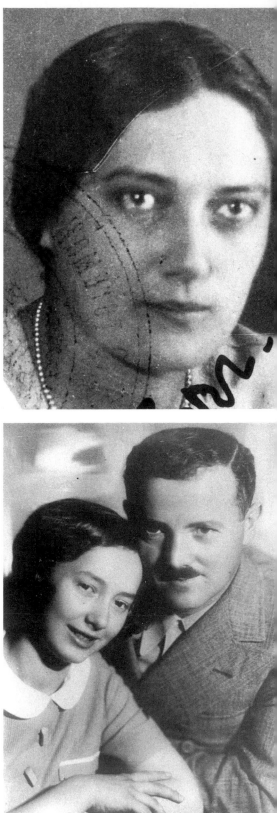

ORLOV THE FAMILY MAN; The dapper and confident NKVD General without his gun holsters at his Barcelona headquarters. Maria Orlov (*upper right*) as she appears in the Austrian passport on which she travelled to Britain in 1934 as Maria Feldbine. Veronica Orlov (*right*) with her devoted father shortly before her illusions were shattered when the family fled from Spain to their American exile in July 1938.

allegations were then used in an attempt to break Zinoviev and Kamenev. Stalin's mounting impatience became evident to Orlov at the Lubyanka when Yagoda and Yezhov personally started making regular rounds of the interrogation rooms in the small hours of the night. "These visits kept the interrogators in a great state of tension and made them work with redoubled energy all night through," Orlov wrote. He himself was able to monitor the slow progress of the inquisitorial "preparation" through his friend Lev Mironov, whom he had served alongside while in the Economics Department.

Mironov was one of the principal NKVD interrogators entrusted with obtaining the necessary confessions and Orlov records how, after a particularly gruelling session with Kamenev one night, Mironov came into his office to tell him that the prisoner explained he could not confess to a role in the alleged conspiracy because he had been under constant surveillance in prison. A despairing Mironov told Orlov that he had been quite unable to answer this, conceding that he feared he would "get into a mess with Kamenev's case".[9]

It was July 1936 before Yagoda and Yezhov finally persuaded Kamenev and Zinoviev to agree to admit their guilt provided Stalin would personally promise them before the Politburo to spare their lives and those of their families. Mironov told Orlov how he had then accompanied the accused pair to the Kremlin, where Stalin convened an *ad hoc* Politburo session and demanded: "Submit to the will of the Party and your life and the lives of those whom you led into the swamp will be spared."[10] Only then did the pair consent to go on trial on condition that none of their old Bolshevik colleagues accused with them would be executed and that no death sentence would be demanded for former members of the opposition.

"That goes without saying," Stalin had offhandedly agreed.[10] The assurance was to prove as hollow as their admission to being part of a monumental Trotskyist conspiracy.

Kamenev and Zinoviev confessed as arranged at their trial, which opened on 19 August. Of the sixteen accused in the Hall of the Trades Unions (before a "public" audience that Yagoda had carefully packed with NKVD officials instructed to shout down any embarrassing testimony), five were NKVD plants, coached in the perjured testimony. After this a guilty verdict was a foregone conclusion, but when the written verdicts prepared pre-trial were handed down at 2.30 am on 24 August, even the red-eyed night shift from the NKVD were stunned to hear the president of the court pronounce death sentences on all the defendants. Flouting Soviet law, Kamenev, Zinoviev and the NKVD's stooges were not permitted the statutory seventy-two hours to petition for clemency. They all faced the same firing squad next morning.

The victims of Stalin's first show trial were followed to their deaths a week later by 5,000 more opposition Communists held in the prison camps. They were secretly executed on the orders of Yagoda and Yezhov at Stalin's instruction. A year later he issued a similar instruction for another 5,000 to be summarily executed as the Great Terror gathered pace.[11]

"How many times that order was repeated I do not know, because in the fall of 1936 I went to Spain as an adviser to the Republican Government," Orlov observed in his starkly drawn memoir of the start of the blood-bath of the Great Purge that engulfed the Soviet Union. "Living abroad I was unable to follow the second and third trials of the old Bolsheviks as closely as I had the first," Orlov wrote, noting how he "learned many valuable behind-the-scenes facts about those two trials from well-informed officers of the NKVD who came on business to Spain and France".[12]

To the American counter-intelligence officers who debriefed him twenty years later Orlov claimed his appointment as assistant to the chief of the Department of Railways and Sea Transport in 1935 was the result of his attempt to distance himself from the centre of power at the NKVD. General Sudoplatov, a contemporary, confirmed that Orlov was indeed at one time head of the Transport Department, but his brief tenure of this relatively unimportant post had more to do with his hope of spending more time with his sick daughter than his fear of being swept up into the bloody power struggle. But, in his testimony before a Senate Sub-Committee in 1955, Orlov ascribed his appointment to Yagoda, who, he said, was not well disposed towards him because of a feud between the NKVD chief and his cousin Zinovy Katsnelson, who had associated himself with the Ukrainian Communist leader V. A. Balitsky.[13]

Like many of Orlov's statements, it does not square with facts in his NKVD dossier. If the NKVD chief had not had full trust in him, it is hardly likely that he would have been appointed to the important post of NKVD chief in Spain a month before Yagoda was himself dismissed by Stalin in September 1936. The decision to dispatch Orlov to Madrid, as he himself records, had actually been taken a month before Kamenev and Zinoviev faced the special court. The first of Stalin's show trials opened in Moscow[14] a week after the insurrection of right-wing military officers had sparked off a civil war in Spain. The Soviet Union, as the self-proclaimed "Workers' and Peasants' State", had a vested – if not vital propaganda – interest in supporting the left-wing Republican Government's efforts to combat a Fascist inspired rebellion. Outside assistance was urgently sought by both sides in a Spain long riven by the rival political factions of left and right.

Falangists and monarchists had both been calling on the army to put down a rising tide of violence as a bickering coalition administration of Socialist trade unionists struggled to govern and contain the spreading anarchist and Communist factions. The rebellion of Spanish colonial army commands, which erupted on 17 July 1936 in North Africa, spread to the garrisons of metropolitan Spain by the time General Franco arrived in a chartered British plane to take command of the troops in Spanish Morocco. The uprising turned the bitterly divided nation into two warring camps. In the north and west of the Iberian peninsula the provinces of Galicia, Navarre and parts of Castile and Seville declared for Franco and the Nationalists, along with most of Andalusia in the south. In the north, Catalonia on the Mediterranean coast and the Basque provinces on the Atlantic, together with the greater part of central Spain, remained loyal to the Republicans after the militias and armed workers had disbanded isolated Nationalist garrisons.[15]

On 20 July 1936, three days after Spain had become the cockpit of the European struggle between the forces of Fascism and the left, the Politburo approved sending Orlov to Spain. According to his own account, it was Yagoda himself who had put his name forward for Stalin's endorsement after it had been approved by the Soviet Foreign Minister. Nominally a political attaché, Orlov was sent to Madrid as NKVD chief in Spain where his "special rank of major of State Security" gave him the authority of a general in the Red Army. The posting indicated not only his prominence in the state security *apparat* but also the importance that Spain had by now assumed in the diplomatic calculations of the Kremlin. As Orlov admitted, he was selected because he alone among the ranking NKVD officers was considered to possess the necessary combination of experience in guerilla warfare, counter-intelligence and foreign operations.[16]

Stalin's authorization for the NKVD to dispatch one of their top spy masters was only one element in the rapid expansion of the Soviet military and diplomatic presence in Spain. It was taken well before the plan for an international Non-Intervention Pact had been promoted by France at the beginning of August, after the Nationalists had appealed for arms and support to the Fascist governments of Italy and Nazi Germany. The French Socialist Prime Minister, Léon Blum, while sympathetic to the request from the Republicans for equal support, faced the hostility of the Radical Party, on which his coalition government depended. The British Government, too, was against sending weapons that might fan the conflagration in Spain into a wider European conflict. Britain joined with France in proposing that no country should sell arms to either side in Spain. The Soviets, anxious to curry favour with the French if not their British ally, then joined with the Germans and Italians on 23 August on a committee that had been set up in London to monitor observance of the "Non-Intervention Pact".

Non-intervention in the Spanish Civil War proved to be one of those international agreements that all parties found it more expedient to honour in the breach rather than in the observance. Before August was out both Hitler and Mussolini, neither of whom ever had any intention of abiding by its terms, cynically began secretly sending aircraft, tanks and troops to bolster Franco's forces. France, in response, discreetly permitted aircraft and arms shipments to reach Madrid. Publicly every European power rushed to shore up the barrier against arming Spain, in support of the British Foreign Secretary, Anthony Eden, who had coined the imperishable diplomatic maxim: "Better a leaky dam than no dam at all."[17]

During the first month of the war the patchwork forces of the coalition Republican Government had proved unable to contain a left-wing revolution, as workers and anarchists seized control of industrial plants in Catalonia and began collectivizing farms. Two weeks before Orlov's arrival in Madrid order had been restored through an uneasy alliance between the Socialists and the Communists which pitted them against the syndicalist trade unionists who had brought Francisco Largo Caballero to power. As a trade union leader and a Socialist, he had been hailed by the left as the "Spanish Lenin" because he made it a condition of assuming the premiership that the Communists would also join his Popular Front administration. Largo Caballero, to humour Stalin, was soon to proclaim his commitment to bring to heel the trade unions, anarchists and a small but vocal Marxist Revolutionary Party.[18]

The Communist Party's participation in the Republican struggle became a strong incentive to the Soviet Government to respond to Largo Caballero's appeals. Caught inconveniently in the midst of initiating his own bloody purge, Stalin was at first reluctant to risk alienating the French by committing Soviet arms or men to fight on the side of the Republicans. At the same time he was unwilling to desert the world revolution as the Trotskyites were noisily predicting he would. Adopting the same duplicity he displayed in the Moscow show trials Stalin, while professing Soviet adherence to non-intervention, secretly approved the immediate dispatch of trained Soviet pilots to fly fighter aircraft supplied by the French. At the same time he put off until October the sending of Soviet aircraft and tanks to Spain. In the meantime Moscow began a rapid build-up of military and political advisers in Madrid under the guise of increasing the staff at their diplomatic legation.

Orlov's arrival in the Spanish capital was preceded by that of a new Soviet ambassador, Marcel Rosenberg, accompanied by a delegation of naval, military and air attachés led by General Jan Berzin, the former head of Red Army intelligence. Artur Stashevsky was made head of the trade mission, effectively acting as Stalin's political commissar, while support at the front-line was assigned to General Emil Kleber. This was the alias of an Austrian-born veteran of the civil war named Moishe Stern. A hardened ex-Comintern agent who had operated in China and the United States, Stern assumed the passport and identity of a Canadian by the name of Kleber to become overall commander of the International Brigade.

On 16 September 1936, when Orlov checked into the Soviet mission in Madrid (which had taken over the Gaylord Hotel near the Prado), he found a cohort of Soviet advisers masquerading as diplomats, journalists and economic advisers. Although he was head of the NKVD station in Madrid, General Orlov was presented to the Spanish Premier, Minister of War and Chief of Army Staff in the Republican Government as a political attaché. The Spaniards were told that the newly arrived brigadier general was to be responsible for "making and submitting reports". In reality Orlov had been given full authority to run counter-intelligence and internal security in addition to supervising the flow of Soviet military aid to the front. As NKVD chief, Orlov had effective control over every Soviet official. As he later admitted to the FBI, his position "made him the top Soviet official in Spain, although the Soviet Ambassador, to the outside world, was the top Russian official".[19]

For all his authority, Orlov's early reports to Moscow reflect his grave doubts about his mission since his first impression of the military and political problems confronting the Republicans was not encouraging. The Loyalist armed forces were run on a committee-militia system that was proving ineffective against the Foreign Legions from Morocco brought over by Franco. This battle-hardened core of the Nationalist army was already cutting its way northwards towards Madrid at a rapid pace. Apart from the resolution of the Communist Party, Orlov found the authority of the Republican Government to be undermined by shifting multi-party alliances and the capricious independence of the provincial administrations. When it came to security and intelligence, the main areas of NKVD interest, it was the same story, according to the pessimistic first report he sent the Centre on 15 October 1936: "There is no unified security service, since the Government does not consider this to be very moral. Each party has therefore created its own security apparatus. In the present Government there are many former policemen with pro-Fascist sentiments. Our help is accepted politely, but the vital work that is so necessary for the country's security is sabotaged."[20]

The Republican Government came close to collapsing on 6 November 1936, when the cabinet decided that the time had come to evacuate the capital. The roads leading from Madrid were flooded with civil servants, ministers and politicians of all parties, and trucks carrying the files of whole Government departments to the safety of Valencia. The proximity of Franco's forces panicked even the Soviet Ambassador into ordering the evacuation of the embassy. The only official whom journalist Louis Fischer found at the Hotel Gaylord later that day was General Orlov, who advised the American reporter, "Leave as soon as possible. There is no front. Madrid is the front."[21]

While the NKVD General was left to prepare single handedly for the defence of the Soviet embassy, his comrade on the front line, General Kleber, saved the Republican army from collapse by marshalling a unified command for the defence of Madrid from the fragmented Loyalist troops and militia units. Anticipating that the Republican Government would fall if the Spanish capital was lost, Comintern leaders from all over Europe rallied to their support and pressed Moscow to send immediate military aid. To their public demands was added the scornful voice of Trotsky, who from his Norwegian exile predicted that Stalin would continue "to betray the Spanish Revolution".[22] It was not the Trotskyists call for the USSR to support the international Communist movement that moved the Soviet dictator, reluctantly, to come to the rescue of the Republicans: it was determination to control the resulting Spanish Government. The NKVD had, in fact, already been directed to arrange for shipments of arms from the USSR by 16 October when Stalin cabled José Diaz, the leader of the Spanish Communist Party: "The Spanish struggle is not a private affair of the Spaniards. It is the common cause of all advanced and progressive mankind."[23]

Sixteen Soviet freighters put to sea from the Black Sea port of Odessa, heading for the Mediterranean. By early November they had safely reached the Republican-held port of Cartagena, where they unloaded more than a hundred tanks and aircraft along with thousands of gallons of badly needed fuel. Although military aid on a far more massive scale was needed to defeat Franco, Stalin's first grudging commitment of Soviet support proved an important morale booster for the Spanish Republicans. Soviet supplies meant that the Loyalists were no longer battling alone against a Nationalist army being supplied with an increasing flood of arms from Germany and Italy.

"Madrid will not now fall," declared Prime Minister Largo

Caballero, "now the war will begin, because we now have the necessary materials."[24] His defiant words were reinforced later that month with the arrival of hundreds of Soviet military personnel and more arms. Orlov and his comrades in the Red Air Force and Army units in Spain resented Stalin's order that military personnel were to "keep out of range of artillery fire". Their T-10 tanks and *Mosca* and *Chato* fighter aircraft proved more than a match for the German and Italian opposition.[25] Even in the hands of hastily trained Republican pilots and crews the firepower and manoeuverability of the Soviet weapons proved superior to Nationalist tanks and aircraft during the December battles for Madrid.

By the beginning of 1937 it had become obvious that Franco's forces had failed to break the Spanish capital's defences which had been entrusted to General Kleber and his Soviet staff officers. Their dogged resistance ensured that by the end of January the Nationalists were still being denied the psychologically important control of the city. The International Brigade troops then arrived to help the Republican forces turn back the tide of the Nationalist assault. These foreign volunteer corps, whose nucleus was 500 refugee Communists sent to Madrid from the USSR, were a Comintern-inspired force recruited under the auspices of the national Communist parties. Thousands of recruits flocked to Spain from Europe, Britain and the United States. Many in the International Brigade were sincere men of left-wing ideals and motivated by conscience who trained and fought largely under the direction of Red Army officers.[26] After Madrid had been held, it was clear that Soviet arms and advisers had tipped the military balance in the Republicans' favour. Stalin then set about making sure that the Spanish Republican Loyalists paid a heavy price for his support. Orlov and the cohorts of Soviet advisers in Spain began a none too subtle process of "Stalinization" that was intended to bring the Republican Government and its armed forces under Moscow's direct control. The authority of the Communist faction in the Government was reinforced by a secret police force, modelled on the NKVD, instructed to intimidate, arrest and eliminate opposition elements. The process was accelerated because the Soviet help in holding Madrid had enormously enhanced the prestige of the USSR, promoting a rapid growth of the Communist Party in Spain.

When Moscow's bill came due, it was to Orlov that Stalin looked to see that the Spanish paid up. The first "collection" was the looting of the international treasury.

The vaults of the Bank of Spain contained the fourth largest gold reserve in the world. While Franco could offer only to barter the mineral resources of the northern territories under his control for Hitler's and Mussolini's help, the Republicans held the country's gold reserves. The bullion in the bank vaults in Madrid amounted to 2,367,000,000 pesetas, worth some $788 million. In August $155 million of this enormous hoard had been shipped to France to provide a branch of credit for the supply of fighters and tanks. This had been frozen by the Non-Intervention Pact and to safeguard the remainder of the nation's gold reserves with the Nationalists' army advancing on the capital on 13 September 1936, Largo Caballero's cabinet gave authority to the Prime Minister and his finance Minister, Dr Juan Negrin, to transfer the gold reserves from the capital "to a safe place". In the weeks that followed the bullion was crated and secretly shipped by a guarded train to a huge cave hewn out of the mountain overlooking the port of Cartagena in southern Spain.[27]

When the military fortunes of the Republic were at their bleakest after the fall of Toledo, at the end of the second week of October, Largo Caballero and Negrin decided to offer the gold as an incentive for Stalin to step up arms supplies. Accordingly they proposed the Soviet Union take custody of Spain's hoard of bullion. Stalin jumped at the opportunity to receive half a billion dollars "on account" against the cost of weapons and advisers. He charged Yezhov, who had just replaced Yagoda as NKVD chief, with overall responsibility for getting the Spanish gold to Moscow. Yezhov sent a secret order to Orlov to make the necessary arrangements.

"The enemy came to within twenty miles of Madrid, people were leaving the city, and the opinion of the Government was that Madrid could not be held and the Government was getting ready to abandon Madrid," Orlov later recalled of the chaotic situation on 20 October, when the cryptogram from Moscow arrived at the Gaylord Hotel. The partially deciphered message was brought to his office by the station's code clerk with the current code book under his arm. Having broken out the first line, "I transmit to you the personal order of the Boss", he realized this meant that Yezhov was relaying an order intended for Orlov's eyes only. After personally completing the decryption process, Orlov was confronted with one of the most unusual orders of his career:

> Together with Ambassador Rosenberg, arrange with the head of the Spanish Government, Caballero, for shipment of the gold reserves of Spain to the Soviet Union. Use for that purpose a Soviet steamer. This operation must be carried out with the utmost secrecy. If the Spaniards demand from you a receipt for the cargo,

refuse. I repeat: refuse to sign anything and say that a formal receipt will be issued in Moscow by the State Bank. I hold you personally responsible for this operation. Rosenberg has been informed accordingly.[28]

It was signed "Ivan Valisyevich", the patronymic Stalin customarily employed to indicate communications of the highest secrecy. Orlov was well aware that the telegram made him personally accountable in the event of failure. After consulting with Ambassador Rosenberg, Negrin was summoned to the Soviet embassy to discuss the logistics of the operation.

"This was my first meeting with Juan Negrin and I saw at once that I was dealing with an intelligent man of vivid mind and pleasant personality," Orlov recalled of the conference. "Negrin spoke perfect German and for a time we conversed in German, but when I learned that he also spoke English, I suggested that we continue in English."[29] The Finance Minister offered the assistance of Spanish troops, but, mindful of Stalin's orders to him, Orlov decided it was safer to use a recently arrived contingent of Red Army tank drivers for the delicate mission. "I frankly told Finance Minister Negrin," Orlov later recalled, "that if somebody got wind of it, if the anarchists intercepted Russians with truckloads of Spanish gold, they would kill my men, and it would be a tremendous political scandal all over the world – and it might even create an internal revolution." He proposed they adopt the fiction that the gold was being shipped for safekeeping "not to Russia, but to England or America". Negrin agreed that Orlov should be supplied with papers identifying him as a representative of a leading English or American Bank.[30]

"In what name should we prepare your credentials?" Negrin asked Orlov, who said that he "reflected for a second and wanted to say 'Mr Black'." He was cut short by Negrin who volunteered "Blackstone! How is that?" Orlov recalled that he "took a good look at Negrin" and wondered how he had "snatched the name 'Black' from the tip of my tongue". He then accompanied Negrin to the Finance Ministry, where he was introduced to the chief of the Spanish Treasury, Señor Mendez-Aspe. According to Orlov's account, he was the only Spanish official, apart from the President Manuel Azana, the Prime Minister and the Finance Minister, who knew about the operation.[31]

Next day Orlov recounted how he had a close brush with death when the Spanish military plane he had arranged to fly him to Cartagena was buzzed and shot at by German fighters escorting a bombing raid over Madrid. He was only saved because his pilot managed to put down at a secret airfield in the surrounding hills, where he transferred to a car and returned to Madrid.

"I no longer had a desire to fly," was Orlov's wry reaction to having to set off on the long 300-mile drive to Cartagena. At the Spanish naval base he met Nikolay Kuznetsov, the Soviet naval attaché to Spain. He decided to take him into his confidence, but not to reveal the true nature of the scheme. He led him to believe that nickel ore from Spanish mines was the "strategic material" for which Soviet tank crews needed the assistance of the local Spanish sailors. Kuznetsov arranged with Captain Ramirez de Togores, the Cartagena naval base commander, to supply sixty reliable submariners for five days of special duty. They were deployed to guard the Aladdin's cave full of treasure that was located some five miles away from the naval base.[32]

Ever mindful of Stalin's injunction and aware that Soviet vessels had been stopped and searched by Italian submarines, Orlov decided to split up the Spanish gold among four ships. Orders were given by Kuznetsov that every Soviet captain who entered the ports of Cartagena or Alicante had to report to him, and he arranged for the Spanish navy to deploy every available warship along the dangerous waters off the coast through which the Russian vessels would have to sail. This entailed taking Indalecio Prieto, the Spanish Minister of Defence, into Orlov's confidence, so he made the risky plane flight back to Madrid to present his case to the Spanish Prime Minister who immediately agreed that Prieto and Negrin would come to Cartagena to make the necessary arrangements.

Orlov flew to the port, which was now subject to heavy bombing attacks because of the newly arrived Soviet freighters tied up at Cartagena wharfs. In defiance of the risks, Orlov personally took charge of the unloading of the cargo of planes and bombs, remembering it as "one of my most unpleasant experiences of the Spanish Civil War". As soon as the German planes commenced a raid, the Spanish stevedores would flee in terror. One bomb hit a freighter, narrowly missing a cargo hold full of munitions, and long hours of coaxing them back to the job were set at naught every time a plane flew over the naval base. One evening air-raid alarm set a mob of stevedores on Orlov, convinced that this foreigner was a spy signalling to the incoming planes by lighting a cigarette. Unable to speak a word of Spanish, the Soviet General was only saved when a bomb that exploded near by sent the hostile stevedores running for cover.[33]

The constant air raids made transferring the gold to the docks a hazardous undertaking. The twenty Russian drivers under the command of the tank regiment's NKVD Commissar Savchenko were ordered to don Spanish army uniforms. Their disguise did not help the five-mile drive up treacherous mountainside roads that had to be made with extreme caution, without lights, by the twenty trucks during a succession of moonless nights. The tank drivers had great difficulty keeping their trucks from a precipitous plunge. According to Orlov they had heavy hands from driving their unresponsive tracked vehicles. Arriving with the first night convoy that nevertheless made the trip, Orlov recorded the awesome spectacle that awaited them:

> I stopped at the entrance to the cave. Before me were the wooden doors built into the hill. These were thrown open. I could see in the dim electric light that it was packed with thousands of neat wooden boxes, all of uniform size, and thousands of sacks, piled one upon another. The boxes contained the gold, the sacks bulged with silver coins. Sixty sailors selected from the submarine fleet were there waiting. This was the treasure of Spain, the savings of the Spanish nation throughout the centuries! The whole scene looked eerie: the strange atmosphere of the cave, the dim lights and lurching shadows, the conspiratorial figures of the sailors and their excited black eyes.[34]

It was obvious to Orlov that the Spanish sailors knew the spectacular value of the treasure they were guarding and he reflected how they could easily have overpowered his Soviet drivers. This made it even more imperative for the Spaniards not to know the destination of the bullion as they helped the tank drivers load up. Each truckload of fifty crates had then to be driven down a treacherously narrow mountain road at night during a total blackout. One vehicle overturned and four trucks took a wrong turning, remaining lost until a worried Orlov found them parked in a nearby village square the following day.

The whole operation took three nights to complete because moving the bullion by day was impossible under continuous Nationalist air raids. The Spanish treasury would also have been blown sky-high if a bomb had hit an adjoining cave where thousands of pounds of dynamite was stored. The intensity of the air attacks became so great that it panicked the Treasury official into fleeing down the mountain after assigning an assistant to supervise the tallying of the boxes. On the second night the Spanish sailors became restless and Orlov arranged for them to be supplied with wine, cards, a record player and a supply of records.

"They were all dance records, foxtrots or tangos, and after the meals, during the rest hour, the Spanish boys surprised me by dancing in pairs as seriously as if they were in a regular dance hall," Orlov recollected, noting how "with all the billions of silver coins around them, they modestly played cards for peanuts".[35]

Each of the boxes weighed 145 lbs and contained a king's ransom in bullion bars, gold *pesetas*, French *louis d'or* and British sovereigns. At dawn on the third day Orlov's final count of 7,900 boxes came out 100 boxes ahead of the official Spanish tally. He decided not to challenge the Spanish Treasury Minister's arithmetic at that point for fear that, if Mendez-Aspe's account proved correct, Stalin would accuse him of embezzling two truckloads of bullion.[36]

When the last box of gold had been put aboard the Soviet steamer *Mologoles*, Orlov recalled how Mendez-Aspe had asked him for a formal receipt. "I knew that this would happen and I dreaded the moment," he wrote, "but I had Stalin's personal order and I had to carry it out." Orlov, "feeling a keen sense of shame", had responded "in a casual tone, as if it were just a matter of formality, that a receipt would be issued in Moscow after a final count". The Spanish official gasped when Orlov repeated that a formal acknowledgement could only be issued by the State Bank in Moscow. To eliminate the quandary, Orlov proposed that Mendez-Aspe send a Spanish Treasury official in each freighter as an observer. Only two accompanied him, so another local volunteer had to be found to leave at half an hour's notice before the freighters put out to sea that night.[37]

It was therefore with considerable anxiety that Orlov recalled how he had watched the four grey-painted Soviet steamships depart from Cartagena. The Spanish navy captains on the warships strung out along the coast had been given sealed orders requiring them to go to the aid of the Russians in the event that they picked up an SOS signal. The sailings were reported to Moscow in two separate coded cables: the first alerted NKVD headquarters that he would be using the word "metal" for "gold".

"What metal are you talking about?" came Yezhov's response to Orlov's second signal notifying him of the freighters' departure. Convinced that "an idiot" was now the head of the NKVD, Orlov sent a third cable: "See my previous telegram. Please report my cable to Ivan Vasilyevich."[38]

"I was waiting for about seven or eight days on tenterhooks," was how Orlov described the long week he spent wondering whether the ships would make safe passage through the Mediterranean blockade. Only when eight days had passed with no alarm did he feel it safe to send a detailed report on the operation to the Centre, informing Yezhov that there was a 100-box discrepancy in the official Spanish account. An immediate query came back: "Ivan Vasilyevich asks whether you are sure of your figure?" To which Orlov responded that he was certain, since the count of boxes made by the captains of the four steamers tallied with his own. He said he later requested to know whether his total of 7,900 boxes was correct, receiving the terse answer: "Don't worry about the figures. Everything will be counted in Moscow." This was followed by another cable from Yezhov: "Do not mention your figure to anybody."[39]

The Soviet convoy reached Odessa without incident on 6 November and the ships were unloaded at night to maintain strict security and put on a special train with a guard of 100 armed officers. The deputy chief of the Ukraine NKVD personally went along to report the successful completion of the mission to Yezhov, his face covered in soot after riding the locomotive cab all the way to Moscow. There the counting began, supervised by the three officials from the Spanish Treasury, who then found themselves prevented from returning home for four years to keep the story of the single biggest gold heist in history from leaking out.[40]

The night the trainload of Spanish bullion arrived in Moscow, Stalin held a drunken party of his closest cronies to celebrate. With the avarice of a modern-day conquistador, the Big Boss gloated over receiving so much capitalist plunder. Later Orlov was to learn from Mikhail Koltsov, then the editor of *Pravda* and a friend of Yezhov who came on a visit to Spain, that at this banquet Stalin had boasted of his coup by recasting an old Russian proverb: "The Spaniards will never see their gold again, as they don't see their own ears."[41]

Stalin was as good as his word. Twenty years later, when Orlov testified in 1957 before the Senate Internal Security Sub-Committee and recounted how he had organized the looting of the Spanish Treasury, Radio Moscow announced that the $420 millions' worth of Spanish gold smuggled to Russia in 1937 had been sent legitimately to "finance the Republican cause".[42] Franco's Government was pressing the Soviets to send back the bullion after Negrin's heirs had returned to Madrid the official receipt for "510,079,243 grams of gold" which the Bank of Moscow had given to the cashiers of the Bank of Spain in 1938.[43]

According to Orlov's testimony, Stalin had never intended to act as a reserve banker for the Spanish Treasury. He recalled how he had been informed of this by his NKVD boss early in 1937, when he was in Paris in the private clinic of Dr Bergère recuperating from a back injury he had suffered in a car accident. At that time he had received a visit from Slutsky, the chief of the Foreign Department, who congratulated him in person on the gold operation, in the course of which he too recounted Stalin's drunken boast that Spain could kiss goodbye to its gold.

Nikita Khruschev, the Soviet President in 1957, certainly was not going to return a single *peseta* of Republican money to the Fascist regime of Franco. This was made clear in a broadcast by Moscow Radio in which the USSR reminded the world that the value of Soviet aid delivered to the Spanish Government during the Civil War amounted to much more than the value of 510 metric tons of gold.

According to the statement the Spanish account with the USSR was still overdrawn because of the Republicans' failure to repay $50 million of an additional $85 million in supplies which they had allegedly been loaned officially.

After the gold episode, Orlov turned his energies and organizational talents to building up a Moscow-controlled secret police force in Spain. His task was to persuade the Republicans to set up a central security service, but records show that the embryo organization, modelled on the NKVD, was disrupted by the evacuation of Government agencies from the besieged capital to Valencia.

"The Government has established a political counter-intelligence organization which has fallen to pieces after the evacuation of this ministry from Madrid," Orlov explained to the Centre in his letter of 29 December 1936. He reported that an anarchist force had arrested Houstinianos, who had been appointed head of the new establishment, after finding 500 kilogrammes of gold and valuable paintings in his car. The Republicans' secret police chief had protested that he had been rescuing, not looting, the gold and paintings. But Orlov had voiced reservations about his honesty. "Nobody can be trusted in this organization," he complained to Slutsky. "I always paraphrase the information which I receive from intercepted telegrams of the local foreign consulates to disguise its source." He went on to explain that in the provinces he had found the situation even more chaotic. Parallel counter-intelligence organizations owing loyalty to different political factions continued to function independently. It had proved impossible to make them follow the Centre's directives, so he asked Moscow to consider, as a matter of urgency, sending him more staff: "The only way out is to attach our advisers to the provincial outfits, to the more important cities and military centres."[44]

At the beginning of 1937 Stalin, with the Spanish Treasury as security, was ready to provide more help to the Republicans. Their military fortunes were also looking up after the Popular Army, as it was now called, had demonstrated new competence and cohesion under Soviet discipline. During the early months of that year, assisted by the growing International Brigade and Soviet tank units, the Nationalists had been beaten back with their Italian allies in two flanking attacks at Jarama and Guadalajara. These setbacks forced Franco to pull back his forces and concentrate on subjugating the northern provinces not yet fully under Nationalist control. To achieve this Franco's army called on German and Italian air power to terrorize the civilian population. The savage bombing of Guernica by the Luftwaffe's Condor Legion on 26 April proved a propaganda disaster for the Nationalists. Although postwar investigation revealed that some of the damage was inflicted by the Republicans' defence of the town, the savagery of the bombing raid brought a shift of international sympathy to the Republicans.

Yet, despite the transformation in the Loyalists' military prospects, Orlov reported to Moscow as early as February 1937 his doubts about the Republican Government's ability to exploit the opportunities opened up by the Nationalist army's withdrawal from Madrid. It proved to be such a prescient forecast of the future course of the war and of the underlying reasons for the eventual Republican defeat that it merits quotation in full:

The Spanish Government possess all the possibilities for waging a victorious war: they have modern weapons, an excellent air force, tanks, a navy and great human resources. They hold a sizeable territory with a war industry base which is more than adequate for supporting such a "small" war (Hispano Suiza's plants and others). Adequate provision base and so on. The number of Government troops outnumbers the enemy considerably. But this whole machine and all these resources are corroded by:
1. Inter-party conflicts in which the energy of most people is devoted to winning authority and power in the country for their own party and discrediting others rather than to the struggle against Fascism.
2. The corrupt composition of the Government, part of which has got nothing in common with the Revolution and which reacts to events passively and whose only consideration is preparing a timely escape in the event of a collapse.
3. The Government's failure to appreciate the real danger of the situation as a result of anxieties and excessive panics. The true threat to the fortunes of the Republican Government of Spain is now perceived by them as a normal state of alarm.
4. Irresponsibility and sabotage by Government bodies and staff in supplying the army and directing its operations.
5. Failure to mobilize hundreds of thousands of healthy men living in cities (Madrid, Barcelona, Valencia and a number of others) for civil works and erecting fortifications.
6. The absence of an experienced Soviet staff with clear authority and the absence of a really prominent adviser on our part. Gorev [the Soviet military attaché] has no military experience. In war affairs he is a child. Grishin [the alias of General Berzin, the former GRU chief] is a good Party member, but he's not an expert – and this is the pinnacle of our [military] command. With such [a lack of] leadership the abilities of a number of our specialists subordinated

to them are brought to naught. (Only the air force and tanks and their heroic personnel are good, but they cannot stand in for an army.)[45]

Orlov's criticism of the military competence of his Russian comrades became even more outspoken when it came to pinpointing the weakness of Spanish intelligence and counter-intelligence operations and the need for more direct Soviet control:

> It seems to me that the time has come when it is necessary to analyze the threatening situation that has come to pass and forcefully present to the Spanish Government (and Party leaders) the issue of the full gravity of the situation and to propose the necessary [corrective] measures – if the Spanish Government really wants help from us: (1) Bringing the army and its command into a healthier state of discipline (shooting deserters, maintaining discipline, etc.) and (2) putting an end to the inter-party squabbles.
> If, in the face of immediate danger, we do not bring the Spanish Government to its senses, events will take a catastrophic turn. The fall of Madrid would bring in its turn the demoralization of the army and rebellions and betrayal by certain regions in Catalonia.[46]

Despite Orlov's accurate assessment of the underlying weakness of the Republicans, his words fell on deaf ears in both Moscow and Madrid. As NKVD chief in Spain his authority extended only to espionage, counter-intelligence and guerilla operations. His brief had been to create a secret police system to counter internal opposition in the Republican Government which was increasingly beholden to the Kremlin. The extent to which Orlov succeeded is detailed by the contemporary NKVD records. Documentation that provides a salutary reminder that if Orlov had been given his way, Spain might have become a Soviet satellite state, like the eastern European nations liberated by the Red Army during World War II only to find themselves chained to Stalin's USSR.

"FORBIDDEN SUBJECTS"

G ENERAL ALEXANDER ORLOV's efforts to build up a secret police force under NKVD control to effect a Stalinization of Spain did not go unnoticed, or unchallenged, by ministers of the Republican administration. In his memoirs the Communist Education Minister, José Hernandez, bitterly and specifically attacked the NKVD chief for his sinister role in establishing and directing the SIM, the acronym for the feared Servicio de Investigaciòn Militar, which he believed was intended to become the mechanism for enforcing a totalitarian state in Spain.[1] In March 1937 General Berzin had sent a confidential report to War Commissar Vorishilov reporting resentment and protests he had received about the NKVD's repressive operations from high Republican officials. It stated that the NKVD agents were compromising Soviet authority by their excessive interference and espionage in Government quarters. They were treating Spain like a colony. The ranking Red Army General concluded his report with a demand that Orlov be recalled from Spain at once.[2]

"Berzin is absolutely right," Slutsky allegedly told another NKVD officer, Walter Krivitsky, who happened to be in Moscow when the General's report arrived. The head of the Foreign Department, he said, went on to assert that "our men were behaving in Spain as if they were in a colony, treating even Spanish leaders as colonists handle natives". When Krivitsky asked what action he was going to take, Slutsky told him it was "up to Yezhov", the NKVD chief.[3]

When in exile in the postwar United States, Orlov repeatedly denounced the assertions of his former comrade Krivitsky as unfounded. He would vehemently deny any personal involvement in repressive secret police operations, nor would he concede that the NKVD in Spain was involved in the brutal suppression of anti-Communist opposition elements in, or outside of, the Republican Government. Orlov sought to portray himself in his books, to the FBI and before the Senate Committees, as a professional adviser to the Spanish Government on counter-intelligence and guerilla warfare. He charged that those who accused him of sinister activities on behalf of Stalin were motivated by Trotskyist sympathies and that he was the innocent victim of lying propaganda.

Orlov's repeated denials are, however, now exposed as lies by the Soviet archival records. Indeed it is a measure of the willingness of the Russian Intelligence Service to serve the interests of history that they permitted the publication of the records which finally confirm the darker side of Orlov's operations as Stalin's NKVD chief in Spain. The charges made by Hernandez and others that Orlov directed a Stalinist purge of Spanish Marxists and Trotskyites can now be corroborated from his actual reports and documents in the archive records.

The *Correspondence of the Rezidentura in Spain* shows how the NKVD directed repressive operations. Like those of its Soviet parent, these were an outgrowth of, and response to, anti-subversion counter-intelligence operations. For example, within two months of Orlov's arrival, his agents had uncovered an outpost of the Deuxième Bureau of the French General Staff in Barcelona. "6,000 documents have been photographed," Orlov reported to the Centre, informing them that "the file of the resident ALEXANDER is interesting. Italian and German agents have been exposed."[4] On 1 March 1937 in another dispatch he noted: "With our assistance in Madrid, two Fascist organizations have been exposed: twenty-seven and thirty-two people. In Valencia, on the basis of the Italian consul's archive, Italians have been arrested [including] the Bogani brothers and Karloti Politi and thirteen Spaniards. Politi confessed that they had been conducting intelligence work since 1930 in Valencia at the direction of the Italian consul."[5]

Orlov's counter-intelligence operations were expanded after a contingent of NKVD officers arrived from Moscow. By May 1937 the General had his Soviet security advisers stationed in the local Spanish security organizations in Madrid, Barcelona, Bilbao and Almeria. From his own headquarters in the Hotel Metropole in Valencia on the eastern coast, Orlov directed not only the NKVD personnel, but also encouraged the growing power of the SIM, the Spanish Republican military secret police. Its location, midway between Barcelona and Cartagena, gave Orlov easy access to travel to the other regions under Republican control and also enabled him to cross the Pyrenees to make his rendezvous with Philby in France.

In May 1937, after scanning the latest results of his expanding counter-intelligence network in Spain, Orlov catalogued his successes, with evident satisfaction:

A spy has been arrested: an International Brigade Lieutenant Maksim Starr, a member of NSDAP, a Gestapo agent, a former member of the SA, a provocateur in the German Communist Party

(KPD). German spies Ernst Klement and Müller have been arrested, a radio transmitter has been taken. The chief of German espionage in Spain, the former attaché ALEX has been discovered in the Dutch embassy and arrested. As a result penetration agent, King Alfonso's nephew, Lieutenant Colonel José Bourbon de la Torres, has been arrested on our instruction. The investigation is uncovering his Fascist contacts. In Valencia an underground stock of arms and 400 bombs has been discovered. A prominent speculator, Markenstein, who received £5,000 from Prieto for supplying weapons has been exposed and arrested.[6]

Reports Orlov received from his growing web of agents suggest that the British intelligence service did not miss any opportunity to spy on both sides of the front line in Spain, by resorting to some ingenious combinations:

An intelligence service agent, the Hindu [Anglo-Indian] Eric Edward Dutt, arrived in Valencia from Salamanca on assignment from the Intelligence Service [MI6] chief in Gibraltar, Murphy. In Salamanca Dutt contacted Gestapo chief Fischer. During the search, a copy of the secret report sent from Salamanca to the Intelligence Service about his activity during the period of his stay on Franco's territory was found on Dutt. On the basis of available information from the [NKVD] agents, the British intelligence officer King also has been arrested. On him was discovered an Intelligence Service questionnaire for filling in information on the state of Republican troops. King's informant, Rudolf Schirman, a German arrested in connection with this case, was a member of an International Brigade.[7]

The four thick archive volumes of operational correspondence relating to the NKVD field station in Spain are full of Orlov's reports of the discovery of spies in Republican ranks whose penetrations were facilitated by the infighting of political factions as much as by the confusion of the Civil War. They also disclose that Orlov achieved considerable successes by launching his own penetration operations, thereby assisting the irregular forces of the Republicans (which he played a leading role in directing) in spreading subversion and confusion in Franco's rear lines.

"The guerilla operations in Spain began in rather a modest way with the organization of two saboteur schools for about 200 men each, one in Madrid and the other in Benimamet, near Valencia. Later four more schools were added, one of which in Barcelona numbered 600 men,"

Orlov recorded in his *Handbook* in which he devoted twenty pages to writing about guerilla warfare.[8] His contemporary reports to Moscow confirm that by April 1937 his training camps were operating in Valencia, Barcelona, Bilbao and Argen, where the school to train guerilla commanders was located. At these camps for young Spaniards in the Republican army, German Communists from the International Brigade and even former Tsarist officers hoping to earn the right to return to their homeland were taught demolition work, marksmanship and how to execute raids and ambushes by living off the land while making long marches carrying twenty-five-pound backpacks. One cavalry and five unmounted assault groups were formed. Orlov himself supervised an armoured group consisting of three captured German tanks and seven German Internationalists who trained alongside a Red Army airborne group of saboteurs for parachute operations in Franco's rear.

"The Republican guerilla force grew fast, and by the summer of 1937 its operations became more sophisticated," according to Orlov. "Guerilla commandos had assignments not only to destroy lines of communications but also to harass the enemy deeper in his territory by attacking arsenals and ambushing moving columns and supply convoys."[9]

Orlov clearly relished directing the *"Marxistu guerilleros"* as the Nationalist press branded the Republican irregular forces, on Franco's orders. For Orlov it was an opportunity to put into effect many of the tactical lessons he had learned in his youthful days commanding the troops on the Polish front during the Russian civil war. His fifty-strong guerilla platoons would operate often 150 kilometres behind the battle front, penetrating deep into enemy-held territory to blow up power lines and bridges. Then they would wait to ambush the Nationalist troops who were invariably sent to the scene. He records how one night operation against an enemy convoy destroyed twelve trucks and on another night Nationalist airfields were attacked by the guerilla group led by his outstanding guerilla fighter, a Captain Nikolayevsky. This blond giant took to wearing a swastika armband to fool Nationalist guards into believing he was a German; the Spanish guards were dismayed to discover that their "allies" were shooting up rows of Franco's parked aircraft.[10]

A rigorous Republican guerilla campaign was conducted by Orlov during the summer and autumn of 1937 with his units penetrating more than 300 kilometres deep into Nationalist territory. Among the mineral mines in Rio Tinto and Aroche, the wild mountains of the Asturias along Spain's north coast proved ideal terrain for such operations. They tied up thousands of Nationalist troops and played havoc with the production of the world's largest copper mines, causing a drop in output of the rich ore which Franco traded for German armaments. More than 3,000 Republicans were eventually engaged in this guerilla warfare, many recruited from the ranks of sympathetic Spanish miners. They proved adept at making mortar bombs out of sticks of captured blasting dynamite. Supplied by air drops from Soviet-built transports, these partisan groups were directed on the ground by Major Strik and Captain Glusko, two of Orlov's most experienced Soviet irregular warfare experts.[11]

These guerilla campaigns not only helped the Republican army tactically retain the military initiative during the better part of 1937, but, as Orlov later pointed out, provided Soviet officers with expertise which was later used by the Red Army in their campaign against the Germans in World War II. A Spanish sabotage group, so vividly portrayed by Ernest Hemingway in his Civil War novel *For Whom the Bell Tolls* finds its echo in Orlov's real-life readiness reports: "A guerilla detachment of thirty-two men is ready. The training has been somewhat delayed since we have managed to obtain combat horses, and cavalry training was needed. Besides, it was necessary to give instruction in the use of explosives. The detachment is equipped with machine guns (heavy and light), carbines, grenades and a supply of explosives and detonators. One day soon the detachment will travel over to the rear [of the line] in the district of Aranjuez."[12]

"The capture of Teruel and the fighting off of Franco's brutal assaults have been a turning point for both the army and the country," Orlov informed Moscow Centre in December 1937.[13] But for all his successes, his acute strategic eye led him to express doubt that the Republican army "had learned how to fight and withstand battles whose ferocity exceeds those of World War I". The Loyalist forces had in fact reached the climax of their offensive phase of the war in December 1937 in capturing the walled city of Teruel that had been a Nationalist stronghold in the mountains of Aragon. But its recapture by Franco two months later was a signal that the enemy had learned to mount effective counter-measures to the guerillas by successfully defending vital lines of communication.

"The subversive work [guerilla operations] remains very important," Orlov informed Moscow, along with a caution that it "was becoming incredibly difficult" to carry out operations since the Nationalists had "begun serious guarding of roads, bridges, railroad tracks and electricity transmission lines". Increasingly his guerilla bands were having to rely on "surgical operations". They now proceeded to raid the enemy's concentration camps with the aim of freeing arrested Communists and Socialist workers, who, according to Orlov, could then be trained to "infiltrate and take over small towns that do not have garrisons like Segovia".[14]

Throughout 1937 Orlov devoted his main efforts to running a successful guerilla war in central and northern Spain, yet the files of his NKVD station show that he did not neglect his first responsibility: intelligence-gathering operations. When he learned that the Republican Government had no organization capable of gathering political intelligence abroad, he had one built up from scratch. By May 1937 he was able to send to Moscow the first intelligence reports gathered by a network of Spanish journalists and diplomats abroad, an *apparat* Orlov co-ordinated through the Information Department of the Ministry of Foreign Affairs.

"The good relations struck up between us and the Ministry of Foreign Affairs," Orlov advised the Centre, "makes it possible for us to read all cryptograms being sent and received by the foreign legations in Spain." Of particular interest to Moscow were the foreign intelligence reports of German troop movements and the identity of their agents, amongst whom was listed a niece of General von Blomberg, Hitler's army Chief of Staff. She was apparently "directing espionage work in Barcelona". Another female agent Orlov identified in Marseilles "was working for Franco, as was the turncoat Spanish Loyalist consul in Montpellier".[15]

These sources which Orlov developed with the aid of the Spanish offered an opportunity for the NKVD to expand the range of its overseas intelligence operations. The networks built up by the Valencia field station soon extended Orlov's reach into Spanish Morocco and France. The NKVD records show that a measure of the trust in Orlov was that he was given an unusual degree of independence. In contrast to other NKVD station chiefs, he did not have to request authorization from Moscow for every major administrative and operational decision he took in Spain. This unfortunately makes it more difficult to track many of Orlov's operations because they were simply not reported and are not detailed in the archive files. Some of the most intriguing cases which he was involved with in Spain are only alluded to cryptically in fragmentary reports. This is the case in an operation referred to in his letter to Moscow of 29 December 1936: "I beg you to send at least two or three radio transmitters. One is needed to provide our network in Gibraltar about which I informed you. The second will be needed for the nephew of Franco's premier (K. code-named NEPHEW) who has been sent by us to the enemy."[16]

What this report does is reveal how Orlov was tapping into a high-level intelligence source within Franco's inner circle. One of his most reliable sources in the Nationalist camp was Kim Philby. As already recounted, Philby was for a time under consideration for an assassination attempt on Franco and Orlov regularly obtained information from the British journalist in person by making trips to Narbonne and other towns along the French side of the Spanish border.[17]

The Spanish *rezidentura* files also reveal that Orlov used his wife, Maria, whose cryptonym was JEANNE, as a courier. One report states that JEANNE "after a two-month gap has now established contact with SÖHNCHEN's wife", indicating that Philby's estranged spouse, Litzi Friedman, who then in Lisbon, was meeting with Orlov's wife. This adds a new twist to Philby's story because, even though she had long been living apart from her husband, Litzi was still maintaining an operational relationship for the Soviet intelligence service.[18] Philby also served as the model for Orlov to exploit other foreign journalists as Soviet agents. This is evident from a letter to Moscow in May 1937 in which he named other potential recruits whom a female Soviet agent operating under the code name of KARO had under cultivation:

About the mission for sending people to Franco's rear, both anarchists and by selecting journalists in England: KARO was sent by me on a mission to Paris, where she communicated the assignment to the Englishman B— E— to select several reliable journalists in London for sending to the other side. B— E— has been recommended to us by our source, an English journalist B—, a representative of the United Press (American). On 24th May I shall have a meeting in Paris with candidates for transferring over to Franco.[19]

The precise identification of the English and American journalists is impossible from the surviving records. Nor is there any evidence on whether Orlov's trip to Paris to recruit them was successful. What is also not clear is precisely what was the outcome of Orlov's intention to tap Winston Churchill's son Randolph, then a prominent journalist, when he visited Spain in the spring of 1937. There is a reference to him in the NKVD Barcelona station files which suggests that he too was approached by KARO. That they discussed an operation in which Churchill appears to have volunteered his help is evident from a paragraph contained in Orlov's report of 4 May 1937: "I draw your attention to the enclosed report about our connection with Lord [sic] Churchill and the valuable service he is ready to render to us. We hope with his assistance to send, through the British Fascist organizations, doctors and nurses to Franco for intelligence purposes." The contact is corroborated by KARO in her account of her work in Spain in the NKVD archives. But what the incomplete records do not reveal is whether this particular plan to exploit the Churchill connection was ever put into effect.[20]

Specific information is also missing on Orlov's more ambitious projects such as his scheme to select and train Germans and Italians fighting on the Republican side for subversive operations in their home countries in the event that Hitler and Mussolini – as he predicted – would unleash another general European war. Another of Orlov's ingenious operations was to arrange for Governor Bretel of Murcia, the province adjoining Valencia, to organize a rebellion through his contacts in Spanish Morocco, the strategic off-shore base from which Franco had launched his campaign and from which he continued to obtain arms and military personnel. The Governor was an avowed Communist, so employing him in an NKVD operation without clearing it with Moscow was strictly against the rules. The Centre nonetheless turned a blind eye to Orlov enlisting Bretel for an operation which, in January 1937, looked very promising. Following Bretel's trip to Morocco, Orlov reported how the Governor of Murcia had set up a six-man group, which reported that it would take only the French Government's consent and "several million francs" to start an insurrection. When the French let it be known that they had grave reservations about an anti-Franco rebellion that might spill over into their own Moroccan territory, the ever resourceful Orlov put into effect what would now be termed an "active measure".[21]

Ingenuity and audacity were typical of Orlov's carefully contrived operations, and this one was no exception. It depended for its success on the fact that, at the very beginning of the war in Spain, the NKVD's Barcelona field station had recruited the Russian emigré Alexander Matveyevich Asangayev, a prominent transport engineer who had emigrated to Spain after building the Murmansk railroad line and a number of foreign seaports. His hour of glory had come in 1936, when Orlov charged him with preparing a scheme "to make up a fictitious plan of German expansion in Spain, directed principally against France". His original intention was to arrange for details of the plan to fall into French hands "accidentally" after being worked up by the Soviet Consul General in Barcelona, Antonov Ovseenko. It was SANGO, as Asangayev was code-named, who developed an elaborate deception and submitted the bogus documentation personally to Orlov for his approval.

"The documents are compiled in such a way that their publication would intimidate the French [General] Staff and public opinion in

France," Orlov assured the Centre, informing them that "Antonov wants us to publish the documents in Paris now to coincide with the League of Nations session".[22] He therefore asked Moscow to certify the "authenticity" of the skilfully forged papers that were designed to show that Hitler was preparing to isolate France both from Spain and her African colonies by sending German troops to occupy strategic points on the Iberian peninsula and in the Balearic Islands. "The documents have allegedly been found by the Spanish authorities on the premises of the German embassy in Madrid," Orlov reported. "We enclose the material consisting of two memoranda: first a military strategic plan (with a chart and a map); second an economic plan."[23]

The deception scheme, which had originally been conceived in December 1936, was finally put into effect with Moscow's approval in the summer of 1937. By September Orlov was able to report to the Centre that information obtained through his own agents in Paris revealed it had been only a partial success. The French General Staff swallowed the bait and made a secret report to the Government underscoring the "fatal impact for France of a victory by Franco", according to Orlov. Orlov wrote that his own reliable sources had assured him that "the French Government is inclined to render active assistance to Republican Spain by supplying weapons", but the Madrid Government had not followed this up. The Republicans, moreover, had repeatedly failed to win French co-operation for anything more than an occasional brief opening of their border with Spain to permit the passage of shipments of weapons.[24]

Orlov was more successful in his clandestine efforts to exploit the soldiers of the International Brigades for Soviet espionage activity. Given the heavy casualty rate among the front-line units who fought in the battle of Madrid under the unrelenting command of Soviet officers answerable to General Kleber, the passports of dead volunteers – especially those of the Lincoln Battalion of Americans – were seized by the NKVD as spoils of war. It was from among the surviving veterans that Orlov picked potential recruits to swell the ranks of the NKVD's international underground networks. Many were young Communists who burned with ideological zeal and anti-Fascist fervour. They provided the raw material from which Orlov handpicked recruits for training as secret underground servants of the world revolution. A secret spy school was set up under his direction for training underground intelligence agents along the lines of the Military School in Moscow, on whose faculty he had served before coming to Spain. Operating under the code name CONSTRUCTION, the first NKVD extraterritorial spy school, unlike their guerilla warfare and subversion camps, was operated clandestinely and its existence was deliberately concealed from the Spanish authorities.[25]

"Taking into consideration that the whole school is illegal," Orlov reported to Moscow at the beginning of 1938, it had been no small triumph to keep it functioning "during the strictest mobilization" and he said that he had trouble preventing his trainee agents from being conscripted. He personally selected candidates for training, International Brigade soldiers whom his Soviet officers had selected as those most committed to the idea of waging a secret war against international Fascism. After a thorough training course in the rules of *Konspiratsia*, secret communications, espionage and underground work, the cream of the CONSTRUCTION graduates were considered too valuable to commit to work for the NKVD in Spain. They were instead taken out through France into western Europe, whence they dispersed on operational assignments in their home countries. The security surrounding the Spanish spy school was so strict that its students were registered only by numbers to protect their identities. Their real names were known only to a very restricted number of people, including Orlov himself. Even for the NKVD such secrecy was unusual. Confirmation of this appears in a letter Orlov wrote on 10 May 1938 to the Centre. "I request that you send the prepared passports to my name marked *Strictly Personal* so that nobody will know their new surnames."[26]

The curriculum of the CONSTRUCTION training programme was supervised by Orlov who therefore became "godfather" to many important secret agents. The existence of the illegal spy school he ran in Spain was another secret that Orlov carefully concealed from the Americans, as were the identities of some of its most promising students. Among those who can now be named were Wilhelm Fellendorf and Albert Hoessler, who later served as underground radio operators for the Berlin branch of the *Rote Kapelle*. One graduate was a United States citizen who went on to become a member of the espionage network that helped the Soviets steal from the United States the production secrets for nuclear weapons.

Orlov's NKVD file reveals that it was he who personally selected, trained and recruited Morris Cohen, a Jewish American from Brooklyn who had volunteered to fight with the Abraham Lincoln Battalion in Spain. A dedicated Communist and a former high school football star, Cohen was selected for training at the secret spy school, where he demonstrated a special aptitude for undercover work. His NKVD file shows that in terms of resourcefulness and longevity,

Cohen's active career rivalled that of Philby.

"In April 1938," Cohen recalled in his KGB autobiography, "I was one of a group of various nationalities sent to a conspiratorial school in Barcelona. Our chief commissar and leaders were Soviets." After returning to the United States and serving in the US army during World War II, Cohen and his no less dedicated Communist wife Lona became involved in the Soviet atomic espionage network. In contrast to Julius and Ethel Rosenberg, who despite their denials of complicity were found guilty and were executed in the electric chair at the New York state penitentiary at Ossining in 1953, Morris Cohen and his wife managed to escape the FBI dragnet which rolled up the Soviet atomic spy ring in 1950. They slipped abroad, where another Cambridge-educated underground Soviet agent, a diplomat named Daniel Patrick Costello, obtained New Zealand passports for them in the name of Peter and Helen Kroger. The couple then travelled to England, where they resumed operations, setting up as antiquarian booksellers in west London. Their suburban bungalow in Ruislip provided radio and technical support for a Soviet espionage ring run by Gordon Lonsdale, a KGB "illegal" whose real name was Konon Timofeevich Molody. Their network stole underwater weapons and submarine secrets from the British naval base at Portland until their second ring was broken up in 1961 after a CIA tip-off from their Polish penetration agent Michael Golienewski.[27]

After the conviction in a sensational espionage trial, the British judge handed down stiff prison sentences on Molody, the Cohens and their associates Harry Houghton and Ethel Gee, the members of the so-called Portland spy ring. Molody served only three of his twenty-five years' sentence before being freed in a spy swap. The Cohens, however, served out the greater part of their prison term before being repatriated to Moscow where they lived in quiet retirement after a turbulent life of espionage, into which Morris Cohen had been initiated in Spain by Alexander Orlov.

Kirill Khenkin was another International Brigade volunteer whose Jewish family had left Russia in 1923. A dedicated Marxist, Khenkin found that French Communists were of little help to a former Soviet citizen "eager to go and fight Fascism". His passage to Spain from Paris in the spring of 1937 was eventually arranged by Serge Efron, a Soviet emigré like Khenkin who happened to be a member of Orlov's French network. "My assignment was to get to Valencia, go to the Hotel Metropole, and ask for Comrade Orlov," was how Khenkin recalled the instructions he was given. Efron had assured him that "anyone could fight in the trenches", but by reporting to this particular Russian General, he would receive an "interesting" assignment, although he had not explained precisely what that "interesting" work would be.[28]

As Khenkin later recalled, he was full of anticipation when he arrived in Valencia, tired and hungry after an overnight train journey in a carriage full of French International Brigade volunteers with whom he had travelled across the frontier. He had no difficulty finding Orlov's headquarters in the eight-storey Hotel Metropole because it was the newest and smartest hotel in the city, adjoining the bull ring and facing the railway station.

"Tanned, fair-haired men in uniform sat in touring cars parked in front of the hotel; armed Serbian guards stood at the entrance," according to Khenkin. "Behind the front desk, along with the hotel employees, stood some men in civilian clothes with piercing eyes – the kind that are the same the world over." He quickly realized he was in the headquarters of Soviet intelligence in Spain when he was escorted up to the sixth floor and into the spacious suite of the General in charge of NKVD operations. His first impression of Orlov was that he was very far from being a typical Soviet military officer. Khenkin's recollection is of a fastidious man, more accustomed to his creature comforts than the rigours of the front line: "When we entered the room, Orlov sat down a considerable distance from me. I was amazed at how well groomed he was. He had just shaved and doused himself with eau de Cologne. He was wearing morning dress: flannel trousers, and a silk shirt without a tie. At his belt was a 7.65 Walther pistol in an open suede holster."

It was not simply the gun, or the strong scent of Cologne that lodged in the memory of the unkempt, dog-tired young volunteer who had just been through an International Brigade boot camp, but the lavish breakfast wheeled in on a trolley by a white-coated servant that "entranced and paralyzed" him. "Orlov buttered some hot toast, bit off one corner and set to work on his ham and eggs, occasionally taking some coffee," Khenkin recalled, noting how the General did not touch the cream. "He listened to me distractedly, sometimes asking questions that were intended to confuse me. But for the most part he didn't interrupt me. As for me, I tried hard not to stare at the food – not to disguise the fact that I was hungry, but in order not to lose face. I hadn't eaten for twenty-four hours." After mopping up the egg yolk with a croissant and draining his coffee cup, Orlov pulled out a packet of Lucky Strikes, lit a cigarette and dismissively informed the dazed Khenkin, "We'll get in touch with you."[29]

The summons from NKVD headquarters never came. After sizing

him up as a potential candidate for the spy school, Orlov had evidently decided that this young Russian emigré from France was not cut out for "interesting work" in the Soviet intelligence service. Khenkin, who would later claim to have trained as an NKVD "illegal" after returning to the USSR, was instead assigned to a guerilla unit in Spain. He encountered Orlov only one more time, in Barcelona the following year shortly before the General's abrupt departure from Spain.

Khenkin may not have made the grade himself, but he became personally acquainted with a number of those in the International Brigade who worked for the NKVD on undercover operations against the Trotskyist factions in Spain. One of them was Lothar Marx, an exiled German Communist who had made the journey with Khenkin from France. Marx, according to Khenkin, never actually served in any of the International Brigades or in any of the partisan units, but periodically visited Khenkin's guerilla outfit and the hostel in the avenida del Tibidabo where the partisans lived. "Orlov would send a car for him and he would go (usually at night) to report to him," Khenkin wrote. "He himself used to tell me that he was serving as a political worker in a Trotskyite unit." Later he admitted that he had managed to worm his way into the leadership of the Trotskyists. Khenkin also met other Russian exiles in Spain who were prominent in Trotskyist units, including one named Narvich, who he remembered was "clobbered in a dark alley" when it was discovered that he was an NKVD spy.[30]

Orlov, as Khenkin learned from Lothar and other comrades working for NKVD counter-intelligence in Spain, controlled penetration agents to infiltrate the Catalonian-based POUM (*Partido Obrero de Unificación Marxista* – The Workers' Party of Marxist Unification). According to what Khenkin learned, "the rooting out of Trotskyism and the destruction of the Trotskyites was done under the direct supervision of Orlov".[31] Ramon Mercader, the Spaniard who in 1941 would eventually succeed in murdering Trotsky in Mexico with a mountain ice axe, was one of Khenkin's comrades in the partisan units which fought behind Nationalist lines. According to Khenkin's account, Mercader had special privileges because he was well regarded by "the higher ups". Ramon's mother, the glamorous Caridad Mercader del Rio, was a friend – some claim was the mistress – of Leonid Eitingon,[32] Orlov's principal deputy in Spain. Apart from running Guy Burgess, Eitingon's main task was directing the partisan operations under the alias of Colonel Naum Kotov. Mercader became a member of Orlov's inner circle and it came as no surprise to Khenkin to learn early in 1938 that Eitingon had arranged for him to be sent to

Moscow for special training.[33] Since it was Orlov who obtained his passport, Khenkin points out that he must have been aware of the mission for which Mercader was being groomed: the assassination of Trotsky.

Orlov, it turns out from the *rezidentura* records, was much more deeply implicated in Stalin's relentless pursuit of Trotsky and his French and Spanish disciples than he ever admitted in his statements to the FBI or the Senate. The principal target of the NKVD's operations in Spain was the POUM, the revolutionary Catalonian group of Marxists who had declared war on Stalin, accusing the Soviet dictator of betraying the Revolution by establishing "the bureaucratic regime of a poisoned traitor". Urged on by their leader Andrés Nin, the radical Spanish Marxists invited Trotsky to live in Barcelona, proclaiming the need to bring down the "bourgeois democracy" of the Communist-backed Popular Front administration of the Spanish Republic.[34] A prominent figure in Trotskyist circles, Nin had gone to Russia after the October Revolution in 1917, where he became a close associate of Trotsky. After Trotsky was exiled from the USSR in 1929, Nin left him to return to Barcelona, where in 1935, together with Joaquin Maurin, he had founded his revolutionary Marxist Party. The POUM threw down the gauntlet to Stalin in 1937, just as the Soviet dictator was accelerating his purge of the Bolshevik old guard in the USSR under the guise of rooting out Trotskyist subversion. What was ultimately to prove a fatal challenge for Nin and many of his supporters was made at the time when Soviet influence over the Spanish Government reached its zenith after the Republican army's victory over the Nationalists at Guadalajara. Moscow's influence was reinforced by the NKVD, which, under Orlov's direction, had established firm control over Spanish secret police operations.

Demonstrating the Spanish Communist Party's obedient loyalty to Stalin, its leader José Diaz, on 5 March 1937, branded POUM members "agents of Fascism who hide themselves behind the pretended slogans of revolutionaries to carry out their major missions as enemies of our own country".[35] At a stormy secret meeting of the Party executive attended by a group of Soviet representatives including Orlov, Comintern representative Stephanov and the Soviet *chargé d'affaires* Gaikin, it was agreed to oust Prime Minister Largo Caballero and replace him with the more pliant Finance Minister, Juan Negrin.[36] A radical revolutionary, Caballero had refused to sanction a purge of the POUM, and was protesting at what he saw as the Stalinist excesses of Orlov's growing NKVD operations. Negrin, on the other hand, supported the Communists and called for a purge of the troublemakers and revolutionary Marxists. While the Republican cabals began working for the downfall of the Prime Minister, Orlov set in motion an elaborate intrigue to discredit the POUM. The rising tide of street violence and terrorism with which the anarchists were undermining the authority of the Republican Government and its Communist supporters in Catalonia provided the NKVD with political tinder to make a flash point for a final showdown with Nin's supporters.

Orlov's agents had already penetrated the leadership of the Federation of Spanish Anarchists and the POUM. His plants reported back to NKVD headquarters on the preparations the two groups were making for an armed insurrection. This was nothing new or surprising to Orlov who reported to Moscow in October 1936 that "the Trotskyist organization POUM, active in Catalonia, can be easily liquidated".[37] After a visit to Barcelona he reported to Moscow in December 1936 "that a militant uprising is being prepared by Trotskyists (POUM) in Barcelona for the beginning of January for the purpose of active penetration into the exposed Fascist organization at the Hispano Suiza plant".[38] This was the same insurrection independently reported to the Centre by the Soviet embassy in Berlin after receiving an anonymous tip-off from their agent Harro Schulze-Boysen. From contacts on the *Luftwaffe* General Staff he revealed that German agents had also infiltrated Trotskyist circles in Barcelona with the intention of encouraging their *putsch*.[39]

The intended insurrection in Catalonia did not, however, erupt until May 1937. It was sparked when Prezident Azana went before the *Generalidad*, the provincial council of Catalonia, which, after a stormy session, voted to send in troops to take over the central telephone exchange the next day. The anarchists, with the backing of the POUM, seized on the order as the excuse to start their violent insurrection against the Republican Government in Madrid.

"It has long been known that FAP [Fascists Anarchists POUMists] are preparing for a *putsch* in Catalonia by provoking it using a variety of means," Orlov informed Moscow on 7 May 1937. He stated that the provincial rebellion had begun with a provincial border incident, which served as the signal for "armed conflict [which] broke out between FAP elements on the one hand and the *Generalidad* troops and units of PSUC (*Partido Socialista Unido de Catalonia* – the United Socialist party of Catalonia)". The fighting had escalated along with political assassinations and murders stirred up by the opposition, which Orlov reported claimed that Nin had called for "an armed insurrection and appeal to poor workers of Catalonia and Marxists" to "join Franco's troops on the Aragon front".[40]

The bloody street fighting of the "May Days" in Catalonia presaged an outbreak of uncontrollable violence throughout the Spanish Republic. Moscow reacted swiftly, ordering the Communists to call for repressive measures against the POUM. This shattered their alliance with the trade unionist Largo Caballero, whose cabinet promptly collapsed. Negrin, the leader of the Spanish Socialist Workers' Party, with the secret backing of the Communists, assumed the premiership on 16 May 1937. This cleared the way for Orlov to launch an NKVD-orchestrated crackdown on dissident anarchists and Marxists in Catalonia.[41] They were accused by the new Premier of sabotaging the war effort, a policy that echoed with Moscow's worldwide campaign against Trotsky and his followers. Having planted no fewer than five of his agents in Nin's Barcelona headquarters, Orlov was able to keep Moscow abreast of their activities from inside the inner councils of the POUM.[42]

The POUM became targets in Stalin's campaign against Trotsky and his supporters. By using his pen to fire broadsides against his old comrade from his Norwegian exile, Trotsky had repeatedly tried to marshal external opposition against the Soviet dictator even as his purge in the USSR was sweeping away all vestiges of internal dissent. The world headquarters of Trotskyism was in Paris, where Trotsky's energetic son, Lev Sedov, ran a study and propaganda centre under the wing of the Nikolayevsky Institute of Social History. It had long been penetrated by NKVD agents dispatched from Moscow.

Trotsky and Sedov were opposed to individual terror even though, like all Leninists, they supported the exploitation of mass terror for political ends. During the first Moscow show trial, in August 1936, a public statement made by Trotsky in 1932 that "It is time to carry out, at last, Lenin's final and insistent advice: remove Stalin!" had been transformed into what the Kremlin charged were secret orders to kill Stalin. Trotsky made his papers available to an international commission that investigated and disproved the charge that he had supported a policy of assassination, and Sedov also answered the false charge in *Livre sur Le Procès de Moscou*. His assistant while writing this book, which was published in 1937, was Mark Zborowsky, a penetration agent whose code name on his NKVD file was TULIP.

Zborowsky had so successfully ingratiated himself into Sedov's circle by 1937 that he was regarded as totally loyal in Trotskyist circles.[43] The TULIP file reveals that it was from Zborowsky that Stalin, in January 1937, obtained material that was claimed to be evidence to renew his charges against Trotsky. But TULIP, who can hardly have been unaware of Sedov's real views, appears simply to have relayed to Moscow information that he believed "The Boss" wanted to hear. For example he wrote to the Centre: "On 22 January L. Sedov, during our conversation in his apartment on the subject of the second Moscow trial and the role of the different defendants, declared, 'Now we shouldn't hesitate. Stalin should be murdered.' "[44]

Stalin's deep fear of assassination would, therefore, have been inflamed by a more detailed report of the intentions revealed by SONNY – as Sedov was known by the NKVD – which Zborowsky dispatched to Moscow on 11 February:

Not since 1936 had SONNY initiated any conversation with me about terrorism. Only about two or three weeks ago, after a meeting of the group, SONNY began speaking on this subject again. On this occasion he only tried to prove that terrorism is not contrary to Marxism. "Marxism", according to SONNY's words, "denies terrorism only to the extent that the conditions of class struggle don't favour terrorism. But there are certain situations where terrorism is necessary." The next time SONNY began talking about terrorism was when I came to his apartment to work. While we were reading newspapers, SONNY said that the whole regime in the USSR was propped up by Stalin; it was enough to kill Stalin for everything to fall to pieces.[45]

Zborowsky's unsubstantiated reports that Trotsky and Sedov were contemplating the assassination of Stalin is contrary to all their public pronouncements and the evidence contained in Trotsky's private papers that were examined by the international commission. That it appears at all in the NKVD files is significant. Even its veracity is open to question and what Zborowsky reported may have been merely an emotional outburst rather than any practical plan and it could have been pure invention to please Stalin. This report was made before Sedov died in the French clinic where he had undergone an apparently successful operation for appendicitis. The presence of Russian émigré doctors, some of whom were suspected of being in the pay of the NKVD, led to rumours that Sedov had been murdered on Stalin's instructions. Zborowsky himself fell under suspicion of being implicated because he was one of the trusted entourage. The claim that he dispatched Sedov with a poisoned orange appears fanciful in the light of a report in his NKVD file. Made shortly after Sedov's death, Zborowsky's letter advised the Centre that an autopsy should be called for, noting that until no evidence of foul play was found it would cause panic among Sedov's former assistants. He proposed that he start a whispering campaign to implicate Krivitsky who had recently defected to Paris that July and whom he referred to by his cryptonym GROLL.

If Zborowsky had indeed poisoned Sedov, it does not seem logical that he would have encouraged an autopsy – unless he was confident that no poison would be found in the body to implicate him. The circumstantial evidence that Sedov was murdered is now far less persuasive than that which shows that Zborowsky had also helped a team of Soviet agents to loot the Trotsky archives from the Nikolayevsky Institute in November 1936.[46]

Three months later when Orlov himself was in Paris in February 1937 he first heard of another plot against Stalin's life. This, he was later to claim, was taking shape within the NKVD. While hospitalized for the treatment of two vertebrae crushed when his car had run over an embankment in Spain in January, Orlov had been flat on his back for a month when he was visited by his cousin Zinovy Katsnelson, then deputy head of the Ukraine NKVD. In the privacy of the private clinic, his boyhood friend he said had tried to enrol him in a plot inspired by a group of NKVD officers who, Katsnelson told Orlov, had uncovered incriminating documentation that Stalin had once been a secret informer of the Tsar's *Okhrana*.[47] Chastened by his personal knowledge of Stalin's ruthless exploitation of the NKVD, which had been confirmed by alarming reports received from colleagues recently arrived in Spain, Orlov declined to become involved. He had already learned the sordid details of the second Moscow show trial, after which Yuri Pyatokov and Karl Radek had been shot together with fifteen other old Bolsheviks after abjectly confessing yet another Trotskyist plot against Stalin. Orlov had good reason to be cautious. When he returned to Spain a few weeks later, he learned that Katsnelson had been arrested and liquidated shortly after he had arrived back in Moscow from his trip to Paris.[48]

Orlov's cousin was only one of many thousands of NKVD officers who fell victim to Stalin's purge a year after he had made Yezhov head of the NKVD. The bloodbath had been foreshadowed in March 1937, when Yagoda was impaled on the blade of the terror he had helped the Big Boss to forge. A little more than two years after the NKVD chief had been hailed as the "avenging sword of the revolution", he had been summarily removed as head of the secret police in September 1936 by Stalin who informed the Politburo that he had "definitely proved himself incapable of unmasking the Troskyite-Zinovievite bloc".[49] Six months later Yagoda was being charged with working for the German secret service. To compound the enormity of such an astonishing crime, he signed a full confession in prison that included the wildly improbable admission that he had planned to poison Stalin, Yezhov and all the other members of the Politburo.[50]

Yagoda's contrived confession, extracted with the express intention of putting all the other NKVD department heads on the spot for their blindness in failing to uncover their chief's astounding treachery, was the work of Yezhov. The boyish features of the new People's Commissar for Internal Affairs masked a methodical brutality that this former Secretary of the Central Committee of the Communist Party demonstrated now that he was Stalin's secret police chief. The first native Russian to head the state security apparatus, Yezhov knew little and cared less about the traditions of the *Cheka*. His loyalty was to the Big Boss, who had tasked him to undertake a massive purge of the state security service as soon as he had installed his own henchmen in key positions.

As a curtain-raiser for the so-called "*Yezhovchina*", that was unleashed on the former *Cheka* cadres of the Lubyanka, the "Dwarf", as Stalin's sinister lackey was known, set about uncovering a vast and imaginary conspiracy amongst the leaders of the Red Army. On 11 June 1937 Muscovites awoke to the stunning news that Marshal Mikhail Tukhachevsky, the Soviet army commander in chief and hero of the civil war, had been arrested along with seven other generals. Next day they were all summarily executed after allegedly admitting their "treacherousness, wrecking and espionage". It was only later that they were branded as both Trotskyists and Nazi plotters, based on forged documentation that supposedly proved that Tukhachevsky had enlisted the aid of the German military in plotting a *coup d'état*.[51]

Stalin's paranoia can only have been fuelled by Yezhov's unscrupulous demand for inflammatory intelligence reports of conspiracies at home and abroad to justify the blood-letting in Moscow. In the spring of 1937 the NKVD was ordered to step up its campaign against Trotsky supporters abroad, and begin liquidating them rather than simply monitoring their activity. Under Yezhov's direction the physical elimination of those who opposed Stalin began, exporting his political vendetta. Since it was impossible to stage sensational court trials and rigged confessions outside the closely guarded borders of the USSR, other methods had to be devised to dispose of Stalin's real and imaginary opposition.

Yezhov directed the Executive Action Department of the NKVD to establish "mobile groups", as they were euphemistically termed. These were "flying squads" of professional assassins, trained to strike swiftly and suddenly so as not to leave any traces of individual terrorism either on the victims or in the form of incriminating reports. In all Orlov's correspondence with the Centre, there can be found only fragmentary references to these liquidation operations, in the form of cryptic code words and elliptical reports that point to when, how and by whom the execution of Stalin's political opponents was carried out. An extract from Orlov's letter to the Centre dealing with the assassination of the Austrian Socialist Kurt Landau, a POUM sympathizer, provides a rare insight into the "wet affairs", as they would later be referred to by the KGB during the Cold War.

"*Liternoye delo* of Kurt Landau turned out to be the most difficult of all previous cases," Orlov informed the Centre on 25 August 1937. Using the contemporary NKVD jargon for a physical liquidation derived from the Russian term for a "special letter", he referred to Landau's withdrawal from public activity: "He went deep underground and in spite of the fact that for ten days we have been keeping under vigilant surveillance a prominent female anarchist who, according to her disclosure to a source of ours, is his courier and sees him every day, we have not so far been able to find him." Orlov advised Moscow that, if surveillance did not yield results in "two or three days", he would arrange a meeting, but not "pick him up" because Landau was "without doubt a central figure in the underground organization of the POUM". If he had been shot at the rendezvous, it would expose the NKVD's source if the police interrogated him. "That is why I suggest we should not 'pick up' Landau at the meeting, but follow him to his residence and take him later in a day or two. As you know, Landau, unlike other foreign *literniks*, has forged close links with local Trotskyist organizations."[52]

"In spite of the tense situation I think that, taking Landau's importance into account, we should not hesitate and that we should also carry out this *liter* (assassination) in such a way as you instructed us," Orlov concluded his report, which still evokes a chill after nearly six decades.[53] This document, together with other similar NKVD records, provides the irrefutable circumstantial evidence that implicates Orlov in the murder apparatus that killed Landau and the other "foreign *literniks*" who vanished mysteriously in Spain that summer.

It follows from the last sentence of Orlov's letter that, in carrying out these liquidations of POUM sympathizers, he was fulfilling secret orders from the Centre – and that meant Stalin. What is grimly remarkable is the cool resolution Orlov demonstrated in pursuing the *liter* missions assigned to him. The meticulous planning involved in these assassinations suggests that he had no hesitation in directing such executions. Like many Soviet intelligence officers whose ethical standards had been forged in the heady cauldron of the Revolution and the civil war, Orlov it seems was quite prepared to murder political opponents in pursuit of what he regarded as the highest ideals of Communism.

The documentary evidence of the NKVD's Spanish operations shows that Orlov deliberately and repeatedly lied both to the FBI and to US Senate investigators by denying any personal involvement in the disappearance of Marxists in Spain and the liquidation of the most prominent member of the POUM central committee. The mystery of what happened to Andrés Nin in June 1937 became a major political scandal for the Spanish Republican Government. It was rumoured at the time to be yet another example of Stalin's murderous vengeance. Now from the Spanish *rezidentura* files it is possible to reconstruct the role that Orlov played in the Nin affair, that has been a matter of speculation for more than half a century.

What emerges is that in the aftermath of the "May Days" insurrection in Barcelona that had been savagely put down by the Republican troops, forged documents were passed to the Communist-controlled Madrid police that pointed to a Falangist connection between Nin and Franco. The incriminating letters containing the false evidence that the Marxist leaders were involved in a fifth column plot served as the justification for Negrin's Government ordering Nin's arrest, along with other members of the POUM leadership. They were all imprisoned prior to standing trial for treason.

The archive records of the NKVD's Spanish station contain the documentation that proves the charges on which Nin was arrested were forged under Orlov's personal direction. They show how, in the spring of 1937, the Republican military counter-intelligence with the help of Orlov's NKVD agents had uncovered a large Francoist intelligence network genuinely being run by agents of the Falange. According to Orlov's reports to Moscow, seven senior members of the Francoist intelligence centre were conspiring with high-ranking Republican officials and officers. The leaders of Fascist cells in Madrid were promptly arrested and two radio stations together with cyphers and intelligence reports on the disposition of Republican army units were uncovered. Military plans of attack along with a large amount of explosives parcelled up for terrorist activity were also recovered in a counter-intelligence operation between the NKVD and the Republicans. This led to 270 arrests for involvement in the alleged widespread Falangist conspiracy.[54]

Not a single member of Nin's organization, however, was implicated. But Orlov's fertile talent for subterfuge encouraged him to seize the opportunity to nail Nin by expanding the genuine Falangist conspiracy to involve the POUM. This is evident from the outline of an ingenious scheme for framing the POUM leadership that Orlov detailed for Moscow's approval in his report of 23 May 1937:

> Taking into consideration that this case, in connection with which the overwhelming majority have pleaded guilty, has produced a great impression on military and Government circles, and that it is firmly documented and based on the incontrovertible confessions of defendants, I have decided to use the significance and the indisputable facts of the case to implicate the POUM leadership (whose [possible] connections we are looking into while conducting investigations).
>
> We have, therefore, composed the enclosed document, which indicates the co-operation of the POUM leadership with the Spanish Falange organization – and, through it, with Franco and Germany.
>
> We will encypher the contents of the document using Franco's cypher, which we have at our disposal, and will write it on the reverse side of the plan of the location of our weapons emplacements in Casa del Campo which was taken from the Falangist organization. This document has passed through five people: all the five Fascists who have admitted passing the document to each other for dispatch to Franco. On another seized document we will write, in invisible ink, a few lines of some insignificant content. It will be from this document that, in co-operation with the Spaniards, we shall begin to scrutinize the documents for cryptographic writing. We shall experiment with several processes for treating these papers. A special chemical will develop these few words or lines, then we will begin to test all the other documents with this developer and thus expose the letter we have composed compromising the POUM leadership.
>
> The Spanish chief of the counter-intelligence department will leave immediately for Valencia where the cypher department of the War Ministry will decypher the letter. The cypher department, according to our information, has the necessary code at its disposal. But, if the department cannot decypher the letter for some reason, then we will "spend a couple of days" and decypher it ourselves.
>
> We expect this affair to be very effective in exposing the role

POUM has played in the Barcelona uprising. The exposure of direct contact between one of its leaders and Franco must contribute to the Government adopting a number of administrative measures against the Spanish Trotskyists to discredit POUM as a German-Francoist spy organization.[55]

Orlov's scheme for planting the skilfully contrived evidence of Nin's involvement with Franco was executed with his customary precision. The proof can be found in the Ministry of Justice communiqué issued after Nin's disappearance that provoked a political furore by announcing that the General Police Directorate had seized from POUM headquarters "cyphers, telegrams, codes, documents concerning money and arms purchases and smuggling". Also discovered were incriminating documents "indicating that the POUM leadership, namely Andrés Nin, was mixed up in espionage".[56]

Confirmation that Orlov's plan had worked perfectly is provided by his own report to the Centre of 25 September 1937, in which he drew "special attention to the interrogation of the Minister of Home Affairs conducted by the court (the examination record is enclosed.) The Minister testified that he had received a photographic copy of the given document [against Nin] through the Madrid police, which considers the document absolutely genuine in its double aspects." The reference to "double aspects" was an allusion by Orlov to the genuine Falangist plan for the bombardment of Madrid, to which the NKVD had surreptitiously added an incriminating letter written in an invisible ink.[57]

On 16 June 1937 Nin and forty other POUM leaders were arrested, their militia battalions were disbanded and their headquarters at the Hotel Falcon in Barcelona closed by order of General Ricardo Burillo, the recently installed head of public order in Barcelona. He was taking orders from Colonel Antonio Ortega, the Republican Director General of Security, a hard-line Communist Party member who later admitted he was following Orlov's directions. The POUM was promptly declared illegal and its newspaper *Battalia* shut down. The most senior officials, including Nin, were transferred from Catalonia, where it was feared revolutionary sympathizers might spring them from jail, to the capital where the Communist-controlled police could be relied upon to hold them in a closely guarded house in the Alcala district of Madrid. From 18 to 21 June Nin and his colleagues were intensively interrogated in preparation for standing trial. But Nin was never brought to court and press reports started surfacing in Catalonia to the effect that he had been murdered.

"Where is Nin?" Spanish newspaper headlines demanded to know.

Prime Minister Negrin, who had already complained to the Communist ministers that the Soviets were acting as if Barcelona was now part of the USSR, was assured by Colonel Ortega that the former POUM leader was safely in prison and under interrogation. But he had vanished.

Nobody had seen Nin since 21 June and rumours had begun to circulate in Madrid and Barcelona that the POUM leader had been taken away the following night from the house in the Alcala. His abductors were alleged to be German-speaking members of the International Brigade who had bundled him off to the El Prado Park north of Madrid, where he was murdered. This was the version Negrin himself gave the President of what he called a "dirty business". Reportedly Azana reacted sceptically by asking, "Was that not a little like a novel?" Meanwhile, some Spanish newspapers carried stories that Nin had escaped. When he did not reappear, the Prime Minister decided to put the best face he could on the "dirty business" by admitting that Nin had vanished, while disclaiming all responsibility and taking care to emphasize the POUM leader's guilt. The same line was taken in the official communiqué issued from the Ministry of Justice on 5 August 1937 declaring that: "After appropriate investigation it came out that Señor Nin, together with other POUM leaders, was arrested by the *Seguridad*, transferred to Madrid and held in a preliminary detention prison specially prepared by the Police Commissioner of Madrid. He disappeared from this prison and up to the present time everything that has been done to find him and his guards has brought no result."[58]

Members of the Republican Government, including Negrin, suspected that Orlov (who was known to have a German bodyguard) was behind Nin's disappearance. In his interrogation by the FBI and again before the US Senate Orlov repeatedly denied under oath the charges explicitly made against him in the published memoirs of former Soviet military intelligence officer Walter Krivitsky and the Communist Minister of Education in Negrin's Government, José Hernandez.[59] These allegations were "absolutely foolish", Orlov assured the FBI, dismissing the charges as a "Trotskyist invention". He insisted he could not have "committed the assassination" because he was only a "political attaché". Had he ordered the killing of Nin, Orlov claimed that "Russia in the eyes of the world would have been discredited". It was his belief that "Stalin had ordered the assassination of Nin and that this order had been executed by the Russian named Bolodin", who, he said, received the Order of Lenin upon his return to Moscow.[60]

What is most telling about Orlov's version is that he eventually conceded that Nin had indeed been murdered on the orders of Stalin –

a fact which, as head of NKVD operations in Spain at the time, he could hardly deny with any credibility. But his effort to pass on the blame to an assassin named Bolodin has now been exposed as a lie by documentary evidence which has surfaced in the NKVD archives. This reveals tell-tale links between Orlov and the operation to discredit the POUM leadership. It also confirms his direct involvement in the other *liter* liquidations, all of which leads to the inference that he was the one who had been entrusted by Stalin with the highly sensitive mission of arranging for the liquidation of Nin.

Whilst no single NKVD report in the Spanish station records constitutes the smoking gun, an accumulation of incriminating evidence, in particular one cryptic letter in Orlov's files, does directly implicate him. This is a report he sent to Moscow on 24 July 1937 detailing an operation whose code name was NIKOLAY. Its contents, together with its timing indicate that its subject can only have been Nin. This report of Orlov's describes, in the characteristically cryptic terms he used for *liter* operations, the manner in which the POUM leader was kidnapped from prison and liquidated by trusted NKVD agents identified only by their initials. Its fourth paragraph is particularly revealing, both details and conspiratorial style being consistent with the established facts of the abduction operation. Moreover, it suggests that Orlov himself was personally involved in executing the plan by which Nin was kidnapped from the Alcala detention house and driven away, stuffed in the trunk of a car:

> About those involved in the NIKOLAY case, the main participants are first L. and second A.F.: I.M. was an indirect assistant when he brought food to the detention centre and the gates were opened for him, our people entered the inner yard. Poltavsky was to report to you from Paris about the departure for Moscow of the last participant of the operation JUZIK. The main encyphered document, which is familiar to you, was written by his hand.[61] He worked for me as an interpreter in connection with this case and was with me in the car at the house from which the object was brought out. We used his policeman's badge to avoid a too thorough inspection of the car on the part of the road patrol when we were taking the cargo out in the car.[62]

Was the "cargo" the drugged body, or corpse, of the kidnapped POUM leader? Russian intelligence experts are inclined to take this view and speculate that Nin was probably still alive at this point. They hypothesize that Orlov may have originally decided to stage Nin's escape in order to confirm his guilt and to discredit POUM still further.

Since there was no possibility that Nin could ever be freed to reveal the truth, Orlov may originally have intended to dispatch him to a Soviet freighter for trans-shipment to Moscow. Whether this was the plan or whether Stalin's orders called for immediate liquidation and elimination of the corpse to prevent any trace of the NKVD's hand in Nin's disappearance emerging can not yet be established for sure. Additional NKVD documentation tying Orlov directly to the Nin assassination consists of a handwritten pencil note, stitched into page 164 of the first volume of his NKVD operational file: "N. from Alcala de Enares in the direction of Perane de Tahunia, half way, 100 metres from the road, in the field. [Present were] BOM, SCHWED, JUZIK, two Spaniards. PIERRE's driver VICTOR."[63]

Unnumbered and undated, with no indication of the authorship, the anonymous note appears to have been part of a hurriedly attempted damage assessment and attempt to cover the traces of the "special operation" or *liter*. There are three good reasons, however, for believing that this is a third surviving document relating to the Nin operation. Firstly, it indicates the presence of both SCHWED (Orlov) and JUZIK, in the case. Secondly, the Madrid suburb of Alcala de Enares was the location of the prison where the accused POUM leaders were confined. Thirdly, the reference to "N" is a clear indication that the note refers to the spot where Nin was buried after being shot.[64]

What the NKVD records do show is that, after destroying the organization of the POUM, Orlov continued his relentless battle against Trotskyism. After Stalin's number one enemy had settled in Mexico in January 1937, Spain served as a reservoir of agents to undertake the task of locating his hide-away. In addition to Ramon Mercader, Trotsky's assassin, Orlov had supplied Moscow with other Spanish agents who crossed the Atlantic and gave reliable addresses in Mexico at the Centre's request. If, as now appears indisputable, Orlov was responsible for the abduction and murder of Nin, his involvement in this and other *liter* operations in Spain explains why he was aware of the fate in store for him one year later when he received a cryptic telegram from Moscow.

"A DANGEROUS GAME"

Barcelona was roasting in the heat of a Mediterranean summer on 9 July 1938, when cryptogram No. 1743 from Moscow Centre arrived at the mansion that served as the NKVD field headquarters in Catalonia. Addressed to SCHWED, Orlov's code name, it peremptorily ordered him to travel as soon as possible to Paris. There he was instructed to rendezvous with Binyukov, the Soviet Consul General, who "might come in handy as a liaison man in connection with the important task that lies ahead".[1] They would then be driven in the embassy car to the Belgian port of Antwerp by 14 July where they would board a Russian steamship named *Svir* for a conference with an unidentified individual who, Orlov was informed, would be "known to him". The initial impression given by the cable was that this was a summons to an important meeting with one of the chiefs of the NKVD.[2]

Yet, as Orlov reread what he later described as a "long and tricky" telegram from the Centre, he realized there was something odd about it. What sense did it make for him, at such short notice, to travel the length of Europe for an unexplained rendezvous? Why not simply call him to Moscow or arrange for the official to meet him in Paris or Spain? What was the significance of a shipboard conference? The *Svir* obviously held the answer.

"It was clear to me that the ship was to become my floating prison," Orlov concluded after realizing that Yezhov had, in fact, given the order for him to be purged. But he was too canny to walk into the trap that had been set for him.[3]

For more than a year reports had been reaching Orlov of the growing purge decimating his old Chekist comrades in the upper echelons of the NKVD. The disturbing news was brought to Spain by every officer arriving from Moscow, who told of the upheaval at headquarters ever since Yezhov moved into the top job at the Lubyanka in October 1936. He had brought with him 300 new officials, who he assigned as assistants to the NKVD department heads in Moscow and the provinces. The changes were explained as necessary to meet the Politburo's demands to raise efficiency to "a higher level". But most of the new men were Party bureaucrats with no professional experience or training in intelligence. After they had become familiar with their new trade by assisting with the preparations for the second round of Moscow show trials that had been staged in March 1937, Yezhov made arrangements to promote his henchmen. Yagoda's former deputies and department chiefs were informed that the Central Committee wanted them to investigate personally the political reliability of regional and local party officials and organizations throughout the Soviet Union. They had dutifully departed from Moscow to conduct their individually appointed missions, but none of them ever arrived at their destinations. At each train's first stop, they were arrested, driven back to Moscow by car and imprisoned.[4]

Weeks had passed before the staff at the Centre had become suspicious. During that time Yezhov had taken care to change all the Lubyanka guards and replace the officers commanding the NKVD troop units in Moscow. Only four department chiefs were spared what proved to be fatal assignments. In addition to Slutsky, the head of the Foreign Department, the fortunate ones were three with close links to the Big Boss: K. V. Pauker, the head of the NKVD Operations Department, who was Stalin's trusted bodyguard; Stanislav Redens, head of the NKVD Moscow Region, who was married to Stalin's sister-in-law; and Mikhail Frinovsky, another trusted crony, who was chief of the frontier troops.

Slutsky was spared at first because Yezhov had not wanted to disturb the operation of the foreign networks while systematically purging the ranks of the *Chekists* at headquarters. As the bloodbath accelerated, and the senior NKVD department heads were put under arrest, Yezhov retreated behind a succession of heavily armed security guards in his third-floor office. Anticipating the fate that awaited them in the basement cells of the Lubyanka, some of the senior officers chose to hurl themselves from their office windows rather than submit to the same grim processes they themselves had employed to extract "confessions" from their own victims. The winter snows of 1937 had barely begun to thaw in the Moscow streets when Stalin's vendetta began to wash bloodily and very publicly outside the Lubyanka. Colonel Feliks Gursky, a ranking member of the Foreign Department who had only just received the Order of the Red Star, jumped through his office window. He was followed by two interrogators of the Secret Political Department.[5] These suicides naturally attracted the attention of ordinary folk passing by at the time, and before long, reports of an impending revolt were flying round Moscow. Yet despite such alarming rumours, all remained calm outside the Lubyanka, while inside confusion reigned; the blood flowed too in the cells, where scores of officers were arrested, accused of Trotskyism, espionage or both, and then summarily shot without formal trial.

"Officers of the Foreign Department of the NKVD who arrived in Spain and France told weird stories of how armed patrols scoured the NKVD apartment houses and how sometimes a knock on the door of one apartment house caused a suicide shot to be fired in an adjacent house," Orlov later wrote, recalling how "inquisitors of the NKVD, who not long before had driven fear into the hearts of Stalin's captives, were now themselves shaking with indescribable terror".[6]

"The top officials and the interrogators of the NKVD were like hunting dogs, too busy with the pursuit of their game to pay attention to the hunter himself," was how Orlov explained the failure of the Chekist old guard to anticipate Yezhov's purge. It was his conviction that Stalin's intention was to exterminate all those who had been involved in, or knew the truth, about the Moscow show trials. But the records show that Yezhov soon expanded the purges to NKVD organizations in the provinces across the length and breadth of the Soviet Union. These hapless officers had little knowledge of and had played no part in the purges of the former members of the Politburo. During 1937 alone it is estimated that more than 3,000 operational NKVD officers were liquidated.[7]

The "Yezhovchina", as it was called, grew fearsomely in 1938 after the guilty verdicts were rendered to order at the third Moscow show trial. One of those executed was former NKVD head Yagoda, who had set the stage for Stalin's reign of terror at the first of these trials only two years earlier. Of the NKVD inquisitors who had helped obtain the confessions that led to the round of guilty verdicts, only Georgy Lyeshkov, the deputy head of the Political Department and Molchanov's assistant in the first trial, escaped execution. He saved his life by defecting to the Japanese in the summer of 1938 after his posting as NKVD chief to the far eastern provinces of China.[8]

The impact of Stalin's purge of the officer corps of the Red Army was also felt in Spain. In February 1937 General Kleber was removed from command of the International Brigades. On Moscow's orders he was assigned to organize the Loyalist defence of Malaga, but he disappeared soon after his arrival there and was never heard from again. He probably fell victim to an NKVD assassination squad, but General Berzin was also ordered home after he had criticised Orlov's high-handed direction of the NKVD in Spain. He fell victim to Yezhov's vindictiveness along with Stashevsky, Stalin's Commissar in Spain, who had also dared to criticize the NKVD.[9]

Officers on foreign assignment were recalled only to disappear without trace and the fear engendered by such a summons from the Centre made it necessary to lure some back to the Soviet Union by subterfuge. One of the first was Smirnov, the Paris *rezident* who had acted as liaison with Philby. This was not Dimitri Smirnov but V. V. Smirnov, whose code name was PETER, and whose real name was Stanislav Glinsky. He had served for four years in France, so neither he nor his wife found it unusual to receive a recall in July 1937. If the wife of another Paris based NKVD officer had not witnessed the arrest of Mrs Smirnov in Moscow, his former colleagues in France would have assumed her husband had been assigned abroad in another post. When it became known Glinsky had been executed for treason, Yezhov ordered his underlings to put it about that Smirnov had confessed to being a Polish spy. His Paris comrades were aware that this was a ludicrous fabrication because the Centre continued using the same codes and none of their agents or sources were betrayed.[10]

Mally was another "illegal" who, Orlov learned in 1938, was among the forty NKVD officers recalled the previous year only to be accused and condemned to death for alleged treason. All but five had obeyed Moscow's order to return, despite a growing apprehension at the fate that awaited them. Some, like Mally, coolly faced the prospect of becoming martyrs. Others believed they would be able to prove themselves innocent of any charges brought against them. Most would have fled to save themselves but for the powerful disincentive to defection posed by the extraordinary law promulgated under Stalin's signature on 8 June 1938. This held the families of NKVD officers hostage by decreeing that the closest relatives of members of the Soviet services who fled abroad were liable for deportation to Siberia. Every NKVD officer was informed of a secret addendum to the law that introduced an automatic ten-year prison term for wives and close relatives of defectors, and they could be put to death if state secrets were betrayed.

Stalin had also instructed Yezhov to take whatever steps were necessary to counter defections of NKVD officers abroad who might expose secrets about Soviet underground operations to hostile counter-intelligence agencies. The "mobile groups" of the Directorate of Special Tasks hunted down defectors who chose to disobey Moscow's orders.

Krivitsky, whose true name was Ginsberg, the NKVD "illegal" *rezident* in the Netherlands who had been running arms into Spain, and Ignace Reiss, "illegal" in Belgium whose real name was Poretsky, were two of those who preferred to take their chances in defying Moscow by staying abroad. Orlov would later admit that he also knew of two other underground NKVD agents who had defected that year, code named PAUL and BRUNO.[12]

The most senior NKVD officer to make a break was Ignace Reiss, who fled in July 1937 with his wife and child to Switzerland after receiving the fatal summons from Moscow. Before leaving his station he dropped off a letter at the Soviet embassy in Paris informing the Central Committee why he had broken with Stalin and announcing that he was "returning to freedom – back to Lenin, to his teachings and his cause". Stalin responded to this "in the eye" gesture of defiance by ordering Yezhov to wipe Reiss and his family off the face of the earth as an example to others. The "mobile group" of NKVD assassins finally caught up with Reiss on 4 September in Switzerland, pumping him full of machine-gun bullets before dumping his body on a lonely roadside outside Geneva, near the village of Chamblades.[13]

Two months later NKVD *rezidentura* chief Walter Krivitsky, who until 1935 had been a GRU officer, decided to flee, having learned of the liquidation of his friend Reiss. Abandoning his station in The Hague, he arrived in Paris with his wife and son to ask the French police for protection and asylum. He, too, would almost certainly have been quickly assassinated by one of Yezhov's "mobile groups" had not the French Government been embarrassed by the recent kidnapping scandal perpetrated by the Soviets in broad daylight on 23 September 1937 when General Miller, Kutyepov's successor as commander of the White Russian veterans organization, ROVS, had been seized by a Soviet hit squad on a Paris street corner. The French Government ordered one of the largest manhunts the country had ever seen, but the General was never found either dead or alive.[14] Orlov, as he would later confide to Feoktistov, had played a part in the Miller kidnapping although he had fallen out with Yezhov because he said he had disapproved of the whole operation. A letter in the correspondence file of the Spanish *rezidentura* reminded Spigelglass that Orlov had chartered the aircraft "in which you and I spirited away FARMER", the code name for General Skoblin, the deputy chief of the White Russian veterans group. Skoblin was "fingerman" (according to Orlov) in an operation that was intended to put him at the head of the organization.[15]

The operation was bungled and Skoblin only escaped thanks to Orlov, a fact that he did not reveal to the CIA twenty-seven years later when he told the story of how the turncoat General's wife was left to be arrested by the Paris police. The French Government had warned Moscow that they would break off diplomatic relations with the

USSR if Soviet agents perpetrated another murder on French soil. With Hitler making increasingly menacing demands on European territory, Stalin had no wish to alienate France at this time. *Realpolitik* may have proved Krivitsky's saviour. There had been two attempts on his life while in France, but he managed to get safely to America. Three years later in 1941 his suicide under mysterious circumstances in a Washington DC hotel was taken by many, including Orlov, as an indication that he had not in the end managed to escape the long arm of Stalin's vengeance.[16]

The "mobile groups" who operated from bases in Europe and Mexico also left a trail of unsolved deaths and disappearances in 1937 of Communists on both sides of the Atlantic. Among those who appear to have been victims of Yezhov's hit list was a leading member of the Ukrainian nationalist underground, Konovalets. He was blown to pieces by a bomb that exploded outside a Rotterdam café to which he had been summoned for a rendezvous. Another probable victim of the NKVD was Juliette Stuart Poyntz, a former activist in the American Communist Party, who disappeared without trace in New York in June 1937. One certain Soviet liquidation victim was the former OGPU *rezident* in Turkey, Georgy Agabekov, who had defected to the British in Constantinople in 1931 and who vanished in July 1937 while en route from Paris to the Pyrenees. Rudolf Klement, the former secretary of Trotsky's Fourth International, disappeared on 12 July 1938.[17] Shortly afterwards the Paris police found what they believed to be his headless corpse floating down the Seine

The first intimation Orlov had that deadly "purification" directed from Moscow might be targeted at him arrived at his Barcelona headquarters in August 1937, in a telegram from Slutsky. This warned him that the Germans and Franco's intelligence services might be planning to kidnap him and extract information about Soviet aid to the Republicans. The Foreign Department chief announced that the Centre would dispatch forthwith a personal bodyguard for Orlov consisting of twelve men to ensure his safety. "It immediately occurred to me that those guards might have orders to liquidate me," was Orlov's reaction. He recorded how he had "wired back to Slutsky that I didn't need a bodyguard because my officers were guarded twenty-four hours a day by the Spanish Civil Guard and that armed agents of the Spanish Secret Police accompanied me on all my travels".[18]

After declining the Russian guards, Orlov, as a precaution, dispatched his assistant Eitingon to the German International Brigade to select out ten of the most trusted KPD Communists to become his chief's personal bodyguard. "These chosen men became my constant companions," Orlov wrote, noting that they "followed me everywhere with tommy guns and clusters of hand grenades on their belts".[19]

Orlov's suspicion that he was moving to the head of Yezhov's liquidation list was reinforced in October 1937, when he received an unexpected visit from Mikhail Spigelglass, the deputy head of the NKVD Foreign Department. Orlov claimed he had arrived from Paris after being sent by Yezhov to personally direct the hunting down of Reiss. The NKVD records show that Orlov was covering up the true circumstances since Spigelglass had been sent to Spain[20] by Slutsky to arrange for Skoblin's escape by plane from France.

Orlov's concern for his own safety increased when he claimed he found out that Spigelglass had met the NKVD agent named Bolodin in Madrid, whom he had been warned had been sent by Yezhov to lead a "mobile group" in Spain. The news made him apprehensive that the operation might be planned involving the kidnapping of his wife and daughter as hostages to ensure that he would return to Moscow when the time came for his recall.[21]

"When that thought occurred to me at twelve o'clock in the night, I drove to the villa and woke them up," Orlov wrote. "I took them to France and hired a villa for them and left them with an agent from the Spanish secret police who knew France because in olden times he used to be a taxi driver in Paris." Orlov in his testimony to the Americans claimed that he had considered defecting himself in 1937, but said that, after weighing the options, he had decided that the time was not yet ripe. "I waited, postponing my break with Moscow, because I felt that by doing so I was prolonging the life of my mother and mother-in-law," Orlov explained. "In the back of my mind a vain hope still lingered that something would intervene, that something would happen in Moscow that would put an end to the nightmare of endless executions."[22]

The nightmare did not end in 1938. It grew even bloodier. Once Yezhov had completed the liquidation of the old guard of the NKVD officers, he no longer had any use for the symbolic figure of Slutsky. On 17 February 1938 the Foreign Department chief was called into the office of Frinovsky, recently promoted as one of the deputy heads of the NKVD. Half an hour later Spigelglass received a summons from Frinovsky only to find his boss slumped awkwardly across an armchair with an empty tea glass at his side. Frinovsky confidently announced that a doctor had already ascertained that Slutsky had died of a heart attack. Several NKVD officers who knew from experience the symptoms of cyanide poisoning observed the tell-tale blue spots on the face of their late Foreign Department chief as his open coffin lay on its bier in the NKVD officers' club. Orlov's own suspicions were aroused after he sent telegrams addressed to Slutsky because his death notice arrived not by cable, but by slow diplomatic mail.[23]

Yezhov, as Orlov knew, was not well disposed to him. The elevation of Spigelglass to replace Slutsky as head of the Foreign Directorate also increased his vulnerability. Nonetheless the contemporary records show that Orlov appeared to go out of his way to irritate the new regime in the Lubyanka. He provided his enemies in Moscow with the justification they were looking for to move against him in the spring of 1938 after he filed a series of incautious reports. One in particular was highly critical of the SIM, the Spanish Republican secret police that Orlov had been instrumental in creating in the image of the NKVD. His accusation against the organization whose reign of terror he had directed against the Trotskyists in Spain did not go down well with Yezhov. But as a thoroughgoing, if ruthless, professional, Orlov felt himself duty bound to point out that the SIM was becoming undisciplined. After playing a leading role in the operations against the POUM, the Spanish secret police careered out of control as its senior officers commenced their own internecine vendetta which led to spilling the blood of Communist Party members loyal to Moscow.

"Spain is unprecedented in Europe in its arbitrary rule of law," Orlov wrote to the Centre, reporting that "any Special Department officer of the Spanish Republican Security Service has the right to arrest anyone without special permission, even the military staff". He complained that "instead of fighting the true fight against spies and Fascists, false cases are being trumped up" and noted in particular that the deputy head of the SIM had just installed an electric chair "on which he tortures detainees".[24]

Orlov's report on the disturbing direction which the reign of terror in Spain he had helped engineer was taking did not go down well at the Lubyanka, where Yezhov's minions were conducting their interrogations in a manner not at all dissimilar to the excesses being practised in the jails of the SIM. The "Dwarf" had been awaiting an opportunity to pay off Orlov for an old grudge resulting from a failed exfiltration operation involving a senior Comintern figure, in which Stalin had taken a personal interest. Yezhov's notorious vindictiveness had been further inflamed when Orlov interceded on behalf of a Polish-born Red Army commander who was about to stand trial for alleged Trotskyist sympathies.

General Svertchevsky, known to the Spanish Communists and members of the International Brigades who fought under him as General Walter, was recalled suddenly to Moscow early in 1938. In a bid to save one of the genuine Soviet heroes of the Spanish Civil War,

Orlov wrote a personal plea to Yezhov that was countersigned by all five of his deputies. It asserted not only that Svertchevsky's loyalty was above reproach, but also that he was immensely popular with the Spanish public. They made their case by enclosing the silver box which had been a gift to the General from the Spanish Young Communist League. Its lid, engraved with a map of Spain, was inset with rubies to mark the sites of the military victories won by Svertchevsky. Inside Yezhov found letters attesting to the General's bravery and skill on the battlefield. It was one of the rare recorded instances when the NKVD chief was persuaded to spare one of his victims. Svertchevsky was exonerated, but the "Dwarf"'s vengeance was redirected towards Orlov, who noted that it was shortly afterwards, on 9 July 1938, that he received his own recall to Moscow.[25]

"When I received the telegram instructing me to go to Belgium and board a ship, ostensibly for a top secret conference where a member of the party would be waiting for me, two of my assistants talked to me privately," Orlov wrote. One had cautioned, "I do not like that telegram." Orlov recalled how a few months earlier he had been ordered to send one of his other assistants back to Moscow, supposedly to be decorated and to report personally to Stalin on the war in Spain. When this assistant had not returned after a month, Orlov and his staff gloomily concluded that their comrade had become another victim of Yezhov's liquidation campaign.[26]

"What do you think, what conference could there be?" Orlov had asked his concerned assistant. He said he had not received an answer, but that the man instead looked away. "He was afraid to talk," Orlov wrote of the officer's final and hesitating response: "Why didn't he come to Spain to talk to you?"[27]

"Everyone felt the danger, everyone was actually trembling," was how Orlov described the reactions of his staff. Eitingon, he noted, had immediately appreciated the significance of the telegram, pointing out that Moscow had not even identified with a code name the supposedly important man Orlov was supposed to meet in Antwerp aboard the *Svir*.

"Yezhov and the men whom he had brought with him to the NKVD from the apparatus of the Central Committee were not as experienced as the old NKVD chiefs whom they had liquidated," Orlov wrote. Even his staff had seen through the cable that it was intended to allay suspicion, but "so clumsily" written was it that Yezhov had betrayed his real intentions.[28] This was indicated by the instruction that Orlov was given that "if for some reason he found it inconvenient to go aboard ship, he should wait in front of the American Express

Company in Antwerp" for five minutes every two hours from 2 p.m. to 8 p.m. "I would be shot in the same way that several of my colleagues were shot," he surmised. "Kotov [Eitingon], to whom I showed the telegram, understood that it was a trap."[29]

Orlov foresaw that if he did rendezvous with the Soviet consular official, he would become an armed guard to ensure that Orlov went aboard the Russian ship in Antwerp. So he decided it was important not to give Moscow or Eitingon and his staff any indication that he intended avoiding the trap, if indeed it was one. "I confirm the receipt of your telegram No. 1743. In order to be in Antwerp on 14 July, I must depart from here on 11 July, or the 12th at the latest," Orlov cabled Moscow Centre, asking "to be informed, before that date, the terms of my meeting with our comrade in Antwerp". He also asked whether Soviet underground agents whom he designated only by numbers 5, 10, 26, 27 and 29 "must, by the 14 July, be in Europe already or can they, for the time being, stay in Spain in a state of readiness?"[30] Moscow responded in the affirmative about the need to maintain the assignments of these agents, but provided no further information about his own meeting.

Then Orlov dispatched a routine response giving no indication that his suspicions were aroused. In it he requested Moscow Centre's directions regarding the dispatch of the four NKVD men and a female agent, who was operating as a journalist under Orlov's command, to the Belgian capital, to conceal his own intention not to keep his appointment in Paris:

> Confirm the receipt of telegram No. 1750. On 12 July I shall register my departure and send LADY JOURNALIST to Brussels and her brother to the city of FIN [Paris]. On 12th or 13th one of the five people mentioned in telegram 1743 will be transferred there. Contact with everybody will be prearranged. Wire whether the brother must take the radio transmitter with him, whether it should be packed, whether diplomatic correspondence and inventory should be destroyed. I shall be in Antwerp on 14 July.[31]

This was to be Orlov's final communication to the Centre in his capacity as a general of the NKVD. The next day he went to his headquarters for what both he and his staff knew would be the last meeting. "When I left my office in Barcelona, my officers came out of the mansion which we occupied, they were gloomy and they felt that I was walking into a trap," Orlov recalled of his departure on 12 July. But his journey did not follow the course they feared or that Moscow intended: "Instead I called up my wife and made an appointment with them at a certain hotel in Perpignan and fled."[32]

After dropping off his trusted German bodyguards at the frontier, Orlov's Spanish chauffeur drove him across the French border to the Grand Hotel in Perpignan. There he collected his wife and daughter to take the overnight train for Paris. They arrived on 13 July, the eve before the annual festivities of Bastille Day. Orlov recalled that his own mood was at odds with the conviviality of the Parisians.

"I felt like a man who had abandoned a ship and got into a lifeboat without plans and with little hope," Orlov wrote. "I knew that the NKVD had powerful connections in France and that within forty-eight hours Yezhov's terrorists would be on my trail. I had to get out of France as quickly as possible because there I could easily be cornered and murdered."[33]

Orlov's extensive network of relatives in America, many of whom he had taken care to look up during his 1932 trip, made the United States an obvious safe haven. But his plan to go there directly fell apart when a phone call to the US embassy revealed that William C. Bullitt, the Ambassador, was out of town. He did not feel confident that he could trust his case to a junior official, so he needed an alternative country to flee to – and fast. "So on the advice of my wife I went to the Canadian embassy and luckily their office was not closed," was how Orlov described his lucky break. The legation happened to be near their hotel and within a short time he had arranged a personal appointment with the Consul General. He knew Canada did not at that time maintain diplomatic relations with the Soviet Union and therefore could not grant him a formal entry visa. The Canadian Consul, according to Orlov, turned out to be "a friendly sort of man" and by a stroke of good fortune also happened to be the former Commissioner for Immigration. The Consul, therefore, wrote a letter of introduction to his country's immigration authorities, noting that the Soviet General was travelling to the United States on a diplomatic passport and had requested permission to take his wife and sickly daughter to Quebec for a vacation before facing the stifling summer heat of Washington, where he would take up his new post.[34]

The Orlovs now had to get to Canada without delay because the alert would surely go out once the General failed to show up next day at the Soviet embassy for the drive to Antwerp. It would only be a matter of time before the Soviets' Foreign Ministry cancelled his passport affording the Orlovs diplomatic status to get into America. Fortune continued to smile on the fugitive family. While waiting in the embassy, Orlov learned from a priest who had struck up a conversation with his wife that a Canadian steamship named the ss

Montclare would be sailing that very evening from Cherbourg to Montreal.

Orlov hurried off to find a travel bureau to book passage for the three of them whilst Maria rushed back to their hotel to collect their bags and daughter Vera. The holiday traffic made their trips across Paris a frantic race against the clock but they met up at the Gare St Lazare with only minutes remaining to catch the train to Cherbourg. An hour after arriving at the port later that afternoon, the Orlovs went aboard the ss *Montclare*. Shortly after sunset, with two mournful blasts of her siren, the twin-funnelled steamer carrying the highest ranking Soviet intelligence officer ever to attempt to flee from Stalin sailed out into the darkening waters of the English Channel and set a westerly course for the Atlantic crossing to Canada.

So began Orlov's fourteen years as a fugitive. The Centre apparently had no idea that the former commander of the Soviet secret police in Spain was already aboard ship on the Atlantic when word reached Moscow next day that SCHWED had failed to turn up at the Paris embassy as scheduled. Forty-eight hours later his NVKD records show that his disappearance had become a matter of personal concern for Yezhov. On 21 July, when the *Montclare* docked in Montreal and the Orlovs stepped from the gangplank on to Canadian soil, the NKVD chief was preparing to send out the "mobile squads" to hunt for the missing General.

The Canadian authorities gave Orlov a friendly reception. After examining his diplomatic passport and reading the letter of recommendation from the head of their consulate in Paris, the immigration officer issued the General with an identification card admitting him for a two-month stay as a non-immigrant. Secreted in their hand baggage, the Orlovs carried a small fortune in US currency. The Soviets would later claim that their cash hoard was NKVD operational funds stolen from the Barcelona *rezidentura* office safe. Supporting evidence is found on page 170 of volume one of the Orlov file which contains a certificate of examination of the safe made out after his disappearance. This records that about $60,000 dollars was missing, presumably taken by Orlov. This was far in excess of the money that Orlov later testified he carried with him when he arrived in North America. Significantly he never accounted for the discrepancy, nor is it clear from the NKVD file whether there was any other explanation for the disappearance of such a substantial sum.[35]

"When I entered the United States I had $22,800," Orlov would later testify, insisting that every cent of it was from his "savings". He assured the US Immigration and Naturalization Service in 1955 that he was "a highly paid official" whose "salary during the last years was $900 a month and my wife's $350 a month". He claimed that the money was always paid to him in dollars when he worked abroad, with no deductions. This made it appear that the total sum the Orlovs brought with them amounted to little more than their combined wages for the two years they spent in Spain. Since this could not have taken into account either living expenses or their daughter's medical bills, Orlov contended that it was supplemented by cash from the fund they had been saving to send Vera to a "school-sanatorium" in Switzerland when she reached sixteen.[36] However he obtained these funds, it was a tidy sum representing over $250,000 in current values. Significantly, one of Mrs Orlov's first actions after reaching Canada was to take advantage of the capitalist system by putting their fortune to work for them earning interest: she opened a savings account with the Bank of Montreal, No. 300937, using the name of Berg.[37]

The passbook was opened in Maria's name so that she could survive independently to look after their daughter in the event that Yezhov's "mobile squads" assassinated her husband. It was a wise precaution in the circumstances since we find that the August 1938 entry in his personal file at Moscow Centre, although it did not earmark him for immediate liquidation, raised the possibility. It noted that the General's "flight was regarded as a result of fear and misunderstanding", but Orlov's senior ranking as an operational officer was high enough that his "fleeing was a unilateral action, bordering on treason".[38]

"It was a dangerous game for me and my family," Orlov later reflected. "I was aware that the Kremlin's terrorists were out to find me and liquidate me." He therefore decided that in addition to going to ground in North America to protect his family, he must also make a move to protect his mother and that of his wife, who were then both living. What Orlov did was to issue a blackmail threat to Stalin: "I wrote a letter to Stalin and to the chief of the NKVD, Yezhov, warning Stalin that if they took revenge on my mother or the mother of my wife or that if they succeeded in murdering me, my lawyer would publish all the data known to me about Stalin's crimes which I enumerated in those two letters."[39]

Orlov records that his duplicate "thirty-seven-page" blackmail letters were written shortly after he reached Canada. According to his published account and later testimony before the US Senate they contained a long list of the Soviet dictator's crimes. Starting with the murder of Kirov and sparing no gruesome detail, he said he set down a catalogue of Stalin's crimes that included the use of the NKVD to obtain the confessions and trumped-up charges for the rigging of the

Moscow trials and the purges of Marshal Tukhachevsky and the other Red Army commanders. To settle his old score with Yezhov, Orlov also claimed he had taken care to tell Stalin how the NKVD agent General Skoblin, one of the kidnappers of General Miller, had ignored the Kremlin's express orders by taking refuge in the Soviet embassy in Paris in September 1937.

"I warned him with all the determination at my command that, if he dared to revenge himself on our mothers, I would publish everything I knew," Orlov wrote with a sense of high drama that would have done credit to a Hollywood screenwriter. "I was confident that Stalin would have to postpone his revenge until he had succeeded in kidnapping me and forcing me to yield my hidden memoirs, thereby making sure the secrets of his crimes would not be published."[40]

This was blackmail on a grand scale. And to pull it off Orlov had to find a way to deliver his demands without revealing his own whereabouts. He achieved this by enlisting the aid of two of his Russian cousins who had emigrated to America.

"When I arrived in Canada from Europe, I called up my cousin Isaac Rabinowitz," Orlov later testified. "I asked him to contact Nathan Koornick and to send him to me in Montreal because I needed the services of Nathan Koornick to take my letters to Paris."[41]

Orlov had become reacquainted with his Koornick cousins while visiting Rabinowitz during his trip to the United States in the autumn of 1932. He had known them as children when the brothers Nathan, Max, Isadore and their sister Florence had lived in Pogorsk, about eighty-five miles from the Feldbin family home in Bobruysk. Travelling even such a relatively short distance was not easy for a Jewish family in Tsarist Russia at the turn of the century and according to Isadore's recollection, the two were only barely acquainted before the Koornicks left for America in 1905.[42] They were therefore hardly close friends and Nathan remembered that he himself had never really spoken to Orlov until they happened to arrive at their cousin Rabinowitz's home in the Bronx one day in September 1932. Orlov was there and they had then chatted for about an hour and a half about Russia. Koornick told the FBI in 1954 that he was not able to establish precisely what Orlov was doing in the United States other than going to Detroit "to buy some automobile parts". It had therefore come as a surprise, Koornick said, when he received a telephone call from Orlov in July 1938, saying he was in trouble and asking him if he would come at once to Montreal.[43]

"I was not absolutely sure that he would be able to do that service for me," Orlov would later admit to immigration examiners who questioned him closely on why so distant a relative and one whom he had not seen for so many years should have immediately placed himself at his cousin's beck and call. His response was that Koornick was "a very good and close relative", who had been "the best friend of my parents" during Orlov's childhood days in Russia.[44] He said that his cousin, who was some twenty years his senior, had helped his father financially. If Nathan had not responded to Rabinowitz's call, Orlov contended that he would have asked "some other relative to come to me". The service he was asking his cousin to perform was onerous, he admitted, but such mutual aid was a tradition amongst the tightly knit family networks who had banded together to survive the pogroms in Russia. It had remained a strong tradition amongst the emigré Jewish community in New York. So a call for assistance on Orlov's behalf from such an influential friend as Rabinowitz could not easily be denied by the Koornicks.

Nathan Koornick himself told the FBI that he "knew and liked Orlov's father", and this was another reason why he had responded immediately by travelling to Montreal. He recalled how he had checked into the Hotel Windsor, as instructed by Rabinowitz. It was in the lobby that he met Orlov, who asked him to go to France to deliver two letters to the Soviet embassy in Paris. Koornick agreed, but first had to return to New York in order to obtain a passport. He was back in Canada by the beginning of August, at which time Koornick said that he gave Orlov $2,000. The loan, he said, was not solicited and his cousin "appeared to live well and did not appear to be in need of any money".[45]

In 1954 Koornick then told the FBI how he had sailed from Montreal on a steamship of the Canadian Pacific Line, reaching Paris five days later. There he took a taxi to the Soviet embassy in the rue de Grenelle and, since it was a holiday, "only one clerk appeared to be on duty". Following his cousin's instructions to keep the taxi waiting, he delivered the two sealed letters and then had the cab drive rapidly away from the legation. He then went to a post office, where he mailed a postcard, pre-addressed and written by Orlov to the Soviet Ambassador informing him of the delivery of his two letters. Koornick said that he also sent a separate telegram, prepared by Orlov, to Moscow, informing the authorities that the Soviet embassy in Paris had received two sealed letters, "one to the head of the NKVD and the other to a personal friend of Stalin for personal delivery to Stalin". The two envelopes delivered to the embassy he said bore Orlov's thumbprint as positive identification. Even though Koornick said he had not seen their contents he had been led to understand by Orlov that they contained a statement of why his cousin was defecting.[46]

This was the version that Orlov gave of his blackmail scheme in all his published writings, and reiterated to the FBI and the Immigration Service examiners. Because his scheme had manifestly succeeded in persuading Stalin to call off his assassination squads, Orlov was never questioned about why Stalin should have caved in to these particular threats, or why his threatened revelations were so potent that they amounted to a gold-plated life insurance policy. Had it simply been a matter of Stalin's so-called "ghastly crimes", the cynical dictator would surely have scoffed them off as the undocumented allegations of an embittered Trotskyist traitor.

The extent to which Orlov deceived the Americans about how he dissuaded the Soviet dictator and his secret police chief from hunting him down or taking revenge against his relatives in the USSR is finally revealed by his KGB dossier. The original letter that his cousin Nathan Koornick went to such great lengths to ensure reached Moscow has survived. It was eleven, not thirty-seven, pages long with a two-page attachment. No trace of the copy Orlov claimed to have sent to Stalin has been found. But though the hand-written envelope containing Yezhov's copy does not have Orlov's thumbprint, it still has scraps of maroon sealing wax clinging to the yellowing paper above the carefully penned Cyrillic characters spelling out "Strictly Personal. To Nikolay Ivanovich Yezhov. Not To Be Opened By Anyone Else."[47] Initialled "from SCHWED", Orlov's operational code name, his letter has been declassified in full by the Russian Intelligence Service – with the exception of two minor deletions of operational information. In Orlov's bold hand, he eloquently explains and defends his motivation for fleeing. Significantly the letter contains not a single reference to Stalin's crimes but it does make clear the substance of the threat that Orlov delivered and which proved such potent blackmail:

Nikolay Ivanovich Yezhov,
I would like to explain to you in this letter how, after nineteen years of unimpeachable service to the Party and to Soviet power and many years of underground work, after the Party and Government awarded me the orders of Lenin and the Red Banner for my efforts for two years of full and active self-sacrifice and struggle under the conditions of ruthless war – how it could happen that I deserted. My life has been one of irreproachable and total service to the interests of the proletariat and Soviet power under the steadfast gaze of the Party and the leadership of our collective people [the Foreign Directorate of the NKVD].
On 9 July I received a telegram which lacked any operational justification. It implied that, for absolutely incomprehensible motives, I was being led into a trap aboard the steamship *Svir* which

had obviously been specially sent to capture me. The telegram instructed me to go to Antwerp on 14 July, where I would be met on board this steamship by a comrade I know personally.

"It is desirable," the telegram stated, "that the first meeting take place on board." This reeked of conspiracy, not only because of the nature of the meeting, but because it ordered that I make the journey by a diplomatic car provided by our embassy in France, accompanied by the Consul General.

Why should the first meeting take place aboard ship? Why, if not to strike me down and transport me there as a condemned enemy? Why should I have to be accompanied by a Consul General in a diplomatic car? Why, unless it was to keep me under surveillance during the journey – or, in the event of some delay near the steamship, to invoke the power of the Consul General to declare me insane after suffering concussion in Spain to claim that I was being escorted back to the USSR under close supervision. Security was the explanation given in the telegram, of the diplomatic car but this was clearly a smoke screen for an insidious trap set for me – a totally innocent man.

It was clear to me that those in the leadership who want me liquidated had overdone their "purge" of the apparatus. Whoever it was who sought to advance his career in expectation of being rewarded for a well-executed operation by trying to portray me as a criminal by such bizarre means must have been operationally illiterate to try to lure me aboard the ship as an "enemy of the people". It was clear to me that my fate had been determined and that death lay in store for me.

I asked myself a question: do I, as a member of the Party, have a right, even under a threat of inescapable death, to refuse to go back home? My comrades who worked with me know well that I have many times risked my life when required for the cause and the Party. I repeatedly exposed myself under heavy bombardment from Fascist aviators for two whole weeks when unloading ammunition ships – even though it was not part of my duties. Many times have I risked my life fulfilling operational tasks known to you. At a distance of three paces I was fired at by a White Guardist who sought to kill me, a hated Bolshevik. When I was in plaster after crushing two of my vertebrae in a car crash, despite the doctor's orders, I did not give up work, but continually drove to various towns at the front in the interests of the struggle with the enemy. Surely the Party never demanded a senseless death from its members? Certainly not in the interest of criminal career makers. But not even a threat of illegal and unjust punishment stopped me from going to that steamship. It was the realization that, after my execution and the exile or execution by firing squad of my wife, my fourteen-year-old sick girl would find herself in the streets. She would have been dogged by children and adults as a daughter of an "enemy of the people". That this should be the fate of the daughter of a father of whom she was proud as an honest Communist and fighter, was beyond my power to endure.

I am not a coward. I would even accept an erroneous, unjust verdict, enduring it to the last, unwanted by anyone, a sacrificial goat for the Party, but to die with the realization of the fact that my sick child is destined for such horrible torment and suffering – that was more than I could stand. Could I count on arriving in the USSR to have a just investigation of my case? No, and once more no.

My rationale is as follows:

1. The very fact that I was not recalled, but that a trap was set for me aboard ship explains it all. Evidently I was listed as an enemy of the people even before I was to have stepped aboard ship.

2. I would have found myself in the hands of a criminal named DOUGLAS [code name for Spigelglass] who, until July 1938, was the deputy head of the Foreign Department. He directed the NKVD assassination squads which accounted for Ignace Reiss, who was shot in 1937. I would have played right into the hands of DOUGLAS, who, out of base personal motives, has already liquidated two most honest comrades.

This is not all. I know that DOUGLAS gave an order to liquidate hero of the Spanish [Civil] War [General] Walter, who voluntarily spent sixteen months at the front. Walter is one of the few names popularly known to every soldier. This order was given by DOUGLAS on the grounds of unconfirmed rumours and hearsay that he, Walter, had "unhealthy ideas which might lead to his refusal to go back home". Honest people did not carry out this criminal order, and Walter, of his own volition, went back home in good heart believing in the Party.

There are many other examples which characterize the criminal nature of the man DOUGLAS whose careerist motives made him ready to liquidate dozens of honest people and Party members with the pretext of creating an impression of operations that were necessary for the success of the struggle against our enemies. In this quest for popularity, the careerist DOUGLAS, in the presence of the majority of my operational officers, has revealed a number of most important service secrets. He even terrorized my officers by reciting the names of the families of our former officers who were shot by firing squad without trial. DOUGLAS's own motives, according to trustworthy officers who arrived from home, should be questioned. It is ironical that officers who should have enjoyed his fullest confidence were found guilty of espionage, while their networks are still working and are intact today. If "P", for example, was a spy, why did he keep working with such a man as TULIP, whom he recruited? How come he did not betray TULIP? Or, if "M" had been a spy, why did he not betray WAISE or SÖHNCHEN or any of the others who are still operational sources?*

In short, these are the reasons which persuaded me, a man devoted to the Party and the USSR, not to walk into the trap prepared for me aboard that ship by the criminal careerist DOUGLAS. I want you, as a human being, to appreciate every step of the tragedy which I now have to endure: a loyal Party member deprived of the Party and an honest citizen deprived of my mother country.

My sole purpose now is to survive to bring up my child until she comes of age. Always remember that I am no traitor to my Party or my country. No one and nothing will ever make me betray the cause of the proletariat and of Soviet power. I did not want to leave my country any more than a fish wants to leave water, but the delinquent activity of criminal people has cast me up like a fish on ice. From my knowledge of other cases I know the identity of the forces which will have been committed to my physical liquidation. Put a stop to the misuse of our people. It suffices to say that they have caused me extreme misery by depriving me of the right to live and fight within the ranks of the Party to enjoy the just rewards of long years of unselfish service.

I have not only been deprived of my mother country, but the right to live and breathe the same air as the Soviet people. If you leave me alone, I will never embark on anything harmful to the Party or the Soviet Union. I have not committed, nor will I commit anything damaging to the Party and our country. I solemnly swear, to the end of my days, not to utter a word which may harm the Party which brought me up or the country in which I grew up.

SCHWED

PS: I ask you to issue an order not to disturb my old mother. She is

* "P" refers to PETER, the code name of Smirnov/Glinsky, the Paris *rezident* who ran TULIP, the code name for Zborowsky, the NKVD agent who penetrated the entourage of Trotsky's son Sedov. "M" stands for MANN, the cryptonym used throughout his career by Theodore Mally who in 1937 had been running Maclean [WAISE] and Philby [SÖHNCHEN] in London.

now seventy; she is innocent. I am the last of her children to survive and she is a lonely and unhappy creature.[48]

By all accounts Yezhov was not the type of individual to be touched by humanitarian sentiments, however eloquently spelled out, but the fury of the NKVD chief and his deputy Beria on reading it would have been all the more volcanic because of the implicit blackmail threat contained within its lines. "P" was a reference to PETER, the code name of S. M. Glinsky, Orlov's friend, who was the former NKVD Paris *rezident* known as V. V. Smirnov. "M" was MANN, the cryptonym of Theodore Mally – both had by 1938 been recalled and charged as traitors on Yezhov's orders. The references to the code names of two members of the Cambridge network, WAISE (Maclean) and SÖHNCHEN (Philby), sent a special signal to Moscow that, should the NKVD death squads hunt him down, Orlov had taken steps to ensure there would be dire consequences for the networks he had built up. By naming TULIP, the cryptonym of Mark Zborowsky, the NKVD agent who had penetrated the entourage of Lev Sedov, Trotsky's son, Orlov knew he would secure the attention of the NKVD Chief. "He was so highly valued that even Stalin knew about him," Orlov later testified, an indication that he knew that TULIP was the NKVD penetration agent earmarked to "become the organizer of the assassination of Trotsky or Trotsky's son at any time". Because of the great trust Trotsky (whose code name was STARIK (OLD MAN)) and his son (whose cryptonym, like Philby's, was SONNY or SÖHNCHEN) had in Zborowsky, the NKVD planned to use him to "help infiltrate an assassin into Trotsky's household in Mexico".[49] The reference to TULIP in Orlov's letter was calculated to reinforce the impact of Orlov's blackmail threat because he knew how much Yezhov and Stalin wanted to settle scores with Trotsky.

Orlov's communication was clearly intended to hold the Soviet intelligence service to ransom and it was reinforced in the wording of the two-page appendix. In it he took care to include mention of the Spanish Gold operation together with "all his considerable work" on Trotsky and his son, and a cryptic reference to the part he played in the political terror in Spain. He also alluded to all the operations he had conducted "in the country of GRAFPEN" (the name of the current London *rezident* and therefore NKVD shorthand for Britain) and "in the country of FIN" (France) when he had been sent to recruit "illegal" penetration networks on both sides of the Channel. Orlov also specified other cases and operations by code names that have yet to be tracked down in the contemporary Soviet records. The very fact that they have proved so elusive to uncover is an indication of their sensitivity and subsequent efforts to expunge references to them from the NKVD files. Altogether his appendix listed a roster of more than sixty agents and operations in addition to TULIP, MÄDCHEN and SÖHNCHEN whose secrets he held.

The roster of NKVD agents represented the "crown jewels" of the Soviet intelligence networks – and it did not require minds so pathologically attuned to suspicion as those of the "Dwarf" and his "Big Boss" to appreciate that an intelligence officer as skilled as Orlov would have taken the precaution of keeping a copy of the blackmail list. They could expect that he would have a copy placed in a bank safe deposit with instructions to his lawyer for this box to be opened in the event of his disappearance or sudden death. This list was Orlov's way of reminding Yezhov and presumably Stalin, to whom it would be shown, that moving against him would put at risk nothing less than the exposure of the most important Soviet foreign intelligence networks. At the same time, it indicated that he was offering to keep his mouth shut in return for an assurance that no harm would overtake his relatives in Russia and the NKVD calling off the hunt for him.

It was a pact of the devil's devising and one which gave the Soviet dictator and his henchmen little choice but to accede and trust Orlov would keep his side of the bargain. This is clear from the NKVD files which show that when Orlov's letter reached Moscow in mid-August, the descriptions of the missing General had already been drawn up by the Centre preparatory to launching a worldwide manhunt for him. The operation to liquidate the missing NKVD General, however, was never given the go-ahead. It was cancelled by a directive "from above", according to Orlov's contemporary, Sudoplatov, who was then a ranking NKVD officer at the Centre. This, he recalled, had come as a surprise to some NKVD officers. Sudoplatov told the authors that the decision to rescind the operation could only have been issued on Stalin's direct authority.[50]

In the NKVD files there is another confirmation of how swiftly Yezhov, and presumably Stalin, caved in to Orlov's blackmail. It is in the Spigelglass file as an item in the very detailed confession that he gave six months after his own arrest for treachery in November 1938: "NIKOLSKY [Orlov] when he became a non-returner, wrote a letter to Yezhov *in which he said that he would expose compromising material as soon as he detected the slightest hint of surveillance* [emphasis added]. After that Yezhov issued a directive not to touch NIKOLSKY."[51]

The stakes were high in Orlov's "dangerous game" and it would have been clear to Yezhov and Stalin that his was no idle bluff. At the time of his defection in 1938 Orlov's dossier indicates that he had knowledge of the major operations involving agents in most of the underground networks in Europe, Britain and the United States. The Oxbridge networks in Britain and the Berlin network in Germany were just two that were to become increasingly important, giving Stalin all the more reason to stick to his side of the bargain. Orlov could not have guessed just how his "insurance policy" would increase in value over the years. But it is significant that he deliberately concealed the true contents of the blackmail letter he had written to Moscow from his American interrogators and that this permitted Philby, Blunt and the Oxford "moles" to continue operating for Moscow in the upper reaches of the British Government.

It is also significant that, despite Orlov's assertion that he had supplied information to Stalin which proved that Yezhov disobeyed his express orders during the kidnapping of General Miller, when Skoblin took refuge in the Paris embassy, it does not appear anywhere in the letter in the KGB files. This, it appears, was another element in the General's monumental deception. Orlov's decision to keep his side of the devil's pact – not to betray Philby and the other agents he listed – became part of the deadly illusion that made the KGB underground networks in Britain such a potent force during the Cold War.

13

"IN CONSTANT FEAR OF THEIR LIVES"

WHEN NATHAN KOORNICK returned to Montreal aboard the *Empress of Australia* in the second week of August 1938, after delivering Orlov's blackmailing letter, he found his cousin had already left Canada. While Koornick was in France, Orlov had put into operation the second stage of his survival plan when he visited the American legation at Ottawa and matter-of-factly requested permission to enter the United States. Presenting his Soviet diplomatic passport No. 3632 and his wife's, No. 3633, he claimed that he was accredited to the staff of the Soviet Ambassador, Trianowsky, in Washington. The American officials dealt with his request as a matter of routine and issued him visa A2 472 620, granting permission for him and his family to enter the United States for an indefinite stay as a foreign diplomat under Section 3-1 of the 1924 Immigration Act. His paperwork was stamped by US border officials when the train from Ottawa stopped at Rouses Point, New York on 13 August 1938, one month to the day after the Orlovs had left Paris.[1]

"I used that passport for my travelling," Orlov told US Immigration and Naturalization Service examiners fifteen years later. But claiming that he was an accredited diplomat he had entered America illegally. Orlov nevertheless maintained that he had "renounced the rights given to represent the Soviet Government, but still my diplomatic passport was valid [until] my official resignation reached Moscow later". His deception, he said, was necessitated by his desire to protect his life and that of Maria and his daughter Vera.[2]

When the family reached New York, Orlov used his cousin's surname, registering himself and his wife as Mr and Mrs Leon Koornick when they checked into the Wellington Hotel at 55th and Broadway. The towering, red-brick edifice may not have been one of the city's smartest hotels, but it was large enough to afford the anonymity the fugitive NKVD General sought because its guests included many overseas visitors. Orlov trusted only his cousin Isaac Rabinowitz with his address, and so it was by contacting

Rabinowitz that Koornick finally managed to arrange a meeting with Orlov on his return to New York. The rendezvous took place not at the Wellington, but at the Hotel St George, Koornick told the FBI. He recalled that after reporting to Orlov on his trip, his cousin had told him that "he had known Stalin very well and that Stalin was a man moved by the spirit of vengeance and that he never forgot an enemy". Koornick said it was his strong impression that his cousin was "generally in fear of Stalin".[3]

According to the account Koornick gave FBI investigators in 1954, he had himself borne the cost of the two trips to Canada, all his hotel bills and the transatlantic return fare to France.[4] That he had accepted this not inconsiderable outlay puzzled the Bureau analysts, since it was at variance with Orlov's account. In his sworn statement to the Immigration and Naturalization Service in June 1955, initialled by Orlov on every page, he had declared "absolutely" that he had reimbursed Koornick for *all* his expenses in 1938. Orlov's memory, according to another boyhood informant, was like a "razor blade". The FBI found it odd that Orlov insisted that he could not remember the total cost exactly.[5]

"It must have been within some $400," Orlov told the examiner. Challenging Koornick's statement that he had not been reimbursed for the trip he declared: "that man is eighty-one years old and he has a very feeble memory, but my memory is good". Considering the value of the service Nathan had performed for him, that he was using his cousin's name and that he had later tapped him again, in 1941, for another $1,000 to open an account with the National City Bank of New York, Orlov's callous remarks are surprising. But, as his FBI record shows, when it came to assuring his own personal survival Orlov had no hesitation twisting facts to conceal the truth from American investigators. For their part, it appears that his Jewish relations from Bobruysk wittingly assisted Orlov in his efforts to draw a veil over his past. Nor it seems did they ask any questions; he was "family" and they continued helping him even when they later learned that he had been a high-ranking official in Stalin's secret police.

George Sokolsky was another of Orlov's boyhood circle from Bobruysk who had emigrated to the United States. They had studied Hebrew together and he told the FBI that he had not seen Orlov from 1917 until September 1938 when they encountered one another at a synagogue in Astoria, Queens, on the Day of Atonement. That evening they had talked, recalling old times, until 2 a.m. But, according to Sokolsky, Orlov would only tell him that he was "on some commercial mission". Sokolsky did not even know at the time that the man he knew as Feldbin now called himself Orlov, recalling only that his friend had seemed "extremely fearful" and "could not sit for a moment before getting up and walking around the room".[6]

Orlov pointedly had left no address or telephone number with Sokolsky, who told the FBI that he did not see him again for fifteen years. Attending the synagogue on Holy Days, as Orlov's voluminous FBI file discloses, was one way in which he made discreet contact with his cousins and Bobruysk friends who lived in the New York area following his arrival in the United States. By adopting the same methodical techniques that had made him a successful spy master, the fugitive General spent the next three months on the move, shuttling his family between New York and Philadelphia, where his cousin Koornick lived. Among the hotels they resided in during their first six months of hiding out in the United States were the Benjamin Franklin, Stratford and the Plaza in Philadelphia, and the Wellington and St George in New York City. All were establishments catering to less affluent tourists and commercial clients and the Orlovs took care never to stay in the same hotel for more than a few weeks, alternating their aliases at each stop, their preference being Koornick and Berg.[7]

Apart from their own safety, the Orlovs' main concern was for the emotional trauma suffered by their daughter, whose physically weak constitution was badly stressed by the constant travelling. "My wife and I never tried to destroy her illusions," Orlov wrote of Vera. "She had the deepest aversion to any kind of violence and an infinite sympathy for those who suffered." Because they knew that her life span would probably be short, her parents had decided it would be dishonest to conceal from her the reason why they had to flee from Stalin's tyranny. Vera had listened to her parents recounting the terrible catalogue of suffering of her fellow countrymen with tears in her eyes, according to Orlov. "The world she had known had suddenly turned into fiction," he wrote. "She was robbed of all her big and little dreams." Vera had known that her father and mother had fought in the Revolution. She felt deeply hurt for them and the way that their dreams had been shattered, Orlov wrote touchingly, declaring that they took comfort that this ailing daughter had grown up and become very adult by the time they reached America.[8]

The family bonds between them were strengthened by the Orlovs' fugitive life-style. They all knew that it was only a matter of time before their diplomatic passports were revoked and, even though they had an indefinite US visa, it would be invalidated once the State Department found out that it had been obtained under false pretences. At some point, therefore, Orlov realised they would be left with no choice but to request asylum, or risk being deported. Applying for permanent residency status would bring him to the attention of the American authorities and this in turn increased the risk that his whereabouts would become known to Moscow. Orlov knew only too well from his time in the Foreign Department at the Centre that the NKVD regarded the United States bureaucracy as invitingly open to penetration by their network of American-based agents. Any formal registration with the Immigration and Naturalization Office would therefore multiply the risk that his family's whereabouts would become known to Moscow. A formal request for asylum would also attract the interest of the FBI, who would insist on an exhaustive interrogation of a former General of Stalin's secret police force.

This would put his secret at risk and so Orlov's survival strategy depended on enlisting the aid of sympathetic US Government officials who would permit him to make a discreet application for residence without revealing his address, or drawing attention to himself. This, in turn, required a lawyer who could act for him, preferably one who possessed high-level political connections to pull the strings of Washington officialdom on his behalf. He sought the advice of his cousin Rabinowitz, who had many Washington contacts from his friends on the board of the American Red Cross Society. With the help of Henry Feld, the husband of one of his Russian-born Koornick aunts, Orlov obtained an introduction to John F. Finerty of the Park Avenue law firm of Olwine, Conolly and Chase.[9]

Finerty was a well-known civil rights attorney, who had been a counsel in the notorious 1921 case of Nicola Saccho and Bartolomeo Vanzetti, the two Italian-born anarchists from Massachusetts who were convicted in a controversial trial and later executed for armed robbery and murder, despite worldwide concern over their protested innocence. Finerty had also been one of the lawyers on the commission into Trotsky set up by Professor John Dewey whose conclusions, published as the book *Not Guilty* in 1937, were that the charges made against him in the Moscow show trials were without foundation.[10]

If Orlov had been frank about his role in hunting down the POUMists in Spain, it is unlikely that Finerty, who sympathised self-evidently with Trotsky, would ever have taken him on as a client. But he *did* become the General's attorney and as a well-connected figure in the Democratic Party, had soon obtained an introduction to James L. Houghteling, Commissioner of Immigration and Naturalization.[11] In September 1938, the Orlovs left Philadelphia, where they were staying in the Benjamin Franklin Hotel, and took the train to Washington accompanied by Finerty. They met with the Commissioner at his office in the Department of Labor and Houghteling referred them to his assistant, Mr Shoemaker. After hearing that the Orlovs had more than adequate funds of $22,800 and American relatives ready to sponsor them, Shoemaker agreed with Finerty that, as his clients' lives were obviously at risk, "the best thing for Orlov to do was to avoid publicity and keep his arrival secret".[12]

The Assistant Immigration Commissioner undertook to make no official record of Orlov's decision to reside in the United States – Finerty would later claim that his clients' trip to Washington was evidence that Orlov had received the official dispensation for them not to register as aliens. The way had now been cleared for the Orlov family effectively to go underground, which they did early in 1939 by heading for the West Coast. In California Orlov not only put more distance between himself and any pursuers sent out by Moscow but the doctors they had consulted about their daughter's rheumatic heart had advised that the state's mild climate could be beneficial for her condition. But before they took the transcontinental train west, there was one other piece of business to which the former NKVD General attended: he contacted Trotsky to warn him of the assassination operation being mounted against him.[13]

Orlov was later to testify that he had decided to alert Stalin's arch-enemy about the plans to have him murdered by a member of his circle, named Mark, after he had learned about Zborowsky's sinister role in Sedov's household. Since the former NKVD General had been an accessory in Spain to Stalin's worldwide vendetta against Trotskyites, it is curious that he should have put himself at some risk – by attempting to issue a warning that would have been construed in Moscow as a direct betrayal of his blackmail pact. It was this concern which led Orlov to camouflage the origin of his warning by inventing a new "legend" for himself as the Russian emigré uncle of the Soviet defector General Lyeshkov. This was the persona he adopted to warn Trotsky that his nephew had written from Japan about "an important and dangerous *agent provocateur* who has for a long time been the assistant of your son Sedov in Paris". Identifying Zborowsky only by physical description and his forename Mark, this "well-wisher" calling himself "Stein" alerted Trotsky that this dangerous NKVD agent had also engineered the theft of his archive from the Nikolayevsky Institute and hinted that he might have also been involved in Sedov's death. According to Orlov's letter, Lyeshkov had "expressed apprehension that now the assassination of Trotsky was on the agenda Moscow would try to plant assassins with the help of this *agent provocateur*, or through *agents provocateurs* from Spain under the guise of Spanish Trotskyites".[14]

"Be on your guard," Orlov concluded. "Do not trust any person, man or woman, who may come to you with recommendations from this *provocateur*." The letter from "Stein", which had been drafted in phonetic Russian on a Latin typewriter, was left unsigned and identical copies addressed to both Trotsky and his wife were posted to their hide-away in a villa at Coyocan near Mexico City. In them

"Stein" invited Trotsky to contact him for more information by placing a notice in the January or February issue of the *Socialist Appeal*, a Trotskyist newspaper in New York.[15]

Trotsky, according to sources close to him at that time, considered the "Stein" letter to be a deliberate hoax by the NKVD aimed at panicking him and disrupting his organization.[16] Nonetheless he arranged for an advertisement to be placed in the *Socialist Appeal* that read: "I insist you go to the editorial offices and talk about it with Comrade Martin." Orlov was later to admit that he had followed this up, without informing his wife who regarded herself as her husband's security guard. He said he had paid a visit to the New York offices of the *Socialist Appeal* to inquire for "Comrade Martin", but that he did not like the swarthy looks of the man who was pointed out to him; his appearance suggested not Russian, but Hungarian origins. "He did not inspire too much confidence in me," Orlov recalled, relating how he had decided not to enter Martin's office to identify himself as "Stein". Instead he had then tried to contact Trotsky by telephone when he reached San Francisco in February. Although he had managed to get through to a secretary on one occasion, Orlov said that Trotsky apparently did not want to come to the telephone because he thought the caller was just another journalist trying to exploit him.[17]

This was as far as Orlov took his bid to warn Trotsky of the assassination threat being mounted against him. Corroboration can be found in the NKVD files that indicates that the news of this warning did reach Moscow from an NKVD agent operating in the entourage of the exiled Soviet leader at the Villa Coyocan. The Centre was taken in by Orlov's deception, crediting General Lyeshkov as the originator of the alarm after news of "Stein"'s letter was relayed via Zborowsky to Moscow almost a year later in a cryptogram from the Paris *rezidentura* of 25 June 1939, which reads:

On 21 June 1939 NEIGHBOUR [Russian *Soseoka*, "female", the NKVD cryptonym for Lilia Estrine, a Russian-born member of the Trotsky circle] returned from America. On the same day TULIP [Zborowsky] had a meeting with her in the presence of Elza and Gershuni [two other members of the entourage]. She said that OLD MAN [Trotsky] had questioned her in depth about TULIP. He had told her that he had received a denunciatory report on him in two letters, one by registered post and the other by ordinary mail. The author of the report was alleged to be a relative of Lyeshkov who lived in San Francisco signing himself Stein. In it he claimed to have had a rendezvous with Lyeshkov after the latter had defected to

Japan and had passed on to Stein some information about the work of Soviet intelligence abroad, and had asked Stein to warn the OLD MAN that there was a traitor in their midst who used the nickname MARK, a spectacle wearer who had a one-year-old child. Until 1938 MARK had been working at the Institute with Nikolayevsky, after surfacing out of the blue. Stein had reported that MARK had ostensibly been a member of the Polish Communist Party, but this was not cross-checked. Lyeshkov did not remember MARK's surname. MARK, however, worked closely with SONNY [Lev Sedov], informed on him to the GPU [NKVD] and stole the Trotsky archives. Stein asked the OLD MAN not to trust anyone who turned up on MARK's recommendation.[18]

Stein had also requested that the OLD MAN give an answer in the newspaper *Socialist Appeal* – which OLD MAN did, but the author [of the warning letter] did not appear.

NEIGHBOUR asserted that the OLD MAN did not believe the report and saw it as a GPU [NKVD] provocation. Elza confirmed that this was indeed a GPU provocation. NEIGHBOUR said that a denunciatory report had been received on her too. It was in a letter from V[ictor] Serge in which she figured as a GPU [NKVD] agent.[19]

Reacting to this report, the Centre had initially considered using Zborowsky to write a letter to Trotsky explaining away the warning about him as a malicious libel. But TULIP rejected this course of action in his reply of 15 July 1939, contending that it could only make the situation worse. He pointed out that "no member of the organization" had ever accused him and that Trotsky himself believed the warning to be a "provocation." Since Trotsky had used Estrine to relay secret instructions to him, he was obviously still held in trust, and also "GROLL [Krivitsky] in his evidence about an agent among the Trotskyists did not have a word against him, but had only made accusations against Serge". Furthermore, he wrote, Elza, who was the Trotsky "expert" on the NKVD, had also excluded him from any shadow of suspicion and continued to recommend him favourably. After considering Zborowsky's points, the Centre concurred that their agent TULIP must indeed be above suspicion and that Trotsky himself had dismissed "Stein"'s letter as an NKVD provocation.[20]

Orlov of course was unaware of all this, but he made no further attempt to warn Trotsky of the approaching danger although files at the Centre indicate that he must have known far more about the anti-Trotsky operations than he chose to pass on in his two letters to the Villa Coyocan. He would assure the FBI and the investigators of the Senate Internal Security Sub-Committee that while he did not know Zborowsky, he had learned that he "received about 4,000 francs a month in 1937" and had read some of his reports from Paris.[21]

While in Moscow, it is more than likely that Orlov would have discovered from Zborowsky's file that he had been recruited in 1933 by an NKVD agent B-138 whose code name was JUNKER.[22] One of the many enigmas of the Orlov case is how much he really had known about Zborowsky, particularly his full name and the background to his operations against Sedov. Was his warning a genuine attempt to save Trotsky or nothing but a carefully veiled and deliberately vague alert to cover himself against criticism if he had not made any effort to warn the victim? The NKVD record leads to the presumption that Orlov must have learned all about Zborowsky. Clearly, Orlov did not pass on all that he could have revealed about "Mark"'s sinister activity. But passing on a more definite warning would have risked the Centre identifying him as the source – and that he was breaking his blackmail pact not to betray TULIP, or any other Soviet penetration agents. Orlov's paramount objective was not to save Trotsky, but to ensure his own survival and secure a future for his wife and sickly daughter in America.

It was shortly after his visit to the *Socialist Appeal* that the Orlovs took the train for California. It is also significant to find that Lilia Estrine reported to the NKVD that the "Stein" letters were postmarked from San Francisco, not Philadelphia as Orlov later asserted in a letter to the Director of Research of the Internal Security Sub-Committee on 10 October 1955.[23] This would suggest that he delayed longer than he claimed in sending the warning since he had arrived in San Francisco early in 1939, before moving south to Los Angeles towards the end of February, where the family were to remain for the next eighteen months.

When Stalin made his infamous pact with Hitler in August 1939 and the flames of war engulfed Europe the following month, the Orlovs were ensconced at the Mayan apartment house at 3049 West 8th Street under the name of Berg. After the defeat of Poland they moved to the Hershey apartments at 2600 Wilshire Boulevard before taking up residence at the Ansonia apartments on 2205 West 6th Street. The following summer, as the *Los Angeles Times*' headlines carried news of the Dunkirk evacuation and the fall of France, the Orlovs were living at the Westbury apartment house on 3360 West 9th Street.[24]

While Europe fell to the Nazi *Blitzkrieg*, the peripatetic family suffered their own great personal tragedy. To her parents' dismay, the California sunshine had come too late to arrest the accelerating decline in the health of their cherished daughter. The rheumatic fever virus, which had been eating away at Vera's heart muscles ever since she succumbed to the chill caught ten years earlier, caused her to be hospitalized on 22 May 1940. She was attended at the Good Samaritan

Hospital by Dr Russell W. Lyster, who recognized that her case was hopeless and discharged her on 7 June. It was he who recalled for the FBI that shortly after his sixteen-year-old patient had returned home, he had received an emergency call from her parents on 15 July 1940 to come to their apartment house on West 9th Street because their daughter had suffered an unexpected relapse. When Dr Lyster reached the Westbury, he found another physician already there who had just given the girl an injection, although convinced she was already dead. Dr Lyster said that his original prognosis was that the Orlovs' daughter would never recover, and he had no hesitation in signing the death certificate of Veronika Berg which was given the registry No. 9452 and filed at the Los Angeles Bureau of Vital Statistics.[25]

Vera's death was a terrible blow to the Orlovs, who had sacrificed so much of their lives in a vain attempt to sustain her. They had nonetheless never given up hope she might miraculously be cured. The loss of their beloved only child served to accentuate the unsettled nature of their lives. Now they could not bear to remain in California and, within a few weeks after their bereavement, the Orlovs packed up their few belongings and headed back east. This time they travelled to Massachusetts, registering at the Hotel Essex in Boston on 5 September 1940 as Mr and Mrs A. Berg. They stayed there only briefly before taking rooms in an apartment hotel across the Charles River at 36 Highland Avenue, an art-deco residence fifteen minutes' walk from Harvard University campus.[26]

The Orlovs had carried with them their most precious possessions. The urn containing their daughter's ashes was interred in a family vault in the local Cambridge cemetery, but it was to a Boston bank vault that they consigned an even more valuable item that guaranteed their own safety. According to the records of the Pilgrim Safe Deposit Vaults, a Mr and Mrs Berg arrived at the bank on 31 Milk Street, a block from Faneuil Hall, on 7 September 1940 giving their address as the Essex Hotel, Atlantic Avenue. They were assigned box No. 7165 at an annual rental of $7.50. The vault log shows that over the next twelve months the Bergs had access to this safety deposit box on eight separate occasions.[27]

What they secreted in their security box, according to a clerk who observed its contents in 1942, was a bank savings book and a quantity of "roll and flat pack" film.[28] That two foreigners should want to keep film under tight security raised the bank official's suspicions that the Bergs were German spies. Under the war regulations then in effect, he was obliged to report the matter to the FBI. Fourteen years later Orlov was subpoenaed by a Grand Jury to produce the film in court. The 35mm rolls turned out to be movies of their daughter and her governess shot in Spain. But he was never questioned, or required to produce the contents of the "flat-pack" film. Precisely what the box contained can only be the subject of conjecture, but it would be entirely consistent with the practice that Orlov had used to ship his confidential reports to Moscow by courier, to hypothesize that the film bore negative copies of the eleven pages he had written to Yezhov with the accompanying two-page list of sixty-two underground agents and important NKVD operations.[29]

The FBI records are evidence for concluding that the letters listing Stalin's crimes that Orlov repeatedly testified he had lodged with his attorney to be opened in the event of his death were nothing more than dummies and that his real "insurance policy" was the "flat-pack" film in the Boston bank vault. This important clue would never have come to light had there not been a wartime revision in the US Treasury Department regulations relating to safety deposit boxes held by aliens. This could not have been anticipated by the Orlovs, who, to leave as few traces of their presence as possible, had carefully avoided opening a US bank account: Maria carefully continued to draw cash from her Canadian savings book.

Keeping the lights on in their apartment for security reasons appears to have been the one extravagance the Orlovs indulged in after their daughter's death had relieved them of her heavy medical expenses. With characteristic attention to detail in budgeting, they had set out to live very frugally.[30] Taking into account utility bills, but forgoing all but essential food and clothing needs, they calculated that their Boston rent of $45–$50 a month would enable them to get by on about $1,500 a year. This would permit them to eke out their cash reserve for more than a decade before Orlov would have to seek some form of work, because if he got a job, he would have to register for Social Security. Employment records would increase the risk of his whereabouts being discovered.[31]

The problems of official registration were to impact on Orlov in the autumn of 1940, when Congress passed the Aliens Registration Act. The bill, a response to the outbreak of war in Europe and a flood of refugees reaching the United States, required all foreigners to register and report annually, giving notification of any change of address within ten days. Registering openly could expose him to additional risk but fearful that, if he did not do so, he would be subject to deportation back to the Soviet Union, Orlov took the train to New York to see his lawyer.[32] Finerty went to work on the case by going right to the top of the Justice Department where he contacted Francis Biddle, the Attorney General of the United States, who happened to be an old friend. It was Biddle who then furnished the Orlovs with an introduction to Earl G. Harrison, the Director of Aliens

Registration, who was instructed to take personal charge of handling this sensitive case.[33]

After arriving in Washington on 19 December 1940, Finerty took the Orlovs to a private meeting with Harrison. Explaining the unusual predicament of his client and the danger of assassination, Finerty mentioned that the Attorney General had agreed it would be best to find some way of registering them without recording their whereabouts. Knowing that Biddle himself had taken a personal interest in the case persuaded Harrison to be accommodating. He verbally agreed to waive the condition laid down by the law, assuring the Orlovs that they need not keep the Immigration Service informed of their address, provided that they could be reached through Finerty.[34]

To ensure there were no snags in this unusual arrangement, Harrison detailed his personal assistant, Sewell, to accompany the Orlovs and their lawyer to the Post Office building on Pennsylvania Avenue. There Richard E. Eggleston, the inspector in charge of alien registration, processed the paperwork and fingerprinted the Orlovs. Under "citizenship" Orlov stated "None – last a citizen of Russia" and gave his aliases as Leon Feldbin and Leon Koornick. The address he gave was the Hotel Wellington, Broadway, New York, and his emergency contact was the Manhattan home of his boyhood friend Rosovsky.[35] Eggleston would recall for the FBI thirteen years later his surprise that Mrs Orlov at this meeting had produced her own blotter from her purse to clean her fingers. He told the FBI that the Orlovs were given "special treatment as a result of a phone call he had received" from the Director of Aliens Registration. He said he was under the impression that these special privileges had been arranged for the Orlovs because "they were distant relatives of Russian nobility".[36] The exceptional consideration given to his clients was also acknowledged by Finerty in letters to the Attorney General and the Immigration Commissioner. Harrison had responded warmly. "The attitude of your friends with respect to compliance with the laws was such that the least we could do was to give everything possible in the way of protection." This written confirmation that the immigration laws of the United States had indeed been bent by high officials in Washington would later save Orlov from deportation when he was called upon in 1953 to defend the irregular circumstances of his registration.[37]

The Orlovs then returned to Boston to resume their spartan, reclusive life in their fifty-dollar rooms at Mrs Connell's apartment building in Cambridge. They were to remain there for another year and a half because Maria had struck up a friendly relationship with the manageress. Mrs Connell later informed the FBI how Mrs Berg had told her that she and her husband had formerly resided in Los Angeles, where her husband had owned a bookstore. She also recalled that for most of the two-year period the Bergs had lived in her building they had stayed in their apartment most of the time, going out only very occasionally.[38]

It was on one of their rare trips across the Charles River into Boston that, on 16 August 1941, the Orlovs received a most unpleasant shock. When they went to open their safety deposit box they were summoned to the office of the chief clerk of the bank vault. It was some six months since they had last had access to their property and in the meantime President Roosevelt had issued an executive order freezing all Axis assets in the United States in response to Japanese aggression in Indochina. To enforce the ban, the proclamation also required that foreigners with safe deposit boxes must produce naturalization certificates or provide the bank with a detailed inventory of the contents of their boxes. After the Orlovs had been informed of the new regulations, the man claiming to be Mr Berg had to admit that neither he nor his wife was naturalized. The bank official's suspicions were aroused when the man said that he had no time to do this immediately as he "was in a hurry". But, after promising to return in ten days, Orlov was permitted to take out two passports and the Canadian bank book, their access supervised by the clerk, who later told the FBI about the films. He added that the Bergs were most anxious to remove this film, but that he had not permitted them to do so.[39]

Ten days passed and the Bergs did not return to fulfil their legal obligations. Mr Berg had told the bank official that he and his wife were Russian, but while they seemed to be "people of some breeding" the clerk told the FBI that he was left with a "very definite impression that they were Germans". His belief that they might be hostile agents and that the film they were so anxious to retrieve was used for spying on nearby naval defence installations was confirmed when the bank's September bill for the second year's rent of the box was returned from the Essex Hotel stamped with the notation "Not Found". Although Mr Berg had informed him that a $20 bill had been left on top of the box to cover the rental and drilling out of the lock if he fell overdue with the rent this had proved unnecessary when on 4 September the Pilgrim Trust Company received a money order for $8.33.[40] The Bergs had still not reappeared five months later by the time that the United States had entered World War II, when a sense of patriotic duty prompted the chief clerk of the Pilgrim Trust Company to contact the Boston FBI office at 100 Milk Street on 24 January 1942.

The report caused the FBI to open its first file on the Orlovs under

"Alexander L. Berg, Maria Orlowe Berg", designated as an "Internal Security G[erman] investigation". This report noted that apart from the couple's registration at the Hotel Essex on 5 September giving their home address as 3360 West 9th Street, Los Angeles, there was "a scarcity of information relating to this pair". The trail had gone cold after the Los Angeles FBI office reported that there was no pre-1941 register available for former residents of that apartment house and that a search of documentation in City Hall had shown "the public records of this city do not reveal these subjects to be now residing in this city". An investigation of Aliens Registration division records turned up nine Alexander Bergs and sixteen Maria Bergs, but none of them registered in the Boston area. The FBI search was widened to include New York after the Pilgrim Trust Company had reported having received a money order from Alexander Berg on 25 June 1942 from the St George Hotel in Manhattan. But the bank's receipt was returned with the notation that the subject was no longer there and had left no forwarding address.[41]

The Orlovs by now had already left Boston. One factor which appeared to have prompted them to uproot again was newspaper reports of the death of Krivitsky. On 11 February 1941 the chambermaid at the Bellevue Hotel, a block from Washington's Union Station, had discovered the body of the Soviet defector with a gun next to the gaping bullet wound in his head. Suicide notes beside the bed in room 532 had led the Washington police investigation to conclude that the Soviet defector's death was indeed the suicide that it appeared.[42]

According to a maxim attributed to the NKVD, "anyone can conduct a murder, but it takes an artist to commit a suicide" and Orlov would have regarded this "suicide" as the artistic handiwork of an NKVD assassination squad. Hard on the news of Krivitsky's death Orlov was dealt another threat to his cover in April 1942, when he came within the US military draft that had been extended to include all able-bodied men over forty-five years of age. Apprehensive that if he did not register for selective service, some patriotic busybody in Highland Avenue might report him to the authorities as a draft dodger, the former Soviet General decided to observe the law before moving on again so that he could not be traced. The Orlovs checked in as Mr and Mrs Alexander O. Berg at the Eliot Hotel in Boston on 25 April. The next day an "Alexander Orlov Berg" registered for selective service at the office on 419 Boylston Street, giving as his address the hotel and stating that he had no place of employment. Having complied with the law, the Orlovs then left Boston two weeks later, once again omitting to provide the hotel with a forwarding address.[43]

This time the Orlovs travelled via New York to Ohio, where they rented for $65 a month apartment 202 in the Bertland building at 2384 Euclid Heights Boulevard on the eastern outskirts of Cleveland. Just why the Orlovs chose to live in this industrial city sprawled along the shore of Lake Erie is not clear, other than it offered them an anonymous urban neighbourhood where the influx of war production workers provided camouflage for new arrivals. The snowy Ohio winters may also have been reminders of their Russian homeland for the two exiles. For the next thirty years Cleveland was to be their home town.

The owner of the Bertland apartments would later recall the Bergs as "very quiet people who kept to themselves and had no visitors", who seemed to be "in constant fear of their lives". The FBI were told how they "kept their doors locked at all times, not admitting anyone to their apartment unless the identity of the caller was known to them". The owner's decision to take over their spacious second-floor apartment for his own use in 1943 he said had prompted the Orlovs to move to the other side of Cleveland. They rented an apartment at 12040 Lake Avenue where they remained in seclusion for the next ten years. Neighbours at Lake Apartments recalled the Bergs as "very quiet tenants who stayed very much to themselves". Over the years, though, they became sufficiently confident to tell one of their neighbours that they had come from Russia. This woman told the FBI how the couple had often expressed a dislike of the Soviet Government because they feared for the safety of their relatives. Another neighbour had a little girl, of whom Mrs Berg with her strong foreign accent grew very fond. She would often give the girl candy and presents, telling the mother how she loved children and how her own daughter had died.[44]

The Orlovs' neighbours found it curious that Mr Berg, who claimed to be a translator, did not seem to have any set working hours. But by 21 December 1942 Orlov had become sufficiently assured that, with an eye on a future career, he had enrolled in a business administration course at the Dyke and Spencerian College. The FBI also discovered that he had offered his services to the local Berlitz School as a Russian and German translator, but was never offered a position.[45]

The only people with whom the Orlovs ever associated were their immediate neighbours in the Lake Apartment building, who noted the Bergs' hostility to visitors. On the one occasion they did make an exception they were almost brought to the attention of the FBI. On 23 March 1943 they had let a war bond salesman come into their apartment and bought a $50 bond. This was so large a sum from such an apparently poor couple that the collector promptly did his patriotic duty by reporting them to the local FBI office. His suspicions, he said, had been aroused because their living room was so sparsely furnished, and that Mr Berg had purchased the bond with cash which he had taken out of the closet after carefully closing the doors to the other rooms.[46]

The Cleveland FBI office, however, did not consider this information sufficiently alarming to warrant investigation. Had they done so and followed it up, it might have had a significant impact on the dormant "Internal Security – G" case still pending in their Boston office. After no further leads had turned up for a year and a half, the Berg file had then attracted the interest of Special Agent Edward A. Soucy after the Pilgrim Trust Company reported receiving a letter from Mrs Berg on 4 September 1943. Postmarked "Pittsburgh, Pennsylvania 2 September", it contained a cheque and a typed note: "Gentlemen: I am enclosing $10.50 (money order) for rental of safe No. 7165 for another year. The safe is rented in the name of my husband, Alexander Berg, and mine. Very truly yours, Marie Berg."[47]

The cashier's cheque No. A-18250 had been drawn on the Potter Title and Trust Company in Pittsburgh, but neither the envelope in which it was sent nor the covering note contained a return address. The childish signature of Mrs Berg precisely matched that on the Mayflower bank vault box rental agreement and Soucy had both shipped off to the FBI laboratory for analysis. In response to his request, the Pittsburgh office sent an agent to the bank which issued the cheque. He reported that the teller at the Potter Title and Trust Company recalled drawing the cashier's cheque for Mrs Berg, whom he had never seen before. The teller said she had mentioned having to pay for a vault, but that he did not connect this with a safety deposit box, assuming that the woman was making a payment on a burial vault.[48]

After Special Agent Soucy had requested FBI headquarters to make a thorough search of their name records under "Berg, Alexander", interviews were conducted with Alexander Berg, the Honorary Norwegian Vice Consul in San Francisco, a seaman by the name of Adolf Berg, a Mrs Ausbjarn Berg and a New Jersey couple of the same name. None of them proved to have any connection with the suspect German couple who had rented the safety deposit box in the Boston vault. An investigation of all the Pittsburgh hotel registers also failed to turn up any trace of the elusive Bergs.[49] Yet Soucy still considered the case important enough to be brought to the attention of the Director of the FBI, in a letter to J. Edgar Hoover dated 14 February 1944.[50]

After lengthy investigation, the Bureau laboratory had reported on 27 July 1944 that it had proved impossible to match the handwriting of Alexander Berg with any known suspect on their files. This did little to allay the suspicions of investigator Soucy in Boston that there must be a reason for the vanished couple to take such elaborate steps to conceal their whereabouts, while at the same time maintaining control of the contents of their safety deposit box. The FBI files indicate that in August 1944 he reviewed the case with Edward D. Hassan, the Assistant US Attorney for Boston, with a view to obtaining legal authority to have the Bergs' deposit box opened to establish precisely what was on the film that the supposed German couple had appeared so anxious to reclaim.[51]

The Federal Attorney, however, decided that it might not be possible to secure a court order for the purpose of having the safety deposit opened "in view of the skimpy information available at the present time with reference both to the contents of the box and the background, particularly the nationality, of both subjects". He therefore advised Soucy to cease further investigation of the case "subject to its being reopened when the Boston field office is notified by the Pilgrim Trust Company of the presence of either individual at the bank or when furnished with a known address on either subject".[52] Orlov never knew how close a call it had been, but now his secrets remained safe in the bank vault at the heart of Boston's financial district as the Red Army marched on to capture Berlin.

The FBI investigation of the Orlovs as suspected German agents was to remain closed for the rest of the war because no additional leads could be developed. The Pilgrim Trust Company reported in August 1944 and again the following year after receiving annual rental cheques from Alexander Berg, both treasurer's cheques drawn on the Union Trust Company of Pittsburgh.[53]

The end of the war in 1945 brought the lapse of the regulations governing the use of safety deposit boxes by aliens – and the FBI no longer had any legal right or interest in pursuing the matter. For the next five years the annual rental cheques from the Bergs continued to arrive at the Boston bank and box No. 7165 remained unopened. Not until 9 May 1950 did Mr Berg arrive in person to retrieve the contents. He then closed the account with the bank, handing in his two keys and giving as his reason for termination that he and his wife were "no longer residents of Boston".[54]

The Orlovs had not resided in the Commonwealth of Massachusetts since 1943, but the fact that he had made his long train journey from Cleveland to retrieve the contents of the safety deposit box was another indication of their significance. If, as appears likely, the film contained a copy of his 1938 blackmail letter to Yezhov, it was essential to recover it because the former NKVD General was planning to effect yet another dramatic transformation in his life.

14

"CLOSELY GUARDED SECRETS"

Aᴏʀ A ᴅᴏᴢᴇɴ years in hiding in the United States, Alexander
Orlov planned to break cover by publishing a damning indictment of the Soviet terror that had forced him to flee to save his life. As
memoir and history of Stalin's purges, the book served a dual
purpose. Apart from its sensational revelations concerning the Soviet
dictator's brutality, it was drafted by Orlov to reinforce the carefully
crafted version of his career that he intended to give the American
authorities. By portraying himself as a victim rather than an
accomplice to Stalin's terror, it would divert attention from his own
role in the NKVD terror in Spain.

The Secret History of Stalin's Crimes was presented in its foreword as
an expansion of the contents of what Orlov claimed was the thirty-
seven page letter he had written to Stalin in 1938 detailing his "secret
crimes". While the case it sets out was damning enough, the alleged
content of his blackmail letter was another of Orlov's deceptions. To
sustain the illusion, however, necessitated that the copy of his eleven
page letter and its two page appendix had to be retrieved before the
book's publication. On the hypothesis that the boxes of film in the
vault contained copies of the blackmail he had sent to Moscow, Orlov
realized it could put at risk the Soviet agents he had listed, including
Philby and Maclean, as well as others who might still be active in
Soviet service. Although the sixty-two agents and operations were
listed only by cryptonyms that the FBI would have had a hard time
cracking, the very discovery of the original letter would have led to
questions about Orlov's claim to be a genuine defector and the
"legend" he had invented to explain why he had been able to
blackmail Stalin.[1]

Like every major operation instigated by the former Soviet General,
the manner in which he emerged from the chrysalis of his secret
American exile was planned and executed with careful precision. The
actual timing of his re-emergence was prompted by financial

considerations which he must have begun taking into account long before 1950. Even with his wife Maria's frugal budgeting, their $22,800 cash reserve had shrunk to only a few thousand dollars by the end of the Forties. Orlov was by then too old to start a second career. His hopes of finding work after his graduation, on 15 June 1945 from the Dyke and Spencerian College in Cleveland, in business administration were shattered when the war ended. The transition from military to civilian work would have been tough enough for a demobilized American officer, let alone a former Soviet General of fifty who would be confronted by a flood of younger men returning from the services to the civilian job market.

In 1945 the Orlovs could calculate that it would be little more than five years before their cash reserves ran out, during which time they had to arrange for an alternative source of income. Obtaining a pension by becoming a paid informant for the FBI was not in keeping with Orlov's character. He had remained dedicated to the Revolution and loyal to the agents he had recruited and directed. There were, however, other lesser secrets he could transform into hard cash by turning to penmanship in a way that would not endanger his fundamental beliefs, or hazard what he would presume was the continuing work of his espionage networks. Orlov therefore never set out to write a tell-all account of his role in Soviet espionage operations, as Krivitsky had done in his book *I Was Stalin's Agent*. If he had, it would have broken the pact he had made in 1938. It was an exposé of how Stalin murdered his way to power.

Soon after the war ended Orlov therefore began work on assembling his personal recollections of what he had learned about the Great Purge. In it he carefully avoided any mention of his own contribution to forging the Soviet secret service police apparatus into a formidable weapon of domestic repression and international espionage. The object of his labour, as he presented it in the foreword to his book, was to expose Stalin and document for history "the crimes he had committed to secure his personal power, the judicial frame-ups which he had organized against the leaders of the Revolution and about his relations with his closest friends whose ruin he plotted".[2]

Drawing on his prodigious "razor-sharp" memory, Orlov set about compiling a damning indictment of Stalin which had to be detailed and shocking enough to lend credibility to his claim that Stalin had succumbed to his blackmail rather than have such grisly secrets revealed. Although fluent in English, Orlov preferred to write his drafts in long hand in Russian. At his Lakewood apartment and in the White Memorial Library in Cleveland he laboured for months writing and researching published works on Soviet history to give his own work veracity. What Orlov produced each day was typed up every night by his devoted wife Maria on a specially purchased Cyrillic typewriter. Starting with the story of the assassination of Kirov in 1934, Orlov set out to explain how Stalin arranged the murder of his potential rival to instigate a purge of his opponents. He detailed the sordid process by which false confessions were extracted from the old guard Bolshevik leaders in order to make them the centrepieces of a sequence of show trials which, in turn, would justify a witch hunt for more traitors and Trotskyites that led to the judicial liquidation of thousands. In his foreword and repeatedly throughout the book, Orlov took great pains to emphasize the credibility of an indictment that although unsupported by any documents was based on his own personal knowledge and on the eyewitness accounts of his NKVD comrades.

"I have written down the directives which Stalin personally gave to NKVD chiefs at the conferences in the Kremlin," Orlov wrote, stressing his authenticity and accuracy. "I have recorded Stalin's personal negotiations with some of his victims and the words actually spoken by the doomed men behind the walls of the Lubyanka Prison. I obtained these closely guarded secrets from the NKVD interrogators themselves, some of whom had, in the past, been subordinate to me."[3]

With its horrendous catalogue of gruesome details, *The Secret History of Stalin's Crimes* relates how the NKVD was exploited by a cunning and ruthless tyrant as the instrument for enforcing an ever widening reign of terror. He explained how Stalin had purged the Politburo, and the Red Army, before turning on the secret police *apparat*. "To commit his horrible crimes Stalin needed trusted accomplices from among the officers of the NKVD," Orlov wrote, explaining that "as the number of his accomplices increased and mindful of his name in history and anxious to conceal his crimes from the world, Stalin in 1937 decided to kill all his trusted aides, lest some of them survive him and become witnesses against him".[4]

Orlov took care however to portray himself not as one of Stalin's accomplices but as an intended victim, but one who had survived to carve his grim testimony on the historical record. After Stalin, through his henchman Yezhov, had orchestrated the liquidation of "almost all of the chiefs of the NKVD" along with thousands of his fellow officers who "might have learned the secrets of his crimes" he had avoided his turn for execution in the summer of 1938. Casting himself as a passive witness to Stalin's monstrous tyranny rather than an active participant was essential to Orlov's legend. This required a delicate balancing of truth and fiction, since the credibility of his own account was based on an inside knowledge of the Soviet secret police *apparat* that he could only have had if he had played a significant role in its operations. As a ranking officer of the NKVD who had known Stalin since 1924 and had been a personal consultant on intelligence in 1935, before obediently and ruthlessly executing the purge of Trotskyist opposition in Spain, Orlov had to conceal the degree of his own complicity as an accessory to the Soviet dictator's tyranny.

The former NKVD General also had to camouflage the major role he had played in directing Soviet foreign espionage penetrations that took on an increasingly important role in postwar confrontation with the United States. As the ideological struggle and the nuclear stand-off between the West and the USSR intensified in the late 1940s, Orlov – as he laboured away in the Cleveland Public Library – could not have been unaware that, had he chosen to reveal his secrets, he might have significantly changed the course of the Cold War. He would have been aware of the significance of his own secrets from the press reports of how the information provided by the GRU cypher clerk Igor Gouzenko, who had defected from the Soviet embassy in Ottawa in 1945, led to the arrest of the British atomic scientist Alan Nunn May a year later.[5]

Orlov would have been following newspaper and radio reports headlining the FBI's campaign against Communist subversion. Under its authoritarian director, J. Edgar Hoover, the FBI, after the final defeat of Germany and Japan, turned its counter-intelligence efforts against the subversive operations of the new enemy of the United States – her erstwhile ally, the Soviet Union. The first real insight into the extent of Soviet penetration of the US government bureaucracy was provided in the autumn of 1945 by the former Party official Louis Budenz and by Elizabeth Terril Bentley, whose confessions were to be followed by that of David Whittaker Chambers. These defectors from Communism detailed the extent to which the Soviets had used American Party members to develop espionage networks within the wartime Washington bureaucracy. Their alarming revelations reinforced Gouzenko's debriefing in November by the counter-intelligence department of the Royal Canadian Mounted Police.[6]

Orlov could not have known how deeply the FBI's investigation had dug into the roots of Soviet espionage operations or the importance of the role played in Cold War espionage by the agents he knew of or had recruited. Even if he did not learn from a newspaper report that Maclean had been First Secretary at the British embassy in Washington since 1944, he might have guessed that at least one of the "Three Musketeers" he recruited from Cambridge was still passing on to Moscow important Allied secrets after the Soviet Union rang the Iron Curtain down across eastern Europe and the Cold War began.

Whether Orlov did or did not learn about Maclean's career or any of the other Oxbridge penetration agents, the fact remains that he did not go to the FBI and make a clean breast of secrets that could have aided its investigations. A decade later he was to admit that he personally knew a number of the ranking NKVD agents operating in the United States during and immediately after the war, including the *rezident* in Washington, Vasili Zubilin, who, with his wife Liza, was responsible for managing some of the most important Soviet networks. In 1945, after Gouzenko's defection had accelerated the FBI's investigation, it had been only seven years since Orlov was in contact with Moscow. The information that he could have provided to the FBI about the inner workings of Soviet intelligence would have been invaluable to Hoover's postwar crackdown on Communist penetration agents in the US bureaucracy.

The FBI's expanding investigation had given its director solid reason to believe that there were very extensive networks of Soviet agents operating in North America. Among more than thirty suspects on the list he drew up were Alger Hiss, the Director of Special Political Affairs in the State Department, and Harry Dexter White, an assistant Secretary of the Treasury. On 26 November 1945 Hoover had sent that list to the White House along with a memorandum warning President Truman: "a number of persons employed in the Government have been furnishing data and information to persons outside the Federal Government, who are in turn transmitting this information to espionage agents of the Soviet Union."[7]

Harry Truman, who had been pitched into the White House after Roosevelt's death six months earlier, was too preoccupied with the global burdens of the presidency to pay too much attention to alleged Communist conspiracies in the administration he inherited. When Hiss was vigorously defended by the Secretary of State, Dean Acheson, who had Truman's ear, the President then let it be known that he was "very much against building up a Gestapo". Rebuffed, the FBI director raised the issue in public the following year with a "Red Fascism" speech that warned of the dangers posed by 100,000 American Communists who were following orders from Moscow. After the Communist take-over in Czechoslovakia and the Soviet blockade of Berlin the following year signalled an intensification of the Cold War, the President decided it was politic to demonstrate that he was not as soft on Communism as the Republicans on Capitol Hill charged. Enunciating the "Truman Doctrine" in 1947, he promised

American aid and military support to check Soviet advances abroad. At home he declared that subversion would be countered by a loyalty check on all federal employees.[8]

The public stage was now set for a Red scare of far greater dimensions than the earlier one that had inflamed Americans in the 1920s. It began with indictments returned against the leaders of the Communist Party of the United States in 1948 and the appearance of Elizabeth Bentley, who was billed in the press as the "Red Spy Queen" when she testified on Capitol Hill. Her allegations of extensive Soviet penetration of US Government agencies by Communist sympathizers such as Dexter White, was reinforced by Whittaker Chambers' accusations against Hiss. Encouraged by Hoover's warnings Republican legislators, including Richard M. Nixon sprang to national prominence by leading the charge against the Democratic administration in the House UnAmerican Activities Committee. White suffered a fatal heart attack after defending himself before the Committee and Hiss vehemently rejected the espionage allegations. The Statute of Limitations wartime espionage charges had run out but Hiss was nonetheless finally indicted on two counts of perjury. He was convicted at his second trial on the evidence of Chambers' Austrian-born Soviet contact, Hede Massing who had defected in 1938 to the US and had been debriefed by the FBI in 1945[9]

Public apprehension about the Red menace was already running high when the stunning news broke in September 1949 that the Soviets had exploded their own atomic bomb. Americans were shocked to find that their country had overnight lost the military superiority that the United States regarded as its legacy from World War II. Within a month American prestige was struck another heavy blow when Mao-Tse-Tung proclaimed final victory after the Communist take-over of China. Recriminations that put the blame for the loss of China on Soviet subversion in the Democratic administration became more shrill seven months later, when the Cold War turned into a hot one in Korea. Republican Senator Joseph McCarthy burst into national prominence with his crusading demagogy against Communism, replete with sensational charges that the State Department was still harbouring fifty Soviet agents. By 1950, when GIs were being killed by Chinese Communist bullets, the testimony that Bentley and Chambers had given two years earlier on Capitol Hill was being revived by the junior senator from Wisconsin as the match he was looking for to ignite a holy war against the Red menace that made his name synonymous with political witch hunting.

It was while McCarthy was helping to write one of the uglier chapters in modern American political history that Orlov completed the Russian version of his manuscript. He then confronted every first-time author's problem: finding a publisher. Sending out his memoir as an unsolicited manuscript was obviously too risky, so he decided to consult Max Eastman, whose own works on the Russian Revolution had been studied by Orlov in the Cleveland library. He travelled to New York in late 1950 to consult with Eastman, who had once been a disciple of Trotsky in the Soviet Union where he had married the sister of Nikolay Krylenko, Orlov's superior when he had worked as a lawyer in the Supreme Court in Moscow. Eastman had subsequently become one of the most outspoken American critics of Stalinism and a force in right-wing intellectual circles. The former NKVD General was cautious, therefore, in his approach, presenting himself not as the author but as his representative. After reading the manuscript, Eastman pronounced it "magnificent" and offered to perform as translator and editor for a third share of the royalties.[10]

Although the Orlovs' financial situation was becoming precarious, after thinking it over for two days, they declined Eastman's offer because his price was too steep. Instead they resolved to translate the book themselves. Returning to Cleveland, Orlov decided to speed up the process by learning to type, enrolling for a year-long secretarial course in March 1951 at the Dyke and Spencerian College.[11] As they reworked the manuscript together into an English text, they had less and less cash to finance themselves. They would later tell the FBI how they were often reduced to a daily diet of cornflakes, the cheapest form of sustenance, as they eked out their money by pawning their few valuable possessions. The last to go into hock was their daughter's camera. With nothing left to pawn in the summer of 1952, Orlov went to New York to see his Koornick cousin, Mrs Florence Kellerman, at her home in Gerard Avenue in the Bronx. She provided him with $1,000, which, she later informed the FBI, she had lent her cousin because "he was her relative and he said he needed it for expenses". Mrs Kellerman added that Orlov had paid her back the full amount after his book was published.[12]

While Orlov attended typing classes by day and helped his wife type up the translation of his manuscript by night, the anti-Communist campaign in the United States was being fanned by McCarthy's accusations. They were given added impetus by a stunning series of spy trials which underscored his warnings of massive Soviet espionage operations against the United States. The enemy was the MGB (the Russian acronym for the *Ministervo Gosudarstvennoy Bezopasnosti* or Ministry of State Security), which in 1946 had assumed responsibility for the NKVD. It only became the KGB (*Komitet Gosudarstvennoy Bezopasnosti*) after Stalin's death in 1953. The Red spy scare had begun in 1950 when the German-born British physicist

Klaus Fuchs confessed to passing atomic bomb secrets to Moscow. He had identified a Philadelphia chemist, Harry Gold, as one of the American contact men used by the Soviets. Investigations of Gold had led the FBI to David Greenglass, a former US army machinist from the nuclear weapons laboratory at Los Alamos. Greenglass in turn incriminated his brother-in-law, Julius Rosenberg, and his wife as key figures in a spy ring which had passed on nuclear secrets to Moscow. Another of the dozen suspected Soviet agents rounded up and indicted in the Rosenberg case was Morton Sobell, but his associate Morris Cohen (whom the NKVD records reveal Orlov had recruited in Spain) fled overseas with his wife Lona before he could be interrogated by the FBI. [13]

The trial of the Rosenbergs in 1951 and their subsequent conviction on espionage charges resulted in public furore when the death sentence was pronounced on the Jewish couple from Manhattan. When their final appeal was rejected three years later, the Rosenbergs became the first American civilians executed for espionage. To many members of the public the couple were innocent victims, judicially sacrificed on the altar of McCarthyism. This impression was encouraged by outraged left-wing opinion and reinforced by the fact that the ultimate proof of their guilt could not be produced in court because it was highly classified and derived from the intercepts the US Army made in 1944 of NKVD cables exchanged between Moscow and their New York consulate. The so-called VENONA traffic was found to contain references to the Rosenbergs and their close associates, Alfred Savant and Joel Barr – both of whom had fled to Czechoslovakia before they could be arrested. The Soviet transmissions had been cracked after many years of work by the US Army. The 1,500 pages of charred one-time cypher pads, found by the Finns, were probably the same code books that the NKVD files show Harnack had warned in 1941 had fallen into enemy hands. [14]

In the light of Orlov's knowledge of Harnack's role in the Berlin *Rote Kapelle*, it was a twist of fate that CORSICAN's warnings had been ignored in Moscow. It was the breaking of the VENONA traffic that led to the unmasking of Maclean. His identification as a Soviet agent codenamed HOMER was only made possible by the discovery in the cables of verbatim reports about Anglo-American nuclear energy secrets. From references to HOMER's travel habits and pregnant wife the British had belatedly homed in on the First Secretary of their Washington embassy as the source of the leaks. But, before Maclean could be interrogated, according to KGB records, the instructions detailing how he would make his escape with Burgess were sent to London on 17 May 1951, eight days before the Foreign Office decided to authorize his interrogation by MI5. The pair made good their flight from England on the night of 25 May. His Britannic Majesty's Government issued repeated denials stating that the pair were not suspected of being Soviet agents, but British and American newspapers confidently reported that the missing British diplomats were already in Moscow.[15]

FBI Director Hoover had immediately ordered a massive investigation into the activities of Burgess and Maclean during their stay in the United States. The Bureau's agents in the Cleveland field office who read the teletyped alert little suspected that in the very same building, on the floor below, occupied by the Dyke and Spencerian College, there was a short grey-haired man of fifty-eight in the typing class who could have given them all the answers. Orlov, however, did not come forward with the truth about Burgess and Maclean, nor did he give the barest hint that he had even been in England. The newspaper headlines made by the disappearance of two of his three Cambridge "Musketeers" evidently steeled their former mentor to do all he could to protect Philby and the other members of the Cambridge network in subsequent interrogations by the FBI.

The English manuscript of *The Secret History of Stalin's Crimes* was completed by the end of 1952, six months after Burgess and Maclean had defected. In February 1953 Orlov took it to New York. To help him find a publisher he looked up George Sokolsky, arriving late one night at his home in the borough of Queens. His Hebrew classmate from Bobruysk, who had last encountered Orlov on Yom Kippur night fifteen years earlier, was now a prominent Russian-born American journalist on the *Washington Times Herald* and a syndicated columnist for the Hearst Newspapers. Orlov told him he had come to seek advice on getting his book published.[16] According to Sokolsky's FBI interview, Orlov had revealed that he now called himself Feldbin, that he was a former General in the NKVD and that for fourteen years he had been in hiding in America. But he gave Sokolsky no details of his activities during this period or any indication of where he and his wife had been living. Orlov appeared extremely nervous and declined to give his New York address or telephone number when Sokolsky promised to contact his friend William L. White, the noted author who might assist him in getting his book published.[17]

Orlov's discussions with White resulted in a meeting with John Shaw Billings, the editorial director of *Life* magazine. His keen understanding of Soviet affairs convinced him of the importance of the former Soviet General's story.[18] Orlov's timing could not have been more fortuitous, for while his manuscript was being read at *Life* the news that Stalin had died two days earlier broke in banner headlines around the world on 4 March 1953.

The death of the Soviet dictator who had become known to millions of American World War II veterans as "Uncle Joe" gave Orlov's memoir a topicality that made it a potential best-seller. But before Billings would accept it for serialization, he wanted positive confirmation that Orlov really was the former NKVD General he claimed to be. For proof of his identity Orlov turned to Louis Fischer, an American journalist, whom he had encountered in Moscow and then in Madrid during the Spanish Civil War. Fischer would later tell FBI investigations how out of the blue he had received a telephone call from Orlov on 17 March "asking if he remembered him". When he said he did, Fischer was summoned to attend a meeting at Billings's office, where he confirmed that Orlov was indeed the former NKVD chief in Spain.[19] The deal was clinched and *Life* paid a handsome sum for the right to run substantial excerpts, which put an end to Orlov's financial problems.

"The Ghastly Secrets of Stalin's Power" was the title of the four articles *Life* published, commencing on 6 April. Illustrated with an artist's graphic rendition of some of the more ugly behind-the-scenes episodes of the Moscow show trials, the pieces created a sensation by revealing the depths of megalomaniac treachery and vicious cruelty to which Stalin's depravity had descended. Hard on the heels of the *Life* articles, Orlov was signed up by Random House to bring out his memoir in book form – it was published that autumn dedicated to the memory of the Orlovs' daughter Vera.

"My only aim," Orlov declared in the book's foreword, "is to present to the public the hidden facts about Stalin's crimes and thus supply the missing links without which the tragic events that occurred in Russia defy understanding and assume the character of an insoluble mystery."[20] Yet, because he carefully avoided his own role in exporting the Stalinist purge to Spain, this was a self-serving justification. Orlov's central thesis was also constructed with a view not only to providing a historical rationalization for the Great Terror but also as a personal expiation for having faithfully served the NKVD, thereby abetting Stalin's bloody tyranny. Moreover, by waiting until the beginning of 1952, Orlov had continued to be a passive accomplice to the mechanism of Soviet Cold War espionage into whose works he might have cast a very large spanner had he chosen to come forward earlier to tell all he knew.

That he did not do so, according to Orlov, was because Stalin had "colossal political influence and hordes of secret agents to throw upon my tail". While this did not explain why he had remained silent for so long, he attributed his ability to survive the fate that had overtaken other NKVD defectors – like Reiss and Krivitsky to his "skill to foresee and discern their tricks, and the devotion and courage of my wife and daughter". The principal factor in thwarting the NKVD assassination squads, Orlov said, had been his 1938 letter threatening Stalin. "I warned him that, if he dared to revenge himself on our mothers, I would publish *everything* that was known to me about him." Only at the beginning of 1953 had he and his wife concluded "that our mothers could no longer be alive and that it would be safe to publish my memoirs without delay". Just how the Orlovs would have found out if the NKVD had taken any action against their aged parents is not clear, especially since he stressed how they had cut themselves off completely from any contact with the Soviet Union during the fourteen years before the publication of his memoir. "All these years we did not write to our mothers or to our friends in Russia, not wishing to endanger their lives," wrote Orlov, adding for good measure, "We did not receive any messages either."[21]

The contradictory elements of his alleged blackmail threat are compounded by another glaring inconsistency in his story: if, as Orlov claimed, he had been targeted by Soviet underground assassination squads for fourteen years, why had he risked making preparations to publish his indictment of Stalin while the tyrant was still alive? Orlov, who admitted knowing Stalin since 1924, was under no misapprehension about his capacity for vindictiveness. He would surely therefore have presumed that the Big Boss would redouble his efforts to hunt him down once he published the information that he claimed had constituted his "life insurance policy". Nor could Orlov have foreseen that Stalin would suffer a fatal stroke the month *after* he had started negotiations with the editors of *Life* magazine.

Orlov's decision to publish and be damned can now be seen to have nothing to do with breaking his pact with Moscow not to betray agents since his 1938 letter had nothing to do with Stalin's crimes. It was therefore gratuitous for him to have commented that he was "enormously disappointed" that the Soviet dictator "did not live a little longer to see the secret record of his crimes laid open before the world and to realize that his efforts to hide them had been futile".[22] His original threat to reveal intelligence secrets still remained potent. It was the gold plate on Orlov's "life insurance", a policy that would have held good even if Stalin had survived to see the April editions of *Life*. Liquidation of the renegade NKVD General would still have been less important to the rulers of the Kremlin than preserving the operational integrity of the surviving members of the "Oxbridge" networks who, like Blunt and Philby, continued to be potentially valuable assets to the Soviet Union.

"The death of Stalin did not diminish the threat to my life," Orlov insisted in his book to reinforce the impression that he was still in real danger. "The Kremlin is jealous of its secrets and it will do everything in its power to destroy me in order to instil fear in the hearts of the other high officials who might be tempted to follow me."[23] The fear of an assassination attempt that Orlov repeatedly raised with his interrogators served as both an excuse and a cover. After Stalin's demise, he must have known that, as long as he abided by his pact and kept secret the names of the Soviet underground agents, he would be left alone. Orlov, however, insisted he was in danger, after he said he had spotted a Soviet hit team led by Konstantin Vladimirov on Manhattan street corners.[24] The main danger that now faced the former NKVD General, as he was soon to discover, came not from Moscow but from Washington; it emanated not from the KGB (which came into being in 1954), but from the FBI. After *Life* magazine hit the news stands on 6 April the Orlov case had landed like a bombshell on the desk of J. Edgar Hoover.

The fall-out started immediately in Washington. The Commissioner of the Immigration and Naturalization Service (INS) wrote the very next day requesting information on Orlov from the Bureau files, advising the Director that an investigation was being opened because their records showed that Orlov had not been legally granted political asylum and was therefore evidently subject to deportation.[25] This was only minor consolation to Hoover, whose fury had been aroused by learning from public print that throughout his eight-year effort to expose and root out Soviet penetration, one of Stalin's top spymasters had been living in America under the noses of his supposedly vigilant agents. The manner in which Orlov chose to break cover made the FBI Director and his organization look very foolish indeed – and Hoover never forgave him. According to one American Government official, the Director's reaction was a "mixture of incredulity, horror and wrath".[26]

"Just who is this NKVD General writing for *Life* magazine?" Hoover angrily penned across the first report on the matter to reach him.[27] With Capitol Hill demanding to know why the FBI had not known that such an important defector had been in hiding in the United States for so long, the Director ordered a full investigation of Orlov, to establish who he really was and what secrets he held about the Soviet intelligence service.

Hoover's determination to restore the FBI's reputation in the eyes of the public and of Congress was his paramount concern. His discovery that the Central Intelligence Agency had found out about the former Soviet General before the FBI also infuriated the Director. The records show that Admiral Roscoe Hillenkotter, the founding Director of the CIA, who had sparred with Hoover from 1947 until his retirement three years later, had been told before the *Life* article appeared about its author by Sokolsky, according to the deposition that the journalist gave the FBI. The Admiral, it appears, had bowed out of a proposed meeting with Orlov, advising that, in his opinion, the General was of such a high rank that he needed careful handling. Hillenkotter told Sokolsky that it was essential "Orlov be not pushed further for information in view of his extreme caution and fear".[28]

The former CIA Director's sound advice was not heeded by Hoover and his FBI interrogators. Pressed to meet their Director's injunction to establish all the facts with the minimum of delay, the kid gloves were put aside by the FBI during the critical first debriefing of Orlov. Instead of trying to win his confidence with subtlety, Hoover's interrogators went like bulls at a gate when interviewing him. For weeks after the appearance of the *Life* articles, a succession of hard-nosed Bureau agents beat an official path to the Orlovs' newly rented New York luxury apartment. The former General and his increasingly protective wife had hoped to enjoy some of the comforts they had long denied themselves, but their new-found financial resources could buy them little privacy. They were subjected to such relentless questioning that little consideration was given to addressing psychological niceties, or the couple's professed fears of Soviet reprisals.

Hoover's agents started out by asking Orlov for immediate answers to thousands of questions. The Director's grudge against Orlov for not coming forward was intensified by the discovery that the Boston field office of the FBI had opened an '"Internal Security-G" file on Orlov eleven years earlier under his alias of Alexander Berg. This file was immediately revised from a "German" to a "Russian" case as Bureau agents fanned out to interview everyone they could find who had been in contact with the former General during the fourteen years of his underground exile.

Embarrassed admissions were quickly obtained from the former Attorney General, Francis Biddle, and Earl G. Harrison, his Director of Aliens Registration. They conceded that they had indeed approved Orlov's irregular registration. Decade-old registers of hotels in New York, Boston and Philadelphia were scoured for traces of a couple registering themselves as Berg or Koornick. Medical details of Veronika Orlov's death were exhumed from Los Angeles and the doctor who had treated her was interviewed. Bank records were examined in Philadelphia, Boston and Pittsburgh, and the clerks who had issued cashier's cheques to the couple for their safety deposit box payments over the years were reinterviewed. Field agents in Cleveland,

Boston and Los Angeles tracked down apartment managers and neighbours to reconstruct a profile of the Orlovs' Spartan life-style and behaviour. The investigatory trail then went cold because Orlov and his wife steadfastly refused to divulge the names of their cousins who had helped them, because they said this might endanger relatives still alive in the Soviet Union.

The rapid expansion of Orlov's FBI dossier in the two years following his public reappearance is a measure both of the scope and the frustration of the Bureau investigation. Despite all this effort, the FBI did not obtain the trophy that Hoover was demanding. Protesting his lack of knowledge, Orlov did not reveal a major Soviet spy ring. Although this is self-evident from the fact that Philby, Blunt and the other members of the "Oxbridge" networks Orlov knew about were not exposed, not one first-hand interview of Orlov by the Bureau has been permitted to be released among the more than 800 pages declassified under the Freedom of Information Act. Nearly half the pages are blank, or blacked, citing administrative excuses for not releasing material that allegedly has "to be kept secret in the interests of national defense and foreign policy".[29] Other items are withheld under exemptions which suggest that the FBI may be reluctant to reveal their interview techniques. The only contemporary interrogation reports on Orlov that have been released are those conducted by the Immigration and Naturalization Service.

In spite of the deletions in the FBI records, an assessment of the information that Orlov did provide can be deduced from the roster of names made by US Military Intelligence from the FBI's 1954 summary analysis of the Orlov file. Declassified under a different set of FOIA rules, this list of sixty-four subjects discloses that none of the names were new to the FBI investigators.[30] Most of them can be identified from the responses of interviewees in the declassified sections of the FBI file and Orlov's later testimony before two sessions of the Senate Internal Security Sub-Committee. Yet to judge from some of the references that do remain uncensored, the Bureau appears to have believed that if Orlov were pressed hard enough, he would yield information about Soviet operations that could have explained unresolved internal "Security-R" cases. For his own part Orlov also set wild geese flying to divert his interrogators. He told the FBI that some time prior to the autumn of 1935, when he was in Moscow, he had seen copies of secret State Department reports that might have been supplied to the NKVD by an unidentified code clerk at the US embassy in Moscow.[31]

To many of the specific questions posed by the FBI it is clear that Orlov simply said he could give no answer because they related to cases that emerged *after* he had severed links with Moscow in the summer of 1938. However Hoover found it difficult to accept that the former NKVD General was not the encyclopaedic source on Soviet intelligence operations he presumed. Like all defectors, Orlov certainly had his own agenda for trickling out the secrets he would divulge to ensure a continuing "meal ticket". He also knew which ones he was not going to yield and, in contrast to most other fleeing Soviet intelligence officers, Orlov had many years to prepare his "legend" and excuses. There had been plenty of time to memorize the version he wanted to give of his career and how best to tell his story by concealing those details he decided should be kept hidden whilst at the same time conveying the impression that he was being forthcoming and honest.

"I never believed I came close to getting all the information that I could have from him," was how Edward McCarthy put it. As one of the first FBI investigators to be put on the case he found that he was confronting a "very strong personality" whose "heavy bows" contributed to the General's formidable bearing. He recalled that Mrs Orlov was never present very often during his long interviews with her husband in the summer of 1953. "There was never any doubt in my mind that he was an impressive character," McCarthy said, recalling how the odds were stacked against the FBI because they did not have any background on Orlov beyond what he had admitted in his book. He said that it had never occurred to him to question Orlov about the recently defected Burgess and Maclean because the FBI had not the slightest inkling that he had ever been in England. According to McCarthy, who was from the New York field office, Bureau headquarters gave priority to trying to find out how much the former NKVD officer could tell them about the Soviet networks in America. "You must remember he was very small potatoes at the time," McCarthy said, explaining that the FBI were at the time focussing on the Rosenberg case and had no idea of Orlov's importance. Orlov, who always "gave very little direction" about the information that he did have, was also very good at conveying the impression that he answered questions to the very best of his knowledge. "On the material I asked him about, I was impressed at the time with his answers," McCarthy said. This, he reflected, may have been because Orlov was able to confirm what the FBI had established about Soviet agents in the United States whose operations had preceded the General's flight from Spain in 1938.[32]

Hoover and his FBI interrogators miscalculated the difficulty of mining information from a ranking NKVD General who had demonstrated his skill at deception and subterfuge by evading their attention for so many years. The FBI also at that time had little first-hand experience of debriefing defectors and Orlov was the most important Soviet official they had ever tried to crack open. Aware of their Director's impatience for results, FBI investigators who succeeded McCarthy erred by adopting an approach that relied more on bludgeoning than finesse. It proved to be a disastrous mis-calculation when it came to the debriefing of a shrewd General who had written the Soviet manual on counter-intelligence and lectured on the techniques of resisting interrogation.

Orlov deeply resented the FBI's approach. He was himself a master of deception who, it can now be seen, turned the crude approach of his interrogators to his advantage to camouflage the secrets he did not want to reveal. It made him deeply resentful of the FBI. According to one of the former CIA counter-intelligence officers who later got to know Orlov as well as anyone in America ever did: "Every time I mentioned that episode, or he thought of it, he almost frothed at the mouth."[33]

Orlov also had Hoover and his agents frothing with frustration. What little information on Soviet operations and networks Orlov did yield up provided no new leads and was yielded with the painful slowness of extracting deeply rooted teeth. This is evident from those sections of his file that have been declassified and corroborates the recollections of McCarthy, his first FBI interrogator, and CIA counter-intelligence officers.

Apart from the sensational revelations behind Stalin's purges, it was clear to the FBI that Orlov had given away little about his own career that was not in the sketchy half-page *curriculum vitae* he gave in the foreword of his book. This stated that he began his career in the Economic Department of the NKVD, and had served with Soviet trade missions in France and Germany. He had then briefly visited the United States in 1932 while serving with the Economic Department of the NKVD. Orlov was unspecific about what this post involved, beyond the fact that it comprised travelling through Europe as a sort of supervisory agent before his 1936 posting to Spain. There he insisted his activity was restricted to advising the Republican Government on counter-espionage and guerilla operations before he fled Stalin's vengeance in 1938.

The passage of time and the FBI's lack of detailed knowledge of the inner workings of the Lubyanka made it relatively easy for Orlov to conceal his role in developing the Soviet penetration networks in Britain and Europe. Since he did not volunteer any hint of what his underground work involved, it remained an unplumbed topic. The FBI, moreover, had no reason to connect Orlov in any way with the recent sensational Burgess/Maclean case in which they – in contrast to the British – had concluded that Philby was involved. As Philby would later tell the KGB with some satisfaction, "He never said a word about me, though the FBI and CIA were interrogating him in a tough manner."[34]

Orlov's ability to conceal the central role he had played in pre-World War II foreign agent operations was aided by his counter-intelligence expertise from which he could measure his interrogators' knowledge from the drift of the questions and adjust his responses accordingly. He had lectured NKVD trainees on the technique of admitting only what the interrogator knew and then deflecting a line of questioning with false information that could not be checked. Orlov was, therefore, able to protect the parts of his career that he was most anxious to hide. Also many years had elapsed since he had last been in Moscow so he was able to deny convincingly all knowledge of the atomic espionage operations that headed the FBI's priority list. Orlov regretted that he could not shed any light on Soviet networks then operating in the United States, beyond confirming that he knew Vasili Zubilin, whose real name was Zarubin, who the FBI had already established was until 1944 the NKVD *rezident* in Washington. He also told them that Zubilin's predecessor, Peter Gusev (Gutzeit), had once been his assistant. Although Orlov knew very well that it did not conform to the actual pattern, he nevertheless agreed with the FBI's theory that in the 1930s the NKVD *rezident* in the United States usually operated through six subordinates. They in turn were believed to have been supported by three assistants from the Communist Party of the USA, who acted as contact men. It was the FBI's estimate that at least eighteen separate spy rings were operating at the time he fled from Spain. Orlov agreed, helpfully pointing out that these NKVD operations were separate from what he guessed were a similar number of espionage networks operated by the GRU. The only one so far uncovered by the FBI was that of Whittaker Chambers.

Adopting a classic "smoke and mirrors" stratagem, Orlov sought to diminish his own dated first-hand knowledge by speculating on the alarming reports by postwar Soviet defectors that he had read about, such as Ege, who had testified to a Senate Committee that twenty GRU rings were still operating in the United States.[35] Orlov indicated that the Soviets would certainly have taken advantage of the wartime alliance to multiply their networks in America and that these must have mushroomed during the Cold War because of the subsidiary operations run by Stalin's eastern satellites.

"I must say that Soviet intelligence services are the most skilful in the world," Orlov was to assure the Senate Internal Security Sub-Committee in 1957. Had it been known how much Orlov held back about his own contribution to that achievement, the Senators would not have been so generous in their praise of his apparent frankness. Orlov could not have known how Philby had accessed the CIA's Cold War secrets while MI6 liaison officer in Washington, or the depth to which MI5 had been penetrated by Blunt and the other "Oxbridge" recruits. But the former Soviet General did predict that the KGB had succeeded in attaining its goal of the "infiltration of the security agencies of the United States and other countries".[36]

Such diversionary tactics did not entirely succeed in pulling the wool over the eyes of the FBI agents digging into Orlov's own record.

One of the areas of suspicion uncovered had concerned allegations about his role in the anti-Trotsky purges in Spain. Their attention had particularly been drawn by a public challenge against Orlov made by the ex-Minister of Information in the Catalan Government in a letter published in the 11 May edition of *Life*. Jaime Miravitales demanded to know whether the former Soviet General who had written the Stalin articles was the NKVD chief in Spain. Orlov had also been accused by the former Republican Minister José Hernandez in his recently published memoir of planning the assassination of Indalecio Prieto, the Republican Minister of War, and carrying out the execution of Andrés Nin "under orders to liquidate Trotskyists in foreign countries".[37]

Orlov's finely honed response was to admit that while he was NKVD chief in Spain, he had played no part in Nin's murder, or in the attempt on Prieto's life. In a denial that smacked of protesting too much, he claimed that he would not have been trusted by Stalin with such a sensitive operation because he himself was already marked down for liquidation. Even had he received such orders, Orlov insisted, his diplomatic status and role as adviser on intelligence and guerilla activities would have precluded his involvement. To dispel any remaining doubts Orlov stated that the assassinations in Spain had not been directed by him but by "a task force of secret liquidators sent from Moscow, one of whom, Bolodin, was probably the agent who did away with Nin".[38]

This was the text that Orlov subsequently reprised with vigour and consistency to the FBI, the Immigration Service, the Senate Sub-Committee and to the CIA whenever the charges made against him in Hernandez's memoirs were resurrected. He had more trouble dismissing the very specific charges made by his old NKVD comrade Krivitsky in his memoir. When he was taxed with these allegations, Orlov produced a line by line rebuttal of Krivitsky's "absolutely foolish" allegations that the NKVD in Spain had "employed all the methods familiar in Moscow of extorting confessions and summary executions". It was "simply invention", Orlov said of Krivitsky's recollection of seeing the letter from General Berzin demanding the NKVD General's recall because he was behaving with "colonial" ruthlessness in Spain. "Absolute invention" was how Orlov rejected the charge that he had been involved in the disappearance of the POUM leader. "Had I killed Nin," Orlov said in the annotation of Krivitsky's text he prepared for the FBI, "Russia in the eyes of the world would have been discredited." He maintained that he knew "nothing concerning their disappearance or murder in Spain".[39]

Orlov's elaborately constructed denials are now exposed as deliberate deceptions by his actual reports in the NKVD files of the kidnapping of Nin and the other so-called *liternoye delo* operations. The FBI made repeated attempts to break through Orlov's barrier of dissimulation, but they failed every time they tried to get the truth in the course of their two-year investigation. A number of witnesses were found who corroborated the allegations of murder and secret police terror Orlov masterminded in Spain, but none could produce any hard evidence to back up what were hearsay claims. Typical of the charges was an unidentified source in Miami who told the FBI that Orlov had a "bad reputation" as NKVD chief in Spain because he had controlled the Spanish secret police, who in turn systematically purged and "put to death persons opposing the efforts of the Republican Government".[40]

Confirmation of the facts of these cases did come from veteran American journalists who covered the Spanish Civil War, including Louis Fischer of the *New York Times* and Paul Wohl, an associate editor of *Christian Science Monitor*. Even Sokolsky, who had helped Orlov get *Stalin's Crimes* published, voiced his own suspicions that there was a darker side to the former General's Spanish activity although he was not interviewed by the FBI until after he announced that he knew Orlov, in his October 1953 review of Orlov's memoir in the *Washington Times Herald*. This he had praised as "a most valuable book" for its authentic portrayal of Stalin's character, which, he wrote, "stands out like a horrible frightening nightmare: this man was devoid of all moral qualities". But in his review Sokolsky had also urged Orlov to write about his role in the Spanish Civil War "to fill in some of the blank spaces in this carnival of murder".[41] Privately, he told FBI investigators that he for one did "not have full confidence in any people like Orlov". Sokolsky said that he had suggested to Orlov that he write a book which revealed how the American volunteers of the Abraham Lincoln Brigade were manipulated by the Communists. According to the FBI special agent's report on this conversation, Sokolsky was highly critical of Orlov for not writing his own autobiography and hiding his own account behind that of Stalin.[42]

"The big story," Sokolsky said was "what Orlov himself did". It was his opinion that his friend from Bobruysk was holding back the real truth about himself "because if he told the full story this might paint Orlov as a criminal".[43] The contemporary NKVD records confirm that Sokolsky was not only correct, but that the emigré journalist had accurately divined the strategic objective of his boy-hood friend. Orlov, as the files demonstrate, *was* responsible for engineering and directing a Stalinist purge of the POUM, that led to the death of Nin and hundreds of Trotsky's Spanish supporters and other opponents of the Moscow-backed Republican Government. But without the documentary evidence that was to surface forty years later in the NKVD archives, the FBI in 1952, despite its conviction of Orlov's complicity in the Spanish purges, had no way of breaking through his barrier of lies. Hoover was all the more chagrined because he had jealously insisted on monopolizing the debriefing of Orlov, fending off all requests from the INS and the CIA who were kept posted only with summaries of the Bureau's slow progress.[44]

Orlov produced an article on Beria for *Life* magazine on 20 July 1953, apparently thumbing his nose at the FBI by going direct to the public with his revelations. This further irritated Hoover, who had fostered the impression that his agency was the true fount of accurate information about the Soviet intelligence service. The FBI had been advised by Sokolsky that, because Orlov had expressed his intention of seeking US citizenship to "become a bourgeois", he believed that "if a way could be found to give Orlov assurances he could stay in this country that it would be possible to get his whole story".[45] The Bureau ignored his advice and piled on the pressure. Since the records show Orlov had not admitted his Communist Party membership during his 1940 aliens registration statements, he was technically liable to deportation. To put pressure on Orlov, the FBI permitted the INS to begin their investigation and Orlov's lawyer was informed in October 1953 that his client was expected to present himself at their New York office. According to the law, if the examining immigration officer concluded that there were grounds for a deportation case, "the warrant for his arrest must be served immediately and Orlov taken into custody".[46]

Alerted to the possibility of deportation by a summons from the Immigration Bureau, the Orlovs arrived on 13 November 1953 at the INS offices on 70 Columbus Avenue armed with an affidavit to apply in person for American citizenship. Their papers had been drawn up by their new lawyer, Hugo C. Pollock. This time around the Orlovs had no need to beg for favours and had retained one of the top New York immigration attorneys thanks to the $44,500 they had received in advances. Articles and book had made Orlov something of a *cause célèbre*, but, as he explained to the immigration officer, he still feared to disclose his current address for fear of Soviet reprisals.[47]

Despite Orlov's claims to special treatment by the Immigration authorities because his life was in danger, there is no evidence in the KGB records of the Centre resurrecting action against Orlov after the publication of his articles and book on Stalin. While it was certainly an irritant, the KGB, like Philby, appears to have remained confident that, despite press headlines, their former General would stand by his word and not give damaging revelations about the agents or operations he had listed in his 1938 letter.

Orlov's rank lent credibility to his revelations about Stalin, which were exploited by the Voice of America for propaganda broadcasts to the Soviet bloc. The following year, 1954, CBS broadcast *The Terror*

Begins, a vivid television dramatization based on his version of the Kirov murder.

All the publicity his alleged defection received meant that Orlov did not lack distinguished public figures who were prepared to come forward to support his citizenship applications. In January 1954 he travelled to Washington to make his first annual registration as required by the Immigration and Nationality Act. He gave as his address the New York apartment of his Bobruysk classmate, Boris Rosovsky, who recalled how he had started receiving letters for Orlov from the United States Congress concerning his immigration status.[48]

Orlov's New York friends had enlisted the aid of Congressman Francis E. Walter of Pennsylvania, an influential Democrat on the House Judiciary Committee, to introduce a citizenship bill on behalf of the Orlovs. That Walter then sought the approval of the FBI Director is a clear indication of the influence Hoover wielded over the legislators on Capitol Hill. His private and confidential "Dear John" letter of 6 January informed the FBI Director that a "group of writers associated with *Life* magazine and with the *Reader's Digest*" had approached him to sponsor the bill because at the time of Orlov's 1940 filing under the Aliens Registration Act the General had been told "not to bother" observing the strict letter of the law, but to "sit tight". Now it appeared that immigration officials were hounding the couple and Walter informed Hoover he was "quite willing to help them if you tell me their records are clear and that you personally (just for my own information) believe that I should go ahead with a private member's bill".[49]

"I regret that I am precluded from making any recommendation concerning Orlov and his wife," the FBI Director responded, advising the Congressman that his hands were tied because, as a former NKVD officer, Orlov was subject to the Foreign Agents Registration Act of 1938. After the Director's aide, Nichols, pointed out that "our letter might be interpreted as being abrupt", Hoover sent him up to Capitol Hill personally to explain to Walter why the FBI "could make no recommendation or interpose objection". The Congressman took this as an indication that the FBI had no objection to his proceeding and on 20 January 1954 he introduced into the House bill number HR 7427 to legalize Orlov's residency in the United States. The impressive array of sponsors for Orlov's citizenship included an associate editor of *Reader's Digest*, his editor at Random House, and the representatives of a number of Russian emigré organizations in the United States, plus the support of the head of the Tolstoy Foundation and the editor of *Life*.[50]

The introduction of Orlov's citizenship bill also triggered an automatic investigation by the Immigration Service. In March the

General received notification that he had to report for another examination to the INS New York office. Until this investigation had been completed the House bill could not be considered by the House Judiciary Committee. Congressional backing for HR 7427 also waned when a string of witnesses came forward to raise objections to Orlov's becoming a citizen because of his conduct as NKVD chief in Spain. The most influential of these objectors was Paul Wohl, associate editor of the *Christian Science Monitor*.[51]

Examiner Denton J. Kerns of the Immigration Service was well briefed when the Orlovs arrived at his New York office on 29 April 1954 for a searching question and answer session. The verbatim transcript of their meeting shows that there were a number of areas in which Orlov held back essential information. He did, however, admit misrepresenting his Communist Party membership to obtain a visa for his 1932 visit to the US, but he denied he had used the trip to establish contact with his American relatives. He also agreed that he had not met the strict reporting requirements of the Aliens Registration Act from 1940 until 1952 because he feared that it would have endangered his life. But it was Orlov's refusal to divulge the name or address of his eighty-year-old cousin who had carried his blackmail letters to Paris in 1938 that persuaded the INS examiner that the subject was being obstructive. From Kerns' repeated questions about the allegations made against him in Spain it is clear the examiner shared the FBI's suspicion that the former NKVD General was deeply implicated in the kidnapping and murder of Nin.[52]

That the FBI was more than merely suspicious is indicated by an April 1954 instruction to its Miami field office: "You should keep in mind that Orlov, as chief resident in Spain for the NKVD, was probably involved directly and indirectly in most of these acts."[53] In the meantime the INS instituted mandatory action to begin deportation proceedings against the Orlovs as required by the Aliens Registration Act. On 16 July Orlov was subpoenaed to appear before the Federal Grand Jury by the INS because he had "not co-operated" by refusing to name his American cousins, to answer written questions about his Communist Party membership, to permit the projection of the roll of 35mm film, or to identify the American journalist whom he alleged was a Soviet espionage agent in Europe in the 1930s.[54]

The answers demanded by the Federal Grand Jury indicated the degree to which the INS and FBI investigations had become interlocked and Orlov was put under physical surveillance from 17 to 20 July. The reporting FBI agent observed "nothing of importance concerning Orlov's activities" during the two days he was examined at the US Court House on Foley Square in Manhattan. Orlov finally agreed to co-operate by giving answers to the four outstanding questions, but he did not disguise his resentment of the Bureau investigation in a statement that explained why he had "decided to give them under oath, not just say to the FBI agent who jots down the details in his own way".[55]

When the reels of film were screened the images proved to be of nothing more sinister than his daughter Vera playing with her governess in Spain. Previously Orlov had refused to let the FBI do more than hold up selected frames to the light, claiming that he was anxious to spare his wife the trauma of motion pictures of her dead child. His obstinacy appears to have been directed to focusing the FBI's attention on the roll of movie film that had originally been brought to their attention by the Boston bank clerk. As a result the investigators apparently showed no interest in contents of the boxes of film that had also been in their saftey deposit box so the Grand Jury never considered the possibility that they might have contained filmed copies of Orlov's blackmailing letter to Yezhov.[56]

Orlov also submitted to the Court's ruling by answering a list of questions about Communism, by providing the addresses of his Koornick cousins and by naming Louis Fischer as the American journalist he alleged had once been an espionage agent. The NKVD records contain no evidence that Fischer was ever anything more than a Comintern sympathizer and since the FBI does not appear to have moved against the journalist, he appears to have been falsely accused by Orlov to cast doubt on the credibility of his claims in his memoir *Men and Politics* that Orlov was implicated in the assassination of Spanish Marxists.[57]

Following the Grand Jury proceedings, the INS had scheduled a second examination of Orlov for 26 July, but the hearing was cancelled when Orlov's lawyer telephoned to report that his client's wife had suffered a heart attack that morning.[58] With Congress about to adjourn, Pollock suggested that he saw no need to press the need for another interview. By October 1954, when neither Orlov nor his lawyer had called to reschedule the examination, the INS decided – according to the report they gave the FBI – that out of consideration for Mrs Orlov's health, they "did not feel they wanted to appear too anxious for the interview". Neither, it seems, was the FBI. Hoover's men needed more time to interview the Koornicks and track down sources who might be prepared to testify about Orlov's activity in the Spanish Civil War.

On 22 September 1954 a special agent from the Los Angeles FBI field station interviewed Nathan Koornick. Despite his 82 years, he had immediately volunteered to come to New York to testify in his cousin's support if his deportation case came to court. Koornick confirmed all the details of Orlov's account but denied his cousin had ever reimbursed him for his trip to France or the loans he had made. The FBI was told that he had not seen his cousin again until March of that year, when despite his advanced years he had flown to New York to make a sworn statement about his 1938 trip to Paris because Orlov said it would "help him to become a citizen".[59]

Koornick's sister, Florence Kellerman, who was interviewed by the FBI in January 1955, said that the Orlovs had visited her every two or three years since arriving in the United States in 1938.[60] Two months later her brother Max (who had changed his surname, from Koornick to Kay) was contacted. Both had been guarded to the FBI and insisted that no other members of their family had been approached by the Orlovs since their arrival in the United States.[61]

While the FBI had been busy checking out Orlov's story with the Koornicks, he himself had taken two more steps to resist deportation. To remove another legal obstacle to his client's application for permanent residency, his attorney Pollock in December 1954 filed his papers with the Justice Department in Washington, complying – albeit seventeen years late – with the 1938 Foreign Agents Registration Act.[62] The official questionnaire was answered by Orlov's *curriculum vitae* as a Soviet intelligence agent in the same sketchy and deceptive form that he had provided in the foreword to his book, listing his successive chiefs of Stalin's secret police *apparat*.

Three months later, on 10 March 1955, a bill was introduced in the Senate on Orlov's behalf by Senator George H. Bender. The previous summer, just before he had been subpoenaed by the INS, Orlov had made a move to win support on Capitol Hill. Judge Robert Morris, the former Judiciary Committee counsel who had played a leading role in Senate investigations of Communist penetration, was contacted by Orlov, who volunteered to give testimony about Fischer and others suspected of being Moscow's agents before Senator Jenner's Committee, then holding hearings on Soviet espionage. In the event, Orlov's appearance before the Federal Grand Jury on the same day had prevented him from going to Washington to testify, but his willingness to co-operate with the Senate investigators had evidently impressed Senator Bender.[63]

If the FBI were correct about Orlov's cynical motivation, then Hoover had every reason to be dismayed when Orlov succeeded in persuading Bender to introduce a bill on his behalf in the Senate. The proposed Senate legislation, however, differed from that which had been stalled for over a year in the House, because, instead of conferring US citizenship, it required only that Orlov and his wife "shall be held and considered to have been lawfully admitted to the United States for permanent residence".[64] Nonetheless the INS investigators still had ultimate control of Orlov's fate, since it was on the basis of their recommendation that the House and Senate Judicial Committees would have to vote to send the respective bills to get them onto the floor. In connection with the pending legislation the INS scheduled a resumption of their postponed second examination of the Orlovs for 23 June 1955.

When Orlov and his wife arrived at the Immigration Bureau in New York that morning, they received a nasty surprise when they were served with parole notices. This was a standard preliminary to a commencement of deportation proceedings and it restricted their movement and forbade them to associate with members of the Communist Party. Taking umbrage that they should be treated as undesirable aliens, Orlov immediately countered with a written statement of his own: if they were served with warrants of arrest, he would seek asylum in another country, probably Switzerland, "within ninety days".[65]

Orlov's gesture of defiance appears to have been a shrewdly calculated move to stir up support for his bill in the Senate since he had also volunteered to appear before the Internal Security Sub-Committee of the Judiciary Committee of the Senate sixty days later in September 1955. Knowing that there were influential Senators on Capitol Hill who were counting on him for star testimony, the former NKVD General let it be known that his final decision to leave the United States depended on the bill introduced to the Senate. If it passed, Orlov announced that he and his wife would not leave but be "very happy to live in this country".[66]

In the event, the bureaucratic high-handedness failed to shake Orlov into any more admissions during two days of questioning by two INS examiners who repeatedly probed at the inconsistencies that the FBI had uncovered in his account. Their verbatim transcript shows that they were particularly interested in knowing why Nathan Koornick had flatly contradicted Orlov's sworn testimony in his previous examination about being reimbursed for his 1938 trip to France. Orlov denied that he had not paid his cousin and that he had held out on naming him in order to prevent the FBI questioning Koornick. He rejected the INS charge that he had flown Koornick to New York (this time at Orlov's expense) so that he could be coached into making an affidavit that supported his account.[67] The INS expressed doubts that Orlov and his wife could have survived on an annual income of $1,500 for over a dozen years and were also sceptical about the telegram from Moscow which had prompted his flight. Why, Orlov was asked, had an investigation of the Antwerp port entry records failed to establish that any Soviet vessel had docked in Antwerp in July 1938, the month Orlov said he was ordered to go aboard the *Svir*? Orlov could only tell his interrogators that his friend Rosovsky, who was himself in Belgium at the time, had informed him that he had been told that the *Svir*'s chief engineer, a classmate from Bobruysk, had been seen passing through the port that summer on his way to Moscow.[68]

The two examiners reserved their toughest questions for Orlov, taxing him about allegations of assassination operations that he had denied running as NKVD chief in Spain. The INS had also sent a letter to Senator Bender proposing that the Judiciary Committee of the Senate might be well advised to investigate the charges made against Orlov by sending a consular official to Mexico to interview the former Spanish Republican Ministers Hernandez and Vidarte. In their examination the INS set out to put the former NKVD chief in Spain on the spot for the part they believed he had played in the Stalinist purge of the POUM leaders. But Orlov was a skilled tactician. Aware that his Spanish cover story was the weakest part of his defence, like any good general, he pre-empted the attack by going on to the offensive. Producing a long typewritten statement accompanied by a photocopy of the relevant pages of the books which accused him of responsibility for the assassination of Nin, he dismissed the charges of Hernandez as "slander". Questioning the credibility of the former Spanish Minister Orlov in a classic Stalinist ploy sought to discredit his accuser by claiming that Hernandez was a Communist agent following Moscow's orders to denigrate him.[69]

"Little additional information" was how the Immigration Service reported to the FBI their failure to shake the truth out of Orlov in a two-day battle of wits in which the former NKVD General may have been outnumbered, but was not outgunned.[70] Orlov was also marshalling supporters on Capitol Hill who began to turn up the political heat on the FBI and the INS by writing to the Attorney General. Among them was Norman Thomas, the chairman of the American Socialist Party, who was himself no stranger to being the target of Red baiting. He was moved to advise the Attorney General he should move to curb the tendency of the FBI and INS to "use various laws rigorously and bureaucratically sometimes in the hope that they can win something out of the victim of their severity". Thomas's laws rigorously and bureaucratically sometimes in the hope that they can win something out of the victim of their severity". Thomas's letter urged the speedy passage of the Bender bill, and insinuated "there seems reason to think the FBI and agencies or agents of the Immigration Bureau have actually been dissuading members of Congress from taking an interest in the case".[71] While there is every reason, based on the information in the FBI dossier, to believe that Hoover would have been delighted if the recalcitrant former NKVD General were deported, the INS finally caved in. A senior official rushed to assure Thomas: "No action has been taken or is contemplated at any time in the future with regard to the aliens named herein above that is not in accord with the laws of the United States."[72]

The INS investigation was halted and the deportation case against Orlov put on hold, pending the outcome of the private bills on Capitol Hill. In contrast to the FBI and INS, Orlov was received very sympathetically by Representatives and Senators. To the politicians adept at grasping the political significance of symbols, their support for the Soviet defector was a potent image to parade before the public. Billed as the most senior officer to defect from the ranks of Stalin's secret police, Orlov's shocking denunciation of the Soviet dictator appeared to indicate his willingness to take up arms on behalf of the United States in the Cold War struggle. The Senate's investigators also believed Orlov had secret information with which they could stoke the anti-Communist political fires that still burned with the American electorate in the waning years of McCarthyism. What the Senators who were backing Orlov's case for permanent residency wanted was some testimony to light a fire beneath suspected Soviet agents such as Mark Zborowsky, who was scheduled to be called before the Senate Internal Security Sub-Committee. Orlov was politically attuned enough to appreciate that there would be a *quid pro quo* for his co-operation at the forthcoming hearings that would get the FBI and the INS off his back and at the same time speed up the passage of Bender's bill to permit him to remain in the United States.

Orlov was scheduled to testify at the September 1955 hearings into the administration of the Internal Security Act. In preliminary discussions with J. G. Sourwine, the Sub-Committee's chief counsel, Orlov went over the evidence he would give that Mark Zborowsky was the NKVD agent who had operated in the Paris circle of Trotsky's son Sedov in the 1930s.[73] Orlov's obsessive fear of assassination was assuaged because his testimony related to a pending federal criminal case and would therefore be delivered in an executive session. His under oath would not be published for seven years.

On the afternoon of 25 September 1955 the former NKVD General, accompanied by his wife, entered room 411 in the Senate office building to appear before the Internal Security Sub-Committee presided over by its chairman Senator James O. Eastland. Orlov stuck to his story of how he had not been able before his 1938 defection to ascertain the identity of Zborowsky, who wrote under the *nom de plume* of Etienne. In his testimony Orlov stated that, when he was debriefed by the FBI the previous year, he knew Zborowsky only by the name "Mark", whom he had witnessed in a meeting with his control officer Alexeeyev in a Paris park in 1937. This information had been given "while talking with the FBI officials and naming a number of spies and talking about the NKVD work". Orlov stated disingenuously "I didn't know his name was Zborowsky and they probably put it in the index under the name Mark."[74]

Orlov maintained that he did not hear Zborowsky's name until the summer of 1954, when he had a discussion on 6 July with David J. Dallin, an eminent writer on the Soviet Union whose wife had worked alongside Zborowsky in Paris before the death of Sedov. Orlov said that, because he knew that Mrs Dallin, as Lilia Estrine, had been a close friend of "Mark", so he had approached the meeting with caution. He therefore did not associate "Mark" with Dallin's question about whether he knew an agent Zborowsky, whom he believed had returned to his native Poland. It was not until a second meeting with Dallin and his wife on Christmas Day that year that the couple had admitted having helped a Mark Zborowsky enter the United States in 1941 and that he was now an American citizen.[75]

Lilia Dallin had at first insisted that Orlov was wrong to accuse her friend of being Stalin's agent who had engineered the burglary of Trotsky's archives in addition to informing Moscow about Reiss's whereabouts and possibly having a hand in Sedov's mysterious death in the French clinic. Only after Orlov had recalled two specific incidents concerning Sedov that Zborowsky had reported to Moscow and which he claimed he had seen in his file, did Mrs Dallin finally concede.

The day after seeing the Dallins, Orlov had visited the US Attorney's office on Foley Square to report that Mark Zborowsky, now a naturalized American citizen, was a dangerous Soviet agent. Later he was able to identify "Mark" positively from a Bureau photographic file. His main concern, he had told the FBI at the time, was that Zborowsky would have been forewarned by Mrs Dallin that Orlov was going to expose him. He therefore did his best to convince the FBI and the Senate Sub-Committee that the Soviet spy he claimed to have exposed was one of the Soviets' "most valuable agents" who had been sent to the United States in 1941 to operate against him.[76]

"It is my firm belief that that man Zborowsky, all through those years, has been in the United States as an agent of the NKVD conducting espionage on a large scale," Orlov declared. "I told the FBI man who used to come to me for information that I am afraid that the Russians might kill me." He said he also shared Dallin's belief that Zborowsky had informed the NKVD of Reiss's whereabouts before his assassination. Orlov said he was told by the FBI not to be afraid because Zborowsky now was co-operating with them.'"[77]

The testimony Orlov provided was later used against Zborowsky, when he was called before the Senate Internal Security Sub-Committee five months later on 29 February 1956. But the available KGB and FBI records, however, indicate that Zborowsky was not "burned" by Orlov, but that he had come to the FBI's attention long before the former NKVD General warned the FBI about him in December 1954.[78]

The facts, as they can now be established, show that Zborowsky arrived in the United States in 1941. He was instructed by the Centre to report through the Sobelivicius brothers, better known by their aliases of Jack Soble and Robert Soblen. The pair had formerly run operations against Trotsky's followers in Germany before shifting their operations to the United States. When Zborowsky became affiliated with this network, his targets among others were the Dallins and Viktor Kravchenko, a Soviet diplomat who had defected in 1944. Zborowsky had continued his contacts after the war when no one in this spy ring was aware that one of its members, Boris Morros, a flamboyant Hollywood producer of Laurel and Hardy movies, had been "turned" by the FBI into an informant in 1947.

Morros had been spotted by Bureau agents in 1943 meeting with Vasili Zubilin, the NKVD *rezident* at the Soviet embassy in Washington.[79] After four years' observation of Morros, the FBI had hauled him in for questioning in July 1947. After he had admitted working for the Soviets using the Boris Morros Music Company, which had offices in New York and Los Angeles, as a cover for intelligence operations, Morros agreed to become a double agent. For the next ten years the FBI was able to monitor the operations of the Soble ring through Morros, before they eventually rolled up the network in 1957.

Zborowsky was identified positively in 1955 as a member of this spy network according to Robert Lamphere. Then a ranking FBI counter-intelligence officer, Lamphere asserted that the Bureau's interest in Zborowsky had peaked after his hunch that his was the code name of the KGB agent sending surveillance reports on the White Russian colony in New York. KANT was Zborowsky's code name while operating in the United States and this had apparently shown up in some of the surveillance reports intercepted in the VENONA traffic of the Soviet consulate in Manhattan. Lamphere also confirms that the suspicions were solidified following the interview of Elsa Bernaut by the Bureau's New York field office. The widow of the slain NKVD agent Reiss had then been tailed to a lonely road in Connecticut where she met Zborowsky to warn that the FBI were enquiring after him.[80]

If Orlov was a factor in exposing Zborowsky, then Lamphere says he was totally unaware of it at the time. This is not clear from the FBI declassified files, which note only that Zborowsky "furnished information concerning his involvement in Soviet espionage" in the course of "a series of interviews conducted on December 2,6, and 10, 1954 and January 14 and 27, 1955". It was unknown to Orlov, however, that the FBI had already interviewed Zborowsky three times *before* he gave his name to the US Attorney in New York on 27 December after meeting the Dallins for the second time two days earlier, when they had finally disclosed Zborowsky's name to him.[81]

Orlov from his talks with the Dallins may have realized that Zborowsky was already under suspicion, using his disclosure to the US Attorney to curry favour. While Orlov may have contrived to make it appear that he was exposing Zborowsky, it is clear from both Lamphere's statements and the contemporary Bureau records that he was not the first to identify "Mark". Nor was Orlov the one who set in motion the FBI interviews of Zborowsky that also resulted in his partial confession of spying activities against Sedov in France. This came in January 1957 when the FBI obtained hard evidence of his involvement in US espionage activities with the Soble network when Morros passed on the letter that Jack Soble wrote to Zubilin (Zarubin), who was then head of the KGB's Illegals' Directorate in Moscow. In it Soble alerted the Centre to the fact that Zborowsky was appearing before the Senate Internal Security Sub-Committee and expressed his concern that a confession would threaten his own network, because since 1954 the FBI "had been working on him [Zborowsky]" to confess.[82] Anticipating his ring was threatened with exposure, Soble urged the Centre to "take the most urgent measures". Moscow evidently decided that neither Soble nor his spy ring merited the effort of exfiltrating him before his arrest a few months later. In March 1957 the leading lights in this long-watched Soviet espionage network in the United States were indicted before a Federal Grand Jury.

Zborowsky's KGB file, however, contains no record of this letter, but does include a warning the Centre received via the Paris *rezidentura* a year earlier that also indicated that by 1954 he was already under suspicion from the FBI. This does not appear to have been considered of great moment in Moscow since his file shows that Zborowsky had not been in direct contact with them since 1945. Nor is there any indication that Zborowsky was as important a contact of Soble's as the FBI believed. This is confirmed by the lack of any entries in his file after 1945, when a note indicates that KANT had been "put on ice". By 1955 Zborowsky was considered a burned out case by the KGB.[83]

Yet Orlov inflated Zborowsky into a top Soviet spy and "the director of several espionage rings" in the US in his testimony to the Internal Security Sub-Committee. Zborowsky, when called before a Grand Jury in February 1957 vigorously denied knowing Soble, who had already named him, along with other members of the ring including his brother, Jack, along with his wife Myra and the other leading members of his Soviet network. They were all tried and convicted of espionage. Robert Soblen later escaped to Israel only to commit suicide in 1962 in London while *en route* to New York in the process of being extradited.[84]

Zborowsky was not indicted for espionage in 1957, because there was no way he could be prosecuted under US law for his pre-war activities in France. But he was subsequently convicted for perjury in November 1958 for denying under oath before a Grand Jury that he knew Soble who had testified that he had paid Zborowsky $150 a month for supplying him with information on "Trotskyites and Mensheviks", the Dallins and the defector Kravchenko. Zborowsky's conviction was overturned a year later by the US Court of Appeals on a technicality involving the denial to his counsel of access to certain pre-trial statements made against him by Soble. But when Zborowsky was retried in 1962, Orlov, in dark glasses, was on hand in court to testify until he was barred from doing so on the ground that his hearsay evidence about Zborowsky's activities in France was not pertinent to the US perjury indictment. In response the Senate then released the testimony the former NKVD General had provided the Internal Security Sub-Committee seven years earlier. Zborowsky's supporters claimed its publication influenced the guilty verdict brought in by the second jury after hearing Soble's damning and detailed testimony. The mild-mannered former NKVD agent, who looked less like a spy than a bespectacled mole, received a forty-seven-month sentence. After his release from the federal penitentiary, TULIP went to the West Coast to marry again and resume his career as a respected cultural anthropologist until his death in 1990.[85]

The lurid allegations that Orlov had given the Senate two years earlier about Zborowsky's possible role in Sedov's death and the liquidation of Reiss had been irrelevant to the conviction for perjury. Nor, as some have argued, can Orlov be credited with providing the information that enabled the FBI to roll up the Soble ring. What is now clear, however, is that Orlov's inflation of Zborowsky's importance before the Internal Security Sub-Committee may well have been motivated by the need to satisfy the Senate's anticipation of his "sensational testimony". The contribution he gave served to ingratiate Orlov with leading members of the Senate and the staff of the Sub-Committee chairman, James O. Eastland. This is evident from Orlov's correspondence in the Internal Security Sub-Committee's records that reveals he had used his testimony against "the Soviet *agent provocateur* Mark Zborowsky" to remind Jay Sourwine, the committee's influential counsel, about his own "immigration problem". His own "unsettled status" and the "hardships" that he and his wife had to endure, Orlov complained, would continue as long as the bill introduced on their behalf by Senator Bender was "awaiting a hearing".

"I am not asking for any special treatment," Orlov pointedly reminded Sourwine, after four months had elapsed since his testimony. As he put it none too subtly, "The only thing which I should like to be done in [*sic*] my behalf is to have an early hearing scheduled on my bill at the Senate Immigration Committee."[86]

Orlov finally received the pay-off for his co-operation with the Internal Security Sub-Committee on 20 July 1956, when the Senate bill allowing him permanent residence was signed into law by President Eisenhower. The Orlovs never did take up American citizenship, but they had won their long struggle with the FBI with the General's most important secrets still untold. Nor did he reveal them at his second appearance before the Internal Security Sub-Committee in February 1957, when he left the Senators agog with his story of how he had spirited all the gold in Spain's Treasury to Russia. Once again, this served to divert attention away from his role in the Stalinist purge of the Spanish Marxists. The questioning was gentlemanly, enabling Orlov to deny the charges of atrocities directed while he was NKVD chief in Madrid.[87]

As Orlov would later assure Feoktistov, nothing that he had ever disclosed to the Americans could have inflicted any damage on the operations of the Soviet intelligence apparatus. Even if it was suspected that Orlov might have had a hand in exposing Zborowsky, it would not have been considered a damaging blow to their intelligence networks since he had been inactivated by 1945. In his testimony before the Senate Internal Security Sub-Committee, just as in his debriefings by the FBI and the INS investigators, Orlov concealed his really important secrets behind a skilfully erected wall of partial truths and lies. Time and again he proved a past master in the art of using disinformation both as a weapon and as a shield. As the former NKVD General would later report to Feoktistov, it had been a relatively easy task to deceive the Americans over the details of his own career because they were waylaid by the dramatic story he had told them about Stalin.[88]

Orlov by elevating Zborowsky to a significance that the Soviet records show he did not warrant, encouraged the belief that he had made a major revelatory contribution to the Congressional investigations. As his 1965 debriefing by the CIA for the French DST confirms, even ten years later Orlov was to embellish and mislead with his damaging accusations against the Dallins and warning that the professor "could have been unwittingly controlled and manipulated by the Soviet Service". He even went so far as to declare that Dallin and his wife had been part of the "Trotskyite elements" who "have pretended to assist" the US authorities but who "have been, and probably still are, deeply penetrated by the Soviets".[89] [See Appendix III]

The extent to which Orlov had succeeded in pulling the wool over the eyes of the CIA is shown by the way that the investigator named Rumsey who drew up this report noted that "Orlov regards Zborovskiy [sic] as a continuing element of Soviet operations in the United States and the relations between Zborovskiy and the Dallins to be of interlocking and continuing significance".[90]

What the Soviet records make very clear is that it was Orlov who "pretended to assist" the US authorities by magnifying the importance of Zborowsky and deceiving them with his convoluted explanation of how he had learned of "Mark"'s sinister activities. Orlov's 1938 blackmailing letter to Yezhov with its references to TULIP makes it plain that he knew all about Zborowsky. In the appendix listing the sixty Soviet agents of which he had intimate knowledge, he threatened to expose "all the work done by TULIP and GAMMA [Boris Alexeeyev, Zborowsky's control officer in Paris]." That he did not know who Zborowsky actually was is given the lie by another contemporary letter in Orlov's file.[91] It was from FIN, the code name of Georgy Nikolayevich Kosenko, the Paris *rezident* in 1938 whose alias was Kislov. Reporting to the Centre on 19 August, a month after Orlov had disappeared from Spain and referring to him by the cryptonym of BEGLETZ (FUGITIVE – the cryptonym used by the NKVD until the plan to search for him was dropped) Kosenko notes: "How to explain the fact that FUGITIVE has two pages of TULIP's report in his possession? He [Orlov] was in contact with him for about a month and a half in late 1937."[92]

Other documents show that Orlov, as NKVD chief in Spain, also controlled the channel of communications that had been established between the POUM and the Trotskyists in Paris. This was operated by an NKVD agent code-named STED who acted as a courier travelling between Barcelona and Sedov's headquarters in the French capital.[93] This points up Orlov's extensive personal involvement with and knowledge of not only Zborowsky, but also the other agents involved in the penetration of Trotsky's organization. In his 1965 CIA debriefing, Orlov added to what he had told the FBI and the Senate Internal Security Sub-Committee by asserting that after he had witnessed the 1937 meeting between Alexeeyev (probably GAMMA) and Zborowsky in a Paris park, he had made his first attempt to warn Trotsky by writing "a letter in block letters addressed to Trotsky, blind, in Mexico City warning him that there was a Soviet penetration agent in his Paris organization".[94]

This struck Rumsey, the CIA interviewer as most significant because it was "ten months before Orlov finally cut the cord in Spain". In answer to his question whether this was not "taking an extreme risk in doing a thing of this kind?" Orlov stated that "it might seem to be the case" but that he had written in "untraceable characters" and "acknowledged that he had never been able to determine whether his first warning had ever reached Trotsky". Since Orlov said that he had "no information at the time regarding Trotsky's precise address", so he had simply addressed it "Leon Trotsky, Mexico City."[95]

Given what we now know to be Orlov's deep involvement with the anti-Trotsky operations of the NKVD, his claim not to know Stalin's arch-enemy's precise address must be as suspect as his denying knowledge of Zborowsky's real name. Like his subsequent attempts to alert Trotsky, this represented only a token gesture, to save him from possible later criticism and suspicion. Had Orlov ever admitted to the FBI or CIA what he really knew or had it been discovered that had fled from Spain with Zborowsky's two page report, then his whole account would have been exposed as the sham that it now appears.

Orlov may have relished the idea of paying Stalin back by revealing Zborowsky's name or sending the TULIP report to Mexico which would immediately have alerted Trotsky to the danger. But that would have identified him as a traitor – and this was one role General Alexander Orlov was determined never to play.

I5

"A PROFESSIONAL TO THE END OF HIS DAYS"

"WE HAVE NO grounds to institute a trial case against Orlov," the head of the Investigation Department of the KGB concluded in his report of 6 December 1955. The four-page memorandum supporting this conclusion indicates the review of this case was prompted by the Centre having learned, from an unidentified source, that their former General had testified in secret before a US Senate Sub-Committee at the end of September. The inquiry was the outcome of a 1 November instruction issued by the head of the First Chief Directorate to the Investigation Department.[1]

The examination and analysis of the relevant archival records took just over a month to complete. Mikhail Malayrov then returned the dossiers with his conclusion that "the Investigation Department of the KGB with the Council of Ministers of the USSR does not consider it expedient to institute a prosecution of the case against A. M. Orlov". The Investigation Department had uncovered no evidence of "criminal activity" by Orlov after his flight from Spain seventeen years earlier. The former General had disobeyed orders. He had deserted his post after appropriating $60,000 from the *rezident*'s office safe, but no evidence had reached the Centre in seventeen years that any one of the sixty agents and operations he knew about in 1938 had been betrayed. The significance of the word "expedient" suggests that the KGB was also aware of the damage Orlov might yet do by revealing the names of agents not so far uncovered by the Western counter-intelligence services. They included Philby and Blunt, whose recruitment by the Soviets was not exposed until after the former's flight to Moscow in 1963.

The KGB dossier also reveals that the case against Orlov was finally laid to rest by none other than A. M. Korotkov, then deputy head of the First Chief Directorate. As chief of the Illegals' Directorate, Orlov's former protégé and colleague in NKVD underground operations in France twenty-one years earlier had ultimate responsibility for some of the undercover Soviet agents. As a former elevator technician in the Lubyanka who had been launched on a remarkable career by Orlov, Korotkov may have been personally pleased, but he was too experienced an intelligence officer to have let personal considerations influence his professional judgement when he signed off on the inquiry into the loyalty of his former mentor.

What the KGB analysis had sought and not found was any evidence that Orlov might have betrayed any Soviet operations, or underground agents, during the fourteen years since his flight from Spain. The sustained flow of information from Philby, Maclean, Burgess and the other Cambridge and Oxford agents was the clearest indication that he had kept his word. Account also had to be taken of the possibility that Orlov might have been instrumental in exposing some lesser agents in order to ingratiate himself with the American counter-intelligence services. While the KGB did not find any evidence of this in their records, they could not be one hundred per cent certain that some very deep game was not afoot when Orlov had appeared before the Senate Sub-Committee that September, to testify that as soon as he "came into the open" he had named "a number of spies" to the FBI.[2]

No names of any agents he claimed to have "burned", except Zborowsky, emerge from the heavily censored FBI files. The inference must be that, if Orlov had exposed operational Soviet agents in May 1953, even if the FBI had played the standard cat-and-mouse game, the KGB would have discovered who he had "burned". The KGB may have had to wait until 1962 to read Orlov's Senate testimony to see what contribution Orlov had made in the Zborowsky affair. But it would have been clear by 1957 that his role was incidental, rather than central, to his exposure. By 1945 Zborowsky was a burnt out case and Orlov simply inflated his importance in order to enhance the contribution he was supposedly making by exposing him. Unless some devious plot was afoot their own files confirmed that Orlov did not disclose all he knew about Zborowsky's operations.[3]

Orlov was to make headlines again on 23 April 1956, when *Life* magazine published his article "The Sensational Secret Behind the Damnation of Stalin". Again his sense of timing was right on the button. Less than a month earlier Khrushchev had delivered a staggering denunciation of the former Soviet dictator to the Twentieth All Union Communist Party Congress. His ill-kept secret speech entitled "The Cult of Personality and Its Consequences" had touched upon some of the criminal acts that Orlov had himself raised in his first book, preempting the Soviet leader's debunking of the Stalin myth.

Prompted by Khruschev's dramatic denunciations, Orlov was soon in print again, this time to declare that the time had come for him to uncover a secret about the former Soviet leader which was too dark even for Khruschev to reveal, namely that Stalin had been an *Okhrana* informant and had betrayed his Bolshevik comrades before the Revolution. In another *Life* article, Orlov claimed he first learned of the sensational evidence from Zinovy Katsnelson. He revealed how his cousin had made a special point of visiting Paris to tell him in February 1937, as he lay flat on his back in the clinic recovering from two broken vertebrae. Katsnelson was then not only deputy chief of the NKVD in the Ukraine, but also an influential member of the Central Committee of the Communist Party.[4]

"In my Paris hospital bed," Orlov wrote, "I shuddered as I heard a story that Zinovy dared to tell me only because of a lifetime of mutual trust and devotion." The tale related to documentation which had supposedly come to light in the voluminous archives of the Tsarist secret police. It had been discovered by an NKVD officer named Stein, who had been charged with researching the *Okhrana* records for evidence that could be used against the defendants in the first of the Moscow show trials. Amongst the papers of Vissarionov, the deputy director of the *Okhrana*, Stein had allegedly found one file containing a photograph of Stalin and a series of reports in his own handwriting confirming that he had been an assiduous informant. According to Katsnelson, one report showed the Georgian had even tried in 1913 to oust Roman Malinovsky, one of the six Bolshevik deputies in the Duma (the Imperial Russian parliament), who was an *agent provocateur* for the Tsar in Lenin's Bolshevik Party organization. Amongst other intelligence furnished by Stalin was a particularly damaging report detailing a conference he had attended in 1913 at Lenin's apartment in Cracow, the part of Poland then in the Austro-Hungarian Empire. Stalin's former role as an informant appeared to explain how he had apparently escaped punishment until 1913, when he was arrested and deported to Siberia. Documents allegedly showed how Stalin had written directly to the Tsar's Minister of the Interior, Zolotarev in an effort to supplant Malinovsky.[5]

Fully aware of the danger inherent in his dramatic discovery, Stein had withheld the explosive documentation from Yagoda, Katsnelson had told Orlov. Stein had travelled to Kiev to show it to his former superior, who was also a trusted personal friend and Katsnelson's boss, V. I. Balitsky, the NKVD chief of the Ukraine. That, as Orlov explained, was how his cousin came to know the contents of the

Okhrana file. In the privacy of the hospital bedroom Katsnelson revealed how they had taken the documents to two of their closest associates, General I. E. Yakir, the commander of all military forces in the Ukraine, and Stanislav Kossior, the Ukrainian Party chief who was also a member of the Politburo and Secretary of the Communist Party. Yakir had then gone to Moscow to brief Marshal Tukhachevsky, the Commander in Chief of the Red Army, who harboured an intense personal distrust of Stalin. Armed with the ammunition documenting the treachery of the Big Boss, Tukhachevsky and the Deputy Commissioner of Defence, Gamarnik, entered into a conspiracy to overthrow Stalin.

"In February 1937 the Red Army generals were still in the process of 'gathering forces', as Zinovy phrased it," according to Orlov, who explained how they "had not reached agreement on a firm plan for the *coup d'état*". The essence of their plan depended on persuading Stalin to summon a conference in Moscow on the military problems of the Ukraine's defence. This would enable the conspirators and their trusted aides personally to seize Stalin in the Kremlin, while two elite Red Army regiments sealed off the approaches to Moscow. When Katsnelson saw Orlov in Paris, the conspirators were still undecided whether to dispense summary justice by shooting Stalin on the spot, or to present the incriminating documents to a plenary session of the Central Committee. Orlov said he had given encouragement to his cousin, cautioning him that to delay widened the circle of plotters, increasing the risk that one of them would betray the conspiracy.[6]

"In case of failure, if Elena and I are shot, I want you and Maria to take care of my little girl," Orlov said Katsnelson had requested as they kissed each other farewell. It was the last he saw of his cousin. Over the coming weeks he listened anxiously for news of the coup, in Radio Moscow broadcasts. On 11 July 1937 when he heard the announcement that Marshal Tukhachevsky and a number of Red Army generals had been arrested on charges of treason and executed, he knew the plotters had been betrayed. Those shot with Tukhachevsky included Yakir. Orlov later discovered that Kossior and his cousin had been executed soon after. When he heard that Gamarnik and Stein had shot themselves too, he took this as confirmation that Stalin had moved swiftly to protect his deadly secret.[7]

The official reason for what developed into a major purge of the Red Army was that Tukhachevsky and his fellow officers had been plotting to overthrow Stalin in league with the Nazis. On the basis of what he had learned from his cousin Orlov believed this was just a convenient cover. It had been easy to fabricate as a result of information

Stalin received from the Czechs a year earlier, when President Edouard Beneš had instructed the Czechoslovak secret service to let Moscow know that they had picked up a Soviet named Israelovich in Prague in 1936 following a clandestine meeting with two German general staff officers. Orlov, who had once had dealings with Israelovich, insisted that he was a loyal NKVD officer, but that it had suited Stalin's purpose – and that of the Czech President – to convey the impression that Israelovich was a GRU spy who had served as Tukhachevsky's go-between with the Nazis.[8]

Orlov's account of Tukhachevsky's conspiracy rests mainly on the information provided to him by Katsnelson. But another article in the same issue of *Life* also charged that Stalin was an *Okhrana* informant. This was put forward by Isaac Don Levine, who had ghost-written Krivitsky's memoirs and who was a tireless researcher into Soviet history. The evidence he cited, however, was based on what is now regarded as a forged 1913 letter to the *Okhrana* chief of the Yenmisiek province of Siberia, where Stalin had been exiled. It passed on information that in 1906 and 1908 the Georgian had provided "valuable denunciatory information" to the Tsar's secret police.[9] The authenticity of this document could not, according to the FBI, be established as "one hundred per cent genuine". Levine, however, was convinced of its provenance because it had been passed to him by influential emigrés and authenticated by reference to the signature of its recipient engraved on a silver decanter given to him by a former Tsarist police official.

Whatever the relative authenticity of the two revelations, the decision of *Life* to publish both in the same issue infuriated Orlov who believed that Levine had tried to upstage him. According to Mrs Ruth Levine, her husband had never trusted the former NKVD General. Her own suspicions had been aroused when, shortly after the publication, the Orlovs had arrived at their Connecticut home bearing a five-pound box of chocolates as a peace offering. It was, she recalled, a gesture that was too extravagant and ingratiating.[10]

What the KGB made of the *Life* articles is not indicated by Orlov's file. However, as Orlov himself pointed out, Khruschev and the Politburo, despite all their denunciations of Stalin, could hardly have admitted the truth about his work for the *Okhrana* because this would have only served to undermine the legitimacy of his successors.[11] He did regard it as significant that one of the victims of the purges Khruschev had gone out of his way to vindicate was the former Ukrainian Party chief, Kossior, whom Katsnelson had put at the centre of the plot.

The KGB investigators, in 1955, appear to have been less concerned with the allegations against Stalin than with looking for any evidence that Orlov might have betrayed Soviet operations or underground agents. What they concluded was that Orlov's assistance was marginal and limited to confirming identifications that the FBI had already made of Soviet spies.

Orlov did not attract KGB suspicions, either, in 1957 during the case of the Soviet "illegal" who, despite holding US passports in the name of Martin Collins and Emil Robert Golfus, identified himself as Rudolf Ivanovich Abel. Microfilm messages found by the FBI amongst his possessions indicated that he was an important KGB officer who had been one of Moscow's links to the atomic espionage network. Abel's arrest in the Latham Hotel, New York, on 21 June was the result of the defection of his assistant in the Soviet underground. He was a disgruntled Soviet "illegal" agent with a Finnish "legend" and an alcohol addiction named Reino Hayhanen. He had walked into the US embassy in Paris to denounce his boss, whom he knew only as "Colonel Mark".[12] For two months Abel was held incommunicado under deportation charges at an aliens' detention centre in Texas, while the FBI unsuccessfully tried to persuade him to turn against the KGB in return for his freedom. It was only after he had been taken back to New York to be indicted on espionage charges that the name of Colonel Abel became public and Orlov contacted the CIA. A photograph of the tall, monkish man accused of being a Soviet spy being escorted by federal marshals into the Brooklyn court for arraignment appeared in the *New York Times* of 7 August 1957. After seeing it Orlov telephoned his contact in the CIA to confirm that Abel was indeed a KGB agent, because he recalled having seen him in the Lubyanka headquarters building some time before 1937.[13] Whether he provided any more information about Abel is not clear because Orlov was not called upon to testify at the trial, which began on 14 October.

Abel's spy paraphernalia and Hayhanen's testimony were more than enough to persuade the jury to agree on his guilt eleven days later. Sentenced to thirty years, he was to serve less than five years in a federal penitentiary in Atlanta. In February 1962 Abel was flown to Berlin for repatriation in a spy-swap that secured the release of Francis Gary Powers, the American pilot whose U-2 had been shot down over the Soviet Union on an ill-fated reconnaissance mission in May 1960.

Once again it appears that Orlov took advantage of a *fait accompli*, by confirming that an arrested spy was a Soviet agent to reinforce his *bona fides* as a true defector. But according to the memoirs published twenty-two years later by Kirill Khenkin, the former NKVD General had known far more about Abel. He said Orlov was aware that Abel was born a British citizen whose real name was William Henry Fisher. Khenkin, claimed that he had learned of the connection through his friendship with Fisher, whom he first met during World War II. After Fisher's repatriation, he had again befriended the spy the West knew as Abel until his death in 1971. Not until the following year, when an American journalist discovered Abel's gravestone in a Moscow cemetery bearing a second inscription in the name of Fisher, did his real name become known to the Western intelligence services.[14]

According to Khenkin, Fisher had adopted the name Abel as a cryptonym in his communications with the Centre and because he was "testing the Swede", as he referred to Orlov, whose operational code name was SCHWED. Precisely what the test involved Abel/Fisher never did reveal to Khenkin, other than that it confirmed Orlov "turned out to be an absolutely decent man". Fisher may have been concerned that his former comrade SCHWED could have revealed his true name and British citizenship to the Americans, but there is a reference that Orlov made in an FBI interview on 19 January 1954 when he mentioned a colleague by the name of Volodya Fisher.

If this was "Willi" Fisher then Orlov was aware of Abel's deception in 1957 when he did not betray his colleague beyond identifying him as a KGB officer. Khenkin also states that Fisher had learned, some five years after Orlov disappeared, that his mother had been spared Stalin's wrath because the General had sent a letter which had "threatened to blow the whistle on the network of agents" to deal a "crushing blow to Soviet intelligence".[15] Since Khenkin made this claim in his book more than ten years before it was confirmed by the release of Orlov's KGB dossier, there appears to be more truth in Khenkin's recollections then he has previously been given credit for.

Corroborative evidence that the true nature of the contents of Orlov's blackmail letter had also become known to others at the Lubyanka was supplied by Vladimir Petrov, the Soviet embassy official who defected in 1954 while KGB *rezident* in Australia. In his published account Petrov recalled how he had been the duty code clerk at the Centre in July 1938, when the cable containing the dramatic news of Orlov's defection arrived from Paris. According to Petrov, it had been reported that the fleeing General had let it be known that, if he was assassinated, his lawyer would publish "all his agents and contacts in Spain and a description of his important and highly secret work on behalf of the Soviet Government".[16] Petrov's account should have alerted the FBI to the real nature of Orlov's successful blackmail of Stalin, although it appears that Petrov had succumbed to embroidering reality. No such telegrams exist in Orlov's file, only handwritten letters reporting how the *rezidentura* had reorganized itself after he vanished. Nor would Petrov have had access to Orlov's blackmail letter, which was addressed personally to Yezhov. It is possible, however, that Petrov learned about the contents in some vague way from whispered rumours in the corridors of the Lubyanka.

Concern that Orlov's successful blackmail might set a dangerous precedent, in addition to the sensitive information his appendix contained on other agents, was sufficient justification for his dossier to be considered such an important secret that even within the KGB it was given the special security classification that it still carries. It was accordingly retained in a separate and doubly secure section of the archives, where the records of other senior defectors were housed, and access to this section required the special authority of the KGB Chairman himself.

Until Orlov could be personally contacted, the KGB – despite its 1955 review – could not be completely certain about his loyalty. Inevitably a certain uneasiness over his case was aroused whenever he testified before the Senate Internal Security Sub-Committee. Even though the CIA records of their debriefing of Orlov have not been made available, the debriefing taken in 1965 for the French DST and information supplied by those who debriefed him indicate that he did not in any way betray his most important secrets.

According to Orlov's FBI file, the CIA were kept at arm's length by Hoover until some time late in 1956. The Agency officials who were then involved in his debriefing made no secret about the fact that they felt their chances of obtaining information from the former NKVD General had been severely prejudiced by the animosity he felt at the heavy-handed treatment he had received from the Bureau. So although the CIA counter-intelligence staff assigned as his contacts tried repeatedly over succeeding years to repair the distrust and rebuild confidence, they had started out at a great disadvantage. They never had a chance to win the co-operation or the information that they suspected he was withholding. The CIA, from the start, realized that they were dealing with a very complex character whose loyalty to the revolutionary cause and his agents was always obscured behind his deep devotion to his wife and the memory of his beloved daughter.

"Perhaps some sense of personal loyalty remained for his friends and colleagues whom he thought he could still put at risk in the 1970s," observed the CIA officer who had maintained the closest links with the former General. "Perhaps after the example of what had happened to Krivitsky, he even feared for himself if he unlocked certain boxes of tricks. One never knew." Recalling one session with Orlov towards the end of his life, his CIA contact said that he had finally learned that his code name had been SCHWED. While reminiscing about his time in Spain, the former NKVD General had also recalled meeting his close friend, the NKVD *rezident* in Paris whose code name was FIN. According to Orlov, FIN, who he did not identify, had told him about a Soviet agent in Franco's entourage who was a British journalist with a speech impediment. The CIA officer suspected that Orlov was dropping a hint that he knew of Philby, who by this time was safe in Moscow, as would have been obvious from 1963 press headlines about his defection from Beirut. This was the only tantalizing hint Orlov ever gave the Americans that he was aware of any members of the Cambridge ring. "One never knew," Orlov's CIA contact reflected wistfully. "On some subjects the curtain would simply come down."[17]

Just how well the inscrutable old General was able to hold the curtain down on his most important secrets also concerned the KGB. Their uneasiness was reawakened in 1963 with the publication of his second book, *A Handbook of Counter-Intelligence and Guerilla Warfare*. A check revealed that all the cases and examples he cited in his effort to re-create the 1935 manual for the Military School were well known, or so carefully camouflaged that they could not possibly have affected current KGB operations. It is significant that Orlov's dossier contains an annotated translation of the contents of his *Handbook* without any annotations as to its merits. But it was not regarded negatively since it is not mentioned in any of the "damage assessments" referring to him, which were all positive for Orlov. Surprisingly his file shows that there was no real damage assessment made on Orlov until 1964, when the first information about his whereabouts in the United States reached the Centre. The analysis was then drawn up in connection with the decision that had to be taken on whether to try and send an officer to restore contact with LEVON, as Orlov's new code name was recorded in the contemporary internal files of KGB correspondence. The summary confirmed that even a full year after Philby's successful exfiltration to Moscow, the old General was still maintaining a tight-lipped silence about one of the most important Soviet agents he had been involved in recruiting:

> In the course of his work in commanding posts in the Centre and in the *rezidenturas* LEVON knew valuable foreign agents [*agentura*]. He was also well informed about many special operations, some of which were executed with his personal participation or under his personal command in Britain, France and Spain. All in all he knew about 60 agents and field officers, including "illegals". There are no grounds for asserting that LEVON, after becoming a "non returner", betrayed to the enemy any of the above mentioned agents or

supplied information about special operations executed by the "organs" at that time. Some of the agents whom he had recruited and whom he knew very well were successfully working from 1952–63, that is until their exfiltration into the USSR.[18]

The use of "their" in this report is significant, because it suggests that Philby was not the only agent recruited by Orlov to "come in from the cold" in 1963. Nor did he ever drop any hint of who that so-far-unnamed Soviet mole might be to the Americans during the final decade of his life. This is confirmed by the final damage report prepared for the KGB Chairman in 1969 after the Centre received Feoktistov's report on his first meeting with the former Soviet General. Dated 9 December, it concludes: "The analyses of the special measures conducted by our organs abroad with his participation shows that he did not betray to the enemy the valuable foreign agents and did not inform them about the 'special measures' conducted by our agents abroad."[19]

Until Orlov had been contacted by one of the KGB's agents, a gnawing uncertainty inevitably persisted at headquarters. It was only after word of where he might be living reached Moscow in 1964 that it became practical to contact him and try to persuade him to return to the Soviet Union. Even with the resources at the KGB's disposal, this was no easy operation. The former General had maintained such a close security concerning his whereabouts that his telephone number was unlisted and his publishers forwarded his mail to his lawyer who sent it on to a series of post office boxes.

In 1962 the Orlovs moved again.[20] After completing work on his *Handbook*, they transplanted themselves from New York to Michigan. Apparently through the good offices of the CIA, arrangements had been made for the University of Michigan to publish his book and give him a teaching post at the Ann Arbor campus. In the course of producing his manuscript he received encouragement from his CIA contacts, for whom he remained a consultant. His lecturing duties in the Department of Law were not to be too onerous, to give him time for research into the Soviet legal system, which he had decided was to be the subject of his next book.

Orlov and his wife had that December moved into their seventh-floor Maynard House apartment, which was considered quite lavish by the standards of their faculty colleagues. The FBI's Detroit field office was given the couple's address because security was still a concern for the sixty-seven-year-old former NKVD General and his fifty-nine-year-old wife. But they now socialized more freely with the teaching staff on the campus. It was at a faculty get-together shortly after the publication of his *Handbook* that, according to a tantalizingly censored report, the host asked Orlov to escort Professor [name deleted] and his wife home on the evening of 23 September 1963.[21]

What began as a social encounter, the unidentified Professor later reported to the FBI, turned into what he later described as a "third degree" interrogation at the hands of Orlov and his wife during the weeks which followed. The Professor, who had favourably reviewed Orlov's *Handbook*, said that this could not possibly have accounted for the way in which Mrs Orlov had pestered his wife with dinner invitations, ignoring her polite refusals. Orlov had also dogged him on campus and while the put-upon professor did not consider himself a likely intelligence target, he suspected he was being pursued because Orlov wanted something from him. Since he had also had wartime security clearance when he served in the Navy and his brother-in-law was a senior member of Admiral Hyman Rickover's team in the nuclear submarine command, the academic felt obliged to report the matter to the FBI because he knew that his pursuer had been an NKVD General. Orlov's persistence, he told them, was even more peculiar given the vigour with which they had "disagreed significantly during their limited social encounters".[22]

The report that the FBI Detroit office sent to the FBI Director is significant because of the Professor's belief that, while Orlov was definitely anti-Stalinist, he was "still a Communist" who was to say the very least "a strong Leninist". This had become clear through Orlov's "violent objection" to his casual comment that Lenin and Stalin were of the same breed. The impression had been reinforced when Orlov declared he was "defaming the Revolution and the integrity of Lenin" when the Professor told him that certain documents in the captured German Foreign Ministry archives showed Lenin had received financial support from Berlin to bring about the Russian Revolution in 1917.[23]

The FBI simply "noted the comments" relayed by Detroit and concluded that, because of Orlov's "strong convictions in some matters", there had been a "personality clash" between the two men.[24] But the unidentified Professor was evidently a distinguished academic and his insight into Orlov's deep-rooted Leninism was a further indication that the former Soviet General had not abandoned his fundamental adherence to Communism.

This would have given great reassurance at KGB headquarters where, a year later, the chiefs decided to initiate a search for Orlov. The only information Moscow had of his whereabouts in 1964 was that the exiled couple were living somewhere in the north-east of the United States. Locating any individual in the United States was problematic because in contrast to the Soviet Union, no registration of residence is required in the US and the lack of any central register made a search difficult and very time-consuming. The Orlovs' KGB dossier shows that it was not until 1969 that information reached the Centre from a "reliable source" (who is named in the files but who Russian Intelligence prefers not to identify) giving his address and telephone number at Ann Arbor where he resided openly using his own name.[25]

The Centre now had to decide who should be entrusted with the delicate mission of travelling to the United States to contact Orlov. There was also the question of how this agent could penetrate what was assumed to be a careful watch the FBI would be keeping over their prized defector. The principal concern was that any approach to this former Soviet intelligence chief by the KGB would arouse his suspicion and hostility, since he could be expected to be haunted by the belief that the automatic death sentence for defectors was still in effect. It was decided that he would have to be approached with extreme caution as Orlov would be unaware that, after the 1955 inquiry, the KGB had decided there was no ground for taking action against him in a Soviet court.

The prerequisite for conducting such a delicate mission was therefore to find someone whom Orlov had known and trusted in Spain. The obvious candidate was Nikolay Arkhipovich Prokopyuk, a former NKVD officer at the Barcelona station Orlov would be very familiar with. The alternative considered for the task was Fyodor Zinovievich Kimochko, the Soviet pilot who had saved Orlov's life when a White Guardist had shot at him from close range. Prokopyuk, the Centre's first choice, had long since retired to write books, but when he was informed whom he would be contacting, Prokopyuk enthusiastically volunteered for the mission.[26]

The decision was taken to dispatch this veteran intelligence officer who in World War II had been awarded the star of Hero of the Soviet Union. The First Chief Directorate had already worked up an operational plan to infiltrate him into the United States when they had second thoughts, concluding that the risks were too great if Prokopyuk were apprehended by the FBI. He had been involved in too many sensitive missions after the war and was anyway considered a little too old for such an operation. Instead, the Centre decided to send a letter from him via another officer, Feoktistov, who was already in the United States operating under the code name GEORG.

"It was I who was chosen to meet with Orlov using Prokopyuk's letter of recommendation," Feoktistov said, explaining, "I was a natural choice – I was a lawyer and investigator by education and training." To prepare him for this delicate meeting with Stalin's former spymaster, who might be expected to be very hostile at first, Feoktistov was fully briefed in Moscow on Orlov's case and absorbed all the details from the General's dossier before returning to his post as a member of the Soviet Mission to the United Nations, lodged in the grey brick apartment building on 67 Street on Manhattan's Upper East side.[27]

Feoktistov, as he later recalled so vividly, was not successful during the initial encounter with Orlov, at Ann Arbor in November 1969. Despite all the carefully laid plans, it had turned out the Centre had completely failed to take account of his fiercely protective wife Maria. She had more than lived up to the assertion by a former CIA executive that Orlov's wife was "his best security guard" by coming to her husband's defence brandishing a gun.[28] At the same time Feoktistov reported that the former NKVD General had not himself produced any evidence of personal hostility during their brief encounter and long telephone conversation. While this had given the Centre no reason to doubt the conclusion of their internal investigation that Orlov was no traitor, there was still uncertainty about precisely how much he might have revealed to the Americans. So they authorized GEORG to make a second trip to Ann Arbor three months later. Feoktistov's report on his visit to the University of Michigan in early 1970, confirming as it did that the Orlovs had been spirited away to a new hiding place was taken as a clear indication they had reported his first visit to the FBI. To give the dust time to settle, the Centre waited for a year and a half before authorizing Feoktistov to make a third trip to Michigan in the summer of 1971.[29]

This time Feoktistov made the long journey by car, taking advantage of the trip to take a family vacation to Niagara Falls. Leaving the August heat of Manhattan behind, he drove north up the length of New York State at the wheel of his Plymouth Valiant. He was accompanied by his very pregnant wife and their five-year-old daughter Leana.

"My plan for locating the Orlovs was to begin by locating the library at Ann Arbor from which they had borrowed their Soviet newspapers and magazines," Feoktistov said, recalling how, on reaching Ann Arbor, he first established that Orlov had not returned to the university campus by checking the list of lecturers on the board in the Physics Department. Then he began to make a systematic round of all the libraries on campus and in the vicinity until his diligence paid off with a lucky break.[30]

"In one of the libraries I actually discovered the Soviet magazine *Communist* number 11 of 1969," Feoktistov explained. "It was the very same one I saw in Orlov's apartment because it had the same ink blot on the cover." When he asked the librarian to check the records, she found that the elderly Russian couple had left town more than a year before, but she told Feoktistov she did not believe they had moved too far because she recalled them telling her they did not want to leave their beloved daughter's grave site. The librarian did not know their new address, but helpfully suggested that Feoktistov, who cast himself as an old family friend, could probably find them either in Detroit, Toledo or Cleveland, the three nearby cities on the shores of Lake Erie.

Feoktistov, a methodical investigator, and one of the KGB's most accomplished "manhunters", decided to drive the 160 miles to Cleveland as it was the most distant of the three from Ann Arbor. After reaching the city and failing to find the Orlovs in the local telephone directory under any of their known aliases, he drove to the main library. He knew the only sure way of rapidly establishing whether they were living there was to gain access to the residential directories for the Cleveland suburbs. Claiming he was looking for long-lost relatives, the KGB officer was directed to the second-floor department where these street directories were kept.[31]

"It was my good fortune to find that the door of this section was not locked," Feoktistov said, recalling that there was nobody to be seen. But from behind a curtained cubicle at the end of the room full of book stacks he heard noises which left him in no doubt that a couple were busily engaged in love-making.

"The curtain didn't quite reach the floor and I could see a pair of black legs belonging to a man and a pair of white ones just as obviously a woman's," was how Feoktistov described the bizarre circumstances as he slipped into the room and silently closed the door with a practised hand. It was already late on Friday afternoon and he wasted no time locating the stack containing the directories he was after. Following a hunch that the Orlovs were now living under their own name, he pulled out the O volume first and had no difficulty in finding their address. Memorizing it along with their telephone number, he then headed out of the stacks for the door. But before he could exit he was spotted by the black man emerging from the curtained cubicle. The clerk had evidently been too preoccupied with his amorous activity to have noticed that Feoktistov was leaving, not entering. Tucking his shirt into his trousers, he was too flustered to do more than make a peremptory request how he might be of assistance. Feoktistov responded that he had a rather complicated inquiry and that he would drop in again the following week.[32]

"That is exactly what the man wanted to hear," Feoktistov observed, recalling how he had then returned to his car and driven about eleven miles from the city to find a motel for the night. It had been his experience that on Fridays motel managers left early for a weekend off, leaving their establishments in the hands of service personnel. The modest lakeside motel he selected for its dowdiness had only a young receptionist in charge. So when Feoktistov was asked to fill in the registration form, he played a standard KGB trick of handing over a $10 bill to cover the accommodation charge, saying that, as he would be leaving early next day, he would leave the completed slip in the cabin.

"Needless to say, I didn't fill in the form, but I did leave at 5 am the following morning before anyone was around," Feoktistov said. "The motel receptionist pocketed the $10, which was what he had been counting on, and I did not leave behind any clues of my stay in the Cleveland area, which was what I was counting on."[33]

Shortly after six on the morning of 10 August 1971 Feoktistov was at the wheel of his Plymouth Valiant driving past the Orlovs' apartment house in Clifton Road on the outskirts of Cleveland. After circling the block, Feoktistov drew up opposite a nearby park, where his wife and daughter could stretch their legs.

"I told my wife that if I didn't return in three hours, she was to phone the Orlovs and ask to speak to me," Feoktistov said, telling her that, if her request was denied, she was to threaten that their apartment would be immediately blown up. He then walked across to the brick apartment house. This time he did not have to wait to gain entry, because a laundry van was delivering linen. Checking the Orlovs' apartment number, he took the lift up to the fifth floor and rang the doorbell of No. 507.

"Mrs Orlov opened the door, but she didn't recognize me even when I introduced myself," Feoktistov said. Her confusion, he explained, was due to the fact that he was "looking rather like a hippie". Unshaven and wearing shorts, sandals and a short-sleeved sports shirt, he had again to produce his passport to identify himself. "When did you break with your Government?" Mrs Orlov demanded, assuming the Soviet agent might also have become a defector.[34] When he assured her that he still worked for the Soviet Government, she insisted that Feoktistov turn and face the wall while she frisked him thoroughly. After examining even his watch and inside his sandals, she permitted him to enter the apartment. There he found Orlov already dressed in light coloured slacks and a jersey. According to Feoktistov, he was not in the least alarmed, but very interested to know how he had been found this time.

"Do you have your people everywhere?" Orlov asked the KGB officer with a broad and knowing grin. As he invited Feoktistov to take a seat on the sofa, Orlov pulled off his sweater and rolled up the telephone in it. Not satisfied that he had fully muffled any listening device that might be hidden in the handset, he suggested they had best go into the kitchen for a private conversation.

According to the version the Orlovs later gave to the FBI, the KGB officer on his second visit "picked up his fawning litany where he had been forced to break it off in Ann Arbor two years earlier".[35] Feoktistov had assured them that Orlov was a hero of the Soviet Union who was greatly admired for his loyalty. The purpose of this second visit was to obtain permission to publish a monograph extolling his great deeds. Feoktistov according to Orlov had reeled off a list of names of old friends who would welcome his return to Moscow. All of them, Orlov later assured the FBI, he knew had been liquidated. He said that he had declined to provide the visitor with a list of friends who might still be living and that Maria too refused the offer to communicate with her sisters.[36]

The FBI was told how the elderly couple bravely fended off each of Feoktistov's advances, including an invitation to meet his wife and daughter. This, the Orlovs claimed, had been a sickening ploy to reassure them and catch them off-guard. They said that their exchanges were limited to telling Feoktistov that he was only doing what his bosses ordered and that they were not going to be lured back to Russia. Their encounter was not only brief, but was terminated by Maria who showed the KGB agent the door after threatening to call the police. Both of them firmly repeated that they never wanted to see the KGB or any other Soviet again.[37]

Feoktistov's account in both the report he filed at the time and his recollections during an interview twenty years later paints a very different picture. He described Orlov as smiling conspiratorially when they went into the kitchen to be at a safe distance from what he had described, with a gesture towards the radio and telephone, as the "modern listening apparatus". According to Feoktistov, their long, detailed discussion lasted almost five hours. At an early stage in their talk he recalled how Orlov happened to mention he had once lived in the Koshenkin Lug (Koshenkin's Meadow), a district Feoktistov said that he himself knew well. He told Orlov how, as a youth before World War II, he was a physical fitness addict who had often gone jogging over the meadow, past the old well, from which he used to refresh himself with cool water brought up in a bucket attached to a long wooden arm. This reminiscence, Feoktistov said, served to dispel Orlov's remaining suspicion of him.[38]

Orlov opened up and admitted that, when Feoktistov had first arrived at his Ann Arbor apartment, neither he nor Maria could be certain whether he was an *agent provocateur*. They thought that he might have been an FBI officer who had been posing as a KGB agent to trick him into revealing all the Soviet intelligence secrets he had withheld from the Americans. Some of their concern had been dispelled after Feoktistov had correctly named his uncle and Maria's sisters, but they still could not be certain they were not falling into a trap.

"The American intelligence know a great deal, but not everything," Orlov now told Feoktistov, assuring him that after he had mentioned the well on Koshenkin's Meadow "all doubts had left him". Neither the FBI nor the CIA could possibly have known such a historic and seemingly inconsequential detail about Moscow.[39]

Once the residual ice of Orlov's distrust had melted, Feoktistov recounted how he began learning all the details about everything that the Centre wanted to know. Orlov had told him about the principal cases in which he had been involved in Europe, naming Philby and four other Cambridge agents who had been recruited into the network before his posting to Spain in 1936. Orlov, he said, had spent hours relating, in the smallest detail, everything that had happened to him and his family after he had received the ill-fated telegram from Moscow in July 1938.

Orlov told Feoktistov that one of the factors which had led to his recall from the Barcelona station in 1938 was his increasing disagreement with the methods adopted by Yezhov. In particular there had been the problems caused to the NKVD's underground operations in Spain by the appearance there of Spigelglass and his "mobile groups" of assassins. On at least three previous occasions, Orlov said, he had aroused the displeasure of the bloodthirsty Yezhov. He recalled how he had protested to Moscow not only about the summary shooting without trial of two of his former colleagues but also that he had raised professional objections to the operation in which the White Guard leader General Miller had been kidnapped from France.[40]

Such outspoken criticism, Orlov was convinced, had made him a target for liquidation because he had already crossed swords with Yezhov. This incident, he told Feoktistov, had directly involved Stalin, whom he had first come to know when he was Party Secretary in the period between 1921 and 1924, when Orlov was an investigator with the Supreme Tribunal of the All Russian Central Executive Committee. Evidently Stalin had been impressed by the efficient way he had handled some important cases, so that when he became the supreme ruler of the Soviet Union, he had often invited Orlov into his Kremlin office to consult him on details of operational intelligence work. It was Stalin, Orlov explained, who had decided that he should drop the alias of Nikolsky and assume the name Alexander Mikhailovich Orlov before he was posted to Spain.

Orlov's professional intimacy with the Big Boss, he assured

Feoktistov, had proved an irritant to Yezhov after Stalin had made him head of the NKVD, and once he had even been recalled from a mission in Italy and told to report to the Kremlin. According to Orlov, Stalin frequently took a personal interest in NKVD operations and on one occasion asked Orlov's advice on Yezhov's plan secretly to exfiltrate to Moscow a prominent European member of the Comintern and his family. After listening to both Orlov and Yezhov on how they proposed to conduct this operation, Stalin decided that Orlov's plan was safer. As soon as they were outside the Big Boss's office, the NKVD chief had angrily turned on Orlov, telling him that he "wouldn't get any credit" for the operation because it was going to be conducted according to his scheme, or Orlov would "pay for it".[41]

Orlov said that he had been left with no choice but to obey the head of the NKVD. The operation had gone wrong and the Comintern leader had been seized while trying to make an illegal border crossing, later dying in prison. Stalin was furious, and encouraged by Yezhov was blaming Orlov. He told Feoktistov how he had then decided to write to him disclaiming responsibility for the debacle. As he later found out, this letter had never reached the Big Boss. Yezhov had intercepted it and from that point on decided to order Orlov's liquidation at the first opportune moment. When the fatal telegram ordering him to go abroad the *Svir* had arrived in July 1938, Orlov recalled how he had agonized over whether to flee to the United States. He declared that, while he himself would have been prepared to return to confront Yezhov and submit himself, like Mally, to his fate, it was the fear of what might happen to his sick daughter that had finally decided him against returning to a martyr's death.

Orlov explained how his diplomatic passport made it easy to pass from Canada to the United States. Thanks to a rich and politically well connected relative in New York, he said he had been able to enlist the aid of an influential Washington friend to obtain permission to become a resident of the United States. It was this same relative who had arranged for his letter to Yezhov to be delivered at the Soviet embassy in Paris without attracting the attention of the French police. Feoktistov also reported that Orlov had also told him that he had never at any time requested permission for political asylum. Nor had the Orlovs ever wanted to become American citizens; although they had only been permitted to remain legally in America after Congress had passed a special citizenship bill which he could not have repudiated without arousing suspicion about his true motivation.

"We were so carried away by our conversation," Feoktistov said, that he did not notice that over three hours had flown by. The time for his prearranged phone call from his wife had long passed when he said he looked out of the kitchen window and saw his car. "Near by my wife was lying on the grass with my daughter beside her." Mrs Feoktistov, who was then seven months pregnant, had found the heat too oppressive.[42]

When Feoktistov explained his wife's predicament to Orlov, he had immediately called in Maria and both had insisted that his wife and daughter should come upstairs for rest and refreshment. Feoktistov protested that this was against sound operational practice, a point Orlov took aboard without demur. Not so his wife. Feoktistov recalled he was having some difficulty persuading Maria not to go down to his car when the doorbell rang. It was a cake the Orlovs had ordered. After Maria brought it into the kitchen, she announced that Feoktistov must immediately take some down to his wife and daughter along with a carton of milk and some apples. After attending to his family, Feoktistov returned to spend another two hours with the Orlovs. During this part of the debriefing they took him through every phase of their life in the United States and listed precisely what had, and had not been disclosed to the FBI and the CIA. All these details Feoktistov passed on to the Centre in a seventeen-page report that constitutes the final section of the Orlov dossier.

According to Feoktistov, Orlov, who had fondly recalled Eitingon, his deputy in Spain and his friend Sudoplatov, brightened visibly on hearing they were both alive and well. Did they not have any problems, he enquired? Feoktistov reported that both had survived lengthy terms in Stalin's *gulags*, but had been rehabilitated and were now drawing KGB pensions in Moscow. Orlov had also asked about Lev Mironov, his former colleague in the Economic Department, whom he had written in his book had fallen victim to Stalin's purges. He was surprised to learn that Mironov had not only survived but that until 1964, he had been head of the Administrative Department of the Central Committee of the Communist Party.

"It is not possible that he was not shot," Orlov interrupted Feoktistov, raising his arms in bewilderment. "I do not believe he was not executed. I was certain that he had been shot. Like myself, he was too fond of telling the truth. Yezhov liked to flatter Stalin and reported to him only what the Boss wanted to hear."[43]

Orlov admitted that ever since his break with Moscow until the occasion of Feoktistov's first visit he and his wife had been living in fear the KGB would some day find them only to liquidate them. It was for this reason he never bought a car, because its registration could be traced and he said he was afraid it could too easily be booby-trapped with a bomb.

One request which Orlov made of Feoktistov was that he promise to try to find and send over a copy of a picture which appeared on the cover of the journal of the Law Institute of the Academy of Sciences that marked the five-year anniversary of the Supreme Court of the USSR.

Orlov explained that he had been in the group photograph and would like it as a memento of old times. He had repeatedly assured Feoktistov that neither the FBI nor the CIA had ever succeeded in obtaining anything of substance about the Soviet "illegal" underground networks from him, although it had been impossible for him to appear totally uncooperative about giving some information. Orlov said that he had given his questioners only harmless historic information in order to demonstrate that he was not wilfully holding out against his interrogators. Anything of value that he might have inadvertently disclosed, he assured Feoktistov, could not possibly have damaged the operational side of Soviet intelligence activities. He had restricted his information to areas of purely historic value, as was the case with his testimony before the Senate Internal Security Sub-Committee in 1955 and 1956.

Orlov proudly claimed to have mastered the art of subtly splicing fact with misleading fiction. This technique he said he had learned at an early stage in his career when he found that disinformation could be a very effective defensive as well as an offensive weapon. It had, he told Feoktistov, been a relatively easy task to gull the FBI and the Senate because his American interrogators appeared more concerned with the general picture than a detailed analysis. For this reason he found that both his FBI and CIA interrogators had been predisposed to take his word because of what he had written about Stalin.

If the Centre had any remaining doubts, Orlov told Feoktistov that the acid test of his loyalty was surely that he had never given any hint or revealed anything about his role in establishing the "illegal" NKVD networks in Europe and Britain before World War II. On the back of his official report to the Centre Feoktistov made a handwritten note that Orlov had named to him five British agents of the Cambridge group which indicated that he had kept abreast of the development of the network after he had left London in 1935.

In both his original reports and in his interview with the authors of this book, Feoktistov declared that he was completely persuaded that Orlov had remained true to his oath as a Soviet intelligence officer, which his file records show he had signed on 1 April 1924:

I, here undersigned, an official of the Economic Directorate of the GPU, Nikolsky, Lev Lazarevich, being in the service, commit myself by this to keep in strict secrecy all the information and data about the work of the GPU and its organs, under no pretext or in no form to make it public or share it, even with my close relatives and friends. Any non-fulfilment, non-compliance or breach of this commitment subjects me to the penalties under paragraph 117 of the Criminal Code.
[Signed] L. Nikolsky
1 April 1924[44]

Orlov, as far as the KGB was concerned, had never betrayed either his oath or his motherland during his long battle of wits with the FBI and later with the CIA. As the old General had repeatedly reminded Feoktistov, had he been the genuine defector the Americans believed him to be, he would have been far better treated if he had revealed all his secrets about the Soviet intelligence apparatus as soon as he had arrived in the United States.[45]

A professional intelligence officer, however, Orlov told Feoktistov in one of several emotional moments in their long talk, had a solemn duty to remain silent in order to protect those who trusted him with their lives. When he heard this, Feoktistov knew he was in the presence of a remarkable survivor of the Bolshevik old guard who had remained true to a resolute faith which had been forged in the heat of Lenin's Revolution. But Orlov also made it very clear that he could never return to the USSR because Stalin had betrayed the ideals for which he had fought and for which many of his close NKVD comrades had died in the purges. Towards the end of their lengthy conversation, Orlov wistfully reflected how, from his reading of the Soviet press, the post-Stalinist regime had been managed by the Boss's former henchmen who were burdened with guilty knowledge. They had been supported by a generation of self-serving Party *apparatchiks* who had played supporting roles in the great crimes that had sold out the Revolution. Fate now demanded that Orlov live out his final years as an exile rather than risk being disillusioned by a Soviet Union which had not kept faith with the ideals to which he had dedicated his life.

"At the end of our meeting Orlov gave me copies of his books and asked me whether he should sign them," Feoktistov recalled. They decided it would be safer not to do so, but agreed that Feoktistov's visit should not be kept a secret from the FBI if there was any question it might compromise the Orlovs' position. The actual contents of this discussion were to be kept secret and a suitable camouflage story concocted. Before taking his leave, Feoktistov said he had been directed by the Centre to ask Orlov about a document he had in his possession. This was evidently a reference to the list of agents and operations Orlov had attached to his 1938 letter blackmailing Yezhov and Stalin.[46]

Orlov denied that he had any such document, only encyphered notes which an outsider would not be able to understand and which were kept in a safe hiding place. "You have nothing to fear in that respect," Feoktistov said Orlov told him, adding as further proof of his true loyalty that he had "put together something interesting" for Moscow Centre. After making some notes, he proceeded to dictate to the KGB agent a long list of names and positions of American officials who he said "could be interesting for the Soviet intelligence service".[47]

Before taking leave of the Orlovs, Feoktistov recalled he had once again offered to arrange their safe return to the Soviet Union, formally communicating the Centre's offer to take them back, secretly if necessary. He said that the "essence of the proposal" was that the Orlovs would return to a General's pension of 300 roubles a month and a spacious two-bedroom Moscow apartment. This offer included the guarantee that, if the couple were not happy after their return, they were free to go back to the United States. In response both the Orlovs agreed that, while they appreciated the offer, there were just too many factors that weighed against their being able to accept. Firstly their daughter was now buried nearby in the United States and they would be too old ever to make the journey back to her tomb. Secondly they believed it was too late to start their life over again and that was exactly what they would have to do if they returned to Russia.[48] "I told them the choice was theirs, but that the offer would be held open," Feoktistov said he had assured Orlov, reassuring him that he "had nothing to fear, since he was still a Soviet citizen and was no longer considered a defector".

"Our parting was touching," Feoktistov said, remembering how emotional the elderly couple had become as he bade them goodbye with the hope that he would see them again soon. As Maria walked him to the lift, he recalled how she had suddenly clutched his arm. "Be true to yourself and never, not for any millions, betray your country," she said with tears welling up in her eyes. "Your mother country is everything."[49]

Feoktistov did not know it at the time, but the closing of the lift door severed the final link between the KGB and the exiled couple. It was with real personal sadness that he learned three months after his visit that Maria Orlov had died of a heart attack on 16 November 1971. Bereft of his devoted companion, Alexander Orlov continued labouring to complete a volume of personal memoirs when he suffered a cardiac arrest on 25 March 1973. Rushed to Cleveland's St Vincent Charity Hospital, for two weeks he surprised his doctor by clinging on to life with the same resolution with which he had lived it for seventy-eight years.[50]

The final pages of the KGB's Orlov dossier contain a letter dated 2 December 1972 which he wrote to one of his relatives, the first and last letter he sent to the Soviet Union in thirty-five years. This letter to Vera Vladislovna, dated 2 December 1972, was that which he wrote to his late wife Maria's younger sister. It was the first and last communication he had with any of his relatives in the USSR after his flight from Spain in 1938. It is largely of a personal nature, recalling the last time he had seen his sisters-in-law, in 1920, when he had been serving with the 12th Army in the city of Rovno. Introducing himself as Lev Nikolsky, he described himself as a "writer" who used the name Alexander Orlov. He explained how he had recently been visited by a Soviet diplomat who had supplied him with her address. Inquiring about life in the Soviet Union, he asked his sister-in-law to respond with news of any of his surviving relatives, giving the Madison Avenue address of his New York lawyer for her correspondence. He particularly wanted to know that the grave of Maria's mother, Ekaterina Ivanova, was properly marked, offering to order and send to the USSR a "gravestone of Polish granite" with an appropriate inscription.[51] If he ever received a reply, there is no record of it in his KGB files. But it is unlikely that a reply to his final effort to reach out to his family in the Soviet Union will turn up among Orlov's private papers. These, together with another uncompleted memoir, were sealed under a Federal Court Order after his death and deposited in the National Archives with instructions that they were not to be opened until 1999. Even when they are opened, it is doubtful whether they will adequately explain how the old General justified to himself the enigmatic role that he had played or give a final answer to the question: what made Alexander Orlov a loyal servant of the Revolution, as the KGB believed and not the most senior Soviet intelligence officer ever to defect, as his American hosts for so long maintained?

There can be no doubt that until 1938 Orlov loyally served his masters in the Kremlin. He played a part in developing both the theory and the practice of underground espionage networks such as the Cambridge ring and facilitated the KGB's reputation for ruthless penetration of Western governments. What the records in the Russian Intelligence Archives give the lie to is the myth that after Orlov fled to the West to save his life he delivered a "priceless legacy" to the Americans in the fight against Communism.

It is now known that Orlov concealed the most valuable part of that legacy by refusing to expose Philby and the other members of the "Oxbridge" networks. So, although Orlov's active operational career as a Soviet intelligence officer may have ended in 1938, by not telling the Americans then, or later, all he knew he continued to make a real, if passive, contribution to the KGB's Cold War operations. It is therefore something of an historic paradox that Stalin's henchmen, but for his successful blackmail, would have tried to liquidate Orlov. At the same time the very success of his blackmail became the reason why this complex man could not betray the Soviet underground networks that he had helped to found.

If Orlov had broken faith with Lenin's Revolution and had given the secret list of underground Soviet agents to the FBI instead of withholding the information, he might single-handedly have changed the course of history. Had he blown the "illegal" networks in 1938 he would have deprived Stalin of vital information from such agents as Philby and the *Rote Kapelle* which played a part in World War II. If he had exposed these Soviet underground networks, Stalin's agents might never have stolen the secrets of the atomic bomb. Orlov's contribution was so far reaching that a former senior CIA officer describes him as "the single most versatile, powerful and productive officer in the seventy-three-year history of the Soviet intelligence services".

"Orlov remained a professional to the end of his days," was the judgement of the CIA official who knew him best and who realized that Orlov had never unburdened all his secrets. "He only revealed what he wanted to reveal and, as a rule, produced facts of his own in response to ours."[52]

To his dying day Alexander Orlov was a secretive man who had become one of the many victims of a profound human tragedy. His encounter with Feoktistov and his first and last letter home in more than thirty years reveal that he died a lonely exile, preferring to remain a steadfast adherent of Lenin's Communist vision. A man of high intelligence and immense practicality, the master of deception never would have admitted that he had fallen victim to the deadly illusion of a Marxist Utopia – an impossible dream that by the time of his own death had already become fixed in the amber of time.

APPENDIX I

THE RED ORCHESTRA

Digest of the Most Significant Messages Relayed to Moscow from the CORSICAN *and* SENIOR *Networks in the Six Months Before the German Attack on the Soviet Union*

January 1941:

"In *Herrenklub* circles the informed opinion is that Germany will lose the war [on the Western Front] and, in the light of this, it is necessary to come to terms with Britain and the United States in order to turn the military forces against the East."[1]

"In the German Air Force General Staff an order has been issued to commence reconnaissance flights above Soviet territory on a large scale with the object of photographing all the frontier [defence] lines. Leningrad is also included in the area of these reconnaissance missions."[2]

"Goering's position is more and more inclined towards reaching an agreement with America and England."[3]

"Goering has given an order about transferring 'the Russian sector' of the *Luftwaffe* ministry to the so-called active section of the Air Force General Staff which is concerned with working out and planning military operations."[4]

"The quartermaster departments of the Imperial Statisticians Directorate has received from OKW the order to compile maps of the industry of the USSR."[5]

March 1941:

"The practicality of anti-Soviet operational plans is being intensively discussed by the German leadership. Confirmation of this is the concentration of German troops on the eastern frontier."[6]

"Operations of the German air force in aerial photography of Soviet territory are in full swing. German aircraft are flying from airfields in Bucharest, Königsberg and from Kirkness in northern Norway. Pictures are taken from a height of 6,000 metres. Kronstadt has been particularly well photographed by the Germans."[7]

"Goering is the principal driving force in drawing up the plans and preparing for action against the Soviet Union."[8]

"The question of a military attack against the USSR in the spring of this year has been decided on the basis that the Russians won't be able to burn the still-green wheat and the Germans could benefit from this harvest. Zechlin [a professor of the *Politische Hochschule* in Berlin who was a member of Harnack's circle] has learned from two German field marshals that the attack is planned for the first day of May."[9]

"According to the German General Staff the Red Army will only be able to put up resistance during the first eight days, after which it will be smashed."[10]

"By occupying the Ukraine, the Germans will be able to deprive the Soviet Union of its main industrial base. The Germans will move east to occupy the Caucasus. The Urals, according to their calculations, can be reached in twenty-five days."[11]

"The attack on the Soviet Union is dictated by Germany's present military advantage over the USSR. When calculating the effectiveness of the anti-Soviet campaign, particular attention is being paid to the importance of the oil fields in Galicia."[12]

"Besides the occupation troops, the only active division [of the German army] is presently in Belgium, which is further confirmation that combat action against the British Isles has been postponed. The German troops are concentrating in the east and south-east."[13]

"The preparation for a blow against the USSR has become self-evident. The location of the concentrations of the German forces along the borders of the USSR confirm it. The Germans are paying particular attention to the railway line from Lvov to Odessa, which has a western European [gauge] track."[14]

"The German Air Force General Staff is carrying out intensive preparations for action against the USSR. Plans for bombing the most important objectives are being drawn up. The plans for raiding Leningrad, Vyborg and Kiev have just been completed. Photographs of cities and industrial targets are being regularly processed by the *Luftwaffe* staff. The German air attaché in Moscow scouts the location of the Soviet electric power stations personally in his car by driving around the areas where the generating stations are located."[15]

April 1941:

"The German Air Force General Staff has completed preparations for the air attack plan against the Soviet Union. The *Luftwaffe* is to concentrate its attack on railroad junctions in the central and western part of the USSR, on the electric power stations in the Donetsk coalfields, on aviation factories in Moscow. The airfields near Cracow are the geographic departure points for the attack on the USSR."[16]

"Rosenberg's expert on the USSR Liebrandt has advised Zechlin that the question of a military attack against the Soviet Union has been settled. Germany's total war with England and the USA cannot be won. That is why a peace treaty with them is necessary. In order to make England more compliant, it is necessary to occupy the Ukraine. This occupation of the Ukraine will force England to make concessions."[17]

May 1941:

"It is necessary to warn Moscow seriously that the question of an attack on the Soviet Union is a settled one. The attack is planned for the immediate future. In the German Air Force General Staff, the preparations for operations against the USSR are being carried out at great speed. In conversations with staff officers, 20 May is often cited as the date for the beginning of the war. Others predict that the attack is planned for June."[18]

"In spite of the Soviet Government's protest note, German aircraft continue to make flights over Soviet territory on photo reconnaissance missions. Now the photography is conducted from the height of

11,000 metres and the flights themselves are conducted with great caution."[19]

"An OKW order of the day of 7 May has been promulgated to the Air Force General Staff which states that the German plans and strategic reconnaissance have become known to the enemy. SENIOR explains this order of the day with reconnaissance flights of German planes over Soviet territory and the note from the Soviet Government."[20]

June 1941:

"All preparatory military measures including plans of Soviet airfield locations and the concentration of German air forces in the Balkan airfields are to be completed by the middle of June."[21]

"The commanders of air bases in Poland and eastern Prussia have received orders to prepare to receive their aircraft. A large airfield in Instabruck is being hastily equipped."[22]

"The appointment of the chiefs of the quartermasters' directorate of the future districts of the occupied territory of the USSR have been made. In the Caucasus it is to be Amonn, one of the senior Nazi Party officials in Düsseldorf; in Kiev, Burandt, a former official of the Ministry of the Economy; in Moscow, Burger, the chief of the Economic Chamber [of Commerce] in Stuttgart. Schlotter, the head of the Foreign Department of the Ministry of the Economy has been designated as General Director of the Economic Management of the Occupied USSR."[23]

APPENDIX II

The CORSICAN and SENIOR Networks after June 1941

Contingency plans to enable Moscow to maintain direct radio contact with Harnack's and Schulze-Boysen's groups had been made two months before the German attack on the Soviet Union on 23 June 1941. Instructions issued to Korotkov by Moscow Centre on 12 April read:

> STEPANOV at his next meeting with CORSICAN is to discuss the question and get CORSICAN's full consent for transfer to him for direct radio contact with Moscow. CORSICAN will then bcome our "illegal" *rezident* and he himself the radio operator. This assignment is urgent. We will provide you with the technical equipment and the means. The pressing necessity of it in the light of the developing situation should be explained to CORSICAN.[1]

When Korotkov approached Harnack with this plan, which required him, in the event of war, to become the fully-fledged "illegal" *rezident* of the Soviet intelligence service in Berlin, he expressed reservations. As it was reported to Moscow: "CORSICAN will undertake the collection of information and control of the radio operation, but refuses to be responsible for making the radio transmissions. That is why this part of the operation will be conducted through SENIOR."[2]

Harnack, a naturally careful individual had been made even more cautious by the Gestapo investigation the previous year. Schulze-Boysen, by contrast, was more co-operative. As Korotkov put it, he was "a more energetic personality" who immediately agreed to accept the risks involved in setting up a communications facility for both groups. This came as no surprise since Korotkov had just discovered that the *Luftwaffe* lieutenant was already living dangerously by keeping up regular contact with members of the Communist underground.

"We have come across a Party line and request your opinion," Korotkov had cabled Moscow on 18 April 1941. This was a serious breach of the NKVD rules of operation, and violated operational procedures that had been in effect since Artusov had laid them down in the late 1920s.[3] The dilemma for the Centre now was that Korotkov did not consider it appropriate to question Schulze-Boysen about his Party activities because he would be interfering directly in Comintern affairs. "What to do?" Korotkov requested, explaining that to take a tough line might prejudice his relations with SENIOR at a critical time and make him unwilling to recruit more sources.[4] In their 25 April response, the Centre instructed Korotkov to "somehow try to influence their activity" while taking care "not to interfere in Party affairs". He was however instructed "to provide for CORSICAN, SENIOR and OLD MAN's isolation from all Party work".[5]

If by "Party work" Moscow Centre was referring to anti-Fascist conspiracies, then their instruction was easier to issue than to enforce. But the NKVD record shows that the chiefs had been sufficiently intrigued by a memorandum from SENIOR to have considered the possibility of using him to tap into the anti-Nazi opposition. According to Schulze-Boysen, there was "a rather strong, scornful attitude to Hitler" among senior *Luftwaffe* officers which was manifested by their ironical use of "Adolf" when referring to the Führer and the way they overplayed their "*Sieg Heils!*". According to SENIOR's memorandum, the failure to defeat Britain in 1940 had increased discontent in certain military circles. While he expressed doubt that such discontent ran deep enough yet to promote a putsch, he believed his opportunity would come "in the case of Hitler's failure to win a war with the Soviet Union".[6]

In the CORSICAN file there is a 1941 chart of the Berlin *Rote Kapelle* networks which indicates Moscow was indeed planning to penetrate and exploit the anti-Hitler opposition. Its focus was to be Kuckhoff's network and the plan was developed a stage further in May 1941 after the Berlin field station sent Moscow a dossier on the Nazi leadership circle which had been compiled by Police Chief Helldorf. Adolf Grimme, another member of the OLD MAN network, was earmarked by the Centre as a potential liaison for opening up Moscow's contacts with the Leichner and Goerdeler anti-Hitler underground groups. Corresponding assignments had been mapped out for Kuckhoff when the scheme had to be shelved after the German invasion of the Soviet Union disrupted communications between Moscow and its Berlin underground networks.

This breakdown in communications lasted for over four months. This was through no fault of Korotkov, who had organized the delivery of two transmitters to SENIOR's group two months before the attack. One was a small battery model and the other a larger mains-powered set portable enough when broken down to fit in a suitcase. The equipment had been shipped from Moscow to Berlin in late May by diplomatic bag along with the new code system to be employed. Korotkov had briefed Schulze-Boysen on the importance of not keeping any encyphered transmissions. To increase security further, the cypher keys were to be memorized so that the actual encoding could be performed using innocent-looking editions of German fiction.[7] The Berlin groups had established several safe locations on the upper floors of trustworthy colleagues' houses in the countryside outside the city where the transmitters could be assembled and their aerials run up into the attics in order to communicate with Moscow. The Centre arranged to keep a listening watch on set hours and days of the month, which were multiples of the numbers four and seven.[8]

Harnack's group selected an AEG engineer named Karl Behrens as their radio operator. He was assigned station identification D5 and the code name STRAHLMAN. Schulze-Boysen picked Kurt Schumacher, a sculptor and woodcarver to be the radio operator of station D6 with the cryptonym TENOR. When his original choice was drafted into the army, he replaced Schumacher with a young factory technician named Hans Coppi, who was given the operational name CLEAN. After receiving instructions from an experienced radio operator from the Berlin NKVD "legal" field station in May, Coppi became an accomplished "musician", as Morse operators were known in intelligence jargon. Between 7 and 16 June 1941 Coppi had successfully made experimental tests of the D6 radio by sending the message "Ein tausend Grüsse an alle Freunde", which was picked up and decoded in Moscow.[9]

After this test transmission the radio section of NKVD Special Department heard nothing more from D6 or D5. The days became weeks and the weeks months, and still no word was heard from the CORSICAN and SENIOR radios, even though Soviet listening posts in the London and Stockholm embassies were directed to tune in to the appointed frequency. After more than three months had elapsed, the NKVD chiefs finally decided in desperation to turn to their comrades in the GRU for help in re-establishing contact.

"In September 1941, in response to our question about assistance in establishing contact through the intelligence directorate of the Red Army, they agreed to assist in restoring communication with our valuable agents in Berlin," Korotkov recorded in his 1946 memorandum on the history of the CORSICAN and SENIOR networks. "The intelligence directorate proposed to arrange this through its illegal operation in Belgium headed by KENT, who was regarded as an absolutely reliable and trusted officer of the Red Army, who had the chance of making the trip to Berlin."[10]

On 11 September 1941 the orders were signed in Moscow to effect this co-operation and the GRU in Belgium was ordered to contact Kurt

Schultze.[11] The agent detailed for the operation was a GRU "illegal" who used a Belgian firm called Simexco as cover for his operations. The Gestapo records show that they identified him as Victor Sukolov, who travelled under the Uruguayan alias of Vincente Sierra. The NKVD files disclose that his real name was Anatoly Markovich Gurevich. Since 1939, using the cryptonym KENT, Gurevich had been handling clandestine radio communications for the Belgian and French networks of the *Rote Kapelle*. Set up by the Red Army, these networks were under the direction of Leopold Trepper, a Polish-born Communist who called himself "*Le Grand Chef*".[12]

Until the NKVD files became available, Trepper, who published a self-serving memoir in 1974, had taken the lion's share of credit for masterminding the *Rote Kapelle*. But what was formerly believed, on the basis of the wartime Gestapo investigation, to have been solely a GRU operation is now revealed as a much more extensive and complex interlock of networks that was run by the NKVD as well as the Red Army. Gurevich's instructions to make contact with the dormant NKVD networks in Berlin were signed both by General Panfilov, the head of the Intelligence Directorate of the Red Army and its Commissar Ilychov, with an endorsement by NKVD intelligence chief Pavel Fitin. The actual telegram (according to a GRU postwar report) was radioed to KENT on 10 October 1941 with an additional cryptogram which read:

> On your visit already planned to Berlin go to Adam Kuckhoff or his wife at the address of 18 Wilhelmstrasse, telephone 83–62–61, the second staircase to the left, on the upper floor, and announce that you have been sent by a friend of Arvid. Remind Kuckhoff of a book which he gave to Erdberg as a present not long before the war and of his play *Till Eulenspiegel*. Suggest that Kuckhoff arrange your meeting with Arvid and Harro, and, if that is impossible, ask Kuckhoff
>
> (1) When will communication begin and what has happened?
> (2) Where and in what position are all the friends? – in particular those known to Arvid: ITALIAN, STRAHLMAN, LEON, KARO and others.
> (3) Receive detailed information for relay to Erdberg.
> (4) Suggest sending a man for personal contact to Istanbul or one who can personally make contact with the trade representative in Stockholm at the [Soviet] consulate.
> (5) To prepare a [safe] house for receiving people.

In the event that Kuckhoff is absent, go to Harro's wife, Libertas Schulze-Boysen, at her address 19 Altenburger Allee, telephone 99–58–47. Announce that you have come on behalf of the person Elizabeth had introduced to her in Markwart. The mission is the same as the meeting with Kuckhoff.[13]

Gurevich's instructions to go to the assistance of the NKVD comrades happened to coincide with orders he had already received to go to Berlin. This required him to make contact with a GRU radio intelligence operator named Kurt Schultze, code name BERG. He served as the channel of communication with another GRU agent code-named ALTA, an official in the Foreign Ministry named Ilse Stöbe, who had also relayed to Moscow warnings about the German attack on Russia. A former journalist, Stöbe had been recruited for Soviet military intelligence in Warsaw in 1931. Instructed to return to Germany in 1939, she obtained a post with the Information Department of the German Foreign Ministry where she formed a group of agents who were to be arrested in the Gestapo round up of 1942.[14]

According to Gurevich, he reached Berlin on 26 October, remaining there for two weeks, during which time he succeeded in contacting Schultze and, through Libertas, meeting Harro Schulze-Boysen. He found that Schultze and the SENIOR network's radio operator, Coppi, had already been put in touch with each other by a mutual Communist acquaintance by the name of Walter Husemann. Together they had tried to repair the malfunctioning transmitters of the SENIOR network. When this had failed, they had vainly attempted to make contact with Moscow using Schultze's set, until this too had broken down.

Gurevich was not able to provide any technical assistance to the two radio operators, but he did pass on to Schultze his new cypher system. KENT was in Berlin from 26 October to 5 November when he returned to Brussels to report the problems with the Berlin radio sets. He relayed the detailed intelligence he had obtained from CORSICAN's and SENIOR's networks in a series of messages sent on 21, 23, 24, 25, 26, 27 and 28 November 1941. The records show that it was from the Intelligence Directorate of the Red Army that NKVD headquarters, by this time evacuated to the city of Kuibyshev in the face of the German advance threatening Moscow, learned that their networks had expanded considerably in the four months since the last reports had been received from Harnack and Schulze-Boysen in June.[15]

"Harro intends to answer all the questions put to him," KENT's 28

November cryptogram from Brussels stated. He reported that SENIOR
had already commenced work to obtain detailed information, but the
information that he did relay from Schulze-Boysen proved
invaluable. It gave heart to the Red Army commanders battling to
defend the gates of Moscow to know that the *Luftwaffe* had already
suffered far heavier losses than anticipated in the Russian campaign.
Even more significant was the news that the *Wehrmacht's* Panzer
divisions were running critically low on fuel and supplies as they
approached Moscow.

> The fuel supply which the German army now has at its disposal is
> only sufficient to last until February or March next year. Those
> responsible for supplying the German army with fuel are concerned
> about the situation which may arise after February/March 1942 in
> connection with this as far as the progress of the German attack on
> the Caucasus and above all on the Maikop, which is expected first.
> The German air force has had serious losses and now has only about
> 2,500 aircraft fit for action. Confidence in a quick German victory
> has evaporated. This loss of confidence has hit the more senior
> section of the officer corps especially hard.[16]

Among other important items of intelligence in SENIOR's report
relayed by KENT was the possibility that the Germans would resort to
unconventional forms of warfare. It also gave the precise whereabouts
of the Führer's headquarters on the Eastern Front and significant
information about important leaks in Allied communications:

> In spite of the fact that the Germans have not yet installed
> generators for conducting chemical warfare in their planes, large
> supplies show that preparations for conducting chemical warfare
> are under way.
> Hitler's headquarters often changes its location and its precise
> whereabouts is known only to a few. Supposedly Hitler is now in
> the vicinity of Insteburg. Goering's HQ is now in the area of
> Insteburg.
> The Germans possess the USSR's diplomatic cypher, which was
> captured in Petsamo, however, the cypher has reportedly not yet
> yielded to the extent that there is an opportunity to decypher any
> large volume of Soviet documents. The chief of German Intelli-
> gence, Admiral Canaris, has for a large sum of money recruited the
> French officer [on] General de Gaulle's staff, to work for the benefit
> of the Germans. [His] recruitment was effected in Portugal. [He]
> was also in Berlin and Paris, and, with German help, has

exposed General de Gaulle's espionage network in France, where important arrests have been made mainly among the officer corps.

The Germans decypher a greater part of the telegrams sent by the British to the American Government. The Germans have also uncovered the entire British intelligence network in the Balkans. That is why SENIOR warns us that it is dangerous to contact the British for joint work in the Balkan countries. The Germans have the key to all the cryptograms sent to London by the Yugoslav representatives in Moscow.[17]

As to the use to which the NKVD put such vital intelligence there is a telling note written for the archive file on 25 November 1941 by Gennady Zhruavlyov, the senior intelligence officer responsible for directing the CORSICAN network at the Centre which expresses his evident concern: "All the reports have been committed to the People's Commissar Comrade Beria on the instruction of Comrade Fitin, *instructions as to the implementation of these reports have not been received* [emphasis added]."[18]

This observation is another indication of the structural weakness of the NKVD when it came to evaluating the intelligence received. Lacking the trained staff to do a proper analysis, the NKVD chiefs were evidently concerned about how much intelligence was squandered by being passed on to the Kremlin in its raw state for NKVD chief Beria and the Big Boss to pick and choose what they thought significant. The record indicates that it was only because the Red Army intelligence directorate was involved in relaying SENIOR's report that any of his information reached the appropriate military commands.

Sustaining radio communications with the Berlin networks of the *Rote Kapelle* continued to pose a problem for Moscow. The CORSICAN and SENIOR files record that by February 1942, the NKVD Special Department responsible for communications reported picking up the D6 call signal on only two occasions. By then it was not possible to use the KENT channel for re-establishing contact because the Gestapo's radio direction-finding equipment had uncovered the Brussels network's transmitter.

Early on the morning of 13 December 1941 the *Sonderkommando* unit set up to track down the *Rote Kapelle*, headed by SS *Sturmbannführer* Friedrich Panzinger, had raided KENT's safe house at 101 rue des Atrebates at Etterbeek. His radio operator Anton Danilov, whose code name was HEMNITZ, was arrested along with a female cypher clerk, VERUNDEN, and his trainee radio operator, DEMI, who had been working the transmitter at the very moment the Gestapo broke in. Trepper, whose arrival for a scheduled meeting at the house in the rue des Atrebates was perhaps too miraculously delayed, managed to escape the German round-up. He was able to alert Gurevich, who fled to France. KENT evaded arrest until 12 November, less than a month before Trepper himself was picked up on 5 December 1942.[19]

Shutting down KENT's field station was regarded as a major success by the Germans because its "musicians" had been the most frequent performers of all the Soviet underground radio stations which comprised the Red Orchestra. Overuse of their radio, according to Gurevich's postwar debriefing by the KGB, was his group's undoing. They had been so burdened with additional radio traffic for other networks, including the NKVD Berlin groups, that his radio operators had no choice but to ignore strict security regulations about limiting their transmissions. In the weeks before the Gestapo raid, KENT's station had been on the air transmitting for five hours out of every twenty-four, making it an easy target for the German direction finders. Gurevich also said that the Gestapo had seized encyphered texts of the station's communications which his operators had neglected to destroy. This was ultimately to prove fatal for the CORSICAN and SENIOR networks when torture was applied to make the radio operators talk. It was only a matter of time before German cypher specialists had obtained enough information about the code keys to break out the names and addresses in the 10 October 1941 message that had directed KENT to make contact with CORSICAN and SENIOR.

Exploiting their radio operator prisoners, the Gestapo set in motion an operation to feed disinformation to Moscow in an elaborate *Funkspiel* radio deception game. This was effected with the direct participation of Trepper. "*Le Grand Chef*" also betrayed members of his network (he claimed on Moscow's orders) before his escape in September 1943 from Gestapo custody while in a Paris pharmacy.[20]

In March 1942 the Centre resorted to alternative methods to restore communications with CORSICAN and SENIOR in Berlin. Their first attempt to succeed was in April when a GRU agent from the Red Army's Stockholm field station whose code name was ADAM was sent to Berlin. He was directed to hand over to Kurt Schultze an encyphered message together with 500 Reichmarks of additional funds. ADAM succeeded in making contact, but out of concern for security he was not authorized to meet either SENIOR or CORSICAN. The message he relayed from the Soviet embassy in Stockholm upon his return described how he had hidden the money with instructions for its retrieval:

Adam buried 500 marks in a brown bottle with a black plastic cap in a designated spot: if one stands at the Brandenburg Gate facing

Charlottenburgstrasse, to the left of the gates there is a path leading to the Tiergarten. Ten metres from the gates there is a sculpture of a wounded lioness. On either side of the sculpture there are four benches. Behind the second bench to the left, as one approaches from the gates, there is a tree at which the lioness looks down, at the base of which on the outer side from the bench, the bottle is buried in a shallow vertical position.[21]

"Your duty begins in the morning" was the contact message to be dropped in Schultze's postbox. On receiving the signal a Soviet courier would be waiting at 6 pm on the same day at the viaduct entrance to the Am Zoo Station of the Berlin S-bahn. The GRU agent ADAM also informed Schultze that he had buried the emergency cash near the Brandenburg Gate under the gaze of a bronze lion.[22]

"We have no anodes. I am trying to get batteries. Hans [Coppi] called you without result. We are trying to do all we can. BERG" was the message Schultze gave ADAM to relay to the Centre through GRU channels.[23] It informed Moscow that Schultze's radio was the continuing cause of the communications breakdown and resulted in plans being formulated to get new and more powerful transmitters to both CORSICAN and SENIOR. This was a difficult mission which Moscow concluded could be best effected by utilizing the offer of co-operation on clandestine operations just made by the British. The disassembled radio sets were to be parachuted with two operatives, who would be flown from England into northern Holland, from where they could be carried east to Berlin. To achieve this delivery two experienced German NKVD agents were selected. Their code names were BRIGADIER and WACHE, the latter a weapons, explosives and radio expert who had carried out many dangerous missions in Spain for Orlov. The NKVD records show that the pair were sent to London at the end of November 1941 for training with the Special Operations Executive (SOE), the clandestine warfare organization for which Philby then worked. They were originally scheduled to be dropped over Holland in December 1941, but the operation was postponed by bad weather. Before their mission could be remounted, WACHE injured himself on a training jump and the whole operation had to be cancelled.[24]

It was not until the summer of 1942 that the Centre was able to prepare and train another pair of German-speaking parachute agents for the mission. This time it was decided to drop them from a Red Army plane over German-occupied Soviet territory, from where they would trek westwards to Berlin posing as German workers. The leader of the two-man team was Albert Hoessler, a former KPD functionary and member of the International Brigade who had trained at Orlov's secret spy school in Spain. Code-named FRANZ, Hoessler was accompanied by Robert Barth, another German-born NKVD agent whose cryptonym was BECK. Once on German soil, they were instructed to split up for the trip to Berlin where Hoessler would contact Kurt Schultze or the Schumachers in SENIOR's network, while Barth was assigned to contact BREITENBACH the Gestapo officer who was a member of CORSICAN's group.[25]

After parachuting safely near the town of Bryansk, close to the old Prussian border, on 5 August 1942, both Barth and Hoessler succeeded in reaching Berlin within a week. Sheltered by the Schumachers in their apartment, Hoessler then made contact with Schultze and, through him, reached the radio operator Coppi. Together they assembled the new set and tried, without success, to raise Moscow, transmitting first from the house of Erika von Brockdorff and then from the home of Oda Schottmüller. As the radio operators fought to get their recalcitrant transmitters to function, neither they, nor Harnack nor Schulze-Boysen were aware the Gestapo was already closing its net around them.[26]

Not until late August 1942 did Schulze-Boysen receive the first hint of danger, from Horst Heilman. He had taken this new recruit to his network for a sail in his yacht in order to question him confidentially. Once safely out in the Wannsee, he told Heilman that he was carrying out intelligence work for the Soviet Union and asked him if he was prepared to assist. He had known his sailing partner since 1940, when he had given seminars in foreign commercial studies at Berlin University, where Heilman was then a student. Under Schulze-Boysen's tuition, Heilman had secretly come to embrace Communism before he had enlisted in the *Wehrmacht* the following year. Out on the sparkling lake Heilman eagerly pledged his co-operation and then revealed that from contacts in the cypher section of Army High Command (OKH) he had already learned that the Gestapo had broken the cyphered radio traffic transmitted by the Soviet underground agents. Steering his boat back to shore, Schulze-Boysen asked Heilman to check out the information as a matter of urgency. It was imperative to know whether any of the intercepted messages revealed that members of his group were under suspicion.[27]

It took Heilman only forty-eight hours to complete his first – and last – mission for Moscow when he made a careful search of the files of OKH cypher section and turned up a copy of the message Soviet military intelligence had radioed to KENT in Brussels eleven months earlier. Classified "a secret of the command", the decrypt represented the product of many months work by the Gestapo's special *Rote*

Kapelle Sonderkommando. Heilman was shocked to find the telegram gave the name and address of his friend Schulze-Boysen, and named his wife Libertas in addition to other members of their network.[28]

Unable to contact Harro, who was working at the time at Potsdam outside Berlin, Heilman managed that same evening to arrange a clandestine rendezvous to warn Libertas Schulze-Boysen. The next day he passed on the warning to Jon Graubenz, another member of SENIOR's network and assisted him to destroy compromising documents. But it was too late. Schulze-Boysen, Harnack and Kuckhoff had already been picked up by the Gestapo. The mass round-up of the other members of their organization began and Heilman himself was soon under arrest.

Paradoxically, the NKVD records show that the first news Moscow Centre received of the exposure of their Berlin networks was from the Gestapo itself. This came on 8 October 1942 in a message that reached Moscow from Hoessler's radio transmitter D6, which suddenly burst on the airwaves. The report, on the correct frequency and on time indicated that he had "established contact with the group", but that "our people are subject to danger" because "arrests are taking place" requiring him to "change his place of residence often".[29] It was only later that Soviet intelligence established it was the Gestapo which had sent the message as part of their *Funkspiel* deception. Concerned that Moscow would soon discover the disruption of their Berlin networks, Panzinger, the *Sonderkommando* chief, had decided to take the initiative in the radio game. The transmission of the alert was therefore intended to enhance the credibility of forthcoming German broadcasts of disinformation.

The NKVD would learn only in February 1944 that they had been fooled. The news was obtained from Harnack's nephew, Wolfgang Havemann, whose code name was ITALIAN. His full involvement in CORSICAN's network was never uncovered by the Gestapo, but his uncle's guilt was cause enough for his transfer from the German navy to an infantry division on the Eastern Front. When his unit was overrun by the Red Army in November 1943, Havemann was taken prisoner. He was then able to identify himself and provide the NKVD with some first-hand details of the break-up of SENIOR's organization. Havemann reported how, during his own interrogation on 5 or 6 October, the Gestapo had shown him a picture of a Soviet agent they identified as Hoessler. Since radio transmission for D6 had continued to be monitored in Moscow after this date, it was clear that the other radio operator, Barth, must have been turned by the Germans and become a pawn in their radio deception game. This was confirmed in

1945, when Barth was taken prisoner by the Americans. The NKVD files indicate that this was another example of their wartime co-operation with British intelligence, since they were the ones who had reported that Barth had worked for the Germans in occupied territory in Europe. He was handed over to the Soviets by the Americans who had captured him. Gestapo interrogation records showed that, following his arrest, Barth had betrayed both Hoessler and the NKVD's Gestapo source BREITENBACH. Hoessler had refused to co-operate and was executed, a fate which also awaited Barth who was shot by the Soviets for his treachery.[30]

One telling indication of the size and scope of the Soviet intelligence networks which had operated in Berlin was that the Gestapo round-up in 1942 resulted in the arrest of 130 members of the Berlin *Rote Kapelle* networks. Six were tortured to death or managed to commit suicide in jail. After summary trial, seventy-one were imprisoned and forty-nine were executed, including Harnack, Schulze-Boysen and their wives. Libertas Schulze-Boysen was retried on Hitler's orders and the death sentence was returned again. She courageously faced death declaring her opposition to Nazism. In a final letter from the Plötzenzee prison she stated that, like Christ, she was "dying for the people".[31]

Soviet records show that the Gestapo round-up accounted for less than half the underground membership of their CORSICAN, SENIOR and OLD MAN networks. The NKVD files indicate that the total figure for their *Rote Kapelle* networks came to close to 400 members, including a network in Hamburg, which was headed by Germans named Robert Abshagen, Franz Jacob and Bernhard Bästlein.[32]

APPENDIX III

A Section of the 1965 Debriefing of Alexander Orlov

The following is a reproduction of one of the summaries of Orlov's responses given during an April 1965 debriefing. The subject is the Dallins and it forms part of a series of "memoranda for the file" (in English) which bear no security classification. They cover a range of subjects on which Orlov was interviewed and parallel his responses in French to detailed questions about his *Handbook of Counter-Intelligence and Guerilla Warfare*. The folder includes the carbon copy of thanks, in French, addressed to "Dear Jim" that indicates that the source of the documentation was probably James Angleton, then chief of counter-intelligence staff at the CIA. The French source who supplied the folder of documents from the French DST counterintelligence agency files has requested anonymity. The documents are cited as ORLOV DST File.

It is a significant indication of their origin that the English memoranda have the name of the source providing the information censored out whenever it appears. It is clear from the context and comparison with Orlov's testimony to the Senate Internal Security Sub-Committee that his is the missing name – and it has been inserted in parenthesis. The text has been set verbatim and any syntactical infelicities and spelling errors are as they appear in the original carbon copy which is in the British author's possession.

> SUBJECT: David and Lidya Dallin
> SOURCE: [ORLOV]
> DOI*: 15–16 APRIL 1965

1. [Orlov] reviewed the highlights of his exposure of Zborovsky & Etienne & Mark. He noted he thought he had seen an indication recently that Zborovsky had been released upon completion of his prison term. [Orlov] felt that David and Lidya Dallin were both compromised wittingly or unwittingly in Zborovsky's activity, that they had contributed wittingly or unwittingly to Zborovsky's promotion as a Soviet agent from Europe to the US, that they had dragged their feet for years to prevent his exposure, and that they had only been stimulated to take an active part in Zborovsky's exposure

[* DOI = Date of Information]

when they realized that Yaseen had the goods on him.

2. The essence of [Orlov's] charge against the Dallins on this score is lodged in the chronology of their conduct. The crux of his allegation is that it was only after [Orlov's] positive identification to the US attorney in New York of Zborovsky as "Mark" that the Dallins took denunciatory action before Senate Committee. He regards this timing as a significant confirmation of their complicity, direct or indirect.

3. [Orlov] went over in detail how he had acquired the information on "Mark" during a visit that he had made from Spain to the Paris *rezidentura* sometime in 1937. He went to Kislov's office and found him reading a contact report from one of the *rezidentura*'s case officers. Kislov passed him the file, with the latest report on top, to read. Orlov flipped through the accumulated reports. He recalled that the last one dealt with events taking place in a clinic in Paris where Sedov, Trotsky's son, was being treated for an abdominal condition. He recalled specifically that among the details it was cited that Lidya Dallin had brought Sedov an orange. Among the file materials were other reports which indicated that the agent, who was cited as "Mark", had set up the burglary operation against Trotsky's files.

4. The case officer came in to recover the file and saw [Orlov] reading it. Later, [Orlov] ran into him in the corridor or anteroom. [Orlov] had to make certain purchases in Paris of a personal nature for himself and his group in Spain. Kislov had assigned "Mark"'s case officer to assist him in making the purchases. When they met in the Embassy, the case officer said that he had a contact to make with the individual who was the subject of the file: would [Orlov] come along to the contact, and after that they could proceed on their purchasing chore? [Orlov] welcomed the suggestion because it presented an opportunity for seeing Mark. He went and observed the contact between the case officer and "Mark", which took place in a small public park. [Orlov] was able to get a very precise, clear visual image of "Mark" during this event. [Orlov] then wrote a letter in block letters addressed to Trotsky, blind, in Mexico City warning him that there was a Soviet penetration agent in his Paris organization. (Comment: This development is significant because it takes place in 1937, almost a full year, or ten months, before [Orlov] finally cuts the cord in Spain.) Wasn't he taking an extreme risk in doing a thing of this kind? [Orlov] acknowledged that this might seem to be the case, but he pointed out that he wrote in what he regarded as untraceable characters. He also acknowledged that he had never been able to determine whether his first warning had ever reached Trotsky. He acknowledged that it might have been rash to have simply addressed the communication blind: Leon Trotsky, Mexico City, and expect that the missive would ever reach him, but he had no information at that time regarding Trotsky's precise address.

5. After his defection, he sent a much more specific warning; in fact, he sent one copy to Trotsky and the other to Sedov. He knows both of the letters arrived because the originals are in the Trotsky archives at Harvard. And, of course, Trotsky complied with the suggestion regarding the placement of an advertisement in the Trotskyite New York publication.

6. Because of concern with his own predicament, [Orlov] continued, he had no knowledge of "Mark" or his activity between these events in 1937–38 and Christmas 1953 [sic – should be 1955] when, as a consequence of discussions that had taken place between himself and Levitas of the *New Leader*, a meeting was arranged between [Orlov] and Dallin in the lobby of the Wellington Hotel in Manhatten. The Dallins had talked with Levitas at Bretton Woods after the publication of [Orlov's] first book. Abramovich, a prominent Russian Social Democrat, was another participant at the talk with Levitas.

7. After listening to [Orlov's] discussion of "Mark" and "Mark's" activity against Trotsky, Abramovich asked whether he had ever heard of a man named Zborovsky, but the question was made in a way that did not relate it to the earlier conversation. The name meant nothing to [Orlov]. Abramovich advised [Orlov] to report fully to Federal authorities, and repeated the name of Zborovsky as the probable identity of "Mark". This was the first time – as far as [Orlov] was concerned – that a name was attached to what he had known up to that moment simply as an NKVD cryptonym.

8. At the Wellington Hotel meeting, the [Orlovs] were most cautious and an unidentified individual was noted by the wife who was in the lobby just before David Dallin came into the hotel from a side entrance. For his own protection, [Orlov] did not protract the stay at the Wellington after a reciprocal acknowledgement of identities and conveyed Dallin out by another entrance into a taxi which Mrs [Orlov] had standing by and they took him to Schrafft's where they continued their discussion.

9. Dallin was reticent and cautious during the conversation. He did not reveal to her the fact that Zborovsky was in the United States, though [Orlov] probed to determine where "Mark" had gone from Paris. When he asked the question obliquely, all Dallin stated was that "Mark" had undoubtedly gotten out of France, but the suggestion he gave was that he had remained in Europe. Dallin attempted to convince [Orlov] that there were two Etiennes, and that they might have become confused with Zborovsky and Mark. [Orlov] was prepared for this because, indeed, there were two Etiennes in the Soviet employ as agents. But that fact did not in any way muddy up the identification of Zborovsky as Mark, he pointed out to Dallin. Dallin made the suggestion that the [Orlovs] come to his house in Central Park West for further discussions. He volunteered he would see to it that his wife was

not present. [Orlov] picked this up immediately and rejoined that he saw no reason why Mrs Dallin shouldn't be present.

10. The meeting at the Dallins' house took place a short time later. Mrs Dallin was introduced and she too began by attempting to suggest that there were two Etiennes, and "Mark" had somehow become confused in [Orlov's] mind. Dallin himself got her off after [Orlov's] indication that this element was irrelevant. To pin down Mrs Dallin after the Etienne episode, [Orlov] said he would cite one detail which he said he was sure would convince her that his charges against "Mark" were based upon factual, direct information. [Orlov] said he then recounted the episode of the orange from Mark's reporting during Sedov's fatal confinement in the Paris clinic. Mrs Dallin was absolutely petrified by the reference, because she recognized that it referred to an event in which she had taken part. Her immediate reaction was: "I believe you now entirely." Security notes that the wife of Mrs Dallin's brother – Mrs Dallin is a Ginzburg – was the head doctor at the place. It was a small, dirty place to which a man in Sedov's condition should never have been brought for treatment. In [Orlov's] opinion, Sedov was done in.

11. Mrs Dallin then suggested tea and Mrs [Orlov] joined her in the kitchen to make sure that nothing was being done to the beverage. During the conversation in the kitchen, Mrs Dallin – apparently still under the impact of the episode about the orange – said her husband had undertaken grave responsibilities, even for her. Zborovsky, she said, was now in the United States and had gotten into the country on the basis of her testimonial which, she said, she had given at her husband's request. Mrs [Orlov] immediately came into the living room and excitably informed her husband of Mrs Dallin's revelation that "Mark" was, indeed, in the US.

12. [Orlov] stresses the timing and the sequence of events. This was the first indication that he had had of the fact of Zborovsky's presence, and he went early the next week to the Federal attorney in New York to formally place on the record his information on Zborovsky. It was only after this that the Dallins made a clean breast of things before the Senate Internal Security Committee. In [Orlov's] opinion, that performance was arranged to get them off the hook as rapidly as possible, and it was accomplished by the Social Revolutionary, Trotskyite elements who have continuously assisted, or have pretended to assist, the US authorities. What the US authorities don't understand is that these Social Revolutionaries and Trotskyites have been, and probably still are, deeply penetrated by the Soviets.*

* [Orlov] attributed difficulties, or more accurately, charges in treatment he was accorded by I&NS at this time and small snags that came up in his own private bill

13. The events thereafter moved rapidly to the own appearance before the Senate Internal Security Committee where he repeated what he had given the Federal attorney in New York and the FBI, and the trial and conviction of Zborovsky himself.

14. In [Orlov's] opinion, Mrs Dallin knew all along Zborovsky's true status as a Soviet agent, and in his opinion she herself was a Soviet agent. During one of their conversations, [Orlov] said that he sprung at her very rapidly the question: "Do you know Brunn?" She immediately became flustered and confused and acknowledged: "Yes, I know him. He comes from the same town as I do." Brunn, [Orlov] said, was the NKVD case officer in Paris handling emigre affairs and, in his opinion, Brunn was Lidya Dallin's case officer.

15. Dallin himself, [Orlov] stated – at least in Berlin – was a Soviet agent. Bazarov was his case officer and Dallin may not have been worked by the Soviets against the emigres at that time. For Bazarov, Dallin was running a source in the First Section of the German Foreign Office. [Orlov] says that it is possible that Dallin broke with the Service when he left Berlin or came to the United States, he does not know and cannot guess about this aspect.

16. Finally, [Orlov] pointed out that it was impossible for him to understand how Zborovsky could now remain in the US after having served a jail sentence directly connected with his activity as a Soviet agent. Why has he not been expelled from the country?* Comment: It was Rumsey's impression that [Orlov] regards Zborovsky as a continuing element of Soviet operations in the United States and the relations between Zborovsky and the Dallins to be of interlocking and of continuing significance. This would imply that there might be something salvageable in Zborovsky if he remains in the US. It also implies that Dallin's work and the history of Soviet espionage activity

---

naturalization proceedings to the machination of these elements. It is not possible to judge the merits of his charges, but certainly [Orlov] still generates considerable heat when he discusses the topic. Apparently he was restricted in his freedom of movement about New York, and I&NS forced him to drop his alias – a concession that had been freely made by the Commissioner and the Attorney General in 1938. Much ado was made about whether the *Svir* had actually arrived in Antwerp in July 1938 as [Orlov] claimed. He said he was told by I&NS that investigation in Belgium had not confirmed his claim. This was absurd. For the price of airmail postage, [Orlov] himself wrote to the Antwerp shipping authorities and received from them a formal attestation that the *Svir* indeed had *arrived* at the time Yezhov's telegram had told [Orlov] to meet it. [Orlov] produced a copy of the attestation before the Senate Internal Committee. The crowning blow – everybody marvelled and suspected the worst because he had been able to secure the documentation!

* Zborovsky acquired US citizenship by naturalization in June 1947.

in the West as revealed in overt cases may have been a part of a damage assessment process in which the Soviet Service was directly interested.

17. It should be underlined that [Orlov] made a clear distinction between his allegation between Lidya Dallin and her husband. He allowed that the Professor may have broken with the Soviet Service before he came to the US. He did not make the same qualification, however, for his wife. Further, he conceded that in his activity in the US Professor Dallin could have been unwittingly controlled and manipulated by the Soviet Service.

18. It is interesting to speculate about the use of scholars in the performance of what are, in effect, damage assessments through overt information access and in this light to consider recent efforts that have been made by journalists and scholars in the West with respect to the Sorge case (Deakin, Johnson etc.), the Noel Field case (Flora Lewis). Note with respect to Mrs Lewis her recently announced intention of doing a book on the Krivitsky case.

19. The real purge in Soviet politics will be possible, in [Orlov's] opinion, when the evidence is finally forthcoming that Stalin had been a Tsarist police agent. [Orlov] believes very firmly in the accuracy of this charge. He recalled that his cousin Katsnelson revealed to him the details of this allegation early in 1937 at their last meeting in Paris when [Orlov] was recovering from a back injury sustained in an automobile accident. It should be recalled that [Orlov] associates the secret executive action taken by Stalin through the NKVD on Tukhachevsky and the military as directly related to the sharing by these individuals of Katsnelson's secret. Katsnelson himself was, of course, purged as the same time. His cousin in their final conversation had assured [Orlov] that he was leaving in the USSR the formal evidence to back up the charge. [Orlov] said he has spent years trying to think of ways of getting at the people and the places that Katsnelson may have chosen to entrust this material. [Orlov] suggested that he had himself contemplated plastic surgery to facilitate his own return, though he said he did not want this on record, nor he said did he want any of this information circulated.

20. It may very well be that a number of individuals that [Orlov] and his wife had cultivated in their stay at Michigan, whom Mrs [Orlov] has trained in the Russian language, may fit into this man's very deeply felt belief in the feasibility of uncovering the elements of this information by contacts and reconnaissance inside the USSR. Clearly [Orlov] has only contempt for Isaac Don Levine's so-called documentary evidence of Stalin's appertenance [sic] to the Okhrana. He regards the material published by Levine as a gross forgery. The material described to him by Katsnelson he believes is authentic.

APPENDIX IV

NOTE ON NOMENCLATURE

The successive names by which the Soviet security and intelligence apparatus was known reflected its complex relationship with the Internal Affairs Commissariat until the KGB was established in 1954 as a separate committee under the council of Ministers. This relationship has been somewhat simplified by using the following titles chronologically in the text:

Cheka – 20 December 1917 to February 1922 – V ChKa – (*Chrevzuychanaya Komissiya po Borbe s Kontrarevolutsiyei i Sabotazhem* – All-Russian Extraordinary Commission to Combat Counter Revolution and Sabotage)

GPU – February 1922 to July 1923 – *Gosudarstvennoye Politicheskoye Upravleniye* – State Political Administration.

OGPU – July 1923 to July 1934 – *Obyedinyonnoye Gosudarstvennoye Politicheskoye Upravleniye* – Unified State Political Administration.

NKVD – July 1934 to April 1943 *Narodnyi Kommissariat Vnutrennikh Del* – Peoples Commissariat of Internal Affairs under which operated the GUGB – *Glavnoye Upravlenie Gosudarstvennoye Bezopasnosti* – Chief Directorate for State Security.

NKGB – April 1943 to March 1946 – *Narodnyi Kommissariat Gosudarstvennoye Bezopasnosti* – Peoples Commissariat of Internal Affairs.

MGB – March 1946 to March 1953 – *Ministervo Gosudarstvennoye Bezopasnosti* – Ministry of State Security.

MVD – March 1953 to March 1954 – *Ministervo Vnutrennikh Del* – Ministery of Internal Affairs.

KGB – March 1954 to November 1991 – *Komitet Gosudarstvennoye Bezopasnosti* – Committee for State Security.

In November 1991 the KGB was dissolved and its internal and external functions separated. The responsibility for counterintelligence and internal surveillance was merged with the MVD – *Ministervo*

Vnutrennikh Del – Ministry of Internal Affairs. What had been the First Chief Directorate of the KGB became the CIS of the USSR – *Centralnoye Sluzba Razvedki* CCCP – Central Intelligence Service of the USSR, then in January 1992 the SVRR – *Sluzba Vneshney Razvedki Rossi* – Foreign Intelligence Service of Russia (Anglicized in the book as the Russian Intelligence Service – RIS.)

For most of these seventy-five years the Soviet foreign intelligence service was under the INO – *Inostrannye Otdel* – the Foreign Department of the GPU, OGPU and the MVD after World War II. It was eventually the First Chief Directorate of the KGB – the predecessor of the SVRR (Russian Intelligence Service):

Soviet Military Intelligence also underwent a similar transformation and name changes. Starting out as the RU – *Razvedyvatelnoye Upravleniye* – Intelligence Directorate of the 2nd Directorate of the Red Army General Staff – in 1921, it was successively under the 5th, then 7th. Then after a brief marriage with the NKVD between April 1937 and November 1938, it was under the 5th Directorate until 1942 when it became the GRU – *Glavnoye Razvedyvatelnoye Upravleniye* – Soviet Military Intelligence – under the 2nd Chief Directorate of the Red Army.

Rezident – Soviet intelligence service station chief.
Konspiratsia – Literally 'the rules of conspiracy' – the name given to the standard practices adopted by Soviet intelligence for preserving secrecy and security in its operations.

Chairmen of the Soviet Intelligence and Security Apparatus

Feliks Edmundovich Dzerzhinsky (*Cheka*, GPU, OGPU)	1917–26
Vyacheslav Rudolfovich Menzhinsky (OGPU)	1926–34
Genrikh Grigoryevich Yagoda (NKVD)	1934–36
Nikolay Ivanovich Yezhov (NKVD)	1936–38
Lavrenty Pavlovich Beria (NKVD)	1938–41
Vsevolod Nikolayevich Merkulov (NKVD)	1941
Lavrenti Pavlovich Beria (NKVD)	1941–43
Vsevolod Nikolayevich Merkulov (NKGB–MGB)	1943–46
Viktor Semyonovich Abakumov	1946–51
Semyon Denisovich Igantyev (MGB)	1951–53
Lavrenty Pavlovich Beria (MVD)	1953
Sergei Nikiforovich Kruglov (MVD)	1953–4
Ivan Aleksandrovich Serov (KGB)	1954–58
Alexander Nikolayevich Shelepin (KGB)	1958–61
Vladimir Yefimovich Semichastny (KGB)	1961–67

Yuri Vladimirovich Andropov (KGB)	1967–82
Vitali Vasilyevich Fedorehum (KGB)	1982
Viktor Mikhailovich Chebrikov (KGB)	1982–88
Vladimir Alexandrovich Kryuchkov (KGB)	1988–91

Chiefs of Soviet Foreign Intelligence

Iakov Kristoforovich Davtian (Davydov) (*Cheka*)	1920–21
Solomon Grigorievich Mogilievsky (*Cheka*)	1921–22
Mikhail Abramovich Trilliser (*Cheka,* GPU, OGPU)	1922–30
Artur Krystianovich Artusov (OGPU, NKVD)	1930–36
Abram Abramovich Slutsky (NKVD)	1936–38
Vladimir Georgievich Dekanozov (NKVD)	1938–39
Pavel Mikhailovich Fitin (NKVD, NKGB)	1939–40

KI – *Komitet Informatsie* – Intelligence Committee

Under the chairmanship of Vyacheslav Molotov, the Soviet Foreign Minister, this committee oversaw the foreign intelligence functions of both the Military and State Security apparatus – the deputies were:

Pyotr Vasilyevich Fedotov (MGB)	1946–49
Sergei Romanovich Savchenko (MGB, MVD)	1949–53
Vasily Stepanovich Ryasnoy (MVD)	1953
Alexander Korotkov (MVD)	1953
Alexander Semyonovich Panyushkin (MVD, KGB)	1953–55
Alexander Mikhailovich Sakharovsky (KGB)	1955–71
Fyodor Konstantinovich Mortin (KGB)	1971–74
Vladimir Alexandrovich Kryuchkov (KGB)	1974–88
Leonid Vladimirovich Shebarshin (KGB)	1988–91

Объединенное Государственное Политическое Управление

При Совнаркоме СССР

НА ТЕМП... УЧЕТ

ОБ... АРХ...

3427..

ЛИЧНОЕ ДЕЛО № 3891хр.

Никольского

Льва Лазаревича

"Швед"

том 2 — приложение (документ фото...
хранится отдельно)

Начато _____ месяца ___ 193 г

Окончено _____ месяца ___ 193 г

32476

32476

3891/хр.

...т. запаса № _3891/хр._   Архив № _____

...e cover of the first volume of the personal File No: 3891XB (original OGPU number stamped "special ...tive") of Nikolayevsky, Leva Lazarevich, code name "SCHWED". Bearing KGB archive No: 32476

116 242

Handwritten notes below the diagram of the French Army Headquarters indicate "O points of our surveillance (where we are positioned visibility is good) 'A' – Main entrance on [Boulevard St.] German from where we have accompanied four female officials.

Keep on carefully and thoroughly maintaining under surveillance.

2. The directorate for Moroccan affairs and the Railway Company of Morocco from which house you took under surveillance a girl has nothing to do with your Firm [*Deuxième Bureau*]

3. We approve the cultivation of a girl leaving the main entrance on the main avenue of the above mentioned number, but we categorically forbid you to use for this purpose local compatriots [members of the communist party] this may lead only to bad results.

4. About STAHL

MANN [Mally] explains that the side entrance is firmly closed. On the lower floor there is a private residence. On the second floor [in Russian sense, first in English] some of the rooms are occupied by the secretariat your Firm [*Deuxième Bureau*], therefore the presence of STAHL in the lower floor of the side entrance raises [suspicion] . . . end of page.

[Orlov File No: 3347 Vol. 11. p. 242]

месте.

Продолжайте осторожно тщательно следить.

2. Управление по делам Марокко и Компания по жел.дор гам Марокко, из дома которого Вы брали под наблюдение вушку, к Вашей фирме не имеет никакого отношения.

3. Обработку какой-либо девушки, выходящей из гла парадного, на главной аллее указанного выше номера, бряю, но категорически запрещаю Вам использование д цели местных земляков. Это только может привести к хим результатам.

4. О Стали.

Ман разъясняет, что побочный вход окончательн В нижнем этаже живут частные жильцы, а на 2-м э которых комнатах помещается канцелярия В/фирмы нахождение Стали в нижнем этаже побочного входа вызывает

Balance 1 February 1934	75043,"	555,555					8892
					Changed into Swiss Franks.		3685
Received from the center according to the budget.	32,000 –				Changed into French Francs.		
					Salary for SCHWED - February	– – – – –	–
					" - March.		340
Received from changing £8,872.			30 124,30		" " DLYNNY - February.		295
					" " JEANNE - February		
Received from changing £3,685.		57 425,75			" " " - March.		240
					" " JOSEPH - March, April.		
					" DLYNNY March, April, May.		
					" SCHWED April.	– – –	
					" JEANNE April.		
					" SOURCE 205 March-April.		
					Paid expenses source 205 for clothes.		
					A trip to Paris, Geneva, and Paris.		
					Hotel		
					French and international driving license.		
					To Vernick		
					For the deposit box in the bank		
					A trip Geneva, Paris and return.		
					Agents expenses for five months.		
					Salary SCHWED - May		
					" SCHWED - June		
					" JEANNE - May		
					Trip to Zurich, Vienna and return.		
					Salary JOSEPH - May-June		
					" DLYNNY - June		
					" JEANNE - June		
					JEANNE's trip to Geneva, Vienna and Geneva.		
					DLYNNY's trip to Switzerland.		
	15043 "	89981,30	30124,20				13432

To the Chairman of OGPU
FE Dzerzhinsky

After the discussions that have taken place with V. A.
tyrne, I express my agreement to co-operate in
incerely providing full evidence and information
nswering the questions of interest to the OGPU
elating to the organization and personnel of the
British intelligence service and as far as it is known to
1e what information I have relating to the American
ntelligence and likewise about those persons in the
ussian emigration organizations with whom I had
ealings.
  Moscow, the Inter Prison,
    30 October 1925
        [Signed] Sidney Reilly

morandum written by Reilly for
erzhinsky on 30 October 1925 (Trust File
: 302330 Vol. XXXVII. p. 300)

tructions from Centre to Orlov for
ducting surveillance of the French Army
neral Staff HQ [Orlov File No: 3347 (left)]

penses of Orlov's group in France 1 February 1934. [Orlov File No: 32476 Vol. II. p. 110]

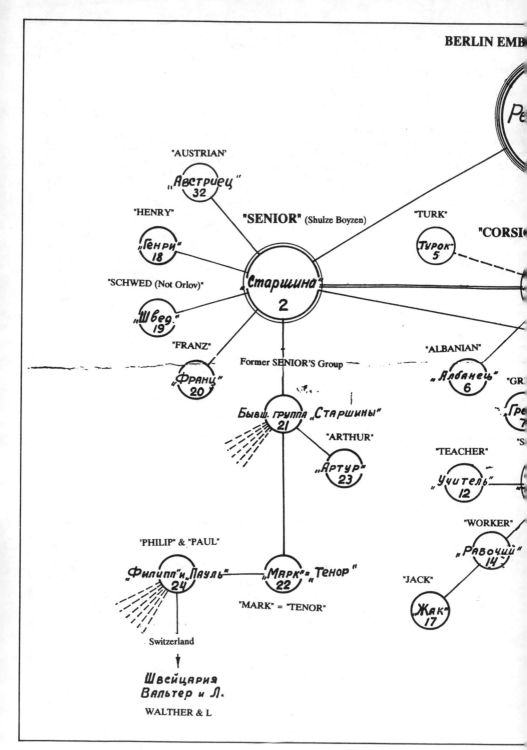

The Centre's chart of the Berlin *Rote Kapelle* networks in May 1941 on the eve of the German invasion of the Soviet Union. The loosely interlinked SENIOR, CORSICAN and OLD MAN groups were its three principal elements, with 28 separate sub-groups radiating out from them [Corsican File No: 34118 appendix to Vol. 11.]

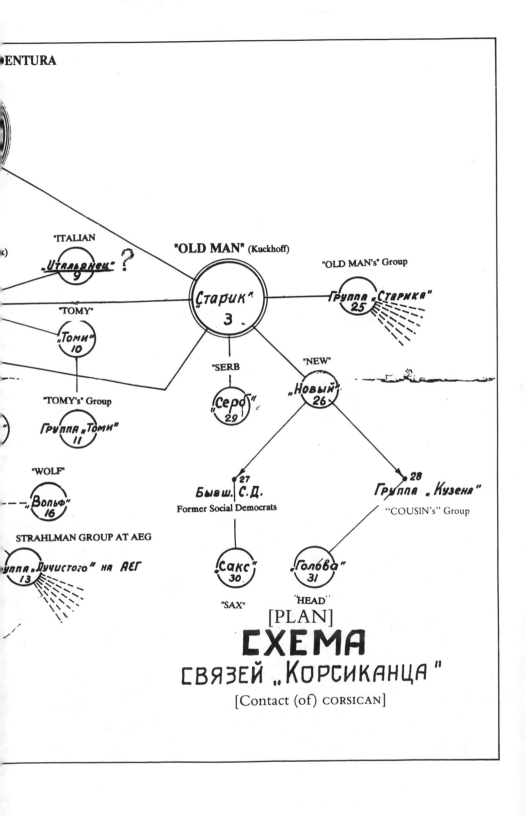

ENTURA

"ITALIAN"
„Итальянец" ?
9

"OLD MAN" (Kuckhoff)

"Старик"
3.

"OLD MAN's" Group
Группа „Старика"
25

"TOMY"
„Томи"
10

"SERB
„Серб"
29

"NEW"
„Новый"
26

"TOMY's" Group
Группа „Томи"
11

"WOLF"
„Вольф"
16

STRAHLMAN GROUP AT AEG
уппа „Лучистого" на АЕГ
13

27
Бывш. С.Д.
Former Social Democrats

28
Группа „Кузена"
"COUSIN's" Group

„Сакс"
30.

„Голова"
31

"SAX"

"HEAD"

[PLAN]
СХЕМА
СВЯЗЕЙ „Корсиканца"
[Contact (of) CORSICAN]

Orlov's letter of assignment to Britain in June 1934 [Orlov File No: 32 Vol. IV. p. 129–131]

The visa and UK immigration stamps on Orlov's US passport in the name of William Goldin shows his movements in and out of the country during the year-and-a-half that he ran the NKVD illegal *rezidency* in London [Orlov File No: 3247 Vol. I. p 227, in envelope]

[Top Left Hand corner] Number 1 [means letter number 1 hand-dated] 19th June 1934.
Dear SCHWED [Orlov's operational code name]

As part of the reorganization of our work you are being assigned to lead our group which has been previously been directed by Comrade ANATOLI.

TASKS of the group: Cultivation, surveillance and penetration into the work of the English intelligence organs in the Centre [London] and on the periphery of our country [USSR] – Latvia, Finland and Estonia. THE PRINCIPAL ASSIGNMENT for the London part of the group is penetration of the [British] intelligence service for illuminating the ways this establishment works on our territory.

The Baltic section of your group has been given the task to penetrate the British intelligence and counterintelligence organs in the above mentioned countries and exposing their work on our territory.

COMPOSITION OF THE GROUP: 1. Your assistant for the central group [meaning London] is Comrade MAR [Ignaty Reif], an officer of the central [Moscow] apparatus personally known to you. 2. Comrade ARNOLD [Arnold Deutsch] – an officer of JACK [an illegal officer in the Paris] *rezidentura* a member of our compatriots group [member of the Bolshevik party], a group leader and a technician in the *rezidentura*. According to his personal and operational qualifications, he can be used as a controller of individual sources as well as acting as an assistant to MAR in liaison matters. 3. GRIMM – a former source of the Berlin *rezidentura* (probably known to you) – [NAME AND IDENTIFICATION DELETED BY RIS] He can be used by you for finding a cover.

COMMUNICATIONS WITH "MAR": The address of MAR following in English, *London 16 Brixton Hill, S. W. 2. Max Wolisch.* Liaison with MAR through ARNOLD: *London W. 14 – Castletown Rd, Leontine Williams für Mr Deutsch.* And through GRIMM [ADDRESS DELETED BY RIS]

PAGE 2 [DELETED BY RIS BECAUSE IT LISTS ALL THE SOURCES OF THE LONDON GROUP] . . .

PAGE 3:–

. . . meeting IGOR so that he could be warned about the meeting with you. The rendezvous for meeting IGOR is known to MAR, but just in case we repeat [LOCATION DELETED BY RIS]

4. It is necessary to first organize a failure-proof and regular communications line with MAR on the ISLE [code word for Britain] as well as with us. For the previous two months we received from MAR two letters in secret ink which could not be developed. This kind of communications of course cannot satisfy us in this form and in the [delays] of timing. You are [therefore] to organize communications with us in such a way that we have opportunities: 1. To receive mail from you and MAR regularly 2. To telegraph to you and receive from you information by cable about the progress of your work.

By this we would not exclude the means of corresponding using secret ink, but this may duplicate your alternative channels. The presence in MAR's group of ARNOLD who is well versed in photographic and secret ink techniques will help you to solve this task. For control letters directly to us, we are giving you and MAR the following direct address and a [chemical] recipe for letters (it is known to ARNOLD) Address Moscow B-Serpukhovka, 7 Serpukhovsky Pereulok, Apartment 7 to M. F. Popova (the initials and the family name on the envelope to be underlined).

5. By return post inform us about the balance of the money that remains with MAR and with you. Draft a budget which is really necessary for your group. In the budget must be shown: (a) The salary of the members of the group (SCHWED, JEANNE [Maria Orlov], MAR, ARNOLD and so on). (b) The pay for the sources, operational expenses of the sources, operational expenses of the group, travel expenses of the group and expenses for the cover.

6. Pending receipt from you of the budget and its approval, we are sending to you an advance for the group in the sum of 100 (one hundred pounds [£'s]) the receipt of which please confirm by a separate receipt.

7. At the time of dispatching this letter to you, we received from MAR, who at present is in Copenhagen, the following [RIS DELETION] information "the group has recruited the son of the Anglo-agent Philby, [King] Ibn Saud's counsellor. Also recruited are a female official of [NAME DELETED BY RIS] which has materials [DELETED BY RIS] MAR established contact and started to work with the following sources: 1. INSPECTOR 2. GOD and 3. PROFESSOR. There are a number of leads and reports. MAR is expecting to establish contact with ANATOLI or to be recalled home [for a short visit]."

We responded by telegraph to MAR and asked him about the possibility of immediately travelling to Paris to establish contact with you and ANATOLI. His recall home is not on our agenda at present. As soon as we receive an answer from him we will inform you by telegraph the date of his arrival Paris and you will be put in touch with him by Comrade PETER.

8. By return post we are expecting a detailed report from you and MAR concerning the work done and the prospective the immediate future.

[Signed] *Artem* [ARTUR – ARTUSOV]

Reif's *spravka* (memo) "For the personal file of 'WAISE' or 'SIROTA' [Maclean]

Through SYNOK [Philby] we established that one of his closest friends, a member of the Compat [Communist Party] organization in Cambridge, son of late Minister of Education Maclean, has g connections in political circles. His work in the Compatriots Organization was known to a very lin circle. In his character Maclean (we gave him the code name SIROTA alias WAISE.) He is a withdrawn reserved person, exceptionally loyal and prepared to help the Compatriots movement with everythin has. We have drafted a plan of bringing "SIROTA" back into the high society [British Establishment. U the cover of an assignment from the Compatriots Organization SYNOK suggested that SIROTA she discontinue any contact with the Compatriots Organization in Cambridge. [He] declared to the comr who knew him in the Organization that he is busy with his studies and therefore does not want to cannot work [for the Party.] After the end of three to four months of such behavior by SIROTA, Compatriots Organization in Cambridge wrote him off as an active Compatriot. SIROTA's rebuilding o contacts in the Establishment, persuaded those persons who knew him because of his work in Compatriots Organization that he had distanced himself completely from the movement. In October 1 it was suggested that SYNOK should put me contact with SIROTA directly. In the name of an antifa organization, I started to instruct SIROTA in the required manner. As Baldwin is a personal friend of Maclean family, SIROTA's mother managed to get a letter from him. (I have personally read the lette which he writes he [Baldwin] will by all means assist SIROTA to embark on a diplomatic career.) mentioned in the letter that Baldwin has let it be known to an appropriate person in the Foreign Offic was personally interested in the SIROTA's advancement. As it is known, in Britain individuals who are g to work in the Ministry of Foreign Affairs must pass appropriate examinations. SIROTA entered the requ courses and in the summer of this year will pass the exams. At the same time SIROTA is culivating person interest to us. In Febuary 1935 I passed [control of] SIROTA over to SCHWED [Orlov.] SIROTA is not getting special salary from us. We give him money according to operational needs. This sum does not exceed £ £4 a month. SIROTA requires better training and instruction. He fulfills our assignments with interest very carefully. He is prepared to make any sacrifices in connection with our work. Lately, he realized tha is an agent of the [Soviet] Union and with even greater desire he gave himself to our work. Uncondition a very prospective source.

13 VII 1935   [Signed] MAR

[Maclean File No: 83791 Vol. 1. p. 44–5]

...morandum for the file by STEPHAN – Arnold Deutsch – on Donald
...clean (LYRIC).

"Spravka [Memo] about LYRIC [Maclean]."

In London I got in touch with Edith [Tudor Hart] whom I knew from my time in Vienna. In the autumn [a slip of Deutsch's memory since it was actually late spring] of 1934 SYNOK [Philby] that is SÖNNCHEN came to Edith with his Austrian wife. This Austrian girl [Litzi Friedman] was an active party worker and introduced SYNOK into this work. SYNOK and his wife told Edith about his opportunities to work for us. In this connection, we instructed Edith to keep them away from the [Communist] Party work in London. In May or June 1934, Edith put me in touch with SYNOK, but I, at that time, did not put the question specifically about our work and only later I finally introduced him into our operations. SYNOK had two friends in Cambridge, both active Party members and both had excellent opportunities and connections. They were LYRIC [Maclean] and MÄDCHEN [Burgess]. As LYRIC seemed to us the better [prospect] we suggested that SYNOK should carefully find out about his opportunities and contacts and should draw him away from active Party work. After what we learned about LYRIC we suggested that SYNOK should eventually recruit him. And that was what he did. In connection with this SYNOK organized a meeting of Reif with LYRIC and Reif had direct contact with him from October to December 1934. After that he was directed by SCHWED [ORLOV] until the 6 October 1935 and then [he was run] by me until my departure.

LYRIC and MÄDCHEN were good friends, but we agreed with LYRIC not to give MÄDCHEN any indication about his contact with us. [THREE LINES DELETED BY RIS] In connection with the fact that LYRIC, on our instructions, started distancing MÄDCHEN and Party work, the latter started suspecting that LYRIC was conducting special work and by way of inquisitive questions and [NAME DELETED BY RIS] he discovered that he [Maclean] was working for us. So that to prevent MÄDCHEN from talking about LYRIC we decided to recruit him (he proved to be a valuable person) and instructed LYRIC for this purpose, about whose contact with us he had already known. LYRIC talked to him and arranged for a rendezvous with STEPHAN [Deutsch]. Thus in January 1935 MÄDCHEN started to work for us. [DOZEN LINES DELETED BY RIS]

[Signed] Stephan

[Maclean File No: 83791 Vol. 1. p. 277–8]

... работы этой организации для начала еще не 1...
... за первые 6 месяцев 25000 ф. ст. и персонал из 4 чел,

... вхожу и я.

...это придается большое значение этому шагу.

...организация была утверждена сэром Уоррен Фишером и премьер

...министром после многочисленных совещаний. Сейчас необходимо ре

...вопрос о сырье, о котором я вам уже сообщал - существуют

...это режим в Германии не подает нам надежды в том, что он

...представит опасности Британской Империи...

...мнение и решение с другой стороны ни в какой степени не

...меняет сознательно выраженного намерения заставить Германию

...помочь ей напасть на Советский Союз.

...подтверждается I. мнением разведки, которая считает это

возможным " и 2. Досоном, редактором "Таймс" /через Берна/,

который считает это "действительно желаемым и возможным".

...дка считает современный режим в Германии на кануне кризи

...а, особенно это относится к позиции Гебельса.

...ветке хотелось бы работать с Герингом, но чувствует , что с

...надежда теряет почву. Гиммлер, на которого полагается Гим

...отнится к борьбе с Герингом. Чемберлен и Досон хотят, чтобы

...еринг приехал в Англию/ или даже в Шотландию, чтоб избежать

...монстрация/., но разветка этому противостоит. Граф Берчтоерд

... обеде с Ротшильдом и /3/ Болдуином подтвердили слабость

...зиция Геринга, которая во всяком случае является причиной

...зования этой организации.

...рез той секции этой разведки , в которой я работаю, всяке оч

...ет , что снятие контроля над суще...твующим режимом в Германии

...лее срочным и необходимым, нежели нападение на Советский Сою

...организация будет работать с разветкой и министерством: ино

...ел. Политическая линия и содержание программы будет намечено

...группой/ из разветки/ и министерством иностранных дел. Я из

...делаю их применительно к мнимой организации путешествия.

Guy Burgess – MÄDCHEN ...
reports the formation of a
secret Foreign Office unit
promote anti-Hitler
propaganda, on the
Anglo-Soviet negotiation
the summer of 1939 and h
approach to Lord Rothsch
regarding the Jewish
question [Burgess File No
83792 Vol. 1. p. 149–205]

An MI6 officer (colonel Valentine
Vivian?) as drawn for Soviet
identification purposes by Guy Burgess
[Burgess File No: 83792 Vol. 1. p. 146]

The scale of work of this organization [the so-called "Travel Bureau" set up by the Foreign Office to disseminate anti-Hitler propaganda to Germany] is for now not very great. It has for the first six months a budget of £25,000 and a staff of four people, among them myself, but nevertheless, a great deal of importance is attached to this step. This organization was approved by Sir Warren Fisher and the Prime Minister after much discussion.

Now it is necessary to solve the question of the Jews, about which I have already reported. The current regime in Germany does not give us any hope that it will not present any danger to the British Empire. Such an opinion and a decision of the other side by no means changes the consciously expressed intention to make and help Germany to attack the Soviet Union.

This is confirmed 1. by the view of the Intelligence Service [MI6] which thinks it's possible. 2. By [Geoffrey] Dawson, editor of *The Times* (through Burn) who thinks that it is really "desirable and possible." The Intelligence Service thinks that the existing regime in Germany is on the verge of crisis especially regarding Goebbels's position. The Intelligence Service would like to work with Goering, but feels that this hope is disappearing. Himmler, on whom Hitler relies, is preparing for the fight with Goering. Chamberlain and Dawson want Goering to come to Britain (or even Scotland to avoid demonstrations) but the Intelligence Service is against it. [German diplomat] Count von Bernstorff at the dinner with Rothschild and [former Prime Minister] Baldwin confirmed the weakening of Goering's position which, in any case, the reason for the creation of this organization [the propaganda unit]. The department of that section of the Intelligence Service where I work still thinks withdrawing control [monitoring] over the regime in Germany is more urgent and necessary than the attack on the Soviet Union. This organization [the "Travel Bureau" propaganda unit] will work with the Intelligence Service and the Ministry for Foreign Affairs. The political line and contents of the programs will be approved by [Major Laurence] Grand (from the Intelligence Service) and the Ministry of Foreign Affairs. I will rearrange them according to [under the guise of] the fake travel service.

Page 149

Page 205 of the same Report of Burgess – not reproduced – continues:–

I would very much like to receive your decision on this question, since it is possible that if I would do this, then we could use my new contacts for feeding false information. [Burgess probably refers to one of the freelance assignments given to him by MI6 which he does not make clear in the report, but which appears to be an approach to the Soviet Embassy.]

Then [David] Footman introduced me to my present chief Major Grand, who according to him, is an important man.

My first mission for Grand was work on the Jewish question and Palestine. My task was to activate Lord Rothschild politically and in the first instance to use him for splitting the Jewish movement and the creation of opposition in relation to Zionism and Dr. [Chaim] Weitzman.

Grand told me that the British Government had decided to go to any length to reach an agreement with the Arabs because they make our position in the Near East dangerous. On the other hand Weitzman is a strong and dangerous figure.

Orlov's Expense Sheet for the London Illegal Station July 1935 (Translation on pp 153–4) [Orlov File No: 32476 Vol. III. p. 123]

№9 Мдунжа [...] April 25ᵗʰ

Dear Comrade,

This is to say first of all how glad I am to be in touch and working again. As you will have heard, I have no reason to think that my position is not quite sound, and I think the arrangements which we have made for work should be alright. The trial of flodding will doubtless have increased watchfulness on the part of the authorities. Certain warnings have recently been issued in my office possibly as a result thereof, namely that "green" i.e. secret papers should as far as possible not be taken out of the office, and that "Red" (i.e. most secret) papers should never be, and also that blotting paper used to blot confidential papers must be carefully destroyed!

With regard to the work, I will get you have, as before, all I can, which will be chiefly the printed despatches + telegrams, + such secret reports and particularly interesting papers as come my way. This time we are sending some despatches + a good many telegrams: it would be useful to know how many of the latter you would like — a lot of them are I think of little value. We have also sent a memorandum by COLLIER, head of the Northern (Russian) Dept about the British policy generally in regard to Spain, together with the comments thereon of the high foreign office authorities. The document is, I think, of considerable interest. Collier takes the more

Letter dated 25 April [1938] from Maclean, shortly after the Soviet *rezidentura* re-established contact with him through NORMA, which he signed using his code name LYRIC [Maclean File No: 83791 Vol. I. pp. 174–6]

or less left-wing anti-fascist line, which, as you will remember, he has long followed, but all the rest of them, who comment, Halifax, Cadogan, Mounsey, Plymouth & Cadogan, are, as was to be expected, unanimously in favour of the present policy of conciliation with Italy + consequent acceptance of a Franco victory. Vansittart, who, as you will see, does not comment is believed to share Collier's views at least in part, (as is indicated in his memorandum), but it appears that his advice is not much sought since Eden left. I may be able to tell you something more on this point later.

With regard to myself, I am being me, as you now I think know, to the Paris Embassy as a 3d Secretary, in all probability in the middle of next October. I do not really know how easy or difficult it will be to do our work in Paris, but I think & hope that it will be much easier than at most places to which I might have been sent. I am therefore pleased — provided that you are too. I shall have to go away for the regular holiday in the summer and have arranged provisionally to do this in September, which leaves 4 clear months for work here. It would also mean in effect that I should go straight from my holiday to Paris. I shall stick to this arrangement unless you prefer

some other.

I have seen Korsekoff (Otto will know who I mean), who was back here for a few days some 3 weeks ago; he is very anxious to be put in touch again & says that the same applies to others who are in Paris. I heard yesterday that his 3rd Musketeer has had a breakdown of some kind and has had to go away for 2 months. I have not seen him myself for many months so do not know if this is likely to be true, but I shall be very sorry if it is.

I don't think I have anything more to say, at present, except to send my best greetings to Otto & Theo, to any others I may know, and to yourself.

LYRIC

P.S. Please let me know if there are any particular things you want to know about & I will do my best. I deal myself only with Spain, as before.

Letter from Maclean to Soviet control officer in Paris dated 19 October [1938]
[Maclean File No: 83791 Vol. 1. p. 161]

Paris, le 19 octobre.

Cher Egereff,
    Ni Norma ni moi ne vous ont pas vu ni entendu depuis longtemps, et nous voulons vivement vous voir et avoir de vos nouvelles, specialement dans ces circonstances si difficiles. Comment allez vous? Nous vous reprochons beaucoup de ne pas avoir nous fri fait signe depuis si longtemps et nous esperons que vous allez prendre contacte avec moi aussitot que possible. Norma vous a ecrit mais elle n'a pas recu de reponse. Elle ne comprend pas pourquoi vous l'avez laissee sans mot comme ca. C'est necessaire donc que vous sortiez de votre silence toute de suite et que vous me donniez un message pour elle. Je vous invite a prendre le petit dejeuner avec moi a neuf du matin chez moi samedi, dimanche ou lundi prochain ou n'importe quel jour pendant la semaine prochaine. Vous avez mon adresse; j'habite au deuxieme etage. Si vous ne pouvez pas venir laissez moi un mot chez moi.

        Toutes mes amities,

            LYRIC.

98

января Л. Седов, во время
нашей беседы, у него на кварти-
ре, по вопросу о 2-м москов-
ском процессе и роли в нем
отдельных подсудимых (Радека,
Пятакова и др.), заявил:
"Теперь колебаться больше нечего,
Сталина нужно убить".
Для меня это заявление было
настолько неожиданным, что
я не успел на него реаги-
ровать. Л. Седов тут же перевел
разговор на другие вопросы.

23 января Л. Седов, в присутствии
моем и также Л. Эстриной,
бросил фразу такого же содер-
жания как и 22-го. В ответ
на это его заявление, Л. Эстри-
на сказала: "Держи язык
за зубами". Больше к этому
вопросу не возвращались.
Л Зборовски.

On January 22 L. [Lev] Sedov in the course of our discussion at his apartment on the question of the second Moscow process [trial] and the role played in it by individual defendants (Radek Pyatakov and others) declared: "There is no hesitating any more now, Stalin must be killed" For me this statement was so unexpected that I had no time to react to it. L. Sedov immediately changed the subject of the conversation.

On 23 January L. Sedov in the presence of myself and also of L. [Lilia] Estrine [Mrs Dallin] dropped a phrase of similar contents of the 22. In response to this statement of his [Sedov] L. Estrine said "Hold your tongue". They did not return to this matter again.

[Signed] M. Zborowsky

Page 17 of Orlov's letter to Moscow from Barcelona of 10 July 1938 showing that he was in contact with Philby [Correspondence of the Spanish *rezidentura* File No: 19897 Vol. III. p. 17]

17

... was handed over to the chief of the special department of Valencia through the chairman of the syndicalist party, Feken. This document contains an insolent proposal to organize a "concession settlement." I passed it over to del Vaya. The document raised a lot of outrage in the government. The American and British consulates said they had nothing to do with this document.

Herewith I attach materials of SYNOK (SÖNNCHEN) [Philby] concerning the dislocation of Franco's military forces. [Crosshatched in red in original.]

All the remaining questions I set out in the general letter.

With best regards. [Signed] SCHWED.

10. VII. 38.

Note indicating the burial place of Spanish Marxist leader Andres Nin [Orlov File No: 32476 Vol. 1. p. 164]

"N. from Alcala de Enares in the direction of Perane de Tahunia, half way, 100 metres from the road, in the field. [Present] BOM, SCHWED, JUZIK, two Spaniards. PIERRE'S driver VICTOR."

rlov's two cables from Barcelona responding to e Centre's instructions to go to Antwerp [Orlov le No: 32476 Vol. 1. p. 120–1]

"I confirm the receipt of your telegram No: 1743. In order to be in Antwerp on 14 July, I must depart from here on 11 July, or the 12th at the latest." Orlov cabled Moscow Centre on 10 July, asking "to be informed, before that date, the terms of my meeting with our comrade in Antwerp". He also asked whether the Soviet underground agents designated "5, 10, 26, 27 and 29 must, by the 14 July, be in Europe already or can they, for the time being, stay in Spain in a state of readiness?'

СОВЕРШЕННО СЕКРЕТН

МЕМОРАНДУМ № 6365

От ШВЕДА   Из БАРСЕЛОНЫ

...рждаю получение телеграммы № 1743. Чтобы быть
...рпене 14 июля, я должен отсюда выехать 11 июля,
...здее 12 июля. Поэтому прошу к этому времени
...щить: 1) Условия моей встречи с нашим товарищем
...нтверпене. 2) Должны ли люди 5,10,26,27,29 к 14 -му
...я уже в Европе или они могут пока находиться в состо
...ти находиться в Испании.

916

ВЕРНО:

СОВЕРШЕННО СЕКРЕТНО
120

МЕМОРАНДУМ № 6400

Из Барселоны От ШВЕДА   Получена 10.УП.38г.
                              Подана 9.УП

...чение телеграммы № 1750 подтверждаю. 12 июля
...рмляю выезд и вышлю "Журналистку" в Брюссель, а
...та в город Фина. 12-го или 13-го июля перебрасы-
...тся туда один из пяти человек, указанных в телег-
...ме № 1743. Со всеми будет обусловлена связь
...афируйте должен ли брат захватить с собой ра
...рат. Нужно ли его запаковывать, уничтожить д
...взять диплисты. Буде в Антверпене 14 июля.

№ 320

ВЕРНО:

Confirm the receipt of telegram No: 1750. On 12 July I shall register my departure and send LADY JOURNALIST to Brussels and her brother to the city of FIN [Paris]. On 12th or 13th one of the five people mentioned in telegram 1743 will be transferred there. Contact with everybody will be prearranged. Wire whether the brother must take the radio transmitter with him, whether it should be packed, whether diplomatic correspondence should be destroyed and the inventory should be brought along. I shall be in Antwerp on 14 July.

The Appendix to Orlov's July 1938 letter to Yezhov listing NKVD cases and operations [Orlov File No: 76659 Vol. 1. p. 301]

Incomplete list of questions and cases.
1. Export of the metal. Details. [Spanish gold]
2. The case of [NAME DELETED BY RIS] Alexei's trip [DELETION.]
3. Czech and his wife [REAL NAMES DELETED BY RIS] their present location. A letter *poste restante*. A failure. The last means.
– [4 – DELETION OF 3 LINES]
–
5. Details of [NAMES DELETED BY RIS] history. The house of [NAME DELETED BY RIS.] A trip. Breakfast with [NAME DELETED BY RIS] Details of negotiations with [NAME DELETED BY RIS] on this case.
6. Details about FARMER. His ring (with the engraving) left to KADI is with me. Have also his letter to [NAME DELETED BY RIS] The key for talks with number
13. The last meetings with ALEXANDER, their trip in the car with a stranger (F) and a frank conversation. The symbolic meaning of packages from DOUGLAS [Spiegelglass.]
– [7 – DELETION]
– [8 – DELETION]
9. All the history of the case of NIKOLAI and NIKO-LAYEVSKY. Have a draft of the cryptogram written by JUSIK and also a draft of the letter written by SIEGFRIED, found later after the operation.
– [10 – DELETION]
– [11 – DELETION]
– [12 – DELETION]
13. A detailed history of all the cases of TULIP

2.

[Zborowsky] Have at my disposal two pages of his report home about the possibility of his failure and people responsible for this. All his deeds (SNEBLIT, LUDWIG, the archives, the OLD MAN [Trotsky], the SON [Sedov].)
– [14 – DELETION 3 LINES]
–
16. The work of GAMMA.
17. TROYAN's trip. It's objective.
– [LINE DELETION]
18–19. All *liter* [liquidation] military operations some substantial evidence and witnesses.
[DELETIONS]
30. Have photographic pictures and real surnames of the participants in the case of NIKOLAI [Nin assassination] and names of those who can identify these photos. The date of their departure for the [Soviet] Union. The photo by three consulates. (Swiss, Austrian and Polish.) [DELETED BY RIS] (DELETED BY RIS)
34–39. All about the OLD MAN and SON. All the considerable work of all [undercover agents] including GAMMA, TULIP etc.
40. About the processes [Moscow Show Trials.]
– [41–44 DELETED]
45. All the [undercover] work in the country of GRAFPEN [Britain.]
46. – – – – – – – – – of FIN [France], etc.
All this will never see the light!

NOTES AND SOURCES

Chapter 1: "People Like Us Hate the KGB"

1 Interview with Mikhail Alexandrovich Feoktistov conducted by Oleg Tsarev in Moscow, February 1992. Feoktistov who is now retired was one of the KGB's most experienced "man-hunters" – undercover agents specializing in tracking down contacts.

2 The photos and description of Orlov had originally been prepared by the NKVD in July 1938 before the cancellation of the search for him after his flight to the United States. They are in the KGB archive file No. 76659 "ALEXANDER ORLOV" Vol. 1, page 2 (hereafter ORLOV file) lodged in Russian Intelligence Service Archive, Yasenevo, Moscow (hereafter RISA).

3 Prokopyuk was one of Orlov's subordinates in Spain. During the Great Patriotic War, 1941–5, he became a prominent commander of an NKVD Partisan Brigade and was awarded the Gold Star of the Hero of the Soviet Union. His portrait with notes on his career is in the Ministry of Security Museum (former KGB Museum) at 2 Lubyanskaya in Moscow. The fact that Orlov denied any knowledge of him indicated his extreme caution in dealing with a stranger rather than forgetfulness. ORLOV File No. 103504, Vol. 1, p. 66, RISA.

4 The account of the confrontation with Maria Orlov is based on Tsarev's interviews supplementing Feoktistov's November 1969 report to KGB headquarters made under his operational code name "GEORG". ORLOV File No. 76659, Vol. 1, p. 2, RISA.

5 *The Legacy of Alexander Orlov.* Prepared by the Senate Subcommittee to Investigate the Administration of the Internal Security Laws of the Committee of the Judiciary (hereafter SISSC), 93rd Congress August 1973. US Government Printing Office, Washington DC (hereafter ORLOV *Legacy*) p. 11. This is a valuable source since its foreword includes information supplied by the FBI and CIA sources who debriefed Orlov *after* his encounter with Feoktistov. In addition it reprinted the testimony Orlov delivered in the closed session to the SISSC in 1955 and 1957.

6 According to the details Feoktistov supplied in his interview with Tsarev, he said he did not mention the gun in his official report to Moscow so as not to alarm the Centre. Feoktistov's assessment of the final outcome of the first meeting was not at all pessimistic and he hoped for permission to meet with Orlov again soon. This is why the story of Maria threatening Feoktistov with a gun does not feature in Tsarev's article on Orlov which appeared in the Soviet Trade Union Newspaper *Trud* on 20 December 1990. This piece had been written from the Orlov KGB archive files which do not mention the incident. Tsarev did not learn the full story until he interviewed

Feoktistov in 1992. He explained that his concealment of the gun episode in his official report was indeed a breach of discipline. But in his job as a man-hunter and with his knowledge of the workings of the Centre's bureaucratic machine, Feoktistov said that he was confident in his professional intuition and prepared to take calculated risks which would and in fact did bring him success. The situation illustrates the common conflict of views between a field operative and a bureaucracy, based on different psychological approaches, that is exploited in fiction and spy thriller films.

7 Feoktistov interviews.

8 Feoktistov report, Orlov File No. 76659, Vol. 1, p. 2.

9 Feoktistov interviews.

10 ORLOV Legacy, p. 11.

11 Report dated 16 December 1969 to FBI from State Dept. – Feoktistov, Mikhail Alexandrovich, UNSEC Translator, ORLOV FBI File No. 115–22869 FOIA.

12 Introduction by Senator James O. Eastland on p. 3 of ORLOV Legacy, pp. 5–8.

13 Orlov's KGB dossier discloses that those who intuitively knew the real details behind Orlov's flight to the West in 1938 never called him a traitor or defector. They employed a Russian term Nevozvraschenez, literally "somebody who didn't come back from abroad", which does not imply treason, or changing sides. In one or two instances in his file where Orlov was actually described as a traitor it was by officers under Stalin's regime who wrote superficially of his case. They were clearly not familiar with all the details of the case and appear to have been ideologically opinionated rather than professionally competent.

14 This according to the CIA officials who had debriefed Orlov, who were consulted by the respected British intelligence writer Gordon Brook-Shepherd and anonymously cited in his study of The Storm Petrels: The First Soviet Defectors, Collins, London 1977, pp. 204–5. One of the sources who provided information to Brook-Shepherd on a confidential basis was consulted by the authors.

15 Orlov's dossier consists of nine volumes of files – including his personal file and those reflecting his operational work in France, Britain and Spain. Parts of Philby, Maclean and Burgess's files are also concerned with Orlov's work in London in 1934–5. The review of Orlov's actual files was restricted to very few people before 1990. Until Tsarev's research for this book it had not been made available in full because of its sensitive nature. Access to files in the First Chief Directorate's archives was in any case restricted on a "need to know basis". Few researchers, even on official internal investigations were given authority to examine more than a few pages or sections of any individual's files. An occasional check on a name in registry would point to certain pages in these files, and then only those individual pages would be shown to the officer who would not have grasped the full dimension of Orlov's work.

Chapter 2: "Sword and Shield"

1 Pseudonyms listed in ALEXANDER ORLOV Internal Security-R FBI File # 105–22869 FOIA and ORLOV File No. 76659 and 32476 RISA.

2 Sworn statement 23 August 1954 of Alexander and Maria Orlov before Mr Joseph J. Gaudino, Inspector of Immigration and Naturalization Service, New York City. In FBI File No. 62–1246 FC ORLOV Internal Security-R File No. 105–22869 FBI Archives, Washington. Obtained under the US Freedom of Information Act (FOIA). Hereafter ORLOV INS Deposition 1954/FBI 105–22869.

3 Testimony given by Isaac Rabinowitz to FBI in ORLOV FBI File No. 105–22869 FOIA.

4 ORLOV FBI File No. 105–22869, Statement to INS, FOIA.

5 ORLOV *Legacy*, p. 3.

6 ORLOV FBI File No. 105–22869, FOIA.

7 Boris Rosovsky's name has been deleted from the declassified report of his interview by a New York-based special agent on 10 January 1954. But his name appears uncensored in a deposition Orlov gave to the Immigration and Naturalization Service on 29 June 1955 – escaping censorship because the photostat copy in the files is a negative image, white on black and badly blurred. In it Orlov identified the boyhood friends who lived in New York. Rosovsky was the only one whom he contacted in 1954 whose biographical profile precisely fits the dates in the FBI report, including having lived in Belgium at the time of Orlov's flight in 1938. Rosovsky recalled his meeting in Antwerp in July 1938 with another Bobruysk classmate by the name Oftzov, who was the engineer of the Soviet freighter *Svir*, to which Orlov had been ordered by Moscow. Rosovsky told the FBI how he and Orlov had been close friends in Bobruysk and that he believed that Orlov, whom he knew as Feldbin, was not born in the town itself. The Rosovsky family who were "members of the wealthy class inasmuch as his father owned a number of large factories", had left Russia at the beginning of the Revolution. Until he received a phone call from Orlov to meet in the lobby of the Park Sheraton Hotel during the afternoon of New Year's day 1954, Rosovsky had not seen Orlov since 1917. On that occasion he said he had encountered his childhood friend wearing the uniform of a second lieutenant at the door of a Moscow department store. SAC New York report 2 October 1954 to Director, Folio 163 ORLOV FBI File; and see sworn statement by Alexander Orlov, US Department of Justice Immigration and Naturalization Office, 23 June 1955, Serial 305, p. 16. ORLOV FBI File No. 105–22869, FOIA.

8 *Ibid.*

9 Boris Rosovsky interview in ORLOV FBI File No. 105–22869, FOIA.

10 Orlov *Legacy*, p. 4; ORLOV File No. 39476 Vol. 1, p. 5, RISA.

11 ORLOV File 39476 Vol. 1, p. 5, RISA.

12 Feoktistov report, ORLOV File No. 76659, Vol 1, p. 2, RISA. See also report of unidentified academic to SAC Detroit that Orlov was still an ardent Leninist, 9 September 1963. Folio 353, FBI ORLOV File No. 105–22869, FOIA.

13 ORLOV's sworn deposition to INS in FBI 105–22869/FOIA.

14 *Ibid* and ORLOV File 39476 Vol. 1, p. 5, RISA.

15 ORLOV KGB File No. 32476, Vol. 1, p. 2, RISA.

16 Orlov *Handbook*, pp. 171–2.

17 Dobrzyhnsky was head of an underground network of the 2nd Department (Military Intelligence) of the Polish General Staff when he was tracked down and captured by Orlov's forces in May 1920. Interrogated by the *Cheka*, he was persuaded by Artusov to become a double agent. Operating under the pseudonym of Sosnovsky, the Pole worked for the *Cheka* as an undercover agent before being taken on to the NKVD staff as an officer of the Special Department. He worked in a succession of important posts in what had now become the OGPU and then the NKVD. Dobrzyhnsky/Sosnovsky fell victim to Stalin's purges when he was arrested and accused of treachery before being executed on 15 November 1937.

18 Orlov *Legacy*, p. 4.

19 Sources include: *Decrees of Soviet Power* Moscow, 1957 Volume 1, pp. 154–5, 165–166, 546; V. I. Lenin, *The Bolshevik Revolution 1917–1923*, London, Allen & Unwin, 1929, Vol. 2; *Lenin's Complete Works* Vol. 35, pp. 156–7, 357–8; George Leggett *Lenin and the VCheka*, p. 100; Nikolay Zubov, *F. E. Dzerzhinsky: Bigrafiya,* Politizdat, Moscow 1971, p. 183; M. Y. Latsis, *Chrezvychanye Komissii po bor'be s Kontrrevolyutsiey*, Gosizdat, Moscow, 1921, p. 12; "Collection of Documents, 1917–1922", Moscow 1987, documents on pp. 18 and 19; Minutes of the CDC Session No.

20 of 19 December 1917 in *History of the VCheka* Vol. 2, p. 17; Agenda for 20 December 1917 meeting of the Council of People's Commissars (*Sovnarkom*) including Dzerzhinsky's report on the *Cheka*, Central Party Archive, Russian Centre for the Storage and Study of Documents of Recent History.

20 Dzerzhinsky as quoted by George Leggett, *The Cheka: Lenin's Political Police* Oxford University Press, Oxford, 1981, p. 11.

21 Dzerzhinsky as quoted by the then KGB Chairman, Viktor Chebrikov, in *Pravda*, 11 December 1987.

22 Marguerite Harrison had been personally interrogated by Dzerzhinsky when she was suspected of being an "enemy of the Soviet State". She described her experiences in *Chicago Tribune*, 1 August 1926.

23 As quoted by George Leggett, *The Cheka: Lenin's Political Police*, p. 11.

24 "For this purpose [to disrupt the Treaty of Brest Litovsk] the Central Committee considers it possible and expedient to organize a number of terrorist acts against the most prominent representatives of German imperialism." Minutes of the Central Committee of the Left Revolutionary Party Session of 24 June 1918, in "Correspondence on Historical Subjects", Moscow, 1989, pp. 218–19. For an authoritative general background see John J. Dziak, *Chekisty: A History of the KGB*, Ballantine, New York 1988, p. 77.

25 George A. Hill wrote about the Envoys' Plot in his memoir *Go Spy Out The Land* Cassell, London, 1932. For Bruce Lockhart's own account see his book *Memoirs of a British Agent*, Putnam, New York, 1934.

26 Robert Bruce Lockhart, *Ace of Spies: A Biography of Sidney Reilly* (Hodder & Stoughton, London, 1967), which was later the basis of an internationally popular television drama series.

27 Lockhart, *British Agent*, p. 276–7

28 The saga of this unfortunate American amateur intelligence operative was first detailed by Dr William Corson and Robert T. Crowley in *The New KGB*, William Morrow, New York, 1985, pp. 47–60. See also D. S. Fogelsang "Xenophon Kalamitiano: An American Spy in Revolutionary Russia", *Intelligence and National Security*, June 1989, p. 151.

29 Reilly interrogation report dated 7 October 1925 in "TRUST" File No. 302330, Vol. 37, p. 241 (from the operational counter-intelligence archive of the former KGB now under the control of the Ministry of Security, Moscow, hereafter MSA).

30 Corson & Crowley, *The New KGB*, pp. 59–60.

31 Interview given by Dzerzhinsky in June 1918 to *Novaya Zhizn (New Life)*.

32 Lockhart, *British Agent,* p. 233. Volodya Merzlyakov is the curator of the KGB Museum in Moscow and is one of the few insiders of his generation to have full access to the secret *Cheka* records. Leggett, *op. cit.* p. 349.

33 The casualties and the figures of *Cheka* strength are those estimated by Western analysts and quoted by John Dziak, *Chekisty: A History of the KGB,* Ivy Books, New York, 1988, p. 36. They have yet to be accurately assessed from the newly released Soviet records. Professor Litvin of Kazan University, CIS is currently working on a book devoted to the Terror – both Red and White – of the civil war. It will be based on archival documentation, including access to the hitherto closed *Cheka* archives.

34 Agenda for 20 December 1917 meeting of the People's Commissars including Dzerzhinsky's report on the *Cheka* (Central Party Archive, Russian Centre for the Storage and Study of Documents of Recent History). Significantly Dzerzhinsky also signed, on the same day in 1920, the order No. 169 setting up the INO (Foreign Operations), *History of the Soviet Secret Intelligence Service* KGB official publication

Moscow, 1982, p. 18. The tradition endures and it remains the practice of the Russian Intelligence Service to keep the same payday.
35 Maria Orlov's sworn statement in ORLOV FBI File No. 105–22869, FOIA.
36 ORLOV Legacy, p. 4 and ORLOV INS deposition FBI FOIA.
37 Ibid, confirmed by Orlov's service reports in the first pages of his personal file No. 32476, Vol. 1, pp. 2–3, RISA.
38 Cited in Paul Aurich, Kronstadt: 1921, W. W. Norton, New York, 1974, p. 241.
39 Minutes of the IX All Russian Congress of the Soviets for 23 December 1921. See also Dziak, Chekisty, p. 172.
40 Letter of 24 December 1942 to Menzhinsky, Dzerzhinsky Archive, Central Party Archive, Russian Centre for the Storage and Study of Documents of Recent History.
41 Ibid.
42 Orlov's file does not contain the details of the case that Orlov referred to in one of his debriefings which is alluded to in Legacy p. 8.
43 ORLOV Legacy, p. 5 and ORLOV Personal File No. 32476, Vol. 1, p. 5.
44 ORLOV Handbook, p. 71. According to the History of the Soviet Intelligence Service, published by the KGB in 1982, subversion was not on the agenda of the INO operations whose mission was formulated as follows:

– penetration of white emigré organizations.
– rooting out anti-Soviet terrorist organizations.
– obtaining information on interventionist plans of Western countries and Japan.
– discovering the government plans of those countries to mount an economic blockade of the USSR.
– obtaining documents on the secret military and political alliances of these countries.
– external counter-intelligence.
– technical, scientific and industrial intelligence.

45 Teodor Gladkov and Nikolay Zaytsev, Iya emu ne mogu ne verit, Politizdat, Moscow 1983.
46 "TRUST" File No. 302330, Vol. 1, MSA.
47 Yakushev's report in "TRUST" File No. 302330, Vol. 1, p. 70, MSA.
48 Report on Schulgin's trip in "TRUST" File No. 302330, Vol. 3, p. 24–5, MSA.
49 Review of OPERATION "TRUST", Moscow, KGB, 1981, p. 49. This classified publication was prepared for the KGB Academy. Orlov, in his 1965 debriefing by the CIA, revealed that Savinkov's mistress, Mme de Aehrental, who was the wife of his assistant, "had been recruited in Paris by the Soviet service by exploiting her love of many". It was she, Orlov declared, who, after receiving instructions, had finally persuaded Savinkov to return to the USSR "to claim his place in history". Mme de Aehrental demanded – and received – $5,000 advance payment from the OGPU which she collected on condition she did not return to Paris. (See Note 69 for citation and source.)
50 Report from Yakushev in "TRUST" File No. 302330, Vol. 1, p. 70, MSA.
51 Savinkov's statement was published in Pravda, 30 August 1924. English translation cited in a footnote by John J. Dziak, Chekisty: A History of the KGB, Ballantine, New York, 1988, p. 210.
52 The account of Savinkov's death was obtained from Colonel Boris Goodze, a former NKVD, later GRU officer. While there is no documented report in the KGB file of Savinkov's suicide, Goodze's version appears more consistent with the circumstantial facts than that given by Oleg Gordievsky, a former KGB agent, which holds that Savinkov was pushed over a stairwell (Christopher Andrew and Oleg Gordievsky,

KGB: The Inside Story, Hodder & Stoughton, London 1990, p. 71).

53 *Ibid.*

54 Undated report from Yakushev in "TRUST" File No. 302330, Vol. 37, p.112, MSA.

55 *Ibid.*

56 Notes in Reilly's handwriting found in his cell, "TRUST" File No. 302330, Vol. 37, p. 37, MSA.

57 Reilly's 30 October letter to Dzerzhinsky is in "TRUST" File No. 302330, Vol. 37, p. 300, MSA.

58 Reilly's notes dated 3 November, "TRUST" File No. 302330, Vol. 37, p. 366, MSA.

59 Reilly's notes 4 November, "TRUST" File No. 302330, Vol. 37, p. 366, MSA.

60 Feduleyev's report, "TRUST" File No. 302330, Vol. 37, p. 355, MSA.

61 Review of OPERATION "TRUST", MOSCOW, KGB, 1981. Tsarev interview with Boris Goodze who took part in the Trust Operation.

62 *Ibid.*

63 Orlov *Handbook*, p. 20.

64 *Ibid.*

65 ORLOV *Legacy*, p. 5; ORLOV INS testimony File 105–22869 FBI; ORLOV Personal File No. 32476, Vol. I, RISA.

66 The story of how Orlov believed his daughter caught the cold that developed into rheumatic fever was told to Brook-Shepherd in *The Storm Petrels*, p. 203. He obtained it from unattributed CIA contacts.

67 The original of the letter purported to have been sent by Zinoviev dated 15 September 1924 has vanished, making it impossible to determine whether it was a forgery or genuine. Western researchers into the affair (N. Grant, "The Zinoviev Letter Case", *Soviet Studies*, 1967, and L. Chester, S. Fay and K. Young, *The Zinoviev Letter Intrigue* London, 1967), confirm the *Sunday Times* findings published in 1965 that the letter was *not* written by Zinoviev. More recent research by the historians of the Russian Ministry of Security have picked up documentary traces that point to Vladimir Orlov, the ex-chief of intelligence of the White Russian General Denikin. Alleged to have been working for the British SIS in Berlin at the time, Vladimir Orlov often met with Reilly. This Orlov – no relation to Alexander Orlov – was known to be an expert in passing off forged Comintern documents. The dates and connections with Reilly have still to be more fully researched before the Ministry of Security publishes its findings.

68 An authorative summary of the main elements in the power play is given by Dziak in *Chekisty*, pp. 45, 56–7.

69 After analyzing Orlov's *Handbook* in 1965 the *Direction de la Surveillance du Territoire* (DST) learned the extent of the French cases he had apparently been involved in. It was arranged for the CIA to question him in detail about the references to pre-war Soviet operations in France in his book. Orlov's responses to some sixteen cases identified by the French counter-intelligence service are covered in a sixty-page report in French together with a series of "memoranda for the file" in English (see Appendix III). The dossier reached the authors through a French source connected with the DST. Included in the file was a 7 July "Dear Jim" letter to James Angleton, who in 1965 was chief of counter-intelligence staff at the CIA. The notation indicates that it was written in November 1965 and based on direct interviews held with Orlov about the operations he had conducted during his two tours in France as "legal" *rezident* with the Soviet Trade Delegation in 1927–8 and then as an "illegal" in 1932. "Cas No. 2", p. 28 in the *Handbook of Counterintelligence and Guerilla Warfare*. (Cited hereafter as ORLOV DST File.)

70 *Ibid.*

71 Orlov in his responses to "Cas No. 5", p. 45 *Handbook*, ORLOV DST File, misled the CIA into believing that this was Alexander Karin who operated as KARI. His NKVD file

discloses that ALEXANDER was his other code-name, which he used as *rezident* in France from 1931 to 1933, when he began working for Soviet military intelligence, then known as the RU.

72 "Reconstitution des "LEGAUX" en France, d'apres Orlov" and "Subject: LORD-CHIPANIDZE [sic] ZAGARELLI" information supplied by Orlov 15–16 April 1965, ORLOV DST File.

73 Orlov *Handbook*, p. 21.

74 *Ibid.*

75 Orlov's reponse to "Cas No. 1", p. 21 in *Handbook* ORLOV DST File.

76 Orlov's response to "Cas No. 3", p. 28 in *Handbook* DST. Although they could find no trace of such an "*affaire scandaleuse*" the French report indicates they suspected that the Minister of Justice in question might have been Marc Rucart. He was a participant in many cabinets in the brokered political alliances that marked the "revolving-door" Governments of the pre-World War II French Republic.

77 Examples of this "tradecraft" vocabulary can be found in the citations of the NKVD archive documents. Orlov himself used some of the nomenclature in his *Handbook*, Chapter "Clandestine Meetings", pp. 110–125.

78 Orlov *Handbook*, pp. 118–119.

79 Orlov's responses to "Cas No. 14", p. 118 *Handbook* ORLOV DST.

80 *Ibid.*

81 Orlov *Handbook*, p. 119.

82 Orlov *Handbook*, p. 82.

83 Orlov's responses to "Cas No. 9", ORLOV *Handbook*, pp. 69–70 ORLOV DST.

84 Analysis of the historic NKVD records makes it possible to see how the information that Orlov supplied in 1965, and presumably in his earlier debriefings as a CIA informant, was camouflaged and tailored to his audience. Orlov added some details to the cases which he admitted deliberately confusing in his *Handbook* – such as identifying the code names of Soviet intelligence officers and their dates of operation in France. It is significant that he could not recall the names of any of the Frenchmen who served as NKVD informants in the Paris Police Department, the *Deuxième Bureau*, the French Army General Staff or the Chamber of Deputies. The DST reports reveal – and the Soviet records confirm – that Orlov *did not* betray the real names of any of those who had served Moscow from within these organizations, even though the request for their identities was the subject of a specific questionnaire supplied to the CIA for his answers. In the absence of any other information to the contrary, it is reasonable to presume that Orlov adopted the same techniques when it came to dealing with the other issues raised by his CIA debriefers.

85 Orlov *Handbook*, p. 70.

86 MI5 Reports on ARCOS Raid supplied to US State Department, 18 July 1927, in US Embassy London, 800B, RG 84 NAW.

Chapter 3: "Industrial Help, Not Espionage"

1 Note on Maria Orlov in Orlov's 1965 debriefing by the CIA in ORLOV *Handbook*, DST.

2 "History of the Berlin *Rezidentura*", File No. 3588, Vol. 1, p. 306, RISA.

3 David J. Dallin, *Soviet Espionage*, Yale, New Haven, 1977, pp. 79–88 *passim*, "The *Handelsvertretung* as Cover". Dallin was in a position to know, according to the DST reports of the debriefing that Orlov gave the CIA in April 1965. He told them that Dallin "at least in Berlin was a Soviet agent" whose case officer was Bazarov. After emigrating to the USA, Dallin became a leading – and well informed – authority on

Soviet espionage. Orlov told the CIA that this "implies that Dallin's work and [sic] the history of Soviet Espionage in the West as revealed in overt cases may have been a part of a damage assessment process in which the Soviet Service was directly interested". 13 page file "Subject David and Lydia Dallin" date 15–16 April whose "DOI" was Orlov, given to the French in 1965 as part of the *Handbook* ORLOV DST File. For details of the Ehrenlieb/WESTWOG operations see Corson and Crowley, *The New KGB*, pp. 278–9.

4 ORLOV *Legacy* pp. 129–131 and Alexander Orlov, *The Secret History of Stalin's Crimes,* Random House, New York, 1952, p. 322.

5 Dallin, *op. cit.,* p. 76.

6 Orlov, *Handbook,* p. 30.

7 *Ibid,* p. 31.

8 Dallin, *op. cit.,* p. 79.

9 Orlov, *Handbook,* p. 31.

10 Dallin, *op. cit.,* pp. 92–9.

11 Orlov, *Handbook,* p. 31.

12 *Ibid,* p. 32.

13 *Ibid.*

14 *Ibid,* pp. 33–4.

15 *Ibid,* pp. 34–7.

16 *Ibid,* pp. 72–3.

17 *Ibid.*

18 The name of the manufacturer – according to Orlov – was embossed in gold on all his pencils and well known throughout Imperial Russia, but he has proved impossible to trace in the fragmentary Soviet intelligence records of that time. Orlov *Handbook,* pp. 98–100. The names and details are therefore as Orlov gave them in his *Handbook* and the assumption is that he was in fact the OGPU agent involved in these cases even though it has proved impossible to confirm this directly from the files.

19 *Ibid,* p. 98. Again it has proved impossible – so far – to locate the name of the secretary in this case in Orlov's records. The files for this period do not appear to have been kept in the same detail with which they were later recorded.

20 ORLOV, *Legacy,* p. 66. Testimony of 15 February 1957.

21 *Ibid,* p. 67. Orlov, *Handbook,* p. 20.

22 Quoted by Dallin, *Soviet Espionage,* p. 76.

23 *Frankfurter Zeitung,* 19 December 1931; Archives of the Security Service, I.G. Farben, Leverkusen, as cited by Dallin, *op. cit.,* pp. 77, 106, 109.

24 *Ibid,* p. 107.

25 *Ibid,* p. 109.

26 *Ibid,* p. 110.

27 *Vossische Zeitung,* 28 July 1931, cited by Dallin, *op. cit.,* pp. 118–208.

28 *Ibid.*

29 *Berliner Tageblatt,* January 1930.

30 Orlov, *Legacy,* pp. 53–6. Testimony of 28 September 1955.

31 Corson and Crowley, *The New KGB,* pp. 318–28 and notes 453, 456–7. During his 1957 testimony before the Senate Subcommittee, Orlov, surprisingly, affected not to remember the name of the banking house, even though the inside story had been published in the US press before the war and detailed in 1939 by his former colleague and GRU defector Walter Krivitsky in *I Was Stalin's Agent,* Foyles, London, 1940, pp. 135–58.

32 For an account detailing Dozenberg's and Tilden's role see Corson and Crowley, *The New KGB,* p. 320–6.

33 ORLOV, *Legacy*, pp. 53–6. Testimony 28 September 1955.

34 *Ibid.*

35 For a summary of the Kutyepov affair see Andrew and Gordievsky, *KGB: The Inside Story*, pp. 116–17 and Dziak, *Chekisty*, pp. 109–110.

36 ORLOV, *Legacy*, p. 6.

37 Serebryansky, according to the version Orlov gave the CIA in 1965, was not "a regular member of State Security" but an operative who was "only brought in for special jobs". He described this OGPU "contract hit man" as a "cool and calculating fellow who knew his work" who usually worked in Moscow at one of the Economic Ministries. Orlov said that Kutyepov had "died on the hands of his kidnappers because of a heart attack" and that his body was disposed of by burial outside the embassy. (Orlov's observations on the kidnapping dated 15–16 April 1965 in ORLOV *Handbook* DST.)

38 Orlov's observations on Grigory Bessedovsky are also from ORLOV DST.

39 Orlov, *Handbook*, p. 40.

40 ORLOV *Legacy*, p. 6.

41 Dziak, *Chekisty*, pp. 62–75 *passim*; Robert Conquest, *The Great Terror: A Reassessment*, New York, Oxford University Press, 1990, pp. 18–20.

42 ORLOV *Legacy*, p. 65; compare with the fuller detail he gave the INS: "Record of sworn statement before the US Naturalization Service (INS), 29 June 1954", p. 49, FBI Files ORLOV Internal Security R 105–6073.

43 *Ibid.*

44 *Ibid.*

45 *Ibid.*

46 Orlov's American passport in the name of William Goldin is in his personal file in the ORLOV File No. 32476, Vol. 1, p. 227, RISA. A complete colour photographic copy of each page was made available to the authors.

47 Orlov's passport shows that after his return from Britain in late October 1935 (entry visa on October 29 1935) his service record confirms that he was indeed appointed assistant Chief of Transport Directorate of the NKVD (ORLOV Personal File No. 32476, Vol. 1, pp. 3–5). This can be explained by the common practice adopted in the service then and later to offer an officer who has just returned a commensurate position in another department or directorate until another posting abroad, or until a suitable position becomes free in the Soviet intelligence service. Staff regulations require that an officer cannot be idle. In the meantime he was assigned to a holding post such as Orlov had in the transport department, but he actually worked in the intelligence service although he received his pay from the assigned section. In Orlov's case he continued to monitor and consult on the work of the Cambridge group and in 1936 he also went on short trips to Estonia and Sweden, where his assignment, according to Spigelglass, was to recruit an ambassador of a western country. This he successfully accomplished. (Spigelglass's testimony 1939, File No. 21746, Vol. 1, p. 148, Ministry of Security Archive (MSA)).

Chapter 4: "Dangerous Guesswork"

1 As head of Section VII (Economic Intelligence) of INO Orlov would have been informed of the ARPLAN visit. Even if the visit was operationally dealt with by the German desk, it was standard practice to brief other interested units of the intelligence service on relevant matters.

2 *The Rote Kapelle: The CIA's History of Soviet Intelligence and Espionage Networks in*

Western Europe, 1936–1945, published by University Publications of America, Maryland 1979, pp. 288–90, (hereafter CIA *Rote Kapelle*). The CIA documentation represents as complete a source on the *Rote Kapelle* as existed in the West since it was based both on the Gestapo records and postwar investigations by US Military Intelligence and the CIA. It is supplemented by Karl Heinz Bienal and Louise Krausher, *Die Schultze-Boysen-Harnack Organization in Antifascistischen Kampf*, Dietz Verlag, Berlin, East Germany, 1975. Although this was a controlled history, it was drawn from Soviet records made available to the East Germans.

3 *Ibid*. Mildred Fish was not Jewish, as was later wrongly asserted by Walter Schellenberg who subsequently misled others. Her ancestry was traced back to 1776 when she joined the "Daughters of the American Revolution" and the papers recording this were vouched for by the American Consul General in Berlin. The authors are grateful to Shareen Brysaac for this and other information she has contributed from her extensive researches that are the basis of her forthcoming book on Mildred Harnack.

4 Comintern report to OGPU, 18 December 1940 in HARNACK (CORSICAN) File No. 34118, Vol. 1, p. 238, RISA. After Hitler's rise to power, Professor Friedrich Lenz travelled to Britain and then to the United States, where he studied at the American University in Washington DC, before returning to Berlin in 1940, when he became a liaison agent for the *Rote Kapelle*, camouflaging his true politics by writing Nazi brochures. He survived the war to become a noted German academic. The CIA investigation into the *Rote Kapelle* membership indicates that Lenz was suspected of once being under direct Soviet control (CIA *Rote Kapelle* p. 309).

5 Minutes of Fifth Department of GUGB of NKVD Departmental Conference, 15 July 1935, CORSICAN File No. 34118, Vol. 1, p. 12, RISA.

6 Harnack's first codename was BALT – because he came from a family of Baltic Germans. It was changed in 1940 to CORSICAN which is the name on his NKVD file. (Hershfeld report to the Centre, 9 September 1935, CORSICAN File No. 34118, Vol. 1, pp. 9–10, RISA.)

7 In March 1938, after the break in contact with Arvid Harnack (CORSICAN) brought about by the turmoil of Stalin's purges in the INO, the Centre decided to resume the relationship with their German agent. To that end they telegraphed an inquiry to the Spanish *rezidentura* asking Alexander Belkin (KADI), Orlov's deputy who had been Harnack's control officer in Berlin from 1935 to 1936, about how to contact him. Belkin replied on 10 April 1938 giving the necessary information and furnishing them with a letter in German recommending the new NKVD officer to him. He also advised restoring the lost contact with STRAHLMAN (Karl Behrens) who worked for the AEG firm. As head of the Spanish *rezidentura*, Orlov read all the incoming and outgoing telegrams and mail according to strict rules of the NKVD. He would therefore certainly have discussed the Harnack case with Belkin. (CORSICAN File No. 34118, Vol. 1, p. 37, RISA.)

8 According to American intelligence sources Mildred Harnack's friend Martha Dodd was also recruited shortly afterwards by a Soviet intelligence officer. She later figured in the Soble/Soblen group which operated in the United States, (see Chapter 15 for details). (CORSICAN File No. 34118, Vol. 1, p. 37.)

9 Report of 9 December 1940, CORSICAN File No. 34118, Vol. 2, p. 77, RISA.

10 The Gestapo records show that they believed that the Red Orchestra networks began playing some three years later on the eve of the outbreak of the European war. This is reflected in the CIA *Rote Kapelle* report although it does allow (p. 289): "It is possible that Harnack and his circle of Communists and left-wing sympathizers were exploited by Erdberg for the GRU some years before the outbreak of the Russo-

German war." Erdberg (who the Soviet files reveal was Orlov's former assistant Korotkov, an NKVD officer) did not take over as control officer of the Berlin networks until the fall of 1940. But it is now clear from the NKVD records that the Red Orchestra had already been playing for Moscow for four years, starting two years earlier than has previously been known. The fact Erdberg (Korotkov) was not a GRU officer, confirms that the *Rote Kapelle*, which has previously been considered entirely a Soviet Military Intelligence operation, had its Berlin section run by the NKVD.

11 CORSICAN File No. 34118, Vol. 2, p. 77, RISA.

12 CORSICAN File No. 34118, Vol. 1, p. 37, RISA.

13 *Ibid.*

14 BREITENBACH File No. 2802, RISA.

15 CORSICAN File No. 34118, Vol. 1, p. 37, RISA.

16 CIA *Rote Kapelle*, p. 275.

17 Gerson had formerly been Dzerzhinsky's secretary responsible for operational missions and had been one of the organizers of the OGPU sports club. (KOROTKOV File No. 32209, Vol. 1, p. 192, RISA.)

18 *Ibid.*

19 In tense times it was not unusual to pick up an agent in a car and drive him away to a quiet place for a talk. CORSICAN was not told in advance that he would be driven to the Soviet embassy, so as not to raise his suspicion that Korotkov's approach was a Gestapo provocation. (CORSICAN File No. 34118, Vol. 1, p. 108, RISA.)

20 CORSICAN File No. 34118, Vol. 1, pp. 57–61, RISA.

21 *Ibid.*, p. 108.

22 Centre to Korotkov, 26 October 1940, CORSICAN File No. 34118, Vol. 1, p. 63.

23 The extent and seriousness of the scores of peace feelers which Hitler and the German Foreign Ministry orchestrated before Hess's abortive 1941 mission are detailed and examined in Costello, *Ten Days To Destiny,* Morrow, New York, 1991.

24 Cryptogram from Korotkov to Centre, 26 September 1940, CORSICAN File No. 34118, Vol. 1, p. 62, RISA.

25 CIA: *Rote Kapelle*, pp. 353–4.

26 SENIOR (Schulze-Boysen) File No. 34122, Vol. 1, p. 132, RISA.

27 Korotkov report to Centre, 31 March 1941, CORSICAN File No. 34118, Vol. 1, p. 217, RISA.

28 *Ibid.*

29 CORSICAN File No. 34118, Vol. 1, p. 327, RISA.

30 CORSICAN, SENIOR and OLD MAN were acquainted with each other and it would have been impossible effectively to departmentalize them. The only other person who knew about the existence of this network and was considered as a second contact man was the NKVD chief of the Berlin station Amayak Kobulov. But according to information obtained from his Gestapo source BREITENBACH, Kobulov was under heavy surveillance and for that reason forbidden by the Centre to contact any of the leaders of the three networks. (CORSICAN File No. 34118, Vol. 1, p. 347, RISA.)

Kobulov became *rezident* in Berlin due to his good contacts with the NKVD leadership. But his meagre intelligence experience and subsequent lack of professional judgement were obvious to the professionals and earned him no credit with them. This is illustrated by a note in his personal file: "If ZAKHAR [Kobulov's cryptonym] is ever mentioned Sudoplatov [deputy chief of the intelligence service] and Zhuravlev [head of the German desk] simply wave their hands." (KOBULOV File No. 15852, Vol. 1, p. 41.)

31 CORSICAN File No. 34118, Vol. 1, p. 183.

32 CORSICAN File No. 34118, Vol. 1, pp. 120, 183–184A, RISA.

33 CORSICAN File No. 34118, Vol. 2, pp. 23–33, RISA.

34 *Ibid.*

35 Korotkov to Moscow Centre, 16 June 1942, CORSICAN File No. 34118, Vol. 1, p. 223, RISA.

36 As published in full, with Stalin's annotation, in the April 1990 issue of the Soviet monthly journal *Isvestia of the Central Committee of the CPSU.*

37 Moscow Centre to Korotkov, 5 April 1941, CORSICAN File No. 34118, Vol. 1, p. 223, RISA.

38 *Ibid.*

39 Müller debriefing in ZAKHAR (Kobulov) File No. 15852, Vol. 1, pp. 65–82, RISA.

40 CORSICAN File No. 34118, Vol. 1, p. 247, RISA.

41 Korotkov to Centre, April 1941, CORSICAN File No. 34118, Vol. 2, p. 29, RISA.

42 Korotkov to Centre, May 1941, *Ibid.*

43 *Ibid*, p. 31.

44 Korotkov to Centre, 14 May 1941, SENIOR File No. 34122, Vol. 1, p. 145, RISA.

45 Korotkov to Centre, June 1941, CORSICAN File No. 34118, Vol. 1, p. 351, RISA.

46 Orlov, *Handbook*, p. 10.

Chapter 5: "A Complete Metamorphosis"

1 Orlov, *Handbook*, p. 39.

2 *Ibid*, p. 40.

3 The British have never released the full list or any of the papers seized in two truckloads of documentation that was driven off after the raid on Soviet House which ARCOS shared with the Soviet Trade Mission. An indication of its scope can be found in the assessments of its significance supplied to the Americans containing a list of safe houses, mailing addresses and names of Soviet couriers who travelled to and from the United States. (MI5 report of 18 July 1927 in US Embassy Files London 800 BRG 84 National Archives.) See also: *Documents Illustrating the Hostile Activities of the Soviet Government and Third International Against Great Britain*, HMSO, 1927.

4 Orlov, *Handbook,* p. 40.

5 *Ibid*, p. 41.

6 *Ibid*, p. 40.

7 *Ibid*, p. 43.

8 Official purpose of his visit attested to by Orlov in his statement in FBI File No. 105–22369 before INS investigator Denton J. Kerns, New York, 29 April 1954. Naturally he did not disclose that he had in 1932 obtained papers of William Goldin to get a genuine passport by fraud with the aid of an underground Soviet agent. (ORLOV File No. 32476, Vol. 1, pp. 3–5, RISA. The actual American passport is attached to p. 227 of the same file.)

9 *Ibid.*

10 *Ibid.*

11 *Ibid.*

12 *Ibid*, p. 47.

13 *Ibid*, p. 79.

14 For a summary of the Cremet and Muraille cases, and Soviet espionage in general in France during its high point from 1928 to 1933, see Dallin, *op. cit.*, pp. 39–47.

15 Operation EXPRESS Operational Directive in ORLOV File. No. 32476, Vol. 2, p. 152, RISA.

16 *Ibid*, p. 154.

17 *Ibid.*

18 KADU had been party to an operation involving the Italian intelligence service which had put him in jeopardy obliging the Centre to order his withdrawal.

The KADU/Red Beard case is another where Orlov carefully refrained from naming the Soviet agent in the *Deuxième Bureau* to the CIA. ("Subject LAGRANGE" in ORLOV *Handbook* DST.)

19 ORLOV File No. 32476, Vol. 2, p. 170, RISA.

20 Orlov, *Handbook*, p. 52.

21 ORLOV File No. 32476, Vol. 2, p. 172, RISA.

22 *Ibid.*

23 Orlov, *Handbook*, p. 111. Though Orlov does not mention himself as the subject, the anecdote is clearly a personal one as confirmed by his answers to the French DST questionnaire. ("Cas 13", *Handbook* ORLOV DST.)

24 Orlov's report to Moscow Centre in ORLOV File No. 32476, Vol. 2, p. 157, RISA.

25 *Ibid*, p. 162.

26 *Ibid*, p. 162.

27 *Ibid.*

28 *Ibid,* p. 163.

29 *Ibid.*

30 *Ibid,* p. 175.

30 *Ibid,* pp. 180–81. Orlov's original report referred to "advertisements", but since the Soviet press did not carry such capitalist items, "items" appears a better interpretation. It is however conceivable that STAHL might have used "advertisements" in a clumsy fabrication.

32 ORLOV File No. 32476, Vol. 2, pp. 164–5, RISA.

33 *Ibid*, p. 255. The actual date the Centre replied is not clear, but in his report of 24 March 1934, Orlov states that, according to the Centre's directive which he notes he received through JACK (the NKVD *rezident* in Paris) he took over both JOSEPH and B205.

34 *Ibid*, p. 168. The nationality of B205 is not clear from the file.

35 *Ibid*, p. 169.

36 *Ibid*, Mally's note to Slutsky.

37 *Ibid*, p. 193.

38 There are three indications so far identified in the Soviet records that link Orlov directly to the case of General Miller. First, he told Feoktistov at their second meeting in 1971 that one of the reasons why he had fallen out of favour with Yezhov was that he had declined to approve the plan for the kidnapping operation. Second, in his letter to Yezhov of August 1938 he said that he had in his possession "FARMER's ring" – FARMER was the code name of General Skoblin, a key figure in the operation. Third, on 10 May 1938, Orlov wrote to Spigelglass from Barcelona about the possibility of buying an aircraft: "For $15,000 we could buy an airplane of the type in which you and I whisked away FARMER." (Sources: ORLOV File No. 103509, Vol. 1, pp. 13–25, 205–221, RISA and "Correspondence of the *Rezidentura* in Spain", File No. 19897, Vol. 3, p. 121, RISA.

39 ORLOV File No. 32476, p. 193, RISA.

40 *Ibid.*

41 *Ibid*, pp. 208–9, 245.

42 *Ibid*, pp. 210–12.

43 Orlov to Centre, *Ibid*, pp. 245, 258.

44 Orlov to Centre, *Ibid*, pp. 258–9.

45 *Ibid.*

46 The operational archives reveal several cryptic NKVD euphemisms including

"*liternoye delo*" ("special letters"), for the special liquidation operations that were later termed "wet operations".

47 Orlov to Centre, File No. 32476, Vol. 2, p. 263, RISA.

48 Orlov to Centre, *Ibid*, p. 264. In his *Handbook*, pp. 102–5, Orlov described a case involving a female Soviet source in place in the French Foreign Ministry who reported that her girl friend had been asked by the Deputy Foreign Minister to become his private secretary. Orlov reported how she had been tapped with the aid of a young British writer from Wales who was claiming to be working on a book on European affairs. The writer might have been Goronwy Rees, one of Burgess's recruits to the Cambridge ring, since Orlov told the CIA in 1965 that the case he was writing about took place in 1936 and was run by his friend Smirnov, the "illegal" NKVD *rezident* in Paris. Orlov said that he had the details from Smirnov including the first meeting at the Comédie Francaise with two "dashing young Englishmen who spoke fluent French". He identifies one as a pianist and the other as a Welshman. (Orlov *Handbook* DST File).

49 Orlov to Centre, ORLOV File No. 32476, Vol. 2, p. 264, RISA.

50 *Ibid*, p. 265.

51 ORLOV *Legacy*, pp. 6–9. Testimony 14 September 1957 before Senate Internal Security Sub-Committee and Orlov DST.

The precise date of this operation as referred to in Orlov's book suggests that it must have been during his time as underground *rezident* in Paris, although in his 1955 Senate Internal Security Sub-Committee testimony – and in his 1965 CIA debriefing for the DST File – Orlov stated it was 1932. This, however, was the year *before* he went to France and since the operation took place in the autumn, it would have conflicted with his trip to the United States which lasted until the end of November. The December 1933 Italian entry and exit stamps on Orlov's American passport are further evidence that his mission to Rome was actually undertaken towards at the end of 1933. This is corroborated by the NKVD records that show he returned to Moscow just before the end of the year for a debriefing. It can be confirmed by reference to his reported discussion with KADU, who was known to be in Moscow at the time.

52 Giuseppe Bottai was the Italian Minister Orlov named in response to the DST questionnaire, in which he also stated that he had been sent to Rome to supervise the recruitment. "Cas 10", pp. 81–82, *Handbook* ORLOV DST File.

53 Date stamps for Italian frontier posts in Orlov's passport as William Goldin in his personal file in the NKVD archives.

54 Orlov, *Handbook*, pp. 81–83. Although he wrote that the unidentified underground *rezident* in France used a Canadian passport, Orlov omitted to tell the CIA in 1965 that this was a deliberately misleading detail. What is significant is that he claimed he had operated using an Austrian passport – understandably he never told the CIA about his alias as William Goldin and his illegally obtained American passport.

55 ORLOV *Legacy*, pp. 68–9, Orlov Testimony 14 February 1957 to Senate Internal Security Sub-Committee.

56 Orlov, *Handbook*, pp. 142–5 and Orlov's responses indicating Korotkov was undercover in Paris as a Czech student in his responses to the DST questionnaire relating to "Cas 15", *Handbook* ORLOV DST File.

57 *Ibid*.

58 *Ibid*.

59 Since Soviet intelligence officers in the Thirties often served as both "legals" and "illegals" it increased the chances of bumping into people who had known them in their previous capacity. This added to the danger that they would be exposed. Dimitri Bystrolyotov, a member of a "flying squad" of trouble-shooting "illegals" gives many examples of such cases in his revealing and detailed memoirs which are lodged in the NKVD archives. Orlov to Centre, ORLOV File No. 32476, Vol. 2, pp. 292–3, RISA.

60 *Ibid.*

61 *Ibid*, p. 294.

62 Orlov to Centre, 8 May 1934, *Ibid*, p. 290.

Chapter 6: "Philby Will Be Called *SYNOK*"

1 Moscow Centre to Orlov, 19 June 1934, ORLOV File No. 32476, Vol. 1, p. 132, RISA. Mail from the London "illegal" *rezidentura* was in the form of secret writing in seemingly innocent letters. The most commonly employed form of invisible ink for secret messages at this time was photographic hypo. Such easily formulated and obtained chemicals were used by Soviet "illegals" because they would arouse no suspicion if discovered during a police search. But as was the case with the London "illegal" station, this invisible writing proved unreliable. Communications from the Centre to the "illegal" *rezidentura* was photographed and sent in rolls of undeveloped photographic film so that it could be easily destroyed in the event of an emergency during transit.

2 Copy of Reif's aliens registration certificate in the name of Max Wolisch in REIF File No. 15486, Vol. 1, p. 108, RISA.

3 It was not unusual NKVD practice for a *rezident* to be based in another country where he would not conduct any unlawful activity and therefore not compromise himself in the eyes of the authorities of the targeted country. The letter, 19 June 1934, from the Centre addressed to Orlov said in the first paragraph: "In order to regroup our work you are assigned an illegal group that has previously been under Anatoly." Anatoly was a Soviet "illegal" *rezident* in France named Evgeny Mitskevich who was nominally in charge of "illegal" work in Britain. But because of the workload he could not devote enough time to the London group. Orlov, acting under the Centre's instructions, was originally to be based in Copenhagen from where he would supervise the penetration of British intelligence in London and its spy-nets in the countries neighbouring the Soviet Union – Finland, Latvia and Estonia – which were used by the British as bases for espionage against Moscow. Though Orlov was supposed to be based in Copenhagen which was a communications point for the London group, just as on his previous assignment to penetrate the *Deuxième Bureau* of the French General Staff, he found it more practical to set up his base in London itself, a decision which was approved in a letter from the Centre, 7 January 1935. ORLOV File No. 32476, Vol. 2, pp. 118, 129.

4 *Ibid*, p. 133.

5 "Transmission of Biographical Letter re H. St John Philby", prepared by the British Foreign Office in 1945 for the First Secretary US Embassy London, State Department, decimal File No. 111 20A/7 RG 84, National Archives.

6 Philby's biographical details as corroborated by a number of published sources including: Bruce Page, David Leitch and Philip Knightley, *Philby, the Spy who Betrayed a Generation*, Sphere, London, 1968; H. A. R. Philby, *My Silent War*, MacGibbon & Kee, London, 1968; Philip Knightley, *Philby: KGB Master Spy*, André Deutsch, London, 1988; Andrew Boyle, *The Climate of Treason*, Hutchinson, London, 1979. Interview with Philby by Philip Knightley, *Sunday Times*, 20 March 1988.

7 By British ethical and legal codes Philby and the members of the Cambridge network were indisputably traitors who betrayed their country. The Soviet intelligence service, however, regards them as penetration agents, whose dedication to Communism determined their loyalties to Moscow *before* they were ever in a position to betray Britain's secrets. They contend that it is therefore inappropriate to describe them as "traitors", especially since they had gained their position of trust in the British

Government while in the service of international Communism. According to the Soviet viewpoint, this set Philby and his comrades apart from "traitors", who achieved such positions of trust *before* switching loyalties to betray their country's secrets.

8 The late Andrew Boyle's investigation of the Cambridge spy network, which had been "inspired" by his Establishment connections and friendship with the late Sir Dick White, the former head of MI5 and MI6, who as a senior member of the British secret service had been a wartime colleague of Blunt. It was published in the United States as *The Fourth Man*, James Wade/Dial Press, New York, 1979, and in the UK as *The Climate of Treason*, Hutchinson, London, 1979.

9 Peter Wright and Paul Greengrass, *Spycatcher*, Viking, New York, 1987.

10 Affidavit sworn by Peter Wright as reported in the *Guardian*, 9 December 1986.

11 Interview with Philby by Philip Knightley, *Sunday Times*, 20 March 1988.

12 TASS quoted by *New York Times*, 12 May 1988.

13 Interview with Philby by Philip Knightley, *Sunday Times*, 20 March 1988, and Philby, *The Spy Who Betrayed a Generation*, Deutsch, London, 1989, pp. 37–47.

14 Notable is the closely documented research of Verne W. Newton, *The Cambridge Spies: The Untold Story of Maclean, Philby, and Burgess in America*, Madison Books, Washington, 1991. This book catalogues from the US Government's records the true dimension of Maclean's espionage.

15 Most notably John Cairncross who passed on from his wartime posting to GC & CS at Bletchley Park the ULTRA material giving the *Luftwaffe* order of battle before and during the critical battle of Kursk in June 1943. Interview with the author 1992. Cairncross debriefing cited by Chapman Pincher, *Too Secret, Too Long*, Sidgwick and Jackson, London, 1984, p. 396 and corroborated by Wright, *Spycatcher*, pp. 221–5.

16 Letter written by Donald Maclean from Paris dated 25 April (1939). (MACLEAN File No. 83791, Vol. 1, pp. 174–5, RISA.)

17 Preface to Orlov, *Handbook*. ORLOV, *Legacy*, p. 67. Testimony 14 September 1957 before Senate Internal Security Sub-Committee.

18 Orlov, *Handbook*, p. 5.

19 *Ibid*, pp. 108–9.

20 *Ibid*.

21 *Ibid*.

22 Philby, *My Silent War*, p. 14.

23 In his letter from Copenhagen, February 1935, Orlov wrote: "From July 1934 to January 1935 we had not a single letter from you and no reply to three mails with materials. Brought to C. [Copenhagen] by HERTA [courier code name]." (ORLOV File No. 32476, Vol. 3, p. 7, RISA.)

24 As early as December 1926 a special commission, consisting of K. Voroshilov (People's Commissar for Defence) and A. Trilliser (INO Chief) and a representative of Comintern, set up to investigate and analyze a case of failure of a military intelligence *rezidentura* and came to an imperative conclusion fixed in its protocol: "Work of members at foreign Communist parties in [Soviet] intelligence units (organs) abroad is utterly undesirable for in case of failures, which in the course of work is unavoidable, the Communist parties are exposed to a blow." The Commission suggested that "utilization of members of foreign Communist parties as agents be prohibited". Despite this there was no proper control over the implementation of their suggestion: a short cut to the objective was too tempting. In the Thirties this question arose again and exemptions were made only to secret members of CPs, when their recruitment was substantially justified. *History of the Soviet Secret Intelligence Service*, KGB, Moscow, 1982, p. 65.

25 Philby KGB Memoir, p. 5. Philby's "KGB memoir" is bound in a volume and was

dictated by him in English around 1985. It is not strictly part of his file and was not given a volume number, although it is kept with the other 18 volumes that comprise his dossier. The tape was transcribed and translated in Russian by the First Chief Directorate and the final text was arranged in one volume of 283 typed pages.

26 *Ibid*, pp. 6–8.

27 *Ibid*.

28 Lord Stamfordham to Lord President of the Council Arthur Balfour, 1 September 1925, Balfour Papers as quoted by Kenneth Rose, *King George V*, Weidenfeld, London, 1983, p. 369.

29 Page *et al*, *Philby*, p. 36. In his KGB Memoir Philby quotes Dobb as having told him, "I can give you a letter of recommendation to a leader of the 'Workers International Relief' – MOPR in Paris." The translator left the English name in the text as quoted, although it is clear that Philby was referring to the International Workers' Relief Organization.

30 Philby KGB Memoir, p. 10. In it Philby claims he could not remember the Italian's name. While there were many Italian Communists working for the front that Willi Münzenberg had set up to provide relief for the Russian famine, it is consistent that Gibarti, who was also one of the most prominent members of the *League Against Imperialism*, would have been the one to whom his letter was addressed. Whether Philby actually saw Gibarti, or was referred to Nepler by an underling cannot be established for sure (Gibarti spent little time in Paris in the summer of 1933 since he was busy organizing the counter-trial in London to the Leipzig trial of Dimitrov.) The authors are grateful to Stephen Koch of Columbia University for drawing this possible link to our attention. See his analysis of Münzenberg and Gibarti in *Double Lives: Espionage and the War of Ideas*, Free Press, New York, 1993.

31 The International Workers' Relief Organization had been founded in Berlin by Willi Münzenberg, the prolific perpetrator and activist of the so-called Communist front organization. After the Nazis had come to power a year earlier, he and his associates had fled, decamping with the headquarters to Paris.

32 Philby KGB Memoir, p. 11.

33 *Ibid*.

34 *Ibid*, p. 12.

35 *Ibid*, p. 13.

36 *Ibid*.

37 *Ibid*.

38 *Ibid*, p. 17.

40 *Ibid*, p. 15.

41 Letter from Mrs Dora Philby to Harry St John Philby was quoted by Page, Leitch and Knightley in *Philby*, p. 45.

42 Professor Dennis Robertson's comments recalled by colleagues, as cited by Andrew Boyle, *Climate of Treason*, pp. 106–7, quoted by Page *et al*, *Philby*, p. 45.

43 Philby KGB Memoir, p. 17.

44 *Ibid*.

45 Page *et al*, *Philby*, p. 86.

46 At the first meeting with Deutsch, Reif's report (quoted on page 137) indicates that Philby was only asked – and gave his consent – to help to penetrate bourgeois institutions. At this stage he did not know for whom he was being asked to work: the Comintern, the anti-fascist underground or the Soviet Union. Moreover, Reif's undated letter to the Centre, that preceded Orlov's arrival in England by a few weeks, specifically states that he was given the impression that it was for anti-fascist work because it was "too early" to recruit him for the Soviet intelligence service. Deutsch's

approach therefore can be regarded as stage one of Philby's recruitment. His actual induction into the Soviet intelligence service therefore occurred under Orlov's direction of the London "illegal" station. That this step was taken sometime after the summer is indicated by the undated letter he wrote to the Centre setting out the plan to get Philby into MI6 by sending him out to India, which was written between 16 July 1935 and Orlov's departure for Moscow on 25 September that year. In it he states Philby had "remarkably progressed in the understanding of his tasks and agent work" for which he demonstrated a "great appetite". That Philby himself realized that it was Orlov who effected that final stage of recruitment into the Soviet intelligence service is evident from his KGB memoir, in which he refers to him as a Bolshevik and the chief of a big operation run from Moscow. The same applies to Orlov's role in the recruitment of Maclean and Burgess because "illegal" operatives such as Deutsch and Orlov were expressly forbidden for security reasons from disclosing that they were officers of the Soviet intelligence service during stage one of recruitment operations. If it was disclosed at all, it was only *after* the "candidates for recruitment", as they were known during stage two, had been thoroughly vetted and tested for reliability.

47 Precisely when Edith Tudor Hart arrived in Britain is not clear from her NKVD file, but it was 1933 and almost certainly May, the year before Philby set out for Austria. She was followed to Britain by her brother, the noted animal photographer Wolf Suschitsky and her mother. She joined the Communist Party of Great Britain and was one of the founders of the "Workers' Camera Club" later the "Workers' Film and Photo League" which documented the social injustices of the Depression. Her studies of miners, working-class women and children appeared in books and in such magazines as *Picture Post, Weekly Illustrated* and the *Listener*. Although her work was well known before the war, Edith Tudor Hart's name was to be eclipsed by her more famous contemporaries such as John Grierson and Cecil Beaton. After she died in 1973 her work was the subject of renewed interest and Liverpool's Open Eye Gallery mounted a retrospective exhibition of her photographs in 1992.

48 In Edith Tudor Hart's file can be found the following profile of her written by Deutsch: "She is modest, diligent and brave. She is prepared to do anything for us, but unfortunately she's not careful enough. This arises from the fact that she became accustomed to legal Party work. . . . She takes up many things at the same time. She is very honest with money (even parsimonious). One has to be very cautious when [arranging] to meet her because she is one of the most well-known children's photographers in Britain. We have to demand more precision and carefulness from her. She has greatly improved in this respect in the period that she's been connected with us [the "illegal" *rezidentura*] because it was strictly demanded of her. Her carelessness can also be explained by the fact that she is very *shortsighted*." (EDITH TUDOR HART File. No. 8320 Vol. 1, p. 52, RISA.)

49 Philby KGB Memoir, p. 16.

50 A note from Reif on Philby indicates his potential value on the eve of his recruitment: "Important factors in the recruitment of SYNOK [SÖHNCHEN] were: 1. position of his father; 2. his [Kim's] intention to enter Foreign Office service." (PHILBY File No. 5581, Vol. 1, pp. 3–4, RISA.)

51 DEUTSCH File No. 32826, Vol. 1, p. 347, RISA.

52 DEUTSCH File No. 32826, Vol. 1, p. 5, RISA.

53 In his autobiography in the NKVD files Deutsch states that he first came to London in February 1934, taking up his permanent position in the *rezidentura* in April 1934. (DEUTSCH File No. 3286, Vol. 1, p. 9, RISA.) Deutsch arrived in London from the Paris *rezidentura* while his wife remained in Moscow. In August 1935 he went on leave to Moscow for the first time in three years of underground work. He returned to

London in November 1935 where his wife joined him in February 1936 before their first child was born. When his student's visa expired, he was employed by his cousin, a film company owner, who tried to get permission for Deutsch to work in Britain. This failed and Deutsch had to leave England in September 1937. But he returned shortly afterwards in November using a new cover and passport, to put his network of agents on ice. (DEUTSCH File No. 32826, Vol. 1, pp. 4–8, RISA.)

54 Ibid.

55 Undated note, report by Reif to the Centre (probably early June 1934), PHILBY File No. 5531, Vol. 1, p. 3. Also see undated note in MACLEAN File No. 83791, Vol. 1, p. 189, RISA.

56 Reif's June report was relayed to Moscow by diplomatic bag from Copenhagen. Telegram No. 2696 was sent simultaneously with the mail but it arrived much earlier than the diplomatic bag. It was accepted NKVD practice to report the most important developments by telegraph and send details of them by mail.

57 Philby KGB Memoir, p. 18.

58 Ibid, p. 19.

59 Ibid.

60 Ibid. The translator left Philby's English expression in brackets in the Russian version.

61 Ibid, pp. 19–20.

62 Undated cryptogram (probably June 1934) from Copenhagen, No. 2696, PHILBY File No. 5581, Vol. 1, p. 3, RISA.

63 In this same period Maclean and Burgess were recruited by Orlov's rezidentura. Also before the Centre got a word about Deutsch's approach to Kim Philby in June 1934, MARR had sent two letters in secret ink which the Centre was unable to develop. So it happened that the first stages of the recruitment of all three initial members of the Cambridge ring were not specifically authorized by Moscow. ORLOV File No. 32476, Vol. 2, p. 124.

64 Philby KGB Memoir, p. 20.

65 "The recommendations from Viennese comrades and Edith herself" in the report cited indicates that Edith must have known Kim as well as Litzi during her time in Vienna before she came to Britain.

66 Interview with Philby by Philip Knightley, Sunday Times, 20 March 1988.

67 Philby KGB Memoir, p. 20–22, RISA.

68 Ibid.

69 Ibid.

70 Ibid.

71 Ibid.

Chapter 7: "A Great Appetite for Agent Work"

1 Orlov to Moscow Centre (no date but it must have been dispatched between 15 and 25 July 1934), PHILBY File No. 5581, Vol. 1, p. 6, RISA.

2 Philby KGB Memoir, pp. 18, 26.

3 Orlov's "William Goldin" American passport that he used for his English trips contains a visa issued at the British Consulate in Stockholm dated 11 July 1934. The first incoming immigration stamp 25 July indicates he spent only ten days during his first visit to England. The next incoming stamp was issued in Newhaven for 18 September 1934, indicating that he must have taken the cross-Channel ferry. Then he appears to have left the country again the following month because there is an

immigration stamp for 16 November for Plymouth, suggesting that his third arrival was again across the Channel by way of Cherbourg. There is an aliens registration stamp given by Bow Street police station on 14 January 1935 and two additional Harwich Immigration Office incoming stamps for 13 March and 26 April 1935, indicating North Sea crossings from Esbjerg in Denmark.

4 On Orlov's file there is a copy of his August 1934 personal request, addressed to Artusov, the Chief of the 5th Department of the GUGB, NKVD (formerly the INO). As it is a copy it is both unsigned and according to Soviet bureaucratic practice leaves the day of the month out. Like the signature this was only filled in on the top copy. (ORLOV File No. 32476, Vol. 2, p. 4, RISA.)

5 Since these two important Government sources have never been identified by the British authorities, the RIS is not yet prepared to name them in accordance with its stated policy. But their significance can be judged from their position on the June–July 1935 account sheet that Orlov submitted to Moscow Centre: ORLOV File No. 32476, Vol. 2, p. 123, RISA, and from his report relating to Philby's offer of a job in India, ORLOV File No. 32476, Vol. 3, pp. 147–9, RISA.

6 Wright's account showed that Edith Tudor Hart was suspected of being a contact of Litzi Friedman and a Comintern agent. According to his account she refused to talk and could not be broken. (Wright, *Spycatcher*, pp. 289, 315.) This is confirmed by the story Philby related about Skardon on pages 20–22 of his KGB Memoir.

7 Companies House did not retain the records for The American Refrigerator Company which became defunct in 1941. But it is listed – and advertises – in the London Trades Directory for the years in which it operated. The year after Orlov's departure the business – which imported American refrigerators and equipment – moved its offices to 135–137 Queen Victoria Street. In 1938 it opened a branch office in the City at 59 Knight Rider Street EC4. Copies of its notepaper and Orlov's business card as Goldin are in his file in the NKVD archives. (ORLOV File No. 32476, Vol. 2, p. 121, RISA.)

8 Orlov, *Handbook*, pp. 64–5. In his 1965 debriefing by the CIA made at the request of the French counter-intelligence service Orlov expanded on the details of what he termed a "fiasco" – although he claimed not to recall the names of the other "illegals" operating on the same batch of Austrian passports other than his former deputy in Paris, Korotkov. According to Orlov, the NKVD, through an agent he named as Rosenfeld, who worked in the Austrian Government bureaucracy, had obtained access to processing false birth certificates for passport registrations. The operation had been running undetected for a considerable time, giving the NKVD great confidence in the scheme which enabled them to get genuine passports for a large number of their agents. When Mally's mishap occurred there was therefore both alarm and debate at the Centre about how to contain the damage. According to Orlov the INO officer responsible for obtaining the passports, an Austrian by the name of Mueller, was very much opposed to recalling the agent involved. He argued that the Austrian Government had neither the inclination, nor the resources to mount an extensive investigation. Also because of the elaborate precautions taken over the birth certificates Mueller did not believe that Mally or the others were in any real danger of discovery and never understood why the chiefs had taken such precipitate action. Orlov's account confirmed that Mueller was correct. After a short period the Austrians ceased their investigations, enabling Mally and the others to go on using their falsely obtained, but genuine, passports. (Details given by Orlov in relation to "Cas 15", ORLOV DST File.)

9 *Ibid.*

10 ORLOV File No. 32476, Vol. 3, p. 41, RISA.

11 Orlov letter to the Centre of 24 February 1935, ORLOV File No. 32476, Vol. 3, p. 13, RISA. One of the reasons why neither the Home Office nor MI5 could come up with anything compromising against Reif (as far as we know without access to his MI5 file) is that Orlov's "illegal" group was very careful about security. For example, this is how Orlov reported to the Centre the way they were running BRAUT (Bride), a woman who in her turn was cultivating a Foreign Office diplomat: "MARR will tell you about the techniques of our meets with BRIDE which completely exclude possibilities of a compromise. She never knew when she was going to see us and all meets were organized in an 'unexpected manner' with surveillance and other devious tricks." (ORLOV File No. 32476, Vol. 3, p. 12, RISA.)

12 Orlov, *Handbook*, p. 132.

13 Orlov to Centre undated, probably March 1935, ORLOV File No. 32476, Vol. 3, p. 41, RISA.

14 According to the Soviet practice the actual process of recruitment followed a strict sequence: spotting, contacting, cultivating, recruiting, training and working. Cultivation might sometimes be dispensed with if the "candidate for recruitment" was expected to give his consent at the first approach – as was the case with Philby when Deutsch asked him openly at their first meeting if he would volunteer for "anti-fascist work". The successive steps in the recruitment process fell into two distinct stages:

> *Stage 1*: Recruitment of the candidate for what was known as a "foreign flag" operation – that is one that was ideologically very close, but not openly identified with Moscow. The Soviet Union was the ultimate embodiment of both communism and anti-fascism so the "anti-fascist work" for which Philby, Maclean and Burgess were initially recruited set the broad guideline under which they could be tested.
>
> *Stage 2*: In the course of their training and tasking with appropriate "anti-fascist missions", the "candidates for recruitment" might eventually prove themselves qualified to be considered as fully-fledged agents of the Soviet intelligence service.

Some candidates were never advanced to Stage 2 and continued to work under whatever "foreign flag" the Soviet service had wrapped around itself when it first tapped them for their cooperation. This might be the IRA for the Irish, white racism for the Ku Klux Klan, or the Communist International for the ardent Marxist undergraduate.

In the case of Philby – and a few months later with Maclean and Burgess – the NKVD records indicate that cultivation was dispensed with. Deutsch – with the approval of Reif (in the case of the "First Man") and Orlov (in the case of the "Second and Third Men" of the Cambridge Group) evidently considered that each was already sufficiently ideologically committed to agree on the first approach to work for the "foreign flag" anti-fascist operation. But it was only after months of training and testing that they advanced to Stage 2 when Orlov – as chief of the "illegal" London station – authorised that all three were to be considered as probationary agents of the Soviet intelligence service. Orlov letter to Centre, 24 February 1935, ORLOV File No. 32476, Vol. 3, p. 14, RISA.

15 Orlov, *Handbook*, pp. 84–5, 89.

16 Psychological assessment of Philby supplied by Deutsch, code name STEPHAN, in DEUTSCH File No. 32826, Vol. 1, p. 348, RISA.

17 Reference to the list of Cambridge names in Orlov to Centre, 24 January 1935, in PHILBY File No. 5581, Vol. 1, p. 14, RISA. Also ORLOV File No. 32476, Vol. 3, p. 15, RISA.

18 Philby, KGB Memoir, p. 29.

19 Boyle, *Climate of Treason*, p. 143.

20 The precise date of their meeting is not recorded, but it can be backdated to December 1934 from the correspondence in the files. In his letter of 24 February 1935 to the Centre, Orlov reported that he had already taken over the running of Philby and Maclean from Deutsch. This was *after* Reif had been summoned to the Home Office and Orlov decided that he should leave England. But as we know from Philby, he, together with Deutsch and Orlov, had by then already discussed the possibility of recruiting Burgess. So Philby and Orlov must have met in December at the latest, since the process of inducting Burgess had already been begun by the end of the year.

21 Philby KGB Memoir, p. 31, RISA.

22 Maclean in his autobiographical note of September 1942: "One of your people with whom I worked was called 'Little Bill'. I did not know his real name and cannot identify him for you . . . Then there was 'Big Bill' who later worked in Spain." (MACLEAN File No. 83791, Vol. 2, p. 206, RISA). Philby in his KGB Memoir, p. 56, states that he knew Orlov as "Bill" (Philby never met Reif, so there was no "Little" and "Big" Bill for him, only "Bill").

23 Philby KGB Memoir, p. 31, RISA.

24 Orlov, *Handbook*, p. 91.

25 Tsarev was given access to the main Orlov files in the summer of 1990.

26 Orlov, *Handbook*, pp. 91–4.

27 *Ibid*, p. 95.

28 ORLOV File No. 32476, Vol. 3, p. 115, RISA.

29 Philby KGB Memoir, p. 11.

30 Orlov to Centre 12 July 1935, ORLOV File No. 32476, Vol. 3, pp. 112–13, RISA.

31 *Ibid*.

32 *Ibid*. Wylie was a Westminster School contemporary of Philby, who had gone to Oxford.

33 *Ibid*.

34 *Ibid*.

35 The amounts recorded are operational expenses which varied from month to month. They do not reflect any direct remuneration. Ledger sheet for June 1935 to July 1935. (ORLOV File No. 32476, Vol. 2, p. 123, RISA.)

36 *Ibid*.

37 Orlov, *Handbook*, p. 97.

38 *Ibid*.

39 Orlov letter to the Centre of 24 February 1935, ORLOV File No. 32476, Vol. 3, p. 13, RISA.

40 Orlov to Centre, 24 April 1935, ORLOV File No. 32476, Vol. 3, pp. 113–15, RISA.

41 Handwritten endorsement on above file.

42 Orlov to Centre, 24 April 1935, ORLOV File No. 32476, Vol. 3, pp. 113–15, RISA.

43 *Ibid*.

44 *Ibid*.

45 *Ibid*.

46 *Ibid*.

47 *Ibid*.

48 *Ibid*, p. 147.

49 *Ibid*.

50 The archive files of the NKVD show that BÄR, ATILLA, NACHFOLGER, and BRAUT (BRIDE) were sources whose identity has never been disclosed. Assurances have been given that they are not a "disinformation" ploy. The fact that their code names occur

in the archival documents confirms this – on the assumption that the documents released are genuine. Given the circumstances under which this co-operative project has evolved, there would be little point in fabrication. But in accordance with protecting unnamed agents, the Russian Intelligence Service is doing no more than the CIA and FBI does to shield sources who might still be living and who it does not wish to reveal. Operational intelligence is exempted, as determined by the agencies concerned, from the Freedom of Information Act.

51 ORLOV File No. 32476, Vol 3, pp. 147–9, RISA.

52 Ibid.

53 Ibid.

54 SCHORR to Centre, 9 October 1935, ORLOV File No. 32476, Vol. 2, pp. 89–90, RISA. Such occurrences were not infrequent for Soviet "illegals", as Bystrolyotov described in his unpublished memoir. The reason for this was the lack of experienced intelligence officers which required the assignment as "illegals" of those, like Orlov, who had previously posed as "legals".

55 Telegram from Centre, 10 October 1935, to Orlov, Ibid.

56 Philby KGB Memoir, pp. 34–5.

57 Ibid.

58 The Tatler & Bystander, London, 19 July, 1936.

59 Philby, KGB Memoir, pp. 34–5.

60 Ibid.

61 Ibid.

62 Ibid.

63 Mally had twice visited London, once in 1935 and again in January 1936 in connection with running the Foreign Office cypher clerk King, whose code name was MAG. Later that year he was ordered to take over Orlov's group and he settled in London in April 1936. ("History of the London Rezidentura", File No. 89113, Vol. 1, p. 76, RISA.)

64 Orlov, Handbook, p 64; Stalin's Crimes, p. 236.

65 Wright, citing his interrogation of Blunt in Spycatcher, p. 205. Blunt also told Wright in his secret confession that Mally had left England before he was recruited. This was not true, since Blunt was taken aboard as a fully-fledged agent of the Soviet intelligence service before Mally was recalled to Moscow in June 1937. Until the KGB archive files were released which showed Orlov's role as the original director of the Cambridge network, the assumption had been that Mally was the éminence grise. This incorrect inference had first been argued by co-author Costello in his book on the Blunt case, Mask of Treachery, Morrow, New York, 1988, pp. 279–80. Two years later Christopher Andrew and Oleg Gordievsky, in their book, Inside the KGB, pp. 156–9 advanced the same theory, supposedly on the authority of the latter author's recollections of his service with the First Chief Directorate. It has been established by Costello and Tsarev in conversations with Gordievsky that his failure to appreciate Orlov's true role was because neither he nor anyone else in the KGB below the highest level had seen the Orlov operational files until the summer of 1990 when the Russian author was given special access. Since it was Orlov's successor whose portrait was hung alongside Mally's in the memorial room, Gordievsky gave Mally the credit for being the mastermind behind the Cambridge network.

66 Orlov, Handbook, p. 64. The alias and passport he used in London was that of Paul Hardt. But in Mally's file it states that he held a Dutch passport in the name of Willy Brochart in 1936 when he was in London. This is incorrect and is either a confusion based on wrong records or because Mally held several passports and may have used both the Brochart and Hardt identity to enter Britain. (MALLY File No. 9705, Vol. 1, p. 14, RISA.)

67 MALLY File No. 9705, Vol. 2, p. 58, RISA.

68 Philby KGB Memoir, p. 36, RISA.

69 *Ibid*, p. 67.

70 *Ibid.*

71 Hugh Thomas, *The Spanish Civil War*, pp. 439–44.

72 Philby KGB Memoir, p. 36, RISA.

73 *Ibid.* According to Mally's letter to the Centre of 24 January 1937, PHILBY File No. 5581, Vol. I, p. 38, RISA, "SYNOK [Philby] . . . received a letter of recommendation from Hausehofer [the German Foreign Ministry official who was later to play a key role in encouraging Hitler's deputy Rudolf Hess to fly to England on his abortive peace mission in May 1941] and two letters of recommendation from the London representative of Franco, Marquis Merry del Val – one to the Lisbon government, the other to the son of the Marquis who is head of military censorship in Talavera."

74 Philby, *Silent War*, p. 17.

75 Mally report dated 24 January 1937, PHILBY File No. 5581, Vol. I, p. 38, RISA.

76 The NKVD had set up training centres for saboteurs in Republican Spain. Orlov, who was in charge of the whole Spanish operation had at his disposal dozens of tough operatives who were much better suited to carry out Franco's assassination than an untrained Cambridge graduate like Philby.

77 *Ibid.*

78 Philby, KGB Memoir, p. 37, RISA.

79 Mally's 24 January letter to the Centre in PHILBY File No. 5581, Vol. I, p. 38, RISA, states, "Communications: his [Philby's] wife is going to Lisbon and either he will travel to her or she will travel to him, his reports being collected by couriers [from Lisbon]." It is not clear from Philby's file whether this system was ever put into operation.

80 Philby KGB Memoir, p. 37, RISA.

81 Philby, *Silent War*, pp. 17–18.

82 Philby, KGB Memoir, p. 37, RISA.

83 *Ibid*, p. 53.

84 *Ibid.*

85 *Ibid.*

86 *Ibid.*

87 Mally to Moscow Centre, 24 May 1937, PHILBY File No. 5581, p. 45, RISA. Although this dispatch does not specifically state that Mally discussed it with Philby, it is possible that he did.

88 Deutsch report in DEUTSCH File No. 32826, Vol. I, p. 349, RISA.

89 *Ibid.* Another example of an irresponsible and unprofessional assignment given to Mally came in the late summer of 1937 after the defection of Ignace Reiss whose code name was RAIMOND. Mally was in Paris when he was ordered to locate Reiss. He succeeded in finding the hotel where he was holed up. Knowing that the two had been friends, the Centre gave Mally instructions to liquidate Reiss on the spot. Two plans were suggested to him by Spigelglass who was in Paris at the time. The first was to deliver a fatal blow to Reiss's head in his hotel room with an iron. The second was to poison him in a café and photograph him as he dropped on the floor. Mally refused, criticizing the Centre and laughing at Spigelglass's suggestions. (Undated report in MALLY File No. 8705, Vol. I, pp. 117–120, RISA.)

90 Philby KGB Memoir, p. 39, RISA.

91 *Ibid.*

92 *Times* memo of May 1937, as quoted by Page, *et al*, in *Philby*, p. 119.

93 Philby KGB Memoir, p. 67 and Mally report in PHILBY File No. 5581, Vol. I, p. 52, RISA.

94 *Ibid.* According to Orlov's 1965 CIA debriefing he typically could only recall that the Paris "legal" *rezident's* code name was ALEXANDER although he must have known Kosenko because he met with him on a number of occasions in Paris in 1937 and 1938. This appears to have been another case where Orlov misled the CIA since the NKVD records show that the "legal" *rezident's* cryptonym was SAM. ALEXANDER was the code name of the assistant "illegal" *rezident* in France from 1933–37, Mikhail Vasilievich Grigoriev. (ORLOV DST File.) Nor is it clear from Philby's NKVD file how all these contacts worked out in practice. The instruction of 4 September 1937 on p. 52 of Philby's file simply states: "To STEPHAN [Deutsch] Establish contact through SAM [the London "legal" *rezident* whose embassy-listed name was Grigory Borisovich Grafpen] contact of SCHWED [Orlov] with SYNOK [Philby] in your presence in Biarritz in the lobby or café of Hotel Miramar." As Deutsch left London in September 1937, in practice another scheme might have been devised. What is not in dispute, however, is that Orlov was put in direct touch with Philby in the autumn of 1937.

95 Philby, KGB Memoir, p. 51, RISA.
96 *Ibid.*
97 Page *et al*, *Philby*, pp. 116–17.
98 Philby KGB Memoir, p. 39, RISA.
99 *Ibid*, p. 40.
100 PHILBY File No. 5581, Vol. 1, p. 50, RISA.
101 Philby KGB Memoir, p. 41, RISA.
102 Page *et al*, *Philby*, pp. 116–17.
103 Philby KGB Memoir, p. 51, RISA.
104 *Ibid*, p. 52.
105 *Ibid*, p. 53
106 *Ibid.*
108 *Ibid*, p. 213. "He [Orlov] was recalled to Moscow at the end of the Spanish war, but instead he went to America. He lived in the States, in Canada. But he never said a single word about me, though of course he was interrogated in a tough way by the CIA and the FBI and he was in constant contact with them . . . As it seems, leaving for the States he decided to give them some information, but far from all his information."
109 Philby KGB Memoir, p. 213.
111 *Ibid.*

Chapter 8: "A Promising Source"

1 MACLEAN File No. 83791, Vol. 1, p. 1, RISA.
2 Philby KGB Memoir, p. 28, RISA. There is a reference to the list of Cambridge names in Orlov to the Centre, 24 January 1935, in PHILBY File No. 5581, Vol. 1, p. 14, RISA. The actual list was either not forwarded to Moscow or has not survived because an extensive search in the relevant files has failed to locate it.
3 Claude W. Guillebaud, Senior Tutor of St John's College, quoted by T. E. B. Howarth, *Cambridge Between the Wars*, Collins, London, 1978, p. 148.
4 Whether Kapitsa was a witting or unwitting agent of Mikhail Abramovich Trilliser's technological raiding operation – and, as has more extravagantly been claimed the "father of the Soviet A-Bomb" – is still of intense partisan controversy. All the evidence indicates that there was an extensive scientific intelligence-gathering operation which Trilliser orchestrated from the OGPU and that it also was contributed to by Soviet Military Intelligence. Abram Joffe's decision to allow his top Soviet physicists to work in Western laboratories appears to have been part of a carefully

managed operation and Kapitsa could hardly have been unaware of the long-term advantages in what would amount to a transfer of technology back to the Soviet Union. His problems obtaining a visa for travel through France and his sponsorship by the Soviet Trade Delegation are further indications that he arrived in England, not as an individual researcher, but as part of a more co-ordinated and sinister scheme. When or whether he decided to break the leash that bound him to Moscow's plan is more a matter for conjecture. For a more detailed review of Kapitsa's case and the views of his leading defenders and detractors see Costello, *Mask of Treachery*, pp. 106–7, 145–9.

5 Orlov, *Handbook*, p. 108.

6 *The Cambridge Review*, March 1934.

7 Boyle, *Climate of Treason*, pp. 58, 96.

8 Philby KGB Memoir, p. 28 and PHILBY File No. 5581, Vol. I, p. 7, RISA, which includes Reif's letter of October 1934 that reflects the recommendations made by Philby: "SCHWED [Orlov] and I decided that he [Philby] should be assigned the task of sounding out all of his Cambridge friends who held the same convictions so that we could use some of them for our work. To tell the truth, we spoke mainly about two of them: Burgess and Maclean. Burgess is the son of very well-off parents. For 2 years he has been a party member, very clever and reliable [ideologically speaking] but in 's's [SYNOK's = Philby's] opinion somewhat superficial and can occasionally make a slip of the tongue. On the contrary Maclean (from now on SIROTA [Russia for WAISE or ORPHAN]) is highly praised by 's'."

9 The most illuminating and factually correct account of Maclean and his background is by his Cambridge contemporary Robert Cecil, *A Divided Life: A Personal Portrait of the Spy Donald Maclean*, Morrow, New York, 1989.

10 Boyle, *Climate of Treason*, pp. 114–17.

11 Orlov, *Handbook*, p. 108.

12 The code names of the Cambridge group were remarkably transparent. Apart from SÖHNCHEN, WAISE and MÄDCHEN (Burgess), one of its later members was assigned the familiar form of his forename, TONY (Anthony Blunt). Also EDITH (Edith Tudor Hart) and ARNOLD (Arnold Deutsch) are easily identifiable – but only if *one knows* the truth. It must be remembered this transparency is only obvious *after the fact*. Strictly speaking, however, there can be no doubt that the early code names used by Orlov did not conform to the strict rules of *Konspiratsia*. Note that Philby was interchangeably referred to as SYNOK, the Russian equivalent of SÖHNCHEN. DEUTSCH File No. 32826, Vol. I, p. 348, RISA.

13 "History of London *Rezidentura*", File No. 89113, Vol. I, p. 112, RISA.

14 See note 18.

15 Philby KGB Memoir, p. 61, RISA.

16 *Ibid.*

17 *Ibid.*

18 Cryptogram to Centre No. 55/4037 from NKVD *rezident* in Copenhagen, 26 August 1934 in MACLEAN File No. 83791, Vol. I, p. 34, RISA.

19 Centre to Orlov, ORLOV File No. 32476, Vol. I, p. 39, RISA.

20 Orlov had had no leave for eighteen months because of his arduous efforts as an "illegal" in France. He therefore took a holiday to be with his wife and daughter who had not yet made their separate way to England.

21 Reif to Centre, November 1934, MACLEAN File No. 83791, Vol. I, p. 37, RISA

22 MACLEAN File No. 83791, Vol. I, pp. 44–5, RISA.

23 Cecil interview by Costello in *Mask of Treachery*, p. 277; see also Cecil, *Divided Life*, pp. 36–7.

24 Reif's report about handing over control of Maclean to Orlov was made on 13 July 1935 and is in MACLEAN File No. 83791 Vol. 1, p. 46. Corroboration is the Centre to Orlov, 7 January 1935, MACLEAN File No. 83791, Vol. 1, p. 39, RISA.

25 Orlov to Centre dated 24 February 1935, ORLOV File No. 32476, Vol. 3, p. 15, RISA.

26 Ibid.

27 Apart from Shuckburgh, who was a regular career diplomat, none of these names appear on the regular Foreign Office lists. This was in keeping with the British practice of not naming MI6 officers because of their secret status, although technically Foreign Office employees. For their identification we are indebted to Robert Cecil, a Cambridge contemporary of Maclean and career Foreign Office diplomat who served as a wartime liaison secretary to Sir Stewart Menzies, the head of MI6, and who has written the authoritative study of Maclean, A Divided Life.

28 When Philby joined MI6 in 1941, Robert Carew-Hunt was a leading member of Section V, as head of the North and South America subsection. When Philby was promoted to take charge of Section IX Soviet Counter-Intelligence in 1944, he selected Carew-Hunt to work under him. After he retired in 1950, Carew-Hunt wrote The Theory and Practice of Communism, Geoffrey Bles, London, 1950. (Nigel West, MI6: British Secret Intelligence Service Operations 1909–45, Weidenfeld, London, 1983, pp. 222, 388.)

29 MACLEAN File No. 83791, Vol. 1, p. 44, RISA. By assigning code names to certain individuals Moscow Centre did not necessarily mean that they were targeted for cultivation to become potential agents. Such cryptonyms did, however, indicate that these individuals were considered potentially important sources of information.

30 Ibid.

31 Reif to Centre, 13 July 1935, MACLEAN FILE No. 83791, Vol. 1, p. 44, RISA.

32 Recollection of Maclean's account given to Andrew Boyle by Lady Grimond and Lady Felicity Rumbold in Boyle, Climate of Treason, p. 117.

33 Reif to Centre, 13 July 1935, MACLEAN File No. 83791, Vol. 1, p. 44, RISA. In his report of 2 November 1935 to the Chief of the INO, Orlov states that he brought with him to Moscow a photographic copy of Lord Simon's letter. It is in an envelope on p. 157 of ORLOV's File No. 32476, Vol. 3 – but with time it has become blurred and unreadable.

34 The full list has still to be disclosed by the Russian Intelligence Service, which now has charge of the NKVD records. But documentation in the RIS archives shows that Deutsch played a key role in the recruitment of most members of the Cambridge and Oxford groups, in addition to a number of agents who provided the London "illegal" station with technical information. The summary appearing on p. 8 of Deutsch's NKVD autobiography indicates that the Oxford and Cambridge groups alone accounted for ten people. DEUTSCH File No. 32826, Vol. 1, p. 8, RISA.

35 DEUTSCH File No. 32826 Vol. 1, pp. 384–9.

36 Orlov, Handbook, p. 109.

37 Andrew and Gordievsky in KGB: The Inside Story, in photo caption over a memorial plaque from a Vienna apartment, ascribe Deutsch's death to his "heroic role in the anti-Nazi resistance" leading to his "execution by the SS in 1942". This is incorrect. Deutsch's file shows that while he did die as a result of German action, it was at sea as the result of a Kreigsmarine torpedo, and not from SS bullets!

Deutsch survived the purges because he did not ever figure in evidence extracted from his colleagues. The only testimony against him was given by head of the International Department of Comintern, Abramov, but since it was widely known that Abramov bore a personal grudge against the Deutsches (he would not let his wife join Arnold abroad when she worked for him in CI) this allegation was not taken seriously.

When the war between Hitler's Germany and the Soviet Union began in 1941, the Centre planned to send Deutsch to recruit agents in Latin America. He set out by ship – ss *Kayak* via the Indian Ocean, but got stuck in Bombay where there were crewing problems. He wrote to the Centre asking them to call him back and let him fight the Fascists at the battlefront. Deutsch was eventually recalled to Moscow, only to find he was reordered to travel to the United States aboard ss *Donbass*. In mid-Atlantic on 7 November 1942 the freighter was torpedoed by a U-boat. Eyewitness reports describe Deutsch's courage when, fatally wounded on deck, he continued to bravely encourage and help others to abandon ship.

Another little known fact is that Deutsch was a prolific inventor. He registered four patents while in Britain, including a device for training pilots which he sent to Moscow. This is referred to in his letter of 24 June 1937. He also invented several operational devices and secret ink recipes. (DEUTSCH File No. 32826, Vol. 1, p. 164 and Vol. 2, p. 37, RISA.)

38 MACLEAN FILE NO. 83791, Vol. 1, p. 56, RISA.

39 Orlov to Slutsky, 22 March 1936, MACLEAN File No. 83791, Vol. 1, pp. 75–82, RISA.

40 Cecil telephone interview with Costello, 7 February 1992.

41 *Ibid.*

42 *Ibid.*

43 The first published analysis of the Oldham case was reconstructed by the former CIA officials Corson and Crowley in *The New KGB*, pp. 140–68. To protect their sources they referred to Oldham as "Scott", the same alias he had used when he walked into the Soviet embassy in Paris. Costello in *Mask of Treachery*, pp. 181–2, correctly identified the source as Oldham and noted that Pieck had become an American informant from information obtained from Igor Cornelissen, *De GPOe op de Overtoom*, Van Gennep, Amsterdam, 1989, p. 158. The identification of Bystrolyotov as Oldham's recruiter is from BYSTROLYOTOV File No. 9529, RISA.

44 King's significance as a cypher expert is confirmed by his NKVD file code-named MAG, KING File No. 21870, RISA.

Access to the secret British Foreign Office cables speaks for itself in terms of its importance for Soviet intelligence. But Maclean also had access to a far wider range of Foreign Office documentation than the cypher clerk King. There was also the significant operational aspect to giving two agents in the same organization access to the same kind of files. First, this guaranteed a flow of secret documentation even if one of them was transferred or in the worst case, exposed. Second, it enabled a check to be kept on the sincerity and performance of each of them. This was essential in monitoring whether or not they were subject to counter-intelligence operations which might turn them into double agents to feed false information. In the case of Maclean and King, the London NKVD station could also divide and co-ordinate their work so as to diminish the risk of either taking too much material out of the Foreign Office at any one time.

45 Orlov memo to Slutsky is in MACLEAN File No. 83791, Vol. 1, pp. 75–82, RISA.

46 Mally to Centre, MACLEAN File No. 83791, Vol. 1, p. 71, RISA. In his letter of March 1937 (no date) Mally wrote describing the material obtained from Maclean and sent with this particular mail that they were forwarding a report by SIS about Soviet Foreign Policy based on the information received from an agent in the NKID (People's Commissariat for Foreign Affairs). MACLEAN File No. 83791, Vol. 1, p. 118, RISA.

According to the rules established by the NKVD, material supplied by agents was subject to a ten-year review, when it was saved or destroyed on merit. As time passed, accretion of an abundance of material of purely historical interest led to its destruction. The NKVD saw no operational value in retaining many of the actual copies of British Government documents stolen by Maclean during the first part of his career in the Foreign Office since no one ever foresaw the possibility that such historic records would ever be published.

47 Orlov report, MACLEAN File No. 83791, Vol. 1, pp. 75–82, RISA.

48 Orlov memorandum, MACLEAN File No. 83791, Vol. 1, pp. 75–82, RISA.

49 *Ibid.*

50 *Ibid.*

51 *Ibid.*

52 *Ibid.*

53 MACLEAN File No. 83791, Vol. 1, pp. 108, 110, 132, 133, RISA.

54 *Ibid,* pp. 70–70A.

55 *Ibid.*

56 Turning the MI6 agent was in accord with Soviet practice (this hypothesis rests on the British author's presumption that there was only one MI6 spy). For an account of the "Gibby's Spy" case, as it has been known until now, see Chapman Pincher, *Their Trade is Treachery,* Sidgwick and Jackson, London, 1981, and Wright, *Spycatcher,* p. 220.

In a letter of March 1937 (no date) Mally wrote describing the material obtained from Maclean and sent with this particular batch a report by MI6 about Soviet Foreign Policy based on information received from an agent of theirs in the *Narkomindel* (NKID) (People's Commissariat for Foreign Affairs). This led to the source being uncovered by the counter-intelligence section.

57 MACLEAN FILE NO. 83791, Vol. 1, p. 115, RISA.

58 The Münzenberg information is particularly intriguing since the internal reports received through MI6's penetration agents show up in MI5 documentation given to the US State Department in 1940.

59 MACLEAN File No. 83791, p. 115, RISA.

60 Mally to Moscow Centre, 24 May 1936, MACLEAN File No. 83791, Vol. 1, p. 75, RISA.

61 *Ibid.*

62 BYSTROLYOTOV File No. 9529, Vol. 2, pp. 119–20, RISA.

63 After his return to Moscow, Bystrolyotov worked at the Lubyanka headquarters and in the summer of 1936 travelled to Denmark on a special mission. He also wrote two chapters of the first textbook on intelligence. He started a training course for his next "illegal" assignment (in his memoir he does not say what it was) but with the purges in full swing, everything slowed down. In January 1938 he was served with a notice that he was suspended from duty. Then in March he was transferred to the Chamber of Commerce and on 17 September arrested. He was convicted of espionage after physical torture and sentenced to twenty years hard labour on 8 May 1938. Bystrolyotov was finally released in 1954 and rehabilitated in 1956. He then worked as a translator and editor of medical literature. He wrote up to twelve volumes of autobiographical memoirs and works of fiction before his death in 1970, among them a colourful and revealing account of his "illegal" work in Europe in the 1930s. (BYSTROLYOTOV File No. 9529, Vol. 2, pp. 216–17, RISA).

64 Mally to Moscow Centre, 24 May 1936, MACLEAN File No. 83791, Vol. 1, p. 75, RISA.

65 Elizabeth K. Poretsky, *Our Own People: A Memoir of Ignace Reiss and His Friends,* Michigan, Ann Arbor, 1936, pp. 128, 214.

66 For a summary of the so-called Woolwich Arsenal case see Costello, *Mask of Treachery*, pp. 281–3, and for Olga Gray's account Anthony Masters, *The Man Who Was M: The Life of Maxwell Knight*, Blackwell, 1982, pp. 30–44.

67 In 1941 the request was made to Blunt to check the Tudor Hart MI5 file by Anatoly Gorsky, then the NKVD's "legal" *rezident* in the London embassy. MI5 records show that the police had decided they could not prove that the Leica camera was Hart's. That they suspected her was significant because the camera had been bought by Percy Glading, a known Communist agent, who had given the bill to Olga Gray, an MI5 penetration agent in Communist Party headquarters who had been seconded to act as an assistant to the Soviet spy ring which operated under Mally's direction in the British Government arms factory at Woolwich Arsenal. EDITH TUDOR HART (code name EDITH) File No. 83820, Vol. 1, pp. 17, 24, 27, RISA. The account attributed to the Soviet defector Oleg Gordievsky in *KGB: The Inside Story*, p. 179, which states that Hart lost her diary which contained cryptic references to Deutsch and his operations is not supported by any such evidence in her NKVD file.

68 NACHFOLGER, ATILLA, BÄR and some of his other sources were part of a far-reaching technical and industrial intelligence network that was put on ice. DEUTSCH File No. 32826, Vol. 1, p. 6–7, RISA.

69 MACLEAN File No. 83791, Vol. 1, p. 154, RISA.

70 ADA's File No. 47435, Vol. 1, p. 89, RISA.

71 *Ibid.* Grafpen (SAM) was "legal" *rezident* in London from 1937–38 and was replaced by Anatoly Gorsky (VADIM) in 1939.

Ironically, Grafpen who directed NORMA later also fell a victim of the purges. He was recalled and sentenced to eight years hard labour. Georgy Kosenko, his contemporary as legal *rezident* in Paris, was less fortunate. He was recalled and shot in 1939.

72 Autobiographical note in MACLEAN File No. 83791, Vol. 2, pp. 204–6, RISA.

73 *Ibid.*

74 Grafpen to Centre, 10 April 1938, MACLEAN File No. 83791, Vol. 1, p. 154, RISA.

75 This is clear from the records which show that NORMA was given authority to make her first approach to Maclean on 3 April 1938 and his letter of 25 April is signed LYRIC.

76 Orlov, *Handbook*, p. 109.

77 Any kind of personal involvement of an officer with an agent (financial, sexual and so on) is forbidden in most intelligence services including CIA and MI6. Of course there are no rules without exceptions, especially when a "love affair" would serve the purposes of operational work – but then it can hardly by described as genuinely personal involvement, since it was entered into with the permission of the Centre.

78 Centre to Grafpen, 17 July 1938, MACLEAN File No. 83791, Vol. 1, p. 206, RISA.

79 Autobiographical note in MACLEAN File No. 83791, Vol. 2, pp. 204–6, RISA.

80 Undated letter from LYRIC in MACLEAN File No. 83791, Vol. 1, pp. 174–5, RISA.

81 Orlov, Reif and Deutsch, it is clear from the NKVD records, did make efforts to insulate one Cambridge agent from another. But they were largely unsuccessful because of the exceptional intimacy of the "Three Musketeers". These efforts created certain myths about the role of Burgess as the originator of the Cambridge ring which the Soviet files reveal were deliberately encouraged by certain operational measures that it is not yet appropriate to reveal.

82 Burgess's vulnerability to VD through his promiscuous homosexual adventures has been confirmed in the interviews with his friends and former sexual partners conducted in 1985 for Costello for *Mask of Treachery*.

83 Deutsch to Centre, 8 October 1936, MACLEAN File No. 83791, Vol. 1, p. 43, RISA.

84 Mally in his letter to the Centre of 29 January 1937 states that Anthony Blunt had already been recruited as a talent-spotter to bring in other potential penetration agents from the Cambridge high-flyers destined for Government service. Letter in BURGESS File No. 83792, Vol. 1, p. 75, RISA.

85 Cairncross letter of November 1991 and as admitted in an interview with Nigel West, *Molehunt*, Weidenfeld & Nicolson, London, 1987, p. 26.

86 *Ibid.*

87 Telephone interview with John Cairncross, 29 November 1992. The authors are also indebted for this introduction and for information from his interviews of Cairncross at his home in the south of France to James Rusbridger, intelligence authority, author and former MI6 operative.

It should be noted that Mally in his letter of 9 April 1937 informed the Centre that MOLIÈRE had already been recruited but that they would not get in touch with him until the end of May 1937. This supports the assertion Cairncross made that he was already in the Foreign Office *before* he actually became a Soviet agent. He must therefore have been talent-spotted by Blunt sometime well before his January 1937 recruitment. MACLEAN File No. 83791, Vol. 1, p. 120, RISA.

88 In the last letter that Deutsch sent from London before his departure for Moscow, he informed the Centre on 9 September 1937 that he had received the first batch of Foreign Office documents from MOLIÈRE. Deutsch to Centre, MACLEAN File No. 83791, Vol. 1, p. 145, RISA.

89 Cairncross correspondence and interviews with Rusbridger.

90 MACLEAN File No. 83791, Vol. 2, pp. 31–3, RISA.

91 ADA to Centre, undated report in MACLEAN File No. 83791, Vol. 2, pp. 31–3, RISA.

92 *Ibid.*

93 FORD to Centre, MACLEAN File No. 83791, Vol. 2, pp. 154–64, RISA.

95 ADA to Centre undated report, MACLEAN File No. 83791, Vol. 2, p. 132, RISA.

96 Interview with Vladimir Borisovich Borkovsky who worked in London with Gorsky and later became Chief of the Directorate of Scientific and Technical Intelligence of the FCD. Philby, in his KGB Memoir recalled Gorsky as "dry in manner and attitude".

97 This according to the article written jointly by Yatskov and Krasnikov, two veteran KGB officers who had played a major part in the Soviet atomic espionage operation, *Intelligence Courier*, Moscow, Spring 1992. Tsarev was unable to find the citation in the MACLEAN file, but he contacted Yatsov (who had not sourced his article) who confirmed that Maclean and not Cairncross was the source of the information. Tsarev is continuing to search for the quoted VADIM cryptogram in the RIS Archives.

98 For a documented account of the damage that Maclean did, see Verne Newton, *The Cambridge Spies*, Madison Books, Washington, 1991.

99 Maclean to Moscow Centre, 29 December 1940, MACLEAN File No. 83791, Vol. 2, pp. 154–64, RISA.

Chapter 9: "An *Enfant Terrible*"

1 This is the sequence of recruitment according to the NKVD records. Costello in *Mask of Treachery*, pp. 200–18, gives the first account to challenge the accepted myth about Burgess being the "first man" and the architect of the Cambridge network. Incorrectly, it turns out he assigned that "honour" to Blunt, instead of Philby.

2 Burgess's florid personal habits described in the many published works about the Cambridge spies are echoed in the sober analytical profile recorded by Deutsch in "History of the London *Rezidentura*", File No. 89113, Vol. 1, p. 350, RISA.

3 Reif report "SCHWED [Orlov] had a plan to recruit WAISE [Maclean] and MÄDCHEN [Burgess] through SÖHNCHEN [Philby]." "History of the London *Rezidentura*", File No. 89113, Vol. 1, p. 112, RISA.

4 Philby's KGB Memoir, p. 29, RISA.

5 Goronwy Rees, *A Chapter of Accidents*, Chatto & Windus, London, 1972, p. 133.

6 Boyle, *Climate of Treason*, pp. 84–5, ascribing his doubts about the truth of the story to a "confidential source".

7 Autobiographical note in BURGESS File No. 83792, Vol. 1, p. 8, RISA. The other details of Burgess's early career have been culled from a variety of published sources as cited in *Mask of Treachery*, including the somewhat suspect account Burgess gave to his friend Tom Driberg in Moscow which was published as *Guy Burgess: A Portrait with a Background*, Weidenfeld & Nicolson, London, 1956.

8 For a fully documented discussion of the Apostles, their society's conversion to Marxism and membership list, see Costello, *Mask of Treachery*, pp. 186–90.

9. Undated letter from Victor Rothschild to J. Maynard Keynes in 1933 file, Keynes Papers, King's College Archives, Cambridge.

10 Autobiographical note written in 1943 in BLUNT File No. 83695, Vol. 1, pp. 231–8, RISA.

11 See Orlov's letter of 16 July 1935 sorting out the Centre's concern about MÄDCHEN: "You showed interest in MÄDCHEN as far back as my last visit to our city [Orlov, after a short stay in London in July 1934 had returned home for a vacation]. I reported to you then that he [Burgess] was coming to our country as a tourist and that he was a friend of [Prime] Minister Baldwin's secretary [Dennis Proctor]. A check through our second section established that he had already left our country, so it was decided to approach him on the ISLE [Britain.]" ORLOV File No. 32476, Vol. 3, p. 120, RISA.

The above communication indicates that Orlov had reported on Burgess as a potential recruit when he was in Moscow in August 1934, but that the Centre had evidently forgotten. This would suggest that Orlov's report had been made verbally to the chief of the Foreign Section and not formally recorded.

12 Philby's KGB Memoir, pp. 29–30, RISA. Philby gives no date for the meeting, but because it related to the problem Burgess was causing as a result of his friend Maclean distancing himself from his Communist friends, it would have been December since this would have been after the first stage of his recruitment in October.

13 Orlov, *Handbook*, p. 16.

14 Philby KGB Memoir, p. 112, RISA.

15 Deutsch to Moscow Centre, undated, BURGESS File No. 83792, Vol. 1, p. 10, RISA. Another reason that prompted Orlov and Deutsch to recruit Burgess was to prevent him from talking. Once he was a member of their network, they hoped to impose discipline that would make him more responsible.

16 Centre to Orlov, 7 July 1935, ORLOV File No. 32476, Vol. 4, p. 51, RISA.

17 Orlov to Centre, undated, ORLOV File No. 32476, Vol. 3, p. 120, RISA.

18 Orlov to Centre, 12 July 1935, ORLOV File No. 32476, Vol. 3, pp. 120–21, RISA.

19 Psychological assessment of Burgess in the "History of The London *Rezidentura*", File No. 89113, Vol. 1, pp. 350–1. A copy is also in the DEUTSCH File No. 32826, Vol. 2, RISA.

20 *Ibid*.

21 Two-page list in BURGESS File No. 83792, Vol. 1, pp. 28–31, RISA.

22 Orlov to Centre, 24 April 1935, ORLOV File No. 32476, Vol. 3, p. 68, RISA.

23 There is no evidence in the NKVD files that either Proctor or Watson were actually ever recruited as Soviet agents despite the long-held suspicions of MI5 and the assertions of Peter Wright's investigation.

24 Orlov to Centre, ORLOV File No. 32476, Vol. 3, p. 112, RISA.

25 DEUTSCH File No. 89113, Vol. 1, pp. 250–1, RISA.

26 For details of Katz's involvement, see Costello, *Mask of Treachery*, pp. 293–5, citing the FBI Files on Rudoph Katz and Christopher Isherwood.

27 Orlov to Centre, 12 July 1935, BURGESS File No. 83792, Vol. 1, p. 121, RISA.

28 Deutsch to Centre, 2 January 1936, BURGESS File No. 83792, Vol. 1, p. 56, RISA.

29 *Ibid.* Hill's exaggerated account of his adventures in the early days of the Soviet Union with Reilly and Robert Bruce Lockhart in the so-called "Envoys' Plot" against Lenin and the Bolsheviks is related in his book *Go Spy Out the Land*, Cassell, London, 1932.

30 Philby KGB Memoir, p. 37, RISA.

31 BURGESS File No. 83792, Vol. 1, pp. 46, 55–6, 61–2, RISA.

32 Page *et al, Philby*, p. 93.

33 Burgess told to Goronwy Rees, *op. cit.*, p. 144, and to Tom Driberg, quoted in Driberg, *Guy Burgess: A Portrait with a Background* Weidenfeld & Nicolson, London, 1956, p. 93.

34 Footman's appearance in the Foreign Office was reported by Deutsch in a letter to Moscow of 8 October 1936, MACLEAN File No. 83791, Vol. 1, p. 43, RISA.

35 Mally to Centre, BURGESS File No. 83792, Vol. 1, p. 68, Deutsch to Centre, *Ibid*, p. 97, "History of London *Rezidentura*", File No. 89113, Vol. 1, p. 245, RISA.

36 Footman had served in the British consular service in the Levant before joining Section 1, the political division of MI6 in 1935. He had written a study of Ferdinand Lasalle, the pre-Marxist Socialist who founded the German Social Democratic Party and was a friend of, and influence on, both Marx and Engels. His years of intense study of the USSR resulted in his postwar publications *Red Prelude* (1944), *The Promise Path* (1946), *Civil War in Russia* (1961) and *Revolutions* (1962).

37 Burgess report, undated, BURGESS File No. 83792, Vol. 1, pp. 100–113, RISA.

38 Deutsch to Centre, undated, BURGESS File No. 83792, Vol. 1, pp. 100–103, RISA. His original reports have mostly been destroyed after their translation into Russian and many do not give a specific date. Mally had not been recalled from London in June 1937 and Burgess's contact with Footman appears to have taken place late that summer and early autumn.

39 Burgess psychological profile in DEUTSCH File No. 89113, Vol. 1, pp. 350–1, RISA.

40 *Ibid.*

41 *Ibid.*

42 Hewitt interviews with Costello, London, 1985.

43 Driberg, *Portrait,* p. 48.

44 Burgess reports, undated, BURGESS File No. 83792, Vol. 1, pp. 114–34, RISA.

45 *Ibid.*

46 *Ibid.*

47 *Ibid.*

48 *Ibid.*

49 *Ibid.*

50 *Ibid.*

51 *Ibid.*

52 Eitingon's last contact with Burgess is reported in his letter of 9 August 1938 in EITINGON File No. 33797, Vol. 1, pp. 104–7. There is not therefore not much recorded

on Burgess's early relationship with Footman between 1937 and early 1938 and since most of his reports are undated anyway, the precise chronology of his contacts is unclear until the resumption of his control by the London *rezidentura*, indicated by Gorsky's instructions from the Centre of 19 March 1939 in BURGESS File No. 83792, Vol 1, p. 150, RISA.

53 Undated 1938 report, in BURGESS File No. 83792, Vol. 1, p. 137, RISA.

54 *Ibid*, pp. 138–9.

55 *Ibid*.

56 Burgess psychological profile in "History of London *Rezidentura*", File No. 89113, Vol. 1, pp. 350–1, RISA.

57 Report on meeting with Grand on 19 December 1938, BURGESS File No. 83792, Vol. 1, pp. 145, 205, RISA.

58 *Ibid*, p. 209.

59 Burgess letter, 28 August 1939, BURGESS File No. 83792, Vol. 1, p. 281, RISA.

60 Burgess report, undated, BURGESS File No. 83792, Vol. 1, p. 302, RISA.

61 For a detailed description of Burgess's curious relationship with Liddell, see Costello, *Mask of Treachery*, pp. 367–97.

62 BURGESS File No. 83792, Vol. 1, p. 392, RISA.

63 "History of London *Rezidentura*", DEUTSCH File No. 89113, Vol. 1, pp. 350–1, RISA.

64 Blunt interview as quoted by Cecil, *A Divided Life*, p. 66.

65 BOB, the cryptonym of Gorsky's deputy Kreshin, to Centre, 14 October 1942, BURGESS File No. 83792, Vol. 1, p. 433, RISA.

66 Burgess psychological profile, File No. 89113, Vol. 1, pp. 350–1, RISA.

67 *Ibid*.

68 Burgess report, 1 July 1939, BURGESS File No. 83792, Vol. 1, p. 229, RISA.

69 This was especially true between the autumn of 1938 and early 1939 with the disruption in communications caused by the purges of NKVD "illegals". An example is Eitingon's running of Burgess in Paris.

70 Burgess report, 12 March 1939, BURGESS File No. 83792, Vol. 1, pp. 183–5, RISA.

71 Undated report (either Eitingon or Gorsky), BURGESS File No. 83792, Vol. 1, p. 215, RISA.

72 "History of London *Rezidentura*", File No. 89113, Vol. 1, p. 351, RISA.

73 Burgess 1952 debriefing in BURGESS File No. 83792, Vol. 1, p. 210, RISA.

74 Autobiographical note of 1943 in BLUNT File No. 83695, Vol. 1, pp. 231–8, RISA. Blunt, like those in the other Soviet groups, did not know his code name, and like them adopted his initials as a crude security measure.

75 List given by Burgess of the Cambridge group and its interconnections in BURGESS File No. 83792, Vol. 2, pp. 8–42, RISA.

76 *Ibid*.

77 List of Soviet sources and reviews of their activity for the year 1940 in "History of London *Rezidentura*", File No. 89113, Vol. 1, pp. 190–201, RISA.

78 *Ibid*.

Chapter 10: "Keep Out of Range of Artillery Fire"

1 Preface in Orlov, *Handbook*. It is possible that the manual was proscribed after Orlov fled to the West. But it is more likely that Orlov only contributed to the textbook, since no veteran of the period recalls a manual by him – nor does his file make any reference to it.

2 ORLOV, *Legacy*. Testimony before Senate Internal Security Sub-Committee, 14–15 February 1957, pp. 65–7.

3 Orlov, *Handbook*, p. 187.

4 Tsarev interview with Feoktistov, Moscow, February 1992.

5 Orlov, *Stalin's Crimes*, pp. 59–81. The details he provides show that he himself must have been present since he noted that the meeting involved "the chiefs of the most important departments of the NKVD and their deputies". Orlov was deputy to Alexander Shanin, of the Department of Railways and Sea Transport.

6 *Ibid.*

7 *Ibid.*

8 *Ibid.* For full details of how Orlov learned the truth about the Kirov affair, see Orlov, *Stalin's Crimes*, chapters 1–3.

9 *Ibid*, pp. 112–3.

10 *Ibid*, pp. 113–4.

11 *Ibid*, pp 160–66.

12 *Ibid*, p. 170

13 Sudoplatov interviews. ORLOV *Legacy*, p. 6.

14 "Record of sworn statement before the US Immigration and Naturalization Service (INS)", 29 June 1954, p. 49, FBI Files ORLOV Internal Security R 105–6073, FOIA.

15 The authoritative and detailed account of the complex causes and tortuous course of the struggle is Hugh Thomas's masterly history, *The Spanish Civil War*, Harper & Row, New York, 1961. See also the more recent work of the same title by Burnett Bolbuten, Harvester Press, London, 1970.

16 Order W 832/in ORLOV File No. 32476, Vol. I, p. 37, RISA and ORLOV *Legacy* p. 41. In an interrogation with the FBI in 1954, Orlov corrected the assertions of Walter Krivitsky in *I Was Stalin's Agent*, London, 1939, pp. 93–7, that the decision to send him to Spain was taken by a special meeting of the Politburo on 14 September 1936, as "pure inventions". The fact that he was in Spain by 9 September appears to confirm Orlov's account given to the SAC of the FBI in New York on 8 July 1954, ORLOV File No. 105–6073, FBI.

17 Thomas, *Spanish Civil War*, pp. 394–5.

18 *Ibid*, pp. 406–8.

19 Orlov's statement quoted in Case File 165–22869, ALEXANDER ORLOV, IS-R report of interviews on 1/11/54, 2/16/54, 3/12/54 and 5/18/54. Report to director dated 8 June 1954, FBI FOIA

20 Orlov to Moscow Centre, 15 October, "Correspondence of the *Rezidentura* in Spain", File No. 17679, Vol. I, p. 20, RISA

21 Louis Fischer, *The War in Spain*, New York, 1941, p. 369.

22 José Hernandez, *Yo, Ministro de Stalin en España*, Madrid, 1954, p. 42.

23 Quoted by Krivitsky, *op. cit.*, p. 110.

24 Quoted by Krivitsky, *op. cit.*, p. 121.

25 Cited by Krivitsky, *op. cit.*, p. 100. In his former role as the GRU field-station chief in the Netherlands, Krivitsky played a role in arranging for arms shipments to be smuggled into Spain.

26 Thomas, *Spanish Civil War*, pp. 470–8.

27 ORLOV *Legacy*. Testimony to SISSC, 14 February 1957, pp. 41–7.

28 *Ibid*, p. 42. Orlov's testimony recalling the telegram's wording. Probably because of its sensitivity, Stalin's cable is not in his NKVD file or the "Correspondence of the *Rezidentura* in Spain" files.

29 Typewritten 24-page account prepared by Orlov for the Senate Internal Security Sub-Committee entitled "The Treasure of Spain" in Orlov, Alexander folder of

Investigative Records of Senate Internal Security Sub-Committee Individual Name Files Box 77 RG 46 NAW (hereafter ORLOV SISSC RG 46 NAW).

30 ORLOV *Legacy*, p. 42, 15 February 1957 testimony to SISSC.

31 "Treasure of Spain", ORLOV SISSC, p.6, NAW.

32 *Ibid*, p. 10.

33 *Ibid*.

34 *Ibid*, p. 12.

35 *Ibid*, p. 12.

36 *Ibid*, p. 15.

37 ORLOV *Legacy*, p. 44.

38 "Treasure of Spain", ORLOV SISSC, p. 21, NAW.

39 *Ibid*, p. 22

40 *Ibid*.

41 *Ibid*, p. 23.

42 *Ibid*.

43 *The Washington Post*, 6 April 1957.

44 Letter from Orlov to Yezhov in which he notes he was writing flat on his back in hospital, dated Paris 14 February 1937, in "Correspondence of the *Rezidentura* in Spain", File No. 17679, Vol. 1, pp. 60–63, RISA.

45 Orlov to Centre, 27 February 1937, in "Correspondence of the *Rezidentura* in Spain", File No. 17679, Vol. 1, p. 28, RISA.

46 Orlov to Moscow Centre, 27 February 1937, in "Correspondence of the *Rezidentura* in Spain", File No. 17679, Vol. 1, pp. 60–1, RISA.

Chapter 11: "Forbidden Subjects"

1 José Hernandez, *Yo, Ministro de Stalin en España*, p. 42.

2 Krivitsky, *Secret Agent*, pp. 124–5.

3 *Ibid*.

4 Orlov to Centre, 29 December 1936, "Correspondence of the *Rezidentura* in Spain", File No. 17679, Vol. 1, p. 50, RISA.

5 Orlov to Centre, 5 March 1937, File No. 17679, Vol. 1, p. 81, RISA.

6 Orlov to Centre, 23 May 1937, File No. 17679, RISA.

7 Orlov to Centre, 8 June 1937, File No. 17679, Vol. 1, p. 130, RISA.

8 Orlov, *Handbook*, p. 172.

9 *Ibid*, p. 174

10 *Ibid*, pp. 175–9.

11 *Ibid*.

12 Orlov to Centre, 29 December 1936, in "Correspondence of the *Rezidentura* in Spain", File No. 17679, Vol. 1, p. 45, RISA.

13 Orlov to Centre, 3 December 1937, ORLOV File No. 32476, Vol. 1, p. 140, RISA.

14 *Ibid*.

15 23 May 1937 Report in "Correspondence of the *Rezidentura* in Spain", File No. 17679, Vol. 1, p. 140, RISA.

16 Orlov to Centre, 29 December 1936, File No. 17679, Vol. 1, p. 52, RISA.

17 See reports cited previously in PHILBY File No. 5581, Vol. 1, p. 52 and also Philby KGB Memoir, p. 67, RISA.

18 Report 9 June 1937 "SCHWED LETTERS" in "Correspondence of the *Rezidentura* in Spain", File No. 19897, Vol. 3, p. 170, RISA.

19 Orlov to Centre, 20 May 1937, File No. 17679, Vol. 1, p. 151, RISA.

20 Orlov to Centre, 4 May 1937, "Correspondence of the *Rezidentura* in Spain", File No. 17679, Vol. 1, p. 161, RISA. There are no more details in the Soviet records of the plan to use Churchill's son, but there is a tantalizing but cryptic reference to his name by Orlov in preparations for his testimony before the Senate Internal Security Sub-Committee.

21 Orlov to Centre, 10 January 1937, "Correspondence of the *Rezidentura* in Spain", File No. 17679, Vol. 1, p. 54, RISA.

Bretel has returned from Morocco: he had two assignments. First, organization of an intelligence group in Morocco for receiving information concerning the transfers of special trains and armaments. Second, studying on the ground the possibilities of a rebellion in Spanish Morocco.

Concerning the first assignment: a group of six has been organized; the first radio message has already been received. Concerning the second assignment: a rebellion in Morocco can be organized if two main conditions are met – first the consent to this of the Spanish and French Governments, second the assignment for this of several million francs.

Though the idea of rebellion surfaced at the beginning of the war, the Spanish Government reaction was negative because of their reluctance to strain relations with France. However, as we had now determined absolutely, the left-wing circles of the French Government more than once gave their blessing to this idea and we were ready to come to terms with the Spanish Government. The failure to exploit these possibilities can be explained not so much by political caution as by sabotage.

22 Orlov to Centre in letter of 29 December 1936, "Correspondence of the *Rezidentura* in Spain", File No. 17679, Vol. 1, p. 45, RISA.

23 *Ibid.*

24 *Ibid.* File No. 17679, Vol. 2, p. 43, RISA.

25 Orlov to Centre, 10 May 1938, "Correspondence of the *Rezidentura* in Spain", File No. 19687, Vol. 3, p. 118, RISA.

26 *Ibid.*

27 Autobiographical account COHEN File No. 92753, Vol. 1, p. 22, RISA. For an authoritative published account of what the FBI established about the Cohens' link to the American atomic espionage network see Robert J. Lamphere and Tom Schachtman, *The FBI–KGB War: A Special Agent's Story*, W. H. Allen, London, 1987, pp. 276–8 and 292. Their role in the "Portland Spy Ring" is documented by their British trial and by Gordon Lonsdale, *Spy*, Neville Spearman, London, 1965, and Harry Houghton, *Operation Portland: The Autobiography of a Spy*, Hart Davis, London, 1972. Before Helen died on 29 December 1992 the Cohens had taken part in a pre-coup 1991 KGB co-produced television documentary which avoided any indication of their role in Soviet atomic espionage operations. For information on Daniel Patrick Costello (no relation), see John Costello, *Mask of Treachery*.

27 Kirill Khenkin, *Okhotnik Vverkh Nogami (Hunter Upside Down)*, Posev, Frankfurt/Main, 1979, pp. 16–17.

Khenkin, who later claimed he had trained as a KGB "illegal", was a leading Jewish *refusnik* who finally obtained a visa to emigrate to Israel in 1974. Khenkin is not regarded in either the RIS or the CIA as a consistently reliable source. His unsupported assertions have therefore to be treated with care. But the account of his encounter with Orlov does, however, fit the picture of him at the time as given to the KGB by Philby in his secret memoir.

28 *Ibid*, pp. 19–21.

29 *Ibid.*

30 *Ibid*, p. 285. There were no "Trotskyite units" as such in Spain. This appears to

be another imprecision by Khenkin who was more likely referring to a POUM faction (see below). The POUM consisted of some former Trotskyites and some Left-Socialists who had merged their support with the so-called London Bureau or Two-and-a-half International which included the British Independent Labour Party (ILP). Trotsky himself had condemned the POUM as traitors to the workers' cause, but this did not deter the NKVD branding the faction "Trotskyites".

31 *Ibid*, p. 284.

32 Eitingon's relationship with Mercader's mother is mentioned in a number of Western sources including Dziak *Chekisty*, p. 69, and Levine, *The Mind of an Assassin*. That Caridad Mercader was Eitingon's mistress is disputed by a contemporary witness who knew them both, General Sudoplatov. In an interview he insisted that it was wrong to describe her as Eitingon's mistress despite accounts that asserted that they were lovers.

33 *Ibid*, p. 286. While the files relating to Orlov's activities in Spain certainly record him sending people to Moscow for training, since they are referred to only by numbers it has so far proved to be impossible to confirm Khenkin's assertion. See for example the numbers cited in Orlov to Centre of 10 July 1935 in "Correspondence of the *Rezidentura* in Spain", File No. 76659, Vol. 2, p. 85, RISA.

34 "The Spanish Revolution", POUM newspaper, 3 February 1937, as cited by Thomas, *op. cit.*, p. 649.

35 As quoted by Thomas, *op. cit.*, p. 649.

36 Hernandez, *op. cit.*, p. 66.

37 In his letter of 15 October 1936 Orlov had explained how to set about this liquidation: "The anarchists with a hint of instruction will get rid of the [POUM] leaders. 'The masses' (about seven thousand people) have in most cases by chance strayed into this organization and can easily be involved into a number of other organizations. This is the view of Ilya Ehrenburg [the famous Soviet writer who was then a correspondent in Spain for the Soviet press] who knows Catalonia well enough." The physical elimination of the POUM was not only under consideration by Orlov but apparently was not seen as a major problem. He appears to have been fully aware that part of his mission was to fulfil Stalin's burning desire for the political discrediting of Trotskyism. This led him into setting in motion his plan to discredit the POUM and its leader Nin.

38 Orlov to Centre, 29 December 1936, in "Correspondence of the *Rezidentura* in Spain", File No. 17679, Vol. 1, p. 44, RISA.

39 See SENIOR (Schulze-Boyzen) File No. 34122, Vol. 1, p. 132, CORSICAN File No. 34118, Vol. 1, pp 220, 318. See also *Rote Kapelle* (Gestapo summary of SENIOR's criminal activity), File No. 9361, Vol 1, p. 43, RISA.

40 As cited by Georges Soria, *Guerre en Espagne 1936–1939*, Laffont, Paris, 1977, Vol. 2, p. 28. Russian Edition: Progress Publishers, Moscow, 1978.

41 Orlov to Centre, in "Correspondence of the *Rezidentura* in Spain", File No. 3691, Vol. 1, p. 52, RISA. (In this series there are a number of files bearing different serial numbers.)

"The main organization of POUM is located in Catalonia. According to more or less proven information, quantitatively it represents the following. In Barcelona about 5,000 people and approximately the same number of sympathizers. In Tarragona about 2,000 people. In Gerona about 1,000, and approximately 3,000 people in other towns and settlements of Catalonia. In addition, in Barcelona they have a regiment of 2,000 men, about 50% armed. For some time there has been an association between POUM and the Federation of Spanish Anarchists taking shape which is directed at anti-Soviet activity associated with the latest Trotskyist trial [in the USSR]. The POUM central committee is situated in Barcelona and consists of five people: Nin, Andrade, Uso and Col." Orlov to Moscow Centre, 22 February 1937.

42 Orlov to Centre, March 1937, in "Correspondence of the *Rezidentura* in Spain", File No. 3692, Vol. 1, p. 76, RISA:

"At present a number of people for terrorist work have been confirmed by the Committee [Central Committee of POUM]. The control of the POUM youth organization has been assigned to first Tedor Sans, second Mendez, third another head of the organization called Lorenzo. All these are experienced in terrorist activity and have participated in various armed raids . . . It was established that Blanco's group [a member of the directorate of the POUM youth organization] was preparing a terrorist act against the former Komsomol [Communist youth organization] secretary of the town of Cordova, Ramon Gorerro, and failed to accomplish it only because Blanco was killed at the front. On the 3rd or 4th of February this year an anonymous letter was received by Muel Sebastiano, secretary of the south district Komsomol in Madrid, in which he was advised to leave the post of Komsomol secretary of the district otherwise he and his family would be murdered. The letter was signed in the following way: 'Long live the Spanish Falange! Long live POUM!'

43 See the authoritative works on Trotsky including Sedov's book.

44 Zborowsky also reported: "On 23 January in the presence of L. Estrina he spoke in similar vein to the 22nd. In reply to his announcement L. Estrina said: 'Hold your tongue.' " Zborowsky to Centre, 8 February 1937, ZBOROWSKY File No. 31660, Vol. 1, pp. 98, 140–2, RISA.

45 Zborowsky to Centre, 11 February 1938, *Ibid.*

46 Zborowsky to Centre, March 1938, ZBOROWSKY File No. 31660, Vol. 1, p. 153, RISA. The question of the poisoned orange peel appears to be a confusion caused by Sedov throwing orange peel around his room when he was delirious. Despite the post mortem conclusion that he died of natural causes, there are those who remain convinced that Trotsky's son was murdered by the emigré doctors working for the NKVD. That Zborowsky also played a hand in setting up the assassination of Krivitsky is more persuasively asserted from the words that he blurted out during his Senate testimony: "May I state, Senator, that I was not given an assignment to lure Sedov to a place for assassination. The idea was at the time, it was told to me the idea was to lure him to a place where he and me together would be kidnapped and brought to Soviet Russia, that was explained to me." Testimony in "Hearings on Scope of Soviet Activity" in the United States, Senate Internal Security Sub-Committee, part 4, 29 February 1956, p. 89. See also Orlov's 1965 CIA debriefing on the Dallins and Zborowsky which touches on Lilia Dallin's alleged role in Sedov's death (Appendix III).

An indication of how the impression was given – even inside the Kremlin – that the NKVD had a direct hand in Sedov's death can be found in Spigelglass's file. The Foreign Department chief at the time of Sedov's death, Spigelglass had been arrested on 2 November 1938 in a new round of NKVD purges. He started giving evidence only from 31 May 1939 after "strong pressure" – an euphemism for torture. He was convicted of treachery on 28 November 1940 and executed on 29 January 1941. In the transcript of Spigelglass's confession can be found the following statement that, if his evidence is correct, sheds a new light on Sedov's death:

"In the first half of 1938 Sedov died in Paris of natural causes. I rang up Yezhov to inform him. He replied, 'Come to my office.' When he read the telegram he said, 'A good operation. We did a good job on him, didn't we?'

"I said nothing to this, but I have no doubt that he reported to the Central Committee that it was us who had liquidated Sedov because a couple of days later I called on the former chief of Department 3, Minaev, who had a visitor, Passov [deputy chief of intelligence] and Minaev asked me the question 'How did you manage to do away with Sedov.' " (SPIGELGLASS File No. 21476, Vol 1, p. 99.) This testimony suggests that Yezhov found it advantageous to take credit for Sedov's death even though, according to Spigelglass, the NKVD was not involved.

47 Alexander Orlov, "The Sensational Secret Behind the Death of Stalin", *Life Magazine*, Vol. 48, No. 17, 23 April 1956. Orlov's story about Stalin as an *Okhrana* agent appeared in *Life Magazine*, April 23, 1956. In the same issue they published an article of Isaac Don Levine which contained a copy of a 1913 *Okhrana* letter identifying Stalin as an agent which is now generally agreed to be a forgery. This whole issue was of considerable interest to the KGB in 1956 in furtherance of Khruschev's demythologizing of Stalin. A search for incriminating documentation was made, but none was evidently uncovered. In the Ukrainian Communist Party files, there is however a translation into Ukrainian from the Russian language Canadian newspaper *Noviy Shlyakh* about the *Life Magazine* article by Orlov and the *Okhrana* document. (The Ukrainian Communist Party archive number is Fond 1, Opis 24 Spr. 4337, pp. 270–72.)

48 ORLOV *Legacy*, p. 7.

49 Cited by Wolfe (ed), *Khruschev and Stalin's Ghost*, p. 130.

50 Orlov, *Stalin's Crimes*, p. 219.

51 *Ibid*, p. 239.

52 Orlov to Centre, 25 August 1937, ORLOV File No. 32476, Vol. 1, pp. 91–2, RISA.

53 *Ibid*. "*Liternoye delo*" – literally "a letter of special significance" had during the Civil War period been used to indicate "special operations" and was used to indicate liquidation cases where subjects were referred to as "*literniks*" – i.e. those earmarked for assassination.

54 "Correspondence of the *Rezidentura* in Spain", File No. 17679, Vol. 1, pp. 154–6, RISA.

55 Orlov to Centre, 23 May 1937, File No. 17679, Vol. 1, pp. 154–6, RISA. One of the agents used in disseminating the forgeries was the French Communist Party official Georges Soria, who served in Spain as a representative of the Comintern and writer for *Imprecorr*. His pamphlet *Trotskyism in the Service of Franco* was published in England in 1937 and contains poor reproductions of the documents we know to be forgeries. The forgeries are also cited as real documents in *Imprecor*, May 17, 1938.

56 ASSISTANT (Nin's NKVD code name) File No. 7862, Vol. 1, pp. 234, 240, RISA.

57 Orlov letter to the Centre, 25 September 1937, File No. 32476, Vol. 1, pp. 91–4, RISA. "The double aspect obviously means that both the plan to facilitate the bombardment of Madrid [and] in addition the letter in secret ink on the back of it are genuine."

58 See Thomas, *Spanish Civil War*, pp. 705–6; ASSISTANT (Nin) File No. 7862, Vol. 1, p. 241, RISA.

59 Krivitsky, *op. cit.*, pp. 93–134, and Hernandez, *Yo Ministro de Stalin en España*, p. 99.

60 A search of the relevant NKVD files has disclosed no Soviet agent or operative named Bolodin suggesting that Orlov either disguised his real name, or invented it for the benefit of his story. Orlov interrogation in November and December 1954 with particular reference to the allegations made by Krivitsky, FBI ORLOV File No. 105–6073, FBI FOIA.

61 In the file are two encyphered reports. One is insignificant, so as to draw attention from the main incriminating document. Orlov to Centre, 24 July 1937, ORLOV File No. 32476, Vol. 1, p. 101, RISA.

62 *Ibid*.

63 Undated and unsigned pencil note, ORLOV File No. 32476, Vol. I, p. 164, RISA.

64 Three documents uncovered in the NKVD records in various files, unrelated to each other when taken together indicate that NIKOLAY was Nin.
The first document is an elaborate plan to compromise the POUM leadership and Nin through the "discovery" of a cryptic message in secret ink on genuine captured Falangist spy documents. The key elements in it are Orlov, the fake contrived message and the target: Nin. The second document is that listing the participants in the NIKOLAY case. Orlov was also the author of the document and the third is the cryptic mesage written by Juzik on the back of the main document. We know from the second document that NIKOLAY was kidnapped and liquidated and this coincides precisely with the date when Nin disappeared from his place of imprison ment.

Chapter 12: "A Dangerous Game"

1 Orlov, *Stalin's Crimes*, p. xii.

2 Although the serial number of the cable can be established, the actual telegram sent to Orlov does not appear in the relevant file and has yet to be located in any of the associated NKVD archival files, possibly because Yezhov ordered it suppressed after his flight. "Correspondence of the *Rezidentura* in Spain", File No. 76659, Vol. 2, p. 85, RISA. The version quoted is the one Orlov gave in his testimony before the US Senate Sub-Committee in 1955. ORLOV *Legacy*, p. 25.

3 *Ibid*. Orlov, *Stalin's Crimes*, p. xii.

4 *Ibid*, p. 214.

5 *Ibid*, pp. 215–6. The suicide is confirmed by Bystrolyotov in his memoir: "Colonel Gursky jumped out of the window of the 10th floor." BYSTROLYOTOV File 9259 Vol. 2, p. 217, RISA.

6 Orlov, *Stalin's Crimes*, p. 216.

7 *Ibid*.

8 ORLOV *Legacy*, p. 18–19, 39

9 Krivitsky, *op. cit.*, p. 124. General Kleber, who was an important figure in Soviet Military Intelligence as well as counter-intelligence, had formerly been involved in Soviet espionage operations in the United States.

10 Orlov, *Stalin's Crimes*, pp. 224–5.

11 *Ibid*, p. 223. The NKVD records reveal no agent or officer named Bolodin.

12 *Ibid*, p. 226.

13 *Ibid*.

14 Orlov told the CIA, in a debriefing on the Miller case on 15–16 April 1965, that he had learned the details "from conversations with the participants". He said that the operation was executed "under the personal direction of the Rezident, Kislov and Spigelglass, deputy chief of the First Directorate who had been sent to Paris for this particular purpose. Also involved was Beletsky and the Embassy chauffeur." The whole plan depended on the survival of the long-range penetration agent, General Skoblin, who was the fingerman in the operation. The plan contemplated that Miller would be removed by kidnapping and Skoblin would succeed him as chief of the ex-Czarist official organization (ROVS). But according to Orlov "no one had foreseen that Miller would reinsure himself by leaving a letter with third parties unknown to Skoblin", which pinpointed him as the man who had sprung the trap.
The actual kidnapping had been executed without difficulty, Orlov said, explaining how Beletsky "had used a massive dose of a drug that was being used in Moscow to

induce twilight sleep in women during childbirth". Miller was anaesthetized with it, put in a box and driven by the kidnap team "at very high speed from Paris to Cherbourg where the box – which bore [a] diplomatic seal – was placed aboard a Soviet vessel. All except the chauffeur went aboard and returned to Moscow." Miller, after interrogation, was then executed.

When Skoblin found out about Miller's letter incriminating him, he took flight, exiting in a panic through the back of his apartment building and abandoning his money, wallet and notes to his wife who was a well-known folksinger. Without funds he walked through the whole night before contacting an ex-Czarist colleague next morning from whom he obtained 200 francs. He then contacted the man at the Soviet embassy that Spigelglass had given him as an emergency contact. Against Stalin's explicit orders not to involve diplomatic staff, Yezhov's man had unwisely sent an embassy car to collect Skoblin and give him refuge in the rue de Grenelle until he could be smuggled out of the country to Moscow. (What Orlov did not tell the CIA in 1965 was that on Spigelglass's orders he hired a plane to fly Skoblin out to Spain.) Yezhov, according to Orlov, had taken full credit for the success of the operation but had kept the embassy's involvement from the Big Boss. As he put it: "If Stalin ever found out, it would be my neck."

The Orlov report notes that he claimed that he had taken steps to inform Stalin of Yezhov's disobedience, in the letter he claimed he had written to him after his flight to Canada. "Throughout all this, Orlov became successively more and more emotional in his statements, especially with respect to Yezhov whom he called a 'bloody killer'," the CIA debrief noted. He finally concluded that "I finally got even with him for the killing of my cousin [Katsnelson] and he deserved his fate." (ORLOV "GENERAL MILLER" DST file)

15 The NKVD records reveal that Orlov's role was not as he described it to the CIA. So far as can be identified there are three separate documents that link Orlov directly to the case of General Miller. First, he told Feoktistov at their second meeting in 1971 that one of the reasons why he had fallen out of favour with Yezhov was that he had declined to approve the plan for the kidnapping operation. Second, in his letter to Yezhov of August 1938 he states that he had in his possession FARMER's ring – FARMER was the code name of General Skoblin. (ORLOV File No: 103509, Vol. 1, pp. 13–25, 205–221.) Third, on 10 May 1938 we find that Orlov wrote about another operation to Spigelglass from Barcelona in which he mentioned the possibility of chartering an aircraft: "For $15,000 we could by an airplane of the type in which you and I whisked away FARMER." "Correspondence of the *Rezidentura* in Spain", File No. 19897, Vol. 3, p. 121, RISA.

16 Zborowsky later admitted to the FBI he had notified Moscow of Krivitsky's address. The KRIVITSKY File discloses that the defector was indeed kept under surveillance by NKVD agents in the US, but only until 11 February 1939. The fact that his file shows that the first news of his death was received from the American media is an indication, though not conclusive, that the NKVD may not, after all, have had a direct hand in his suicide. *Spravka* summary dated 6 February 1941 in KRIVITSKY File No. 15485, Vol. 9, pp. 22–37, RISA.

17 Dziak, *Chekisty*, p. 81; Orlov, *Stalin's Crimes*, pp. 227–8; ORLOV *Legacy*, p. 76.

18 Orlov, *Stalin's Crimes*, p xi.

19 ORLOV *Legacy*, p. 25

20 SPIGELGLASS File No. 21746, Vol. 1, p. 199, RISA.

21 Orlov, *Stalin's Crimes*, p xii.

22 ORLOV *Legacy*, p. 26.

23 Orlov, *Stalin's Crimes*, p. 232. Also detailed by Orlov to the CIA in April 1965 in

"SLUTSKY" in which he states, "Slutsky was poisoned in 1938 by Frinovsky who was ostensibly his best friend and deputy. Orlov recalled that he kept receiving cables in Slutsky's name in February 1938 dated after his death. There was an apparent attempt by this device to conceal the fact that Slutsky had met his end by foul play. (Orlov DST File)

24 Report by Orlov to Foreign Department of NKVD dated July 1938. ORLOV File No. 32476, Vol. 1, p. 112, RISA.

25 Letter of 24 May 1938 in "Correspondence of the *Rezidentura* in Spain", File No. 19897, Vol. 3, pp. 158, 160, RISA. File No. 76659, Vol. 2, p 85, RISA

26 Orlov's testimony to Senate Sub-Committee, *Legacy*, p. 75. His chief's flight appears to have had no deleterious effect on Eitingon's career. The Soviet records show that it was Eitingon who ran the Trotsky assassination operation. During World War II he served under General Sudoplatov, who ran NKVD partisan activities. Eitingon remained in Stalin's favour for years and was only arrested after Stalin's death and Beria's fall.

27 ORLOV *Legacy*, p. 75.

28 Orlov, *Stalin's Crimes*, p. 27.

29 Orlov's sworn statements in answer to interrogation by the US Immigration and Naturalization Service, 23 June 1955, Serial 305 FBI ORLOV File No. 105–22869, FOIA.

30 The numbers were those Orlov assigned his agents who were graduates of his espionage school in Spain. Orlov to Centre, undated, but probably 9 July, ORLOV File No. 32476, Vol. 1, p. 120, RISA. Orlov sent his first reply, telegram No. 316, on 9 July which was received by the desk officer at the Centre on 10 July 1938.

31 Orlov to Centre, 10 July 1938, *Ibid*, p. 121. This was Orlov's second confirmation, telegram No. 320. While the Spanish originated cables from Orlov have survived, Moscow's original telegram to Orlov recalling him to the *Svir* has evidently not. That it has apparently disappeared may well have been the result of the stinging criticism of Yezhov for sending such an amateurish missive, in Orlov's letter sent to the NKVD chief from Paris.

32 ORLOV *Legacy*, p. 26.

33 Orlov, *Handbook*, p. xiii.

34 Orlov INS testimony, p. 48, FBI ORLOV File No. 105–6073, FOIA; Orlov, *Stalin's Crimes*, pp. xiii–iv.

35 ORLOV File No. 32476, Vol. 1, p. 129, RISA

36 Orlov INS testimony, p. 48, ORLOV FBI File No. 105–6073 FBI FOIA; Orlov testimony to INS, 27 June 1955, in Serial 303, p. 13, ORLOV FBI File No. 104–22869, FOIA.

37 Detail of bank book given in FBI report, 29 March 1954, reference NY 105–6073, summarizing interview with the clerk of the Pilgrim Vault Company Boston, with whom the Orlovs rented a safe deposit box. Serial 186, p. 10, ORLOV FBI File No. 104–22869, FOIA.

38 August entry in ORLOV File No. 32476, Vol. 1, p. 170, RISA.

39 Orlov testimony to INS, NY 105–6073, ORLOV FBI File No. 104–22869, FOIA.

40 Orlov, *Stalin's Crimes*, p. xiv.

41 Orlov's sworn statement to INS investigators J. J. Caudio and S. E. Mason, 27 June 1955, Serial 303, ORLOV FBI File No. 104–22869, FOIA.

42 FBI report of interviews of Isadore Koornick and his sister, Mrs Florence Kellerman (uncensored), 31 January 1955, in Investigative Records Repository Records (IRR) "ORLOV, Alexander" C8 04 31 16 RG 319 Records of Army Staff National Archive, Washington.

43 Report from Los Angeles SAC of interview of Nathan Koornick, 8 October 1954, Serial 246 LA 105–01608, ORLOV FBI File No. 105–22869, FBI FOIA.

44 *Ibid*.

45 *Ibid.*

46 Orlov's sworn statement to INS investigator Mason, 27 June 1955, Serial 303, ORLOV FBI File No. 104–22869, FOIA.

47 The envelope containing Orlov's thirteen-page letter and two-page attachment is in ORLOV File No. 76659, Vol. 2, p. 85, RISA.

48 There is no evidence to be found in the NKVD files that Orlov addressed a separate copy of his letter to Stalin. Accompanying it is the note to "Surits or Burnukov" at the Paris embassy instructing them to forward the enclosed sealed missive to the chief in Moscow. That there is no evidence of any attempt by him to make direct communication to Stalin is significant in the light of Orlov's repeated claims to have done so in his American testimony. Corroboration that there was no such missive appears in the discovery of two copies of the note that Orlov sent accompanying his letter to Yezhov. They are addressed to Kislov, the Paris *rezident:* "Today I have handed to a concierge at the Embassy two packets addressed 1) to Kislov 2) to Ambassador Surits. Both are to be forwarded to Nikolay Ivanovich [Yezhov]. signed Schwedov" (ORLOV File 76659, Vol 1, p. 98, RISA).

Why did Orlov go to such great lengths to maintain he also sent a copy of a letter to Stalin along with a note revealing that Yezhov had disobeyed orders not to get the embassy involved in the Miller kidnapping? It is conceivable that he wanted to enhance his importance and make his case seem more dramatic. Moreover, if his letter was the one he claimed – detailing Stalin's crimes instead of the list of NKVD agents and operations that he actually sent – logic would have required him to have addressed it to Stalin. Hence the pretence and the false assertion. Another possibility is that Orlov was confusing the blackmail letter with the letter he had written earlier to Stalin disclaiming his role in the operation to exfiltrate the Comintern leader that went awry – as Orlov told Feoktistov in 1971 – as a result of Yezhov's bungling interference with the approved plan.

Certainly two copies of Orlov's letter addressed only to Yezhov have been found in the files. It is clear that one was also seen by Beria. But it is impossible to know from the surviving records whether he showed it to Stalin. Corroboration for this being another of Orlov's inventions was that in his 1971 interview with Feoktistov he mentioned that the only time he personally wrote to Stalin was in connection with Yezhov's failure in an operation to exfiltrate a prominent European Comintern member. In his blackmailing letter Orlov repeatedly blames Spigelglass for many criminal blunders by way of letting Yezhov know that he was aware that the NKVD was really responsible.

49 Zborowsky was a Pole who had been recruited late in 1933 by NKVD agent B–138 ZBOROWSKY File No. 31660, Vol. 1, p. 1, RISA; ORLOV *Legacy*, p. 16.

50 Oleg Tsarev interview with Lieutenant General Pavel Sudoplatov, 2 June 1992.

51 SPIGELGLASS investigation File No. 21746, Vol. 1, pp. 198–9, MSA.

Chapter 13: "In Constant Fear of Their Lives"

1 Orlov's sworn statement to INS investigators 27 June 1955, NY 105–6073 Serial 303, ORLOV in FBI File 104–22869, FOIA, (hereafter ORLOV INS FBI 27 June 1955).

2 *Ibid.*

3 *Ibid.* Los Angeles FBI field office report of interview with Nathan Koornick on 22 September 1954, File No. LA 105–1608, ORLOV FBI File No. 105–22869, FOIA, (hereafter KOORNICK FBI).

4 *Ibid.* Information provided to the FBI by confidential informant T–3 (cross referencing to contents to serial 101 indicates that the source was George Sokolsky) Serial 88 NY 105–60732, 12 May 1953 SAC New York (105–60732), Serial 126 ORLOV File FBI No. 105–22869, FOIA (hereafter SOKOLSKY FBI).

5 Record of Sworn Statement with J. J Caudio and S. E. Mason INS "Q & A Statement of Alexander & Maria Orlov" taken New York 27 June 1955 Folio 299 in ORLOV FBI No. NY 105–675 in ORLOV FBI 105–22859, FOIA (hereafter ORLOV INS Q & A June 1955 FBI).

6 SOKOLSKY FBI.

7 ORLOV INS 27 May 1955 FBI.

8 Orlov, *Stalin's Crimes*, p. xiv.

9 ORLOV INS 27 May 1955 FBI and ORLOV FBI.

10 John Finerty *et al, The Case of Lev Trotsky*, New York, 1938.

11 Information given by Finerty to FBI in Serial 30, ORLOV FBI File No. 104–22869, FOIA.

12 *Ibid.*

13 Orlov's movements listed by FBI on the basis of information supplied by Orlov, Serial 147, p. 1, ORLOV FBI File No. 104–22869, FOIA.

14 Copy of Orlov's letter to Trotsky signed STEIN and dated 27 December 1938, submitted as part of his testimony to SISSC September 1955 reproduced in full in ORLOV *Legacy*, p. 38.

15 *Ibid.*

16 Information supplied by David J. Dallin in testimony to SISSC in Orlov *Legacy* p. 29.

17 According to Orlov's testimony in ORLOV *Legacy*, p. 30.

18 FIN (Paris *rezident* Georgy Kosenko alias Kislov) to Centre 25 June 1959 cryptogram in ZBOROWSKY File No. 31660, Vol. 1, pp. 262–64, RISA.

19 *Ibid.*

20 Cryptogram from Paris *rezidentura* to the Centre dated 15 July 1939, ZBOROWSKY File No. 31660, Vol. 1, pp. 262–64, RISA.

21 Undated memorandum from "BOB" to "BEN" reporting Orlov's reaction to reading Zborowsky's statements in Senate Internal Security Sub-Committee investigatory records, ZBOROWSKY File RG 46 NAW.

22 Report in ZBOROWSKY FILE NO. 31660, Vol. 1, p. 1, RISA.

23 Letter to Benjamin Mandel, 10 October 1955, in ORLOV file Investigatory Records of Senate Internal Security Sub-Committee, RG 46 NAW.

24 Los Angeles SAC report 4 February 1954 File No. 105–1608, Serial 162 in ORLOV FBI File No. 104–22869, FOIA.

25 *Ibid.* Report on interview with Dr Lyster.

26 Report of 3 March 1942 in "Alexander Berg Internal Security-G (German)" Serial 1 in ORLOV FBI File No. 104–22869, FOIA.

27 Interview of name-deleted clerk of the Pilgrim Trust Company reported by FBI Boston, 3 March 1942, File No. 62–1246, Serial 1 ORLOV FBI File No. 104–22869, FOIA.

28 *Ibid.* Report from FBI New York File No. 105–6073 to director FBI, 9 October 1954, Serial 250, ORLOV FBI File No. 105– 22869, FOIA.

29 Letter and enclosure addressed to Nicolay Ivanovich (Yezhov) signed "Schwedov" (ORLOV File 76659, Vol. 1, p. 98, RISA.)

30 Report from FBI Boston Office, 1 August 1943, noting a report filed in 1942 by telephone from Mrs. J. E. Connell, File No. 105–1024, Serial 63 in ORLOV FBI File No. 104–22869, FOIA.

31 Orlov INS, 23 June 1955 in ORLOV FBI File No. 104–22869, FOIA.

32 Report from FBI Boston office, 3 March 1942, "Alexander Berg – Internal Security – G", Serial 1 in ORLOV FBI File No. 104–22869, FOIA.

33 Information furnished to FBI by John F. Finerty, Serial 64 in ORLOV FBI File No. 104–22869, FOIA.

34 Ibid.

35 Orlov in his first examination by the INS claimed that he could not remember whether he gave their lawyer or his friend Rosovsky as their contact. Although the actual name is blanked out in the released records, it is clear that it must have been Rosovsky, since Finerty's legal firm was too long a name to fit in the deleted space.

36 June 1953 report on interview of Eggleton NY 105–6073, Serial 39, p. 11, in ORLOV FBI File No. 104–22869. The detail of Orlov's Aliens Registration fingerprint card No. 2 472 620, 19 December 1940, given in FBI memo to Tolson, 29 April 1953, ORLOV FBI File No. 104–22869, FOIA.

37 FBI Eggleton report Ibid.

38 Information supplied by Mrs Connell to Boston FBI, 13 August 1953, Serial 63, p. 2, ORLOV FBI File No. 104–22869, FOIA.

39 Interview of name-deleted clerk of the Pilgrim Trust Company reported by FBI Boston, 3 March 1942, File No. 62–1246, Serial 1, p. 2, ORLOV FBI File No. 104–22869, FOIA.

40 Ibid.

41 Ibid. Philadelphia FBI field office report, 17 September 1942, File No. 100–11986, Serial 5 ORLOV FBI File No. 104–22869; FBI Boston report, 1 September 1942, File No. 62–1246, Serial 2, ORLOV FBI File No. 104–22869, FOIA.

42 Krivitsky's NKVD file, as previously reported, shows that NKVD surveillance of him ended in 1939, but the suspicion that his death was not suicide remains. The most detailed recent analysis that points to foul play is given by Verne W. Newton, op. cit., pp. 30–2.

43 Boston FBI field office report, 18 August 1953, File No. 105–1024, ORLOV FBI File No. 104–22869, FOIA.

44 Report from Cleveland FBI field station, 16 July 1953, File No. 105–639, FBI Serial 48, ORLOV File No. 104–22869, FOIA.

45 Ibid.

46 Ibid. Anonymous informant cited in the above report from FBI field station Cleveland.

47 Photocopy of original note in Pittsburgh FBI field station report, File No. 100–91869–19, Serial 17, ORLOV FBI File No. 104–22869, FOIA.

48 Reports and letters originated in Boston and Pittsburgh under BERG Security Matter G, 11 September 1943, Serial 7 and 8, ORLOV FBI File No. 104–22869, FOIA.

49 Information and reports in Serials 8–15, ORLOV FBI File No. 104–22869, FOIA.

50 Special agent Soucy to FBI Director, 14 February 1944, enclosing copies of the Berg letter and Pilgrim Vault agreement, Serial 10, ORLOV FBI File No. 104–22869, FOIA.

51 Report from Boston FBI field station, 6 August 1955, ORLOV FBI File No. 104–22869, FOIA.

52 Ibid.

53 Pittsburgh FBI reports, 26 December 1944, 11 September 1945, Serial 16 and 17, ORLOV FBI File No. 104–22869, FOIA.

54 Report from Boston FBI field station, 13 August 1953, File No. 105–1024, Serial 63, p. 5, ORLOV FBI File No. 104–22869, FOIA.

Chapter 14: Closely Guarded Secrets"

1 Orlov, *Stalin's Crimes*, Preface.

2 *Ibid.* p. x.

3 *Ibid.*

4 *Ibid.*

5 Igor Gouzenko defected on 5 September 1945. The principal published source on his revelations is *The Report of the Royal Commission*, 27 June 1946, Ottawa. See also Gouzenko's own account *Iron Curtain*, Dutton, New York, 1948.

6 For Bentley's testimony see her signed statement of 30 November in FBI No. 65–56402 and the updated version of her own account *Out of Bondage* annotated by Hayden Peake, Ivy Books, New York, 1989. A recent thorough and objective analysis of the convoluted Whittaker Chambers case is given by Allen Weinstein in *Perjury, The Hiss-Chambers Case*, Knopf, New York, 1978.

7 Hoover report, 25 November 1945, introduced as evidence in the House Committee hearing on Un-American Activities, Communist Espionage in the United States, 80th Congress, 2nd Session (1948), pp. 113–14 (hereafter HUAC 1948).

8 Truman and Hoover quoted by Robert J. Donovan in *Conflict and Crisis: The Presidency of Harry S. Truman 1945–1948,* Norton, New York, 1977, p. 174.

9 For Bentley's testimony, see above sources. For an analysis of the unproven case against Harry Dexter White, see the FBI documentation cited by David Rees in *Harry Dexter-White: A Study in Paradox*, Coward McCann & Geoghegan, New York, 1973. Hede Massing's account is given in her statements to the FBI and her book *This Deception*, Duell Sloane & Pearce, New York, 1951. For an analysis of the evidence against Hiss, see Weinstein, *Perjury*. The RIS has declined to make available any material on Hiss on the ground that it does not have any. Until the actual files are released by the GRU it will be impossible for Western historians to pass final judgment whether Hiss wittingly or unwittingly assisted the Soviets as both Bentley and Whittaker Chambers alleged in sworn testimony.

10 Information supplied from US counter-intelligence sources who knew Orlov to Brook-Shepherd, *The Storm Petrels*, Collins, London, 1977, p. 218.

11 Cleveland FBI field office report 105–639, 31 January 1955, IRR ORLOV File Army Staff Record RG 319 NAW.

12 Interview with Florence Kellerman (née Koornick) New York, 31 January 1955, FBI New York 105–6073 Serial 257, in ORLOV FBI 105–22869 FOIA.

13 For a recent re-appraisal of the Rosenberg case see Ronald Radosh and Joyce Milton, *The Rosenberg File*, Holt, Rinehart & Winston, New York, 1983. An authoritative summary of the secret evidence of the case against Cohen, Elitcher and Gray and of the Rosenbergs' involvement in Soviet atomic espionage operations obtained from the intercepted VENONA traffic is given by the FBI counter-intelligence officer Robert Lamphere in *The FBI-KGB War*, pp. 183–290.

14 An authoritative account of the VENONA/BRIDE code-breaking was provided by Lamphere in *FBI-KGB War*. Despite repeated calls by such distinguished American historians as Arthur J. Schlesinger Jr for the release of the historically important decrypts, both the NSA and GCHQ refuse to sanction their release on the grounds that they are still yielding useful operational information.

15 Centre to London Station 17 May 1951, BURGESS File No. 83792, Vol. 4, p. 298. For detailed account of the Burgess/Maclean escape see Costello, *Mask of Treachery*. But this must be revised in the light of the information in the KGB files.

16 Sokolsky FBI interview. Although the released files have his name deleted, that he was the subject is clear from comparing the information in the statements made that

are repeated in his review of Orlov's book in the 30 October *Washington Times Herald*. See Memorandum LB, Nichols to Tolson, 17 October 1953, Serial 101; New York teletype, 2 November 1953, Serial 102; Report on interview, 5 November 1953; Report on interview, 17 November 1953, Serials 108 and 119, ORLOV FBI File No. 105–22869, FOIA.

17 Orlov testimony at first INS hearing, , 29 April 1954 in FBI ORLOV File No. 105–22869, FOIA. Sokolsky was the FBI source designated T–3 in the administrative records. FBI New York field office report on interview File No. 105–6073, 1 December 1953, Serial 126, ORLOV FBI File No. 105–2286, FOIA. He had contact with the intelligence community through Admiral Hillenkotter, the former Director of the Central Intelligence Agency, to whom he immediately reported Orlov's account of his defection and motivation.

18 *Ibid*, SOKOLSKY FBI.

19 Fischer interview 19 May 1953 in FBI New York Field office report, File No. 105–6073, Serial 30, ORLOV FBI File No. 105–22869, FOIA.

20 Orlov, *Stalin's Crimes*, Foreword p. ix.

21 *Ibid*, p. xv.

22 *Ibid*.

23 *Ibid*.

24 A search of the relevant Soviet records shows that no KGB agent by the name of Vladimirov was operating in New York in the summer of 1953. He appears to be another potential assassin like Bolodin who Orlov 'invented' to bolster his contention that his life was in danger.

25 Director FBI to Commissioner of INS, 7 May 1953, quoting the 7 April letter about Orlov. Serial 4, ORLOV FBI File No. 105–22869, FOIA.

26 Unnamed official interviewed and cited by Brook Shepherd, *The Storm Petrels*, p. 225.

27 FBI ORLOV FILE No. 105–22869, FOIA.

28 Report on interview with T–3 (Sokolsky), 5 November 1953, FBI New York field office file No. 105–6073, ORLOV FBI File No. 105–22869, FOIA.

29 Most of the FBI deletions from the Orlov file are so marked (b) (1) under SubSections of Title 5, US Code Section 552.

30 ORLOV File C8 04 31 16, IRR Army Staff Records RG 319 NAW. The FBI's p. 116 summary file, 29 March 1954, of which only the contents page (which it enables to be used to identify sources deleted in the FBI's more heavily sanitized version) was not removed by the military declassification process. ORLOV File C8 04 31 16 IRR Army Staff Records RG 319 NAW.

31 Hoover to State Department, 20 July 1959, ORLOV FBI File No. 105–22869, FOIA. The suggestion that this code clerk might have been Tyler Gatewood Kent was not borne out, however, by Costello's investigation of the case records and lengthy interviews. Kent did not in any case become a code clerk at the US embassy in Moscow until 1938! See *Ten Days to Destiny*, William Morrow, New York, 1991.

32 Interview with Edward McCarthy, February 1992.

33 Confidential source (also interviewed by the author) who confirmed making this statement to Brook-Shepherd who cited it anonymously in *The Storm Petrels*, p. 236.

34 Philby KGB Memoir, p. 118, RISA.

35 Orlov 1957 SISSC testimony in *Legacy*, p. 72–8.

36 *Ibid*. Ege had defected in Turkey on 3 June 1942.

36 *Ibid*.

37 *Life* Magazine 11 May 1953, "Letters to the Editor".

38 *Ibid*. Bolodin's name cannot be found in the NKVD files.

39 SAC New York letter to Director FBI, 8 June 1954, reporting on the question of Orlov on Krivitsky's book *I Was Stalin's Agent*, File No. 105–6073 in ORLOV File No. 105–22869, FOIA. Intriguingly Orlov's answers which appear in a version of this report released in the 1970s have been excised from the authors' 1992 FOIA release!

40 New York FBI field office File No. 105–6073 reports on interviews with Fischer, 3 March 1953, Serial 172 ORLOV File No. 105–22869, FOIA.

41 Sokolsky's review *Stalin's Crimes* in *Washington Times Herald*, 30 October 1953.

42 Report to Director FBI from New York File No. 105–22869, 5 November, Serial 103 Memo from Nichols to Tolson, 17 October 1953, Serial 101, ORLOV FBI File No. 105–22869, FOIA.

43 *Ibid.*

44 The CIA was mentioned in the letter of 30 June 1953 from the Washington INS office, Serial 44, ORLOV FBI File No. 105–22869, FOIA.

45 Sokolsky FBI interview, 5 November 1953.

46 Memo to Hoover's aide Tolson from L. B. Nichols, 17 October 1953, Serial 101 and heavily censored and undated memorandum apparently of October 1953 citing telephonic discussion with Mario T. Noto of the Central Office of the INS in Washington, Serial 86, ORLOV FBI File No. 105–22869, FOIA.

47 FBI 116-page summary report of Orlov case, 29 March 1954, Serial 186 and Sokolsky interview in ORLOV FBI File No. 105–22869, FOIA.

48 Orlov's sworn statement to INS and Rosovsky interview by FBI cited on p. 113, summary report of Orlov case, 29 March 1954, Serial 186, ORLOV FBI File No. 105–22869, FOIA.

49 Francis E. Walter to J. Edgar Hoover, 6 January 1954, Serial 151, ORLOV File No. 105–22869, FOIA.

50 Hoover to Hon. Francis E. Walter "Personally Confidential", 12 January 1954, ORLOV FBI No. 105–22869, FOIA.

51 Summary report in ORLOV FBI 105–22869, FOIA.

52 Orlov sworn INS testimony 29 April 1954, ORLOV FBI File No. 105–22869, FOIA.

53 SAC Miami from Director FBI, 22 April 1954, File No. 105–651, Serial 175, ORLOV FBI File No. 105–22869, FOIA.

54 New York File Office report to Director 23 August 1954, Serial 237, ORLOV FBI File No. 105–22869, FOIA.

55 Sworn statement by Orlov in INS examination, 27 June 1955, p. 15, Serial 303, ORLOV FBI File No. 105–22869, FOIA.

56 Summary Report on Grand Jury proceedings in FBI New York, 7 September 1955, FBI File No. 105–6073, ORLOV FBI File No. 105–22869, FOIA.

57 *Ibid.* See Louis Fischer, *Men and Politics*, p. 428. The FBI did not pursue Fischer, not only because they already knew of his strong Communist sympathies and activities but because he co-operated with their investigations of Orlov. No information has come to light in the NKVD files to suggest that Fischer was a Soviet intelligence agent. His pro-Communist activities are recorded since he was a correspondent of *Nation* magazine in the USSR from 1922 to 1937. In 1937 he left Moscow, ostensibly on a Comintern mission to organize an aid campaign for Republican Spain. He is described in one NKVD report as a Trotskyist sympathizer (untitled surveillance file on Trotskyists. File No. 26429). In another report from New York dated 10 February 1937 it is noted that the journalist had arrived there after briefly visiting France and Spain on his way over from Europe. In New York it is recorded that he got in touch with the Socialist Committee to Aid Spain whose members included many Trotskyist elements as this report noted (untitled surveillance file on Trotskyists and their sympathisers. File No. 27446, Vol. 8, p. 391, RISA).

There is also a contemporary reference to material obtained from French intelligence files (presumably from a Soviet penetration agent) which describes Fischer as "a Russian agent who by ministerial decree was banned from living in France".

Orlov encountered Fischer when he visited Spain, on a mission for the Comintern. In the light of the references to the journalist's strong Trotskyist sympathies it is highly unlikely that Orlov or any other NKVD officer who valued his career would have attempted to recruit him at that time.

58 Report from FBI New York File No. 105–6073 to director FBI, 29 October 1954, Serial 250, ORLOV FBI File No. 105–22869, FOIA.

58 Ibid.

59 Los Angeles FBI field office report of interview on 22 September 1954, with Nathan Koornick, File No. LA 105–1608, ORLOV FBI File No. 105–22869, FOIA.

60 FBI New York field office report on Kellerman interview, 31 January 1955, File No. NY Serial 257 105–6073, ORLOV FBI File No. 105–22869, FOIA.

61 FBI Summary report Serial 274, 31 March 1955, ORLOV FBI File No. 105–22869, FOIA.

62 This required "persons having had training in or assignment on or having knowledge of espionage or related activities" to complete a questionnaire. Orlov's notarized answers did not yield any new information to the FBI because he stuck to career details he had already admitted in his book, listing "Felix Dzerzhinsky, Henry [sic] Yagoda, Vyacheslav Menshinsky, Nikolay Yezhov and A. Slutsky" as the "persons under whom the assignments were carried out". FBI summary report, 31 March 1955, File No. NY 105–6073, Serial 274, ORLOV FBI File No. 105–22869, FOIA.

63 Summary report on Orlov by Director FBI to Liaison representative with the RCMP in Ottawa, 19 July 1955, Serial 293, ORLOV FBI File No. 105–22869, FOIA.

64 Senate Bill Serial 1627, 84 Congress 1st Session Bill S.1627 which was read twice and referred to the Committee on the Judiciary.

65 FBI New York field office report to headquarters, 23 June 1955, Serial 23, ORLOV FBI File No. 105–22869, FOIA.

66 Ibid.

67 Ibid.

68 Orlov INS Q & A examination, 27 June 1955 Serial 303, ORLOV FBI File No. 105–22869, FOIA. Later he wrote to the Part of Antwerp authorities and established that the Svir had indeed docked there. DST ORLOV (see Appendix III).

69 Ibid, and FBI New York field office report, 30 September 1955, Serial 303, ORLOV FBI File No. 105–22869, FOIA.

70 Ibid.

71 Letter to the Hon. Herbert Brownell from Norman Thomas, 1 July 1955, quoted in SAC New York to Director FBI, 30 September 1955, ORLOV FBI File No. 105–22869, FOIA.

72 Letter to Norman Thomas from Almanza Tripp, Acting Director INS New York, 4 September 1955, Ibid.

73 Sourwine to Orlov in Orlov Folder, SISSC, RG 46 NAW.

74 Orlov testimony, 25 September 1955, to SISSC in Legacy, p. 21.

75 Ibid.

76 Ibid.

77 Ibid, p. 23.

78 This is advanced by Herbert Romerstein and Stanislav Levchenko, The KGB against the "Main Enemy" – How the Soviet Intelligence Service Operates Against the United States, Lexington Books, Massachusetts, 1989, p. 179.

79 Ibid, and see Boris Morros in My Ten Years as a Counterspy, Viking Press, New

York, 1959, asserting he was the one who went to the FBI, but this is less plausible than the FBI version.

80 Interview with Robert Lamphere October 1992 amplifying his statements in *The FBI–KGB War*, pp. 87–88.

81 "Mark Zborowsky, 2451 Webb Avenue, Bronx, New York in a series of interviews conducted on December 2, 6, 10, 1954 and January 14, 27 1955, furnished . . . information concerning his involvement in Soviet espionage." FBI Report No. NY 105–17490 undated in ORLOV FBI File.

82 The report that cannot be located in Zborowsky's KGB File was produced in evidence at his trials and is cited by Romerstein and Levchenko on p. 197.

83 In 1945 whatever meagre correspondence there had been after his arrival in the US ceased and it records he was "frozen". Zborowsky File No. 31660.

84 Reports of the Zborowsky trials in the *New York Times*, 21 November 1958, 21–28 November 1962.

85 *Ibid*. After his release Zborowsky went to the West Coast and resumed his career as a medical anthropologist. He was for a time a visiting lecturer at the University of California and attached to the Mount Sion Hospital in San Francisco before his death, 12 May 1990.

86 Letter from Orlov to Jay Sourwine, 23 January 1956, in Orlov Folder. Investigatory Records of the Senate Internal Security Sub-Committee RG 46 NAW.

87 Orlov testimony to SISSC February 1955 in *Legacy*, pp. 33–85.

88 Interviews with Feoktistov.

89 "Subject: David and Lydia Dallin" from Orlov DST File.

90 *Ibid*. Rumsey was one of those conducting the interviews of Orlov which took place on 15 and 16 April 1965.

91 Orlov's letter and attachment are in ORLOV File 76659, Vol. 1, p. 98, RISA.

92 Kosenko to Centre, 19 August 1938 in ORLOV File No. 76659, Vol. 1, p. 101, RISA.

93 "Through agent DON who had left, as you suggested we have introduced in the underground Trotskyist group in Barcelona agent STED who is known to you. Thus we have retained in our hands the illegal communications channels between this group and the Trotskyist centre in Paris – STED will receive the first batch of correspondence in the next few days." Orlov letter of 24 May 1938, "Correspondence of the *Rezidentura* in Spain", File No. 19897, Vol. 3, p. 156, RISA.

94 "Subject: David and Lydia Dallin" from Orlov DST File.

95 *Ibid*.

Chapter 15: "A Professional to the End of His Days"

1 Report in ORLOV File No. 103509, Vol. 1, pp. 85–9, File No. 16659, Vol. 1, p. 150, RISA.

2 Orlov's testimony to SISSC on 25 September 1955, in *Legacy*, pp. 21–2.

3 ZBOROWSKY File No. 31660, Vol. 1, p. 187, RISA.

4 Orlov, *The Sensational Secret Behind the Damnation of Stalin*, *Life* Magazine, Vol. 48, No. 17, 23 April 1956.

5 *Ibid*.

6 *Ibid*.

7 *Ibid*.

9 Isaac Don Levine, *A Document on Stalin as a Czarist Spy*, *Life* Magazine, Vol. 48, No. 17, 23 April 1956.

10 Interview with Mrs Ruth Levine, Washington, March 1992.

11 *Life* Magazine, 23 April, 1956.

12 The full extent and significance of Abel's activities in the United States were never fully established and he made no confession. But his importance as a high-level underground *rezident* was established from documents and decrypted messages in his possession and information provided by the confessions of his disgruntled assistant. In addition to radio sets and hollowed-out nails and coins for concealing microdots, the microfilmed messages he carried were translated with the cyphers supplied by Hayhanen, which hinted at the wide extent of Abel's network. He had photographs of the Cohens. Hayhanen also admitted he had stolen the refunds that he had been instructed to supply to the "wife of STONE", the code name the FBI knew was used by the Soviets for Mrs Sobell, the wife of the Rosenbergs' co-defendant Morton Sobell. Published accounts of the Abel case include that of his US attorney, James B. Donovan, *Strangers on a Bridge*, Atheneum, New York, 1964; Sanche de Gramont, *The Secret War*, G. P. Putnam's Sons, New York, 1962; Louise Bernikow, *Abel*, Trident Press, New York, 1962; Kirill Khenkin, *op. cit.*; Edward Van Der Rhoer, *The Shadow Network: Espionage as an Instrument of Soviet Policy*, Charles Scribner's Sons, New York, 1983. Articles by Abel were also published in Soviet newspapers including *Trud* 127, February 1966. Lamphere also covers his involvement in the case in Lamphere and Shachtman, *op. cit.*

13 Information supplied by US intelligence veterans.

14 Romerstein and Levchenko, *op. cit.*, p. 259. Fisher was born on 11 July 1893 in Newcastle, England, the son of Genrikh Matveyvich Fisher, a Russian emigré radical who had been an associate of Lenin. In 1921 the family returned to the Soviet Union, according to Khenkin's account, living in the Kremlin along with Lenin and the rulers of the new state. Although Fisher had a penchant for art, he became a radio engineer and, after service in the Red Army, joined the NKVD and went through training school, where he met a fellow student, Rudolf Ivanovich Abel, whose name he was eventually to adopt.

Khenkin, however, claimed that Fisher told him that he used his British passport to undertake a mission to England "in the late twenties", accompanied by Orlov, whom he used to report to in a succession of London pubs where he "behaved like a conspirator in a grand opera". (Even if Khenkin is correct, he appears confused over the dates since Orlov did not take over the NKVD residency in London until 1934.) The object of Fisher's mission was supposedly to persuade the eminent Soviet physicist Pyotr Kapitsa to abandon his Cambridge laboratory and return to work in the Soviet Union. Kapitsa did return and Stalin's withholding of his exit visa in 1935 brought protests from the international scientific community. Fisher, according to Khenkin, returned from England in 1931 and was sent on underground operations to Denmark, returning to Moscow in 1938, where he survived the purges.

On the outbreak of war Fisher trained radio operators for the Fourth Department of the NKVD for partisan operations; one of these was Konon Molody. Then, in 1948, under an assumed identity in a communication network, he instructed the Cohens, among others, in the techniques necessary to relay information to Moscow. In 1950, when the FBI rolled up the atomic espionage network in which the Cohens and the Rosenbergs were said by the Americans to be involved, Fisher's cover was too deep to be blown. It was a measure of his increased importance to Moscow that he was then assigned an assistant, Hayhanen, whose own carelessness, womanizing and fondness for the bottle contributed to Fisher's undoing. Van Der Rhoer, *op. cit.*, which draws heavily on Khenkin, reconciles some of his more obvious conflicts.

15 Khenkin, *op. cit.*, private translation, pp. 274, 281.

16 Vladimir and Evdokia Petrov, *Empire of Fear*, Praeger, New York, 1956, p. 56.

17 CIA officer as cited by Brook-Shepherd in *The Storm Petrels,* p. 238, and confirmed in interviews with American counter-intelligence veterans by the author.

18 The RIS does not wish to identify the source who put them on to Orlov, who in the autumn of 1964 supplied the information that he had recently met a former Soviet citizen who was a lecturer at a university in the north of the United States. According to this source, Orlov had admitted to being a high-ranking NKVD officer in Spain from 1936–9, when he had fled to the West. Orlov had shown the informant his collection of books about the USSR and said that he had been living under his real name for the last three years – but he did not say where his home was. See the Damage Assessment in ORLOV File No. 103509, Vol. I, p. 160 RISA.

19 December 1969 damage assessment report in ORLOV File No. 103509, Vol. I, p. 160, RISA

20 SAC New York to Director FBI included a reference to a letter, 10 December 1962, notifying them that Orlov was now at apt. 703, 400 Maynard Street, Ann Arbor, telephone 665–4871, and noted that he was employed at the University of Michigan. File NY 105–6073, Serial 354, ORLOV FBI File No. 105–22569, FOIA.

21 SAC Detroit to Director FBI, Serial 353, ORLOV FBI File No. 105–228659, FOIA.

22 *Ibid.*

23 *Ibid.*

24 File NY. 105–6073 Serial 354, ORLOV FBI File No. 105–228659, FOIA.

25 Report to ORLOV File No. 103509, Vol. I, p. 162, RISA.

26 ORLOV File No. 103509, Vol. I, pp. 205–21, RISA.

27 Feoktistov interview.

28 Confidential source.

29 ORLOV File No. 103509, Vol. I, pp. 205–21, RISA.

30 Feoktistov interview.

31 *Ibid.*

32 *Ibid.*

33 *Ibid.*

34 *Ibid.*

35 ORLOV *Legacy*, p. 12.

36 Feoktistov interview and ORLOV File No. 103509, Vol. I, pp. 205–21, RISA.

36 *Ibid.*

37 ORLOV *Legacy*, pp. 12–13.

38 Feoktistov interview.

39 *Ibid.*

40 *Ibid.*

41 Feoktistov interview and ORLOV File No. 103509, Vol. I, pp. 205–21, RISA.

42 *Ibid.*

43 *Ibid.*

44 ORLOV File No. 32476, Vol. I, p. 34, RISA.

45 Interview with Feoktistov.

46 *Ibid.*

47 *Ibid.*

48 *Ibid.*

49 Feoktistov operational report in ORLOV File No. 103509, Vol. I, pp. 205–21, RISA.

50 ORLOV *Legacy*, p. 13.

51 Letter from Orlov to his Russian sister-in-law, 2 December 1972, ORLOV File No. 103509, Vol. I, pp. 244–9, RISA.

52 US counter-intelligence officer who wishes his name to remain confidential, but

who has not changed his opinion since this unattributed quote was published in Brook-Shepherd, *Storm Petrels,* p. 238.

Appendix I

1 CORSICAN File No. 34118, Vol. 2, p. 23, RISA.
2 *Ibid.*
3 *Ibid.*
4 *Ibid.*
5 *Ibid.*
6 *Ibid.*
7 *Ibid*, p. 24.
8 *Ibid.*
9 *Ibid.*
10 *Ibid.*
11 *Ibid*, p. 25.
12 *Ibid.*
13 *Ibid.*
14 *Ibid.*
15 *Ibid.*
16 *Ibid*, p. 26.
17 *Ibid*, pp. 27–8.
18 *Ibid*, p. 30.
19 *Ibid*, pp. 31–2
20 *Ibid.*
21 *Ibid.*
22 *Ibid*, p. 33.

Appendix II

1 *Spravka*, Moscow Centre to Berlin, 12 April 1941, CORSICAN File No. 34118, Vol. 1, p. 249, RISA.
2 Cryptogram Korotkov to Moscow Centre, 12 April 1941, CORSICAN File No. 34118, Vol. 1, p. 346, RISA.
3 CORSICAN File No. 34118, Vol. 1, p. 22. The leaders and members of the Berlin network considered themselves in the first place anti-Fascists who saw in Communism and co-operating with its physical embodiment – the USSR – the only way to save Germany from Hitlerism. Therefore their strong ties with the Communist underground increased the danger of intelligence work.
4 Cryptogram Korotkov to Moscow Centre, 8 April 1941, CORSICAN File No. 34118, Vol. 1, p. 262, RISA.
5 Cryptogram Moscow Centre to Korotkov, 25 April 1941, CORSICAN File No. 34118, Vol. 1, p. 270, RISA.
6 Memorandum by Schulze-Boysen, CORSICAN File No. 34118, Vol. 1, p. 233, RISA.
7 Two books were to be purchased and one sent to Moscow. It must have been a simple cypher with one "slogan" word as the key, since SENIOR's transmitter was assigned the code word "schraube" and given 38745 as the number to use when transmitting letters into figures and vice versa.
8 CORSICAN File No. 34118, Vol. 2, p. 20, RISA.

9 *Ibid.*

10 Korotkov memorandum, April 1946, CORSICAN File No. 34118, Vol. 2, p. 120. RISA.

11 *Rote Kapelle* File No. 593621, Vol. 1, pp 20–23, RISA.

12 Trepper was a Pole who, after joining the Zionist movement in Palestine, in 1928 went to France, where he became a member of the Communist underground. Escaping the police operation that rolled up the so-called *Phatomas* network, Trepper went to Moscow, where he was trained by the GRU before being returned to Belgium, where he took over the underground network funded by the Foreign and Excellent Trenchcoat Company front. After the German occupation of Paris, Trepper, always managing to keep one jump ahead of the Gestapo, moved his headquarters to Paris, where from 1940–2 he acted as *"Le Grand Chef"* responsible for seven networks of Soviet agents, who the Germans believed constituted the principal part of the Red Orchestra. Finally arrested by the Gestapo in 1942 after a long hunt initiated by the interception of Moscow's message to KENT in the autumn of 1941, Trepper betrayed some of his collaborators and doubled for the Nazis during their *Funkspiel*, which succeeded in rounding up a large part of the *Rote Kapelle*. Trepper claimed he did this on orders from Moscow and thereby saved the most important section of the networks under his command. He escaped from the Gestapo in 1943 and by 1944 succeeded in smuggling himself back to Poland. In 1945 he was taken to Berlin along with his principal Gestapo adversary, Heinz Pannwitz, for interrogation. Imprisoned in the Lubyanka for eleven years, he was finally released and returned to Poland, still professing himself an ardent Communist patriot. His self-serving account of his wartime espionage operation, which has hitherto been regarded as an authoritative history of the *Rote Kapelle*, was published in France as *Le Grand Jeu*, Albin Michel, Paris, 1974.

13 Cryptogram GRU to KENT, 26 September 1941, File No. 93621, Vol. 1, p. 26, RISA.

14 *Rote Kapelle* File No. 593621, Vol. 1, pp. 20–23, RISA.

15 When Korotkov re-established contact with Harnack in 1940 his organization numbered some sixty members, the hard core being fifteen absolutely reliable people. In the autumn of 1942 the Gestapo arrested hundreds of people of whom 129 stood trial. This indicates a nine-fold growth in the intervening two years in the Berlin *Rote Kapelle* network. CORSICAN File No. 341188, Vol. 1, p. 108 and *Rote Kapelle* File No. 93621, Vol. 1, pp. 9–10, RISA.

16 Cryptogram KENT to GRU, November 1941, CORSICAN File No. 34118, Vol. 2, pp. 64–6, RISA.

17 *Ibid.*, pp. 54, 65–6.

18 Memorandum, 25 November 1941, CORSICAN File No. 34118, Vol. 2, p. 53, RISA.

19 This Soviet version, culled from the reports in the NKVD files and the postwar Soviet interrogations, gives a different perspective of the *Rote Kapelle* than Trepper's own version or that of Giles Perrault, *L'Orchestre Rouge*. It was clearly written to conceal his co-workers' names. The NKVD files clarify many important details found in the Gestapo records which formed the basis of the CIA's declassified analysis.

20 Trepper, p. 276.

21 Report for GRU Stockholm dated 24 June 1942. CORSICAN File No. 34118, Vol. 2, p. 106, RISA. The bottle may still be there today!

22 *Ibid.*

23 Stockholm cryptogram relayed via GRU, CORSICAN File No. 34118, Vol. 2, p. 111, RISA.

24 *Rote Kapelle* File No. 93621, Vol. 1, p. 202. The little-known wartime co-operation between SOE and the NKVD was initiated after the British representative Sir

Charles Hambro was "prepared" for a mission to Moscow for exploratory discussions in the autumn of 1941. An arrangement was reached by the end of September. The head of the SOE mission to Moscow was George Hill, Sidney Reilly's World War I colleague (and husband of Elizabeth, whom Burgess had targeted for recruitment under Orlov's direction in 1935) (see Chap. 7). Hugh Dalton, the Labour Minister responsible for SOE to the War Cabinet, informed Churchill in late September 1941 that, while the Russians had expressed "extreme willingness to co-operate on a subversive matter", it was essential to keep the SOE NKVD link very secret. So secret was it kept that very few details have ever emerged in the British histories about the twenty Soviet agents dropped into Europe by the RAF between 1941–2 and it appears that the mission was one of the first attempts at collaborative operations. See the reference in David Stafford, *Britain and European Resistance, 1940–45: A Survey of the Special Operations Executive with Documents*, University of Toronto Press, Toronto, 1980, pp. 69–70.

25 *Rote Kapelle* File No. 93621, Vol. 1, p. 202, RISA.

26 *Ibid.*

27 *Rote Kapelle* File No, 480677, Vol. 6, pp. 60–61, RISA.

28 *Ibid.*

29 D6 transmission to Moscow Centre, 8 October 1942, CORSICAN File No. 34118, Vol. 2, p. 124, RISA.

30 Barth co-operated with the Gestapo and worked for them on the Western front, which was confirmed later by the British. After he was captured by the Americans in 1945, he was passed over to the NKVD, interrogated and then tried before being shot for treason. *Rote Kapelle* File No. 93621, Vol. 1, pp. 202–3, RISA.

31 *Rote Kapelle* File No. 80607, Vol. 6, p. 17, RISA.

32 *Ibid.*

AFTERWORD

WHEN I APPROACHED KGB headquarters for the first time on a bone-chilling January day in 1991, I was struck by the whimsical quality of an edifice which belied the Lubyanka's grim reputation. Perched ten storeys above a custard-coloured façade banded by layers of chocolate-painted window pediments, the finials of the ornate clock appeared as candles atop a child's monstrous birthday cake. The fortress-like quality of its dark granite base was the only indication that there might be a sinister power lurking within the block-long building at "Number One Lubyanka Street".

It was only when crossing the square that then bore the name of the founder of the Communist Party's secret police system, that this forbidding force manifested itself in the fixed bronze stare of the statue of Feliks Dzerzhinsky. Now banished to a Moscow park along with the other gods of the Soviet pantheon, that morning the blackened forehead of "Iron Feliks" bore a snowy white mantle, while the traffic circling around his plinth mushed the delicate flakes as remorselessly as Dzerzhinsky and his successors had squashed all dissent in Soviet society for more than three-quarters of a century.

The very name "Lubyanka" had for so long been an embodiment of malign Soviet authority that when I came up to tug on the bronze handles of the unmarked entrance door, it brought to mind images from Tolkien's *Lord of the Rings*. Any fanciful images of cavernous chambers lit by flickering braziers abruptly vanished on entering the cramped white vestibule which was furnished with prosaic wooden chairs upholstered in the obligatory dull red of all Soviet-made office furniture. The entrance was guarded not by menacing dwarves and fire-breathing dragons, but by two smartly turned-out soldiers with the sky-blue KGB lapel flashes who seemed scarcely old enough to be out of school. They saluted smartly even though Colonel Oleg Tsarev was not wearing a uniform. My blue British passport and his red KGB pass appeared all that was needed to get me in without any attempt to search my bulging briefcase.

"Maybe it is easier to check into the Lubyanka than check out," I quipped as we entered the elevator, recalling the American television advertisements for the sticky insect traps named "Roach Motels". Oleg, whose sense of humour I had discovered the previous evening as we drove in from Sheremetyevo airport in a curtained KGB limousine, smiled. He explained that we had yet to enter a secure section of the building. That may have been the case, but getting into the KGB headquarters involved none of the security checks and computerised passes necessary to visit the CIA. Just to get into the main lobby of their modernistic headquarters at Langley near Washington, a visitor is required to pass through a battery of scanners, which I had discovered to my embarrassment were far more sensitive than those at any airport. They were capable of detecting magnetic recording material as insignificant as a long-forgotten microcassette cartridge in my jacket pocket.

Similar security checks – Oleg assured me – were in force at the Soviet intelligence services' headquarters at Yasenevo. No foreign visitors were permitted to enter the First Chief Directorate's main compound outside Moscow. That, he explained, was why the files I had asked to see on Rudolf Hess had been brought to the Lubyanka from the archives. When he fetched the so-called "Black Bertha" dossier from his office safe and placed it on the table in front of me, it was a moment of high anticipation for me, far exceeding any I had experienced in more than twenty years of researching the archives in Britain, the United States, France and Germany. Although the first Westerner to set eyes on actual volumes of KGB files, I could not help wondering if I was being permitted to do so for some ulterior reason that had yet to be explained to me.

The sight of Philby's actual reports about the British Foreign Office's secret response to the arrival of Hess in May 1941 sent the same shiver of anticipation down my spine that I imagine explorers experience on setting foot for the first time on uncharted territory. I yearned to bring out my camera from my briefcase and photograph the scene as proof that I really had been inside the KGB headquarters looking at historic files – later, with Oleg's permission, I did.

Sitting alongside Oleg, we turned the pages of the thick file as he translated. Now and again I noted that an occasional line or paragraph was covered with a slip of paper held in place by tiny Soviet-style paper clips. This he said was information that I could not be permitted to see for "operational reasons". According to Oleg, this was an all-embracing definition of why he had to deny me access. Since I could not read Russian, the precaution appeared to be somewhat unnecessary. Was this flimsy attempt at censorship perhaps an elaborate attempt to impress me? I asked myself. But when I found that only half a dozen sections had been covered up in the entire 250-page dossier, I realised that any such deception would have been on a larger scale.

Six weeks earlier when I had first seen photocopies of some of these documents I had been unaware that the notations were written in coloured inks. But this had not diminished my sense of excitement when I opened the sealed blue envelope that Oleg had sent to me via the Soviet mission to the United Nations. It had been brought to my apartment on 26 November by a Russian, who had telephoned earlier that Thanksgiving Day eve, to say he had been instructed to deliver the "documents I had requested from Moscow".

At first I was so surprised that I did not grasp what this man, who had identified himself as a Soviet journalist, was talking about. My immediate reaction was that I was being made the subject of a practical joke. Then I remembered six months earlier I had written to the KGB requesting documents. At the time I had been finishing the manuscript of *Ten Days to Destiny*, the result of a six-year investigation into how close the wartime British government really had come to making terms with Hitler. So when I read in the London *Sunday Times* a report of a Soviet newspaper article about Hess, whose mission was central to the theme of my book, my interest was aroused. New material on Hitler's deputy had been hard to come by because of the obsessive British secrecy surrounding the affair, but I had just received a hitherto unknown report of October 1941, which had recently been declassified by US military intelligence in response to a Freedom of Information Act application I had made a year earlier. My interest in the Soviet account peaked, for although its claims had been rubbished by the British historians asked to comment on the *Trud* article, they appeared to be corroborated by the information in a confidential briefing given by Churchill's intelligence aide to the US military attaché in London five months after the Hess flight. That very day I had therefore fired off a *pro forma* letter to KGB headquarters asking for their documentation.

I had no expectation of receiving a reply, so I was not quite able to believe my eyes when I opened the package that had arrived so unexpectedly from Moscow. In it I found a letter, in English, from the Deputy Head of the KGB Press Department, Oleg Tsarev. He wrote that he was sending me photocopies of the principal contemporary reports on which he had based his article, along with a copy of *Trud* in which it was printed. The Russian emissary, when he saw its contents, was evidently as surprised as I was. That much was clear from his startled reaction when I handed him a document originating from Philby, identified by Oleg's yellow "Post It" slip – it appeared that the KGB relied on American office products – as a "*spravka*". This, I was informed, was a technical term which my Soviet visitor could not explain, but he none the less agreed to give me a verbatim translation because he realised that the assumption made by "headquarters" that I was fluent in Russian had left me at a helpless disadvantage. He then read into my tape recorder a word-for-word translation of what appeared to be an identical report on Hess to the US army one I had received under the Freedom of Information Act. Also included was a 1942 memorandum from Lavrenty Beria addressed to Stalin and Molotov that quoted information received from a Colonel Moravetz, after he had seen an MI6 report on how Hitler's deputy had been lured into flying to Britain.

Oleg's handwritten letter proposed, as a *quid pro quo*, that I should send him a copy of the American report. Aware of the Soviet record of trapping the unwary as potential agents, I assured my Russian guest that I would have to consider this request. As he was scheduled shortly to return to Moscow, he said that I could communicate with the KGB Press Office via the Soviet mission to the United Nations on East 68th Street. I was supplied with the name and telephone number of an official who I was told could arrange for any correspondence to be sent directly to Moscow by diplomatic bag, since the US mail "was not trustworthy".

To guard against the possibility that I was being "set up" by the KGB, just as soon as I had said farewell to my Russian visitor, I made a series of telephone calls to contacts in Washington. While researching *Mask of Treachery*, my book on Anthony Blunt and the Cambridge spy ring, I had been introduced to many former members of the American intelligence community. These informed professionals who had contacts in the FBI and CIA provided advice that was once again to prove invaluable. While it was possible that I was being suckered into some devious disinformation plot, their opinion was that it was unlikely, given that I had made the first approach to the KGB. Since it would be obvious that I would have the documentation checked before publishing it, there would be no purpose in passing out forgeries. My Washington friends shared my astonishment on the release of the Philby paraphrased cryptograms and the Moravetz material. They found the correlation between the Soviet and the recently declassified American version convincing, but not proof positive, that the KGB documentation was authentic, advising that the documents should be studied by experts.

Since the declassified US Military Intelligence report that Tsarev had requested was now in the public domain, I was assured that there was no reason not to forward it to him. I was also encouraged to follow up the offer to go to Moscow as soon as possible and see the Hess file for myself, since a handful of photocopies hardly constituted a representative cross-section of a single Soviet intelligence dossier. To this end I wrote a carefully worded response that I sent the KGB headquarters, along with a copy of the American military attaché's report. Under the watchful electronic eyes of surveillance cameras – both Soviet and American as I later found out from contacts in the Washington FBI – I was observed handing in my letter to the Soviet mission on East 68th Street. Ten days later, shortly before I left to spend Christmas in England with my family, I received a telephone call from my Soviet contact, informing me that the KGB press office would issue an official invitation to me to go to Moscow during the first week of the New Year.

My first appreciation of the KGB's all-pervasive authority came after I returned to London, when two days before the Christmas weekend, I telephoned the Soviet consulate about issuing a visa. I was at first told they had closed that afternoon for the holidays and assured that it would be impossible for me to go to Moscow at such short notice because Intourist required a minimum of two weeks' notice to arrange a hotel in Moscow. It was only after I explained the KGB invitation that the consulate's attitude changed abruptly and I was requested to come to the office right away.

The London policeman on duty outside the dour Bayswater mansion watched with some surprise as I was buzzed in through the iron gates. I was personally greeted by an official, whom I took to be the *rezident*, who addressed me familiarly as 'John' and personally copied the pages of my passport. He arranged for the necessary paperwork to be processed overnight so that I might pick up the visa next day. Regretting his organisation could not arrange a hotel, he suggested, as Intourist had been so unhelpful, that I contact American Express. That did not come as a surprise. Once while lunching with a group of former CIA officers in Washington's exclusive Hay Adams Hotel, they identified as the KGB *rezident* a swarthy diner who paid for his meal with a Gold Amex Card. It seemed that Soviet intelligence operatives were never allowed to leave home without this vital piece of plastic!

As the iron gate clanged shut behind me, I smiled sheepishly at the "bobby", hoping that I would not be reported to MI5 as a potential Soviet spy recruit. Taking a taxi to the Haymarket bureau of American Express, I was assured by a nonplussed reservations clerk that they could never organise a hotel for me in Moscow at such short notice. Yet even American Express, it appeared, were willing to try once they were told that the KGB had invited me to Russia.

They booked my flight immediately and dispatched a telex advising their Moscow bureau to contact Oleg Tsarev at KGB headquarters for confirmation. The very next day they telephoned to say that a reservation had been made for me and that I would be met at the airport.

I had not had any direct communications with my host for weeks, save a cryptic telegram awaiting my arrival in London. But the week after Christmas when I set off for Moscow I was at least confident that American Express would come to my rescue even if the KGB did not come through. My concerns proved groundless when a stranger pushed forward through the crush of people in the gloomy arrivals hall at Sheremetyevo airport and greeted me warmly. He introduced himself as Oleg Tsarev. His quilted winter coat, pixieish smile and French cap somehow did not fit my impression of a Colonel in the KGB, but there was no doubt about the official-looking chauffered car which he had waiting to take me to the Mezdunrodnya Hotel.

Located on an unpicturesque bend of the Moscow river below the striking white Russian Parliament building, the equally modern but less architectually impressive 'Mezh' is located downwind of an electricity generating station constantly belching steam. This Soviet clone of a Hyatt hotel had all the amenities, but none of the style or service of its American model. I noted that the ubiquitous floor ladies outside every elevator were more elegant and youthful than the severe babushkas I remembered from my visit to Leningrad ten years earlier. Moreover, they now appeared to spend less time on surveillance of the traffic than watching television which was carrying CNN's blow-by-blow coverage of Saddam Hussein's brazen defiance of the UN ultimatum to pull the Iraqi invasion forces out of Kuwait.

Thanks to satellite, I was able to keep abreast with the Gulf Crisis next morning before Oleg arrived to take me to KGB headquarters. Stepping out into a snowy blast, I was fortified against the cold by the prospect of being the first Western historian to see Soviet intelligence files. After a memorable day in the Lubyanka examining documents that I never in my life ever expected to see, I treated Oleg to a depressing Soviet version of a Japanese dinner at the hotel. The next day being Saturday, I spent the afternoon checking out the amateur capitalists on the Arbat before deciding to celebrate that evening at the Bolshoi.

I took my chair in the box anticipating that an authentically Russian combination of Pushkin and Tchaikovsky would produce a memorable performance of *Eugene Onegin*. It was only when the curtain went up that I realised I had made a mistake about the Pushkin. As the orchestra wound its way into yet another performance of *Swan Lake*, I soon found it difficult to resist dozing off. In an effort to keep awake during what proved to be a saccharine, if mechanically polished performance of the familiar ballet, I began reflecting on what

Oleg had told me about his projected book on Alexander Orlov. By the time I was confronting the undulating white tutus of Act II, it suddenly struck me that there might be an opportunity for me to do more than simply help him with research in the FBI files. How, I wondered, would he react if I offered my services as a full collaborator?

Resisting the impulse to rush back to the hotel and telephone Oleg at home, I decided to mull over the idea during the weekend. I felt I might have already pressed my luck by asking him if it would be possible to make a television film about the Hess dossier. I had explained that close-ups of the "Black Bertha" file, with its heavily annotated pages hand-stitched into the yellowing cardboard binders, could demonstrate the veracity of the documentation in a way that no black-and-white copies ever could.

On Monday morning I telephoned Oleg to ask if it would be possible to drop into KGB headquarters on the way to the airport to discuss an important matter. Since the proposal for this joint collaboration was entirely my initiative – and it took Oleg by surprise – it was not a "put up job" contrived by the KGB. Moreover, it was, I said, to be based on a straightforward 50/50 business arrangement. To further safeguard my independence it was essential for the Western publishers to exercise full editorial control over the final manuscript and for all documentation to be checked in advance of publication. I was relieved that Oleg not only understood the reasons for such conditions, but saw that such a collaboration would add to the credibility and significance of the book. Since such a co-operation was quite unprecedented, he said that it might take some time for him to win approval "at the highest level" of the KGB.

We started none the less to discuss the details of the project and became so engrossed that the time for my afternoon flight to London was rapidly approaching. Since Sheremetyevo is notorious for its two-hour check-in times, Oleg volunteered to come out to the airport to speed up the formalities. He continued to take notes on the details of our proposed collaboration on the way past the dour clusters of high-rise apartment buildings towering up out of the gathering winter gloom on the outskirts of Moscow. Despite the dramatic changes that *Glasnost* had brought to the USSR, I could not forget that for all Oleg's seeming good nature and frankness he was a Soviet intelligence officer. There were further reminders of the all-pervasiveness of the organisation for which he worked at the airport. When I could not find currency control documents to be handed in before leaving the USSR, a powerful flash of Oleg's KGB pass removed what might otherwise have been a road block to my departure. As the guard waved me through the final security post, Oleg grinned at his remark, later telling me that the young soldier had asked whether I was a member of the "organisation". Although I laughed as I made my farewell, it occurred to me that the bearer of the British diplomatic passport behind me could well be a Secret Intelligence Service officer. I hoped that Special Branch would not pick me up for questioning at Heathrow. It was now too late to take the advice of my Washington friends to acquaint their opposite numbers in British intelligence of the reason for my mission to Moscow. But although I had the telephone numbers of the FBI counter-intelligence chief and had lectured inside the CIA, I had no way of contacting MI6, whose existence was at that time still not acknowledged officially. All I could do was trust that in the event of any problems, I would be able to rely on the Americans to vouch for my *bona fides*.

After working with my London publisher to rush through a new final chapter for *Ten Days to Destiny* based on the Soviet documents, I flew to the United States to discuss the Orlov project with my friends in Washington. Oleg had given me his home telephone number because he could not receive overseas calls at his office. Overseas calls to the KGB headquarters, as I found to my surprise, could only reach a duty officer who proved very unco-operative about taking messages! Indeed just getting through to Moscow was – still is – a frustrating process, often requiring a half-hour, or more, of repeated redialling to get through the beep-beep busy signal. I was therefore relieved eventually to get through to Oleg, who told me cheerfully that my request to film the documents had been approved and that he expected to have a favourable decision on our joint project very soon. In fact when I called back a few days later to arrange my return trip to Moscow with a film crew, he reported that he had just received the go-ahead for our collaboration on Orlov from the "highest authority".

The Chairman's decision came as something of a surprise to some of my intelligence contacts in Washington. In order to make a convincing case that Orlov had never been a true defector, the KGB would have to make available a substantial amount of documentation to justify their claim. What puzzled them was why Vladimir Kryuchkov would sanction this first-ever large-scale declassification of Soviet intelligence records. He had himself been the foreign intelligence chief before becoming Chairman and was known in both the USSR and the West as a hard-line communist with a record for successful disinformation operations.

Was this book collaboration to be yet another KGB ploy, or a sincere attempt to produce a genuine history? To try and ascertain what I was letting myself in for, I consulted Dr Ray Cline, a former CIA deputy Director and acknowledged expert on KGB operations. He is the Director of the Washington-based National Intelligence Study Center, which had honoured me in 1986 with its "Intelligence Book of the Year Award" and he himself had just made headlines as part of a group of former senior CIA officials who had recently met with a high-level KGB delegation in the United States under the banner of *Glasnost*. Dr Cline and his colleague Colonel Hayden Peake were intrigued by the proposed co-operative history venture. But they both cautioned me on the need to be on my guard, since experience had taught them that the KGB never acted without having an operational objective. The credibility of the book would depend on the documentation, and their considered opinion was that my involvement was coincidental to the strategy that Kryuchkov was implementing, to give the KGB a "friendly" public face and political legitimacy. This was manifested by his authorizing the setting up of a press office which had already collaborated with foreign television productions including documentaries on Philby and the Krogers. The Western press had even reported its efforts to mount a "Miss KGB" contest, although as I found out from Oleg, this had actually been organised as a spoof by a KGB summer youth camp.

The primary concern was how selective the KGB would be in releasing archival material. Would the documentation they declassified for the book be slanted to putting historical events in a most positive light? The release of the "Black Bertha" file was not inconsistent with such a policy, since it allowed the Soviets to claim to be serving the interests of history with documentation that appeared to show that Churchill and subsequent British governments had covered up the real reasons behind Hess's flight. Would the proposed book also serve to burnish the image of the Soviet intelligence service by showing how Orlov had been the mastermind behind the Soviet Union's penetration of British intelligence, who then went on to hoodwink the CIA and FBI? If this really was the truth, then the KGB would have to demonstrate it with convincing documentary evidence. This would require it to declassify many supporting files from its archive – and this in turn could only serve the interests of intelligence history.

Each party to the collaboration would therefore be balancing its own interests. One very senior active counter-intelligence officer, whom I consulted in an unofficial capacity, believed that there were certainly advantages to be gained by encouraging KGB to release documentation. But another distinguished retiree in the same field warned me that I was "putting my head into the lion's maw". He made no bones about his concern that I might be suckered into joining with the arch-enemy in a new conspiracy to belittle the Western intelligence services.

Good deceptions are, however, difficult to sustain since history cannot be denied the truth forever. It was clear to me that the truth about Orlov's story would stand or fall on the documentation the KGB chose to release. The range of evidence needed for a credible account was such that it could readily be checked against his own writings, the information in his FBI files and Congressional Record. The KGB would therefore have to produce a wide range of documents to make their case that he never was a true defector and this would require the release of material ranging from his passports, his operational reports and the contemporary documentation that would establish the role he played with Philby and the recruitment of the Cambridge spies. Its veracity by itself would, *ipso facto*, demonstrate the degree to which Orlov had – or had not – been able to deceive the CIA: he had clearly never betrayed Philby or the former MI6 officer would have been exposed long before his flight to Moscow in 1963.

Aware of the caveats and the historic opportunity, I returned to Moscow in mid-January 1991.

When the local TV crew I had hired was ushered into KGB headquarters, I was not sure whether the anxiety of the burly Russian cameraman named Misha was the result of his apprehension that he might not be let out of the infamous Lubyanka, or concern that by moonlighting from the airport he would miss covering the return of Primakov, Gorbachev's envoy to Saddam Hussein. I suspected that Misha was more concerned about losing face with the American networks, for whom he worked as a stringer. Earlier that morning, after fortification from the bottle of Red Label whisky I had brought to lubricate our co-operation, we had braved the snow flurries in Red Square. Misha had demonstrated his contempt for Soviet authority by setting up his tripod and filming without an official permit, counting on my assurance that we would be interviewing a KGB Colonel who would guarantee our immunity from arrest.

Unfortunately we did not bring the rest of the "Johnnie Walker" into KGB headquarters that afternoon. We could have used some fortification as the crew laboured on without a meal break well into the evening, filming page after page of the Hess and Moravetz files. Oleg had arranged for us to interview him in a deputy chairman's office overlooking Dzerzhinsky Square, where it was obvious from the richly panelled room with its adjoining sauna and bathrooms that rank carried a very special privilege in the Lubyanka. The massive mahogany desk was armed with a battery of ivory, green and red telephones attesting the former occupant's elevated status. Unable to resist the opportunity, I asked Oleg's permission to put a call in to a friend who was a counsellor at the American embassy. I wagered that she would never guess from where I was making the call – and won the bet!

Towards the end of the long taping session, I put to Oleg, on camera, the questions that were uppermost in my mind as the result of the conversations I had had with my Washington friends.

"Why had the KGB only now decided to release the Hess file and what was its operational purpose?"

"There were two main reasons," Oleg responded. "One was that fifty years had passed and those agents and sources such as Moravetz, who had provided the information about Hess, could not now be compromised." His second reason indicated how the tidal wave released by Gorbachev's political reforms was finally washing over the previously impenetrable bastion of the Soviet system.

"Lately we have changed our attitude towards the history of the KGB," Tsarev said, adding with what I took to be an understatement, "We are looking at it from a new approach."

The new approach of which I was now a part was a clear indication of the degree to which even the autonomous KGB *apparat*, for whom Oleg was the official spokesman, was being forced to transform itself to conform to the political realities of *Perestroika*.

"Why provide them to me?" I pressed. The response that I received made it clear that the KGB had not specifically targeted me as a vehicle for a disinformation operation.

"You were the first to ask for the records," Oleg said, explaining that it was simply my good fortune that my letter had reached headquarters in advance of other requests, and his article on "The Last Flight of Black Bertha" had made it possible to declassify the Hess documents.

"Why should we believe Soviet intelligence record?" I demanded. The reports in the "Black Bertha" file contradicted the accepted version, and according to the Soviet sources, Hess had been lured by an MI6 deception to fly to Scotland. He apparently had not only done so with Hitler's knowledge, but with a genuine offer of a final peace deal before the impending attack on the Soviet Union.

"You have been allowed to film the most important parts of these files," Oleg responded, his tone indicating an irritation that I doubted the evidence in the documents before him on the table. They were, as I could see, corroborated by the American archives and wartime Vichy

French intelligence reports that the Red Army had captured from the Germans at the end of the war. It would not be practical, he insisted, to have manufactured such old-looking files, whose pages bore original handwritten annotations and which had been stitched, in sequence, into the yellowing bindings.

"The KGB", I interrupted, "has a long track record of producing skilful forgeries."

"That would be impossible," Oleg insisted. While it was technically possible, I agreed that it was improbable given the current political situation. Apart from the enormous investment of time and resources that would have had to have been committed to such a deception, it would be highly damaging to the new image of Soviet openness to begin manufacturing historical forgeries whose only purpose would be to discredit me and my forthcoming book.

After we had completed the filming, I explained to Oleg how ironic it was that I found myself inside the KGB headquarters questioning the veracity of Soviet documents – including a stolen British MI6 report – when my own government refused to release *any* such intelligence records. I told him of my concerns that there would be a sceptical reception because the British Government would never permit the declassification of the MI6 files which would be the ultimate test of the veracity of the "Black Bertha" dossier. The Soviets might be embarking on a new era of "openness" but Britain's Official Secrets Act – despite its recent amendment – had been specifically tailored to maintain the confidentiality of all the intelligence service records.

As predicted, the credibility of the KGB records as a valid historical source came under immediate challenge when *Ten Days to Destiny* was published in the UK three months later. The battle was joined in print with accusations in *The Times* that the KGB had "lied about the mystery flight" by claiming that the Duke of Hamilton had been involved in a plot to lure Hess to Scotland. Oleg's intended visit to London to explain the KGB documents at first hand had to be cancelled when he was denied a visa, although the BBC interviewed him live from Moscow in a news broadcast which included clips of the film I had shot of him explaining the significance of the material in the "Black Bertha" file. The publication in *The Times* of my letter pointing out the inconsistencies of the British position opened the way for an exchange of letters which rumbled on for a month, concluding with Oleg's appeal for the relevant MI6 files on Hess to be released. This was the first letter – and as it turned out the last – ever published in the newspaper from an official of the KGB from the Lubyanka headquarters.

The debate prompted the British Government to initiate a review of the extensive number of Hess files still being withheld. But the documentation that was released the following year to the Public Records Office *did not* include Major Morton's report of his interviews with Hitler's Deputy, a copy of which I had obtained from both the US and KGB archives. Official assurances that nothing was being withheld which would give credence to the Soviet and American reports on Hess provided no substitute for releasing the actual documents.[1] If there was no conspiracy, then what prevents them putting the documents on the table and giving the lie to the Soviet version?

There is a regrettable irony that the ending of the Cold War has prompted the opening up of the historic intelligence files of the USSR while the British Government seems more determined than ever to keep the final truth of the Hess affair locked in the closet of official secrecy.

The controversy stirred up by the book only served to underscore the challenges that Oleg and I would confront with the Orlov project. But as I pointed out to him, it was an unfortunate but unavoidable fact that the legacy of seventy-five years of Soviet confrontation and conspiracy against the West inevitably raises suspicion about any documents from KGB archival sources. In contrast to files declassified by the British or American governments, which by and large tend to be accepted at face value, those from Soviet sources are regarded as tainted and condemned as unhistorical. The belief appears to prevail, especially in Britain, that any and all Soviet intelligence files must be treated as selective disinformation at best – and at worst as skilful forgeries designed to continue the Cold War by covert historical measures. The double standards by which the Hess material was judged were the inevitable result of decades of Soviet "active measures" of the past. It is a matter of record that the KGB and its predecessors had a long and notorious history of orchestrating the dissemination of forgeries to deceive the West. The most recent example was the effort to persuade the world that the shooting down of the Korean airplane in 1983 was the result of a deliberate US-orchestrated provocation of Soviet air space. Yet whether it was over the fate of Flight 007, or the wartime lie that it was the Germans, not the Red Army, who were responsible for the massacre of Polish troops in the Katyn Forest in 1941, or the elaborate hoaxes of the Trust and Syndicate operations of the 1920s, the Soviet record invites circumspection and distrust.

---

[1] One senior Foreign Office official with whom I exchanged correspondence in 1991 even went so far during a telephone conversation as to cast doubt on the US military attaché's version of Major Morton's report. While not admitting that the original might still exist, he declined to comment on my question that if the American document was a distortion of the truth, why could not the actual contemporary record be made available?

How to confront and dispose of this unfortunate historical legacy has been one of our major preoccupations in writing the Orlov book. It was a topic of discussion when Oleg came to New York in June 1991 to discuss the project with potential publishers and address the National Intelligence Study Center about the release of the Hess material in *Ten Days to Destiny*. That was why we chose to announce the Orlov project at a Washington press conference so as to invite questions that would give Oleg a chance to explain in person the KGB's decision to provide historians with hitherto secret historical evidence. Since there can never be a wholesale declassification, the question of whether such controlled access could contribute to a serious and scholarly attempt to set history straight is a parallel issue. Concern that the KGB might be mounting a carefully controlled and selective release of certain files to put a favourable spin on its own history was also addressed at meetings with intelligence veterans and publishers. In the course of extensive discussions it was agreed that the decision to release Soviet intelligence records was one to be welcomed in principle and carefully reviewed in detail.

So by the time we met with the senior executives of the Crown division of Random House, who had expressed a great interest in *Deadly Illusions*, James Wade, the highly regarded editor of a number of my previous books, appreciated that the project had support from American intelligence experts. While the professional expertise of these former CIA counter-intelligence officers, who had spent their careers duelling with the KGB, could not guarantee that the Soviet material was comprehensive, nor that it was not being slanted, their advice could act as a check against attempts to mislead me with partial truths, or deliberate misrepresentation. A number of the veterans consulted had had the advantage of having had access to the still classified CIA Orlov files, or were once personally involved in his debriefing. So they started out with a healthy scepticism for the Soviet contention that he was never a real defector from communism. Satisfying their demanding criticism was to be an essential test of our book's validity since the FBI, regrettably, could only be persuaded under FOIA to declassify less than half of their available archive files on Orlov – and none of the CIA records was made available to the project officially.

All the *caveats* were measured and the deal concluded. But no sooner had Oleg returned to Moscow and enlisted the aid of the Yasenevo records staff to mount a full search in their registry index than his efforts were disrupted by the August 1991 *coup* against Gorbachev.

On the afternoon of the first day of the dramatic events in Moscow, I picked up the telephone and managed to get through to

Oleg. Sounding remarkably collected in the midst of an upheaval, he assured me that whatever the outcome our project would survive because he already had sufficient files in his office safe at the Lubyanka to begin working up a Russian draft of the chapters dealing with the recruitment of the Cambridge ring. Cryptically, he advised me not to read too much into the Western news reports. But neither I, nor our publisher in New York to whom I immediately relayed his comments, initially entertained such confidence in the survival of our collaborative venture.

We could, however, take some comfort that we were able to remain in touch with Oleg as the storm broke around the Lubyanka and Dzerzhinsky was toppled by the mob from his plinth. It was apparent even to us that since the hardline communists of the Politburo who were behind the *coup* attempt had not been able to cut off telephone lines to the outside world then their conspiracy was neither as extensive, nor as well supported and orchestrated, as it had appeared from the first news reports. When Kryuchkov and the others appeared at the podium for their first televised news conference appealing for calm while obviously themselves shaken and insecure, it became clear Oleg had known more than we did about the conspiracy's shallow roots. Within seventy-two hours the Red Army tanks had been turned back from the Moscow Parliament building and the KGB chairman (who had sanctioned our project) was under arrest for his part in masterminding the failed *putsch*. His removal marked the beginning of the end for the KGB as the once impregnable state-security apparatus was swiftly taken apart after Boris Yeltsin emerged as the triumphant saviour of Gorbachev. It was first renamed the Central Intelligence Service of the re-installed President's proposed Federation of Socialist Countries.

In the aftermath of the attempted *coup*, Oleg was preoccupied with dealing with a flood of Western media correspondents with whom he had become familiar during his trip to the United States. Somehow despite the turmoil, he managed keep researching and writing in every spare moment, so that by the beginning of October he arrived at the Frankfurt International Book Fair with draft chapters and an impressive folio of new documentation. The annual gathering of publishers from around the world coincided with the KGB's demise as it was voted out of existence by the Soviet Congress. This peaked the interest in our project. Within two days Zolnay Verlag had emerged as the victor in a hectic round of bidding among major German publishing houses.

The Orlov book was back on track by the end of the year, by which time the Central Intelligence Service had undergone yet another transformation. The KGB's former internal and external operations had been separated and Oleg became deputy chief of the Press Bureau of the newly established Russian Intelligence Service. This was the organisation, approximating to the CIA or MI6, which assumed responsibility for foreign intelligence operations and for most of the staff of the former First Chief Directorate (or FCD) of the KGB. It was put under the charge of Yevgeny Primakov, who had been Gorbachev's special diplomatic envoy to the Middle East.

The new directorate not only gave its approval for Oleg to continue his collaboration with me but also for him to explore the possibility of developing other books based on their historic archives. *Deadly Illusions* therefore became the inspiration and model for a unique publishing collaboration intended to make it possible to release material from the KGB's intelligence archives for Russian historians, as well as those in the West. This is an unprecedented action for an intelligence agency to initiate, since secrecy is a precondition of their function. This fact of intelligence life was acknowledged in the summer of 1992 by the Russian Parliament when the FCD archive was constitutionally exempted from a "Freedom of Information" principle in the legislation that grants access to the other state archives of the former USSR, including the so-called "rehabilitation files" of the internal organs of the KGB, merged into the Ministry of Security.

Contemporaneously, in June 1992, representatives of the Russian Intelligence Service, Crown, the National Intelligence Study Center and the John M. Olin Institute for Strategic Studies of Harvard University came together in Washington to announce this break-through publishing arrangement. That agreement was reached on such a unique venture was in large part due to the Orlov project, by then nearing its completion, which had demonstrated that it was possible to reconcile the conflicting demands of historical scholarship with the sensitivity inherent in the controlled declassification of KGB intelligence records.

Paradoxically, it had become clear by then that the inhibiting factors on the Russian Intelligence Service were precisely the same as those on the CIA. Neither were primarily concerned to protect the nature of the technical, military and political secrets obtained from their spy networks but with the need to preserve the identity of sources and the methodology by which agents obtained and relayed that information. The rationale is that intelligence gathering in the future would be made more difficult if the tradecraft by which it is obtained, or the names of potential sources, are disclosed. Some degree of confidentiality is essential in the conduct of intelligence business between states. As Oleg has succinctly put it in an interview with

Pravda: "What foreign state or what political leader will dare to conduct any confidential talks with Russian leaders when there is no guarantee that the subject of the discussion will not be made public knowledge in two or three years, if not months?"

It was precisely the same justification for keeping sources secret that I was given by the FBI's Head of Counter-Intelligence. Both the Bureau and the CIA frequently resort to section B (1) of the Freedom of Information Act to excise names of even deceased sources when releasing documentation, to prevent the stigma attaching to surviving family members. This is permitted under the executive order by which these agencies are granted wide discretion to protect "operational" information "in the interest of national defense or foreign policy". But while the Freedom of Information Act permits federal agencies to "sanitise" sensitive American intelligence documents under strict rules requiring the reason for each censoring to be identified, shared intelligence, such as MI5 and MI6 reports supplied to the United States, are subject to the UK/USA agreement which permits them to be removed in their entirety. Such wholesale excisions make it impossible to follow a paper trail, whereas "santitising" leaves the title pages and many portions of a document to give valuable clues to what lies under the censor's black pen. With the exception of a cache of MI5 reports I uncovered in the files of the US embassy in London, only very infrequently does a bureaucratic oversight by the "weeders" permit an occasional intelligence report to escape into the open files.

Our access to the KGB archival records, controlled and selective though it has had to be, nevertheless has now opened a new door to intelligence history, based on a wide range of primary Soviet sources. For the first time it has been possible to have a peek at what was really going on in the enemy's camp on the other side of the secret intelligence war that continued, non-stop, during the most turbulent decades of the twentieth century. Thus we do not have to speculate about what transpired in the upper reaches of the Lubyanka by relying on reconstructions made with the assistance of the imperfect recollections of KGB defectors, who might have been overanxious to appear all-knowing in order to ingratiate themselves with their Western hosts.

We have based our book on verbatim quotes from summaries of the contemporary files, whose existence could only formerly be surmised from selective reflections in the distorting mirror of "official" Soviet history. As for the veracity of the cited documentation, it has been possible to measure some of the KGB archival files from the information they contain from formerly classified British Government records. For example, it is possible to check the reports Donald Maclean photographed for Moscow against Foreign Office files in the Public Record Office.

There will, of course, be those sceptics who will continue to deny that any voluntarily released Soviet document represents the truth. This can now be shown to be an unreasonable position to sustain in the light of corroborative evidence that can be matched against certain KGB records, such as Maclean's reports on British Cabinet decisions in 1936 or the 1941 Morton report on Hess which parallels the one in the US Army Intelligence archives. Yet by its very nature, there can be no absolutes in intelligence assessments – especially with the British still insisting that their records must remain forever closed. The opening up over the last decade of most US wartime intelligence files and now the controlled access to the KGB archive, finally wedges the door open and makes it possible to begin to piece together a more accurate history of intelligence in the twentieth century.

To "tell it like it was" has been one of the principal opportunities afforded by the Orlov project because his active career as a Soviet intelligence officer and his knowledge of Soviet operations and agents spanned the entire period from the establishment of Dzerzhinsky's *Cheka* to the opening moves in the Second World War. That is why Oleg and I decided that the interests of history could best be served by extending the strict boundaries of Orlov's personal story to include sections based on new documentary material from the Soviet files. These cover such major operations as *The Trust*, as it related to the fate of Sidney Reilly; the development of the Berlin section of the *Rote Kapelle* (hitherto regarded as being run by Red Army intelligence) and a history of the first operational successes achieved by the "Three Musketeers" from Cambridge, whose recruitment and initial operations Orlov had personally supervised.

Historians ideally insist on unrestricted research access to sift and weigh a documentary archive. Outsiders, however, can never be granted full access to the intelligence archives of the RIS, any more than to those of the CIA, because they are considered an essential adjunct of the operational data base. Yet, whereas I had to rely on my contacts in the US intelligence community and the Freedom of Information Act to obtain the American side of the Orlov story, Oleg, as a serving intelligence officer, had the access and authority to see whatever files in the KGB archive he needed to pursue his researches. So although I was not permitted to see every file he examined, we had agreed from the outset that this would not be an "as told to" account because at least one of the co-authors of this book *has* seen all the material. And even if it was not permitted to make every document public, copies of all substantive documentation relating to the text will be declassified to coincide with the publication of *Deadly Illusions*.

Our *modus operandi* required Oleg to conduct a comprehensive research programme in the KGB files. Because the "need to know" principle was strictly enforced by the KGB, before he began his research, it would be fair to claim that no one had ever been granted such extensive access to so many files. Research parameters and boundaries were constantly expanding, as my probing questions on the documentation he was mining prompted him to pursue the documentary lode of Orlov's career ever deeper in the Soviet archival files. He then assembled the factual record of Orlov's operations – *in its entirety* – before submitting it to the vetting process on a chapter-by-chapter basis. In this way Oleg was able to argue the necessity of keeping vital information intact whenever the question of with-holding sensitive material arose. This has been crucial to securing the release of more, rather than less sensitive documentation. Copies of the source documents against which the quoted passages in the text could be compared for accuracy were translated and supplied as the narrative was written. Comparison and analysis from the information in Orlov's FBI files and other sources, including my interviews with American intelligence veterans, required that Oleg had often to go back to the archives to research new leads afresh. Many questions arose during this process, especially when the Soviet record appeared to omit or conflict with Orlov's debriefing and the testimony he gave to the Americans. For my part the process can be best compared to researching the KGB archive at one stage removed, like conducting a survey of the moon from Earth by sending and receiving radio messages from a lunar lander.

The irony was that communicating with the robot explorer on the moon was rather easier for Houston Space Center twenty years ago than getting through to Moscow on an almost daily basis in 1992. Nor was it only the political constraints that would have made it impractical to write this book before the advent of fax machines and express air-courier services transformed global communications. In the year-and-a-half that it has taken to write this book, we have invested more than a hundred hours in telephone conferences and shipped dozens of pounds of paperwork between the United States and Russia. The collaborative process has worked out remarkably smoothly, thanks to Oleg's patient work with his archivist colleagues, who have clearly thrown themselves wholeheartedly into the project. In the case of the FBI and CIA records relating to Orlov, I was unable to obtain more than half of the extant files which continue to be withheld despite the filing of repeated FOIA requests and appeals. It has, however, been possible partially to reconstruct a broad outline of what was in the missing sections of FBI and CIA files as a result of two strokes of good research fortune.

The first breakthrough came when I found a full index to the main Orlov file, censored in the Bureau version, duplicated in full in the US Army's Intelligence Records Repository at Fort Meade. The second stroke of luck came when extensive clues to the contents of the CIA Orlov file (which has never been declassified) appeared in the interview reports and correspondence the Agency conducted with the French DST counter-intelligence agency in 1965. These were made available by a trusted source who – for obvious reasons – wishes to remain anonymous. Agency veterans who have examined these interviews conducted by the CIA with Orlov have confirmed their authenticity. With the exception of this Franco-American material which is unsanitised, the principal targets for excisions and deletions in all "officially" declassified Orlov files are the sections dealing with information provided by sensitive sources and intelligence methodology. The deletions for "operational reasons" appear to have been significantly less extensive in the former Soviet material, as can be seen from the samples supplied in the book.

Where such deletions have been made, or sources cannot be named or cases discussed for "operational reasons", this has been clearly stated in our jointly written text. Oleg has assured me that the excisions have been made in good faith – for the same reasons as the sanitisations of the US records – and not as contrived provocations. In the case of the FBI files, however, it has often been possible to deduce what has been removed from the flow and content of contiguous passages. The recollections of veterans, or parallel information in other agencies' reports which were subject to lighter censorship enable many other gaps to be filled with confidence. However rational such guesswork, some clues, like those in a teasing crossword puzzle, inevitably lead to logical but totally incorrect conclusions. In the case of the KGB archives, by contrast, my co-author is aware of precisely what he has been asked to omit. So while Oleg was scrupulous in not betraying any significant details, he has been able to restrain his fellow writer from making any wild flights of speculative fantasy.

Since it is the mission of the historian, not the censor, to determine what is historically significant, in this section, which is not subject to the constraints of joint authorship, I offer some observations emerging from this first exploration of the historic Soviet intelligence archives. First I should stress that any inferences or conclusions that I draw here are entirely my own deductions and are not made with the implied authority of my Russian co-author.

In general, both I and those members of the American intelligence community with whom I have consulted, have been reassured by the objectivity displayed by the *Commissia po rassekrevchivaniyu materialov razvedki*, the so-called "Committee for the Declassification of Intelligence Materials", established in 1992 by the Russian Foreign Intelligence Service. They do not appear to have just released documentation that shows the positive side of Orlov's career. The acid test of the historical objectivity of the "Declassification Committee" was demonstrated after Oleg had discovered the cryptic operational reports Orlov sent to Moscow on the so-called *liter* operations which he directed to liquidate the Spanish Marxist opposition. Confronted with the documentary evidence that there was "blood on his hands" after all, the "Declassification Committee" nevertheless decided to permit the release of the documentation that would finally solve the half-century-old controversy over Nin's death. Since Orlov had always denied them as a Trotskyist fabrication, and had repeatedly testified under oath that he was never involved in such liquidation operations, they could have held back the information. That they did not, even though it put an indelible stain on Orlov's character, has revealed the awful truth about yet another sordid episode of the Stalinist era.

This decision to permit Oleg to assemble the indisputable evidence he had uncovered in the Spanish *rezidentura* correspondence file – that Orlov had been involved in murder operations – was a clear indication that the Russian Intelligence Service would not hold back historic records simply to cover up an unpleasant truth. For the historian this was a critical decision. It gives grounds for confidence in believing that the declassification criteria adopted by the Russian Intelligence Service are being applied consistently. So too does the decision to release a substantial number of operational files, which include many of Orlov's handwritten reports on the recruitment of the "Cambridge group", their psychological profiles and the cables exchanged between the Centre and their agents in the field. They have also supplied photographs of every page of Orlov's American passport with its revealing exit and entry stamps, together with copies of residency permits and other such "operational" documents that would never have been released by US agencies. We have also been allowed full access to Philby's own fascinating personal memoir to compare it with the contemporary operational reports in his personal file. Such a wide range of inter-related documents, selected not solely by the Russian, but also at my request, permits the kind of extensive cross-checking that has proved impossible with FBI and CIA files.

The Russian Intelligence Service has therefore set a new level of openness and has advanced the boundaries of intelligence and counter-intelligence history writing. Indeed, a page-by-page analysis of the FBI and KGB documents that form the basis of this book shows that the RIS has made considerably fewer deletions than the Bureau. What has been excised for "operational reasons" appears to be mainly names or operations. This is in accordance with the publicly stated RIS decision not to name sources who are still alive, and have not been identified by the Western counter-intelligence agencies, or by their own admission. To protect these sources, only their cryptonyms have been released.

It is always tempting to read a special significance into evidence that has been removed or left out. The door marked NO ENTRY always invites special attention, whether it is in the declassified American or Soviet records. Hence the FBI's removal of all Orlov's personal interrogation records, with the exception of his statements to the Immigration and Naturalisation Service, could indicate that omission was made because to release the full documentation would expose both the Bureau's interrogation methodology and its failure to break Orlov.

Similarly, the Russian decision not to release any of the information on what now appears to have been a very extensive espionage network in the Government munitions plant in Woolwich Arsenal, for which Orlov assumed operational responsibility in 1935, also invites speculation. My personal conclusion, based on the references to the Soviet agents involved that appear in the MI5 reports sent to the United States at the time, is that the Soviet penetration was far more important and extensive than the British ever discovered, or are prepared to acknowledge. The principal Soviet ringleaders were never caught in the final round up, although the charges of espionage brought against the British workmen involved in supplying armaments secrets were presented as a great triumph for the British secret services. In this context Orlov's July 1935 accounting records from the London "illegal" station indicate that one of the prominent members of the Woolwich network was named NACHFOLGER – or SUCCESSOR. Given that the codes assigned their sub-agents at that time often contained a clue to their identities, who was the predecessor agent to whom NACHFOLGER was the "successor"? That Orlov also ran three other unidentified British recruits known as BÄR, ATILLA and PROFESSOR suggests that opening up the full story of the Woolwich

Arsenal would expose another major Soviet penetration of the British Government apparatus.

The existence of a hitherto unknown "Oxford Group", which paralleled the well-known Cambridge spy ring, is the most intriguing issue opened up by the declassification of the Orlov dossier. Who were its members and was the information they supplied as damaging as that passed to Moscow by Philby and his contemporaries? These are questions that still have to be answered from the information in the Soviet files. But by one measure at least, they proved even more successful than their Cambridge counterparts because none of the Oxonians who joined the ranks of Stalin's Englishmen has ever been officially exposed. Their names and dates of recruitment can be found detailed in Arnold Deutsch's history of the London "illegal" *rezidentura*, for which he enlisted and ran no fewer than seventeen British spies for the Soviet intelligence service. Since his was the expert hand that had helped land Philby, Maclean, Burgess, Blunt, Straight, Long, Cairncross and the still unidentified Cambridge university comrades codenamed ABO and MAYOR, it is logical to conclude that he applied the same techniques as the prime recruiter of the Oxford ring.[2]

According to the Soviet records, Deutsch was involved in the recruitment of ten members of the Cambridge "Group", and a high proportion of the other British agents he brought into the Soviet fold who made up the nucleus of the Oxford "Group", before he was obliged to leave England in 1937. In his history he records that he gave the codename SCOTT to the "First Man" – the "Philby" of the Oxford "Group". Given Deutsch's propensity for choosing cryptonyms for all these agents that reflected something about their backgrounds, it is not without significance that there were two 'T's in the code name of this Oxford-educated Soviet spy who, undetected throughout his career, rose to prominent positions in British Government service. Since the prime targets among the Cambridge "Group" were high-flyers like Maclean and Cairncross destined for the Foreign Office, it can be deduced that of the half-dozen original members of the Oxford ring, several were destined for diplomatic careers.

Stalin's Oxford "moles" must have burrowed up the same tunnels into the British Government as did their Cambridge contemporaries. But since it has never been the intention of the Orlov project to indulge in "mole" hunting, I have not drawn up a short list of names

---

[2] It is not without significance to find that in his history he included Goronwy Rees as part of what he defined as the "Cambridge Group". This was because this Welsh socialist, although a Fellow of All Souls, Oxford, was recruited in 1938 through recommendation and his close association with Guy Burgess.

from the Oxford Registers from which SCOTT or his fellow-comrades can be run down. Most have taken the secrets of their undercover service to Moscow to their graves. But when the time comes for the Russian Intelligence Service to open its files, I predict that it will not be to smear dead men's bones with accusations of treachery. It will be to provide a documented record of their view of the contribution they made to changing the course of history by passing information about British policy to the Soviet intelligence service over a period of many decades. For example even if it were not known that Maclean had been a Soviet agent in 1936, it would be possible to identify him and the department in the Foreign Office for which he worked by following the paper trail of British Government documentation back from the reports in his agent's file in the Russian Intelligence Service's archive.

One of the most tantalising clues that has dropped out of the KGB Orlov dossier appears in the 1964 "damage assessment report" which finally absolved the runaway General of treachery. It records that agents whose names Orlov "knew very well" continued to operate from the time he surfaced in the United States in 1953 until 1963, "that is until their exfiltration into the USSR". Since the only known "exfiltration" was that of Philby in 1963, it is not impossible that he was followed by other British comrades, whose names appear in the Oxford Register for 1938.

JOHN COSTELLO
London, New York, Moscow, February 1993

SELECTED BIBLIOGRAPHY

Agabekov, G. *G.P.U.* (*Zapiski chekista*) Izdatel'stvo 'Strela', Berlin 1930.

Akhmedov, Ismail *In and Out of Stalin's GRU: A Tartar's Escape from Red Army Intelligence.* University Publications of America, MD. 1984.

Aleksandrovskaya, S. M. *My Internationalisisty.* Politizdat, Moscow 1975.

Alexeeva, Ludmilla *Soviet Dissents: Contemporary Movements for National, Religious and Human Rights.* Wesleyan University Press, Conn. 1985.

Alliluyeva, Svetlana *Only One Year.* Hutchinson, London 1969.

Andrew, Christopher and Gordievsky, Oleg *KGB: The Inside Story.* Hodder & Stoughton, London 1990.

Andrew, Christopher *Secret Service: The Making of the British Intelligence Community.* Heinemann, London 1985.

Antonov-Ovseyenko, Anton *The Time of Stalin: Portrait of a Tyranny.* Translated by George Saunders. Harper & Row, New York 1981.

Ardamatskiy V. I. *Vozmezdiye.* Molodaya Gvardiya, Moscow 1968.

Avrich, Paul *Kronstadt 1921.* W. W. Norton, New York 1974.

Baczkowski, Wlodzimierz *Toward an Understanding of Russia: A Study in Policy and Strategy.* Lipshutz Press, Jerusalem 1947.

Bailey, Geoffrey *The Conspirators.* Harper Bros., New York 1960.

Bamford, James *The Puzzle Palace.* Houghton & Mifflin, Boston 1982.

Barron, John *KGB: The Secret Work of Soviet Secret Agents.* Readers Digest Press, New York 1974.

– *KGB Today: The Hidden Hand.* Readers Digest Press, New York 1983.

Bazhanov, Boris G *Avec Staline dans le Kremlin.* Les Editions de France, Paris 1930.

Bentley, Elizabeth *Out of Bondage.* Ballantine Books, New York 1988.

Bethell, Nicholas *The Great Betrayal.* Hodder & Stoughton, London 1984.

Bittman, Ladislav *The Deception Game.* Ballantine Books, New York 1981.

Bor-Komorowski, T. *The Secret Army.* Victor Gollancz, London 1950.

Boyle, Andrew *The Fourth Man.* Dial Press, New York 1979.

Brook-Shepherd, Gordon *The Storm Petrels.* Collins, London 1977.

Brook-Shepherd, Gordon *The Storm Birds.* Weidenfeld & Nicolson, London 1988.

Calvocoressi, Peter *Top Secret Ultra.* Cassell, London 1980.

Canadian Royal Commission *The Defection of Igor Gouzenko.* Report of 27 June 1946, 3 vols.

Carr, E. H. *The Bolshevik Revolution 1917–1923.* Macmillan 1953.

Cecil, Robert *A Divided Life: A Biography of Donald Maclean.* Wm. Morrow, New York 1989.

Central Intelligence Agency *The ·Rote Kapelle: The CIA's History of Soviet*

Intelligence and Espionage Networks in Western Europe, 1936–1945. University Publications of America, Washington D.C. 1974.
Chamberlin, William Henry *The Russian Revolution*. Grosset & Dunlap, New York 1965.
Cohen, Stephen F. *Bukharin and the Bolshevik Revolution 1888–1938*. Oxford University Press, New York 1980.
Conquest, Robert *The Great Terror*. Macmillan, New York 1973.
 – *The Harvest of Sorrow: Soviet Collectivization and the Terror Famine*. Oxford University Press, 1986.
 – *Inside Stalin's Secret Police: NKVD Politics, 1936–1939*. Hoover Institutions Press, Stanford 1986.
 – *The Soviet Police System*. Praeger, New York 1968.
Cornelissen, Igor *De GPOe op de Overtoom*. Van Gennep, Amsterdam 1989.
Corson, W. and Crowley, R. *The New KGB*. Wm. Morrow, New York 1985.
Costello, John *Mask Of Treachery*. Wm. Morrow, New York 1988.
Costello, John *Ten Days To Destiny*. Wm. Morrow, New York 1991.
Costello, John *Virtue Under Fire: How World War II Changed Social and Sexual Attitudes*. Little Brown, Boston 1985.
Costello, John (with Admiral Edwin T. Layton and Captain Roger Pineau) *"And I Was There" – Breaking the Secrets of Pearl Harbor and Midway*. Wm. Morrow, New York 1985.
Costello, John *The Pacific War*. Rawson Wade, New York 1981.
Dallin, David J. *Soviet Espionage*. Yale University Press, New Haven 1952.
Debo, Richard K. 'Lockhart Plot or Dzerzhinsky Plot?' *Journal of Modern History* 43, No. 3 (September 1971), pp. 413–439.
de Jonge, Alex *Stalin and the Shaping of the Soviet Union*. Collins, London 1986.
Denikin, Anton I. *The White Army*. Jonathan Cape, London 1930.
Deriabin, Peter *Watchdogs of Terror*. University Publications of America, Frederick, Md. 1984.
Deutscher, Isaac *The Prophet Outcast: Trotsky, 1929–1940*. Oxford University Press, New York 1963.
 – *Stalin: A Political Biography*. Vintage Books, New York 1962.
Donovan, James B *Strangers on a Bridge*. Atheneum, New York 1964.
Donovan, Robert J *Conflict and Crisis: The Presidency of Harry S. Truman 1945–1948*. Norton, New York 1977.
Driberg, Tom *Guy Burgess: A Portrait with a Background*. Weidenfeld & Nicolson, London 1956.
Dziak, John J. *Chekisty: A History of the KGB*. Ballantine, New York 1988.
Emelyanov, A. *Sovietskiye podvodnye lodki v Velikoi Otechestvennoi Voine*. Voyenizdat, Moscow 1981.
Epstein, Edward J. *Deception: The Invisible War Between the KGB and the CIA*. Simon & Schuster, New York 1989.
Erickson, John *The Road to Stalingrad*. Harper & Row, New York 1975.
 – *The Soviet High Command*. St. Martin's Press, London 1962.
Feliks Edmundovich Dzerzhinsky 1877–1926. Marx Engels Lenin Institute, 1951.
Finerty, John, et al. *The Case of Leon Trotsky*.
Fischer, Louis *Men and Politics: An Autobiography*. Duell, Sloan & Pearce, New York 1941.
Fischer, Louis, *The War in Spain*. New York 1941.
Fomin, F. T. *Zapiski starogo chekista*. Politizdat, Moscow 1964.
Gehlen, Reinhard *The Service*. World Publishing, New York 1972.

Gerson, Leonard D. *The Secret Police in Lenin's Russia*. Temple University Press, Philadelphia 1976.
Gilbert, Martin *Winston Churchill*. Vols IV; V; VI. Heinemann, London 1976–1986.
Gitlow, Benjamin *The Whole of our Lives*. Charles Scribner's Sons, New York 1948.
Gladkov, Teodor and Zaytsev, Nikolay *I ya enu ne mogu ne verit'*. . . . Politizdat, Moscow 1983, 1986.
Gladkov, Teodor and Smirnov, Mikhail *Menzhinsky*. Molodaya Gvardiya, Moscow 1969.
Gless, Anthony *The Secrets of the Service*. Jonathan Cape, London 1987.
Gnedin, Evgeniy *Iz istorii ostnosheniy mezhdu SRR i fashitkoy Germaniey*. Izdatelstvo "Khronika", New York 1977.
Goerlitz, Walter *Der Zweite Weltkrieg, 1939–45*. Steingrubon-Verlag, Stuttgart 1952.
Golinkov, David L. *Krah vrazheskogo podpol'ya: Iz istorii bor'by s kontrevolyutsiyecy v sovetskoy Rossi v 1917–1924*. Izdatel'stvo Politicheskoy Literatury, Moscow 1971.
Golinkov, David *The Secret War Against Soviet Russia*. Progress Publishers, Moscow 1981.
Golitsyn, Anatoly *New Lies for Old: The Communist Strategy of Deception and Disinformation*. Dodd, Mead & Co., New York 1984.
Gorodetsky, Gabriel *Stafford Cripps' Mission to Moscow 1940–1942*. Cambridge University Press, 1984.
Gouzenko, Igor *The Iron Curtain*. E. P. Dutton, New York 1948.
Gramont, Sanche de *The Secret War*. G. P. Putnam's Sons, New York 1962.
Grant, Natalie *Dezinformatsiya*. Unpublished manuscript.
Grigorenko, Petro G. *Memoirs*. Translated by Thomas P. Whitney. W. W. Norton, New York 1982.
Gromyko, Andrei and Ponomarev, B. N. (eds) *Soviet Foreign Policy 1917–1980*. Progress Publishers, Moscow 1981.
Gross, Babette *Munzenberg, A Political Biography*. Michigan University Press, Ann Arbor 1974.
Gsovski, Vladimir *Soviet Civil Law, Vol. I*. University of Michigan Law School, Ann Arbor 1948.
Hanson, Philip *Soviet Industrial Espionage: Some New Information*. Royal Institute of International Affairs, London 1987.
Haslam, Jonathan *Soviet Foreign Policy 1930–3*. Macmillan, London 1983.
– *The Soviet Union and the Struggle for Collective Security 1933–1939*. Macmillan, London 1984.
Heijenoort, Jean van *With Trotsky in Exile*. Harvard University Press, Cambridge, Mass. 1978.
Heller, Mikhail and Nekrich, Aleksandr M. *Utopia in Power: The History of the Soviet Union from 1917 to the present*. Summit Books, New York 1986.
Hernandez, José *Yo Ministro de Stalin en España*. Madrid 1954.
Hilger, Gustav and Meyer, Alfred G. *The Incompatible Allies*. Macmillan, New York 1953.
Hill, George A. *Go Spy Out the Land*. Cassel, London 1932.
Hingley, Ronald *The Russian Mind*. Charles Scribner's Sons, New York 1977.
– *The Russian Secret Police: Muscovite, Imperial Russian, and Soviet Political Security Operations, 1565–1970*. Simon & Schuster, New York 1971.
Hinsley, F. H., et al *British Intelligence in the Second World War*. 3 Vols. HMSO, London 1979.
Hood, William *Mole*. W. W. Norton, New York 1982.

Houghton, Harry *Operation Portland: The Autobiography of a Spy*. Rupert Hart Davis, London 1972.

Howarth, T. E. B. *Cambridge Between The Wars*. Collins, London 1978.

Hunt, Carew *The Theory and Practice of Communism*. Geoffrey Bles, London 1950.

Johnson, Paul *Modern Times: The World from the Twenties to the Eighties*. Harper & Row, New York 1983.

Kahn, David *The Codebreakers*. Macmillan, New York 1967.

– *Hitler's Spies*. Macmillan, New York 1978.

Karski, Jan *Story of a Secret State*. Houghton Mifflin, Boston 1944.

Katkov, George "German Foreign Office Documents on Financial Support to the Bolsheviks in 1917." *International Affairs* 32 No. 2.

– *Russia 1917: The February Revolution*. Harper & Row, New York 1967.

Kessler, Ronald *Moscow Station*. Scribners, New York 1989.

Kettle, Michael *Sidney Reilly: The True Story*. Corgi, London 1983.

Khruschev, Nikita S. *Khruschev Remembers*. Introduction and Commentary by Edward Crankshaw, translated and edited by Strobe Talbott. Little Brown, Boston 1970.

Knight, Amy *The KGB: Police and Politics in the Soviet Union*. Unwin Hyman, London 1988.

Knightley, Philip *Philby: KGB Master Spy*. André Deutsch, London 1986.

Koch, Stephen, *Double Lives: Espionage and the War of Ideas*. Free Press, New York 1993.

Koestler, Arthur *The Invisible Writing*. Hutchinson, London 1969.

Kozlov Yu M., et al *Sovetskoye administrativnoye pravo*. Izdatel'stvo "Yuridicheskaya Literatura" 1968.

Kravchenko, Victor *I Chose Freedom*. Scribners, New York 1946.

Krivitsky, Walter *I Was Stalin's Agent*. Hamish Hamilton, London 1939.

Krivitsky, Walter *In Stalin's Secret Service*. Reprint. University Publications of America, Frederick, MD 1985.

Lamphere, Robert J. and Shachtman, Tom *The FBI-KGB War: A Special Agent's Story*. Random House, New York 1986.

Langhorne, Richard, ed. *Diplomacy and Intelligence During the Second World War: Essays in Honour of F. H. Hinsley*. Cambridge University Press, 1985.

Lazich, Branko and Drachkovitch, Milorad M. *Lenin and the Comintern*. Vol. 1. Hoover Institution Press, Stanford 1972.

Leggett, George *The Cheka: Lenin's Political Police*. Oxford University Press, Oxford 1981.

Lenin V. I. *Collected Works*, Vols. 26, 27, 31, 45. Progress Publishers, Moscow 1964, 1966.

Lenin V. I. *The Bolshevik Revolution 1917–1923*. Allen & Unwin, London 1929.

Lenin, V. I. *Selected Works*, Vol. 3. Foreign Language Publishing House, Moscow 1961.

Levine, Isaac Don, *Stalin's Great Secret*. Coward MacCann, New York 1956.

Levytsky, Boris *The Uses of Terror*. Coward McCann, New York 1972.

Litvinov, Maxim *Notes for a Journal*. Introduction by E. H. Carr: prefatory note by General Walter Bedell Smith. William Morrow & Co., New York 1955.

Lockhart, Robert H. *Bruce, British Agent*. G. P. Putnam's Sons, New York 1933.

Lockhart, Robin Bruce *Reilly: The First Man*. Penguin Books, New York 1987.

Lonsdale, Gordon *Spy*. Neville Spearman, London 1965.

Lyons, Eugene *Assignment in Utopia*. Harcourt Brace & Co., New York 1937.

McSherry, James E. *Stalin, Hitler and Europe*. Vol. 2. World Publishing Co., New York 1970.

Martin, David *Wilderness of Mirrors*. Ballantine Books, New York 1981.

Massing, Hede *The Deception*. Ivy Books, New York 1987.

Masters, Anthony *The Man Who Was M: The Life of Maxwell Knight*. Blackwell, Oxford 1982.

Matthews, Mervyn, ed. *Soviet Government: A Selection of Official Documents on Internal Politics*. Taplinger Publishing Co. Inc., New York 1974.

May, Ernest R., ed. *Knowing One's Enemies*. Princeton University Press, 1984.

Medvedev, Roy A. and Zhores A. *Khruschev: The Years in Power*. Columbia University Press, New York 1976.

– *Khruschev*. Anchor Press, 1983.

– "New Pages from the Political Biography of Stalin." In *Stalinism: Essays in Historical Interpretation*. Edited by Robert C. Tucker. W. W. Norton, New York 1977.

– *The October Revolution*. Translated by George Saunders. Columbia University Press, New York 1976.

– *Let History Judge: The Origins and Consequences of Stalinism*. Translated by Colleen Taylor. Alfred A. Knopf, New York 1972.

Melgounov, S. P. and Tsyavlovskiy, M. A., eds. *Bol'shviki: Dokumenty po istorii bol'shevizma s 1903 po 1916 got byushego Moskovskogo Okhrannogo Otdeleniya*. Zadruga, Moscow 1918.

Melgounov, S. P. *The Red Terror in Russia*. J. M. Dent & Sons Ltd, London 1926.

Mironov, Nikolay R. *Ukrepleniye zakonnosti i pravoporyadaka v obschenorodnom gosudarstve: Programmnaya zadacha partii*. Izdatel'stvo "Yuridicheskaya Literatura" Moscow 1964.

Moravec, Frantisek *Master of Spies*. Bodley Head, London 1975.

Morros, Boris *My Ten Years as a Counterspy*. Viking Press, New York 1959.

Nekrich, Aleksandr "Stalin and the Pact with Hitler" in *Russia*, No. 4 (1981), p. 48.

Newton, Verne *The Cambridge Spies*. Madison Books, Washington 1991.

Orlov, Alexander *The Secret History of Stalin's Crimes*. Random House, New York 1952.

Orlov, Alexander *A Handbook of Intelligence and Guerilla Warfare*. University of Michigan Press, Ann Arbor 1962.

Page, Bruce, Leitch, David and Knightley, Philip *Philby: The Spy who betrayed a Generation*. Sphere Books, London 1977.

Philby, H. A. R. *My Silent War*. Panther Books, London 1969.

Pincher, Chapman *Their Trade is Treachery*. Sidgwick & Jackson, London 1981.

– *Too Secret Too Long*. St Martin's Press, New York 1984.

Pipes, Richard *Russia Under the Old Regime*. Scribners, New York 1974.

Poretsky, Elizabeth K. *Our Own People: A Memoir of Ignace Reiss and His Friends*. University of Michigan Press, Ann Arbor 1936.

Radosh, Ronald and Milton, Joyce *The Rosenberg File*. Weidenfeld & Nicolson, London 1983.

Rees, Goronwy *Chapter of Accidents*. Chatto & Windus, London 1971.

Reilly, S. G. *The Adventures of Sidney Reilly, Britain's Master Spy*. E. Matthews & Marrott, London 1931.

Rhoer, Edward Van Der *The Shadow Network: Espionage as an instrument of Soviet Policy*. Charles Scribner's Sons, New York 1983.

Romerstein, Herbert and Levchenko, Stanislav *The KGB against the Main Enemy*.

How the Soviet Intelligence Service Operates Against the United States. Lexington Books, Mass. 1989.

Rositzke, Harry *The CIA's Secret Operations.* Readers Digest Press, New York 1977.

Sawatsky, George *Gouzenko: The Untold Story.* Macmillan, Toronto 1985.

Shultz, Richard H., and Godson, Roy *Dzinformatsia.* Pergamon-Brassey's, New York 1984.

Solovyov, Vladimir and Klepikova, Elena *Behind the High Kremlin Walls.* Translated by Guy Daniels. Berkley Books, New York 1987.

Solzhenitsyn, Alexander *The Gulag Archipelago 1918–1956.* Translated by Thomas P. Whitney and Harry Willetts. Harper & Row, New York 1980.

Stafford, David *Britain and European Resistance, 1940–45: A Survey of the Special Operations Executive With Documents.* University of Toronto Press, Toronto 1980.

Straight, Michael *After Long Silence.* Collins, London 1983.

Steinberg, I. N. *In the Workshop of Revolution.* Victor Gollancz, London 1955.

Struve, G. V., Shulgin, V and Voytsckhovskiy V. "New About the Trust." *Novyy Zhurnal,* No. 125 (1975), pp. 194–214.

Suvorov, Viktor *Soviet Military Intelligence.* Hamish Hamilton, London 1984.

Tatu, Michael *Power in the Kremlin.* Translated by Helen Katel. Viking Press, New York 1968.

Thomas, Hugh *The Spanish Civil War.* Harper & Row, New York 1961.

Tishkov, A. V. *Perviy chekist.* Voyenizdat, Moscow 1968.

Trepper, Leopold *The Great Game* Michael Joseph, London 1977.

Trotsky, Leon *Stalin: An Appraisal of the Man and His Influence.* Harpers, New York 1946.

Tsvigun, S. K., et al. *V. I. Lenin i Vcheka: Sbornick documentov (1917–1922).* Politizdat, Moscow 1975.

Tucker, R. C. and Cohen, S. F., eds. *The Great Purge Trials.* Grosset & Dunlap, New York 1965.

Ullman, Richard H. *Anglo-Soviet Relations 1917–1921.* Vols I-III Princeton University Press, Princeton 1972.

Vereeken, Georges *The GPU in the Trotskyist Movement.* New Park Publications, London 1976.

Viktorov, I. V. *Podpol'shchik, voin, chekist.* Molodaya Gvardiya, Moscow 1976.

Volensky, Michael *Nmenklatura: The Soviet Ruling Class: An Insider's Report.* Translated by Eric Mosbacher. Doubleday & Co., New York 1984.

Volkogonov, Dimitry *Stalin: Triumph and Tragedy.* Grove Weidenfeld, New York 1992.

Voytsekhovskiy, S. L. "Conversation with Opperput" in *Vozrozhdeniye,* No. 16 (July-August 1951), pp. 129–137.

– *Trest Vospomininaniya i dokumenty.* Zarya Publishers, London, Ontario 1974.

Watt, Donald Cameron *How War Came: The Immediate Origins of the Second World War 1938–1939.* Heinemann, London 1989.

Weinstein, Allan *Perjury: The Hiss-Chambers Case.* Knopf, New York 1978.

West, Nigel *MI5.* Bodley Head, London 1981.

– *A Matter of Trust.* Weidenfeld & Nicolson, London 1982.

– *MI6.* Weidenfeld & Nicolson, London 1983.

– *GHCQ.* Weidenfeld & Nicolson, London 1986.

– *Molehunt.* Weidenfeld & Nicolson, London 1987.

Williams, Robert Chadwell *Klaus Fuchs, Atom Spy.* Harvard University Press, Cambridge, Mass. 1987.

Wolfe, Bertram D., ed. *Khruschev and Stalin's Ghost: Text, Background and Meaning of*

Khruschev's Secret Report to the Twentieth Party Congress on the Night of February 24–25 1956. Atlantic Press, London 1957.

Wolin, Simon and Slusser, Robert, eds. *The Soviet Secret Police.* Praeger, New York 1957.

Wolton, Thierry *Le KGB en France.* Bernard Grassett, Paris 1986.

Wraga, Richard "Cloak and Dagger Politics" in *Problems of Communism* 10, No. 2 1961.

Wright, Peter *Spycatcher.* Viking Penguin Inc., New York 1987.

Yakovlev, I. K., et al. *Vnutrenniye voyskya sovetskoy republiki (1917–1922). Izdatel'stvo "Yuridicheskaya Literatura."* Moscow 1973.

Zhukov, G. K. *The Memoirs of Marshal Zhukov.* Jonathan Cape, London 1971.

Zinoviev, Grigori *History of the Bolshevik Party: A Popular Outline.* Translated by R. Chappell. New Park Publications Ltd., London 1973.

Zubov, Nikolay I. *F. E. Dzerzhinsky: Biografiya.* 3rd ed., Politizdat, Moscow 1971.

INDEX

Abakumov, Viktor Semyonovich, 413
Abel, Rudolf Ivanovich (William Henry
    Fisher, Martin Collins, Emil
    Robert-Golfus), 371–2
ABO, 246
Abraham Lincoln Battalion, 164, 275,
    276, 349
Abshagen, Robert, 405
Abwehr, 87, 88, 172, 190
Abyssinia, 240
Acheson, Dean, 335
ADAM, 401–2
AEG, 57, 63, 77, 396
Agabekov, Georgy, 298
Alba, Duke of, 165, 173
ALEX, 269
ALEXANDER, 268
Alexeeyev, Boris (GAMMA), 358, 363,
    364
Aliens Registration Act (US), 324, 351,
    352
Alliluyev, Pavel, 8, 56–7
Alliluyeva, Nadezhda, 57
All Russian Central Executive
    Committee, 382
All Russian Congress of Soviets,
    Ninth, 28
All Russian Co-operative Society
    (ARCOS), London, 39, 43, 54, 90,
    203
Alma Ata, 46
Almeria, 268
American Refrigerator Company Ltd,
    The, 143
American Socialist Party, 356
AMTORG, 43

Angleton, James, 406
Anglo-German Fellowship, 160–61,
    163, 230
Anglo-Russian Trade Gazette, 159–60
Anglo-Soviet trade accord, 31
Ann Arbor Michigan, 1, 9, 10, 375–7,
    378
Antwerp, 293, 301–2, 303, 309, 356,
    410
Apostles, Society of the, 181, 222, 246
Angels, 227
Archangel, 21, 26
Argen, 270
ARPLAN (*Arbeitsgemeinschaft zum
    Studium der Sowjetrussichen*), 73, 74,
    75
Artusov, Artur Krystianovich (ARTUR),
    26, 31–2, 35, 36, 42, 62, 68, 69, 75,
    95, 109, 141–2, 187, 394, 414
Asangayev, Alexander Matveyevich
    (SANGO), 274
Asturias, 270
Athens, 104
ATILLA, 142, 145, 153, 154, 207
Auden, W. H., 184
Australia, 372
Austria, 31, 54, 126–9, 134, 143–4, 185
    See also Vienna
Austro-German Immigrant Help
    Committee, 126
Azana, President Manuel, 259, 281, 290

Baldwin, Stanley, 54, 191–2, 201, 227,
    228
Balitsky, V. I., 368
Ball, Joseph, 227

Baltic states, 115
  See also Estonia
Bank of Spain, 257–8, 263
BÄR (BEAR), 142, 145, 190, 207, 508
Barcelona, 83, 265, 268, 269, 270, 277,
  279, 280, 281–2, 287, 289, 290,
  293, 302, 304, 365, 377, 382
Barr, Joel, 338
Barth, Robert (BECK), 403, 404–5
Basset, John Retallack, 221
Bästlein, Bernhard, 405
Battalia, 289
Bazarov, 410
Behrens, Karl (STRAHLMANN), 77–8,
  396, 397
Beirut, 116, 374
Belkin, Alexander (KADI), 75, 76
Bender, Senator George H., 354–5,
  356, 357, 362
Benes, President Edouard, 370
Bentley, Elizabeth Terril, 71, 334, 336
Berg, Igor, see Orlov, Alexander
Beria, Lavrenty, 43, 211, 312, 350, 400,
  413, 490
Berlin, 35, 47, 98, 109, 335, 410
  Kapp putsch, 73
  Soviet Trade Delegation
    (Handelsvertretung), 54, 55–9
    passim, 64–7 passim, 110
  Technical High School, 58, 60
  Rote Kapelle, Berlin section, 72, 73–
    90, 276, 313, 338, 389, 390–93,
    394–405
Berlinks, Orest, 88
Berman, Boris (YELMAN), 49, 109
Bernal, J. D., 181
Bernaut, Elsa, 360
Berzin, Colonel Edouard, 21, 23
Berzin, General Jan (Grishin), 255, 265,
  267, 295–6, 348
Besanov, Max, 18
Bessedovsky, Grigory, 68
Biarritz, 171
Biddle, Francis, 324–5, 343
Bilbao, 268, 270
Billings, John Shaw, 339
Binyukov, 293
Blackett, P. M. S., 181
Blagonravov, Grigory, 30
Blaitsky, V. A., 252
Blau, Colonel, 88

Blum, Léon, 253
Blunt, Anthony (Maurice, TONY,
  JOHNSON), 118, 203, 207, 214, 220,
  222–3, 241, 242, 243, 244–5, 314,
  344, 366, 490, 509
  MI5 post, 245, 347
Bobadilya, Pepita, 34, 40
Bobruysk, 13, 14, 306, 316, 317, 356
Bogani brothers, 268
Bogwood, 53
Bolodin, 290, 291, 299, 348
Bolshevik Party, 16, 19, 20, 21, 24, 25,
  368
BOM, 292
B-138, agent (JUNKER), 322
Bonham Carter, Lady, 192
Boris Morros Music Company, 359
Boston (Mass.), 323–4, 325–7, 329,
  330, 343, 344
Bottai, Giuseppe, 109, 110
Bourbon de la Torres, Lieutenant
  Colonel José, 269
Boyle, Andrew,
  The Climate of Treason, 118
Brecht, Bertolt, 55
Brest-Litovsk, Treaty of, 21
Bretel, Governor, 274
Briantsev, 30
Brickendonbury Hall, 241
BRIDE, 155
Britain,
  opposition to Bolshevik regime, 21,
    24, 34
  Envoys' Plot, 21–4
  Anglo-Soviet trade accords, 31
  1924 general election, 45
  1927 expulsion of Soviets, 54, 91
  anti-Soviet policy, 1930s, 240
  and Spanish Civil War, 253–4
  World War II, 177–8, 390, 391, 392,
    395, 400, 402
  Communist Party, see Communist
    Party of Great Britain
  intelligence services, 32, 35, 36, 39,
    141, 148, see also MI5; MI6; co-
    operation with NKVD, 402, 405
  See also under particular ministries and
    organizations
British Broadcasting Corporation
  (BBC), 230, 231, 232–3, 234, 235,
  236, 498

Brunn, 410
BRUNO, 297
B 205, agent, 103, 108
Budapest, 128
Budenz, Louis, 334
Bukharin, Nikolay, 29
Bullitt, William C., 303
Bunakov, Nikolay, 36
Bund Geistiger Berufe (BGB) (Union of
   Intellectual Professionals), 74, 75,
   77, 80
Burgess, Guy Francis de Moncy
   (MÄDCHEN), 120, 123, 149, 152,
   153, 158, 162, 183, 189, 205, 212,
   213, 219, 279, 312
   background of, 221
   Cambridge career, 220–21, 221–3
   recruitment of, 220, 223, 224–9
   given cryptonym, 145, 225
   Deutsche on, 226, 228–9, 232, 239,
     242, 243, 244
   control by Orlov, 145
   probationary agent, 229–31
   BBC post, 230, 231, 232–3, 234, 235,
     241
   Gibraltar assignment, 167, 231
   cultivation of Cairncross, 214, 246
   fully-fledged agent, 231–45
   MI6 involvement, 230–31, 232–41,
     243–4
   Foreign Office Access, 240
   MI5 involvement, 241–2, 243–4
   Foreign Office post, 243
   on recruiting agents, 244–5
   Mally on, 232, 240
   flight to Moscow, 117, 138, 338–9,
     346
   1952 debriefing, 246
Burillo, General Ricardo, 289
Burtan, Dr Valentine, 66
Bystrolyotov, Dimitri (Hans Gallieni,
   HANS), 198, 204–5

Cairncross, John Alexander Kirkland
   (MOLIÈRE), 213–14, 218, 220, 246, 509
Cambridge, University of, 74, 179–83,
   245
   Trinity College, 116, 182, 184, 214,
     221, 222, 230, 246
   Society of the Apostles, 181, 222,
     227, 246

Marxism at, 180, 181–2, 184–5, 222–3
Cambridge spy network, 72, 117–18,
   120–21, 122–3, 138, 179, 188, 207,
   213, 219, 225–6, 238, 242, 244,
   245–6, 313, 335, 339, 367, 382, 385,
   490, 510
   Orlov as *éminence grise*, xvii, xix,
     121–3, 132, 142, 145, 150, 185,
     188, 189, 192–3, 220–21, 223–6,
     227, 242, 248, 374
   order of recruitment, 220, 246
   expansion of, 245, 246
   See also under Blunt; Burgess;
     Cairncross; Long; Maclean; Philby;
     Straight; Rees
Camrose, Lord, 227
Canada, 303, 306–7, 315
Canaris, Admiral, 399
Capri, 109
Carew-Hunt, Robert, 190
Cartagena, 256, 258, 260, 262, 268
Catalonia, 253, 254, 281, 282, 289
   See also Barcelona
Cecil, Robert, 189, 190, 192, 196, 197
Central Intelligence Agency (CIA), xxii, 9,
   117, 121, 142, 277, 342–3, 249, 346,
   350, 389, 490, 500, 503, 505–6, 508
   debriefing of Orlov, *see under* Orlov,
     Alexander
Central Military School, Moscow, 121,
   248, 275
Centre, The, *see* Moscow Centre
Chamberlain, Neville, 215
Chambers, David Whittaker, 71, 334,
   336, 347
Chance, Sir Roger, 148
Chatfield, Richard, 192
Cheka, 412
   birth of, 19–20, 150
   given expanded powers, 20, 24, 28
   assassination of German ambassador,
     21
   expansion of, 21, 25
   and Envoys' Plot, 21, 23
   "organized terror", 24–5
   Foreign Department (INO), 25, 31
   Counter-Intelligence Department
     (KRO), 25, 31
   and Kronstadt rebellion, 27–8
   abolition and rebirth as GPU, 28
   Counter-Intelligence Department, 31

Sindikat (Syndicate) and *Trest* (Trust) operations, 32–5
China, 336
Christie, 103–4
Churchill, Randolph, 174, 273–4
Churchill, Winston, 37, 39, 86, 201, 495
Cleveland (Ohio), 328–9, 330, 332–4, 337, 339, 343, 379–80
Cline, Dr Raymond, 495
Cohen, Lona (Helen Kroger), 277, 338, 495
Cohen, Morris (Peter Kroger), 276–7, 338, 495
Cold War, xiii, xv, 132, 218, 286, 334–6, 337–9, 340, 347, 388, 499
collectivization of farms, 46, 69–70
Columbia University, 71
Comintern (Communist International), 37, 44–5, 49, 74, 126, 128, 133, 134, 158, 185, 187, 190, 202, 236, 256, 257, 383, 395
Commissariat of Defence, Soviet, 61
Commissariat of Foreign Affairs, Soviet, 248
Commissariat of Foreign Trade, Soviet, 58
See also under Berlin; London; Paris
Commissariat of Heavy Industry, Soviet, 60
Commissariat of Light Industry, Soviet, 62
Committee for Aiding Refugees from Fascism, 128
Communist, 5
Communist International, *see* Comintern
Communist Parties, 54, 123
Communist Party, Austrian, 126, 127–9, 133, 134
Communist Party, French, 108
Communist Party, Spanish, 254, 255, 256, 257, 280, 282, 289, 300, 301
Communist Party of Bolsheviks, 311, 368, 369
Tenth Congress, Russian, 27
Twentieth All Union Congress, 367
Communist Party of Germany (KPD), 59, 65, 74, 75, 80, 81, 83, 268, 270, 298, 394, 403
Communist Party of Great Britain, 123, 124, 130–131, 133, 134, 136,

141, 183, 186, 187, 188, 189, 193, 194, 206, 236, 237, 238
Communist Party of the United States, 67, 71, 334, 335, 336, 347, 355
Connell, Mrs, 325–6
Constantinople, 298
Constituent Assembly, 20
Constitutional Democrats (*Kadets*), 19
CONSTRUCTION, 275–6
Continental News Service, 165
Copenhagen, 114, 115, 137, 154, 187, 188, 200
Coppi, Hans (CLEAN), 396, 398, 402, 403
Cornelius, 60
Cornford, John, 182, 222
Costello, Daniel Patrick, 227
Costello, John, xvii, xix–xx
counterfeiting operations, Soviet, 65–7
Coyocan, Villa, 319, 320, 321
Cracow, 368
Cranborne, Lord, 173
Cready, Sir Robert, 152
Creative Intelligentsia, 84
Cremet, Jean, 54, 95
Curgess, 104, 105
cypher systems, 92, 198, 202–3
Czechoslovakia, 31, 177, 210, 215, 234, 335, 338, 370

Daily Worker, 184, 186
Daladier, Edouard, 215, 234
Dallin, David J., 358, 359, 360, 361, 363, 365, 406–11
Dallin, Lidya (Lilia Estrine, NEIGHBOUR), 320–21, 322, 358, 359, 360, 361, 363, 365, 406–11
Danilov, Anton (HEMNITZ), 400
Danzig, 177
Davtian, Iakov Kristoforovich (Davydov), 47, 414
Dawson, Geoffrey, 170
"Decembrists", 185
de Gaulle, General, 399–400
DEMI, 400
Democratic Centralist Group, 28
de Monzie, Herbette, 47, 48
Denikin, General, 17, 34
Denmark, 79, 114, 115
Derol Oil, 56

Deruta Deutsche-Russische Transport Gesellschaft, 56
Deutsch, Arnold (STEPHAN, LANG, ARNOLD, OTTO), xix, 134–7, 138, 141, 142, 145–6, 149, 150, 152, 153, 154, 162, 163, 164, 168–9, 170, 185, 186, 188, 205, 209, 211, 212, 213, 214, 216, 222, 223, 224, 225, 226, 229, 230, 231, 232, 233, 242, 509
  on Philby, 146, 193–4
  training of Philby, 147, 151
  on Maclean, 193–4
  on Burgess, 226, 228–9, 232, 239, 242, 243, 244
  runs London *rezidentura*, 159, 160, 161, 199
  record in recruitment, 193
  and Oxford network, 247
  MI5 identification, 206
  leaves Britain, 195, 206, 207
Deutsch, Josefine (Liza Kramer), 134
Deutsche Bank, 66
Deuxième Bureau, 96, 97–109 *passim*, 110–11, 268
Dewey, Professor John, 318
D5, station, 396
Diakanov, General, 48
Diaz, José, 256, 280
Dickens, Ralph, 170, 178
Dienstbach, Karl, 64
Dobb, Maurice, 125–6, 181, 182
Doble, Lady Frances ("Bunny"), 173, 177
Dobos, Ladislas (Louis Gibarti), 126
Dodd, Martha, 76
Dolfuss, Dr Engelbert, 126, 127, 129
Dozenberg, Nicholas, 67
D6, station, 396, 404
DST (*Direction de la Surveillance du Territoire*), 47, 48, 49–50, 52, 363, 406, 506
Dukis, 40
Dunkirk, 178
Dutt, Eric Edward, 269
Dyke and Spencerian College, Cleveland, 328, 332, 337, 339
Dzerzhinsky, Feliks Edmundovich, xiv, 19–21, 24–5, 26, 27–30, 31, 36, 39, 40, 42, 44, 45, 413, 501

Eastland, Senator James O., 358, 362

The Legacy of Alexander Orlov, 10–11
Eastman, Max, 337
Eden, Anthony, 212, 254
Efron, Serge, 277
Ege, 347
Eggleston, Richard E., 235
Egypt, 240
Ehrenlieb, Aaron, 56
Ehrenlieb, Abraham, 56
Eisenhower, President, 362
Eitingon, Leonid (PIERRE, Colonel Naum Kotov), 237, 279–80, 292, 298, 301, 302, 384
Elliott, Nicholas, 117
Elza, 320, 321
Emir Saud, 155, 157
Engels, Friedrich, 222
England, *see* Britain
ENIGMA code machine, 86
Envoys' Plot, 21–4
Erdberg, Alexander, *see* Korotkov, Alexander
Espionage, language of, 50
Estonia, 39, 41
Estrine, Lilia *see* Dallin, Lidya
Eton College, 221, 226, 237
European Court, 119
Evening Standard, 165
EXPRESS (Arnold Finkelberg), 96, 98, 103, 105, 106
Extraordinary Committee for Counter-revolution and Subversion, 20

Federal Bureau of Investigation (FBI), xxii, 8, 9–10, 66, 117, 142, 220, 246, 316, 317, 318, 323, 326, 328–9, 334, 335, 336, 359, 360, 361, 362, 370, 371, 376, 381, 386, 490, 500, 503, 505–6, 508
  investigations of Orlovs, *see* Orlov, Alexander
Federal Reserve bank, 66
Federation of Spanish Anarchists, 281
Fedonov, Andrei Pavlovich, 34
Feduleyev, 39, 40
Feld, Henry, 318
Feldbin, Anna, 13
Feldbin, Lazar, 13
Fellendorf, Wilhelm, 276
Feoktistov, Mikhail Alexandrovich (GEORG),

1969 encounter with Orlovs, 1–10, 12, 13, 375, 377–8
1971 search for Orlovs, 378–80
1971 meeting with Orlovs, 248–9, 297, 363, 380–87, 389
Feoktistov, Dimitri Petrovich, 5
Finerty, John F., 318–19, 324–5
Finland, 28, 36, 37, 338
  intelligence service, 36, 39, 41
Fischer, Franz, 66
Fischer, Louis, 256, 340, 349, 353, 354
Fisher, Volodya, 372
Fisher, William Henry, see Abel
Fitin, Pavel Mikhailovich, 217, 397, 400, 414
Five Year Plan, first, 46, 57, 58, 60, 61, 67, 69
Footman, David, 205, 232–7, 238, 241
FORD, 216
Foreign Agents Registration Act (US), 351, 354
Foreign Ministry, Soviet, 248
Foreign Office, British (ZAKOULOK), xv, 116, 122, 172–3, 178, 186, 187, 188, 189, 190, 191, 195–205, 209, 210, 211–12, 213, 214, 240, 246, 338, 488, 499
  security at, 196–7, 211
France, 30, 46–53, 95–109, 110–13, 177, 200, 201, 204, 214–18, 272, 297–8, 299
  opposition to Bolshevik regime, 21, 24, 34
  intelligence services, 32
  counterintelligence agency, see DST
  Ruhr occupation, 57
  attempt to penetrate Deuxième Bureau, 95–109, 110–11
  and Spanish Civil War, 253–4, 258, 274–5
  Vichy, 497–8
Franco, General Francisco, 164, 172, 173, 176, 177, 212, 254, 255, 258, 264, 270, 271, 272, 273, 274, 275, 287, 288, 289
  plan to assassinate, 165, 168, 273
Franco Agency, 166
Freedom of Information Act (FOIA) (US), xvii, xix, xxii, 11, 344, 504, 506
Freikorps, 72
Friedman, Litzi, 127, 129–30, 133, 134, 157, 164, 166, 174

FRIEND, 97, 102, 103, 106
Frinovsky, Mikhail, 294, 299
Frischau, Mitzi, 128
Fuchs, Klaus, 138, 174, 338
Fulford, Roger, 230
Funkspiel, 401, 404
FÜRST (Berlin network), 79

Gaikin, 280
Gamarnik, 369
Gamow, George, 181
Garnitskaya, Nina, 100, 101
Gee, Ethel, 277
Gegner, Der (The Opponent), 82
General Electric Company (US), 63
General Motors, 70, 71
Geneva, 98, 99
Geopolitics, 165
George V, King, 125
Germany, 20, 30, 55–67, 73–90, 376
  Communist insurrections, 44, 55, 57
  Weimar Republic, 55, 56, 57, 63, 73, 74, Soviet industrial espionage in, 57–65, 98–9
  Nazi, 13, 64, 72, 74–90, 95, 128, 185, 204, 369, 370, 390–93, 394–405, Imperial Ministry of the Economy, 74, 76, 77, 80, 89, Air Ministry, 83, 85, Nazi-Soviet pact, 78, 81, 216, 240, 246, Rote Kapelle (Red Orchestra), see Rote Kapelle and under names of individual agents, plans for attack on USSR, 85–90, 390–93, disinformation measures against USSR, 88, influence on Austria, 126, 127, 129, Britain and, 160–61, 200, 201, 229–30, and Spanish Civil War, 164, 173, 176–7, 253, 254, 256, 258, 264, 281, 288, 289, Munich agreement, 177, outbreak of World War II, 177–8
Gershuni, 320
Gerson, Veniamin, 79
Gertz, 83
Gestapo, 13, 76, 77, 78, 79, 80, 81, 82, 88, 90, 268–9, 394, 396–7, 398, 400–401, 403, 404–5
Gibarti, Louis see Dobos, Ladislas
"Gibby's spy", 203
Gibraltar, 167, 213, 269, 272
Gibson, Harold, 203

Giessen University, 73, 74
Ginsberg, *see* Krivitsky
Glading, Percy, 206, 211
Glasnost, 119, 493, 495
Glebov, 64
Glinsky, Stanislav (V. V. Smirnov,
    PETER), 296, 311, 312
Glusko, Captain, 271
Goebbels, Josef, 84
Goerdeler, Karl, 84, 395
Goering, Hermann, 82, 83, 85, 390,
    391, 399
Gold, Harry, 338
Golienewski, Michael, 277
Gollancz, Victor, 236
Goodze, Boris, 35
Gorbachev, Mikhail Sergeievich, xii,
    xx, 119, 497, 501
Gorev, 265
Gorsky, Anatoly Borisovich (VADIM,
    HENRY), 218, 242
Gouzenko, Igor, 334, 335
Government Code and Cypher School
    (GC & CS), 202–3, 246
GPU (State Political Directorate), 28, 412
Grafpen, Grigory (SAM), 207–8, 209,
    210–11, 218, 238, 242, 312
Grand, Major General Laurence D. (Mr
    Francis), 239–41, 243
Graubenz, Jon, 404
Gray, Olga, 206
"Great Illegals", 150, 162, 195, 207, 237
Great Purge, 8, 27, 78, 150, 177, 195,
    204–5, 206, 207, 209, 232, 249–52,
    254, 280, 282, 284–6, 293–302,
    305–6, 309, 318, 332, 333, 368–9,
    386, 411
  in Spain, 268, 277, 279–82, 286–92,
    295–6, 300, 331, 334, 340, 348–9,
    352, 353, 356, 362
Greece, 104
Greenglass, David, 338
Gregor, Major, 83
Grimme, Adolf, 84, 395
GRU, *see under* Red Army
Guadalajara, 264, 280
Guernica, 264–5
gulags, 205, 237, 384
Gurevich, Anatoly Markovich (Victor
    Sukolov, Vincente Sierra, KENT),
    397, 398, 399, 400, 401, 403

Gursky, Colonel Feliks, 294
Gusev, Peter (Gutzeit), 347
GYPSY, 232

Haden-Guest, David, 182, 185
Hague, The, 198, 297
Haldane, J. B. S., 181
Halpin (VASYA), 190, 191
Hambro, Angus, 227
Hamburg, 59, 65, 405
Hamilton, Duke of, 498
Handelsvertretung (Soviet Trade
    Delegation, Berlin), 54, 55–9
    passim, 64–7 *passim*, 110
Hankey, Sir Maurice, 201
Hardt, Lydia, 162
Harnack, Arvid (BALT, CORSICAN), 73–
    9, 83–90 *passim*, 338, 390, 391,
    394–405
Harnack, Mildred (Mildred Fish), 74,
    76, 80
Harrison, Earl G., 324–5, 343
Harvard University, John M. Olin
    Institute for Strategic Studies,
Hassan, Edward D., 330
Hatton, Peter, 227
Haveman, Wolfgang (ITALIAN), 77, 397,
    404
Hayhanen, Reino, 371
Helldorf, Graf Wolf von, 84, 395
Heilman, Horst, 403–4
Hemingway, Ernest, 271
Henlein, Konrad, 234
Hernandez, José, 267, 268, 290, 348, 356
Herren Club, 75–6, 390
Hershfeld, Alexander, 74, 75, 79
Hess, Rudolf, xv–xvi, xvii, xix, xx,
    488–90, 491, 493, 495, 496, 497–9,
    500, 504
Hewitt, Jack, 234
Hill, Brigadier George A. (IK8), 231
Hill, Elizabeth, 230–31
Hillenkotter, Admiral Roscoe, 343
Hindenburg, President, 64
Hindle, William Hope, 148, 160
Hispano-Suiza, 265, 281
Hiss, Alger, 335, 336
Hitler, Adolf, 56, 64, 74, 78, 80, 87, 88,
    89, 90, 115, 129, 160, 161, 164, 17,
    201, 210, 214, 216, 234, 241, 254,
    258, 275, 298, 395, 399, 497

Hoessler, Albert (FRANZ), 276, 402–3, 404, 405
Holsmann, General, 32
homosexuality, 223–4
Hoover, J. Edgar, 329, 334, 335, 336, 342–3, 344–5, 346, 349–50, 351, 352, 353, 355, 357, 373
Houghteling, James L., 318
Houghton, Harry, 277
Husemann, Walter, 398
Houstinianos, 264

Ibn Saud, 115, 153, 155–6, 158
Ibragim, 40
I. G. Farben Industrie, 47, 64, 77
Ilychov, Commissar, 397
Immigration and Nationality Act (US), 351
Immigration and Naturalization Service (INS) (US), 318, 350
  Orlov's statement to, see under Orlov, Alexander
Imperial Defence Committee, 200–201
India, 116, 157, 158, 159
Indian Civil Service, 157, 158
industrial espionage, 31, 57–65, 98–9
industrialization, Soviet, 46
Interior Ministry, Soviet, see under NKVD
International Brigades, 164, 173, 182, 255, 257, 264, 268, 269, 275, 276, 277, 279, 290, 295, 298, 300, 403
International Workers Relief Organization (MOPR), 126, 128, 194
Israel, 14
Israelovich, 370
Istanbul, 54
Italy, 31, 109–10, 200, 212, 235, 240
  and Spanish Civil War, 176, 235, 253, 254, 256, 258, 260, 264, 268
Ivanchikov, Andrei, 30
Ivanova, Ekaterina, 388
Ivan the Terrible, 25, 28

Jacob, Franz, 405
James, Dennis, 236
Jarama, 264
Jenner, Senator, 354
Jews,
  in Tsarist Russia, 14, 16, 306, 307
  Zionism, 239–40

Johnston, Kemball, 241
Joint Broadcasting Commission, 240
JOSEPH, 103
Jouhaud, 399
JUNKER (agent B-138), 322
Junod, 104, 105
JUZIK, 291

KADU ("Red Beard"), 97, 103, 105–6
Kalamatiano, Xenophon, 23, 24
Kamenev, Lev, 45, 249, 250–51, 252
Kapitsa, Pyotr, 181
Kaplan, Fanya, 24
Kapp, Wolfgang, 73
Karin, Fydor Alexandrovich (JACK), 48
KARO, 273, 274, 397
Katsnelson, Zinovy Borisovich, 15, 30, 31, 252, 284, 368–9, 370, 371, 411
Katz, Rudolf, 229
Kell, Sir Vernon, 205
Kellerman, Florence (Koornick), 306, 337, 354
Kerns, Denton J., 352
"Kersakoff", 212, 213
Kessler, Erich, 241–2
Keynes, John Maynard, 226, 227
KGB, 3, 4, 6, 8, 9, 10–11, 19, 26, 79, 286, 337, 342, 350, 412–13
  Orlov dossier, 12, 13, 373, 388
  "damage assessments" on Orlov, 374–5, 510
  contacts Orlov, 376–8. See also under Feoktistov, Mikhail Alexandrovich
  Investigation Department, 366, 371
  Lubyanka, see Lubyanka
  press office, xiv, 489, 491
  Yasenevo headquarters, xi, 12, 150, 162, KGB archive, xi–xiii, xiv–xv, 487–510 passim
Khenkin, Kirill, 277–80, 372
Khruschev, Nikita, 5, 263–4, 367, 370
Kiev, 368
Kimochko, Fyodor Zinovievich, 377
King, Captain John Herbert (MAG), 198, 199, 200, 202, 203, 204
Kirov, Sergei, 250, 305, 333, 351
Klammach, 84
Kleber, General Emil (Moishe Stern), 255, 256, 257, 275
Klement, Ernst, 269
Klement, Rudolf, 298
Klugman, James, 184, 187, 214, 222

Kobulov, Amayak, 88
Kohlman, Israel and Gisella, 127
Kolchak, Admiral, 17
Koltsov, Mikhail, 263
Konovalets, 298
Konspiratsia, 50, 136, 143, 167, 186, 187, 213, 225, 276, 413
Koornick, Isadore, 306
Koornick, Max (Max Kay), 306, 354
Koornick, Nathan, 14, 306–7, 308, 315, 316, 353–4, 355
Korean War, 218, 336
Korotkov, Alexander (Alexander Erdberg, Rajonetsky, SASHA, DLINNY, STEPANOV), 78–90 *passim*, 96, 103, 110–11, 366–7, 394–6, 414
career of, 79, 112
Kosenko, Georgy (FIN, Kislov), 170, 171, 364, 374
Kossior, Stanislav, 369, 370
Kravchenko, Victor, 359, 361
Krivitsky, Walter (Ginsberg, GROLL), 198, 267, 284, 290, 296, 297, 298, 321, 327, 332, 348, 370, 373, 411
Kroger, Peter and Helen, *see* Cohen
Kronstadt rebellion, 27–8
Krupp, 57, 60
Krylenko, Nikolay Vasilievich, 27, 337
Kryuchkov, Vladimir Alexandrovich, xx, 150, 414, 494, 495
Küchenmeister, Walter, 83
Kuckhoff, Adam (OLD MAN), 84, 90, 395, 397–8, 404, 405
Kuckhoff, Greta, 84
Kuibyshev, 398
kulaks, 46
Kutyepov, General Alexander, 35, 36, 41, 67–8, 104, 111
Kuznetsov, Nikolay, 260

Labouchère, 195
Labour Party (Britain), 241
LADY JOURNALIST, 302
Lagrange, 97
Lamphere, Robert, 359–60
Landau, Kurt, 286
Largo Caballero, Francisco, 254, 256–7, 258, 260, 280
Laval, Pierre, 49
Lazarevsky Institute, 15
League Against Imperialism, 203–4
Le Carré, John, 50, 118

Lees, Jimmy, 182, 183
Legacy of Alexander Orlov, The, 10–11
Lehman, Willy (BREITENBACH), 78, 79, 403, 405
Leischer, Wilhelm, 84, 395
Lenin, 16, 17, 19, 20, 21, 24, 25, 27, 28, 29, 43, 44, 131, 181, 182, 185, 222, 249–50, 297, 376, 388, 389
Leningrad, 36–7, 85, 390, 392
See also Petrograd
Leninism, 70
Lenz, Professor Friedrich Bernhard, 74
LEON, 397
Levine, Isaac Don, 370, 411
Levine, Mrs Ruth, 370
Liberal Democrats Organization, 34
Liddell, Guy, 241
Liebrandt, 392
Life magazine, 6, 176, 339–40, 341, 342, 343, 347, 349, 351, 367, 368
Lippner, 64
Lisbon, 166
"Little Council", Soviet, 248
Litvinov, Maxim, 13, 23
LIZA, 76
Llewellyn-Davies, Richard, 222
Lloyd George, David, 31
Lockhart, Robert Bruce, 22, 23, 24
Lomovsky, Mikhail, 53
London,
Soviet Trade Delegation, 39, 54
All Russian Co-operative Society (ARCOS), 39, 43, 54, 90, 203
Orlov as "illegal" *rezident*, 113, 114, 120, 121, 132, 138, 140, 141–3, 144–5, 146–59
Soviet embassy, 115
London, University of, School of Slavonic Studies, 230–31
London Central News, 165
Long, Leo (RALPH), 246, 509
Lonsdale, Gordon, *see* Molody
Lordkipanadze, Dimitry (Zagarelli), 48
Los Alamos, 338
Los Angeles, 322–3, 343, 344
Lowenstein brothers, 59
Lozovsky, Solomon Abramovich, 16
Lozovsky Group, 16
Lubimov, Mikhail, 110
Lubyanka, xi, 23, 30, 35, 37, 69, 79, 294–5, 333, 346, 371, 487, 496–7, 499

Luftwaffe, 80, 82, 83, 85, 86, 173, 176–7, 201, 264, 281, 390–93, 395, 399
Lyeshkov, Georgy, 295, 319, 320
Lyster, Dr Russell, W., 323

McCarthy, Edward, 345, 346
McCarthy, Senator Joseph, 336, 337, 338, 357
MacDonald, Ramsay, 184
Maclean, Donald (WAISE/SIROTA (ORPHAN), LYRIC, STUART, HOMER), 120, 123, 149, 153, 154, 162, 179, 183–4, 225, 226, 232, 311, 312, 331, 509, 510
approach by Philby, 148, 186–7
given code name, 186
recruitment of, 186–91, 192–4, 220, 224–5
control by Orlov, xix, 145, 189
gains Foreign Office post, 191–2
Deutsch on, 193–4, 226
espionage in Foreign Office, 172–3, 178, 195–7, 199–205, 207, 209, 210, 211–13, 248, 504
and NORMA (ADA), 208–11, 214–17
letters to Moscow Centre, 210, 211–12, 219
assigned to Paris, 212, 214, 215–17
marriage, 217
return to England, 218
continues Foreign Office espionage, 218–19
Washington embassy post, 218, 334, 338
exposure and flight to Moscow, 117, 138, 338–9, 346, 361
Maclean, Lady, 184, 189, 191
Maclean, Sir Donald, 183
Macmillian, Harold, 117
Macnamara, Major Jack, 227, 229
Madrid, 177, 252, 255, 256, 257, 258, 259, 260, 264, 265, 266, 268, 269, 287, 290, 340
Maisky, Ivan, 238
Malaga, 295
Malayrov, Mikhail, 366
Malenkov, Georgy, 248
Malinovsky, Roman, 368
Mally, Theodore (Paul Hardt, Willy Broschart, Peters, PAUL, THEO, MANN), 97, 103, 106, 108, 143–4,

145, 149, 198, 204, 211, 212, 237, 242, 311, 312
London *rezident*, 162–70 *passim*, 199–200, 202, 204, 205, 209, 213, 214, 230, 232
and Oxford network, 247
on Burgess, 232, 240
MI5 identification, 206
death of, 206, 207, 296
Mao Tse Tung, 336
Markenstein, 269
Marling, Melinda, 217–18
Martin, Comrade, 320
Marx, Karl, 118, 125, 141, 180, 222
Marx, Lothar, 279
Marxism, 236
in Cambridge, 180, 181–2, 184–5, 222–3
Massing, Hede, 336
Maurin, Joaquin, 280
May, Alan Nunn, 334
MAYOR, 246, 509
Mendez-Aspe, Señor, 259, 262
Menshevik Party, 19, 28
Menzhinsky, Vyacheslav Rudolfovich, 29, 45–6, 60, 96, 249, 413
Mercader, Ramon, 279–80, 292, 322
Mercader del Rio, Caridad, 279
Merkulov, Vsevolod Nikolayevich, 86, 413
Merry del Val, Pablo, 165
Merzlyakov, Volodya, 24–5
Metropolitan Police, Special Branch, 142, 207, 236
Mexico, 292, 356
MGB (Ministry of State Security), 337, 412
Michigan, University of, 1–2, 375, 378
MI5 (HATA), 39, 114, 118, 125, 132, 142, 145, 171, 205, 206–7, 220, 230, 347, 503
identification of Mally and Deutsch, 206
Burgess and, 241–2, 243–4
Philby interrogation, 117, 138, 139
Blunt and, 245
Mikoyan, Anastas, 203
Milan, 96
military intelligence, Soviet, *see under* Red Army
Military School, Moscow, 248, 276

Miller, General Yevgeny, 32, 41, 104, 105, 230, 297, 306, 314, 382
Miravitales, Jaime, 348
Mirbach, Count, 21
Mironov, Lev, 30, 384
MI6, xv, xvii, 22, 34, 39, 104, 148, 155, 156, 158, 164, 170, 190, 191, 205, 347, 490, 494, 498, 503
    tapped by Maclean, 200
    and Burgess, 230–31, 232–41, 243–4
    Passport Control Office, 233, 234
    Department of Statistical Research, 239
    activity in Spain, 269
    Philby's career in, 116, 117, 151, 178, 190–91, 235, 241, 347
Molchanov, 249, 295
Molody, Konon Timofeevich (Gordon Lonsdale), 277
Molotov, Vyacheslav, 90, 248, 414
Monarchist Organization of Central Russia (MOR), 32, 33, 35, 41
Montevideo, 201
Montreal, 306, 307, 315
MOPR (International Labour Defence Organization), 126, 127, 194
Moravetz, Colonel Frantisek (Moravic), xvii, xix, 490, 496, 497
Morris, Judge Robert, 354
Morros, Boris, 359, 360
Morton, Major Desmond, xvii, 499, 504
Moscow, 22, 344
Moscow Centre (The Centre), 8, 9, 92
Moscow Law School, 27, 30
Moscow Municipal Credit Association, 35
Moscow Radio, 263, 369
Mukalov-Mikhaylov, 37
Müller, 269
Müller, Siegfried, 88
Munich Agreement, 177, 215
Münzenberg, Willi, 203–4
Murmansk, 22
Mussolini, Benito, 109, 110, 164, 235, 254, 258
MVD (Ministry of Internal Affairs), 412, 413

NACHFOLGER (SUCCESSOR), 142, 145, 153, 190, 207
Narbonne, 171

Narvich, 279
National Archives (US), 388
National Intelligence Study Centre (Washington), xx, 495, 500, 502
National Socialist Union of Lawyers, 75
Nazi Leaflet, 163
Nazis, 56, 61, 62, 64, 101
    See also Germany, Nazi
Nazi-Soviet pact, 78, 81, 216, 240, 246
Negrin, Dr Juan, 258, 259, 260, 280, 282, 287, 290
NEPHEW, 272
Nepler, Georg, 126–7
New Economic Policy, 27, 28, 30, 31, 35, 42, 43, 46
New York, 307, 315–17, 325, 337, 343, 355–6, 371, 375, 407, 408, 409
    AMTORG, 43
Nicholas II, Tsar, 16
Nicolson, Harold, 227
Nikolayev, Leonid, 250
Nikolayevich, Grand Duke Nikolay, 32
Nikolayevsky, Captain, 270
Nikolayevsky Institute of Social History, 282, 284, 319, 320
Nin, Andrés, 280, 281, 282, 287–92, 348, 349, 353, 507
Nixon, Richard, M. 336
NKGB (People's Commissariat of Internal Affairs), 412
NKVD (People's Commissariat of Internal Affairs), 28, 29, 249, 412, 413
    receives warnings of German attack, 85–90
    changes to "illegal" operation, 91–5
    one-time cypher pad system, 92
    passport desk, 93
    attempt to penetrate Deuxième Bureau, 95–109, 110–11
    running of Berlin section, Rote Kapelle, 79, 84–5. See also Rote Kapelle
    Miller kidnapping, 104, 297–8
    Italian operation, 109–110
    school for undercover intelligence officers, 121
    recruitment strategy and procedure, 1930s, 121–3, 135, 137–8, 150–51, 188

treatment of informants, 149–50
"illegal" station, costs of, 153–4
counter-intelligence operations, 203
Great Purge, 8, 27, 78, 249–52, 284–
6, 291–302, 333, 386. *See also under*
Spain
Beria appointed deputy chief, 210
repression in Spain, 267, 279–82,
286–92, 296, 300, 348–9, 362, 382
operation against Sedov, 282–4
conspiracy against Stalin, 284, 368–9
"mobile groups", 285–6, 296–8, 299,
304, 348, 382
evacuation from Moscow, 398
co-operation with British
intelligence, 402, 405
VENONA traffic, 338
comes under MGB, 337
Chief Directorate of State Security
(GUGB), 75
"Non-Intervention Pact", 253–4, 258
NORMA (ADA), 208–11, 214–18
Norman, E. P. G., 235
Norway, 31, 79

Observer, The, 116
Odessa, 256, 263
Official Secrets Act, 119, 240, 498
OGPU (Unified State Political
Directorate), 28, 29, 412
Economic Directorate (EKU), 30–31,
42–3, 63
Frontier Guard Division, 30
Foreign Department (INO), 31, 44,
45, 57, 58, 61, 69, 71, 95, 413
Counter-Intelligence Department
(KRO), 31, 42, 95
Syndicate and Trust operations, 32–
42
conflict with Comintern, 44, 45, 49
under Menzhinsky and Yagoda, 45–6
involvement in collectivization, 46,
69–70
involvement in industrialization, 46
Berlin base of, 47
rezident's agenda, 1920s, 49
foreign intelligence reorganization,
54, 69
industrial espionage in Germany,
57–65, 98–9

Economic Intelligence Department,
58
pass apparat (passport factories), 59,
65
counterfeiting operations, 65–7
Valuta section, 67
Kutyepov kidnapping, 68, 104, 111
OKH, 403
OKW (Oberkommando Wehrmacht),
77, 82, 86, 88, 390, 393
Okhrana, 20, 21, 25, 284, 368, 369, 370,
411
Oldham, Ernest Holloway, 197–8, 204
OLD MAN network, *see* Kuckhoff
O'Neil, Con, 227
Operation Barbarossa, 85–90
Operation EXPRESS, 96–109
Operation NIKOLAY, 291–2
Operation Trust (*Trest*), 32–3, 35–42
Opperput, Alexander Eduardovich
(Staunitz-Upelnitz), 33–4, 37, 41
oprichniki, 25, 28
Order of Young Germany
(*Jungedeutsche Ordnern*), 82
Orlov, Alexander (Leiba Lazarevich
Feldbin, Lev Lazarevich Nikolsky,
Lev Lazarevich Feldel, William
Goldin, SCHWED, Leo Feldbin, Leo
Nikolayev, "Big Bill", Leon
Koornick, BEGLETZ (FUGITIVE),
LEVON, Igor Berg), xii–xiii, xvi–
xvii, xxii
birth and upbringing, 13–15
move to Moscow, 15
drafted into army, 15–16
joins Bolshevik Party, 16
joins Red Army, 17
in Russo-Polish war, 17–19, 270
joins *Cheka,* 25–6
adopts name Nikolsky, 26
marriage, 26
legal training and work, 26–7, 29–30,
337, 382
acquaintance with Stalin, 382–3
birth of daughter, 27
1924 oath, 385
work for OGPU Economic Directorate
(EKU), 30, 42–3
command in Transcaucasia, 43–4
move to Foreign Department, 44

"legal" *rezident* in Paris, 46–53, 67–8
Berlin posting, 54, 55–67
recall to Moscow, 65, 67
OGPU reorganization, 69
USA visit, 1932, 70–71, 93, 306
return to Russia, 71–2
head of OGPU Section 7, Economic
  Intelligence, 73, 74
starts "illegal" career, 91
attempt to penetrate *Deuxième
  Bureau*, 72, 95–109, 110–11
Italian operation, 109–10
forced to leave Paris, 111–13
London *rezident*, 113, 114, 120, 121,
  132, 138, 140, 141–3, 144–5, 146–
  59, 183, 187, 188, 189–91, 192–3,
  209, 213, 230, recruitment
  strategy, 1930s, 121–3, 150–51,
  éminence grise of Cambridge
  network, xvii, xix, 121–3, 132,
  142, 145, 150, 185, 188, 189, 192–3,
  220–21, 222, 242, 248, 374, 504, 507
  control of Philby, 145, 146, 147–9,
  151–2, 177, 223, 244, 296
in Moscow, 192, 196, 197, 200, 201,
  205, 230, 248, guides Oxford
  network, 247, 248, consulted by
  Stalin, 8, 248–9, work for Central
  Military School, 121, 248, at
  Department of Railways and Sea
  Transport, 252
NKVD chief in Spain, 164, 167, 174–6,
  252, 253, 255–7, 257–66, 267–82,
  286–92, 293, 298–302, 348–9, 352,
  365, first report from, 255–6,
  meetings with Philby, 170–71,
  174–6, 268, ships gold to USSR,
  258–62, 312, 362, Paris
  recuperation, 263, 368, and
  Republican secret police, 265, 267,
  280, 287, 300, 348, foils
  assassination attempt, 175–6,
  reports on Republican prospects,
  265–6, 271, directs Stalinist purge,
  268, 279–82, 286–92, 318, 331,
  334, 340, 347–9, 352, 353, 356,
  362, 507, and death of Nin, 288–92,
  507 directs guerilla warfare, 269–72,
  spy school, 275–6, Khenkin's
  description of, 278, and Miller
  kidnapping, 297–8, 382, summons

to Antwerp, 293, 301–2, 303, 409,
  flight from purge, 7, 195, 302–4
in Canada, 304, 306–7, 315
letter to Stalin, 305–6, 307–8, 331, 341
letter to Yezhov, xvii, 305–6, 307–14,
  324, 331, 363, 372, 383, 386
enters USA, 304, 315, 383
in New York, 315–17
in Philadelphia, 317, 318
visit to Washington, 318–19
warnings to Trotsky, 319–22, 364–5,
  367, 407–8
in California, 319, 322–3
in Boston, 323
safety deposit box, 323–4, 326–7,
  329–30, 353
Aliens Registration, 324–5, 351, 352
in Cleveland, 328–9, 330, 332–4, 337,
  339, 379–88
wartime FBI investigation, 326–7,
  329–30, 343
discovered by CIA, 342–3
examinations by US Immigration,
  70, 304–5, 315, 316, 344, 348, 350,
  351–2, 353, 355–7, 363, 409–10, 508
investigation and debriefing by FBI,
  xix, 11, 68, 176, 267, 287, 290,
  307, 308, 321, 331, 339, 343–50,
  352–5, 357, 358–9, 363, 364, 372,
  373, 384, 385, 386, 389, 508
article on Beria, 350
subpoena by Grand Jury, 323, 352
testimony to Senate, 1955, 1957, 10,
  62–3, 66, 67, 68, 69, 110, 252, 263,
  267, 287, 290, 305, 321–2, 344,
  347, 348, 355, 357–9, 361, 362,
  363, 366, 367, 373, 385, 406, 410
and Zborowsky conviction, 357–62,
  363–4, 365, 367, 406–10
and Abel, 371–2
KGB "damage assessments", 374–5, 510
debriefing by CIA, xix, 11, 47–8, 49–
  50, 51, 52–3, 68, 97, 176, 298, 345,
  346, 348, 364, 373–4, 384, 385,
  386, 406–11
in Ann Arbor, 1–9, 375–7
1969 encounter with Feoktistov, 1–
  10, 12, 13, 375, 378
move from Ann Arbor, 9, 10, 378
1971 meeting with Feoktistov, 248–9,
  297, 363, 380–87, 389

1972 letter, 387–8
death of, 387
NKVD manual, 121, 248, 374
Secret History of Stalin's Crimes, xx, 6,
  7–8, 162, 176, 331, 332–4, 336–7,
  339–42, 348–9, 385
*Handbook of Counter-Intelligence and
  Guerilla Warfare*, 8, 49, 50–52, 52–
  3, 54, 91, 99, 109, 121, 122–3, 143,
  144, 145, 149, 150–51, 154, 162,
  182, 185, 210, 224, 270, 374, 375,
  376, 406
use of pseudonyms, 13
as "Great Illegal", 150
adherence to Leninism, 376, 388, 389
Orlov, Maria (Maria Vladislavna
  Rozhnetsky) (Marguerite Feldbin,
  JEANNE, Maria Feldbiene, Mrs
  Leon Koornick),
  marriage to Alexander Orlov, 26
  birth of daughter, 27
  in Georgia, 44
  Berlin post, 55
  Deuxième Bureau operation, 96, 97
  in London, 143, 144, 145
  courier in Portugal, 273
  flight from purge, 299, 303–4
  in US, 315–30 *passim*, 332, 333, 358,
    378, 411
  and Dallins, 408–9
  1969, encounter with Feoktistov, 3–
    6, 8–10
  1971, meeting with Feoktistov, 380–
    82, 384, 387
  death of, 387
Orlov, Veronika, 97, 142, 143, 144,
  145, 252, 299, 303, 304, 305, 310,
  317, 319, 324, 340, 373, 379, 383,
  387
  birth of, 27
  accident and illness, 44
  death of, 322–3, 343
Ortego, Colonel Antonio, 289, 290
Ottawa, 315, 334
Oumansky, 49
Ovseenko, Antonov, 274, 275
Oxford, University of, 74, 195, 245
  spy network, 120, 138, 238, 246–7,
    248, 314, 367

Palestine, 14, 239–40
Panfilov, General, 397

Panzinger, Franz, SS *Sturmbannführer*,
  400–401, 404
Paris, 35, 126, 130, 166, 167, 171, 234,
  244, 263, 282–4, 293, 296, 297,
  302, 306, 307, 358, 361, 364, 368,
  371, 383, 406, 407–8
  Orlov "legal" *rezident*, 46–53, 67–8
  Orlov's 1933 mission, 72, 99–109,
    110–13
  Orlov's 1937 visit, 284
  Orlovs' flight from, 303–4
  Soviet Trade Delegation, 47, 48, 52–
    3, 98, 106, 111, 112–13
  Café Osner, 51
  Brasserie Duval, 99
  Maclean assigned to, 212, 214–17
Passport Control Office, 233, 234
passports,
  forgery and doctoring of, 59, 65, 93
  fraud in obtaining, 143–4
Pauker, K. V., 294
PAUL, 297
Peake, Colonel Hayden, 495
Pearl Harbor, 87
Peking, 54, 91
People's Commissariat of Foreign
  Affairs, 203
Perestroika, xii, xiv, 497
People's Commissars (CDC), 19, 20
Perpignan, 175, 303
Peschanoe, 36
Pétain, Marshal (MARSHAL), 104, 105, 106
Petrograd, 19, 20, 22–3
  See also Leningrad
Petrov, Vladimir, 372–3
Petrovich, Alexander, xii, xviii
Petsamo, 338, 399
Pfeiffer, Edouard, 230, 234
PFEIL (HERTA), 153, 154, 188, 200, 205
Philadelphia, 317, 318, 322, 343
Philby, Dora, 130
Philby, Harry St John Bridger, 115–16,
  126, 130, 133, 146, 149, 152, 155,
  169–70
Philby, Kim (Harold Adrian Russell
  Philby) (TOM, SÖHNCHEN),
  background and education, 115–16
  Cambridge career, 124–6, 182
  visit to Vienna, 124, 126–9, 131, 185
  marriage and return to England,
    129–30

attempt to join Communist Party, 124, 130–31, 133, 134, 136, 141
recruitment of, 123–4, 131–40, 220, 382
given code name, 137
control by Orlov, 145, 146, 148–9, 151–2, 177, 223, 244, 296
Deutsch on, 146, 193–4, 228
training by Deutsch, 147
probationary agent, 148–9, 151–3, 154–60, 179–80, 183, 186, 188, 223, 228
fully-fledged agent, 160–62, 311, 312, 314
missions to Spain, 163–77, 273, 374
Times Spanish correspondent, 170, 171–4
meetings with Orlov, 170–71, 174–6
Times chief military correspondent, 177, 241
work for SOE, 241, 402
reports on Hess, xv, xvii, 488, 489, 490
MI6 career, 116, 117, 151, 178, 190–91, 235, 241, 347
1952 interrogation, 117, 138–9
protected by Orlov, 11, 176, 331, 339, 344, 346, 350, 367, 388, 389
defection of, 116–17, 366, 374
1988 interview, 119–20
death of, 119
My Silent War, 120, 123, 124, 132, 139, 166
on Burgess, 224
Moscow lectures, xiii
Pieck, Henri Christian (Hans) 198
Piklovich, Andrei, 65
Pilgrim Trust Company, 323, 326, 327, 329, 330
Pittsburgh, 329, 330, 343
pogroms, 14, 16, 307
Poland, 33, 34, 35, 177, 216
intelligence services, 18, 32, 39, 41, 54
Russo-Polish war, 17–19, 26, 31
Politburo, 8, 29, 43, 60, 248, 249, 250, 253, 284, 285, 294, 333, 369, 370
Politi, Karloti, 268
Pollock, Hugo C., 350, 353, 354
Poltavsky, 291
Popular Army (Spain), 264
Poretsky, Ignace, see Reiss, Ignace

Poretsky, Mrs, 206
Portland, 277
Poskrebyshev, A. N., 248
POUM (Partido Obrero de Unificacion Marxista), 279, 280–82, 286–92, 300, 318, 349, 356, 364
Powers, Francis Gary, 371
Poyntz, Juliette Stuart, 298
Prague, 98, 128
Praslov, Yury (KEPP), 52–3, 61
Pravda, 5, 263, 503
Prieto, Indalecio, 260, 348
Primakov, Yevgeny Maximovich, xxi, 496, 502
Proctor, Dennis, 222, 227–8, 234, 242–3
PROFESSOR, 142, 230, 508
Prokopyuk, Nikolay Arkhipovich, 3, 377
PSUC (Partido Socialista Unido de Catalonia), 281
Public Records Office (Britain), 499, 504
purges, see Great Purge
Pyatokov, Yuri, 284

Rabinowitz, Isaac, 14, 306, 307, 315–16, 318
Radek, Karl, 284
Radical Socialist Party (France), 230, 253
Radio Moscow, 263, 369
Rakovsky, Christian, 47
Ramirez de Togores, Captain, 260
Ramishivili, N. V., 48
Random House, xx, 340, 351, 500
Rapallo, Treaty of, 56
razvedka (secret intelligence), 87, 88, 89, 122
Reader's Digest, 351
Red Air Force, 257
Red Army, 17, 18, 25, 26, 28, 57, 86, 90, 120, 246, 257, 270, 271, 285, 295–6, 333, 391, 399, 404
conspiracy against Stalin, 369–70
12th Army, 17–19, 26, 388
Military Intelligence Department ((RU RKKA (later GRU)), 47, 59, 77, 79, 82, 92, 95, 248, 347, 370, 396, 397, 398, 400, 401, 402, 413
Fourth Department, 57
Redens, Stanislav, 294
Red Orchestra, see Rote Kapelle

Rees, Goronwy (GROSS), 221, 245, 246, 509
Reif, Ignaty (MARR, Max Wolisch), xix,
    114–15, 123, 124, 135, 137–8, 140,
    143, 144–5, 149, 155, 186, 187,
    188–9, 189, 191, 192, 194, 209, 224
Reilly, Sidney George, 22–3, 24, 33, 34,
    36–41, 231
Reiss, Ignace (Ignace Poretsky), 114,
    206, 297, 299, 310, 358, 359, 360,
    362
Review of Reviews, 148, 160
Revoi, Andrew, 242
rezidentura, "illegal", 92, 93
RGO, 64
Ribbentrop, Joachim von, 88, 160, 161,
    172, 240
Rickover, Admiral Hyman, 376
Robertson, Dennis, 130, 227
Roisenman, 68
Romania, 68, 82
Rome, 109
ROSANNE, 106
Rosenberg, 392
Rosenberg, Julius and Ethel, 277, 338,
    345
Rosenberg, Marcel, 255, 258–9
Rosovsky, Boris, 14, 15, 325, 356
Ross, 156
Rote Kapelle,
    Berlin section, xviii, 72, 73–90, 276,
        313, 338, 389, 390–93, 394–405
    Hamburg network, 405
Rote Kapelle, The (CIA history), 78
Roth, Paul, 66
Rothschild, Victor (Lord), 222, 229,
    235, 239–40, 241
Roumanian-American Films, 67
Rovno, 388
ROVS (Russian General Military Union),
    35, 68, 104, 230, 297
Royal Automobile Club, 235
Royal Canadian Mounted Police, 334
Rozhnetsky, Maria Vladislavna, see
    Orlov, Maria, 26
Rumbold, Lady, 192
Rumbold, Anthony Claude, 195–6
Rumsey, 363, 364, 410
Rupp, Hans (TURK), 77
Russia,
    1905 Revolution, 14
    1917 Revolutions, 16, 19, 376

civil war, 17–19, 26
    Soviet, see USSR
    Jewish community, 14, 16, 306, 307
Russian Foreign Intelligence Service
    (SVRR, RIS), xxi, xxii, 24, 32–3,
    142, 150, 158, 213, 218, 246, 268,
    377, 502, 504, 507–8, 510. KGB
    archive, see under KGB
Russian General Military Union (ROVS),
    35, 68, 104, 230, 297
Russian Monarchist Council, 35
Russian People's Army, 17, 33
Russian Political Committee, 33
Russo-Polish war, 17–19, 26, 31
Rykovsky, Vladimir Alexandrovich
    (JUAN), 100–102, 103–4, 106

St Ermin's Hotel, 234
St Petersburg, see Leningrad; Petrograd
San Francisco, 322
San Sebastian, 174
Sass & Martini, 66
Saudi Arabia, 115, 155–6
Savant, Alfred, 338
Savchenko, Commissar, 260
Savinkov, Boris, 17, 33–5, 36
Schirman, Rudolf, 269
SCHORR, 159
Schottmüller, Oda, 403
Schukin, 36, 37
Schulze, Kurt (BERG), 396, 398, 401–2,
    403
Schulze-Boysen, Harro (SENIOR), 82–3,
    83–90 passim, 390, 393, 394–405
Schulze-Boysen, Libertas, 83, 281, 398,
    404, 405
Schumacher, Elizabeth, 83, 403
Schumacher, Kurt (TENOR), 83, 396, 403
SCHWED, 83
Scoones, 189, 192
Scotland Yard, 39
SCOTT, 247
Sedov, Lev (SONNY), 282–4, 312, 319,
    321, 322, 358, 360, 362, 365, 407,
    408, 409
Semmelmann, Georg, 65
Senate, US, Internal Security Sub-
    Committee, Orlov's testimony to,
    see under Orlov, Alexander
Senkovsky, Colonel, 18
Serebryansky, Yasha, 68
Serge, Victor, 321

Servicio de Investigaciòn Militar (SIM), 267, 268, 287, 300
Seville, 166
Sharp, Venerable J. H., 229
Shebarshin, Leonid Vladomirovich, xvii, xviii, 414
Shoemaker, Mr, 318
Shuckburgh, Evelyn (MANYA), 190, 191
Shulgin, Vasily, 33
Simon, Lady, 190
Simon, Sir John, 190, 192
Skardon, Arthur, 138–9
Skoblin, General Nikolay, 68, 297, 299, 306, 314
Slavatinski, 157
Slutsky, Abram Abramovich, 61, 196, 200, 265, 267, 294, 298, 299–300, 414
Smirnov, Dimitri Mikhailovich (Dimitri Mikhailov, VICTOR), 48, 94, 296
Smirnov, V. V., *see* Glinsky
Smolny Institute, 250
Sobell, Morton, 338
Soble, Jack, 359, 360, 361, 362
Soble, Myra, 361
Soblen, Robert, 359, 361
Social Democrats, Austria, 127
Socialist Appeal, 320, 321, 322
Socialist Workers' Party, Spanish, 282
Social Revolutionary Party, 17, 19, 24
Society of Old Bolsheviks, 250
Sokolsky, George, 316–17, 339, 343, 349, 350
Sosnovsky, Ignaty Ignatievich (Dobrzyhnsky), 18
Soucy, Edward A., 329–30
SOUND, 93
Sourwine, J. G., 357, 362
Soviet Jurisprudence Weekly, 27
Sovnarkom, 20
Spain, 157, 163
    Civil War, 5, 159, 164–77, 182, 212, 235, 252–66, Falange Party, 172, 287, 288, gold reserves shipped to USSR, 258–62, 312, 362, Popular Army, 264, Republican secret police, 264, 266, 267, 268, 280, 287, 300, 348, Barcelona insurrection, 281–2, 287, 289, Stalinist purge, 268, 277, 279–82,

286–92, 295–6, 300, 331, 334, 340, 348–9, 352, 353, 356, 362, 507, guerilla warfare, 269–72
Spanish Morocco, 253, 272, 274
Spanish Young Communist League, 301
Special Branch, Metropolitan Police, 142, 207, 236
Special Operations Executive (SOE), 241, 402
Spectator, The, 222
Spigelglass, Mikhail (DOUGLAS), 297, 299, 300, 310–11, 313, 382
STAHL, 98–9, 100–107
Stalin, Joseph, xvi, xvii, 5, 13, 16, 18, 29, 41, 42, 43, 48, 53, 57, 60, 69, 109, 110, 161, 210, 216, 218, 222, 282–3, 298, 312, 313–14, 316, 322, 376, 384, 385, 386, 490
    possible *Okhrana* involvement, 368–70, 411
    acquaintance with Orlov, 8, 248–9, 382–3
    achieving of dictatorial power, 45, 46, 70
    currency counterfeiting, 65, 66, 67
    Great Purge, *see* Great Purge
    and Spanish Civil War, 164, 176–7, 253–63 *passim*, 264, 280. *See also under* Great Purge
    1937 plot against, 284
    and *Rote Kapelle* intelligence, 85, 86–7, 88, 89, 90
    as intelligence analyst, 90, 122, 400
    Orlov's letter to, 305–6, 307–8, 331, 341
    cancels hunt for Orlov, 313
    death of, 340, 341, 342
    Khruschev's denunciation of, 367–8, 370
    See also Orlov, Alexander: *Secret History*
Stansfield, M. S., 143
Starr, Maksim, 268
Stashevsky, Artur, 255, 296
STED, 364
Steffen, Erich, 64
Stein, 368, 369
Stephanov, 280
Stern, Moishe, *see* Kleber
Stöbe, Ilse (ALTA), 398

Strachey, Oliver (SONYA), 190, 203
Straight, Michael Whitney (NIGEL), 220, 246, 509
Strik, Major, 271
Styrne, Colonel Vladimir Andreyevich, 37, 38, 39
Sudoplatov, General Pavel, 252, 313, 384
Sukhumi, 43
Sunday Times, xv, 131, 489
Supreme Court, Soviet, 27
Supreme Military Tribunal, 24
Sûreté Générale, 53, 95, 100, 111, 112
Svertchevsky, General (General Walter), 300–301, 310
Svir, 293, 301, 308, 356, 383, 410
SVRR, see Russian Foreign Intelligence Service
Sweden, 31
Sykes-Davies, Hugh, 222
Syndicate (Sindikat) operations, 31–2, 33–5, 41, 42
Syroezhkin, Grigory, 35, 40

Taitinger, Pierre, 104
Talbot, Stafford, 159–60
Terror Begins, The, 350–51
Teruel, 271
Ter-Vangayan, V. A., 16
Thatcher, Margaret, 117
Thomas, Norman, 356–7
"Three Musketeers, The", see Burgess; Maclean; Philby
Tiflis, 44, 48
Tikhon, Patriarch, 23
Times, The, 169–70, 171–2, 173, 177, 230, 498
Tizien (ALBANIAN), 77
Toledo, 258
Tolstoy Foundation, 351
"Tradecraft", 50
Transcaucasia, 43–4
Travellers' Club, 196
Trepper, Leopold, 397, 400–401
Trevelyan, Professor G. M., 227, 230
Trianowsky, 315
Trilliser, Mikhail Abramovich, 31, 45, 53, 95, 414
Trotsky, Leon Davidovich (STARIK (OLD MAN)), 17, 18, 44, 45, 46, 249, 250, 256, 280, 281, 282, 283, 292, 318, 337

Orlov's warnings to, 319–22, 364–5, 407–8
Trotskyites, Trotskyism, 282–4, 285, 295, 298, 359
Spanish, 268, 279–82, 286–92, 300, 319, 334, 348–9, 356, 364, 507
Trud, xv, xvii, xviii, xxi, 150, 489
Truman, President, 218, 335
"Truman Doctrine", 335–6
Trust (Trest), Operation, 32–3, 35–42
Tsarev, Oleg (ALEC), 4, 120, 150, 487
Tudor Hart, Alex, 133
Tudor Hart, Edith (EDITH), 133–4, 135–6, 137, 138–9, 142, 154, 207
Tukhachevsky, Marshal Mikhail, 285, 306, 369, 411
Turkey, 103

Ukraine, 68, 69, 86, 88, 89, 368–9, 391, 392
ULTRA intelligence, 86, 120, 245, 246
Union for the Defence of the Motherland and Freedom, 34
Union of German Industries (Reichsverband der Deutschen Industrie), 63
Uranium Committee (Britain), 218
USA,
  Nazi intelligence against, 85
  Pearl Harbor warnings, 87
  Soviet espionage in, 276–7, 334–6, 337–9, 347
  World War II, 390, 391, 392
  prestige of, 93
  Army Intelligence Records Repository, Fort Meade, 506
  CIA, see Central Intelligence Agency
  FBI, see Federal Bureau of Investigation
  Freedom of Information Act, xvii, xix, xxii, 11, 344
  Government Bureau of Engraving and Printing, 66
  House UnAmerican Activities Committee, 336
  Immigration and Naturalization Service, see under Orlov, Alexander
  Military Intelligence, 344
  Moscow embassy, 344
  National Archives, 388
  Senate, Immigration Committee,

362, Internal Security Sub-Committee, 357, 360–61, 409. *See also under* Orlov, Alexander
State Department, 120, 246, 335
USSR,
first constitution, 29
trade missions, 32, 91, 92. *See also under* Berlin; London; Paris
collectivization, 46, 69–70
industrialization, 46
first Five Year Plan, 46, 57, 58, 60, 61, 67, 69
British policy against, 1930s, 240
Nazi-Soviet pact, 78, 81, 216, 240, 246
plans for German attack on, 85–90, 390–93
atomic bomb, 336, 337–8, 371, 389
Glasnost, 119, 493, 495
Perestroika, xii, xiv, 497
August 1991 *coup*, 500–501
See also under particular state institutions

Valencia, 256, 264, 265, 268, 269, 270, 288
van der Oster, Major, 172
Vansittart, Robert, 201, 212
VENONA traffic, 338, 360
Vernik, 112–13
Versailles, Treaty of, 56, 59, 74, 177
VERUNDEN, 400
VICTOR, 292
Vidarte, 356
Vienna, 96, 98, 113, 114, 126–9, 130, 131, 134, 135, 137, 143, 144, 161
Vissarionov, 368
Vivian, Major Valentine, 235–7, 238
Vladimirov, Constantine, 342
Vladislovna, Vera, 387–8
VOKS ("Association for the Maintenance of Cultural Relations Abroad"), 74
Volgoda, 22
von Brockdorff, Erika, 403
von Bülow, "Count" Enrique Deschow, 66
von Fries, Werner, 227
von Pollnitz, Gisella, 83
Voroshilov, Klement, 57, 267
Voynovich, Vladimir, 198
Vyachi, Toivo, 37

Vyshinsky, Andrei, 27

Wade, James, xx, 500
Walter, Francis E., 351
Walter, General, *see* Svertchevsky
War Office (Britain), 152–3, 178, 235
Department of Statistical Research, 239
Warsaw, 54
Washington, 117, 318–19, 346
British embassy, 218, 338, 347
Washington Times Herald, 339, 349
Watson, Alister, 182, 222
Wehrmacht, 399
Weill, Kurt, 55
Weitzmann, Dr Chaim, 240
Welman, 50–51
White, Dick, 139
White, Harry Dexter, 335, 336
White, William L., 339
White Russians, 17, 18, 19, 24, 25, 32–7, 41–2, 48, 54, 68, 77, 104, 360
Military Union (ROVS), 68, 104, 297
Wilson, Horace, 240
Wohl, Paul, 349, 352
Wohlzogen-Neuhaus, Baron (GREEK), 77
Woolwich Arsenal spy ring, 206, 508–9
Wood, Barrington, 170
World War II,
outbreak of, 216
fall of France, 217–18
German attack on USSR, plans for, 85–90, 390–93
Rote Kapelle, 1941–2, 394–405
"Worm", 60
Wostwag (*West-Oesteuropaeische Warenaustausch Aktiengesellschaft*), 56
Wright, Peter, *Spycatcher*, 118, 119, 142, 203
Wylie, Tom (HEINRICH, MAX), 152–3, 158, 159, 227, 228, 229

Yagoda, Genrikh, 29, 36, 37, 39, 45–6, 79, 249, 250, 251, 252, 253, 258, 284–5, 294, 295, 368, 413
Yakir, General I. E., 369
Yakushev, Alexander A., 32, 36–7
Yanovic, 68
Yelansky, 47

Yezhov, Nikolay Ivanovich, 204, 206,
207, 209, 210, 249–52, 258, 262,
263, 267, 284–5, 293–302, 303,
304, 333, 365, 382–3, 384, 410, 413
Orlov's letter to, 305–6, 307–14, 324,
363, 372, 383, 386
"Yezhovchina", 206, 285, 295 See also
Great Purge
Young Monarchist's Union (France),
108
Yudenich, General

Zborowsky, Mark (KANT, TULIP,

Etienne), 282–4, 311, 312, 319,
320–22, 357–62, 363–4, 365, 367,
406–10
Zechlin, 391, 392
Zhruavlyov, Gennady, 400
ZIGMUND, 137
Zinoviev, Grigory, 44–5, 249, 250–51,
252
Zionism, 239–40
Zolnay Verlag, 501
Zolotarev, 368
Zubilin, Liza, 335, 346
Zubilin, Vasili (Zarubin), 335, 359, 360